Citrix® XenApp™ Platinum Edition for Windows: The Official Guide

Citrix® XenApp™ Platinum Edition for Windows: The Official Guide

BRIAN **CASSELMAN**
TIM **REESER**
STEVE **KAPLAN**

Mc
Graw
Hill

New York Chicago San Francisco
Lisbon London Madrid Mexico City Milan
New Delhi San Juan Seoul Singapore Sydney Toronto

The McGraw·Hill Companies

Library of Congress Cataloging-in-Publication Data

Casselman, Brian.
  Citrix XenApp platinum edition for Windows : the official guide / Brian Casselman,
  Tim Reeser, Steve Kaplan.
     p. cm.
  ISBN 978-0-07-154597-6 (alk. paper)
  1. Computer networks--Remote access. 2. Client/server computing.
  3.Citrix XenApp. I. Reeser, Tim. II. Kaplan, Steve, 1955- III. Title.
  TK5105.597C37 2008
  004'.36--dc22

                              2008046421

McGraw-Hill books are available at special quantity discounts to use as premiums and
sales promotions, or for use in corporate training programs. To contact a special sales
representative, please visit the Contact Us page at www.mhprofessional.com.

Citrix® XenApp™ Platinum Edition for Windows: The Official Guide

1234567890 FGR FGR 0198

ISBN   978-0-07-154597-6
MHID   0-07-154597-2

Sponsoring Editor	**Indexer**
Wendy Rinaldi	Ted Laux
Editorial Supervisor	**Production Supervisor**
Patty Mon	Jim Kussow
Project Editor	**Composition**
Rachel Gunn	Apollo Publishing Services
Acquisitions Coordinator	**Illustration**
Mandy Canales	Apollo Publishing Services
Technical Editor	**Art Director, Cover**
Orestes Melgarejo	Jeff Weeks
Copy Editor	**Cover Designer**
Bart Reed	Pattie Lee
Proofreader	
Word One New York/Jen Larsen	

ABOUT THE AUTHORS

Brian Casselman is a principal consultant and a lead Citrix architect for 3t Systems, a Citrix Platinum Partner located in Denver, Colorado, and has provided Application Delivery solutions to customers for over ten years. He leads a consulting team that specializes in secure remote-access architecture and deployments utilizing Microsoft and Citrix technologies. He holds MCSE, CCEA, and CCIA certifications. Brian is published in *Redmond Magazine* as well as a contributing author for *Citrix Access Suite for Windows Server 2003: The Official Guide* and *Citrix MetaFrame for Windows Server 2003: The Official Guide*.

Tim Reeser is an industry speaker, author, and partner at 3t Systems, a Citrix Platinum and Microsoft Gold partner headquartered in Denver, Colorado. Tim is coauthor of *Citrix XenApp Platinum Edition for Windows: The Official Guide*, as well as the previous two editions of *The Official Guide* and a previous edition of *The Advanced Concepts Guide*. He has written articles for industry trade magazines and has spoken worldwide at industry conferences and events, including Ingram Micro's Venture Tech Network, Citrix's Solutions Summit, iForum Europe, and various industry trade groups and consortiums. Tim has been in the Information Technology Channel business since 1994 and a Citrix partner since 1997. He holds a B.S. in mechanical engineering from Colorado State University.

Steve Kaplan, Vice President of Data Center Virtualization Practice for INX, formerly co-founded and ran AccessFlow, which was acquired by INX in June 2008. Steve previously co-founded and ran RYNO Technology, which was named the Citrix Partner of the Year for the United States before being acquired by MTM in 2001. He spent years as a regular columnist for three different channel magazines and has worked with multiple hardware manufacturers and ISVs to help them develop channel and market-positioning strategies. Steve has sat on the advisory boards of several industry leaders, including a position on the Microsoft Partner Advisory Council, and was a Microsoft MVP for Terminal Server for four years. He has authored scores of published books, articles, and white papers on various IT topics, including security and disaster recovery. Steve is a frequent speaker across the globe and delivered the keynote address at 2006 ThinPower in Norway. He holds a B.S. in business administration from U.C. Berkeley and an MBA with an emphasis in both marketing and finance from Northwestern's J. L. Kellogg Graduate School of Management.

About the Technical Editor

Orestes Melgarejo is the Director of Product Management for the XenApp product line at Citrix Systems. He has been with Citrix for eight years in various capacities within the Product Management team. In the past he has been responsible for product definition of key XenApp releases and technologies, such as MetaFrame XP, Presentation Server 3.0, 4.0, and 4.5, and Application Streaming and Isolation. More recently he leads the team responsible for ensuring the success of the XenApp product line from definition to delivery.

AT A GLANCE

CONTENTS

Part II

Designing an Enterprise Citrix Solution

Part III

Installation and Configuration

Part IV

Delivery, Management, and Administration

FOREWORD

Do you have a strategy for connecting critical business applications to the users that need access to them wherever they may be? Today, more than at any other time, businesses run on applications. Whether they are for business intelligence, CRM, ERM, Financial reporting, compliance management or personal productivity, businesses would be crippled if their employees were not able to get access to applications (or application updates) wherever they may find themselves. At the same time, the distance between users and applications is widening. More than ever, employees and contractors are working a great distance from the corporate head office as trends like globalization, flex work locations, branch expansion and user mobility continue to pervade. There are also more constraints on firms than ever before with increasing regulatory compliance rules, security concerns and consolidation pressures. Many IT organizations take the old approach of deploying applications to end user devices and hard-coding everything. We spend lots of money on the best servers, networks, and PCs and then lock things down to prevent costly changes to the environment. Over time the entire system becomes slow, non-responsive to change and everyone from users to IT and management is dissatisfied. Consequently, the reaction is to buy newer and faster infrastructure but that is only a stopgap that leads to a new cycle of dissatisfaction with the status quo.

At Citrix, we distinguish the term *delivery* from the term *deployment*. To deploy implies heavy lifting and hard-coding, which is difficult to undertake and results in a static environment that is shackled with inertia. The alternative is to have a strategy that *delivers* via application delivery infrastructure. This type of approach provides our customers with a platform that allows them to be agile in the face of a quickly changing environment, maintain a high level of compliance, intellectual property containment and security while providing a superior class of instant access and high performance for their users.

The key concepts that we employ are *separation* and *centralization*. The simple act of separating applications from desktops and managing them centrally in the data center is the powerful step that allows IT organizations to be much more agile and adaptive to change than ever before. We call this separation application virtualization and call out two distinct kinds—server-side or *hosted* application virtualization and client-side or *streamed* application virtualization. Each has its own merits and they are covered extensively in this book. The hosted approach is the classic model whereby applications are installed on central servers and accessed from any device over a remoting protocol. This is still the lowest cost approach for application delivery and management. The streamed approach involves delivery of the application to the end point and execution in an isolated bubble at the end point to avoid conflicts with other applications. In both cases the power for IT lies in the leverage one achieves by being able to manage just a few instances of application packages on central servers versus having to manage hundreds or thousands (or even hundreds of thousands) of instances on end-user devices. The ultimate power and flexibility comes into play when you combine the two approaches by streaming hosted applications to central servers and end-point devices. This reduces the job of application management from thousands of instances spread around the entire globe to a single package found in the central App Hub. Imagine rolling out a new CRM application to 30,000 users overnight or updating 10 business critical applications for your users in a single afternoon by simply touching 10 packages in the central Hub and not touching a single end point device.

All of this and much more is possible today with Citrix XenApp Platinum Edition, the industry leading world-class end-to-end application delivery infrastructure solution. The product's roots lie in the old remote access solutions that Citrix brought to market (WinFrame, MetaFrame, Presentation Server, etc.) but today's XenApp offers a much more complete end-to-end approach to application delivery and management. No longer is XenApp strictly about hosted applications for remote access. Today XenApp can also be used to manage all applications including those that run at the user's endpoint device. XenApp is one complete solution for all Windows application delivery needs whether the applications are accessed centrally or on end user devices.

XenApp Platinum Edition goes beyond application virtualization to provide the end-to-end platform needed to build out a comprehensive application delivery infrastructure. It includes SmartAuditor for recording and playback of user sessions for training and regulatory compliance purposes. It adds user connection licenses for the Citrix Access Gateway SSL/VPN and the Smart-Access capability, which enables secure, policy-based granular control over the resources that a user may access. Platinum also includes user connection licenses for WANScaler which ensures optimal performance for branch-based workers and licenses for EasyCall, a utility that allows users to dial any phone number from any document or application found on the desktop (either local or remote). The award-winning EdgeSight product is also included in XenApp Platinum to enable system administrators to have an end-to-end view of application performance from end point to application server to back-end systems and everywhere in between. Platinum also includes Password Manager for single sign-on of all user applications and self-service password reset to eliminate costly help desk calls.

We are very excited at Citrix to be able to offer the marketplace the most comprehensive, end-to-end application delivery solution that enables IT to meet their objectives while maintaining a flexible and highly dynamic environment that can adapt to change. Things have never been more exciting with the XenApp team than they are today and we look forward to continuing to build out the solution that enables our customers to transition from tactical deployment to strategic delivery of their applications across the enterprise.

Scott Herren
Vice President and General Manager, Application Virtualization Group
Citrix Systems, Inc.

ACKNOWLEDGMENTS

To my wife, Joey, for keeping me on task and for her patience during this process; it's finally done. To Tim Reeser, a great friend, who took a chance on me ten years ago and allowed all this to happen. Thank you very much! To Chris Hampton and Jim Varner for their "mad" writing skills. To Alan and Lindsay—you were both RIGHT! To Tim, Alan, and Steve for allowing me the opportunity to work on this release.

—*Brian Casselman*

To all the readers who read the 690+ pages of the last book—*Citrix Access Suite 4 for Windows Server 2003: The Official Guide*—and have come back for more. To my wife, Lindsay, brother, Ben, and many friends and colleagues who have supported me and contributed to all my books.

—*Tim Reeser*

To my wife, Wendy, for all of her support, inspiration, and so much laughter.

—*Steve Kaplan*

INTRODUCTION

Over the next five years, Russell will likely realize more than $5 million in savings from implementing Citrix software and an additional $4 million in future cost avoidance from outsourcing IT operations.

—Tom Hanly, Chief Financial Officer, Frank Russell Company

Ever since Citrix unveiled the first widespread version of a PC-based multiuser operating system almost two decades ago, the architecture of corporate-based personal computing has continued to evolve. Thin-client computing transitioned into server-based computing, which then morphed into access infrastructure and next into on-demand computing. With XenApp application delivery, Citrix has gone beyond the PC box and enabled a comprehensive architecture for fulfilling the key role of IT—efficient delivery of applications to users anywhere, anytime, anyplace, over any device.

The Citrix product line is comprehensive, ranging from XenApp to bandwidth management to application acceleration. The XenDesktop and XenServer lines, in particular, add another huge dimension to corporate computing by enabling full desktop and server virtualization. Citrix Provisioning Server for Desktops delivers a standard desktop image to both physical and virtual desktops from a network service.

Providing detailed coverage of the entire Citrix product suite is far too ambitious a product for a single book. We therefore continue our tradition of the first three *Official Guide* editions of focusing on the XenApp product, which is the latest incarnation of the Presentation Server/ MetaFrame software that extends the Terminal Server platform. We focus on the business aspects of an enterprise application delivery platform, such as building a case for implementation and preparing your organization for rollout. The book also covers specific attributes of application delivery, such as security, monitoring, management, and disaster recovery.

WHAT'S NEW IN THE FOURTH EDITION

This book is a continuation of the third edition written two years ago by Steve Kaplan, Tim Reeser, and Alan Wood. We include updated coverage of topics such as Citrix policies, printing, XenApp client configuration, application installation and configuration, and profiles, policies, and procedures. We dive into Citrix Password Manager as well as the new capabilities of XenApp Platinum, including Application Streaming and Citrix EdgeSight for XenApp.

The authors of this book have been evangelizing the virtues of an application delivery platform since its roots as thin-client technology. We have worked for firms representing thousands of successful server-based computing installations at every type of enterprise—from Fortune 500 companies to small businesses with only ten employees. Even with this broad success, however, we daily engage with organizations that have little or no knowledge of the powerful benefits of embracing an enterprise application delivery architecture. A significant number of enterprises still have not made the jump from looking at their IT infrastructure as a cost department, to looking at it as an automation and enabling department. Many enterprises are still hesitant to throw out what they believe to be the safe approach of continuing down the familiar (and unending) road of constant PC upgrading and maintenance.

Although this book will speak to those businesses that have not seriously considered an application delivery platform, its text is more specifically aimed at helping those who have made the decision and are looking for industry best practices and practical tips to find the greatest success with this technology.

THE COMPOSITION OF THIS BOOK

This book provides the framework to design and implement a successful access infrastructure for an on-demand enterprise. Our focus is on using Windows Server Terminal Services and the Citrix XenApp Platinum Edition to accommodate hundreds or thousands of users running their desktop applications from one or more central data centers. We address the myriad technical, design, and implementation issues involved in constructing this environment, and assume readers already have a good working knowledge of networking and system administration for Windows Server.

The book is divided into four parts. Part I is an overview of Citrix application delivery. This section reviews Citrix XenApp Platinum Edition and includes justifications for enterprise deployments. Part II covers the design of a XenApp application delivery platform and ranges from planning and internally selling the project to providing guidelines for data center and WAN architecture, file services, remote access, security, network management, and thin-client devices. Part III covers the installation and configuration of the Citrix Application Delivery Platform and includes project management, installation, automation, server farms, profiles, policies and procedures, printing, and migration methodologies. Part IV covers the delivery, management, and on-going administration of an enterprise XenApp environment.

Writing a book about such a rapidly evolving technology poses a challenge. By the time this book is published, additional tools and practices will be coming on the scene. Fortunately, the methodologies and approaches we describe should be relatively timeless, and should prove very useful as you begin your own enterprise server-based computing project.

WHO SHOULD READ THIS BOOK

We have written this book to speak to two audiences: The business decision makers (that is, CFOs, CEOs, CTOs, CIOs, and IT directors) who are evaluating enterprise IT options, and the IT administrators who are considering or will be implementing and maintaining a server-based computing environment. We recommend that the business decision makers focus on Chapters 1, 2, 3, 7, and 8, because these chapters specifically address business issues. All other chapters tend to be more implementation and technically focused, although we worked to keep them relevant and readable by providing a multitude of graphics, pictures, charts, and tables.

In addition to the audience just mentioned, this material will provide a compilation of best practices for enterprise deployment of on-demand computing, and therefore should also appeal to the engineers and consultants of the thousands of Citrix partners worldwide. IT and project managers can benefit from the sections on change control, customer care, and migration strategies.

INTERACTING WITH THE AUTHORS

We welcome your feedback and will incorporate appropriate suggestions into further releases of the book. You can contact Brian Casselman at bcasselman11@gmail.com, Tim Reeser at timreeser@TorqueResearch.com, and Steve Kaplan at steve.kaplan@inxi.com.

PART I

Overview of Citrix Application Delivery Platform

CHAPTER 1

Introducing the Citrix Application Delivery Platform Alternative

More than 200,000 organizations worldwide use the Citrix Application Delivery Platform every day to work more productively and run their IT departments at a lower cost. The Citrix Application Delivery Platform is an integrated, end-to-end system that seamlessly delivers application resources to users, devices, and networks. Instead of a piecemeal approach to application delivery, using an infrastructure approach enables businesses to take a holistic view of application delivery. Within this framework, they can create and execute an overall delivery strategy that addresses the heterogeneity and strategic impact of all applications and the strategic impact of all access scenarios.

The Citrix Application Delivery Platform consolidates management and access into a central location for more efficient and effective control. It automatically adapts to a broad array of application delivery scenarios. It adjusts access rights to enable users to roam seamlessly between locations, networks, and devices—without interrupting their workflow and without their having to understand the underlying access complexities. The end result is easy and instant on-demand application delivery for any user accessing any resource from any network via any device. This result enables secure, efficient, cost-effective, and well-managed application delivery for IT administrators responsible for meeting the information-access needs of the business.

While the Citrix Application Delivery Platform continues to evolve with an increasing number of strategic products, the cornerstone is Citrix XenApp Platinum Edition. Citrix XenApp Platinum Edition includes XenApp along with Citrix Password Manager, Citrix Application Access Gateway, Citrix EdgeSight, SmartAuditor and EasyCall. Citrix XenApp Platinum Edition enables an organization to implement on-demand infrastructure for optimizing ubiquitous access to applications and data.

This chapter introduces the concept of the Citrix Application Delivery Infrastructure. We consider the many economic benefits of on-demand application delivery and the major industry trends that are accelerating its acceptance. We'll look at the six keys to successful application delivery: delivering Windows applications, delivering desktops, delivering web applications, enabling secure application access, accelerating application delivery to branch offices, and monitoring of the end-user experience. We also consider other application delivery infrastructure advantages, such as enhanced security, helping to facilitate compliance with government regulations, improved disaster-recovery capabilities, and being more environmentally friendly. The main components of an enterprise application delivery infrastructure are analyzed. Finally, we discuss the process of designing an enterprise application delivery infrastructure, which we will build upon in the chapters that follow.

ON-DEMAND APPLICATION DELIVERY

The Citrix Application Delivery Platform addresses the broad access area of on-demand access. This book focuses on Citrix XenApp Platinum Edition, which specifically is geared toward optimizing the client/server and desktop-based application environment. The Platinum Edition of XenApp enables a true enterprise application delivery infrastructure by adding Citrix EdgeSight for application performance monitoring, SmartAccess granular control access policies with Citrix Access Gateway, single sign-on with Citrix Password Manager, enhanced regulatory compliance with SmartAuditor, and the ability to initiate calls from within any application with EasyCall. The Platinum Edition of XenApp also features all the many enterprise benefits of the Advanced and Enterprise Editions, including graphics acceleration, application isolation, and application virtualization and streaming.

Graphics-Intensive Application Virtualization

The new SpeedScreen Progressive Display technology improves performance of graphics displays in Windows-based applications by up to 15 times, thus making it possible to virtualize delivery of even the most graphics-intensive applications with no compromise in end-user experience. This capability now makes it possible to virtualize many more applications, and therefore complete desktops, within most organizations.

Server-Side Application Virtualization

Instead of IT administrators installing, managing, updating, and securing a vast array of heterogeneous clients for every user, a single instance of the application is installed on or streamed to each "presentation server" in the data center. This server "virtualizes" application delivery by passing to the client only screen pixels, and receiving back keystrokes and mouse movements across the network instead of actual data. This process is transparent to end users, who have the same application experience as if they were using locally installed applications, and IT administrators have a far more cost-effective, easy-to-manage, and secure method for providing access to these centralized applications.

Through virtualization, presentation services increase access speed, application performance, and network security. They also reduce network bandwidth consumption by eliminating the traditional requirement of transferring application data over the network.

Client-Side Application Virtualization

Client-side application virtualization reduces the cost of testing, installing, and supporting applications for both laptop users and PC users still running local applications. Together with application isolation technology, Application Streaming is the enabler of application virtualization on the client. Rather than applications being installed on each user's PC, applications are streamed to a protected isolation environment on their client device. Application conflicts are eliminated while the cost of regression testing, deployment, maintenance, and upgrades is significantly reduced.

Mainframe Model Similarities

In an enterprise implementation of Microsoft Windows 2003 Terminal Services and Citrix Presentation Server, most applications execute at one or more central data centers rather than on individual PCs. This entails a paradigm shift back to mainframe methodologies, procedures, and discipline, while still utilizing technology and environmental aspects unique to the PC world. It requires a much more resilient, reliable, and redundant network infrastructure than in a conventional client/server WAN. Myriad decisions must be made regarding building this infrastructure as well as several ancillary items such as choosing the right terminals, prioritizing WAN traffic, consolidating storage, enabling redundancy, and migrating from legacy systems.

An on-demand application delivery infrastructure has other similarities with the mainframe model of computing. For example, IT control of the desktop and application standards, reduced infrastructure costs, and much lower staffing requirements are attributes shared with the mainframe environment. Unlike with the mainframe model, though, users do not have to wait six months in an MIS queue in order to have IT produce a report for them. Instead, they can create it themselves in minutes by using Excel or any application to which IT gives them access.

On-demand application delivery combines the best of both the mainframe and PC worlds. It incorporates the inexpensive desktop-computing cost structure of the mainframe model while allowing users the flexibility and versatility they are used to having with their PCs and applications. The matrix in Figure 1-1 compares on-demand access with both mainframe and PC-based computing, with respect to cost and flexibility.

Benefits of an Enterprise Deployment of the Citrix Application Delivery Infrastructure

On-demand access utilizing Microsoft Terminal Server and the Citrix Application Delivery Infrastructure is reshaping corporate computing by driving costs out and facilitating control of IT. A 2003 Gartner study of 23 Citrix customers across five continents determined that the average risk-adjusted payback for the firms participating in the study occurred within seven-and-a-half months of deploying the Citrix Application Delivery Infrastructure on an enterprise scale. Although the economic justification for Citrix alone is compelling, many organizations are transitioning to this architecture primarily to take advantage of other strategic benefits, such as improved security, enhanced disaster recovery/business continuance, faster time to market, increased productivity, universal information access, and faster organizational growth.

On-demand Application Delivery Concerns

An on-demand application delivery infrastructure enables organizations to deliver applications as a utility-like service, where you pay only for what you use. In this environment, building a robust, reliable, and scalable architecture is essential. The data centers must operate with the discipline used by mainframe shops to control changes, limit access, and implement well-defined policies and procedures. Implementing or maturing IT service and support processes is an important part of an enterprise application delivery infrastructure project. Frameworks such as ITIL and COBIT offer guidance in defining

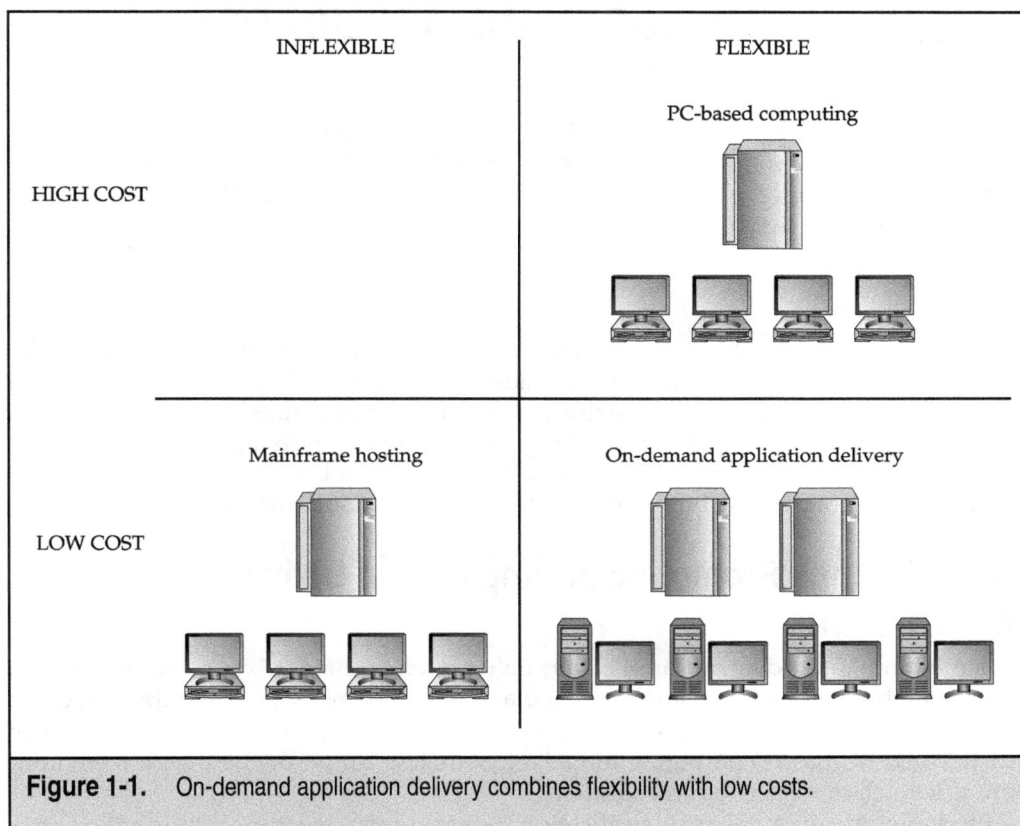

	INFLEXIBLE	FLEXIBLE
HIGH COST		PC-based computing
LOW COST	Mainframe hosting	On-demand application delivery

Figure 1-1. On-demand application delivery combines flexibility with low costs.

service and support processes, including change, release, and configuration management to provide rigorous offline testing of all new applications before their controlled introduction into the production environment.

Despite the continuing huge success of Citrix Application Delivery Infrastructure and the overwhelming advantages of on-demand application delivery, it is still a long way from being universally accepted as the corporate computing standard. The reason for this is that organizations tend to move slowly in adopting new technology paradigms. A myriad of educational, historical, cultural, and, of course, political factors influence an organization's decision of whether or not to implement an application delivery infrastructure. Different departments, for example, may control their own budgets and have their own IT staffs. They may resist ceding computing control to a centralized corporate IT department. Users who distrust a network's reliability because of a history of frequent downtime are going to be extremely reluctant to place all their computing eggs in the IT department's basket.

JUSTIFICATION FOR ON-DEMAND APPLICATION DELIVERY

Our solution utilizing Windows Terminal Services and Citrix has enabled us to deploy our Computerized Patient Record System (CPRS), Microsoft Office, and other applications to our users without requiring a huge investment in new PCs. We eliminated the overhead associated with desktop support while reducing server administration.

—Ray Sullivan, CIO,
VA Medical Center VISN 20

It can be argued that the primary purpose of most IT departments is to efficiently deliver applications. Citrix has become the leader in application delivery by developing a suite of products that enable IT departments to fulfill this role more effectively and with less budget than traditional PC computing. In order to embrace an enterprise application delivery platform though, IT personnel typically must build a compelling case for management incorporating both functionality and economic benefits.

Economic Savings Promoting an Application Delivery Infrastructure

Implementing an on-demand application delivery environment is not inexpensive. In addition to the licenses, hardware, design, planning, implementation, and training costs, this infrastructure usually requires a more robust data center architecture than that of a distributed PC-based computing model. Nonetheless, an on-demand access environment is a much more economical solution.

By deploying an enterprise application delivery infrastructure built on the Citrix XenApp, organizations no longer need to expend a majority of their resources on peripheral devices such as PCs and remote office servers. Information processing, servers, data and application delivery are consolidated at central data center(s), where resources are much more effectively deployed. Organizations achieve economies of scale by utilizing a much smaller number of competent IT staff to manage their entire IT infrastructures.

Consolidating both servers and storage in a central data center enables organizations to significantly reduce their expenditures on hardware and associated maintenance. Moreover, the process of centralization also provides the architecture and economies to utilize more efficient types of hardware, such as network-attached storage (NAS) or storage area network (SAN) devices. It enables a more efficient and economical implementation of software such as the AppSense and PowerFuse products, which aid in the control of which applications users are able to launch.

Personal Computers

Personal computers tend to have a maximum lifespan of only a few years for most organizations. Upgrading a PC is an expensive task that includes not only the cost of the machine and its operating system software, but also the expense of ordering, delivering, and configuring the PC. Data files often need to be transferred from the old unit to the new one, and the user suffers from downtime during the process. Application streaming to workstations allows simplified PC configurations requiring only a base operating system and client. On-demand application delivery extends the life of PCs, because many-to-all applications are processed on central server farms. And, in some cases, users can utilize inexpensive Windows terminals that are set up in minutes.

Suppose, for example, an organization with 6,000 users can run 100 percent of their common user applications with the Citrix Application Delivery Infrastructure for half of their users. Suppose also that as PCs break or require upgrading, this organization replaces one-third of its user workstations with $300 Windows terminals. These Windows terminals simply plug into the network and require little-to-no configuration.

In order to calculate the estimated savings for the 3,000 PCs that can go 100-percent "thin," let's make the following assumptions:

▼ Each PC costs $1,000, including taxes and shipping.

■ Installation of each PC costs $70 (two hours at $35/hour for an average weighted PC technician salary).

■ PCs are replaced every three years.

▲ Disposal costs of a PC average $70.

Over a five-year period, replacing 3,000 PCs with Windows terminals results in the following savings:

{3,000 Workstations ($1,000 Purchase + $70 Installation + $70 Disposal) / 3 Year Life}5 Years = $5.7M

This scenario results in a $5.7-million savings over a five-year lifespan. Including the cost to purchase 4,000 Windows terminals reduces the savings by $900,000 but still leaves a net savings of $4.8 million.

For the remaining 3,000 workstations, let's examine the cost savings:

▼ Each remaining workstation will run the majority of corporate applications via the Citrix Application Delivery Suite. This ensures applications are delivered and data is stored centrally in a secure administrator-controlled environment.

▲ With the majority of corporate applications running on the Citrix Application Delivery Suite, the setup and preconfiguration costs are reduced by half. Each machine requires little more than an initial imaging process prior to deployment. Individual application configuration is not required per workstation.

Over a five-year period, therefore, the organization can expect the following installation-related savings on the remaining 3,000 PCs:

{3,000 Workstations ($70 Installation / 2) / 3 Year Life} 5 Years = $175K

Homogenizing Clients

Citrix Application Delivery Infrastructure 4.5 lets users run the latest Microsoft applications utilizing a wide variety of clients, including Macs, most types of UNIX, Linux, many handheld devices, smart phones, DOS, all flavors of Windows, and even OS/2. This eliminates the requirement of multiple desktops for certain users.

Better Laptop Management

Many organizations give employees laptops primarily to work between the office and their homes, or between remote offices. Traveling workers in the past had limited access to Citrix-based applications. Client-side application virtualization with Citrix XenApp allows local execution of virtualized applications while disconnected from the network. With Citrix client-side application virtualization, employees see their desktop and applications no matter where they are—both online and disconnected—with the reliability of local application execution. Companies can now benefit from the savings network-connected Citrix clients have enjoyed for their laptop users, too. Remote users with network access can avoid the much higher expense of laptops by simply purchasing Windows terminals or less expensive desktop PCs for their employees to use at home.

Administration

Because administration is the largest component of a PC's total cost of ownership, on-demand access saves organizations huge amounts of money by reducing and centralizing IT staffing requirements. This comes primarily from the elimination of the requirement to locally install or push install new applications to desktops. For example, US Oncology has a network administrator who supports 5,000 Citrix XenApp users. This compares to a standard PC-based computing average of around one administrator per 100 users. Contra Costa County's former deputy CIO, John Forberg, commented that Citrix enabled the county to upgrade a large ERP package for hundreds of users literally over lunch.

NOTE: ABM Industries is a Fortune 1000 company that migrated entirely to an enterprise on-demand access model. Prior to implementing Citrix, the IT staff presented three alternative scenarios for migrating the company's 2,500 Lotus Notes users around the country from R4 to R5:
Scenario a: 24 months and $3.0M
Scenario b: 18 months and $3.5M
Scenario c: 9 months and $4.5M
After a companywide migration to on-demand access, the actual time to upgrade to Notes R5 was only *18 hours, with no added cost.*

Maintenance

Maintenance expenses associated with PCs are greatly reduced because users and application conflicts no longer cause problems. Misbehaving software applications are isolated in their own execution environments running without installation, or without alteration to the operating system or other collocated applications. If a PC breaks, it can often simply be replaced with an inexpensive PC with a base operating system for client-side virtualization or a Windows terminal for delivering server-based virtualized applications.

Help Desk Staffing

An application delivery infrastructure often reduces the requirement for help desk support because of the IT staff's ability to instantly "see" and manage the user's screen through Citrix XenApp shadowing. They can then provide remote support by taking control of the user's screen, mouse, and keyboard. Client-side virtualized applications, if corrupted, can be cleared from the local cache and restreamed to the client to repair any local execution problems.

Help Desk Delays

Organizations often document their cost of providing help desk support. They seldom quantify, though, the amount of lost productivity as users either struggle to fix the problem themselves or wait for the help desk to handle it. Users may also waste other employees' time by asking for help from them instead of from IT. An enterprise deployment of Citrix Application Delivery Infrastructure provides easier access to help desk support, and a shorter time to incident resolution and service recovery, thus resulting in less downtime for users.

Employee Productivity

Productivity losses occur when users stop work while their personal computers or applications are upgraded. Incompatible software versions sometimes make it necessary to do time-consuming data conversions in order to share information with other employees. The ability to virtualize applications with Citrix XenApp thus enhances productivity by significantly reducing the downtime associated with PCs.

Training Costs

Many organizations, particularly those with remote offices, do not have the time or resources to provide training to users on new applications or application upgrades in a distributed PC architecture. Presentation Server's one-to-many shadowing feature enables trainers to conduct remote training sessions for users throughout the enterprise. The users can shadow the instructor's machine while simultaneously participating in a conference call. Not only can this significantly reduce the cost of training, but by increasing the amount of training users receive, help desk calls and peer support can be reduced, thus increasing employee productivity.

Electricity

Windows terminals tend to use only about 1/7th of the electricity of PCs. In states such as California with high electricity costs, the savings can run into tens or even hundreds of thousands of dollars annually for organizations with lots of PCs.

Eliminating the Need for Local Data Backup

Many organizations rely on users and remote office administrators to do their own data backups, or they contract this function out to third-party services. Centralizing corporate data in a secure data center eliminates the time, risk, and expense associated with distributed data backups.

Remote Office Infrastructures

In a PC-based application environment, even small remote offices often require not only domain controllers and file servers, but also e-mail servers, database servers, and possibly other applications servers such as fax. An example of a PC-based computing environment in a remote office is shown in Figure 1-2. The remote offices also require associated peripheral software and hardware, including network operating systems software, tape backups, tape backup software, antivirus software, network management software, and uninterruptible power supplies. Someone needs to administer and maintain these remote networks as well as ensure that data is consistently synchronized or replicated with data at headquarters.

In a server-based application delivery model, remote-office servers and their peripherals can usually be eliminated entirely by simply running all users as clients of a central server farm. Powerful as well as low-end PCs, Windows terminals, Macintoshes, and UNIX workstations can be cabled to a low-bandwidth hub and then connected with a router to the corporate data center through a leased line, a frame-relay cloud, or the Internet, utilizing Access Gateway for Citrix or another VPN product. Figure 1-3 shows a typical small remote office in an enterprise application delivery infrastructure.

Naturally, when the remote office servers and associated network infrastructures are eliminated, the corresponding support and maintenance costs are eliminated as well. Suppose, for example, an organization spends $17,000 every three years on upgrading each server in a remote office (including associated software, UPS, tape backup, travel time, network reconfiguration, and troubleshooting). Suppose this company also spends $3,000 per server per year in administration costs and $2,000 per server per year in ongoing maintenance. If there are 100 remote offices with an average of three servers per office, the company would then save $3,200,000 just in their remote office expenses every three years by migrating to on-demand access.

Remote Office Bandwidth

It is not uncommon for an ERP package to require 128KB of low-latency bandwidth (or more) per user, making it very expensive and resource intensive to connect remote-office users in a PC-based computing environment. An application infrastructure utilizing Citrix XenApp to deliver server-side virtualized applications requires only 10KB to 20KB of bandwidth per concurrent user to run a Citrix Independent Computing Architecture (ICA) session. Rather than a local area network (LAN) infrastructure being built at each

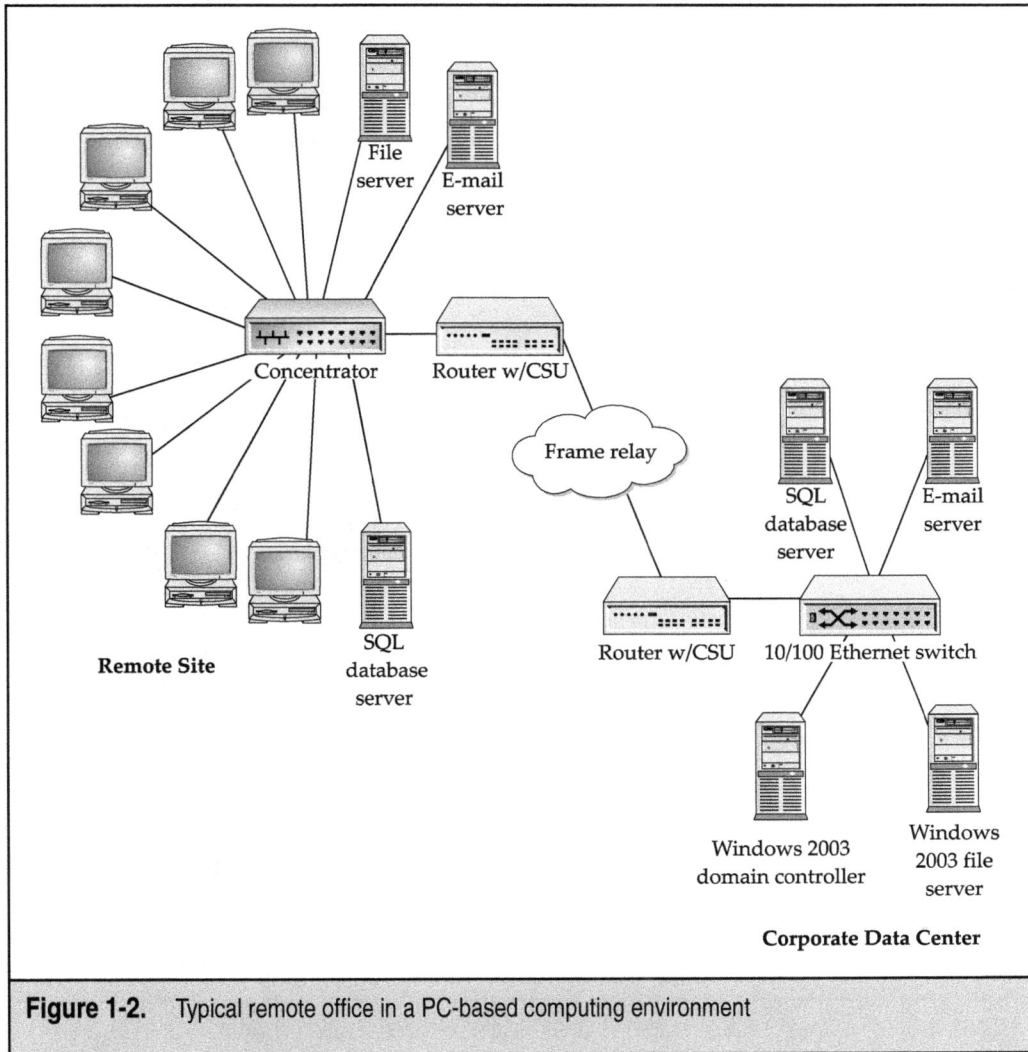

Figure 1-2.   Typical remote office in a PC-based computing environment

remote office that requires data replication with headquarters, the low Citrix bandwidth requirements enable remote-office users to simply run all of their applications from the corporate data center. The Citrix "VPN everywhere" solutions included with the Citrix Application Delivery enable employees to use the Internet as an even less expensive bandwidth medium for enabling on-demand access.

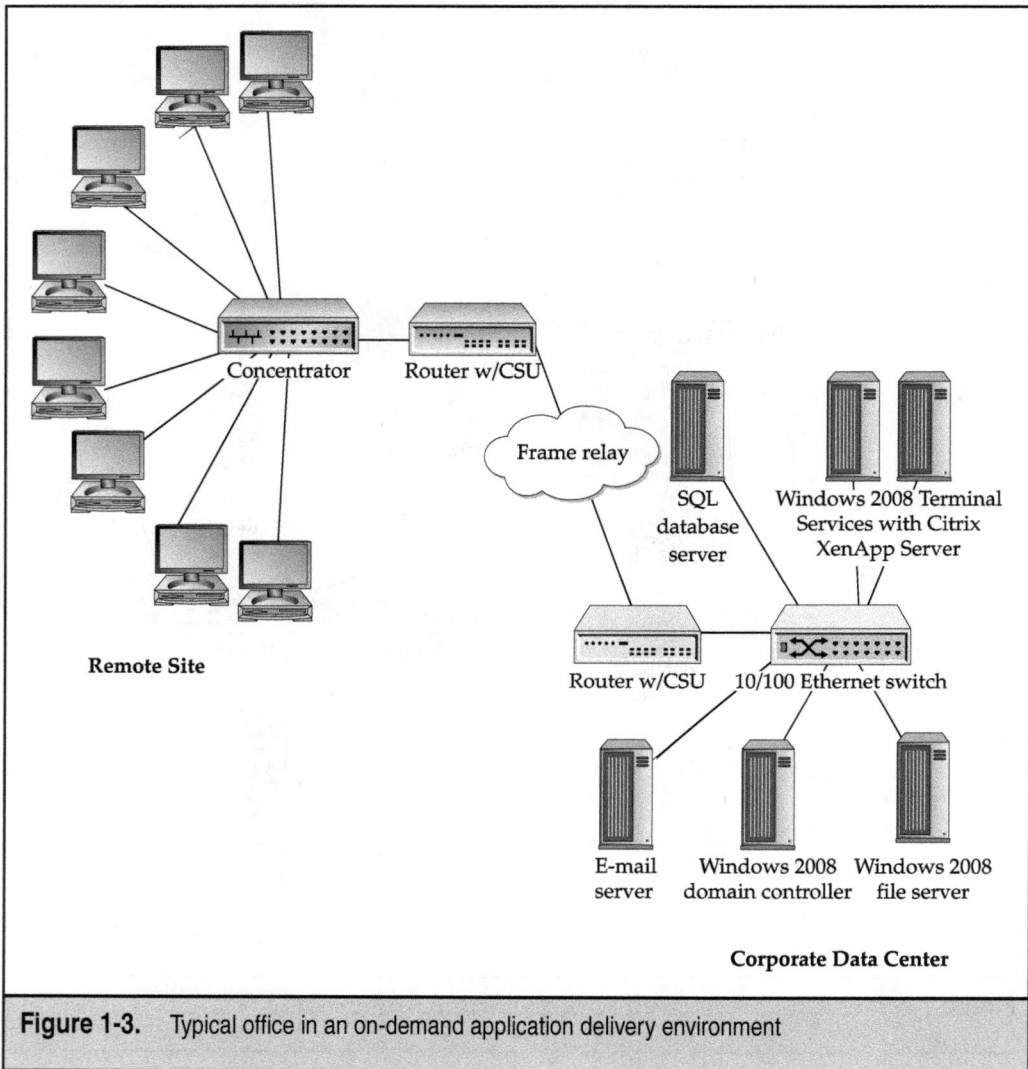

Figure 1-3. Typical office in an on-demand application delivery environment

Topologies

PCs increasingly require faster LAN bandwidth of 2, 4, or even gigabit switching to every desktop. Users of PCs and Windows terminals operating Citrix XenApp see only low-bandwidth screen prints. Although a fast server backbone is a must, legacy topologies of older Ethernet can typically continue to be used to connect workstations with no degradation in performance.

Windows Server 2008 Migration

An on-demand access environment typically simplifies Active Directory design and implementation by eliminating the requirement for remote office servers. When PC users access their desktop via Citrix Application Delivery Infrastructure, they see the same interface that they would when running Windows applications locally (assuming they are not viewing their applications published through a browser). When client-side application virtualization is used, the applications run locally with an identical experience to traditional desktops. This means that an organization can essentially upgrade all of their users to the latest version of Windows without upgrading (or in some cases even touching) a single desktop.

Exchange 2008 Migration

An application delivery infrastructure simplifies Exchange 2008 design and implementation by eliminating the requirement for remote office Exchange servers and the associated replication with headquarters. This enables users around the enterprise to all utilize a centralized Exchange server (or clustered servers) in the data center.

Application Management

Management applications are often utilized to push-install new applications to desktops. These packages tend both to be expensive and to require significant administration resources because the changes do not happen in real time. They also typically do not enable the distribution of certain applications such as new operating systems, and they still depend on the individual PCs having the processing and memory capabilities to adequately run the new applications.

An on-demand application delivery platform reduces the requirement to push applications to the desktop. Because applications can be streamed to the desktop in real time or virtualized on Presentation Servers, processing shifts to the central server farm. Because the emphasis shifts from the desktop as an application source to the data center, asset management can also be made easier. Also, it is much easier to track true IT expenses rather than having them hidden in various cost centers, such as individual expense accounts and remote office contractor costs.

The administration tools of Citrix Application Delivery Infrastructure enable administrators to produce reports showing application usage by user and by access method, including the time online as well as server resources consumed. This can be used to help facilitate compliance with federal regulations such as HIPAA, CJIS, and others to enable billing by resources utilized, or potentially even to reduce licensing fees for some software manufacturers. Network management with Citrix Application Delivery is covered in Chapter 6.

Business Pillars Driving On-demand Application Delivery

Citrix Application Delivery Suite and Microsoft Windows Terminal Services enabled us to reduce our transaction time for our primary advertising order-entry application from minutes to seconds for our remote users. Furthermore, Citrix allowed us to quickly extend our headquarters IT capabilities to our remote offices for a fraction of the cost required if we had chosen an alternative deployment method.

—Jonathan Hiller, CIO,
San Francisco Chronicle

Early "killer" applications that people just couldn't do without, such as VisiCalc and desktop publishing, drove the initial sale of PCs and Macs. Today, we are seeing applications similarly driving the march into enterprise application delivery infrastructure. An organization's existing PCs, for example, may be inadequate to run a popular application such as Microsoft Office 2007. Rather than spending the huge amounts of money and labor required to upgrade or replace existing PCs, an organization can implement Citrix XenApp Platinum Edition and simply publish the Office 2007 icon to all users.

Enterprise Resource Planning (ERP) and Customer Resource Management (CRM) applications such as SAP, PeopleSoft, Oracle Enterprise One, and Siebel can typically be deployed much less expensively and more effectively utilizing on-demand access. This was the case for California's Contra Costa County. When the Department of Information Technology received a mandate to implement PeopleSoft for the county's 360 human resources (HR) users, the county was faced with replacing many dumb terminals and upgrading most of the remaining PCs. They also would have had to apply expensive bandwidth upgrades to 60 different buildings. Instead, the county set up a XenApp farm to deploy PeopleSoft, Kronos Time & Billing, Microsoft Office, Lotus Notes, and other applications to all HR users without requiring any PC or bandwidth upgrades. Windows terminals replaced the dumb terminals and the low-end PCs.

Application Deployment

The ability to rapidly deploy applications to all users through web applications, server- or client-side virtualized applications, or virtual desktops throughout the enterprise enables organizations to provide faster responses to their customers or bring new products to market more quickly.

Universal Access

Citrix Application Delivery enables information, via web and Windows applications or remote desktops, to be delivered through a browser-based interface. It enables users to quickly access all the information and applications they need to execute their job responsibilities. This single point of access, and the bringing together of information in new ways, enables users to draw new conclusions and work smarter. Citrix Application Delivery enables users to enjoy the rich client interfaces native to their applications delivered over the Web, and integrated with the other resources they need. This topic is covered more thoroughly in Chapter 13.

Single Point Access to Multiple Server Farms

Citrix Application Delivery Suite enables highly scaled application provisioning by aggregating application sets from multiple farms in the Application Hub. Users need only to authenticate with their ID and password once in order to access both XenApp for Windows and Citrix for UNIX applications from multiple server farms. This topic is covered more thoroughly in Chapter 5.

Collaboration

The delegated administration features of Citrix Application Delivery enable users to work together on documents with different access rights, depending on their authorization, no matter where they are located. A sales manager, for example, might collaborate with a networking consultant and a salesperson to finish up a Word document late at night when all three are working from home.

Embracing Corporate Standards

With an application delivery infrastructure, control of applications and the desktop shifts from the user to the IT staff, making it relatively effortless to implement corporate software standards. This reduces inefficiencies resulting from data-sharing problems and helps to eliminate duplication of work. It also enables IT to present a common user interface, whether Windows or browser based.

Unlicensed Software

A PC-based computing environment can expose an organization to large fines because of the difficulty of preventing unlicensed software use. Even worse, the corporate information is much more susceptible to loss or to theft because it is stored on hard drives of individual PCs and servers distributed throughout the enterprise. With server-side application virtualization, all the corporate information is housed in corporate data centers, where it is secure, managed, backed up, and redundant.

Eliminating Games and Other Personal Programs

If desired, IT can completely eliminate the ability to load games or other productivity-sapping personal programs.

Reducing Virus Risk

Eliminating or restricting users' ability to add software via their local floppy or onto their local hard drive means that the network antivirus software should eliminate most computer virus problems. Centralizing all access into the network enables IT to implement measures that can virtually eliminate the threat of macro viruses. This topic is discussed more thoroughly as part of Chapter 8 on security.

Helping to Prevent Theft of Intellectual Property

Because users see only screen prints of data, IT can more easily prevent employees from copying corporate information files. This can be important in staffing industries, for example, where applicant databases constitute the company assets and are frequent targets of theft by dishonest employees.

Eliminating the PC as a Status Symbol

Identical performance for everyone means that the PC loses its value as an organizational status symbol. The *personal* computer becomes the *corporate* computer. This eliminates the common, and very inefficient, tendency to shuffle PCs between users as new units are introduced.

Employees in remote offices often feel like the company's "stepchildren." They frequently do not get access to the same level of support and services as headquarters users, let alone access to essential databases such as ERP or CRM applications.

An application delivery infrastructure gives remote office users the same capabilities as they have when sitting in the main office. On-demand application delivery through a corporate WAN or a Secure Access Gateway makes remote office employees more effective because they can see "their" desktop no matter which PC or Windows terminal they use and no matter where they use it. They have access to their data whether at home or at a hotel across the world.

Users at remote offices are more productive because on-demand access enables them to access not only the corporate databases, but also the same network services—such as e-mail, color printing, and network faxing—as headquarters users.

Security

In a PC-based computing environment, the corporate information is susceptible to loss or to theft when it is stored on hard drives of individual PCs and servers distributed throughout the enterprise. An application delivery infrastructure enables all corporate information and virtual desktops to be housed in corporate data centers where it is secure, managed, backed up, and redundant. Network entry points to the central data center(s) are limited, thereby reducing the vulnerability that accompanies access to the corporate network through servers located in remote offices. Security is addressed more thoroughly in Chapter 8.

> *TIP:* Here is an important question to ask when comparing Citrix Application Delivery with traditional PC-based computing: Do you want your corporate data sitting on hard drives of individual PCs and servers distributed throughout your enterprise, or do you want it all to reside at your corporate data center, where it is protected, backed up, redundant, and managed in a secure environment?

Messaging

Citrix Application Delivery enables consolidation of e-mail servers at the data center, thereby eliminating the requirement for remote servers and replication. Data consolidation also makes it much easier to manage and access the data store.

Network Faxing

Citrix Application Delivery Infrastructure vastly reduces the cost of implementing a network fax solution by enabling fax servers to be consolidated in the data center rather than distributed to remote offices. Most fax server products, such as industry leader Captaris RightFax, are designed to run with Terminal Services and with XenApp. Employees can thus send faxes from their PCs and receive incoming faxes as e-mail attachments whether at headquarters, at a remote office, or at home working through the Internet.

Facilitating Growth

On-demand access enables faster organizational growth by making it easy either to open remote offices or to assimilate offices of acquired companies into an organization's electronic information system. Servers do not need to be configured and set up in the remote offices. Users need only low-bandwidth connectivity to the data center, and IT can then publish application icons to their desktops.

Eliminating Theft of PCs

When organizations utilize Windows terminals instead of desktops and laptops, they remove the attraction for thieves to steal the devices, because they are both inexpensive and useless without being connected to the secure Citrix environment.

Workforce Mobility

Citrix solutions extend access to a company's networked resources beyond the traditional office environment—to anywhere, on any device, over any connection, including wireless devices such as PDAs, smart phones, and tablet PCs. The low bandwidth requirements of Citrix Application Delivery often make wireless connectivity practical without rewriting applications or implementing expensive infrastructure upgrades, and without compromising security.

Telecommuting

With Citrix Application Delivery, users see only screen prints of applications, or virtual desktops, and the screen prints use very little bandwidth. Employees can effectively telecommute by coming in securely through the Internet utilizing the VPN components of the Citrix Access Gateway. A cable modem or DSL connection will often enable speeds equivalent to those obtained when using a fat-client PC at headquarters.

IT Flexibility

Citrix Application Delivery gives IT departments flexibility in terms of adopting an application strategy without concern for developing a corresponding desktop deployment strategy. For instance, IT departments can purchase PCs or laptops without worrying about whether they will have the power and capacity to adequately operate a new set of unknown future applications. Even a seemingly simple task such as upgrading a companywide browser version changes from a very time-consuming and expensive endeavor to a nonissue.

Business Continuity/Disaster Recovery

The majority of businesses that suffer a catastrophe such as a fire or flood are, as a result, out of business within two years.

—The Meta Group

A PC-based computing environment has limited redundancy. A catastrophe at headquarters can leave hundreds or thousands of employees unable to do their work. Failure of a server in a remote office can mean a day or more of downtime until a replacement unit can be secured and installed. On-demand access makes it easily affordable to build redundancy into the corporate data center. Citrix Application Delivery Suite 4 furthermore includes server farm failover utilization of redundant data centers. If the primary data center should fail, users can automatically be redirected to a secondary data center and continue working. If a disaster at headquarters or a remote office leads to displaced workers, they can securely access their applications or virtual desktops and data remotely over the Internet from alternative locations—including their homes. This enables much better continuity protection for all headquarters and remote office users than is practical in a PC-based computing environment. Disaster recovery and business continuance are covered in Chapter 8.

Network downtime is also reduced. In fact, because server-side application virtualization and virtual desktop users are dependent on a network, continuous uptime is mandatory. Fortunately, the efficiencies of an on-demand access environment and the centralization of resources enable organizations to build extremely robust, reliable, and redundant network infrastructures.

Other Benefits of Application Delivery Infrastructure

In addition to the enormous economic and business justifications for an application delivery infrastructure, there are also positive environmental and regulation compliance benefits.

Supporting the Environment

The rapidly declining prices of new, more powerful PC models are increasing the rate of PC obsolescence while simultaneously making it difficult to give old units away. Over 100,000 tons of old PCs are junked each year. Disposing of them in a landfill can cause lead, mercury, and cadmium to leach into the soil. Incinerating them can release heavy metals and dioxin into the atmosphere. Virtualizing applications and desktops extends the lives of PCs and often enables their replacement with long-lasting Windows terminals.

Complying with Government Regulation

Regulations such as HIPAA, Sarbanes-Oxley, California Senate Bill 1386, No Child Left Behind Act, and others have enormous implications for the way organizations conduct business. The information security aspects of these acts demand that organizations re-think their IT infrastructures, particularly whether or not they can afford the liability that is an inherent part of a distributed PC architecture. The Citrix Application Delivery platform can ensure compliance through a "secure by design" network architecture and granular control of enterprise resource access based on user, device, location, and network connection. Information is controlled automatically by determining whether users may download, edit, print, or preview documents The likelihood of sloppy password management causing security breaches is reduced, while application access and password change events are all tracked.

Application Delivery Platform Concerns

When considering the implementation of enterprise server-side application delivery, it is important to address concerns about network infrastructure reliability and single points of failure. We have also discussed application virtualization as if the only option were to utilize both Microsoft Terminal Services and Citrix XenApp. We need to address concerns about using only these technologies.

Network Unreliability

Enterprise application delivery may be a new concept for your organization, but it is dependent on your existing network infrastructure. It is senseless to take on an application delivery infrastructure project unless your organization is willing to make the necessary investment to bring your network infrastructure up to an extremely reliable and stable condition.

A history of network unreliability may have created the perceptions that users require their own departmental servers or must keep applications on their local hard drives to enable continued productivity in the event of network failure. In reality, users are becoming so dependent on network applications, such as e-mail and browsing, that network failure means a loss of productivity in any case. Beyond this misperception, it is more prudent to spend a smaller amount of corporate resources building a redundant and reliable network than it is to devote a large amount of resources to maintaining an extremely inefficient PC-based contingency plan.

Citrix Application Delivery saves so much money on the client side that organizations should have the financial resources required to build world-class data centers and network infrastructures. Alternatively, they can utilize the infrastructures already in place at already-established telecommunications or hosting companies. This option also generally makes it easier to utilize an existing data backbone to provide a secondary backup data center.

Single Point of Failure

Concentrating all your former PC-based computing into a central data center leaves your remote offices, in particular, exposed to potential downtime risks that they formerly did not face. These risks can be mitigated by building reliability and redundancy into the data center that go well beyond anything the remote offices could do on their own. Establishing a secondary redundant data center enables remote offices to continue working through virtualized applications, desktops, or web applications, even in the event of a major catastrophe at the main production data center. In a PC-based computing environment, the remote offices are extremely unlikely to have access to a redundant "hot site" that could enable their users to keep working should their own server setup meet with disaster. Finally, redundant bandwidth connections should be implemented to enable at least key remote-office employees to keep working in the event of a communications failure. These topics are discussed more thoroughly in Chapters 3, 5, and 8.

Everything Is Going Web-Based Anyway

Software manufacturers are increasingly writing web-based interfaces to their applications. The reality, though, is that it is still difficult to create a rich interface in a web application. Most users prefer the dynamic and robust Windows interface to the static web server HTML interface. Additionally, a browser requires a deceptively fat client in order to accommodate complex Java scripts and browser plug-ins. The browser, in fact, becomes an application that must itself be managed along with various plug-ins. This is complicated further by the use of embedded objects and client-side scripting as well as by applications that call other "helper applications" such as Microsoft Word, Excel, and Outlook. They may require specific versions of these helper applications in order to operate properly.

If the client-side browser is used to access business-critical information and applications, then security of the browser also becomes a concern. IT needs to develop methodologies for installing the numerous IE security updates and for locking down the browser and ActiveX controls.

When certain organizations are pressed as to why they would prefer web-based applications, the reasoning is typically to lower total cost of ownership, to centralize application deployment, to simplify and enable cross-platform application access, to enable faster application deployment times, and to lower maintenance at the desktop. But Terminal Server and Citrix XenApp provide all those benefits today with legacy Windows applications, thereby avoiding the huge expense and time involved in rewriting them for the Web.

Citrix provides the NetScaler product to deliver and accelerate web applications when they are used. Additionally, when web applications are utilized, it still typically makes sense from an administrative perspective to deploy them securely via Citrix Access Gateway, with the browser hosted on the XenApp farms. Because a web application generally utilizes some combination of HTML/XML, client-side scripting, server-side scripting, and embedded controls to send data to the client device, deploying it via XenApp can help alleviate bandwidth concerns. It is not uncommon for organizations to find significant improvements in performance by running the browser within a Citrix session rather than directly on the client workstation.

Citrix is committed to deploying all applications effectively through an on-demand access environment. While not part of XenApp Platinum Edition, Citrix NetScaler complements it by optimizing the delivery of mission-critical web applications.

It makes more sense to implement an application delivery infrastructure that will work for both Windows and web-based applications than it does to continue investing in a bloated PC-based architecture that is inefficient today and that will be even more inefficient in the future.

Microsoft Is Going to Make Citrix Obsolete

Server-based computing is great. It's happening. It's part of our strategy.

—Steve Ballmer, Microsoft CEO,
Wall Street Journal,
July 21, 1999

Microsoft is very supportive of Citrix and is a Premier Plus member of the Citrix Business Alliance. Microsoft recognizes that Citrix drives an enormous amount of Microsoft software sales by freeing up customer economic and staffing resources for investment in its suite of .NET server products—in fact, Microsoft named Citrix the 2008 ISV Partner of the Year. Whereas Microsoft Terminal Server provides the base for an application infrastructure, Citrix XenApp Platinum is the enabling technology. Citrix supplies the capabilities required and expected of an enterprise solution. These capabilities include versatility, usability, scalability, and manageability, along with enhanced security. The value that Citrix XenApp Platinum Edition adds to Terminal Services is discussed more thoroughly in Chapter 2.

Although the cost of Citrix software is not insignificant, it pales in comparison to the savings that will be realized from implementing an enterprise application delivery infrastructure. Such a solution is a serious and complex undertaking utilizing relatively new technology on constantly changing platforms. It is imperative that sacrifices not be made in the quality of the data center and networking infrastructure. This is also true for the Citrix XenApp component. Delaying the decision to implement application delivery infrastructure access in order to see what the future may bring means the continuation of huge unnecessary expenditures in the present.

COMPONENTS OF AN APPLICATION DELIVERY INFRASTRUCTURE

An on-demand application delivery infrastructure has three major components: one or more data centers, clients (at both headquarters and remote offices and possibly at home offices), and wide area network connectivity.

Data Center

The data center is the heart of an enterprise application delivery platform. Not only are most applications and corresponding data hosted in the data center, but in server-side application and desktop virtualization environments, 100 percent of the hosted application processing occurs within the data center as well. The major data center components include the XenApp farm, virtual desktop servers, file servers and/or network-attached storage (NAS) or storage area network (SAN) systems, other application servers, host systems, a fast server backbone, and a backup system. Figure 1-4 shows a sample data center running an enterprise application delivery environment.

XenApp Farm

Server-side virtual application execution occurs on servers running Microsoft 2008 Terminal Services and Citrix XenApp or Citrix XenDesktop when virtual desktops are being run. Because of the high demands made on these servers, and to satisfy basic high availability practices, it is prudent to utilize at least two load-balanced servers at all times. The XenApp load-balancing software is recommended over other solutions because of its sophisticated ability to share server resources while providing good redundancy. If a user should be disconnected from the server, when they log back in, XenApp load-balancing software will find the server in the farm where the user's session is running and reconnect them to it. Note that data is never stored on the XenApp servers. Data is always stored on back-end file servers, application servers, NAS systems, or SAN systems.

File Servers

The file servers run a network operating system such as Windows Server 2008 or Novell. The servers feed files to the XenApp farm, maintain directory services, and sometimes handle printing functions. For larger Citrix implementations, a separate high-end print server should be dedicated to handle the printing function, as described in Chapter 16.

Storage Area Networks and Network-Attached Storage Systems

A storage area network (SAN) is created when host servers access remote block storage using SCSI commands encapsulated in a networked protocol. The two commonly used SAN transport protocols are Fiber Channel (FC) and iSCSI, which encapsulate SCSI commands in the Ethernet protocol. Configurations can include clustered file servers, RAID arrays connected through a controlling server, or any storage scheme that relies on a host to pass data and control traffic. Windows Server 2008 includes links to SAN technology built into the file system, making it easier than ever to build a large-scale storage network. A network-attached storage (NAS) device is a disk array that connects directly to a network via a LAN interface such as Ethernet or FDDI. Popular SAN and NAS devices include products by companies such as Hewlett-Packard, IBM, Pillar Data, and EMC. Either SAN or NAS enable very fast data access, and many models have storage capacity measured in terabytes. Because most, if not all, of the organization's data will be hosted in the data center, such a storage scheme is often essential. In some application delivery architectures, a SAN or NAS will supplement the file servers, allowing organizations to store and access large amounts of data more efficiently. In others, the SAN or NAS may

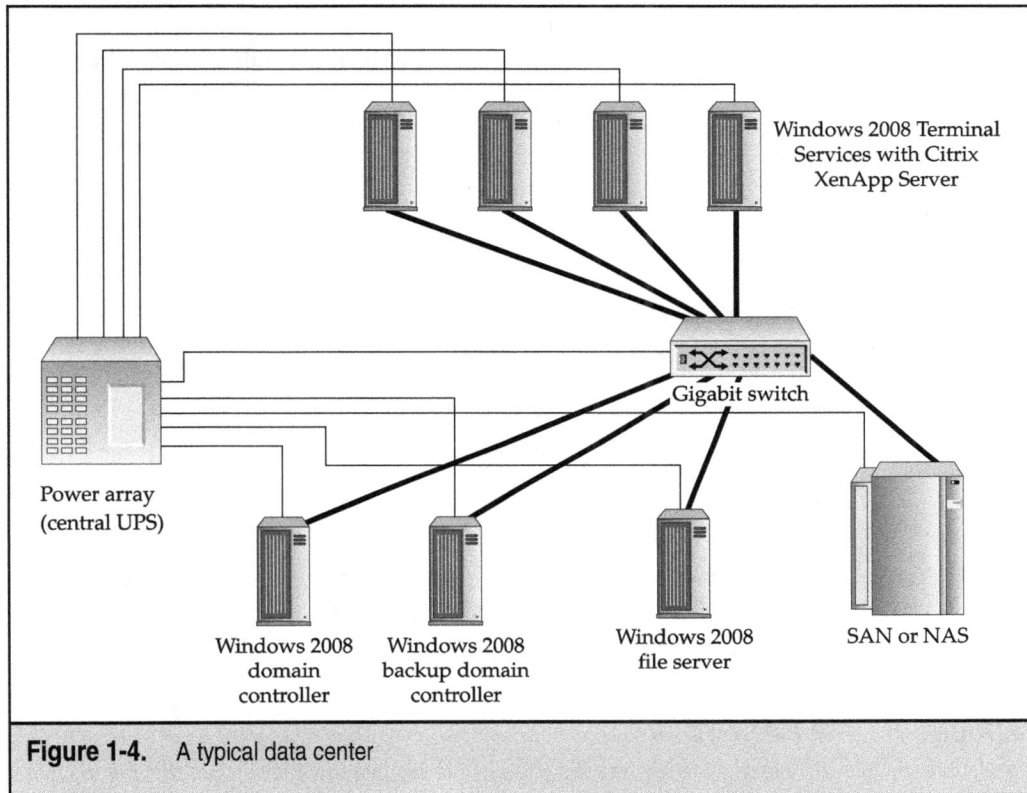

Figure 1-4.   A typical data center

take the place of clustered back-end file servers and still provide mainframe-like reliability and redundancy along with superior performance and scalability. The best solution for your organization depends on both your application environment and your user file-sharing needs. This topic is discussed more thoroughly in Chapter 4.

Application Servers

The rule of thumb is to have your XenApp farm located wherever your data is stored. Therefore, e-mail servers, SQL database servers, and all other application servers ideally should be located within the data center. At a minimum, they must be connected to the file servers and XenApp farm through a very fast backbone. The XenApp farm hosts virtual applications for server execution or streaming to desktops. Virtual desktops can be hosted and accessed through the ICA protocol using the Citrix XenDesktop Server. While users see only screen prints of the applications or desktop at their workstations or Windows terminals, real data is traveling back and forth between the XenApp farm and the file servers and application servers. An inadequate server backbone will cause an immediate data traffic jam that will result in performance degradation for all users. Application servers, including print servers, are covered more thoroughly in Chapters 4, 13, and 16.

Host Systems

Mainframe and minicomputer systems should be housed in the data center, where they can be managed along with the Terminal Services hosting infrastructure. This enables organizations to leverage both their data center environmental resources and their support staffs.

Server Backbone

A very fast backbone should connect the XenApp farm, the back-end file servers, and all other servers in the data center. This backbone should be either switched gigabit Ethernet, FDDI, or ATM. As with all data center components, a redundant server backbone is desirable. This topic is discussed more thoroughly in Chapter 6.

Backup System

A backup system should enable automatic backups of all servers. Tapes should be rotated off-site or data replicated off-site.

Security

Application delivery enables enhanced security by centralizing data and network access. It is still essential to design and implement an enterprise security strategy. Third-party applications, firewalls, VPNs, identity management, and authentication are some of the measures to consider. This topic is discussed more thoroughly in Chapter 6.

Number of Data Centers

The number of data centers utilized depends on many variables, including bandwidth availability as well as business and geographic segregation. For instance, if a corporation's European operations utilize entirely different software than the U.S. businesses, and bandwidth is expensive between the continents, separate data centers make more sense than a single, central one. In general, though, savings will be greater when data centers are fewer. This is a result of the economies of scale realized by centralizing as much application delivery, hardware, software, and administration labor as possible. This topic is covered in Chapter 4.

Disaster Recovery/Business Continuity

A single data center, despite internal redundancy, leaves a corporation's headquarters and remote operations vulnerable to a single point of failure. One strategy for mitigating this risk is to utilize multiple data centers with failover capabilities. Another strategy is to use one corporate data center and then contract with a disaster-recovery provider to maintain a geographically distant facility that mirrors the XenApp farm and other crucial components of the corporate data center. This topic is discussed more thoroughly in Chapter 8.

Clients

Application delivery users will often work at headquarters, at remote offices, and at home. At times, they will be in hotels or at customer sites. They will utilize PCs, laptops,

Windows terminals, tablets, and handheld devices. Increasingly, they will use specialty display devices that incorporate the Citrix ICA protocol to take advantage of the inexpensive computing capabilities provided by Citrix Application Delivery. Clients are covered in Chapters 5, 14, and 15.

Personal Computers

PC users can access applications hosted at the data center in multiple ways. When PCs have a full-time connection to the data center (through Ethernet frame relay or the Internet), XenApp enables application publishing. Employees see icons of both local applications (if any) and applications hosted on the XenApp farm to which they have access. These icons can be part of their start-up file, and it is not obvious whether they represent local applications or applications hosted by the server farm. Users who run all applications from the server farm may receive their entire desktop as a published application. The lower the number of local applications accessed by a PC user, the less administration costs are borne by the IT staff. This topic is discussed more thoroughly in Chapters 5 and 14.

Laptops

Laptops typically run client-side virtualized applications when connected or disconnected from the network. When connected to the network by any connection, their cached applications and license information can be updated. An application delivery environment providing applications virtualized on both the client and the server often result in users abandoning laptops except when on planes or in motels. They find it less cumbersome to simply use a PC or Windows terminal both at the office and at home.

Windows Terminals

Nearly every major PC manufacturer, along with many specialty companies, now makes Windows terminals. Figure 1-5 shows one of the many models of Wyse Windows terminals. Windows terminals are typically display devices with no moving parts of any kind. Some models, such as one manufactured by Wyse, have no local operating system and boot right to the Citrix ICA client. Others utilize Windows CE, a version of Windows NT, or even Linux. Some models such as those by Wyse and Hewlett-Packard include a version of embedded Windows XP for running local browsers. Windows terminals typically have built-in local host emulation, and sometimes browsing, in order to offload these character display functions from the XenApp farm. Some manufacturers also have wireless devices that enable users to access their complete desktop remotely.

Because Windows terminals often have mean times between failure measured in decades, their maintenance expense is extremely low. If a Windows terminal does fail, IT simply delivers a replacement unit to the user. The user plugs in the Windows terminal, turns it on, and sees their desktop. Windows terminals significantly reduce the cost of supporting telecommuters. Unlike PCs, Windows terminals do not allow users to destroy their unit configuration by loading games or screensavers or other potentially damaging software. This makes the Windows terminal a particularly ideal device for telecommuters who may have families that like to share any personal computers in the home. Windows terminals are discussed more thoroughly in Chapter 5.

Figure 1-5.   Wireless Neoware Windows terminal

Other ICA Clients

Most UNIX workstations and Macintoshes can access XenApp servers by running the Citrix ICA client. Many wireless handheld units such as Blackberry, Windows Mobile, and Palm-based devices are capable of running an ICA client.

Increasingly, expect to see manufacturers come up with specialty ICA devices. For instance, a time clock system could be built as a Windows terminal using buttons instead of a keyboard. Employee time stamping could then be directly entered into the corporation's Windows-based time and billing system. Client configuration is covered in Chapter 14.

Application Access Through the Internet

As the Internet's pervasiveness continues to grow, more organizations prefer to utilize browser interfaces. The Citrix Access Gateway component of Citrix XenApp Platinum Edition provides a secure, always-on, single point of access to all applications and protocols. It has all the advantages of both IPSec and SSL VPNs, without their costly and cumbersome implementation and management. With the Advanced Access Control option, Citrix Application Access Gateway finely controls both what enterprise resource can be accessed and what actions can be performed. This topic is discussed more thoroughly in Chapter 16.

Wide Area Network Connectivity

XenApp requires between 10KB and 20KB of bandwidth per user session. This does not include additional bandwidth for large print jobs or for downloading or uploading files to and from a local PC. When remote office applications are hosted at a corporate data center, they are completely dependent on access to the XenApp servers for all of their processing. An application delivery architecture must include both adequate and reliable bandwidth connections along with redundant contingencies.

A frame-relay circuit has traditionally been the most popular method to provide connectivity to multiple remote offices, though organizations increasingly utilize MPLS, virtual private networks, or straight Internet connectivity. Telecommuters, in particular, are using inexpensive fixed-fee Internet accounts to connect to corporate data centers. Bandwidth management is often desirable in order to prioritize ICA traffic. Bandwidth management devices such as Citrix's WANScaler will prevent a user's large print job or file download, for example, from killing performance for the remaining users at a remote office. Regional headquarters and certain remote offices may be too large to gain an economic advantage by centralizing their servers at a corporate data center. This is particularly true if the number of users is large enough that they require their own servers regardless of location. Utilizing software applications largely independent of those used at headquarters is another reason for not centralizing servers. In these cases, it is often more practical to have regional XenApp farms. A common corporate database application, such as an ERP package, can still run off the XenApp servers at the corporate data center. The regional offices can access this application by running the corporate ICA session within their own ICA session. This topic is discussed more thoroughly in Chapter 14.

DESIGNING AN ENTERPRISE APPLICATION DELIVERY ARCHITECTURE

A successful enterprise application delivery implementation depends on a comprehensive project design. A detailed and in-depth plan needs to address all aspects of the application delivery migration, including data centers, disaster recovery, bandwidth, systems management, policies and procedures, security, applications, migration strategies, clients, and support. Unanticipated problems will occur even with the best-laid plans. Diligent work up front, though, will minimize any potential for big disasters and help ensure a successful implementation.

Windows 2008 Terminal Services is far more desirable and stable than a distributed PC-based computing environment, but PC users are often particularly unforgiving of problems because they are initially reluctant to give up the "personal" part of their personal computers.

The considerable technical and cultural challenges make in-depth project planning absolutely essential to a successful application delivery implementation. The first step is to set up a proof-of-concept pilot to ensure that the crucial applications will run acceptably on Presentation Server. Next, assemble a project planning team to prepare a project definition document. The definition document will include the project goals, scope, roles, risks, success criteria, and milestones. The third step involves a comprehensive infrastructure assessment that will both ensure support for an enterprise application delivery implementation and enable a meaningful planning process. Finally, a comprehensive design plan for migrating from locally installed PC-based applications to an application delivery environment will serve as a roadmap for the project managers and implementation teams. These steps are covered more thoroughly in Chapter 3.

CHAPTER 2

Citrix XenApp— Features and Technology

Citrix XenApp, formerly known as Citrix Presentation Server (the Presentation Server nomenclature will remain with version 4.5 and all previous versions), is an application delivery system that offers client-side and server-side application virtualization. Application virtualization provides for the delivery of secure applications as a service. Today, XenApp (and its predecessor Presentation Server) serves over 100 million users at 200,000 customers worldwide, facilitating application delivery with a seamless and secure user experience in complex and heterogeneous computing environments with an endless variety of applications, access scenarios, and network scenarios. Citrix XenApp runs with Windows Server 2003 and 2008 as well as a variety of UNIX flavors.

XENAPP AND MICROSOFT WINDOWS TERMINAL SERVICES

The first question that everyone seems to be asking is, "Do we still need Citrix now that Windows Server 2008 is out?" Although it is a relevant question, it is not new, as many people posed similar questions after the releases of Windows Server 2000 and Windows Server 2003. Then, just as now, the answer is, "Probably, but it depends." This section will address this question. Microsoft has made significant feature progress with Windows Server 2008 (compared with Windows Server 2003), but Information Technology and end-user expectations have continued to evolve as well, and Citrix has built a reputation around building cutting-edge solutions to enable IT departments to keep up with the ever-increasing complexity.

Simple or Complex IT Environments

Microsoft Windows Terminal Services is the underlying platform for the Windows version of Citrix XenApp. Windows Terminal Services provides excellent base-level functionality designed for low-complexity environments. Terminal Services is designed for low-complexity environments that have

▼ A few well-behaved applications accessed by a common group of users.

■ Smaller deployments of up to three to five servers.

■ A high-speed network with low latency, such as a LAN.

▲ Homogenous Windows Server and Windows client environments on the latest versions.

Although we often correlate complexity with the number of users, even small deployments can be complex in nature, and thus benefit from XenApp. Here are some typical challenges the administrator of a complex environment face:

▼ The need to provide instant, easy, and secure access to applications across the organization

■ Meeting the end-user demand for a consistent access experience to information

- Reducing the complexity of delivering and maintaining applications
- Supporting incompatible applications and multiple types of devices
▲ Increasing data security and controlling access to business information

XenApp's Five Primary Areas of Extending Microsoft Windows Terminal Services

Citrix XenApp extends Windows Terminal Services by adding value in five main areas to address complex, business-critical environments. The illustration and descriptions show how Citrix XenApp and Terminal Services work together:

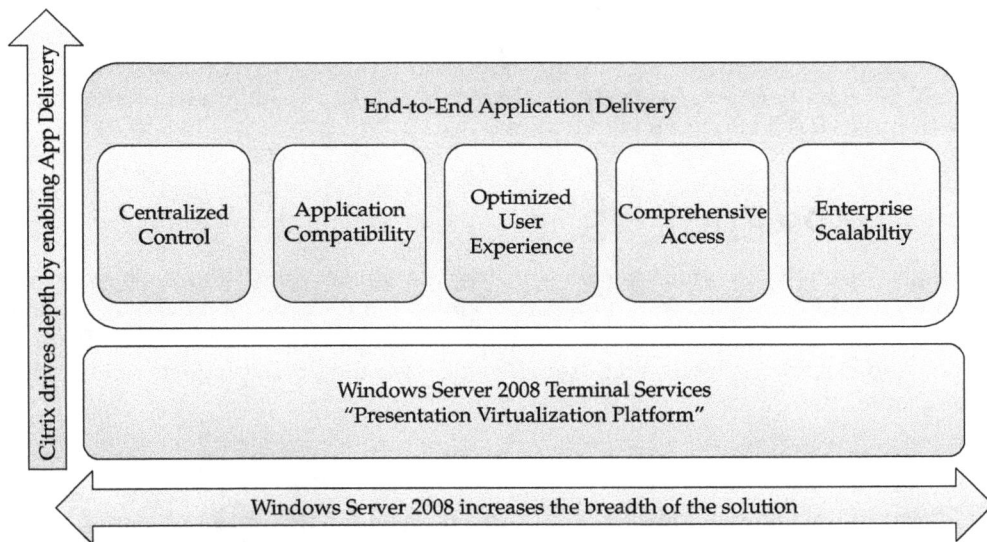

▼ **Centralized control**   Centralized management and monitoring tools put IT organizations in control of their application delivery infrastructure. The result is more control, less downtime, and a better user experience.

- **Application compatibility**   Citrix XenApp addresses the needs of today's heterogeneous IT environments with technologies that ensure applications can work together in a secure manner on a variety of OS platforms. Application virtualization technologies allow the IT administrator to control where and how applications are deployed to provide the best access experience for the end user.

- **Optimized user experience**   IT organizations need to support and manage a wide range of client-attached devices, network types, and access scenarios while still providing users with the best usability and performance available. Citrix XenApp provides a set of technologies that provide significant productivity and performance enhancements for server-based applications. This results in higher user satisfaction and eased support requirements for IT.

- ■ **Comprehensive access**   Citrix XenApp is designed to integrate with the existing IT infrastructure and provides support for a wide variety of client platforms—including Windows, UNIX, Macintosh, Java, and many common mobile platforms. Built-in policy management provides the control IT administrators need to ensure that technologies are not abused by users, but rather allow the appropriate level of access.

- ▲ **Enterprise scalability**   Citrix XenApp enhances Terminal Services with a set of mature and easy-to-use management and monitoring tools and industry-leading performance technologies.

Appendix A contains a chart comparing the features of Windows Server Terminal Services 2003 (without XenApp), Windows Server 2008 Terminal Services (without XenApp), and the features that XenApp adds to both versions of Windows Server Terminal Services. Although Microsoft has made significant strides with Windows Server 2008 Terminal Services, it is obvious from the chart that XenApp is still critical for both complex enterprise and complex small environments.

CITRIX XENAPP EDITIONS

As was the case with previous versions of Presentation Server, Citrix XenApp is available in three editions—Platinum, Enterprise, and Advanced (previous versions also included the Standard edition, which is no longer available). The Enterprise and Platinum editions also include the UNIX platform. We will cover the UNIX platform in detail later in this chapter.

XenApp for XenDesktop

In addition to the generally available XenApp packages, Citrix released a new version of XenApp in May 2008 specifically designed to run in conjunction with XenDesktop, logically named XenApp for XenDesktop. XenDesktop is Citrix's Desktop Virtualization Delivery solution that provides virtualization of the desktop (Windows XP or Windows Vista). In early testing, we found that virtualizing the applications (XenApp) separately from the desktop virtualization resulted in 40% better performance overall. So not only will desktop virtualization not replace application virtualization, but we believe that the combination, albeit a virtual mouthful, of XenApp and XenDesktop will be very popular in the years to come.

New Features Available in all Editions of XenApp

The latest version of XenApp offers core technology enhancements and features that are available in all editions, and it introduces industry-first new functionality in the Enterprise and Platinum editions. The core technology enhancements available to all editions of XenApp include the following capabilities:

▼ **Record and report all XenApp configuration changes**   Track changes made to the XenApp farm, by whom, and at what time to simplify and accelerate troubleshooting. Configuration logging is invaluable for auditing and ensuring accountability when multiple administrators are maintaining XenApp servers and applications.

■ **Provide business partners with federated web access to any application**   Citrix has made it easier to extend application access to trusted partners with support for Active Directory Federation Services (ADFS) through XenApp's web interface. No longer is ADFS limited to web applications—now you can provide federated access to any Windows application delivered by XenApp.

■ **Accelerate graphics performance with SpeedScreen Progressive Display**   SpeedScreen dramatically improves the performance and usability of graphics-intensive applications with new Progressive Display technology. You can centrally manage graphics-intensive applications such as CAD (Computer Aided Drawing), healthcare PACS (Picture Archiving and Communication Systems) and GIS mapping applications, while providing the speed and anywhere-access flexibility that users need. Figure 2-1 illustrates graphically and generically how SpeedScreen improves link performance.

■ **Seamlessly join servers into the XenApp farms**   Ensure a consistent user access experience while bringing new servers online. Load throttling automatically adjusts the server load to prevent new servers from overloading when they first join the farm, and then it gradually returns the load to normal.

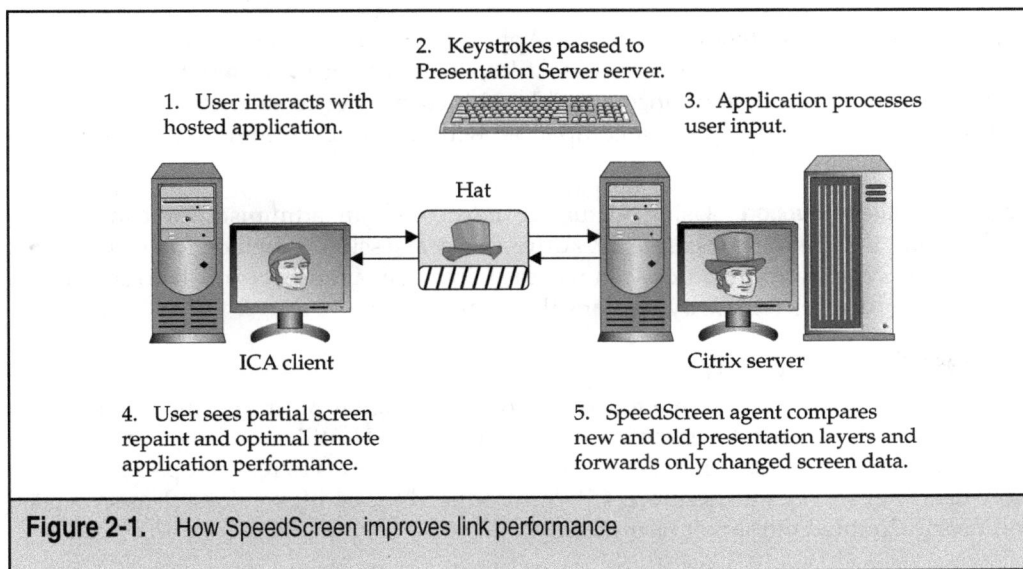

Figure 2-1.   How SpeedScreen improves link performance

- ■ **Provide easy, secure application access from locked-down devices** Eliminate the need to give users "Administrator" privileges in order to install the XenApp client with the Non-Administrator Client Installation feature. This not only makes it easier for users to access virtualized applications from any device, such as kiosks and business centers, but it also eliminates the security and management risks of raising user privileges on their desktops.

- ▲ **Increase security by controlling which servers users can access** Prevent users from accessing unauthorized servers. Similar to Internet Explorer's "trusted websites" feature, Trusted Server Configuration helps lock down environments and increases administrator control.

Quick Review of Previous Enhancements

Although the new features in XenApp are critical, many of the features that Citrix included in the 4.0 release in 2006 remain critical to the success of an Application Delivery Center. As a review, here are some of the feature enhancements that remain core to the solution today (see the previous version of this book, Citrix Access Suite 4.0 for Windows Server 2003: The Official Guide, for more details on Citrix's product history).

Broader Application Support

Many applications were not originally designed for server-based deployment. Some conflict with others when installed on the same server. Some require dedicated IP addresses to run. Citrix released new features, including application isolation environments and virtual IP address support, in 2005 that are critical for success and not available with Terminal Services 2008.

Application Isolation Environment Citrix's Application Isolation Environment provides a virtualized environment for access to files, Registry settings, and named objects, allowing applications that are incompatible with each other to safely run side by side. It allows applications that are not compatible with a multiuser environment to run on Citrix Presentation Server.

Virtual IP Address Support Using virtual IP addresses, an administrator can publish applications that require separate IP addresses per session, whether for technical or licensing reasons. Administrators can use the Citrix management console to set aside a block of IP addresses for use by sessions that require them.

Increased User Density

Organizations continue to strive for lower costs and higher return on their technology investments. Citrix introduced new features such as CPU utilization management and virtual memory optimization in 2005 that allow organizations to realize up to 25 percent more users per server. Furthermore, Citrix introduced the 64-bit version released in 2006 and nearly doubled the server user density.

Improved Printing

Users need to be able to quickly and easily print where they are and leverage the capabilities of new printers. IT needs to reduce network congestion. The Universal Print Driver (UPD) Citrix released in 2005 made printing up to four times faster, while reducing bandwidth and memory, and Citrix continues to improve the technology in the latest XenApp release. Users can use almost any printer and leverage advanced printer functionality such as trays and stapling. Users can more easily print to the closest printer while roaming from device to device, as in a hospital or manufacturing plant.

Citrix XenApp Platinum Edition

Appendix B compares the features of XenApp 4.5 across the Platinum (P), Enterprise (E), and Advanced (A) editions with previous versions of Presentation Server.

For the purposes of this book, we will focus on the Platinum edition, because the other editions are simply subsets of the Platinum edition, and due to attractive pricing and features, a majority of clients are purchasing the Platinum edition today. The following software feature sets are included with XenApp Platinum edition:

▼   Client-side application virtualization

■   Application performance monitoring with EdgeSight

■   Secure remote access with SSL VPN and SmartAccess

■   Strengthened application security with single sign-on

■   Increased regulatory compliance and improved risk management with Smart-Auditor

▲   Integrated communications into applications with EasyCall

Client-side Application Virtualization for Flexible Delivery Options

XenApp provides centralized management of desktop applications, and it provides administrators with the option to isolate applications as well as stream them to users. Isolation and streaming together largely eliminate the historic issues that have nagged application virtualization since its inception by resolving application incompatibility with Terminal Services as well as application incompatibility with other applications on the server. With XenApp, administrators dynamically choose whether to host an application virtually or to stream the application to a user based on the specific user, application, device, and network. You have the flexibility to stream applications to mobile users who need the local CPU resources, require local peripherals, or work offline. Alternatively, for maximum control and security, you can virtualize delivery of applications that access confidential data to the server and execute them in the data center. With the addition of client-side application virtualization, Citrix XenApp is the most flexible and complete end-to-end application delivery system available.

Application Performance Monitoring for Visibility into the Access Experience

The Platinum edition of XenApp includes Citrix EdgeSight software. EdgeSight provides the monitoring and reporting capabilities to enable IT administrators to quickly pinpoint and troubleshoot server, network, and application programming issues that impact the user experience. EdgeSight is a comprehensive application infrastructure that can also integrate into other enterprise management suites such as IBM Tivoli NetView, Hewlett-Packard OpenView, and Computer Associates UniCenter TNG. Chapter 12 of this book is dedicated in its entirety to the topic of EdgeSight.

SmartAccess for Access Security and Control

Powered by the Citrix Access Gateway product line of SSL VPN appliances, the new Access Gateway solution provides SmartAccess granular access control policies and integrated endpoint analysis. Citrix Access Gateway and SmartAccess are discussed later in this chapter and in full depth in Chapter 11.

Single Sign-On for Strongest Application Security

XenApp Platinum includes Citrix Password Manager for single sign-on. With automated application logons, password policy control, and self-service password reset, you can enhance the security of all password-protected Windows and web applications delivered by XenApp. Citrix Password Manager is discussed in depth in Chapter 10.

SmartAuditor for Ensuring Regulatory Compliance and Improving Risk Management

Citrix SmartAuditor, included in XenApp Platinum edition, uses flexible policies to trigger visual recordings of XenApp sessions automatically. IT (with appropriate permissions) can now monitor, record, and examine user activity. Monitoring and recording activity demonstrates internal control, which is a key factor in ensuring regulatory compliance and successful security audits of applications—including financial operations and healthcare patient information systems. SmartAuditor also improves technical support through faster problem identification and time-to-resolution.

EasyCall for Integrating Voice Communications into Applications

EasyCall, included in XenApp Platinum, is powered by the Citrix Communication Gateway and enables users to click on any telephone number, look up anyone in the directory, or just type in a number and make a call using the regular telephone network. Users specify the number EasyCall will call them at before making the outbound call to the desired party.

Health Assistant for Enhanced Reliability

XenApp Platinum also bundles a system resiliency tool called Health Assistant that performs continuous server health checks and automatically initiates recovery procedures, thus minimizing the need for administrator intervention.

Increased Server Performance for Maximum Return on IT Investment

Citrix XenApp Platinum includes CPU management and virtual memory optimization, and it leverages the 64-bit platform to get the maximum number of users on every server. The cumulative effect of all these optimizations has been so significant that Citrix *eLabs* recently demonstrated acceptable performance of 500 users on a single quad core 64-bit server. This dramatic increase in users per server is key to the virtualization revolution, because it significantly reduces hardware acquisition costs, electricity and cooling costs (some organizations estimate that electricity and cooling costs now eclipse the cost of the server itself), and management and maintenance.

Improved User Experience and Faster Graphics Performance

The only way to really comprehend the speed increases (and accompanying bandwidth use decrease) from Citrix's new SpeedScreen Progressive Display technology is to see it firsthand. Citrix's new SpeedScreen Progressive Display technology is mind-blowing for anyone who has worked with Terminal Services or previous Presentation Servers and run graphics-intensive applications. The spinning of a CAD model, the zooming of an X-Ray, or the enhancement of a GIS map have all gone from painful to beautiful. Not only is the user experience now excellent, but there is a significant reduction in network bandwidth costs. CAD, GIS, and PACS users can now enjoy the freedom of working from anywhere, and IT can centrally manage these applications.

PLATFORM CHOICES

Although XenApp's primary solution set has always been Windows based, Citrix has offered a UNIX-based solution for five years now, and has a strong contingent of customers that use the solution. Now, with Citrix allowing customers to use either platform without a requirement to purchase additional or separate licenses, we expect many customers to take advantage of both platform options.

Citrix Presentation Server for UNIX

Although this book is primarily focused on Citrix XenApp for Windows Server 2003 and 2008, UNIX-based applications continue to be a mainstay of many large enterprise environments, and Windows and UNIX users alike can benefit from seamless, single-point, web access to these applications. Because of the overall value of the Citrix Delivery Center in providing web-based seamless access to all applications from any device, for all users, we felt strongly that XenApp for UNIX should be covered in this book. A large majority of the features and infrastructure discussed in these pages will apply equally to XenApp for UNIX and XenApp for Windows 2003 and 2008 Server. Features and tools such as Web Interface, Secure Gateway, Load Management, and any-device access are further promoted by bringing the UNIX applications to the Citrix Delivery Center fold.

Who Needs Citrix XenApp for UNIX

Although some longtime UNIX administrators argue that UNIX has supported multiuser functionality for years through the X Window System, and thus Presentation Server for

UNIX is not needed, they are missing out. X Windows is a tremendous bandwidth hog (even compressed X Windows) and therefore is totally useless over WAN connections. Additionally, the X Windows System does not support Citrix features such as shadowing, copy and paste between windows, and most importantly, Web Interface integration with Windows and web applications.

XenApp for UNIX is included in the Enterprise and Platinum editions of XenApp and cannot be purchased separately. XenApp customers receive both Windows and UNIX platforms along with Unified Licensing—which means that users can now access both Windows and UNIX applications and only consume one Citrix concurrent user license. The product, which at present supports IBM AIX, Sun Solaris (SPARC and x86), and HP-UX platforms, as well as virtually any custom or commercially packaged UNIX applications, offers the same value as XenApp for Windows, but with a UNIX/Java twist: low-bandwidth, universal client access over any network connection to any UNIX or Java application.

How XenApp for UNIX Works

At the core of the XenApp for UNIX product is a modified X11R6.3 server. This does not replace the X11 server supplied with most UNIX operating systems, but is specifically used to enable ICA-connected sessions running on XenApp for UNIX. XenApp for UNIX runs all standard X11 applications using the modified X server rather than the native X11 server.

In operation, the modified X11 server talks to a UNIX-ported ICA stack (Winstation Driver, Protocol Driver, and Transport Driver), which performs an X-to-ICA conversion. This is key to delivering applications seamlessly to clients from all XenApp platforms.

In addition to the modified X11 server and ported ICA stack, XenApp for UNIX also provides an ICA browser for use in load balancing and client browsing, a "listener" to intercept incoming ICA connections, and a "Frame Manager," which manages all the sessions currently running on the server.

The Benefits for Java and UNIX Application Users

The same core functionality used by XenApp for UNIX to deploy X11 and other applications hosted on UNIX servers can also be applied to Java applications. At first, this capability may seem redundant: In theory, Java applications are already portable to any device. In reality, however, Java client-side application deployments still confront numerous challenges.

Downloading Java applications entails the use of the available client/server network protocol, which is often not optimized for low-bandwidth connections. This results in the major complaint about Java applications that they are sometimes incredibly slow to download for operation. Operating the Java application, which is executed locally on a server, over a bandwidth-optimized ICA connection provides a higher-performance solution to this issue.

Java applications also fall prey to peculiarities in the Java Virtual Machine (JVM) that runs on the client system. Not all JVMs are the same, and it is often the case that a Java application that runs perfectly in one JVM behaves very differently in another. Presentation Server for UNIX solves this problem by executing Java applications within the server's JVM environment.

Utilizing a single, server-based JVM also saves time and money when developing and testing Java applications developed in-house. Once the application is working in the server JVM, it can be deployed instantly to any ICA client device.

In summary, Presentation Server for UNIX operating systems can be an important adjunct to Windows-based Presentation Server servers in heterogeneous server environments. Presentation Server for UNIX can be included in server farm and load-balancing schemes, and applications hosted on Presentation Server for UNIX systems may be published individually or as part of integrated Web Integration portals for integrated access by end users. Citrix Presentation Server for UNIX currently supports Sun Microsystems' Solaris 8, 9, and 10; Hewlett-Packard's HP-UX 11 and 11i; and IBM's AIX 5.1, 5.2, and 5.3.

XENAPP—ITS ALL ABOUT THE USER EXPERIENCE

One of the key differentiators of XenApp (and XenDesktop as well) is Citrix's Independent Computing Architecture protocol (ICA). As depicted in Figure 2-2, the Citrix ICA presentation services protocol transports only keystrokes, mouse clicks, and screen updates to the client. The protocol has been demonstrated to operate consistently with 20 kilobits per second of network bandwidth and provide real-time performance with 30 kilobits per second for office automation applications. This enables even the latest 32-bit and 64-bit applications to be operated remotely across low-bandwidth links while delivering performance comparable to local execution on existing PCs, Windows-based terminals, network computers, and a host of evolving business and personal information appliances.

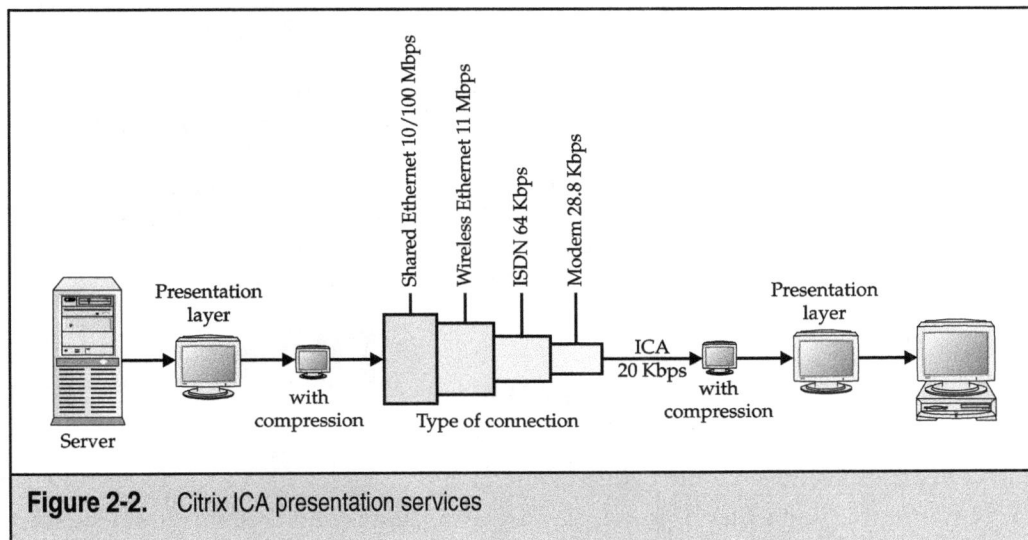

Figure 2-2. Citrix ICA presentation services

The Citrix ICA protocol was designed with low-bandwidth connections in mind, making it a robust performer on both large- and small-capacity links. Moreover, the ICA protocol responds dynamically to changing network, server, and client operating conditions. It takes advantage of available network and server resources and adapts automatically when conditions are more restrictive, often without generating any noticeable changes in the end user's experience. Much of the performance of the ICA protocol can be attributed to the use of intelligent caching and data compression techniques, and to technologies such as SpeedScreen. ICA is a nonstreaming protocol, meaning that if a user's screen has not changed and they have not moved the mouse or keyboard, no traffic will be passed (versus Terminal Server's RDP protocol, which is a streaming protocol). This feature can substantially help larger environments operating over a WAN link, because many users will not be using any bandwidth at certain instances, allowing much better utilization of the bandwidth as a whole.

The Citrix Client Environment

In addition to the contributions of XenApp and the ICA protocol to application delivery performance, XenApp also enhances the basic multiuser client/server environment. XenApp embodies numerous innovations designed to facilitate a broad range of hosted application environments. Considerable effort has been invested by XenApp designers to enable all applications, whether remote or local, to operate and interoperate as though they were local to the end user. This approach increases the user's comfort level and decreases the required training time.

The XenApp User Desktop

The XenApp desktop is designed to provide a user experience that is on par with a Windows PC running locally installed and executed applications. XenApp enables complete access to local system resources, such as full 16-bit stereo audio, local drives, COM ports, USB ports, scanners, and local printers, if available.

The mapping of local resources can be performed automatically or by means of administrative utilities. Specialized client capabilities such as modem dial-up are also supported.

Additionally, mapped resources can be shared with the XenApp server, if desired. Configuration of these mappings is built into the standard Windows device redirection facilities. The client mappings appear as another network that presents the client devices as share points to which a drive letter or printer port can be attached.

Connectivity

Citrix XenApp and the ICA protocol support more than 200 client types, providing excellent flexibility and choice in edge device access.

Citrix Web Interface

Citrix Web Interface enables users to integrate applications and data that are published into customized web portals for the end user, who then can access applications via a web browser.

In addition to publishing applications to the familiar web browser interface, another popular use of Web Interface for XenApp is to deploy the ICA client itself. Web Interface provides for automatic download and updates of the ICA client, largely transparent to the user, upon user logon. This provides a very fast and clean deployment and update mechanism for first-time XenApp users and remote users.

Using Web Interface, the presentation layer elements of multiple applications can be combined on a single page for exposure to the end user as a single, unified application. A simple wizard is provided to aid the administrator in defining the portal contents, which may include applications hosted on XenApp Windows and UNIX servers. Support for XenApp for UNIX enables the Web Interface for Presentation Server portal to be used to integrate both Windows- and UNIX-based applications and data.

Web Interface for XenApp portals can be customized through a wizard-driven interface to meet the needs of individual users, who access their applications in accordance with a user or group account logon, or general-purpose portals that can be fielded for access by anonymous users. Either way, the portals, like other XenApp applications, are managed via the same set of XenApp utilities used to manage and control other applications published through Citrix Presentation Server.

The Access Gateway—SSL VPN Appliance

The Citrix Access Gateway is a 1U SSL VPN appliance that includes policy-based Smart-Access control. In addition to providing VPN services and SmartAccess control, this device is also integrated with Citrix XenApp to allow Citrix customers to run both applications that are deployed via XenApp and applications that are provided through client/server and N-tier deployments via VPN.

Citrix XenApp Platinum includes all user connectivity licenses required for the Access Gateway, but the Access Gateway appliance unit(s) must be purchased separately. The Access Gateway unit has a list price of $2,995 at the time of this writing and can be purchased by itself or in a high-availability pair bundle.

The most talked-about feature of the Access Gateway is its simplicity. The small-footprint user client is much simpler than standard IPSec clients, does not require manual client updates, and the device itself is based on a simple Linux kernel.

Although the device is simple, the SmartAccess component is necessarily as complex as the policies you choose to put in place. SmartAccess allows the administrator to extend the policies to include information about the connection path and information gathered at the endpoint through an extensible Endpoint Analysis client. SmartAccess technology allows administrators to control both access and actions based on the user and the endpoint device. For example, a user may have full access (read, save locally, print, and so on) to a set of files when utilizing their laptop in the office, but may be restricted to "read-only" access when connecting through an unrecognized WAN. Similarly, if an employee tries to log into the corporate network via a home PC that does not have an active antivirus update service, that employee may not be able to access certain mission-critical systems.

It is important to note that the Access Gateway does not include Web Interface capabilities. So in most cases, you will want to utilize a Web Interface Server to provide web-based access to XenApp users.

CITRIX LICENSING

The XenApp license is more than an agreement describing the cost to the user and revenue to the vendor. It is a technical licensing implementation in which licenses are pooled by the XenApp servers themselves and used to calculate authorized use of the software. In short, if the license provides for 20 users to connect to a XenApp server farm, user number 21 will be locked out by the farm.

Citrix delivers XenApp licenses in four ways: shrink wrap, Easy Licensing, corporate licensing, and flex licensing.

The Shrink Wrap Method

Administrators can purchase the base product and licenses for 20 concurrent users. As configurations expand, bulk user packs can be purchased to meet changing needs. Additional XenApp user licenses can be added in increments of 5, 10, 20, or 50 concurrent users.

Easy Licensing

Easy Licensing is designed for customers with up to 500 concurrent licenses who wish to take advantage of electronic licensing. On-demand licensing allows administrators to purchase what is needed when it is needed. This licensing also allows for auto-activation for rapid deployment. Another advantage to Easy Licensing is that it does not have a complex paper contract but rather uses a "click to accept" online agreement.

Corporate Licensing

Corporate licensing programs are available for large license quantities. This program uses a point-based system with four discount levels for corporations and a special education discount level. In addition, special pricing is available for corporate customers who adopt a "long-term strategic use" posture. In this case, cumulative purchases drive discounts. This program is designed for customers with 500 to 5,000 concurrent seats.

Flex Licensing

Flex licensing is designed for companies with more than 5,000 concurrent seats. Flex licensing requires a custom contract, called a Global 2000 agreement, reserved for enterprise customers. The advantage of flex licensing, in addition to a very significant discount, is that Citrix provides additional license automation to make it easier to install and activate XenApp licensing across a large number of servers.

Subscription Advantage

Subscription Advantage provides customers with a convenient way to keep their Citrix software current and maximize their IT investments. As a customer, you receive software upgrades, enhancements, and maintenance releases that become available during the term of your subscription. Subscription Advantage is for a one-year term and can be renewed each year.

PART II

Designing an Enterprise Citrix Solution

CHAPTER 3

Preparing Your Organization for an Application Delivery Platform Implementation

Constructing an application delivery platform requires extensive planning and resources. In addition to the technical challenges, political and cultural factors inevitably play a part in an enterprise application infrastructure implementation. This chapter covers the steps involved in building a Citrix-based delivery platform. We start the process with a small proof-of-concept pilot program to ensure application compatibility with the various infrastructure components. We then look at putting together a feasibility committee to define the project's scope and objectives as well as to seek executive sponsorship and determine financial justification. A guide to performing an infrastructure assessment is followed by a project-planning outline. The steps involved in planning an application delivery platform are as follows:

1. Establish a nonproduction proof-of-concept pilot program.

2. Establish a production proof-of-concept pilot program.

3. Assemble a feasibility committee.

4. Recruit an executive sponsor.

5. Justify the project financially.

6. Assemble a project planning team.

7. Create a project definition document.

8. Perform an infrastructure assessment.

9. Generate a project design plan.

10. Expand the pilot to beta stage.

Feasibility	Test	Manage Organizational Change	Deploy

Application Delivery Infrastructure Migration

Proof of concept	Production pilot	Project definition	Infrastructure assessment	Project design plan	General implementation design	Beta

Project goals

Project scope

Project roles

Project risks

Success criteria

Project milestones

Scalability

Redundancy

Security

Terminal Services design

Windows Server 2008 design

Network design

Policies & procedures

Client design

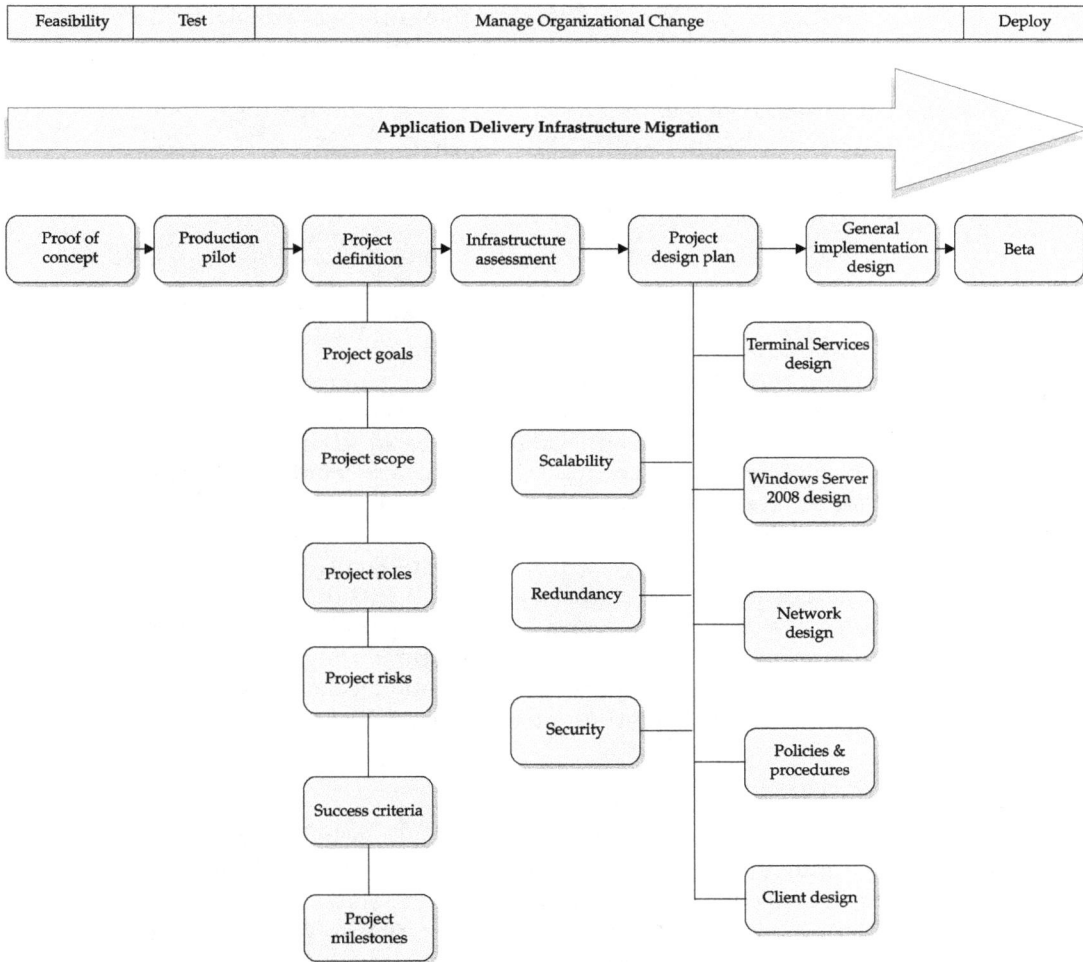

THE PROOF-OF-CONCEPT PILOT PROGRAM

Applications are the reason that we need an application delivery platform. It makes little sense to go through the expense and trouble of planning for an enterprise implementation until you know that your organization's applications will run adequately within this environment. An inexpensive proof-of-concept pilot program enables you to test application compatibility both individually and when running with the various Citrix components (the Platinum components, NetScaler, Gateway, and so on). It also enables you to measure performance and to more accurately gauge the resources required to implement an enterprise application delivery environment.

Starting with a Nonproduction Pilot Program

Although you may ultimately wish to deliver all of your organization's applications through Citrix XenApp, the decision of how much emphasis to put on XenApp architecture generally depends upon successfully running a small number of critical applications. These are the applications that should first be loaded and validated on a server running Terminal Server and XenApp offline. If the results are not acceptable, adjustments to the applications or operating system may be required. Once the crucial applications are running well on XenApp, other less-crucial applications can be added, if desired. If XenApp users will be using foreign-language versions of Terminal Server and XenApp, separate proof-of-concept pilot programs should be set up for each language because different versions and updates are often required.

A pilot program should also be initiated for any non–XenApp applications (such as web applications and legacy applications) to test both feasibility and performance impacts of other application delivery components such as NetScalers and other enhancements. Performance improvements for web applications run through the Citrix NetScaler can be up to 1000%, but there are a myriad of optimization techniques that should be tested in the pilot stage to ensure that results are maximized.

Expanding to a Production Pilot Program

Once the offline pilot program is stable, you can expand it to include a small number of pilot users. Great care, though, should go into the selection of these participants. A natural inclination of IT people is to choose from two types of users. The first type is a user who has an immediate computing need that the pilot program will solve, such as a requirement for extended remote access. The second type is a user who is known to be difficult because requirement for constant help or due to a particularly demanding demeanor. The thinking here is that if Citrix can make a difficult user happy, it can make anyone happy. Using these selection criteria, though, is toying with disaster. A pilot program is likely to have some bugs that need to be worked out. The wrong participant may loudly complain about the problems of working with new technology. If the complaint reaches the ears of an executive, the whole application delivery platform initiative could be killed. The organization might then lose the opportunity to reap the benefits and savings of the centralized application delivery platform simply because of poor selection of participants.

Pilot users should be a representative sample of those who will ultimately use the applications, but they should be friendly to the concept and have a thorough understanding of the pilot testing process, including the likelihood of encountering initial problems until IT works them out. Avoid choosing people for any reason other than testing the concept.

Goals of the production pilot include measuring the time it takes for loading the various applications, reviewing methods for performance tuning, and focusing on user issues such as usability and functionality.

Capacity Planning

Most organizations do not convert their entire infrastructure to a complete Citrix application delivery paradigm at once. Almost inevitably, though, the Citrix components become increasingly utilized once implemented and as the benefits begin to manifest themselves. It is important, therefore, to adequately plan for growth and to implement a system that is scalable. A pilot deployment is a great opportunity to gather capacity metrics in a controlled environment with actual users. It also allows administrators to monitor all components of the implementation, such as server capacity, bandwidth utilizations, Directory Services integrations, peripherals, and file storage. A good practice is to build a pilot environment that contains 30 to 40 percent more capacity than the expected user load for the pilot. The extra capacity gives the administrator an adequate buffer for unexpected bottlenecks that may arise during testing. When the pilot is converted to a beta, the additional resources will undoubtedly be used. Therefore, resources are not wasted.

Hybrids or Pure Thin Clients

Operating in a hybrid mode occurs when users continue to run one or more applications on their local PCs (although the data may still be centralized at the datacenter). If pilot participants will be operating in hybrid mode, make sure their desktops are configured so that they know whether they are in a local session or in a XenApp session. This can be accomplished using application publishing (as explained in Chapter 13).

Even if Windows terminals (also referred to as "thin clients") are not in your organization's application delivery plans, we recommend securing one for the pilot program. Because a Windows terminal is completely dependent on the Terminal Services platform to operate (although many of them have a native web browser), installing one contributes to a deeper understanding of the new platform. You may find that the Windows terminal "brick" has uses that you hadn't previously considered, such as serving as an employee's home "PC."

CAUTION: If you are going to have pilot users run legacy PCs, make sure the PCs are high-quality, reliable models (though they do not need to be powerful machines). In one of the authors' projects, a teacher became frustrated because her extremely cheap PC's keyboard broke when she became a pilot XenApp user. Unfortunately, she had grown attached to her low-end keyboard, and despite our best efforts, we could not convince her that her keyboard's failure had nothing to do with Terminal Server. She ended up poisoning the entire project by warning the other teachers not to let Citrix into their classrooms "because it breaks keyboards."

Headquarters and/or Remote Office Users

If you have hybrid pilot users in a remote office who are connected by limited bandwidth, it is essential that you instruct them in proper usage. You do not want them, for instance, to back up files from their local hard drives to the XenApp farm at headquarters. This will chew up bandwidth and may cause performance degradation for other users in the remote office. As discussed in Chapter 5, you might also consider setting up bandwidth management as part of your pilot program in order to ensure adequate WAN performance.

TIP: Even if you have no intention of putting headquarters users onto Citrix, you should consider setting up at least one corporate IT person as part of the pilot program. Again, this will help to foster understanding of the concept of Citrix application delivery and enable your IT staff to experience it firsthand.

Change Control

Many organizations really struggle with how to keep up with change control. It is important for the success of the pilot that a focus is made on maintaining a stable environment, on consolidating and scheduling updates, on obtaining sign-off authority for changes, on proper regression testing, and on maintaining a detailed rollback plan in the event that new applications disrupt the pilot. Implementation support is extremely difficult when too many people or teams have their hands in the pot. It is also very difficult to monitor the systems when servers are frequently down for maintenance.

If you don't have change control procedures in place for IT infrastructure changes, we recommend creating a simple Excel spreadsheet with a tab for each server. On that tab you can have columns for Date, Change, Changed By, and Approved By. Another option is to create a mail-enabled public folder in Exchange. Allowing administrators to e-mail any change to an address, such as citrixchanges@company.com, would then make the changes easily available for review.

Documenting Performance

Document your expectations of the pilot program before you begin. If at all possible, client-side application performance should be recorded prior to application virtualization. These performance baselines can be used for comparison if application performance concerns arise. Success criteria should be determined up front, including what it will look like and how it will be measured. After the pilot program, create a report on whether the success metrics were met. Document any problems encountered along with their solutions. Document any open issues along with the actions being taken to resolve them.

Pilot Server(s)

Ideally, two load-balanced servers and two load-balanced NetScalers will be utilized for the production pilot program in order to provide redundancy and, more importantly, to test failover and system resiliency. In most cases, though, organizations will probably use only one server in order to keep expenses lower during the proof-of-concept phase. The server should still be close enough to your expected production rollout model to make the results meaningful. For instance, using a Hewlett-Packard server with only two CPUs and half the RAM of your ultimate intended Hewlett-Packard XenApp is probably okay. Using a different brand with different CPU and memory configurations is not a good idea.

Applications

If you are running anything other than 32- or 64-bit applications, be prepared for less-than-optimal performance. Make users aware of what they can expect from various applications. The use of Citrix EdgeSite is absolutely critical in order to gather performance metrics, identify bottlenecks, and optimize performance. (EdgeSite is covered in depth in Chapter 12.) Performance should be monitored and evaluated as each application is added to the XenApp. If performance is less than expected, try removing questionable applications to see if a particular product is causing problems.

THE FEASIBILITY COMMITTEE

Once you have determined that the proof-of-concept pilot program is workable and that performance expectations have been met, it is time to determine whether an enterprise deployment makes sense for the organization—and if so, which Citrix components (if not all) should be used. The decision process of whether to implement a platform should include an evaluation of the proposed project's impact on the organization from operational, financial, cultural, and political perspectives.

A feasibility committee made up of IT personnel and employees from other appropriate departments should assess the merits of the changes. The first task of the feasibility committee will be to broadly define the project's scope, along with its benefits. The committee must then consider the upcoming business and technology needs and drivers to evaluate the strategic fit of an enterprise application delivery platform within the organization. The next steps include finding an executive sponsor and preparing a financial justification for the project. The committee's resulting report can then be utilized to help guide the planning team's work should the Citrix project move forward.

Project Scope

The Citrix Application Delivery Platform might be limited to deployment of a single application, or it may encompass the entire desktop. It might be utilized only in certain departments or regions, or it may be implemented as the new corporate standard. In general, the more extensively an organization implements Citrix, the more money it will save compared with using client-centric computing. (In Chapter 1, we covered the composition of these savings as well as many other benefits of an on-demand enterprise.) The feasibility committee must determine whether a complete strategic enterprise rollout is practical or a scaled-back tactical implementation is more appropriate.

Corporate Culture Considerations

The economies achieved from implementing an application delivery platform inevitably make it much less expensive than decentralized PC-based computing. A hidden potential cost, though, is the turmoil that may result from introducing such huge changes into the computing environment without identifying the potential problem areas and properly preparing the organization for the changes.

Centralized Standards

The nature of client-centric computing makes it difficult for organizations to enforce IT standards. Typically, corporate IT is unaware of many applications that users run locally or departmentally. Although XenApp offers IT the flexibility to allow users to run local applications, it also makes it easy to lock down desktops. Because greater client-side control equates to less administration, IT will tend to exploit this advantage. Even if IT decides to host only a few critical corporate applications, these particular programs now will be outside the direct control of users.

In many organizations, greater IT control is taken for granted as an advantage. Banks, for instance, typically have a tradition of mainframe hosting and readily embrace computing standards for PC users. A software development firm, on the other hand, may decide that the creative benefits of unbridled individual computing outweigh the lower costs obtained from enforcing centralized standards.

The feasibility committee needs to evaluate whether standardization is an acceptable condition within their organizational environment.

Understanding User Perceptions of the Network Infrastructure and IT

The distribution of economic and IT resources mandated by distributed processing often results in a network infrastructure that is plagued with performance and reliability problems. In these environments, users will be reluctant to give up control of their desktops to IT.

NOTE: The feasibility committee must call attention to a networking infrastructure that suffers from performance or reliability problems, but this does not mean that the Citrix project should be abandoned. On the contrary, as long as IT can fix the existing problems, an uncompromising first review presents an opportunity to drive rapid project acceptance. IT should initially implement smaller beta projects that deliver better reliability and performance to thin-client or hybrid users than to their fat-client peers. This strategy can quickly build enthusiasm for the new technology and, in turn, help enable IT to plan an enterprisewide implementation of Citrix.

Political Considerations

In many organizations, the disparate nature of distributed processing has led to control of IT budgets by different departments or divisions. Creating a centralized application delivery infrastructure is a costly endeavor that affects users throughout the organization. The feasibility committee needs to determine whether the organization will be able to marshal the resources to implement such an encompassing project.

Reduced IT Staff

Gartner Group reported that the staffing required to support a fat-client environment is five times greater than the staffing required to support a thin-client environment. An on-demand enterprise utilizing Citrix can eliminate the need for remote office IT personnel, or even for entire regional IT departments. It is the job of the feasibility committee to evaluate whether the corporate culture will permit elimination of unnecessary network administration, help desk personnel, and PC technician positions.

IT Staff Salaries

Because the majority of organizational processing under Citrix takes place at central data centers, the network administrators must be quite skilled. They may require higher salaries than their peers in many distributed processing environments, perhaps even higher than their managers. The feasibility committee must assess whether these types of administrators are already on staff and, if not, whether the organization's salary structure will allow for hiring them.

TIP: An application delivery platform is too encompassing and too vital to efficiency (and eventual savings) to allow for skimping on anything in the data center—including the people who run it. If higher wages for a select network administrator would wreak havoc on the IT department's existing salary structure, consider alternative solutions, such as outsourcing the position.

Finding an Executive Sponsor

Gaining an executive sponsor and executive support is, without question, the single most important thing I did for this project. The challenges that followed during the next nine months would have been difficult, if not impossible, to overcome without the complete backing of the most senior folks in our company.

—Anthony Lackey,
Vice President of MIS,
Chief Technology Officer,
ABM Industries

Many people simply resist change, particularly if they feel they are giving something up. Executive sponsorship is essential for successfully transforming into an on-demand enterprise. Upper management must make it absolutely clear that the application delivery platform initiative is something that will happen and that everyone is expected to make work. Ideally, the CIO and other selected executives should begin using the new platform in order to show their complete support for the project.

Justifying Citrix Financially

As the feasibility committee members discuss the scope and organizational ramifications of building an application delivery platform, they are likely to become more aware of the enormous savings and compelling benefits it will provide. In order for the project to move forward, they need to convey this information to management. Most corporate decision makers will require an in-depth financial analysis of the specific impacts of migrating to a Citrix platform. They will primarily be interested in the estimated cost of the project and the return on the required investment. A reasonable timeframe over which to calculate these figures usually ranges from three to five years.

Although it may seem both very difficult and impractical to estimate project costs without first doing a detailed infrastructure assessment and in-depth planning, this is not the case. The components of a Citrix Application Delivery Platform are not difficult to estimate on a "big picture" basis. And because the resulting savings over client-centric computing are likely to be very high, broad estimates are all that is required for a revealing financial analysis.

We recommend taking a four-pronged approach to building a financial analysis. First, present the hard cost savings. This can be done by comparing the estimated costs of staying with client-centric computing over a period of three to five years versus the estimated costs of implementing Citrix. Hard costs include easily identified expenditures such as hardware purchases and help desk personnel salaries. In most cases, the hard savings alone will more than justify the entire project. This will isolate the feasibility committee from detractors who might try to take shots at the financial analysis.

Next, present the estimated soft cost savings. These are real savings, but their quantification may be harder to agree upon. For instance, how much does it really cost the organization when users suffer downtime as their PCs are upgraded? Presenting them as part of the financial analysis gives management a better idea of the ultimate economic impact of migrating to an application delivery platform.

The third component is a list of the expected benefits from Citrix. These benefits can sometimes be quantified, but often have just as big an impact if they are listed without specific numbers. As described in Chapter 1, the business benefits of building the platform often have more strategic importance to the organization than the hard and soft savings combined.

The last element is a qualitative high-level description of the specific benefits the platform can provide in terms of enhanced security and the much greater disaster-recovery and business continuity potential. This can also include the ability to more easily comply with regulations such as Sarbanes-Oxley and HIPAA while lowering the cost of discovery and the risk of litigation.

TIP: When preparing an ROI analysis for an application delivery platform, try to involve the finance folks at an early stage. They may be able to provide valuable input as to the format they would like to see. Even more important, be sure to get their agreement to review the ROI analysis. Their validation of the results will be instrumental in building a case for on-demand Citrix application delivery to senior management.

THE PROJECT PLANNING TEAM

Once an executive sponsor has been identified and management has accepted the feasibility committee's financial analysis of implementing an enterprise deployment of Citrix, a planning team can be assembled.

The project planning team will be primarily composed of IT staff, including hands-on technical people. It should also include some members from the feasibility committee and possibly representatives from multiple departments or divisions. This will help ensure that the organization's enterprise goals are met with this enterprise deployment.

Each member's role and expected contributions should be defined. Also, accountability should be established.

Consultants

Because much of the technology appears to be Windows-like or Windows-based, many organizations are inclined to plan the entire process internally and use only existing staff. This is probably not an optimal utilization of resources. We recommend seeking out Citrix specialists who have designed and implemented multiple large-scale application delivery platforms. The experience they bring to the table should pay for their fees many times over.

Depending on the size of the project and organization, it may also be worthwhile to consider using a change management consultant who is very experienced in helping implement organizationwide change. As with all consultants, we recommend requesting and checking references.

NOTE: Citrix has stratified its reseller channel into three categories: silver, gold, and platinum. Platinum resellers represent approximately the top one percent of all Citrix resellers. They must have a minimum of six Citrix certified engineers on staff, and they are the most likely to have the resources and experience to successfully implement an enterprise application delivery project. Of course, you should carefully check the references and ascertain the capabilities of any consultants you engage.

The Project Definition Document

The first task of the planning committee is to prepare a document defining project goals, scope, roles, and risks, along with success criteria and milestones. This will be a living document that will guide the planning team through the infrastructure assessment, design, and implementation stages. As expectations, requirements, and conditions change, the planning definition document will serve as a touchstone for keeping the project on track.

Project Goals

Although saving money is likely to be an important objective, the strategic advantages and other benefits described in Chapter 1 may be even more important considerations. Clearly defined project goals serve as a benchmark as the project rolls out.

Project Scope

The preliminary work done by the feasibility committee combined with management's reaction to the financial analysis enable the planning committee to identify the parameters of the Citrix project. In particular, the committee must select the applications to be run via Citrix along with expectations for stability and for upgrades during the implementation process. Adding a new application, for example, requires extensive testing as well as the creation of a new server image. What's known as "scope creep" is inevitable, and guidelines need to be established for an approval process when requests for additional applications or features are made. Allowances must also be made for delays caused by these changes.

Project Roles

Keeping the project's executive sponsor closely informed of progress will help garner upper-management support when needed. The project also requires both an IT owner and a high-level business owner who can intercede to work through any problems that may arise. A project manager needs to be assigned along with a backup project manager who can make decisions in the event the project manager is unavailable. Outlining escalation procedures for contacting the appropriate decision maker in the event that the project manager is unable or unwilling to solve a problem helps to keep things on track. If the rollout is large enough, both a quality assurance person and a training coordinator should be assigned to the project as well.

Project Risks

Identifying risks such as scope creep, unavailability of resources, and lack of user acceptance helps the committee include strategies for reducing the risk of problems with the project. Contingency plans should also be included.

The Criteria for Success

Identifying the criteria by which the project will be judged a success enables the planning and implementation teams to better focus their energies. If user satisfaction is a requirement for success, for example, user surveys should be designed, along with a mechanism for their distribution, collection, and tabulation. We recommend simple electronic forms allowing users to grade the Citrix project on items such as performance, functionality, and reliability. Figure 3-1 shows a sample of the Lotus Notes–based survey forms that ABM e-mailed to their users.

Project Milestones

Infrastructure assessment and upgrade, the design document, beta implementation, enterprise rollout, and administrator and user training are examples of project milestones.

Change Management

Organizations are first and foremost social systems. Without people, there can be no organization…. Organizations are hotly and intensely political.

—Fred Nickols,
Change Management Expert

The analysis prepared by the feasibility committee regarding corporate culture and politics should be incorporated into a plan for successful organizational change. Potential implementation of new application standards, user perceptions of IT, reductions in IT staff and IT salaries, and other political considerations need to be addressed and solutions for them found. For instance, one of our customers created an organizational change plan that began with a meeting of the presidents of all the business units. By explaining the benefits of the technology platform, he turned the presidents into allies who helped smooth the process of organizational change.

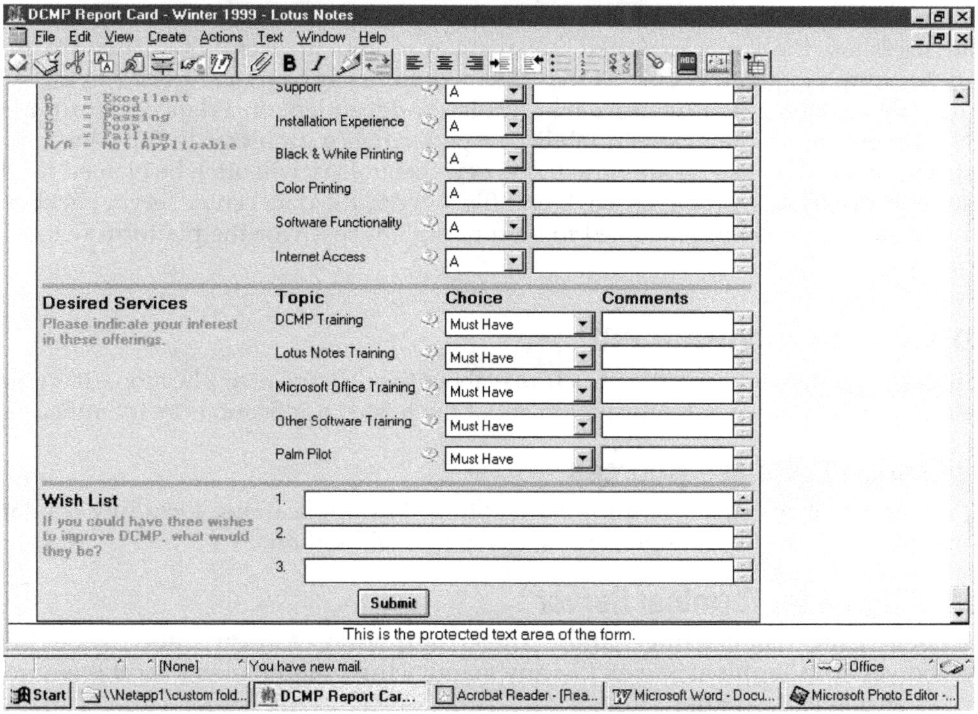

Figure 3-1.   ABM's user survey form

INFRASTRUCTURE ASSESSMENT

To produce a meaningful Citrix application delivery platform planning document, a detailed infrastructure assessment must first be completed. This assessment includes identifying the appropriate contacts for each category and conducting meetings with them.

Another purpose behind the infrastructure assessment is to discover and remedy any infrastructure problems prior to an application delivery platform rollout. In a client-centric environment, employees are often used to things being sloppy. Although the network might have some performance or downtime problems, users tend to be somewhat understanding because they commonly save files to their local hard drives anyway. When users destroy their PC configurations by adding a software utility or deleting an INI file, they often ask a peer for help rather than making an embarrassing support call to IT. Because users work on *their* personal computers and departments run *their* own servers, they are less likely to complain to IT staff or management even when problems arise that are not of their own making.

In a centralized application delivery environment, employees' *personal* computers become *corporate* computers. While vastly more efficient from an organizational standpoint, users lose the status conferred by having ever more powerful PCs. They are more likely to complain about problems that they would never have mentioned in a client-centric environment. Because users are completely dependent on a data center for most or all of their applications, any instability or performance problems in the network infrastructure will instantly be amplified. The new technology will often be blamed for the existing infrastructure problems. Back-end file servers, the data center server backbone, and wide area connectivity all need to be running flawlessly or the platform will be in jeopardy of failing.

The Application Environment

A Citrix application delivery infrastructure is about the delivery of applications. It is therefore crucial that all relevant information about the hosted applications be identified.

Application Database Sources

List the source of any database information utilized by applications, including the database application, the host system, and its geographical location.

Operating under Terminal Server

Describe whether manufacturer support exists for running each application under Windows Server 2008 Terminal Server. List any manufacturer requirements for this environment as well as any caveats.

Application Composition

Describe the language of each application as well as whether it is client, server, or Telnet.

Application Architecture

Determine whether or not the application is built for a multiuser environment.

> **TIP:** Custom applications can be particularly tricky. You will want to make sure that the applications use a Microsoft multiple-user architecture that utilizes roaming profiles. This means that the applications are user specific and that users have their own separate settings and will not be sharing them (HKEY_CURRENT_USER versus HKEY_LOCAL_MACHINE). The applications should also have subordinate files, such as log files or temp files, that can be redirected to the user's Windows directory and/or Temp directory. A program that is not user specific but has global settings means that a user making setting switches will affect all users on that server. If the application is not written as user specific, you will need to lock those keys in the Registry to prevent users from changing them.

Manufacturer Support Contracts

If manufacturer support contracts exist for any of the applications, include the relevant information along with phone numbers and the appropriate identification authorization.

Application Requirements

List specific operating conditions for each application, including the following:

- ▼ Memory requirements
- ■ Disk space requirements
- ■ Sound requirements
- ■ Drive mapping requirements
- ■ Any patches or service packs
- ▲ Location of the install files

Application Issues

List any application issues that could affect performance within a Terminal Server environment. For instance, if an application tends to cause blue screens when running in a client-centric environment, the planning committee must be aware that similar problems are likely to occur under Citrix XenApp.

Application Packaging

Describe how the application is distributed to users within the existing client-centric environment. How often is the application revised? How is it packaged? For instance, can users install updates with a single mouse click?

Internal Application Support

Identify any internal support contacts for all internal and line-of-business applications. Identify any internal application owners who are responsible for deploying new versions of applications.

The Hardware Environment

The planning process will be based on knowledge about the existing hardware environment for servers and host systems.

The Data Center Environment

Evaluating existing data center sites for power, cooling, and physical security will let the project planning team assess whether they are adequate for hosting the Citrix data center(s). See Chapter 5 for more detail on data center requirements and design.

The System Management Environment (SME)

Evaluating the existing SME enables the planning committee to incorporate it into the application delivery infrastructure design. This includes identifying any existing tools for measuring metrics, such as HP OpenView, as well as spending some time with Citrix EdgeSite to see how it integrates with current solutions and how else it might add value.

The Support Structure and Processes

Determining the different levels of support resources available will help the planning team arrive at a strategy for providing support during the implementation. Also define the way support calls are placed and relayed. What help desk package is in use, if any? How will the current incident, problem, change, and configuration management processes be affected by the Citrix application delivery project? Are any service-level agreements (SLAs) currently defined? How is support localized in remote offices?

The Testing Environment

Creating a testing environment is crucial to implementing and successfully maintaining an application delivery infrastructure. The planning team needs to know if a current formalized testing environment exists and if testing labs are available. We strongly recommend the use of Citrix XenServer to virtualize some nonproduction lab environments for testing and training purposes.

Change Control Procedures

What change control policies and procedures are in place today? What kind of approval process is required for making changes? Does the organization maintain a configuration management database or other methods for recording all changes to critical systems? Is there a quality assurance group?

TIP: In many organizations, the IT administrators learned their trade on a PC rather than in a host systems environment. They may be used to making changes on the fly and not recording the changes they make. This approach will cause a data center–centric solution like the application delivery infrastructure to fail. A mainframe shop mentality with rigorous change-and-release management processes are essential for success.

The Training Environment

Is there a formalized training group? Are classrooms available? What kind of training is commonly used for IT people? For end users?

The Windows Server Environment

Identifying components such as protocols and ports used, the existing domain structure, naming conventions, and partitioning is essential planning information.

Network Architecture

Defining the existing network architecture is crucial to designing a solid Citrix infrastructure, including routers, switches, protocols, policy servers, bandwidth allocation policies, remote office servers, existing redundancy options, and remote capabilities. Any existing network reliability or performance problems such as client latency issues need to be identified and ultimately resolved prior to the rollout.

The Security Environment

In order for the planning committee to design the proper secure environment, they need to know the following: What firewalls are in place? How is dial-up security currently handled? What internal policies are in place on Windows servers? How is lockdown of NTFS partitions handled? Is there a security group?

The Backup Environment

The planning committee needs to know what kind of data backup and replication mechanisms and backup policies exist today.

The Printing Environment

Microsoft has said that printing is the number-one customer support issue across the board, and with any new infrastructure, it is certain to be one of the hottest issues. Does printing take place through locally attached printers or only on the network? What network protocols are used? What are the types and number of printers? What print drivers are required? Are print servers used in remote offices today?

The Client Environment

Define the client environment of the participants. This includes categories of users, their location, and whether they have access to a local server. Also describe the details of the specific clients, such as device (PC, laptop, UNIX workstation, handheld), model, local O/S, and any existing performance or reliability issues. Nonstandard PC hardware peripherals should also be noted for testing.

THE PROJECT DESIGN PLAN

The project plan incorporates all aspects of the design. This plan includes both the project definition document and results of the infrastructure assessment. The financial analysis performed by the feasibility committee should be fine-tuned throughout the planning process until the final planning document includes a solid estimate for project costs.

The planning document should clearly convey the organization's application delivery migration strategy and be suitable for presentation to both executives and auditors. It discusses the various options that the planning team considered for each major component of the project, along with the rationale behind the team's ultimate decision.

Incorporated as part of the plan should be the considerations given to capacity, availability, redundancy, and security planning. The tremendous advantages accruing from the centralization that an application delivery infrastructure enables can become huge liabilities if scalability is not easily incorporated, a crucial data center component without a redundant part should fail, or the system's security is compromised.

The project plan also serves as a roadmap for the project managers and implementation team as they work to institute an enterprise Citrix environment. Detailed explanations of the design plan are discussed in the remaining chapters in this part of the book. An overview of the design plan follows.

XenApp Design

Designing the XenApp environment will be difficult for organizations unfamiliar with the basics of application delivery platforms. We recommend that the appropriate IT personnel take courses in Microsoft Terminal Server, XenApp, and Advanced XenApp before beginning the design process. Because XenApp consolidates processing into a central data center (or data centers), it is important to plan for redundancy of all key components. The XenApp farm with load-balancing has built-in redundancy, but special awareness should be given to implementing it for other servers such as Windows Server 2008, SQL, e-mail, and Web Services. Redundancy should also be included for other critical components such as network switches, load balancers, routers, storage units, and bandwidth management devices.

Application Architecture Design

Define the strategy both for deploying the application delivery infrastructure and for handling legacy applications that will not be supported. Users may be allowed, for instance, to run legacy applications locally indefinitely. Alternatively, they may be given a deadline for transitioning to corporate-approved and -supported applications.

Data Center Architecture Design

The planning team needs to determine the number of data centers, based on demographic, geographic, disaster recovery, and business requirements. They must evaluate site considerations, including power, cooling, fire suppression, and physical security. They also must evaluate options for either hosting the centers internally or using co-location centers, such as AT&T or Cable & Wireless. (Data center architecture is discussed more thoroughly in Chapter 5.)

Disaster Recovery/Business Continuity Design

The events following hurricane Katrina in New Orleans clearly demonstrate the importance of enabling effective business continuity. Because millions of people were evacuated from New Orleans for large periods of time, employees were unable to access their applications and data. Even though their data may have been successfully recovered, they were unable to access it because replacement workstations lacked the necessary secure connectivity to that data.

A Citrix application delivery platform decouples the desktop from the workstation. A disaster may preclude employees from accessing their normal workstations, but with Citrix XenApp, applications, the Citrix-enabled "desktop" and any critical browser-based applications can be delivered to the employees securely through a web browser. This remains whether the "desktop" is running in the normal data center or at the disaster recovery site. If employees are prevented from entering their office due to a natural disaster, they can still continue working from another office, from home, or even from an Internet café. (A variety of disaster recovery options are discussed in Chapter 8.)

Network Backbone Design

Each data center requires a high-speed backbone connecting the XenApp server farm with other servers in the data center. Small organizations may be able to get by with 1GB Ethernet. Large firms will likely require ATM or 10GB Ethernet. Redundant network interface cards (NICs) and switches should be incorporated as part of the design. (Data-center connectivity is discussed more thoroughly in Chapter 5.)

Server Farm Architecture Design

The findings from the proof-of-concept pilot program will enable the planning committee to select server quantity, type, sizing, and configuration for the Terminal Server implementation. The Citrix EdgeSite data can help determine server scalability requirements.

File Services Design

When users store all their data at corporate data centers, unique problems arise in handling file services efficiently. The project team should evaluate the different options, including clustering of general-purpose file servers, storage area networks (SANs), and network-attached storage (NAS). Archive systems and backup software and services must also be selected.

Print Server Architecture Design

Printing tends to be one of the most difficult and time-consuming parts of an enterprise application delivery infrastructure implementation. Decisions must be made about the configuration of one or more central print servers at each data center as well as the type and quantity of print servers in remote offices. Just a few of the other printer-related decisions the team will have to make include integration of host system printing, local PC printing, printer auto-creation to create temporary printer assignments for mobile users, trusted print sources, lockdown of registries, and control over printer access. (Printing is discussed in detail in Chapter 17.)

User Profiles Design

Most Terminal Server implementations utilize either mandatory or roaming profiles, but we recommend that organizations use scripting and policies, or a third-party product such as RES PowerFuse to enable desktop lockdown while allowing users the flexibility to select default drives and printers. (We present our lockdown and profile techniques in Chapter 16.)

Login Script Design

To minimize administration, there should be one script that works for both fat and thin clients. Additionally, login scripts should be designed to run very quickly and efficiently.

Automation Design

You will want to automate application installation and updates, server imaging processes, and client installations using products such as Citrix Installation Manager and Symantec Ghost. (Automation design is covered exhaustively in Part III of this book.)

Windows Server Design

Designing a Windows server infrastructure to support Terminal Server is a key part of the planning process. The following components are included.

Active Directory Design

Active Directory planning and configuration tends to be much simpler in an enterprise application delivery environment. This is because there is generally no need to worry about intersite replication since all domain controllers are in the data center. Another concern that is eliminated is the need to accommodate authentication over the WAN by users in small offices without local domain controllers.

Backup Architecture Design

If the infrastructure assessment reveals inadequate backup systems to handle the demands of centralized data storage, the archive systems and backup software and services require selection.

Back-end Database Design

The size and configuration of a back-end database in a application delivery computing environment, where all users will be hitting one database at one time, will often be different from a distributed database model, where several database servers are located across the enterprise. The distributed servers would handle a relatively small number of users and have replicated data backed up and stored at a central point. The Citrix Application Delivery Platform model might require far more powerful database server(s) or clustered servers at the data center, depending on usage, as well as middleware application changes.

Network Design

A sound network infrastructure is vital to supporting an application delivery platform. In addition to remedying any shortfalls discovered during the infrastructure assessment, the following issues should be addressed.

WAN Architecture

An application delivery infrastructure requires a robust, scalable, and highly reliable WAN design because remote office users are completely dependent on centralized servers and network infrastructure at the corporate data centers. The planning team must evaluate the different connectivity options, including the Internet and redundancy options. During the transition from PC-based to server-based computing, residual traffic will chew up an inordinate amount of bandwidth. The project plan must allow for this temporary increased bandwidth requirement during the migration process. (Bandwidth management, including packet prioritization, is often essential in order to ensure adequate performance.)

Alternative bandwidth capabilities should also be designed into the system. For instance, if the primary connectivity to remote offices is frame relay, alternative DSL connections to the Internet should be available for backup. The ultimate redundancy is to utilize the unique capabilities of the Citrix application delivery platform to build a disaster recovery solution with multiple failover data centers.

Remote Design

The project planning team needs to choose the appropriate remote strategy, whether using leased lines, frame relay, or the Internet.

The Systems Management Environment

If the infrastructure assessment indicates that a network management package is already utilized as part of the existing client-centric environment, the planning team should extend it to encompass the Citrix architecture. The team should also decide on how the existing network management package, or a new one, can best be configured to work with software such as Citrix EdgeSite. (Citrix EdgeSite is covered in detail in Chapter 12.)

Metrics Design

As part of the systems management environment, the planning team should determine which metrics are to be collected and analyzed in order to develop strategies for expansion and for limiting bottlenecks. Citrix EdgeSite is a good tool to use in this capacity because it integrates well with existing utilities such as HP OpenView.

Policies and Procedures Design

As is the case with the mainframe model of computing, clearly defined policies and procedures are essential for enterprise application delivery infrastructure success. Adding an application or making a small change to a central router can have severe consequences for hundreds or thousands of users. Although we continue to emphasize the numerous advantages of an enterprise application delivery environment, it does require that the days of the network cowboy come to an end.

Having been raised, from an MIS perspective, in the midrange and micro eras of computing, my staff had a hard time rethinking the way they do things. For example, while "maintenance windows" were commonplace in the days of the mainframe, they've seemingly disappeared in the PC era. My network technicians were used to shutting a system down minutes after announcing it. We all had to relearn what the MIS personnel we replaced 10 to 15 years ago knew as second nature.

—Anthony Lackey,
Vice President of MIS,
Chief Technology Officer, ABM Industries

Data Center Policies and Procedures Design

The planning document should include the organization's strategy for managing environmental changes.

TIP: Depending on the current policies and procedures as revealed in the infrastructure assessment, new requirements may be necessary. For example, a workflow-enabled database should track all changes by administrators and implementers to the application delivery infrastructure.

User Policies and Procedures Design

Decisions must be made about data, device access, and adding new devices. For example, will users be allowed to access local devices from a Citrix session? If so, this policy can have unanticipated ramifications, such as security concerns. (Policies and procedures are discussed more thoroughly in Chapter 16.)

Client Design

The planning committee should identify the different client categories and the levels to which they are expected to utilize Citrix services. They must further decide how to specifically set up the clients and how to configure user desktops. Choices must be made regarding policies for local browsing, emulation, drive mappings, PC local operating systems, and local hardware peripherals. If Windows terminals will be used, the planning team must evaluate the different options and choose the brand and models most appropriate for their organization. (Client implementation is discussed more thoroughly in Chapter 5.)

Client Operating Systems

A primary benefit of centralized computing is the standardization of applications. Although standard client equipment and operating systems make administration easier, one of the most compelling strengths of a Citrix Application Delivery Platform is its ability to effectively manage a heterogeneous environment. Still, different operating systems do have different ramifications for functionality.

User Interface Design

Users can launch entire Citrix XenApp desktops, or they can simply click icons generated through Citrix Program Neighborhood. The Citrix Web Interface component enables application publishing to a browser. Citrix application delivery allows access to all features of the Web Interface component of XenApp as well as the ability to aggregate information from across the enterprise, the Internet, and other data sources and to present it to users in a secure, personalized manner.

Integration with Local Devices

Design strategies must be included for client integration with local printers, handheld units, scanners, bar code readers, and cash drawers.

Non-Windows Client Design

XenApp enables UNIX workstations, as well as Linux and Macintosh users, to run Windows applications without requiring a separate PC. XenApp for UNIX (UX/AIX/Solaris) adds the functionality of the X Windows protocol. Users can subsequently launch either Windows or UNIX applications from the same screen.

Data Organization Design

When users use an application delivery platform, policies will need to be set about where their data will be stored for different applications (central server storage versus local storage). Creating broad policies that extend across all application delivery infrastructure users will greatly facilitate the ability of help desk personnel to provide prompt support.

Client Application Design

Different application strategies may be appropriate for different categories of users. For instance, mobile users will likely have some local applications, whereas office users may have none.

Other Client Design Considerations

Groups, drive mappings, and login script strategies must be designed for the different categories of users.

Security Design

Although security should permeate all aspects of the project design plan, a specific security strategy should be identified. Firewall integration, account management, auditing, and the Terminal Server Registry and Active Directory Group Policies should all be included. (Security is discussed more thoroughly in Chapter 6.)

General Implementation Design

The implementation plan should cover training, user communications, data migration, project management, change management, and customer care.

Training Plan

A training plan needs to be designed for support personnel, system administrators, and end users.

TIP: Once end users are set up to their desktop through the application delivery platform, you can coordinate a more formal introductory training class by using the XenApp shadowing capabilities. The trainer can have several users simultaneously shadow her PC. Setting up a concurrent conference call provides the audio to describe the visual orientation.

Support Personnel The low administrative requirements of the application delivery infrastructure combined with features such as shadowing will enable help desk personnel to support many more users once the migration is complete. During the transition, however, increased staff and training will likely be necessary to handle the demands of the new architecture while supporting users on the old client-centric platform.

End Users Distribution of rainbow packets for general information and at-a-glance documents for frequently asked questions are an expedient way to provide quick user orientation to the new platform. A *rainbow* document is modeled after the colorful organizational wall charts found in many hospitals for quick reference to services and locations. The rainbow document literally contains a rainbow of colored sheets, each a bit narrower than the other, providing easy reference to the topics on the exposed edge. Some relevant topics might be "Getting Help," "Finding Your Files," "Glossary of Terms," and "Your Thin-Client Desktop."

Project Management

The planning team should incorporate the essentials of project management as part of the plan. Implementation teams must have well-defined tasks, and required resources must be identified. An estimated timeline for the project beta testing and rollout should be included as part of the planning document.

An enterprise migration requires project manager authority, stakeholder buy-in, project reporting and tracking, task assignment, project change control, scope creep control, organizational change management, and timeline management. (Project management is discussed in detail in Chapter 7.)

Change Management

The planning document should include the organization's strategy for managing environmental changes in order to enhance management and end-user benefits. Administrator and end-user training, user reference guides, asset tracking, and a frequently asked questions (FAQs) database should all be incorporated as part of the project. The planning team should include survey forms for gathering information prior to implementation and for measuring user satisfaction as the rollout takes place.

A method for communicating migration plans to users is a very important component of change management. Although an application delivery infrastructure will provide users with enhanced capabilities and support, it still involves change. Advanced orientation and education will make the process go much more smoothly.

Customer Care

The help desk department will be able to handle many more users once the migration to the application delivery platform is complete. During the transition, however, increased staff may be necessary to handle the glitches of the new architecture while supporting users on the old client-centric computing platform.

Migrating to an Application Delivery Platform

The planning document should include a roadmap for migrating from a client-centric environment to the application deliver platform. Also clearly documented should be strategies for consolidating data from both PCs and remote office servers, thus minimizing downtime, and creating a "virtual call center" based on skill sets.

Expanding the Pilot Test to a Beta

The planning team must decide at what point the proof-of-concept pilot test will be expanded to a beta implementation, and they must decide the parameters of the beta. Objectives should be defined and results measured in order to allow adjustments to the team's migration strategy, if required. A scope variance process needs to define who has authority to sign off on out-of-scope items, for example, including a new application as part of the beta.

CHAPTER 4

Citrix Platform Data Center Architecture

In this chapter, we discuss the importance of building and running an application delivery and virtualization infrastructure in a secure, reliable data center facility. The need for this approach may be obvious to IT personnel with a background in host systems, but we will define the data center in the context of building a delivery platform. This centralized computing model often entails a new paradigm for network administrators whose IT experience is limited to running distributed networks based on traditional PC technology. The data center plays a far more important role with enterprise application delivery than it does in a distributed network environment, especially in a business world of zero acceptable downtime and the expectation of anytime, anywhere business continuity. The components of Citrix XenApp Platinum Edition, in conjunction with Citrix NetScaler, Access Gateway, XenDesktop, and XenServer, were all designed not only to support, but to sponsor zero downtime and business continuity. However, regardless of the components, if the data center is not purposefully architected and managed, the entire solution will fail.

This chapter discusses several key considerations—including the environment, network, and deployment—for the data center architecture. Chapter 8 will carry the concepts of this chapter forward, detailing a redundant data center solution that solves the business-continuity and disaster-recovery concerns of all businesses today.

WHAT IS A DATA CENTER?

An application delivery *data center* in this context is a central site or location that houses the application and desktop delivery infrastructure for a company. This site is characterized by limited physical access, superior network capacity, power capacity, power quality, and a degree of internal redundancy for these computing resources.

In the following sections, we present some important considerations in designing, building, and running a centralized data center environment utilizing the latest Citrix technology.

DESIGNING A DATA CENTER APPLICATION DELIVERY PLATFORM: OVERALL CONSIDERATIONS

For the purposes of this chapter, the design of the datacenter must encompass and service two key areas:

▼   Facilities

▲   Data center network infrastructure

Both of these key areas can be serviced by your organization internally (using internal resources and facilities) or externally by service providers who provide these services and facilities in an outsourced arrangement to your organization. You will want to perform an assessment of your ability to host and/or manage a data center using some of the criteria presented in this chapter. Let's look more closely at the advantages and limitations of outsourcing a data center.

Here are the potential advantages of outsourcing:

▼ Facilities built specifically for data center hosting already exist, and in fact, many data hosting facilities currently have excess capacity. Thus, new construction is rarely necessary.

■ Redundant power sources, such as UPS systems, backup generators with automatic transfer switches (ATSs), redundant power grids, online as well as backup cooling systems, intruder detection systems, secure access, and fire suppression are often already in place and can be leveraged across multiple organizations, reducing the cost to each individual organization.

■ Physical security is usually better than the individual companies' internal security. Guards on duty, biometric authentication, escorted access, and other measures are typical.

■ Hosting facilities are often built very close to the points of presence (POPs) of a local exchange carrier (LEC). In some cases, they are built into the same location as an LEC, which can dramatically decrease WAN communication costs.

■ Managed services that can supplement a company's existing staff are usually available. These services are invariably less expensive than hiring someone to perform routine operations such as exchanging tapes and rebooting servers.

■ Hosting facilities typically are SAS 70 certified and carry liability insurance, which can help with compliance and often can have a significant impact on the cost of business-continuity insurance.

▲ Many facilities can customize the service-level agreement they offer or bundle hosting services with network telecommunication services.

Limitations of outsourcing include the following:

▼ A company's access to its equipment is usually restricted or monitored. Outsourcing puts further demands on the design to create an operation that can run unattended.

■ WAN connectivity is limited to what the hosting center has available. It can be more difficult to get upgraded bandwidth because the hosting center has to filter such requests through the plans in place for the entire facility.

■ It may be more difficult to get internal approval to outsource the expense because the hosting services appear as a bottom-line cost, whereas many information technology costs are buried in other areas, such as facilities and telecommunications.

▲ If unmanaged space is obtained, it may be difficult or impractical for a company to have one of its own staff onsite at the hosting facility for extended periods of time.

Facilities—Power, HVAC, Fire Suppression, and Physical Security

Statically, downtime due to facilities problems (power, HVAC, fire, and physical security) has dropped dramatically over the last ten years, as large UPSs, generators, and water-free fire suppression solutions have become commonplace. That said, though, all of these items require management, maintenance, and monitoring. It is important to have a process to ensure that the management and monitoring is in place (even it is outsourced). If you are considering building a new data center or getting a new outsourcing arrangement, the following sections should help in determining the size and costing requirements for power, HVAC, and fire suppression.

Power

The utilization of an emergency or standby generator is essential when considering power outages that may affect a data center. Outages caused by the local utility that last no longer than 15 minutes will typically be supported by an uninterruptible power supply (UPS). However, a standby emergency generator is necessary to support longer outages.

Each component has a power rating, usually in watts, that it requires for continuous use. At best, inadequate power will strain the power supply of the component. At worst, it will cause a production failure and likely corrupt data. If the facility has a UPS, it must have adequate capacity now as well as the ability to handle future growth plans. Another consideration is, how long can the UPS keep the systems running in the event of a sustained power failure? Is there a backup generator? Does it run on natural gas or fuel? If it is a fuel-based generator, how many gallons of fuel will it support, and how many hours of operation will that yield, and how quickly can you get more fuel to it? During a power failure, it may be difficult to gracefully shut down all of the servers and equipment. Liebert, Tripp Lite, American Power Conversion (APC), and other vendors provide good data center solutions, including software and hardware components for power backup, generator switchover, and server shutdown.

Assessing Your Power Requirements The first step in assessing the actual power requirements and the resulting UPS/generator need is to estimate the load. This is done in slightly different ways for different equipment, but it comes down to estimating the operating voltage, the load (in watts), and a factor for how often the unit is in operation at this voltage and load—sometimes called a "power factor." Here's an example for a high-end server:

> Operating voltage = 120 volts; load = 400 watts; power factor = 0.75 (it is in continuous operation at nearly peak utilization)

This information should be readily available from the server manufacturer either in printed documentation or from their website. A company should collect and total this information for all of their equipment. Using this example, 15 servers would require 4,500 watts (400 * 0.75 * 15), plus a "safety factor" in case multiple servers suddenly run at peak loads (5,000 to 5,200 watts would be wise).

Next, the site voltage should be determined. Data center facilities can often handle multiple voltages, but 230V/400V is common. An organization needs to consider how much room for growth they will need, and make sure there are adequate connections to support future equipment.

NOTE: Facilities at an LEC might also supply 48 volts DC power.

Uninterruptible Power Supply   Organizations selecting an uninterruptible power supply (UPS) need to determine how long they need their equipment to remain functional after power fails. A UPS vendor will be able to provide you an estimate of runtime after power failure based on the total number of watts for your equipment. UPS systems are usually rated in volt-amps. The conversion from watts to volt-amps is $V*A = W / 0.8$. Using the earlier example, 5,200 watts would require 6,500 volt-amps (5,200 / 0.8).

NOTE: It is important not to power up all data center components simultaneously, because the start-up consumes more power and will thus create a spike in power requirements.

HVAC Units for Cooling and Humidity Control

We have been called in to many organizations to resolve unstable software and server problems, only to discover that the temperature where the servers were running was well over 90 degrees Fahrenheit. Servers and telco equipment generate a great deal of heat and will function inconsistently and often sustain permanent damage if their environment has significant temperature variations or remains consistently warm (typically, 66 to 70 degrees Fahrenheit is considered optimal, with temperature variations of no more than +/–5 degrees per day). The less the variation and the cooler the temperature (but not below 65 degrees), the longer the equipment will operate optimally. Cooling should be sufficient for normal operation as well as have adequate backup. The ideal situation is to have a redundant cooling system with sufficient power backup (UPS and generator) to support it.

The cooling system utilized must not add excess moisture to the environment. Industrial evaporators are available to avoid this potential problem. Many higher-end cooling systems have built-in moisture suppression. Detectors should be installed to provide an alert when moisture exceeds recommended levels. Keep in mind that a dry environment means that people working in the data center should drink adequate amounts of water; thus, water fountains should be placed at convenient locations. A dry environment also leads to higher potential for electrostatic discharge, so personnel should be provided with antistatic discharge tools and techniques and be trained how to use them properly.

Heating, Ventilation, and Air Conditioning Evaluation When evaluating heating, ventilation, and air conditioning (HVAC) units, the following factors should be considered:

▼ The temperature and humidity tolerances of the equipment.

■ The amount of space to be cooled (in cubic feet).

■ The period of operation (evenings? weekends?).

■ Seasonal needs. (Are some months much hotter than others?)

■ Whether people will be working for prolonged periods in close proximity to the equipment.

▲ Location of unit: Inside produces excess noise and possible exposure of equipment to a line burst; outside is susceptible to the elements and requires more overhead to install.

NOTE: Route all liquid-carrying lines away from the data room to ensure that a leak will not damage the servers or other data center components.

Fire Suppression

Data center–certified fire-suppression systems are extremely important in any operational facility. These systems use some type of mechanism to extinguish fires while limiting damage to hardware or facilities. Today's fire-suppression systems must comply with environmental concerns regarding ozone depletion and human safety. This is an important consideration if the data center will be staffed and there is a potential for the fire-suppression system to be activated while people are present.

Fire-Suppression System Types Many types of systems are available that comply with environmental requirements and use different agents to suppress fires. We recommend comparing the quality of the different types of fire-suppression systems to determine which one best fits the data center setup. Table 4-1 lists the advantages and disadvantages of some of the different systems currently available.

Seismic and Other Environmental Activity

For data centers in California or other seismically active areas, adequate facility bracing is a must. Facilities should meet or exceed the earthquake regulations for the area. In addition, computer hardware racks and cabinets, and other equipment, should have their own bracing and be able to pass inspection. Other geographical areas have different environmental concerns that should be planned for—for example, possible hurricanes in Florida and major snow storm–based power outages in some northern states.

Physical Security

If most, or all, of an organization's computing infrastructure will be housed at a data center, it is imperative that physical access be restricted and monitored. Many outsourced hosting facilities have security guards, card-key access, motion sensors, and silent alarms.

Type of System	Chemical Agent	Advantages	Disadvantages
Precharge sprinkler	Water	Provides the best suppression of all fires and protection for structures. No water sits above sensitive equipment.	Extra plumbing is required, including lines and routing of pipes to avoid the data center and sensitive equipment. Major water damage is likely when discharged.
Wet sprinkler	Water	Provides the best suppression of all fires and protection for structures.	Accidental discharge from human or environmental factors can occur. Major water damage is likely when discharged.
FM-200	Heptaflouropropane	Doesn't displace oxygen, so it is safe when people are present.	High cost.
Inergen	Argon, nitrogen, and CO_2 (stands for *Inert gas and nitrogen*)	Allows storage or flow over data center room. Inergen leaves enough oxygen for people to breathe.	High cost, large storage space.

Table 4-1. Comparison of Commercial Fire-Suppression Systems

Despite tremendous amounts of time and money spent protecting a network with hardware and software security, data can still be at considerable risk if physical security is not considered. I have heard many cases where a critical server was simply stolen, never to be seen again. The worse part of these stories is that physical security is typically the least expensive risk to mitigate. We discuss security in more detail in Chapter 6.

Data Center Network Design

In the next sections, we discuss some important factors to consider when planning the data network connections into a data center. Chapter 6 of one of our previous books, *Citrix Access Suite 4 for Windows Server 2003: The Official Guide*, is dedicated to network design for Application Delivery and provides much more detail on these and other topics.

User Geography and Location of the Data Center

The geographic dispersion of the user community plays a major role in the site selection for a data center. Whether a company has only domestic or domestic and international offices has a profound influence on data center aspects, such as availability for WAN bandwidth and hot sites. Ideally, the chosen site should yield the lowest overall network cost from the national exchange carriers while meeting all the other requirements mentioned in this chapter. One of the single largest cost items in building your data center will be the data network. Anyone who has ever ordered a data line from a local or national carrier knows that the distance from their office (demarcation point or demark) to the carrier's point of presence (POP) can translate into hundreds or thousands of dollars per month. A data center is no exception.

Time Zones Microsoft Windows Server 2003 and 2008 and all Citrix products support time-zone translation—meaning that the client machine will display the time based on its local time zone rather than the time zone of the server. This is a critical feature for organizations whose users may be in physically disparate time zones relative to where the servers are physically located.

Bandwidth Availability

Another consideration in planning network connections is bandwidth availability in the area where the data center is located. The required circuits may be easily ordered now, but what about in six months or a year? It is vital that a company understands the capacity available, usually from the LEC, and its growth plans. We have seen many customers experience delays in their entire data center build-outs because there were no additional circuits available from the LEC, and no one thought to check in advance (or they were overpromised by the LEC when they did enquire).

TIP: It has been our experience over many years that telecommunication carriers are often overly optimistic when estimating the time required to install a circuit. They are similarly overly optimistic about the time required to make an installed circuit work smoothly. It is important to build extra time into the schedule for getting the circuit in and working.

Bandwidth Management Due to the nature of Internet Protocol traffic, any amount of network bandwidth can be swallowed up by a variety of both important and unimportant applications, with no respect to priority. Thus, having the tools in place to manage, understand, report, and prioritize bandwidth is critical. A discussion of tools for managing and prioritizing bandwidth is included in Chapter 6 of one of our previous books, *Citrix Access Suite 4 for Windows Server 2003: The Official Guide*.

Reliability

An unreliable network can kill a project. It is crucial that an organization ensure that its bandwidth carrier can provide detailed reliability statistics of the circuits to be used. Especially in the case of newer topologies, incorrect assumptions of flawless performance may lead to project failure. It is wise to get customer references, and ask those companies how the carrier's product is working for them. Organizations should also allow adequate time for their own testing to make sure the circuits are sufficiently reliable to meet their needs.

Network Redundancy

It makes little sense to design all of the components of a data center with failover capability if the network represents a single point of failure. Users will rely on the network to reach one or a few data centers; it must be resistant to production outages. Buying a redundant circuit can be expensive, but carriers are often able to sell access to a circuit to more than one company for far less than the circuit itself would cost. In case the primary circuit fails, they can switch customers to this backup so that they can continue operation. If a secondary live circuit is not practical or affordable, another option is putting a second type of lower-bandwidth circuit in place. These backups will not provide as much bandwidth, but some access always beats total downtime.

Using the Internet as a Redundant Network   Because most businesses and many households today have Internet access, the Internet makes an obvious choice (assuming it can be secured) for access into the data center or as a backup network access path into the data center if private line access is lost. Since the release of Citrix Access Gateway (CAG), it has been easy for organizations to utilize the Internet as an access point into the data center. With the CAG, all data traversing from the Internet to the data center (and back to the Internet) is encrypted using SSL encryption (port 443), and no additional firewall port holes or client-side software is required. The CAG is covered in depth in Chapter 11.

Virtual private network (VPN) technology may also be utilized for this same purpose. In the case of VPN technology, we strongly recommend the use of hardware encryption devices at the data center rather than software termination. Additionally, we have found that VPNs tend to require a significant amount of administrative overhead due to the complexity and update requirements of the client-side VPN software.

DISASTER RECOVERY AND BUSINESS CONTINUITY

Nearly every organization today gives lip service to disaster recovery, but from industry statistics, less than half of all organizations have a tested business-continuity plan. We will examine disaster recovery and business continuity at length in Chapter 8, but we touch on them briefly here because they are such important topics in today's world.

When initially considering the consolidation of distributed corporate servers, an organization may be concerned about "putting all their eggs in one basket." In most distributed computing environments, a single network link failure probably affects only a small group of people. When everyone is connected to the same data center, however, a network failure impacts every user and every application. Fortunately, Citrix provides a very flexible and cost-effective approach to building redundancy across multiple geographies, power grids, data access grids, and user access points. Chapter 8 will provide greater detail on why we strongly recommend organizations utilize two data centers (one main data center and one geographically separate data center) and how to technically configure this solution. For the purposes of this chapter, though, the requirements we have discussed should be applied to the first data center, with the assumption that additional data centers will be similar (albeit scaled down if your DR plan does not require full-scale operations in the case of a disaster).

NOTE: Citrix XenApp is a redundant, but not a failover solution, because data that is residing in memory within a session that has not been written to disk will be lost when a user is moved to another server due to hardware failure, a server reboot, or a server blue screen.

Outage Mitigation Strategies

Having a good disaster-recovery plan in place is small comfort to users if they are experiencing regular interruptions in service. Centralizing computing resources makes it that much more important to incorporate a high degree of resilience into a design. Companies must take a global view of the entire infrastructure and make the following assessments:

▼ *Identify single points of failure.* Even if the database server is clustered, what happens if the WAN connection fails?

■ *Implement redundancy in critical system components.* If one server is good, two are better. If possible, they should carry balanced loads or, at the very least, have an identical backup server to put online in case one fails (a "cold spare").

■ *Implement Citrix EdgeSite with alerting and escalations.* Even when multiple redundant solutions are in place, it is important to have visibility to when one part of the redundancy has failed. We have seen many instances where the primary resource went down and failed over to the backup with no visibility, and when the backup eventually failed, a critical failure occurred. Citrix EdgeSite is covered in depth in Chapter 12.

■ *Establish a regular testing schedule for all redundant systems.* Many organizations have backup plans that fail when called upon. Therefore, it is important to test and document the backup systems until you are comfortable that they can be relied upon in a time of crisis.

■ *Establish support-escalation procedures for all systems before there is an outage.* Document the support phone numbers, customer account information, and what needs to be said to get past the first tier of support.

■ *Review the vendor service levels for critical components, and assess where the vendor may need to supplement them or have spare parts on hand.* Is the vendor capable of meeting their established service level? What is the recourse if they fail to perform as promised? Is support available somewhere else? Is the cost of having an extra, preconfigured unit on hand in case of failure justified?

■ *Establish a process for management approval of any significant change to the systems.* Two heads are always better than one when it comes to managing change. Companies should ensure that both peers and management know about, and approve of, what is happening at the data center.

■ *Document any change made to any system.* For routine changes, approval may not be necessary, but companies should make sure there is a process to capture what happened anyway. Citrix SmartAuditor, released with Update 1 for Platinum Edition 4.5, provides rule-based recording and playback for detailed auditing. The audit trail can be invaluable for troubleshooting. SmartAuditor is covered in Chapter 14.

■ *Develop a healthy intolerance for error.* An organization should never say, "Well, it just works that way." They should obtain regular feedback from the user community by establishing a customer survey concerning perceived downtime, system speed, and so on, and give feedback to their vendors and manufacturers. This is another area where Citrix EdgeSite will be invaluable, because it monitors end-user application performance. It is important to keep pushing until things work the way the users want them to work.

▲ *Build some extra capacity into the solution.* Being able to try a new version of an application or a service pack or a hotfix without risking downtime of the production system is extremely important. Leveraging Citrix XenServer virtualization can provide an economical way to support multiple test environments.

Offsite Data Storage

Even with a secure and reliable data center, data backups should be taken offsite to a hardened location or copied to an offsite location (or second data center) daily. A *hardened* location is one in which proper fire and moisture protection has been ensured, as well as physical security for data storage media. During a production failure or disaster involving a loss of site, such backups can mean the difference between a quick recovery and no recovery at all. Many national and regional firms specialize in data storage. Other firms will use a frame-relay connection or the Internet to back up data to a secure offsite location. If a company is outsourcing its data center, they must make sure they have tape exchange or electronic vaulting as part of the service-level agreement (SLA) with their vendor. Otherwise, one of their own people will have to travel to the data center daily to change tapes.

OTHER CONSIDERATIONS IN DATA CENTER DESIGN

A number of issues may apply to a company when considering the centralization of their application delivery infrastructure. It is not possible to anticipate every conceivable issue of designing a data center, but the following topics cover some issues we have run into in the past that may help in your planning.

Legacy Hosting

Will users need access to data or programs on legacy systems? (Enterprise resource planning, database query and reporting tools, and terminal emulation are all examples of such applications.) If this is the case, the legacy systems and Citrix servers should be co-located to optimize the network bandwidth required between these systems, as shown in Figure 4-1.

Rogue Servers and Applications

An organization should determine whether their group or project team is in control of all the servers in the enterprise that may be affected by a project. Especially in a large enterprise, it is likely that some servers and applications have been set up regionally without their knowledge. Unless the company actively investigates beforehand, the first time they hear of such systems may be when they disable a network circuit or otherwise cut off the regional users from the rest of the network. It is wise to develop a plan to have a "sunset period" in which these locations are given a certain amount of time to phase out such systems and begin to access their applications from the new data center.

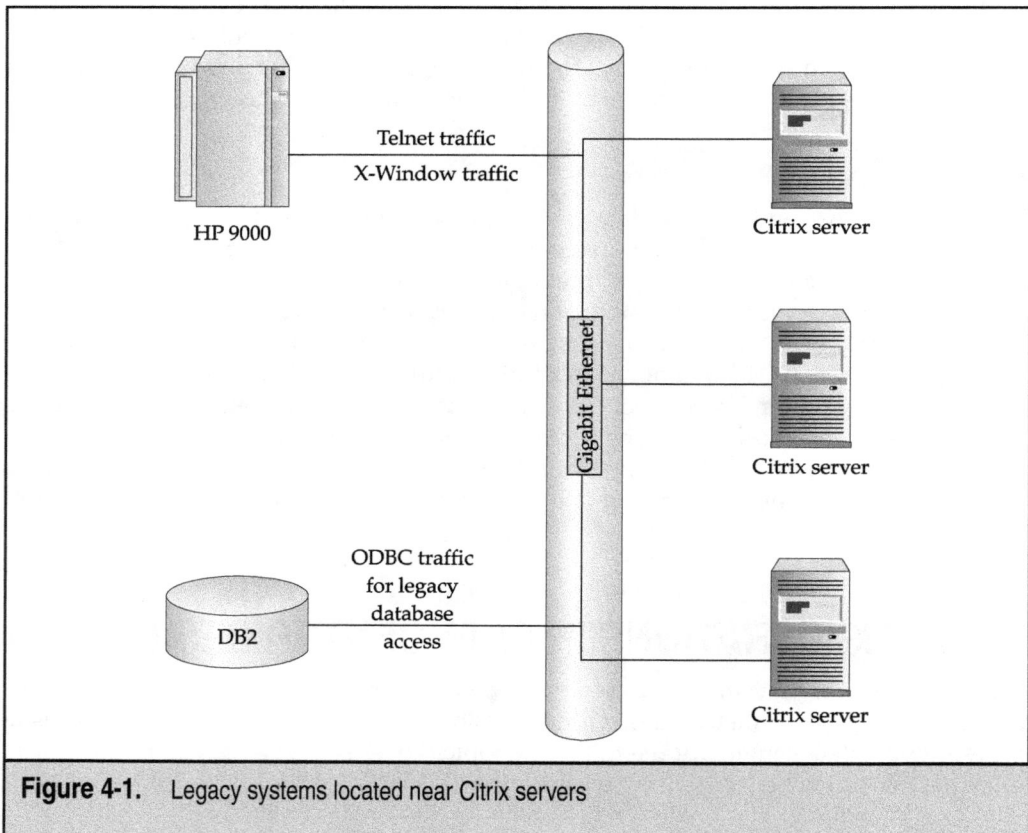

Figure 4-1.   Legacy systems located near Citrix servers

Organizational Issues

Whether an organization decides to outsource the data center or run it themselves, it is crucial they not underestimate the organizational impact of moving toward centralization. Unless such a center is already running, the following needs to be done:

▼   Come up with a three-shift staffing plan (or at least three-shift coverage).

■   Decide whether the current staff has sufficient training and experience to manage the new environment.

■   Determine whether the current staff is culturally ready to deal with the discipline required to make the centralized application delivery infrastructure reliable. In other words, can they manage the systems using rigorous change control and testing procedures?

■   Decide which of the existing staff needs to be onsite and when.

■   If outsourcing, determine which services the vendor will be providing and which will be handled internally.

▲   If outsourcing, make sure there is a clean division and escalation procedure between internal and external support resources.

CHAPTER 5

The Client Environment

In this chapter, we will discuss the three categories of client devices: local devices, remote devices, and hybrid devices. Each of these categories may include some or all of the client device types: thin clients ("toaster" devices such as Wyse or HP terminals or fully locked-down PCs dedicated to running only a web browser and/or Citrix client), desktops or workstations, laptops, and mobile devices running a Palm OS or Windows Mobile OS. We also discuss some of the areas of influence for delivering applications to users and the types of applications to deliver (for instance, when to use desktops versus published applications). Finally, we discuss strategies and provide installation tips not covered by the standard documentation from the manufacturers, and we introduce some advanced concepts and considerations when distributing your client environment throughout your company.

When it comes to choosing the best client device to use in your environment, you'll need to take into account several things. In general, companies tended to lean toward the simplest (or "thinnest") client device available to take full advantage of the savings derived from lower upfront costs, lower setup costs, significantly reduced software maintenance, reduced hardware maintenance, and fewer repairs. Although the concept and approach of thin clients has not changed much since the inception of server-based computing, price and performance have both improved dramatically. It is now possible to procure a simple thin client device for $299 (monitor is extra). A more complex thin client device can be had for $1,000 (running Windows Embedded XP OS) from several manufacturers, including Wyse, HP, Neoware, and others. Recently, desktops and laptop prices have been dramatically reduced in price throughout the industry. This begs the question, "What type of device should my company purchase?" When comparing thin clients and PCs, be fair and make sure you are comparing "apples to apples." Although we have heard many people argue that they can procure PCs for about the same cost as thin clients, we have never discovered that to be true. Even though many consumer-based retail outlets advertise $600 PCs, corporations today often spend over $1,000 per PC in order to get a fully configured PC with the Windows XP Professional operating system, networking, and a three-year warranty. Table 5-1 provides a comparison between the costs of a PC and a Wyse terminal thin client.

The numbers from Table 5-1 are very conservative by most industry standards. The Gartner Group estimates that most enterprise organizations spend closer to $7,000 per PC per year, because the number of nonautomated reconfigurations and software installations is much greater than the numbers used here. Additionally, the internal billable rate ($50 per hour) is lower than most enterprise organizations experience for fully loaded costs. Regardless, we wanted to use conservative numbers to make our case inarguable. For an organization considering a technology-refresh of 100 PCs per year, even if all "soft costs" are ignored, the upfront savings for just the initial procurement and setup costs will be $64,750 per year. If soft costs are included, and a three-year cost outlay is looked at for the enterprise organization, the savings are very significant.

Task	PC: Dell Optiplex with Windows Vista BE, Three-Year Warranty	Wyse Terminal: S-Series S10 (Thin Client), Three-Year Warranty
Initial procurement cost.	$599.	$349 (includes license for management software).
Initial configuration and installation time. (Assume ghost imaging for the PC, but include ghost image setup and maintenance time.)	3 hours @ $50/hour internal billable rate = $150.	15 minutes @ $50/hour internal billable rate = $12.50.
Operating system upgrade price. (Assume one new revision of the Windows operating system over the three-year period.)	$200 + 2 hours @ $50/hour internal billable rate, for a total price of $300.	$0. Wyse S10 is Wyse Thin OS–based and firmware updates are pushed from management software.
Software upgrade time. (Assume one new revision of MS Office and one new revision of other desktop applications per year that must be installed and configured.)	6 hours @ $50/hour internal billable rate = $300.	$5. Software updates will be done once at the server for all clients; assuming hundreds of clients, the cost per client is very small.
Assume one local workstation touch per quarter required for maintenance and security patching of operating systems and web browsers. Assume management software will be used to push out patches (SMS for PCs, Wyse Rapport for Winterms).	8 hours per year (24 hours over three-year period) @ $50/hour internal billable rate, for a total cost of $1,200 to configure and manage the management software.	2 hours per year (6 hours over three-year period) @ $50/hour internal billable rate, for a total cost of $300 to configure and manage the management software.
Hardware repair—assume one warranty repair is required over the three-year period, necessitating a reload and reconfiguration.	3 hours @ $50/hour internal billable rate = $150.	15 minutes @ $50/hour internal billable rate = $12.50.
Total three-year cost	**Approx $2,399**	**Approx $679**

Table 5-1.   Three-Year Price Comparison: PC vs. Thin Client

All that being said, there is still a compelling reason to purchase and use desktops and laptops for client devices throughout the organization. Even though the thin-client technology is a good fit for many users in the environment, not all models are as versatile as their PC counterpart—for instance, when you have mobile users or your environment calls for a hybrid deployment (applications are installed locally on the machines and used along with Terminal Server applications). Also, some organizations may not be able to fully convert to thin clients.

Organizations that may not be able to replace all PCs with thin clients include the following:

▼ Organizations that have large numbers of newer PCs (less than two years old) that cannot be easily discarded. (Some organizations are leasing their desktop PCs, and the terms of the lease will dictate whether it is advantageous or impossible to get rid of the PCs.)

■ Organizations still supporting 16-bit or DOS applications that won't run effectively in a XenApp environment, and therefore must be run using the processing power and operating system of a "local" PC.

▲ Organizations that will only be supporting a portion of their users or applications in a XenApp environment.

A large number of organizations end up running a mix of clients and client devices, at least for a period of time, for these reasons. As such, it is necessary to explore complementary technologies to make hybrid and mobile users take on as many of the desirable characteristics of the thin client as possible. The most significant gain of the thin client—that of not having to install, manage, update, or repair local applications—can be realized from any client device, with the correct configuration and management tools. In discussing these hybrids, we will describe the available technology and techniques needed to accomplish this.

CLIENT CLASSIFICATIONS

The different client device types are shown in Table 5-2. Although client devices tend to be evaluated more on their category and how they will be used more commonly than their actual client type, it is important to note a great deal of overlap exists today with client types. That is, both software and hardware exist today to convert a PC into a full "thin client," and many of the new thin clients have local web browsers, Windows Embedded XP operating systems, and fully supported client peripherals (via USB, parallel ports, and/or serial ports). Therefore, they can be considered a good fit for some hybrid situations. Additionally, with the large number of new device types coming on the scene, such as tablet PCs, handheld devices, Linux devices, and Windows CE tablets, it is useful to discuss using more than one type of client device in your organization for each of the categories of use.

Client Types	LAN Published Applications	Secure Remote Access	Local Web Browser	Local Applications	Support of Local Peripherals	Local File Sharing
Thin client only	×		×		−	
Desktops	×		×	×	×	×
Laptops	×	×	×	×	×	×
Mobile devices		−	×	−		

× indicates that the device meets the requirement.
− indicates that the device *could* meet the requirement.

Table 5-2.   Client Categories

The matrix of client types is meant to provide an idea of how client devices can be used throughout an organization. Today, there is overlap when it comes to the functionality of PCs and thin clients in the application delivery model. For example, a thin client that supports a local web browser, peripheral devices, and a complex local OS (such as Windows Embedded XP), fits into the hybrid category. Although it will be more expensive to procure, configure, manage, and maintain than a thin client that simply supports an ICA client, it has nearly the same functionality as the simple lower-end laptops and desktops. It is also important to note that this client matrix does not define operating systems. If Citrix XenApp will be used, its support of hundreds of operating system variations ensures the use of Linux-based devices, Windows CE–based devices, as well as the more common assortment of Windows 95– through Windows XP–based devices. If only Windows Terminal Services will be used, the device choice becomes more limited.

Because total cost of ownership is not the only consideration when choosing which client type and client devices to support, a significant task in designing an access platform is to figure out which client types and devices will be procured and supported.

CLIENT DECISIONS—WHAT TO BUY?

The process of designing and deploying the user's desktop environment can be a traumatic experience for both the IT staff and the end user. PCs have long been organizational fixtures, often being used as part of a corporate rewards system (those who have been around the longest get the best PCs). Unless the situation is handled correctly, users will fight hard against any change toward a different or more simple client environment. Usually, end users will not be able to see how the change benefits them or their company, especially when they are used to having more freedom on less-secure, non-locked-down devices. In order to help sell the idea and ensure nonbiased decisions are made, a client decision matrix should be used. Defining such a matrix will provide the following benefits:

▼ By applying the same set of criteria to the classification of each user, you will avoid making decisions based on political or nontechnical reasons.

■ When the decision-making process is communicated to users, they will not feel they are being singled out, but rather that they are subject to the same rules as everyone else.

▲ Users can be classified *en masse* relatively quickly, and decisions about the number of clients of each type, necessary upgrades, or disposition plans can then be made.

Start out with some basic evaluation questions, as described here.

▼ *Does the user require access to only Citrix XenApp–based applications?* In other words, does the user only need access to the applications already slated for hosting in a XenApp environment? If so, the categorization of that user can be easily made.

■ *Is the user's existing computer a XenApp–compatible device?* Because the Citrix clients are so thin, a large majority of devices in use in organizations today will work well in nearly any client role. For the purposes of this text, the term "PC" includes any common device, regardless of operating system, that is capable of running the Citrix ICA clients.

■ *Does the user need access to applications outside the local area network (LAN)?* Will this user be accessing applications at the office and from a remote location such as from home, a hotel, or branch office?

▲ *Does the user require offline application use?* Is the user traveling and unable to gain access to the LAN or WAN for extended periods of time? Do they require localized applications? For example, mobile users may be allowed to run applications locally if they do not have consistent access to the Internet or wireless WAN (T-Mobile HotSpot, Sprint, Verizon, Cingular, and others).

Table 5-3 shows the resulting decision matrix, with deployment plans for each category of user.

Category	Deployment
User requires only XenApp–based applications and currently does not have a XenApp–capable device (the user may have a very old PC or green screen, for example).	User gets a standard thin client. The existing PC goes through disposition (disposal or donation).
User requires only XenApp applications and currently has a XenApp–capable device.	User gets a standard thin client. The device gets rebuilt with minimal requirements to run ICA client, or it gets placed in the reassignment pool (see the next item in this matrix).
User requires both XenApp and non–XenApp applications and currently does not have a XenApp–capable device.	User gets a XenApp–capable device from the reassignment pool or a new purchase is made.
User requires both XenApp and non–XenApp applications and currently has a XenApp–capable device.	IT staff disables or uninstalls applications from the PC that exist in the XenApp environment.
User travels with the device and needs access to both XenApp and non–XenApp applications.	User gets a laptop or mobile device, with specific applications and lockdown software.

Table 5-3.   Client Decision Matrix

Thin Clients

Thin clients are available from a variety of manufacturers, with many variations on the same theme. Most thin clients have no moving parts, except perhaps for a fan, and all the operating system and client software is stored in hardware. They typically run Windows CE, Linux or a BSD UNIX variant, or Embedded Windows XP as the operating system, and implementations of other software are proprietary to the device. They are capable of running Windows, Java, Linux, UNIX, and web-based applications safely on Microsoft Windows Terminal Services, Citrix Application Delivery Infrastructure, and Citrix XenDesktop using thin display protocols. This, and the fact that they have different CPUs and graphics capabilities, contribute to the performance differences among the devices. In no particular order, some of the devices we've tested and used in production are the Wyse Thin Client, HP Compaq Thin Client T Series, and Neoware m100 Series. Most of the thin clients have a very small form factor. Some are built into a CRT or flat-screen monitor, whereas others have the look and feel of a laptop. Additionally, all of the devices are low-power consumption devices, a feature that can add to the savings over PCs for large enterprises with thousands of devices. Here are two examples of what a basic thin client setup looks like:

Wyse X90e and X90   Wyse S10

In addition to offering the necessary ICA or RDP software to connect to the XenApp farm, most thin-client models offer emulation and connectivity software such as legacy terminal emulation clients (IBM 3270 and Telnet, for example). Local browsing is also available with either proprietary browsers or OEM versions of Mozilla and Microsoft Internet Explorer. There can be a significant advantage in cost and ease of use in having multiple connectivity software in the device when integrating the terminal into an environment where legacy functions as well as the new features of XenApp must be supported. This is a key differentiator among products.

Thin Client Management

Another key differentiator that is not always clear when evaluating different thin clients is how they are managed. Most manufacturers have developed or purchased their own proprietary management software that can monitor the terminals and report errors as well as provide software updates via automatic download on bootup. Additionally, some manufacturers provide hooks to integrate the terminals into a management framework, such as HP OpenView. Manufacturer-supplied software can work as long as it is sufficiently scalable to handle the network infrastructure in your company. If it can't, consider a solution that integrates into a management framework. At the very least, the terminal should send SNMP messages and supply an MIB for your management software.

Although the key point of a thin client is to keep the desktop simple and reduce desktop administration costs to zero, a certain amount of administrative overhead is associated with a thin client (updating the Citrix client every six months, for example). Therefore, a thin client with good management software can further reduce administrative costs. Wyse, HP, and Neoware all have remote management software packages that monitor the terminals, integrate with SNMP management software, and remotely provide the terminals with software updates.

Functional Differences

The Citrix client for Windows CE and Windows Embedded XP supports all of the functions of the standard 32/64-bit ICA client for Windows, as does the client for Linux on thin clients. Here's a list of the differences between running the client on a PC versus a thin client:

▼ **Client software updates** Although most terminals now provide management software that will automate upgrades to the embedded software, these upgrades remain challenging given the newness of firmware management software applications. Upgrades are typically done via an automatic or scheduled download. Some terminals support the Citrix Auto Update feature, which can be a significant timesaver when a new version of the Citrix client needs to be deployed. At the very least, look for a terminal with management software that supports a centralized method for downloading software (either operating system images or applications) and rebooting the terminal without user intervention.

■ **Local browsing** Embedded browsers are limited with regard to storing local data and using plug-ins. They offer a limited bookmark list and, of course, do not allow plug-ins or other downloads.

■ **Java** Standalone Java applications (those that do not require a browser to run) require a Java Virtual Machine (JVM) to be installed on the thin client firmware. The JVM must be the correct version, and the Java application must also be loaded into firmware in order to execute.

■ **Auto-login** Auto-login can be used when you want to present a limited number of choices to the user when logging in. When auto-login is enabled, the user is limited to one terminal session—either a desktop or a specific, published application. If you want the user to have access to multiple published applications at login, auto-login should be disabled.

▲ **Configuration security lockout** Whatever configuration settings the terminal offers, it is important the users are prevented from changing them once they are established. If the configuration cannot be protected, you run the risk of configuration-related support calls driving up the TCO.

The Desktop—Otherwise Known as the PC

The problem that arises when updating so many desktops is what to do with all the replaced devices. This can be a significant problem for an organization that is committed to being as secure and as easy to manage as possible. PCs that are no longer appropriate for a given user may still have book value, and the company will need to see some kind of return on them. The following sections include some ideas for dealing with this, given what we have seen at other companies.

Reassignment Pool

As the preceding client decision matrix indicates, even if a PC is considered "XenApp capable," it may be removed from a user's desktop strictly through consideration of the user's need. Why do this? When the total cost of ownership is examined for any desktop PC versus any thin client, the reason becomes clear. Even a new PC with plenty of book value costs far more to support than a thin client. The gist is that a PC is far more prone to spawn a call to the help desk due to an application or operating system problem than is a thin client, on which very little can go wrong.

The idea behind a reassignment pool is to create a standard for PCs to be used in your organization and assign the PCs to those users with a legitimate need. As PCs come in, they can be evaluated for reuse, rebuilt to the proper specifications, and cloned with a standard image of the operating system, web browser, and the ICA client. The standard image contains the base operating system in as locked down a state as possible, the Citrix client, a web browser, and whatever other minimal applications are needed. The user's specific application can then be loaded. This sounds like a lot of work, and it is. But it is far less work in the long run to deliver a PC in a known state than to deal with one in an unknown state later in the field.

PC Disposal

Now that there is a plan to reuse PCs that have some value—either financial or technical—what do we do with PCs that have no book value, are outdated, or are broken in some way? The two obvious choices are donation and disposal.

Many nonprofit organizations accept donated PCs, but quite often their minimum requirements are high, because many of them aren't using XenApp and thus need reasonable computing power to run a newer operating system and applications. Nevertheless, it is worth discovering whether your old gear is worth something to someone else. One nonprofit organization that helps with this process is the National Association for the Exchange of Industrial Resources (NAEIR). See their website at http://www.naeir.com/.

The disposal option has also become more complicated, because most computer parts are considered low-level hazardous materials. Contact your local landfill for information on computer disposal.

Carefully consider how to dispose of old hard drives. Even though there are many methods out there that "remove" data from a hard drive (format, magnet, and so on), data can still be obtained from the drive. If you are donating the PC, take the time and format the drive, and even install a new OS on it. Until it is overwritten, data can still be recovered off the drive. Most charities do not have the type of people, or for that matter, the equipment to go after your valuable information, so just a format and rebuild is safe. If you are the type of person who wishes to be overly cautious and take no chances, the only real safe method of protecting the data from being stolen is to destroy the drive.

Many programs are available that will stomp, crush, or melt your drive into unusable piles of scrap metal to ease your mind. A quick Internet or Yellow Pages search will provide you what you need. When searching for this type of service, be sure to check for listings that state the following:

▼ Complete computer and electronic destruction.

■ Complete elimination of information.

■ Destruction process that meets or exceeds all federal, state, and global requirements (WEEE, Sarbanes-Oxley, GLB, FACTA, and HIPAA).

▲ Environmentally friendly handling of electronic waste (100% recyclable).

So far in this chapter, we have talked a lot about getting rid of or reusing the PCs in an organization. This may or may not be an acceptable approach for your particular situation, but it is an optimal one in terms of TCO. If you lean toward keeping PCs and just running applications in a XenApp environment, it is important to understand that this decision will have a big impact on the overall value returned by the project. The following are some advantages and limitations to consider if you plan to keep most of the PCs in your organization.

These are some of the advantages of keeping PCs:

▼ PCs are ubiquitous. It is likely that your organization already has a large number of PCs with residual book value and would like to use them if possible.

■ The skills necessary to support PCs are already available. Supporting other types of devices may take additional training.

▲ PCs are multipurpose platforms that can perform many functions outside those required for a XenApp environment.

Here are some of the limitations of using PCs:

▼ Public studies show that PCs are significantly more expensive to administer than thin clients.

■ PCs have many moving parts that are far more prone to failure than a solid-state device.

■ PCs are prone to obsolescence, which also contributes to the high TCO. This problem is somewhat mitigated by using the PC as a thin client, but if you plan to run *any* applications locally, you still must deal with the constant hardware upgrades required when upgrading software.

▲ PCs require additional configuration and possibly additional software to approach the level of security and stability of a thin client. PCs should only be delivered in your organization if first locked down in a manner that prevents users from making detrimental changes to the Registry or loading unauthorized software.

Does all this mean that you should completely eradicate all the PCs and go "thin" all the way? The hard, definitive answer is…possibly.

In the last few months, there has been a downtrend in the price of PCs—this includes all forms, laptops, desktops, and any device capable of running an OS. Truth is that PCs are still viable options for client devices. Thin clients have their place, but the majority of users these days are more mobile than in years prior. Mobility is the trend in infrastructure. Applications are further and further away from the users, but there is still the need for fast, on-demand access. This leads us away from thin clients and desktops and introduces laptops and mobile devices into the equation.

Laptops and Mobile Devices

Laptops have been around for years, and the prices are dropping every day, which makes them a viable choice for mobile users. Laptops are robust enough for the right price to give users access to applications both on the LAN/WAN and off the LAN/WAN. I know what you're thinking: We just finished discussing the TCO of PCs and how they are prone to this and that, and the blah, blah, blah of PC shelf life. The truth is, that was yesterday's thinking. With new software and cheaper hardware, we can do a double-take on the PC role in the enterprise. How exactly can we make laptops easy to mange and be flexible in the organization?

Picture this: A new user is hired at your company. This user will be a traveling user. A company-issued laptop is built and provided for the new hire to use for work. They sit down at their desk, power up, and log into the network. Upon a successful login, the user sees a beautiful new desktop with all the applications that have been assigned to this user specifically to do their job. This user works all day creating and saving documents and sending e-mails and then logs off and goes home. The next day a coworker calls them up and says they both need to be at the new branch office right away. They head out to the branch location and sit down and begin to work.

Problem: The newbie forgot their laptop at the other office.

Solution: Another laptop is pulled off the shelf and given to the newbie so they can work. When the user logs in, all the same applications and features are present.

How is this possible, you ask? All the laptops in the organization are built exactly the same. Using third-party software such as Enteo's NetInstall or RES Software's Wisdom products, each laptop is formatted and rebuilt according to written policies and procedures. Once discovered by the software suite, a new OS, all the applications, and the updates are packaged and deployed to the client device when the unit is powered on without the involvement of IT! Let me say that again: without the involvement if IT (other than the push of a power button). Because this is a traveling user and there is always the odd chance that the laptop could be stolen or lost, we certainly do not want valuable data and programs located on this device.

This laptop's build consists of a basic OS install, Internet Explorer, Citrix's Program Neighborhood Agent client, and the XenApp Streaming Client, and nothing else. Here is the flow:

The user logs into the laptop and is presented with a secure locked-down desktop using shell replacement software such as RES PowerFuse. Program Neighborhood Agent passes through the logon information to the XenApp Server. The user is authenticated to the Citrix server farm, and a list of this user's available applications is generated. This user, because they are a traveling user, requires both remote applications (applications served up by Citrix XenApp) as well as offline applications (applications streamed to the client by XenApp 4.5 Streaming Client) to use while on the road. Program Neighborhood Agent places shortcuts to the XenApp applications on the desktop and Start menu and begins to stream the offline applications down to the desktop. When the user is ready to go, they log out and take the streamed applications with them for use at a later time, perhaps at the hotel or on the plane.

What we have created here is a dynamic client device. If we were to hand this laptop to another user, they would get the applications assigned to them. There's no need to customize a device for each and every user. This is just one example of how PCs and laptops can continue to be useful across the enterprise.

Lastly, consider the mobile device. For the sake of argument, a mobile device is any device that is running a mobile OS such as Palm OS or Windows Mobile. Personal digital assistants and smart phones make it easy to access personal data from pretty much anywhere a connection is available—and from the guy on TV, we know that is pretty much all over the world. Mobile devices are more capable that they have been in the past, and they provide access to a broader range of applications, thus increasing productivity in the workforce. No longer can the excuse be used, "I was out of the office and did not get your info."

Remember the days when a phone was simply a phone? These days you can listen to music, watch TV, retrieve e-mail, keep track of your schedule and your contacts, browse the Internet, and manage business documents using mobile versions of your enterprise applications such as Microsoft Outlook and the Office suite. Well then, why not remote access? Some phones are Java enabled or can run an ICA client and let you gain access to your corporate resources. Citrix's SmartAccess detects a connection spawning from a mobile device and delivers a mobile-ready interface for users to interact with without the clutter and unnecessary content of standard access methods. These devices are not something you want to work on for hours at a time, but in a pinch such access to applications can be handy, especially for the IT staff. It sure beats the hour drive to the office or home and the disruption of your plans simply to unlock a user account when you are at a Colorado Rockies game!

APPLICATION LOCATION—DO YOU NEED APPLICATIONS ON THE CLIENT DEVICES?

In every organization, IT administrators struggle with the decision "to install or not to install?" That is their question. Whether or not to install apps on the client devices is an age-old dilemma for IT admins around the globe. There is a lot to think about here. For instance, is the application Terminal Server compatible? Will it cause performance issues on the Terminal Servers? Does it "play well" with other apps? On the other hand, is it too much effort to deliver applications to the users' desktops and laptops? Almost every organization deals with this decision.

There is no simple answer to these questions, but here is some food for thought when you're having these discussions with fellow IT staff and upper management to help decide whether you should roll applications out to your users' local machines or keep everything on the Citrix servers.

Simple

When considering delivering applications to your users, think about the type of users you have. We mentioned earlier about considering the locale of the user base in the organization as a part of the client device decision. This same thought process should also help determine how applications are delivered. Take the local users, for example. Because these users do not move their client device around and for the most part stay in the same location each day, they are more than likely using thin client devices, and these devices do not have the resources for application installation. Therefore, you will need applications from the XenApp servers that can accommodate their daily workflow needs. These users—HR, support staff, some administration staff, and so on—we refer to as *simple* device users. The devices they work from will not need any local applications installed on them, except the OS of the device and an access client of some kind, such as Java, ICA, or RDP.

Today, companies are investing dollar after dollar trying to simplify IT administration overhead. It is no secret that internal IT does not make money. They usually are the ones spending it. So the only way to make IT affordable—and we all know it can be expensive—is to find ways of lowering the costs associated with IT. The money people upstairs do not want the IT staff running around installing applications on all the computers and then maintaining them afterward. This takes a significant amount of time and is inefficient. Thin clients help alleviate this problem because no apps can be installed on the device. All applications are located on the Citrix XenApp Servers, and the thin clients provide a "window" into the farm to launch the applications. Also, many other devices can take advantage of this connection, such as tablet PCs and mobile devices running Windows Mobile or Palm OS.

Complex

The sales force and sales engineers might need some access to local or offline applications because they travel and do demonstrations for clients (refer to Chapter 9 for more information on streaming offline applications). These users will be in hotels and on planes, at the coffee house, at the client's facility, and working over dinner where there is no remote connection to their internal resources. (For those of you who are married and wish to remain so for any length of time, we highly recommend that you keep the "working over dinner" to an absolute minimum unless you're dining solo.) At the same time, these users are also in the office from time to time and need access to the internal resources and secure applications not available from outside the LAN. When thinking about local applications, design an environment that keeps the administration of the devices as minimal as possible. We are not trying to create a custom build for each user who gets a laptop. Part of the success of rolling out client devices is that we are trying to standardize the build process; otherwise, we are spending far too much time maintaining PCs and not improving the user's experience.

One way to approach this is to develop a standard image for all the laptops that includes all the applications common to the users who will need to be both at and away from the office. Then you can utilize the XenApp Servers to publish and stream the rest of the applications to the devices while they are connected to the LAN. This way, the laptops do not get "stuck" with a particular user. Each laptop will contain the applications common to all the users, and they will get the rest of their apps dynamically through XenApp based on credentials. If a user has a problem with their machine or they find themselves at the office without their assigned laptop, they are still able to borrow one or get a replacement and continue to work without major delays.

This approach also lowers the number of calls into the help desk when there are problems with the PC. The help desk can simply replace the user's machine with a new one and they can get back to work. The old one can be reimaged at a later time and placed back into the pool for the next person.

The Hybrid Environment

The term "Hybrid" is appropriate for the last section because with the movement to consolidate, not many situations have all the applications running on client machines nor are they all centralized on the XenApp servers. All data is now centralized and replicated across multiple locations; no longer do companies want their users out and about the countryside with internal data and applications loaded on their PCs. However, like any other rule, there is always an exception. IT staff and certain sales engineers and consultants have a need to run quite a bit of software on their machines. However, these are users who will also not burden the help desk with calls about application problems and configuration changes. The networking team at our office has a repertoire of several applications they use to connect to routers, firewalls, and switches as well as network tools for identifying problems over the LAN and WAN. These applications not only would be useless when accessed from the Citrix server, but there are different flavors of those apps used among the different staff, and everyone has an opinion as to which one is the best. It is impractical to try to support all those apps for each of the users across an enterprise. Because these users tend to be the more savvy ones in the organization, there is generally more freedom for installing *most* of the apps locally for them to use.

As always, use your discretion for these users and try to keep this type of deployment to a small number of users when it make sense for their job roles.

When to install and when not to install applications on the users' local machines is becoming a frequent debate in organizations. The real solution is to take a hard stance and force conversations about "why" applications need to be installed locally. Figure out what your users are trying to accomplish, how they work, where they work from, and what they actually need to get their jobs done and then decide on the best method of installing the applications for their devices.

APPLICATION DELIVERY—HOW DO USERS GET TO THEIR APPLICATIONS?

Citrix provides XenApp administrators the option of publishing to end users a full desktop interface to the XenApp Servers—effectively providing desktop users with a window that looks identical to that of a desktop PC running Windows XP, or providing the user with individual applications, launched from within their local desktop or web browser environment. Which to choose depends on the overall environment, the number of applications to be delivered, and whether thin clients, desktops, laptops, or mobile devices will be used. The decision whether to publish individual applications or the entire desktop has many ramifications, ranging from end-user experience and performance to security. Both of these options are available in any client type or device scenario.

Publishing Individual Applications

In the case where a XenApp farm is used to deploy only one application or a small selection of applications to end users, the published application option has many benefits. A published application can be published directly to a user's Windows desktop using Citrix Program Neighborhood or directly to a web browser interface using Citrix Web Interface.

Citrix offers three options for delivering published applications to a desktop or laptop: Citrix Program Neighborhood, Citrix Program Neighborhood Agent (PN Agent), and Web Interface. Program Neighborhood Agent addresses many of the issues that existed with the original Program Neighborhood. With PN Agent, an administrator simply points the agent to the Web Interface server, and when users connect, PN Agent populates users' desktops, Start menus, or system trays with all their published applications. Additionally, Program Neighborhood Agent addresses the problem of the local operating system's not knowing to open files using a published application rather than a local application. Program Neighborhood Agent changes all the local desktop MIME type associations to the appropriate published application from the server (Content Redirection).

The Program Neighborhood Agent can be controlled by an administrator with their deployment method of choice (Active Directory, for example) with no user changes available. The administrator may also allow the user to make some configuration changes such as where the Web Interface server is or where the icons are placed in their environment. The advantage of using PN Agent as well as Web Interface for application delivery is that both methods use a centralized configuration source. Unlike Program Neighborhood, all the settings for getting users to their applications are held on the server and not the client. This makes it easy for administrators to make changes to the environment without having to touch all the clients. The other benefit is that the users cannot make changes to the client either, which keeps "curious" users from disrupting the connections.

Published applications are more secure than a published desktop, because users are not granted access to administrative or desktop tools, or to basic operating system tools such as the Start menu. Without this access, it is very difficult for users (authorized or unauthorized) to do harm to the system, although a hacker can find back doors in some published applications (such as Internet Explorer).

Published applications also tend to use system resources on the server far more efficiently, because less memory and processor power are required when the desktop is not being used. Also, users tend to log out of their sessions more often in a published application scenario, because they often close applications without logging out of their desktop. The significant downside to published applications, though, is that they can be confusing to end users—users find it difficult to distinguish between applications that are running locally and applications published from the XenApp farm. Additionally, the fact that users cannot access configurations such as printer settings can cause challenges, because the user is only running the application and not the full interface, which provides access to the printer Control Panel.

Publishing the Desktop

For environments in which all or most applications will be provided to users via the XenApp Servers, and infrastructures with a majority of thin clients, we strongly recommend publishing the full desktop as opposed to just the applications. Although publishing the full desktop requires the desktop lockdown discussed in the next section, the published desktop is simpler and more intuitive for end users. With a published desktop, end users see the full interface they are accustomed to seeing, whereas from a hybrid client a user will see two Start menus (if the published desktop is set up to run as a percentage of the screen size) to make it more obvious whether they are using an application locally or from the XenApp farm. Additionally, thin clients based on Linux do not intuitively switch between published applications, whereas if the desktop is published, the normal hot keys and windowing controls hold true to what users are accustomed to.

In the past, the recommendation used to be to shy away from the published full desktop. Using GPOs to secure a desktop is still a challenge for IT administrators. It takes days to get a desktop environment in a safe and secure state. Today, with third party add-ons such as RES PowerFuse and Enteo, locking down the desktop is not as daunting a task as it has been. What used to take days can now be done in hours and with less frustration. This will make delivering a full desktop a viable option for application delivery.

Other desktop delivery methods that are worth a quick mention but are outside the scope of this book are XenDesktop from Citrix and VDI (Virtual Desktop Infrastructure) from VMWare. These technologies take another approach to desktop delivery and might provide some nice alternatives to traditional published desktops. For more information go to www.citrix.com and www.vmware.com, respectively.

Desktop Lockdown

Because most organizations will utilize PCs either in full thin-client mode or in hybrid mode, locking down the PCs is critical to keep them from continuing to be an ongoing source of help desk calls. Additionally, these same methods are useful for locking down the published desktop environment of the XenApp farm. Although the tools we recommend for locking down PCs are quite good and will dramatically reduce the administration and maintenance required, desktop hardware failure will still be a cause for lengthy support issues.

According to several studies, including one by the Gartner Group, the PC operating system is the source of most of the support requests from users. Even though the Citrix client runs on a variety of operating systems, including Mac OS and Linux, this discussion will be focused on Windows client devices, because they are the most common (and, therefore, most in need of being locked down).

The methods for locking down Microsoft desktops have evolved over the years, although as we discuss next, there is still ample room for third-party providers to intervene and offer good solutions for securing desktop and server environments. For Windows Vista and Windows XP, user and group policies are reasonably powerful and easy to change through the Policy Editor, but can be cumbersome to maintain and troubleshoot when things don't work according to plan. One challenge when locking down the user's base application is how to address the "exception" in the organization. This is the person who belongs to all the security groups in AD but is "immune" to the lock down rules. If you are an IT admin reading this, you know who this person usually is…the boss. (If you are the boss reading this, we have no idea who the IT admin is talking about.) RES PowerFuse and Enteo provide unique solutions by offering policies and security based on Active Directory security groups. With this model, you can enforce an overall policy at the domain level but create a subset or a different policy at the user or group level. Or perhaps you only want to apply the policy at the time the application is launched. Another possible scenario is to apply security based on a geographical location in the organization. This comes in handy when you are trying to limit the number of printers to a particular floor (zone printing). Citrix has a similar function in XenApp called session-based printing, which we cover in more detail in Chapter 17.

Overall, the published desktop environment can once again be considered a viable option for application delivery to your users without feeling like you're leaving the pasture gate wide open and allowing the animals to run free.

Third-party Software for Desktop Lockdown

In the last three years, several software providers have built tools to automate the lockdown of PCs and the PC user environment. Third-party software packages for restricting user activities present a friendlier interface than Policy Editor and Regedit32, and they can be used to track and roll back changes as well as provide myriad management and performance optimization features. We have utilized tools from two software vendors that provide lockdown for both the server user environment and the desktop environment. Although there are many other vendors, the couple we have used and can recommend for server and desktop lockdown are RES Wisdom and RES PowerFuse from Real Enterprise Solutions (RES) and Enteo's Management Suite. Applications from these providers can be used to make user profile, policy, and direct Registry changes to a workstation based on either a standard image or a centralized rules database. The rules can be assigned by user, group, application, and even time schedule. Although the result of these activities is to change the Registry on the client device's operating system—something that can be done manually—these applications do it in a way that is easy to manage and scales across a large organization. Perhaps most important, these applications are compatible with both distributed and centralized application hosting. They can impose the same restrictions on an application hosted from a XenApp farm as they can on one running on a local desktop.

OTHER CONSIDERATIONS

The client environment has many types of clients to choose from. Choosing the best type depends on several aspects of the user. The location of the user's profiles and whether or not a locally attached printer is necessary can also affect the client type that is chosen. The following are some additional considerations to help determine what type of client to roll out.

Profiles

Although profiles will be the main topic of Chapter 16, they are worth a quick mention in this section, because they impact the overall client design. Windows Server 2003 utilizes user profiles to specify a variety of user environmental and applications settings. Important items such as startup scripts, Registry data, shortcuts, menus, browser bookmarks, user data files, and MAPI and ODBC settings are maintained in the user profile. Because of their importance to user functionality as well as their tendency to grow fast and large (like prepubescent elephants), user profiles represent a difficult challenge in the design of the system. For instance, they can be configured as mandatory, roaming, or a hybrid of mandatory and roaming. A great deal of industry work has gone into creating some best practices for hybrid user profiles, as well as the development of best practices for roaming profiles. Even the lockdown applications discussed earlier address user profiles, and some of them claim to alleviate the need for roaming profiles altogether.

We recommend using roaming user profiles but have ourselves used the tips and tricks provided in Chapter 16 to keep a tight rein on the size and storage of the roaming profiles. For the purposes of network design, refer to the steps laid out in Chapter 6 of the book *Citrix Access Suite 4 for Windows Server 2003: The Official Guide* to ensure sufficient network bandwidth and disk space are allocated to support roaming profiles. From a purely client device standpoint, it is nice to note that thin clients are not affected by user profiles, although any published applications they log onto will be. On the hybrid PC side, administrators should be careful to keep the PC profiles separated from the Terminal Services profiles, as discussed in Chapter 16.

Software Distribution and Server-Based Computing

Because many enterprises today utilize infrastructure automation software such as Microsoft's SMS, Enteo's NetInstall Server, and RES Software's Wisdom product, questions arise about how these will integrate and how this function will be performed in a XenApp environment. The answer is threefold:

1. One of the clear advantages of XenApp is that we no longer need to install, configure, and maintain applications on the desktop. Therefore, unless the desktops will be used in a hybrid environment, the software distribution headache and accompanying software tools will disappear at the desktop level.

2. The only exceptions to the first point are Internet Explorer, Java, and/or Citrix clients, which must be distributed, configured, and maintained on all client desktops. Software distribution tools can be used for this purpose and can be

scripted or automated to make this fairly simple and repeatable. You can also use Citrix Web Interface to deploy the Citrix clients. When a desktop user uses a web browser to navigate to the Citrix Web Interface, site links to the client can be configured to help automate the ICA client delivery.

3. Software distribution automation can be a significant timesaver at the server level for large enterprises with a significant number of servers. In a XenApp environment, the applications must be installed on all the servers that will serve these applications, which can be a significant undertaking for organizations with ten to 1,000 XenApp Servers. Citrix provides a tool for this purpose called Citrix Installation Manager, which is embedded in the Enterprise version of XenApp. We will cover this tool in more detail in Chapter 13.

Local Peripherals

Local peripherals can be automatically mapped from the desktop to the server, but not without a price. The data stream used by the device must travel over the network from the server farm to the client device. This can cause excessive bandwidth utilization unless measures are taken to control it. We discuss methods for accomplishing this with Citrix policies in Chapter 17.

NOTE: ICA COM and LPT port redirection allows a variety of local peripherals to be used, but many require tweaking because the ports do not work exactly as they would if they were local ports. For example, we have found that excessive latency over a WAN connection can cause redirected devices to behave erratically, and in fact these devices can exacerbate the bandwidth problem and cause other network services to fail.

Other Client Devices

Thus far, we have discussed PCs and thin clients as the most common devices used to access the Citrix server farm. Since the ICA protocol has been ported to Windows CE, Linux, and even some cell phones, the server farm can be accessed from a variety of client devices. We are seeing integration with devices ranging from tablet PCs in the medical field to proprietary devices running global positioning systems for transportation companies. Although it is generally not practical to run a Windows desktop on the tiny 320×260 screens of some of these devices, it can be very useful to run a small, published application. Imagine a warehouse in which each stockperson has a handheld Pocket PC device with wireless networking and a physical inventory application that feds directly into the corporate inventory database. Perhaps your company has a large number of hourly employees who can use a thin client touch screen to punch in and out of a virtual time-clock application. As an example of sales force automation, perhaps a field salesperson could use their handheld computer to wirelessly connect to the home office and check stock before filling an order, or check and approve special bulk pricing for an important customer.

Once an organization has committed to deploying an access platform, there are innumerable ways to extend the information infrastructure to remote employees, customers, and even the public.

CHAPTER 6

Security, Monitoring, and Management

I n the days of small workgroup LANs, it was relatively easy for a system administrator to keep tabs on the security and status of desktop PCs, servers, and the network simply by looking at the lights on the front of the equipment. As these networks grew in complexity and scope, it became more than any person, or group of people, could do to manually manage the security and know the status of all parts of the network at all times. This problem provided the challenge for the first network management system (NMS). The early NMS software was little more than a log reader, similar to the Event Log and Viewer in Windows Server 2003. Today, the Citrix monitoring and management package, Citrix EdgeSight as well as Citrix SmartAuditor, and Single Sign-On Powered by Password Manager are all included with the Platinum edition of XenApp, and are key reasons that many customers purchase the Platinum edition.

Although Citrix architecture provides a more centralized and architecturally simpler approach than distributed computing, because this centralization creates more focus on the data center and more potential single points of failure, it is critical to establish service-level agreements for services and security and to use centralized tools, such as Citrix EdgeSight and single sign-on, to manage them. This chapter discusses general security concepts and general monitoring concepts and design, including monitoring and reporting for the Application Delivery Infrastructure.

THE NATURE OF SECURITY

The meaning of "security" as it relates to information systems is often diluted to include only security related to clients and servers. This narrow view can be a fatal flaw in corporate information security. One of the early definitions of security for computer networks came from the IBM Dictionary of Computing, published in 1994 by McGraw-Hill, Inc.:

Information Security *The concepts, techniques, technical measures, and administrative measures used to protect information assets from deliberate or inadvertent unauthorized acquisition, damage, disclosure, manipulation, modification, loss, or use.*

This chapter deals primarily with security concepts, components, and design elements. In that light, many of the concepts and discussions are beyond the scope of what an Application Delivery Infrastructure systems administrator will directly control; however, that system administrator must be able to accurately represent security requirements to other staff members who are responsible for design and implementation. Today's enterprises require that all staff are cognizant and vigilant with security, and the on-demand and in-control enterprise requirements dictate that security be a planned consideration and not an afterthought to any IT solution.

As in a chain, the security of the whole computer system is only as strong as the weakest link. A global or systemic model is critical to the formulation of an effective approach to security in the enterprise. It is not uncommon for large companies to decide, almost arbitrarily, that a particular area of their network is open to attack and invest tens of thousands of dollars to "patch the fence" without realizing that someone could walk right through the front gate. In one case we worked with, a company invested $50,000 in an

Internet firewall without setting up a system to enforce strong passwords. With the firewall in place, no one could enter the system from the Internet—that is, unless the intruder could guess that the system administrator's password was his daughter's first name.

Taking a global view of security for the enterprise can be intimidating, which may account for the woefully inadequate attention paid to the subject by many companies. It is important to realize, however, that the effects of securing your infrastructure are *cumulative*. Even a few simple changes to secure certain access points to the network can make a huge difference. For example, installing an effective Internet firewall can be a strong deterrent to the casual hacker. Before deciding to install such a system, however, you need to assess the overall security posture of the infrastructure. Without such an assessment, you could be securing part of your network while leaving another part open to attack. When getting started, it is useful to ask yourself what you are trying to protect.

What Are You Trying to Protect?

The generic answer, more often than not, is "corporate data." Corporate data must be protected from the following:

▼ **Data access** Access must be limited only to appropriate users without impacting authorized access to data or application performance when manipulating data. Figure 6-1 shows the correlation between the level of security and its impact on a user's ability to work. The three security paradigms—Open, Restricted, and Closed—are discussed later in this chapter. The common criteria linked to data access are Authentication, Authorization, and Accounting (AAA), which are described as follows:

■ *Authentication* The ability to positively identify the authorized user, often via two or more factors (username and password, plus biometric, one-time security code tokens). Single Sign-On Powered by Password Manager provides a key solution that integrates with second factor authentication to ensure a positive identification with the least amount of user confusion.

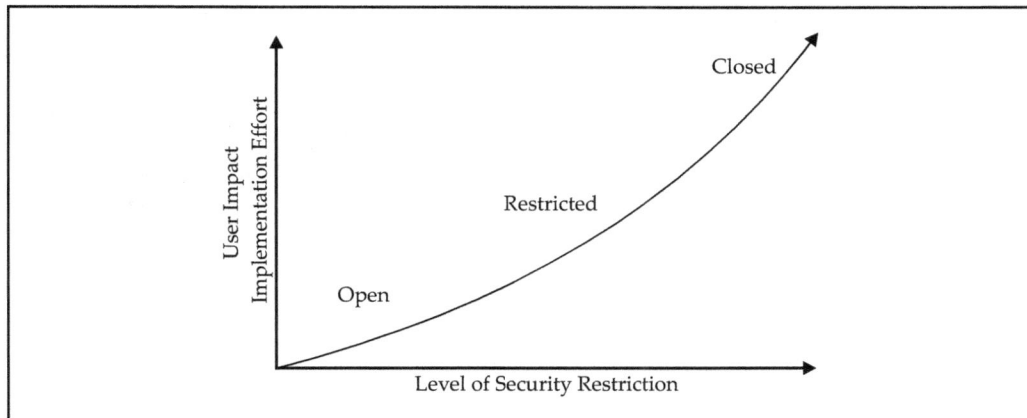

Figure 6-1. Security model vs. user impact

- *Authorization*   The determination of which resources an authenticated user may access, and what rights or permissions they have for each resource. This can be very broad as in file and directory permissions, or very granular as in record-level access controls within a structured database. Citrix SmartAccess, provided through the Access Gateway, offers an industry-leading solution for authorization.

- *Accounting*   The ability to track what a user did or attempted to do. This is particularly critical with regard to audit trails required in most regulated industries. Citrix SmartAuditor (provided with Platinum Version 4.5, Update 1) is the newest solution addition to the suite and a unique solution for auditing.

- **Data integrity**   Data must not be modified or altered except by authorized individuals or processes. AAA rules determine which individuals have the right to perform these operations on the data, and can record what modifications were actually made. Data integrity during transport becomes a serious problem when classic client/server applications are deployed over nonsecure (unencrypted) media. A "man-in-the-middle" attack may compromise data integrity yet remain undetected. In an SBC environment, transaction information remains within the local network, and screen updates and data input (mouse clicks and keystrokes) are contained within the RDP or ICA data stream. The nature of an ICA session makes "man-in-the-middle" or session hijacking attacks extremely difficult to complete because attackers cannot easily synchronize with the video stream.

- **Network resources**   Both processing capability and network capacity must be protected to ensure business continuity. Inappropriate or unauthorized use of processing power may deny service to legitimate applications or processes. Improper control of data storage may allow unauthorized data to consume storage capacity. Network bandwidth and access must be protected from intentional and inadvertent disruption. Denial of service (DoS) events may be intentional (directed at corporate servers, firewalls, and so on) or unintentional (a side effect of unauthorized use of resources). As an example, when a customer used Citrix to deploy Geographic Information Systems (GIS) data to a large remote customer, overall performance of Internet access and Citrix access slowed to a crawl. The cause was isolated to saturation of the customer's Internet T1 by FTP downloads from an internal web server. The server had been hacked, hidden directories created for bootleg copies of a non-English version of Windows 2000, and the download instructions circulated through a European chat room. A single incident deprived the company of processing power (the hacked server), application services (Citrix access was unstable), storage capacity (drive space), and network access bandwidth. Further, it created a potential for liability, because their FTP site hosted bootleg software, and possible expensive legal action.

■ **Liability, reputation, business continuity** These categories are included because companies may actually have to close their doors if certain data becomes public. Engineering designs, business merger and acquisition plans, or other data that constitutes a competitive advantage, if exposed, could have a crippling effect on operations. If it can be proven that a company's officers knew about the lack of security and were negligent in correcting it, they could be liable for damages to the stockholders. A company that allows its security weaknesses to be used to exploit another company or network could be liable for damages. Corporate image and reputation are extremely sensitive for some businesses. For instance, who would keep their money in a bank with a history of security problems? Worse yet, what if security weaknesses allow a business's website to host child pornography, and the business's servers and data were seized as part of a criminal investigation?

▲ **Passwords and strong authentication** The Single Sign-On Powered by Password Manager feature of Platinum improves security in interesting ways beyond integrating with strong authentication. Commonly known as the product category Enterprise Single Sign-On (ESSO), this feature removes the burden of remembering passwords from the end user. Security is actually improved with this approach, because users are less inclined to document their passwords (often on a sticky note under their keyboard or on their screen in plain view). In addition, strong password policies are more reasonable because the ESSO feature is securely "remembering" passwords rather than the user. As an added benefit, password expiry periods and strong password policy can even be added to legacy applications that don't have that capability natively.

The key to securing the corporate infrastructure is a comprehensive security policy. Although addressing all aspects of information security is well beyond the scope of this book, a basic understanding of the breadth of security issues and the security measures necessary in a corporate data center environment is essential knowledge. Most governmental entities, "regulated" industries (banking, stock trading, healthcare services), and many large businesses mandate certification and accreditation processes, with a concise written security policy as a prerequisite for certification or accreditation. Examples of these mandates include

▼ Defense Information Assurance Certification and Accreditation Process (DIACAP), which is the successor to Department of Defense Information Technology Security Certification and Accreditation Process (DITSCAP)

■ Health Insurance Portability and Accountability Act (HIPAA)

▲ Gramm-Leach-Bliley (GLB) Act of 1999 (Financial Services Modernization Bill)

Toward that end, a number of leading vendors and industry groups have produced methodologies and guidance for developing and implementing a corporate security policy. Among the leaders are:

▼ ISO /IEC 27001:2005 Information technology—Security techniques—Information security management systems—Requirements

■ ISO/IEC 17799:2005 Information technology—Security techniques—Code of practice for information security management (complex and detailed, analogous to ISO 9000 for security)

■ Internet Security Systems' ADDME (Assess, Design, Deploy, Manage, Educate) Security Lifecycle Methodology, based on ISO 17799 (www.iss.net)

▲ The SANS Institute (www.sans.org)

All these methodologies vary in complexity and depth, but maintain the same two-part theme: policy and process. The policy component must provide a comprehensive security policy that includes a combination of physical security measures, technical security measures, and administrative security measures to protect the information system. The process component must provide an iterative process to monitor and maintain the policy and associated measures. Cisco Systems' Security Wheel, shown in Figure 6-2, provides a superb illustration of the iterative security management process.

SECURITY DESIGN TECHNICAL CONSIDERATIONS

In a typical distributed network, computing resources are dispersed throughout the enterprise, as shown in Figure 6-3. This means that sensitive information resides on the hard drives of employees' personal computers and on workgroup servers at several locations. If physical access to data is one area of concern for securing that data, it can be said that such a distributed model is less secure than a centralized model.

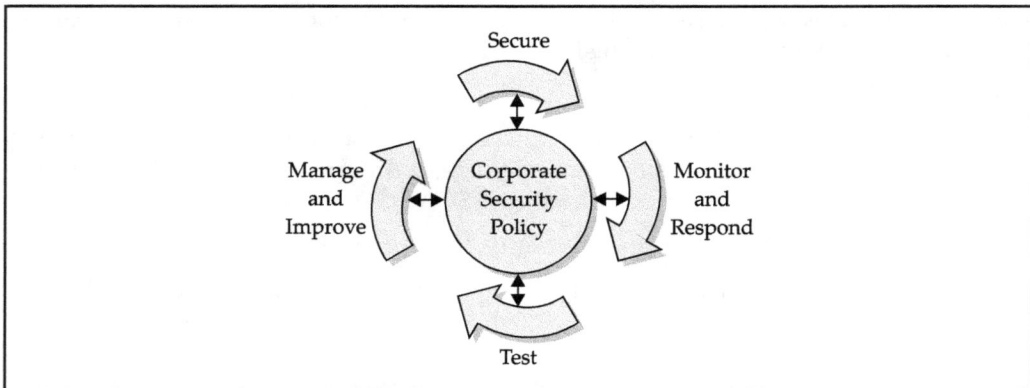

Figure 6-2.   Cisco Systems' Security Wheel

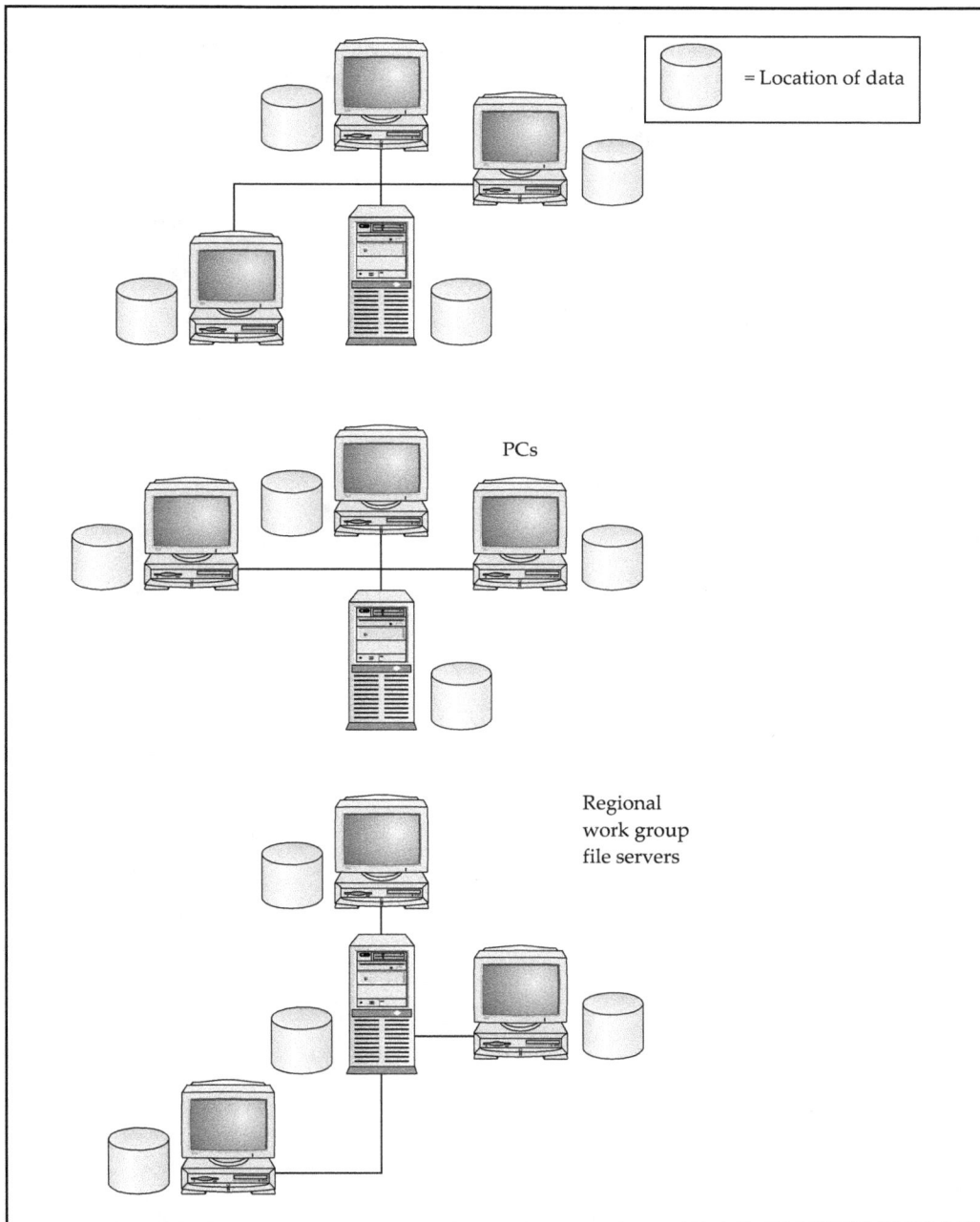

= Location of data

PCs

Regional
work group
file servers

Figure 6-3.   A distributed network in which each regional worksite has its own resident file server

In the centralized model, shown in Figure 6-4, the bulk of computing resources are concentrated in one or just a few data centers. As a result, physical access to that data is much more restricted. Does this mean that a centralized Application Delivery Infrastructure is inherently more secure than distributed computing? It may seem so, but there are numerous areas of concern that make such a blanket assertion shortsighted.

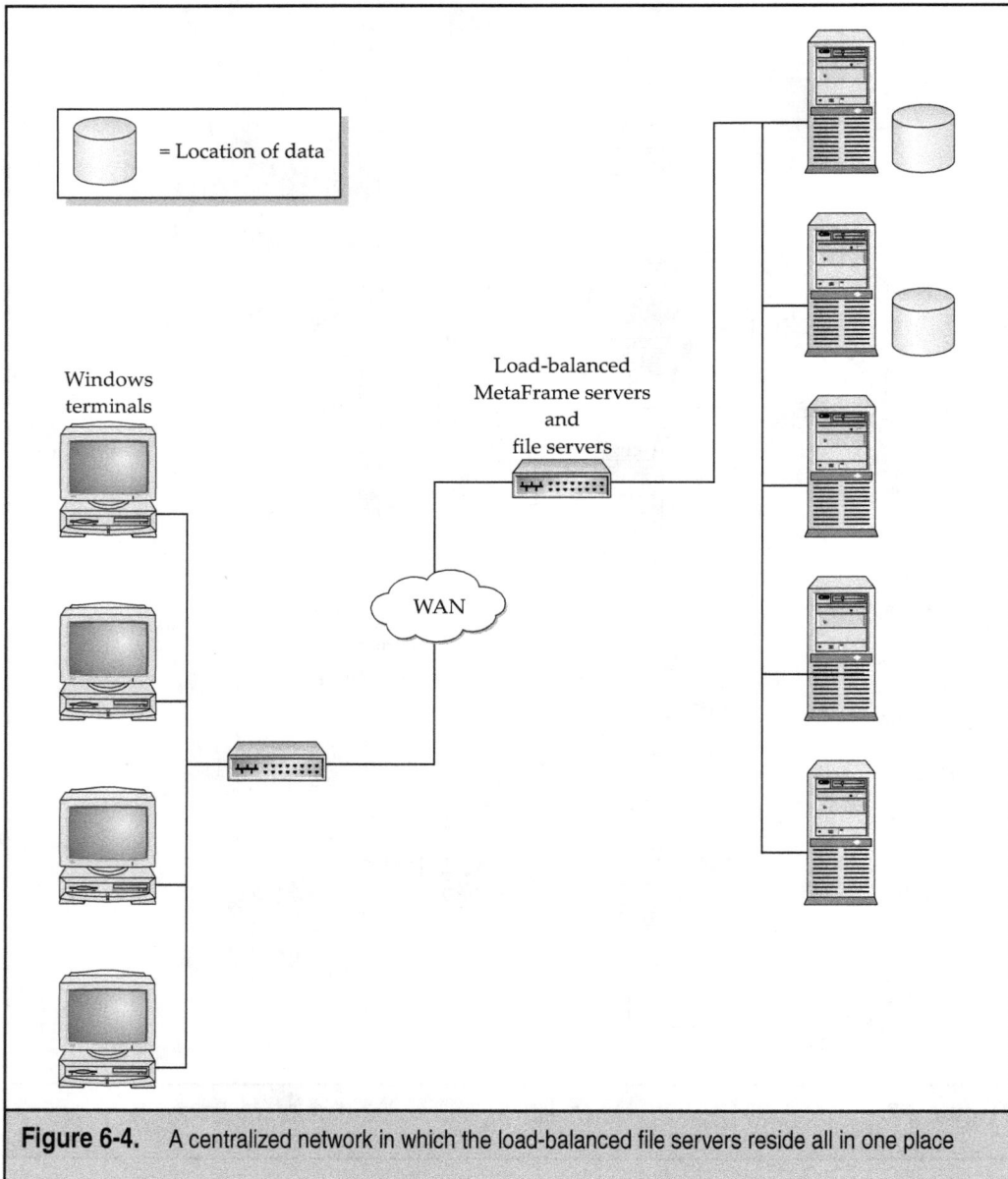

Figure 6-4. A centralized network in which the load-balanced file servers reside all in one place

Technical Measures

This section provides more detail on suggested technical measures to ensure enterprise security. Measures addressed are the most commonly needed and employed technologies, but the list is not all-inclusive.

Firewalls

Network firewalls are the primary line of defense against external security threats; however, a firewall is not a panacea of network security. A firewall is a system or group of systems that enforce a boundary between two or more networks. In the classic implementation, shown in Figure 6-5, the firewall system is composed of a packet-filtering perimeter router, an isolation LAN (screened subnet) with a dual-homed bastion host, and an interior packet-filtering router.

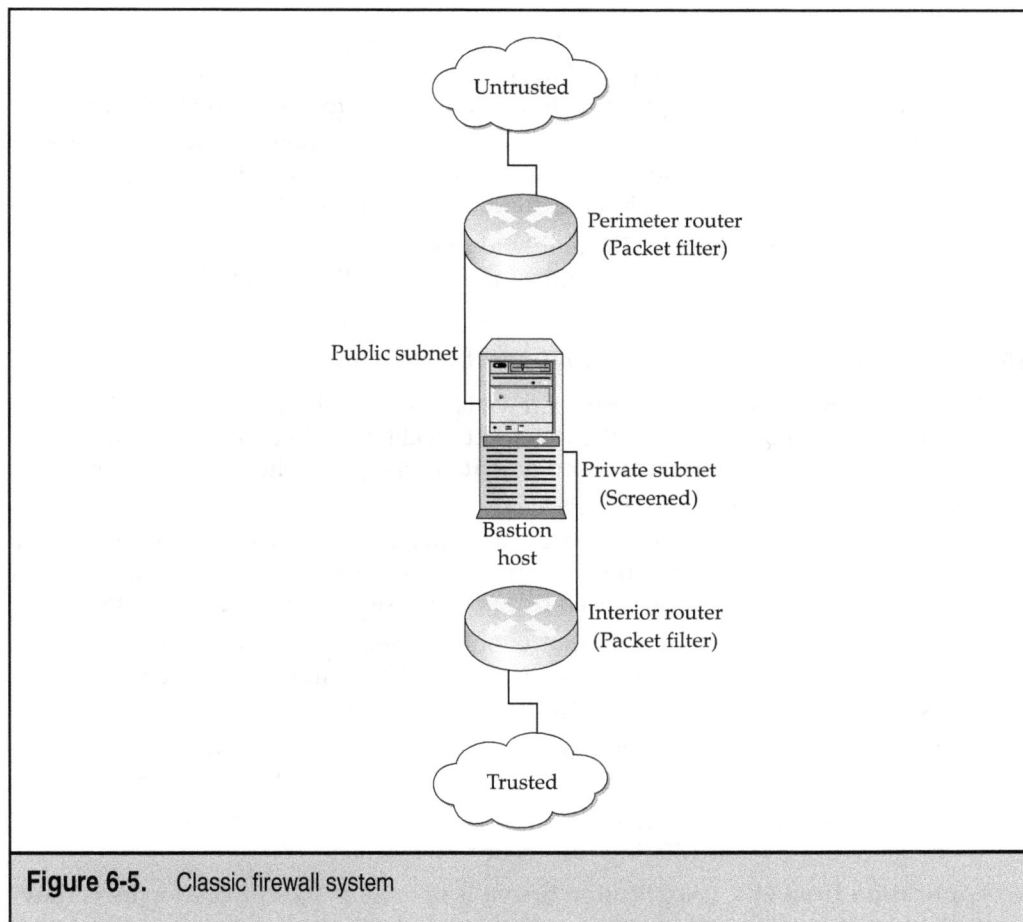

Figure 6-5. Classic firewall system

Most firewalls perform a number of different functions, but the following are common capabilities:

▼ **Protection of internal resources**   Hides internal addressing schemes and hosts from external detection

■ **Authentication**   Uses strong authentication techniques to verify a user's identity before granting access to corporate information

■ **Privacy**   Protects, via encryption, sessions and data streams destined for a remote network segment over untrusted networks (VPNs)

▲ **Auditing**   Provides detailed logging and accounting of communication attempts and other relevant metrics

In addition to these common features, firewall solutions should offer the following:

▼ **Attack and intrusion detection**   The ability to detect common attacks and intrusion attempts such as denial of service and spoofing.

■ **Content security**   A firewall should be "application aware" for a minimal set of common Internet applications (FTP, SMTP, and so on). It should be possible to define access rules based on the application that is attempting to pass through the firewall.

■ **High availability**   The firewall systems should be hardened enough to protect themselves from being brought down by an attack or simple mishap. More critical, firewall implementations should be redundant, with automatic failover.

▲ **Electronic countermeasures**   The ability to mitigate common attacks and intrusion attempts such as denial of service and spoofing, as well as the ability to protect the firewall from direct attack.

Types of Firewalls   Two general types of Internet firewalls are in common use today:

▼ **Packet-filtering firewalls**   Filtering firewalls screen packets based on address and packet options. They operate at the IP packet level (Layer 3) and make simple security decisions (drop or forward) based on data in the packet header. Packet-filtering firewalls may be one of three subtypes:

     ■ *Static filtering*   This is used on most routers. Filter rules must be manually changed and are composed of source and destination pairs as well as protocol and port values. No logic is used to determine session state or packet sequence.

     ■ *Dynamic filtering*   In this subtype, an outside process changes the filtering rules dynamically, based on router-observed events (for example, one might allow FTP packets in from the outside, if someone on the inside requested an FTP session).

     ■ *Stateful inspection*   A technology that is similar to dynamic filtering, with the addition of more granular examination of data contained in the IP packet.

     Dynamic filtering and stateful inspection firewalls keep a dynamic state table to make changes to the filtering rules based on events.

▲ **Application firewalls**   Application firewalls operate at the application level (Layer 7) and can examine information at that level. Application firewalls protect web applications from the growing number of application-layer attacks, including buffer overflow exploits, SQL injection attempts, and cross-site scripting attacks. Decisions are made based on address pairs, application content (for instance, URLs), and application data, such as commands passed within FTP or SMTP command channels. Few vendors provide application-aware firewalls capable of managing RDP or ICA traffic, and enhancements to RDP or ICA require a revision of the firewall source code. One notable exception is the Citrix Application Firewall. As of this writing, the Citrix Application Firewall is the industry leader in application firewall performance.

Firewalls for Application Delivery Infrastructure Packet-filtering firewall systems, in conjunction with an application firewall, are strongly recommended for Application Delivery Platforms. Industry leaders in firewall technology include Cisco Systems (ASA), CheckPoint (NG/NGX), Fortinet (FortiGate), and Citrix (Application Firewall). The firewall system, as shown in Figure 6-6, should include a perimeter router capable of static or dynamic packet filtering (to offload simple filtering and protect the firewall from

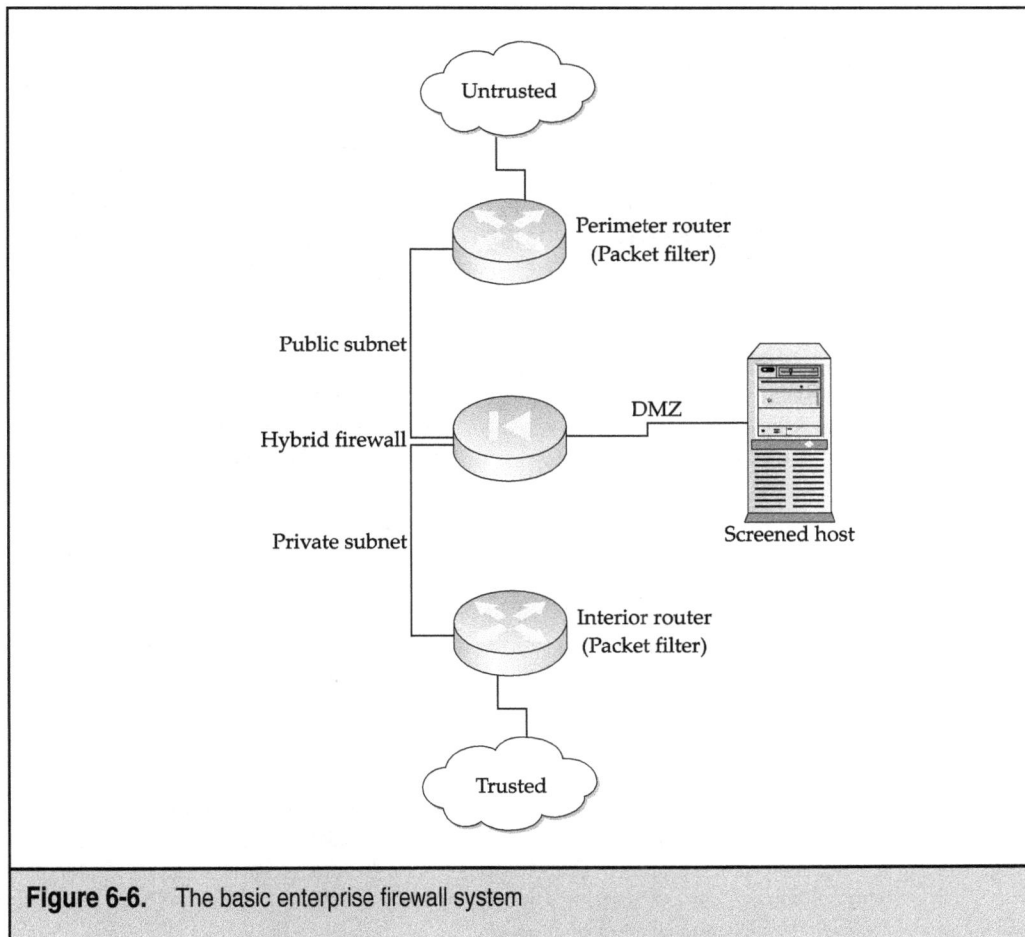

Figure 6-6. The basic enterprise firewall system

direct attack), a packet-filtering firewall element using stateful inspection, an application firewall, and an interior router capable of static or dynamic packet filtering.

Enhancements to ICA since the early MetaFrame versions eliminate the need for firewalls to support UDP pass-through for ICA browser services (UDP port 1604). Stateful inspection firewalls must "approximate" a session state for UDP by using timers because UDP is a stateless protocol. XenApp now supports TCP-based XML services in lieu of ICA browser services.

Encryption

Using the Internet as part of the corporate WAN infrastructure has obvious security implications. The Internet is a public network, and as such it exposes an enterprise's private information to unauthorized individuals by its very nature. The Internet is often an integral part of delivering applications to remote users in a server-based computing network, however. Internet delivery provides virtually universal access to clients, built-in resiliency, and dramatic cost reductions as compared to dedicated media. There are two basic encrypted transport methodologies used for Application Delivery Infrastructure network connectivity: virtual private networks (VPNs) and Public Key Infrastructure (PKI) encryption via Secure Sockets Layer (SSL) or Transport Layer Security (TLS).

Encryption Standards   Encryption standards define both the mechanics of the encryption process and the complexity of the key. For all at-risk data transmissions (anything traversing the Internet), strong encryption should always be used. For SSL/TLS, use a minimum 128-bit key (RC4 with 128-bit encryption and MD5 message authentication, yielding 3.4×10^{38} possible key values). If security is paramount, consider Triple-DES (3DES with 168-bit key and SHA-1 message authentication yields 3.7×10^{50} possible key values) or step up to AES (where AES-128 offers 3.4×10^{38} possible 128-bit keys, AES-192 affords 6.2×10^{57} possible 192-bit keys, and AES-256 provides 1.1×10^{77} possible 256-bit keys). When SSL is used, avoid SSL 2.0 implementations and instead use SSL 3.0 or TLS.

There are two basic types of encryption algorithms: symmetric (or private key) and public key. Private key encryption requires that the same key used to encrypt the data be used to decrypt the data. This is most commonly seen in VPN configurations. The advantage is speed, because less computation is involved than in other methods. The main disadvantage is that the key must be distributed to the intended recipient through some secure mechanism; the symmetric algorithm itself provides no way to distribute the key. The second type of algorithm, the public key, calculates a list of keys, some of which can only encrypt the data and some of which can only decrypt the data. The encryption key is the public key, and the decryption key is the private key. A message encrypted with the former can only be decrypted by the latter. A major advantage of this scheme is that the encryption key can travel in the open without compromising security. Having the public key will not allow someone to decrypt the data.

▼

NOTE: In some applications, such as Secure Socket Layer (SSL), the public key is made freely available to any client requesting it. The client machine uses the public key to encrypt the data before sending it over the unprotected network. Only the possessor of the private key will be able to decrypt it. This is how e-commerce sites can function: Any customer who comes to the site can obtain the public key without any special arrangement or mechanism.

Several encryption algorithm and transport standards have arisen that have been adopted by Microsoft, Citrix, and others. Understanding them will allow an administrator to judge for themselves whether a specific standard is appropriate for their server-based computing project. By implementing an encryption algorithm and transport method in the network backbone, the task of authenticating and securing the network session is made further transparent to the end user. Cisco, Nortel, and other vendors facilitate this seamless authentication by their adoption of one or more security standards.

Encryption for Application Delivery Infrastructures   Both ICA and RDP support basic encryption services through their respective client and server configurations. RDP generally requires what many enterprise security administrators consider to be a "nonstandard" port (TCP 3389) to be open through the firewall, and does not support authentication prior to connecting to the target server (secure application proxy). ICA has variable levels of security, and can be encapsulated to operate on a "standard" port that is usually permitted through enterprise firewalls—TCP 443 (HTTPS). By default, the ICA protocol adds little to the security already existing in Terminal Services. ICA uses a very basic method to encrypt (or more accurately "scramble") the data stream by using a key. It is really meant to help ensure that clear-text is not visible in the data stream. When the 128-bit encryption option for ICA connections is invoked, the ICA session is encrypted with a 128-bit key RC5 encryption algorithm from RSA Data Security. RC5 uses a combination of symmetric and public-private key algorithms. The XenApp client and server use the Diffie-Hellman key agreement algorithm with a 1,024-bit key to generate RC5 keys. Citrix bills this client as being safe enough to run sessions over the Internet, and indeed many companies use or base their products on the RC5 encryption algorithm. Windows Server 2003 Remote Desktop Connection (RDC) services use 128-bit, bidirectional RC4 encryption. Windows Server 2003 (with the encryption module), Windows Server 2008, and Citrix XenApp are now certified as FIPS 140–compliant for use in federal government information systems. In either case, the direct connection from client to target server creates additional concerns, even when passing through most stateful inspection firewalls.

The Citrix Access Gateway (shown in Figure 6-7) replaced the MetaFrame Secure Gateway and adds significant improvements in features, functionality, and security. The Citrix Access Gateway (CAG) consolidates Secure Gateway onto a hardened-OS appliance form-factor and provides not only the SSL application proxy, but also a universal SSL VPN that transparently supports virtually all ports and protocols (including UDP-based Voice-Over-IP soft phones). When deployed with Advanced Access Control (AAC), the CAG provides real-time endpoint analysis to dynamically control which XenApp applications are accessible to remote users based on identity, source address, originating device security, and other factors. Additionally, AAC can control access to application behavior per user session (for example, the right to view, edit, or print) based on the same endpoint analysis criteria.

The actual implementation (network and security architecture) of the Citrix Access Gateway and Web Interface components determine which transport connections are encrypted. For design and deployment considerations for Citrix Access Gateway (CAG), see Chapter 11.

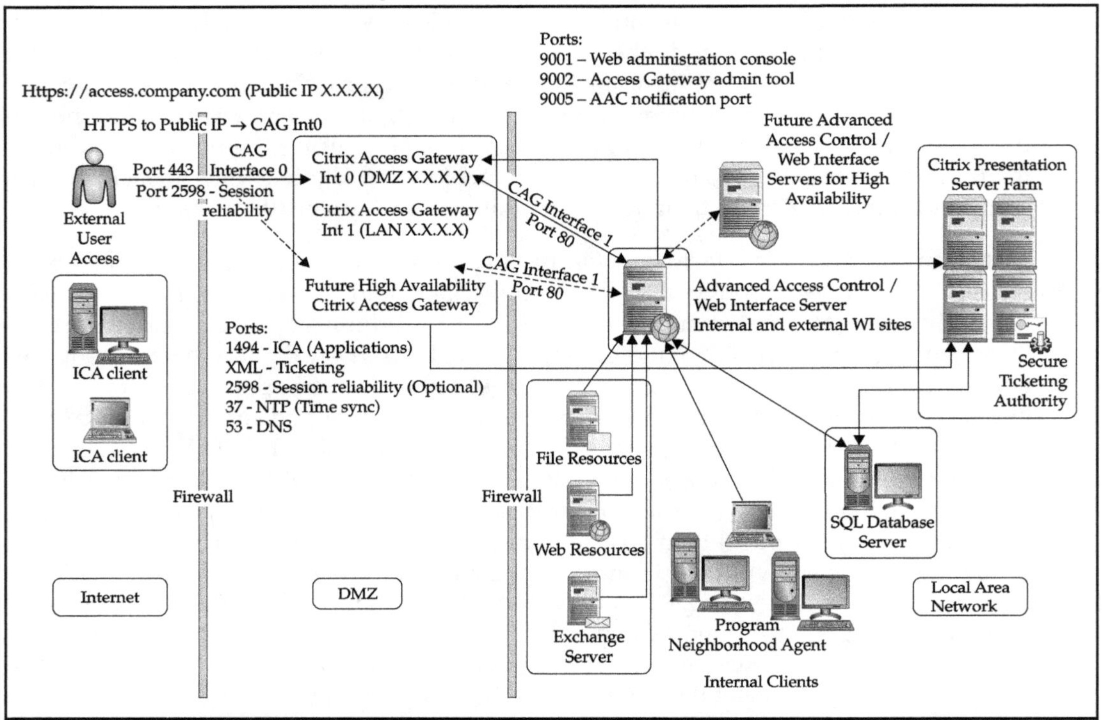

Figure 6-7. Citrix Access Gateway

Authentication, Authorization, and Accounting Services

Authentication, Authorization, and Accounting (AAA) services provide the means to identify a user, grant access to specific resources, and document what the user did and when they did it. The vast majority of AAA services in a Windows Server 2003 server environment are provided by the Windows security model with authentication in the form of user account/password settings, authorization provided by discretionary Access Control Lists (on files, shares, and other OS-controlled resources such as print services), and accounting provided through event logs and event-auditing policies. Windows Server 2003 Terminal Services and XenApp 4.5 both support two-factor authentication (smart card). More robust authentication such as three-factor authentication requires third-party software.

TIP: In Windows Server 2003 and 2008, you can add users and groups directly to the Remote Desktop Users group to allow RDP or ICA access.

Auditing

Citrix SmartAuditor was released with Update 1 to Version 4.5 XenApp Platinum edition. SmartAuditor is a secure auditing tool that does no key-logging but instead provides record and playback of specific application sessions. Figure 6-8 shows a brief synopsis of

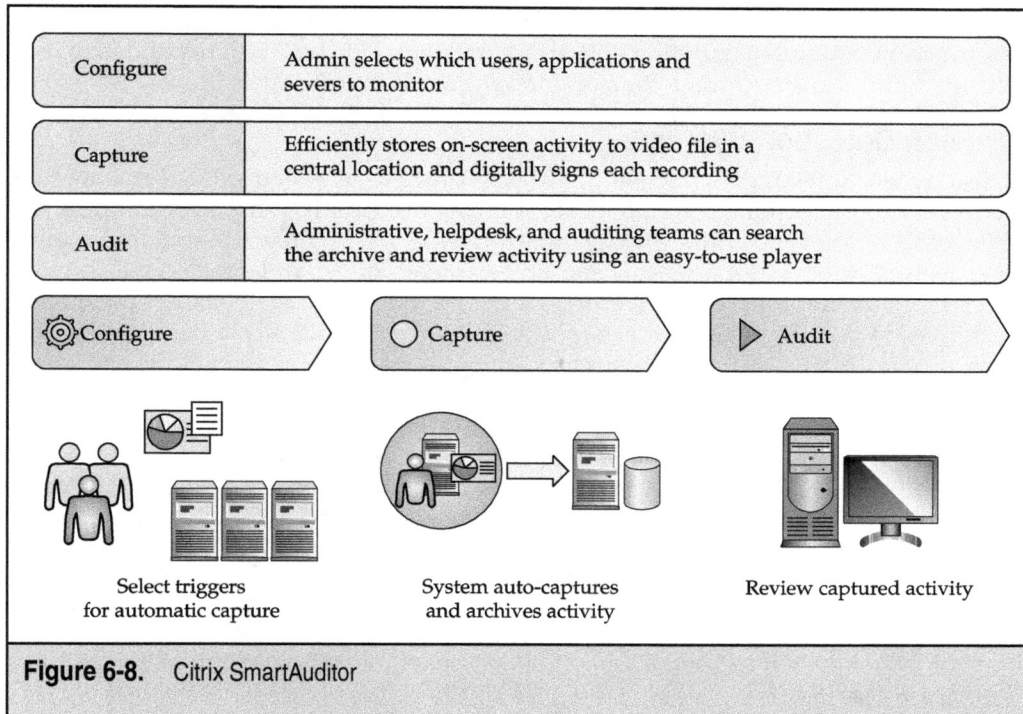

Figure 6-8.   Citrix SmartAuditor

the use of the tool. Using this tool, XenApp administrators can set policies that record specific application sessions based on a user's role, the application being accessed, or the sensitivity of the application transaction. When activated, SmartAuditor acts like a digital video recorder to capture screen activity from a user's computer and store it in a small, digitally signed, time-stamped video file that can later be analyzed and logged. By recording only relevant user sessions, SmartAuditor is far more efficient and practical than add-on auditing solutions, which often have large storage requirements, are difficult to manage, and can be unwieldy to analyze during an audit.

In addition to SmartAuditor, basic auditing should be provided by server event logs and system logs from firewalls and routers. Most database applications can support record-level auditing and transaction logging. Basic auditing by itself is a nice feature for 20/20 hindsight, but is of little use unless audit events are configured to generate administrative alert and notification messages.

Windows Server 2003 provides additional auditing capabilities to meet common government requirements and supplement intrusion detection mechanisms. Notable changes include operation-based auditing (analogous to accounting in AAA services), per-user selective auditing (by name), and enhanced logon/logoff and account management auditing (logon/logoff events now contain IP address and caller information).

The Microsoft Audit Collection System (MACS), a client/server application released in support of Windows Server 2003, provides real-time security event collection and stores event data in a SQL database for ready analysis. MACS can create a security boundary so that event-log data can be independently audited without the possibility of users or administrators tampering with the event data. This type of independent collection and auditing are becoming the norm for regulated industries.

Intrusion Detection Systems

Intrusion detection systems (IDS) and intrusion prevention systems (IPS) are now built into many firewall products. A fully evolved enterprise IDS/IPS should encompass network-based sensors and enforcement points implemented on firewalls, routers, or appliances, as well as host-based sensors and enforcement points implemented via software services on vulnerable servers. Enterprise IDS/IPS services go well beyond the built-in capabilities of most firewalls. For example, Cisco's PIX firewall recognizes less than 100 attack profiles (natively), has only limited autonomous response capability, and attack signatures are not regularly updated. When coupled with Cisco's IDS/IPS appliances, thousands of attacks are recognized, signatures are updated much like antivirus software, and the IDS appliance can dynamically issue configuration change commands to the firewall to block attacks as they occur. Host intrusion detection systems (**HIDS**), on the other hand, functions much like a firewall at the OS kernel level: Any API or kernel call that is not specifically preapproved by the administrator requires explicit authorization. Calls that are not "authorized" are blocked by default, which means HIDS can block and log as-yet-"undefined" attacks. Newer-generation firewall appliances, including the Citrix Application Firewall, now contain built-in IDS/IPS.

Content Filtering

Although not a technical security measure per se, filtering and management of Internet content (more specifically, filtering of user access to web content) and electronic mail content filtering and management are used to address two of the biggest liability and reputation issues in business today. Uncontrolled employee access to inappropriate (as determined by the corporate acceptable use policy) Internet sites not only can damage the corporate image and risk civil and legal prosecution, but can be a precursor to internal attacks on network security and resources. Case in point: an employee who surfs hacker websites may be looking for tools to use, or they may be technologically illiterate and download malicious logic that compromises the network. With regard to electronic mail, businesses may be concerned about unacceptable mail content originated or received under the corporate identity, spam that consumes storage resources, or originated content that divulges sensitive information. E-mail filtering is usually accomplished both on a bastion host in an Internet DMZ (ingress filtering of objectionable content and spam) and on the corporate mail server itself to control employee-to-employee and employee-to-external content. An additional "filtering" capability can be provided by a network WAN management device such as the Citrix WANScaler or Packeteer PacketShaper. Because these devices recognize applications such as chat and instant messaging programs and protocols (MS-Chat, AIM, MSN Messenger), peer-to-peer sharing applications (Napster, Gnutella, BearShare, LimeWire), and commonly abused Internet bandwidth hogs (Windows Media, QuickTime, Real Media), these applications can be assigned a policy of zero bits per second or "never admit" to block access by application. Chat programs are of particular concern because they often use dynamic ports and are one of the most active vectors for malicious logic ("bots").

Virus Protection

Enterprise virus protection is a "must have" in any computing environment. A single uncontrolled outbreak can cost tens of thousand of dollars in PC disinfection costs alone. Heavily infected networks must often be isolated from the Internet and taken out of service to allow IT staff to get ahead of rampant infections. Although most enterprise antivirus solutions offer similar capabilities, the solutions' effectiveness is determined more by implementation and maintenance ease than actual protection. The system must be universally installed, employ a locked configuration to prevent software from being disabled, and support centralized real-time reporting and alerting. Virus protection products must work seamlessly on all the enterprise computer systems.

Server Hardening   Server hardening measures are specific to the server OS and applications. In a XenApp environment, extensive modifications to the Registry, directory and file permissions, and Registry permissions were required to "secure" the server. Server hardening in general can be risky—although standard security lockdowns may work with terminal servers and well-behaved applications, most legacy applications do not fully comply with Microsoft's Terminal Services API and will experience problems.

To fully harden a Terminal Server (as in the DoD C2 Trusted Computer System Criteria), some changes are still required. Microsoft and Citrix have online databases and security sites that detail changes in server configuration, from file and directory permissions, to password and authentication methods, to configuration of server-side protocol stacks. Additional changes to baseline security configurations can be implemented with Microsoft's Security Configuration Editor. For those who want government-type security restrictions, configuration guides and preconfigured *.inf files for the Security Configuration Editor may be downloaded from the National Security Agency's (NSA) System and Network Attack Center (SNAC) at http://www.nsa.gov/snac/.

▼   *CAUTION:*   Never run automated lockdown tools such as the Security Configuration Editor on production servers. Always test first.

Patching known vulnerabilities and exploits with hotfixes and service packs is really fundamental software maintenance, and yet is often overlooked. Built-in features such as Windows Update are more robust in Windows Server 2003 and 2008. Supplemental tools such as the Baseline Security Analyzer, which includes a command-line hotfix checker (HFNetCheck), can help verify the state of the server.

Microsoft supplies a wide variety of built-in tools to help secure the terminal server. In Windows 2003, policy-based enforcement (group policies) is expanded to include Terminal Services–specific policies.

One interesting feature introduced in XenApp 4.5 is the ability to protect the terminal server from "rogue" applications (accidental or intentional). Administrators can define resource consumption limits for applications, and XenApp will police the application to prevent denial of service.

User Environment Management

Because the user environment and experience in an Application Delivery Infrastructure environment exist on the server, lockdown can be easier than in a distributed computing environment. Conversely, there is a far greater need for such security measures.

In relatively simple (from a security standpoint) Windows networks, Windows group policies are an effective means of controlling the user environment. In Windows Server 2003, the cumbersome Windows AppSec tool for locking down application availability has been replaced with built-in software restriction polices.

In a Citrix XenApp environment, many lockdown tasks are mitigated by Citrix's ability to publish applications and content directly, without the complexities and security problems associated with a full windows "shell." When possible, running only published applications obviates the need to lock down many settings associated with desktops and menus—applications run in a seamless window with no exposure of the underlying windows shell (explorer.exe).

As the number of users, different policies, and nested policies grow, the viability of group policies diminishes rapidly. Not only are complex nested policies hard to understand and decipher, excessive nesting can slow logon times substantially. Even the Citrix published applications are not suitable for all environments. Users may need, or legacy applications may demand, access to window shell components. In the worst-case scenarios, applications may be dependent on "desktop" functionality, but incapable of running correctly when standard group polices are applied. In complex situations, third-party lockdown products such as RES PowerFuse greatly simplify administration. Users and applications can be provided in a dynamic and secure user workspace, complete with an alternate (more secure) windows shell component. PowerFuse adds a number of essential features, such as the ability to control the spawning of a child process or an executable, for example, blocking Internet Explorer from launching from an embedded URL within an e-mail message.

MONITORING AND MANAGEMENT—PEOPLE, PROCESSES, AND PRODUCT

Utilizing a monitoring tool such as Citrix EdgeSight is only part of an organization's overall System Management Environment (SME). An SME consists of the people, processes, and product (the "three Ps") within an organization that effectively manages their computing resources. "Product" is more accurately "technology," but "two Ps and a T" doesn't have the same punch as "three Ps." We find the simplest way to think of the interrelationship among the three Ps is in terms of service-level agreements (SLAs).

SERVICE-LEVEL AGREEMENTS

An SLA in this context is an agreement between the IT staff and the user community about the services being provided, the manner in which they are delivered, the responsibilities of the IT support staff, and the responsibilities of the users. An SLA serves many important functions, including setting the expectations of the users about the scope of services being delivered and providing accountability and a baseline of measurement for the IT staff. The established SLAs in your organization also provide the framework for the SME. After all, if you don't first figure out what you are managing and how you will manage it, what good will a tool do you? In addition to incorporating the three Ps, a service-level agreement should address the following three areas of responsibility:

▼ **Availability**   This section should explain when the services are provided, the frequency (if appropriate), and the nature of the services.

■ **Performance**   This section describes how the service is to be performed and any underlying processes related to the delivery of the service.

▲ **Usability**   This section should show how to measure whether the service is being used effectively. For example, a measure of success could be infrequent help desk calls.

Ideally, the SLA is an extension of the overall business goals. Defining a group of SLAs for an organization that has never used them can be a daunting task. The following tips will help you with the effort:

▼ Start by deciding which parts of your infrastructure go directly to supporting your business goals, and define exactly how that happens.

■ Do not define an SLA in terms of your current support capability. Think "outside the box" regarding how a particular service *should* be delivered. The result will be your goal for the SLA. Now work backward and figure out what has to be done to reach the ideal SLA.

▲ Rather than starting at the ground level with individual SLAs for particular services, try laying down some universal rules for a so-called "master SLA." After all, some things will apply to nearly every service you deliver. A good place to start is with the help desk, where all user calls are taken. Decide how the help desk will handle, prioritize, and assign calls. The problem response time, for example, will be a standard time for all nonpriority calls. Once that is established, you can think about whether different services may need different handling for priority calls. Decide what the mission and goals are of the IT staff overall and how they support the business. Work backward from that to how the service management function must be defined to align with those goals.

Establishing a viable SLA for the user community—whether corporate users or fee-for-service (ASP) users—mandates equivalent SLAs with your providers. For example, most WAN providers (Qwest, Sprint, AT&T) will guarantee various parameters (availability, bandwidth, latency) that impact your ability to deliver service to users. Ensure internal SLAs do not invoke more stringent quality and reliability guarantees than external SLAs.

The subject of defining and working with SLAs is adequate material for a book all its own. Our intention here is to get you started in framing your network management services in terms of SLAs. You will find them to be not only a great help in sorting through the "noise" of information collected, but also an invaluable communication tool for users, IT staff, and management alike.

SYSTEM MANAGEMENT ENVIRONMENT FOR APPLICATION DELIVERY INFRASTRUCTURE

In an Application Delivery Infrastructure environment, where information resources are centralized, the need for tools and procedures that serve to decrease the frequency of unscheduled downtime is more important than ever. The organizational mandate for an application delivery platform and full, secure control of the environment dictates that the operations necessary to support the environment have more in common with the Network Operation Center (NOC) of an Internet service provider (ISP) or commercial hosting service than with a traditional, distributed corporate network. It is no longer acceptable for IT staff to discover problems after they occur, as an audit function. They must have tools and procedures in place to perform predictive analysis on potential problems and to isolate and contain problems during the troubleshooting process. An effective systems management environment will address these needs through measurement of the various systems and through the enforcement of service-level agreements. The data collected during measurement can be used in troubleshooting and making corrections. For example, if a XenApp Server crashes due to an application fault, the EdgeSight package will have recorded which applications were running at the time of the crash. Without this information, it would be challenging to find the crash's exact cause. An effective SME has the following objectives:

▼ Improving the availability and performance of the server and network resources.

■ Lowering the cost of IT maintenance and support services.

▲ Providing a service-level view of server and network resources.

The "people" part of the three Ps is made up not only of users and IT staff, but also any group affected by the services being delivered. For many organizations, this means external customers, business partners, and even competitors. The SLAs associated with the services being delivered, and the associated reports, are the "process" part of the three Ps and are, collectively, the tool that shows whether the preceding objectives are being met. The "product" consists of all the hardware and software necessary to deliver the information needed to measure the SLAs. Any technology utilized in the SME should meet the following basic requirements:

▼ *Provide a central point of control for managing heterogeneous systems.* A "central point" refers to one tool or collection mechanism used to gather information from all sources. The actual data repository could be distributed to multiple locations where administrative activity takes place.

■ *Allow event management across heterogeneous systems and network devices.* The toolset should support all the common operating system and network hardware platforms and provide enough extensibility for custom interfaces to be configured, if necessary.

▲ *Provide service-level views of any portion of the infrastructure.* A "service-level view" is an aggregation of lower-level events that correlate to show the impact of various failures in terms of an established SLA. A message stating "Server 110 has crashed with an unknown error" has far less meaning than "Application service capacity has decreased by 10 percent" or "Application services for users in the San Antonio region have been interrupted."

To further refine these requirements, more detail on the exact duties to be incorporated in the SME is needed. Defining in specific terms what will be measured and how it will be measured will greatly aid in the selection of the proper technology. We will discuss SME tools later in the chapter.

Configuration Management

Arguably, the most common problem in managing distributed computer systems is configuration management. Even companies with very organized IT staffs can have complete chaos on the desktop with regard to which application or application versions are installed and which changes to the operating system are allowed. In an application infrastructure environment, the chaos, so to speak, is limited to the data centers, but the need for configuration management is even greater. If a user changes a setting on their PC that causes it to crash, that user experiences unscheduled downtime. If an administrator makes a change to a Presentation Server that causes it to crash, every user currently logged onto that server experiences unscheduled downtime. An effective SME must have in place controls to restrict and audit changes within the data center. A configuration management system should have the following characteristics:

▼ **A clearly defined operational baseline**   The baseline defines the starting point for the management process.

■ **A change tracking system**   A process for requesting, submitting, prioritizing, approving, and testing changes to the operational baseline. Once a change has completed the process, it becomes part of the baseline.

■ **Defined categories and priorities for changes**   For example, some changes need to be tracked, such as changes to group membership and administrative rights, but can be safely implemented as an extension of the current baseline. Others must be implemented very quickly and may disrupt user activity, such as critical security patches. From a software management perspective, most organization configuration management systems differentiate between patches, enhancements, and major revisions, and often employ a "release" process where any or all of these must be tested and certified in a development/test environment before implementation in production systems.

▲ **Implementation procedures**   Necessary steps that must be taken before implementation, such as how to save the current state before a change, how to decide if a change is not working, how to back out of a change, and how to use collected information to modify the original change request and resubmit it.

Modern computing environments are far too complex for an automated tool to check and restrict any change. A combination of an effective automated tool and "best practice" procedures for change management is the key to a successful configuration management function.

Security Management

Security management serves to ensure that users only have access to the applications, servers, and other computing resources they are authorized to use. Again, a combination of automated tools and employee policies are called for. The implementation of an Internet firewall to prevent unauthorized external access will do nothing to prevent a disgruntled employee from accessing and publishing confidential information. Only the combination of automated internal system limitations, effective monitoring, published "acceptable use" policies, and committed enforcement of those policies can serve to deter such unforeseen incidents.

Alerting

As we discussed previously in this chapter, it is not enough simply to log attempts to bypass security within the environment. An effective SME should include a network management tool that will actively alert the appropriate personnel if a security breach of sufficient severity is detected. For example, say an employee discovers the Registry settings where their group information is stored and figures out how to change that value to Admin without using the management console. First, the Registry should not allow the change to be made by that user because it has been locked against changes by anyone not currently in the Admin group. However, if the change is somehow made, the system should log the event (auditing). The management agent program on that system should watch the event log, detect the event, and send a page to the security administrator.

Using Service-Level Agreements

As we mentioned earlier, a service level agreement defines the policies and procedures that will be used within the SME. The execution of those policies and procedures will rely in equal parts on automated tools and "acceptable use" policies that the employees within the organization must abide by. Employing SLAs within the SME will have the following effects:

▼ *User expectations will be much closer to the reality of how a particular service is delivered.* Many users see the network as a public utility that has 100-percent uptime. This is a good goal but often is not realistic. Publishing an SLA will show the users what *is* realistic and what their options are if the service delivery doesn't conform to the SLA. After all, very few public utilities can show a track record of sustained 100-percent uptime.

▲ *IT service quality will increase.* When the service is well-defined and understood by users and service personnel alike, the delivery of that service will be more consistent. This happens for a couple of reasons. First, the people trained to administer the systems have more time to pay attention to their effective management because they spend less time fighting fires. Second, the users' expectations of the service will be more in line with its delivery, which will reduce the number of complaints. A relatively new concept, Application Quality-of-Service (Application QoS) is a measure of how effectively applications are delivered to the user and thus can be one measure of

IT service quality in an SBC environment. Application QoS service-level views can be found in some of the network management tools we discuss later in the chapter.

System Management Environment Architecture

With what has been defined so far, we can now look in detail at some specific duties covered by an effective System Management Environment (SME) for the data center, as shown next. The overall architecture should include, at a minimum, the functions described in the following sections for the entire SBC infrastructure.

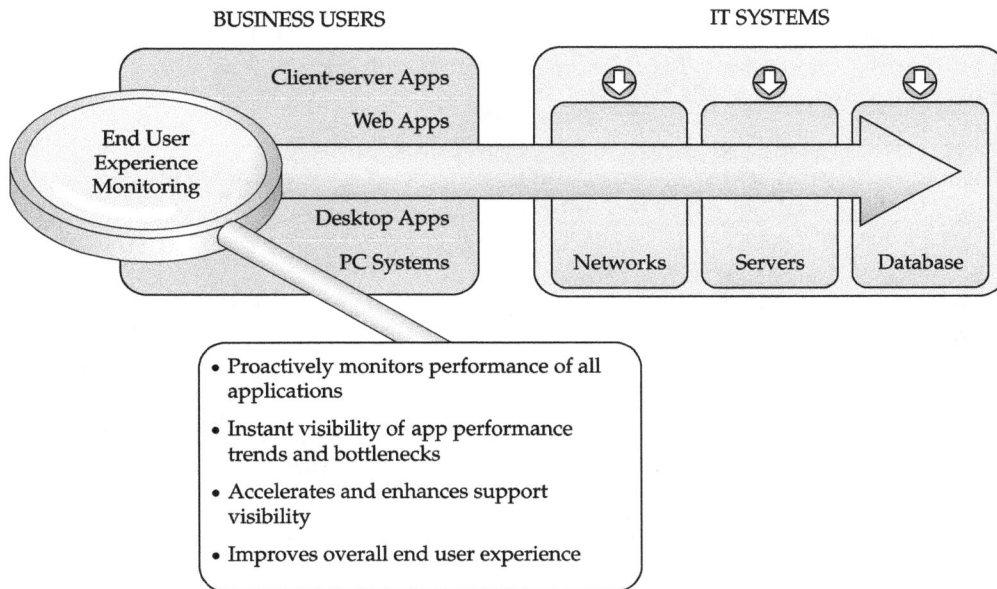

Network Discovery

It would be incredibly tedious if you had to enter information about each node before it could be managed. Fortunately, nearly every modern NMS tool provides the ability to actively discover information about nodes on the network. Though most polling is TCP/IP based, an effective NMS uses a variety of other methods to discover nodes, including NetBIOS and SAP broadcasts. The basic philosophy is "anything that will work." The majority of nodes will respond *somehow*, and those that don't can be handled as an exception and entered manually. Network discovery is a function shared by both the agent and the manager.

Hardware and Software Inventory

This function is similar to node discovery in design but is much more detailed. Once a node is discovered and identified, the discovery process will interrogate the device to find out about the software and hardware configuration. If fat clients must be used, this can be an invaluable tool to "meter" software—that is, to find out if the number of licenses purchased matches the number of licenses in use. It can also aid in creating inventories of hardware that need to be upgraded for a particular project. Similar functionality is available for peripheral and network devices. Hardware and software inventory data is usually rolled into the overall configuration management process.

Monitoring and Messaging

The most common agent function is to "watch" the system and look for problems as defined in a rule base. Ideally, this rule base is administered centrally and shared by all similar agents. The agent's job is to send an appropriate message whenever an item in the rule base is triggered, as illustrated in Figures 6-9 and 6-10. These items can consist of both errors, or traps, and collections of information such as traffic thresholds, disk utilization, and log sizes.

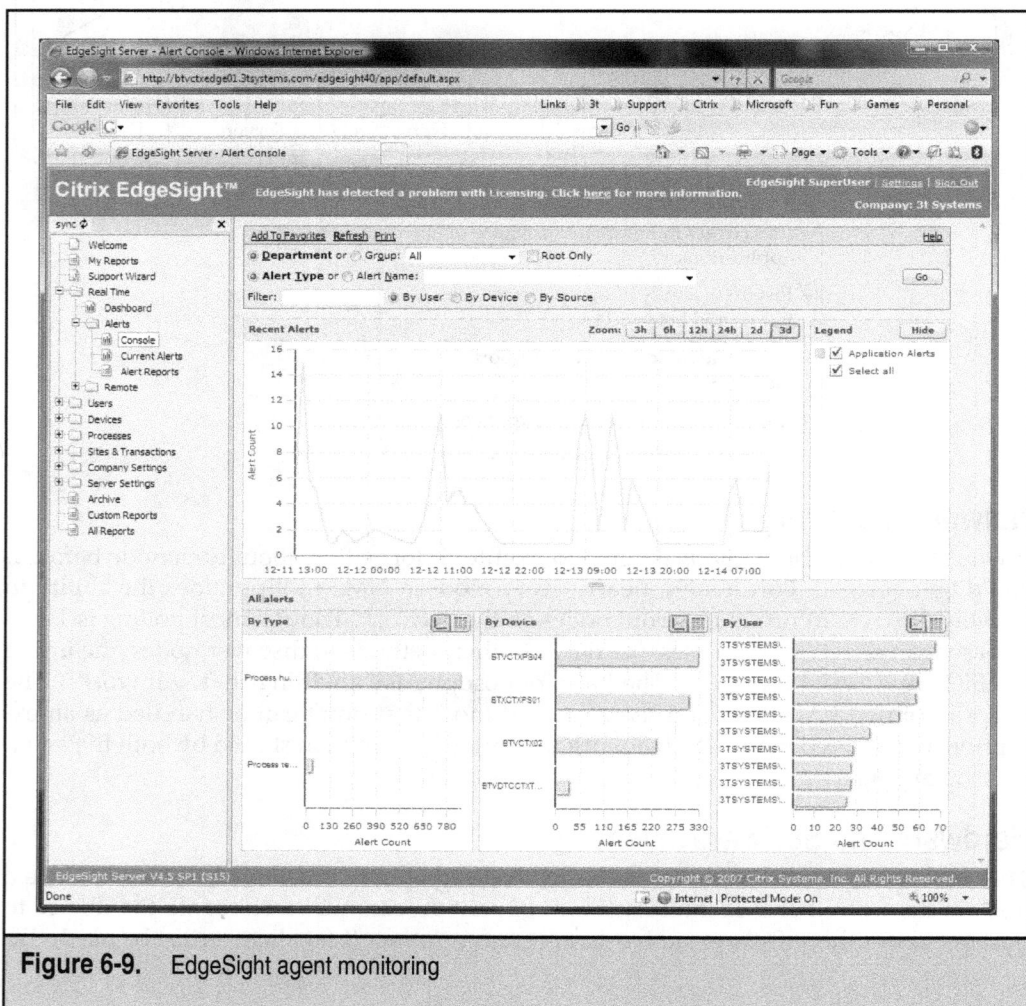

Figure 6-9.   EdgeSight agent monitoring

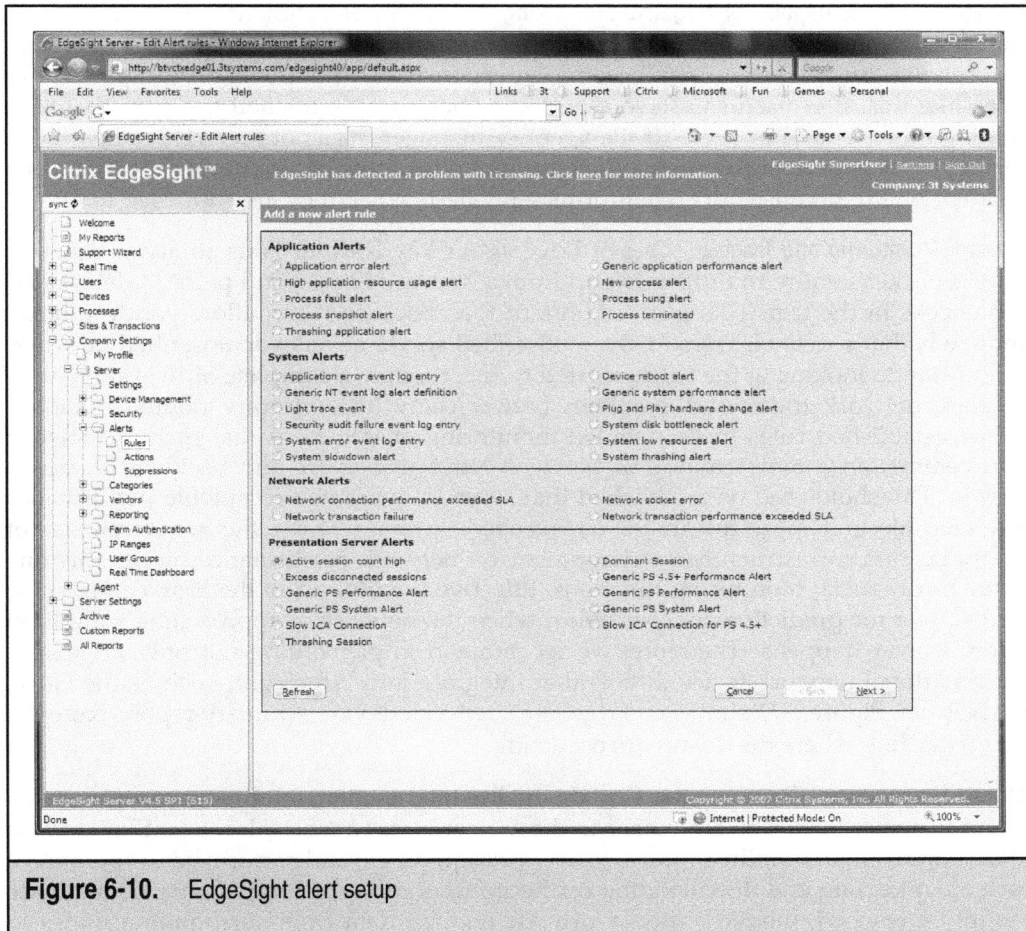

Figure 6-10.   EdgeSight alert setup

With SNMP-based systems, the agent processes events and sends messages with little to no filtering or processing on the local system. This is acceptable because SNMP messages are typically small and not likely to flood the network. In systems with more intelligent agents, where much more detailed information can be collected, the agent has the added task of collating or summarizing the data before sending it to the manager. Otherwise, the added traffic caused by unsummarized messages could cause a bandwidth utilization problem.

NOTE: SNMP uses standard UDP ports 161 and 162. Port 162 is reserved for traps only. As a result, it can be made subject to bandwidth utilization rules in a router (queuing) or in a device such as the Citrix WANScaler or Packeteer PacketShaper. Similarly, CMIP reserves UDP and TCP ports 163 for the agent and 164 for the manager.

Management by Exception or Negative Monitoring   This can be a function of an agent or a manager. Sometimes *not* receiving a piece of information from a system is just as critical as receiving one. A system may become unresponsive without ever sending a trap. In cases like this, it is useful to have a periodic "heartbeat"—a small message that says nothing more than "I'm here." If the agent or manager does not receive this heartbeat, an alert is generated for follow-up. We have found this type of monitoring to be a crucial part of the SME because not all platforms send alerts when they are supposed to.

Network Monitoring and Tracing   One of EdgeSight's key features is its ability to examine an ICA packet's entire roundtrip to and from a XenApp Server, and point to delays and bottlenecks in the trip. This is an important tool, because it can allow you to quickly know whether a delay is from an oversubscribed server or an oversubscribed network. In addition to looking at the Citrix-related traffic, though, a complete SME system must measure network traffic and problems between any two arbitrary points. It should follow established rules to do detailed monitoring on critical paths, such as between data centers, an Internet router, or between XenApp Servers and back-end database servers. Thresholds can be established that serve to guarantee acceptable performance and send alerts if those thresholds are reached. In many ways, the heavy reliance of an application infrastructure's environment on network performance makes this one of the most crucial monitoring functions. Effective monitoring in the SME can provide critical data for predictive analysis about when the network is approaching saturation before it ever happens. Therefore, we recommend implementing not only EdgeSight but additional network-focused tools that integrate into EdgeSight, such as the Citrix WANScaler. Figure 6-11 shows an EdgeSight network device summary report. Note the data regarding where the delays are occurring.

Remote Diagnostics   By using the Citrix's shadowing function, administrators can attach to and run a user's session anywhere on the network from a central location. Similarly, an SME should offer the ability to attach to network equipment and perform basic operations, such as uploading and downloading configurations and rebooting. If a particular node cannot be reached, the SME should provide enough data from surrounding nodes to determine what is wrong with the unresponsive equipment.

Data Collection

Whereas monitoring is the primary duty of the agent, data collection is the primary responsibility of the manager. The manager must record all incoming information without filtering; otherwise, auditing could be compromised. Relevant information can be easily extracted from the manager's database using query and reporting tools.

NOTE: Although having service-level views into problems is extremely useful, sometimes getting the information as soon as it is sent by an agent is more desirable. It is perfectly acceptable to define certain key events from key agents so that they travel the entire escalation path directly to an administrator for follow-up. It is even possible to define some agents so that they send a page at the same time that a trap is sent across the network. (Sometimes bad news needs to travel faster than good news for an SLA to be met.)

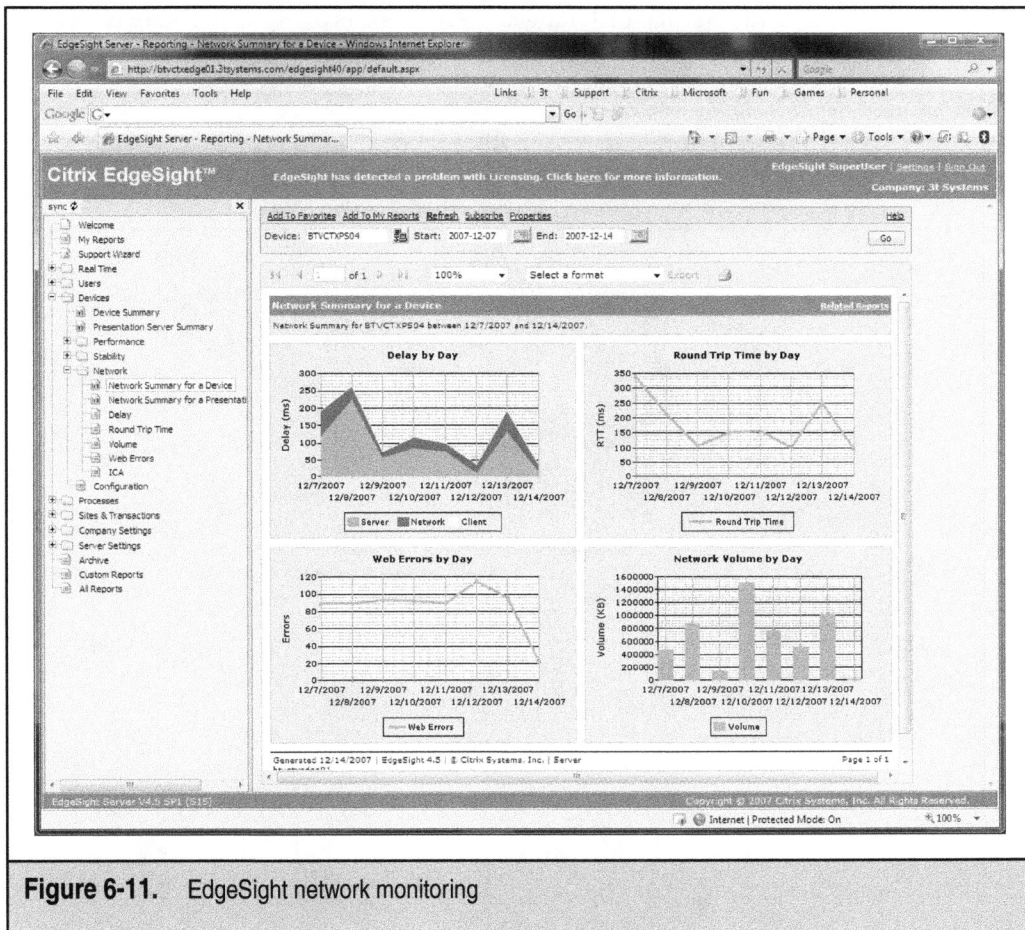

Figure 6-11. EdgeSight network monitoring

Other SME Functions

A few additional functions common to an SME take on slightly different roles when applied to the SBC infrastructure. We discuss these next.

Software Distribution/Unattended Install In terms of thin clients, XenApp Servers perform the function of software distribution. There is no reason to distribute an application any further than the server farm when nothing is running on the desktop except the ICA client. Therefore, the need for unattended installation of desktop software loses its importance (security updates and core OS updates remain important). Even with a server farm containing 50 servers, it is not that difficult to install applications manually if necessary. This would be a far different proposition, however, with 5,000 desktops.

NOTE: Fortunately, it is not necessary to install applications manually on your server farm. We will discuss methods for streamlining this process in Chapter 13.

If you don't have the luxury of taking the entire enterprise to thin-client devices, software distribution and installation are more important and should be considered a critical part of the SME. We will discuss this function as part of the tools discussion later in the chapter. Figure 6-12 shows software distribution in a thin-client network, whereas Figure 6-13 shows the same function in a traditional distributed (or fat-client) network. The Citrix Provisioning Server product, as well as third-party solutions such as Front

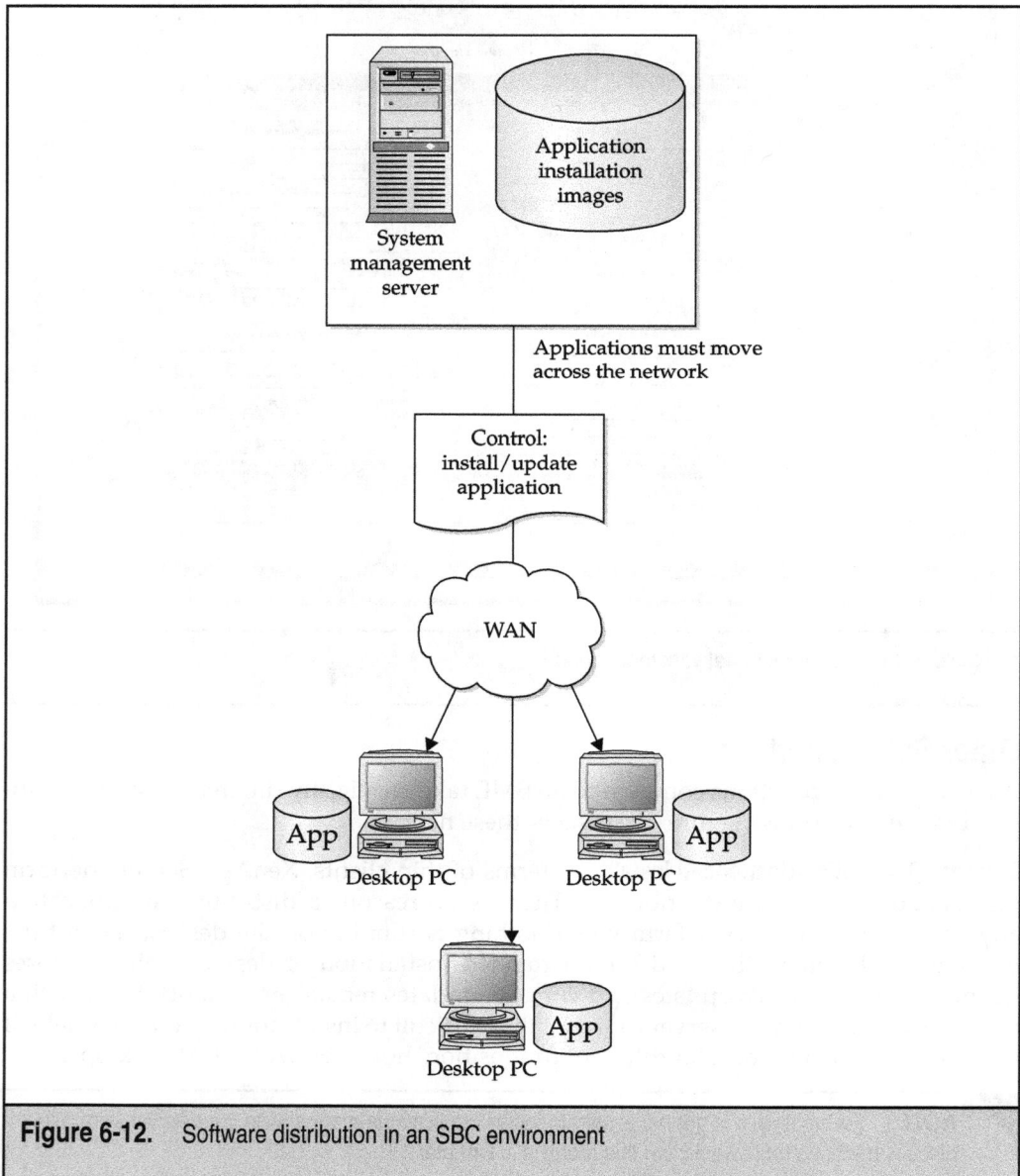

Figure 6-12.   Software distribution in an SBC environment

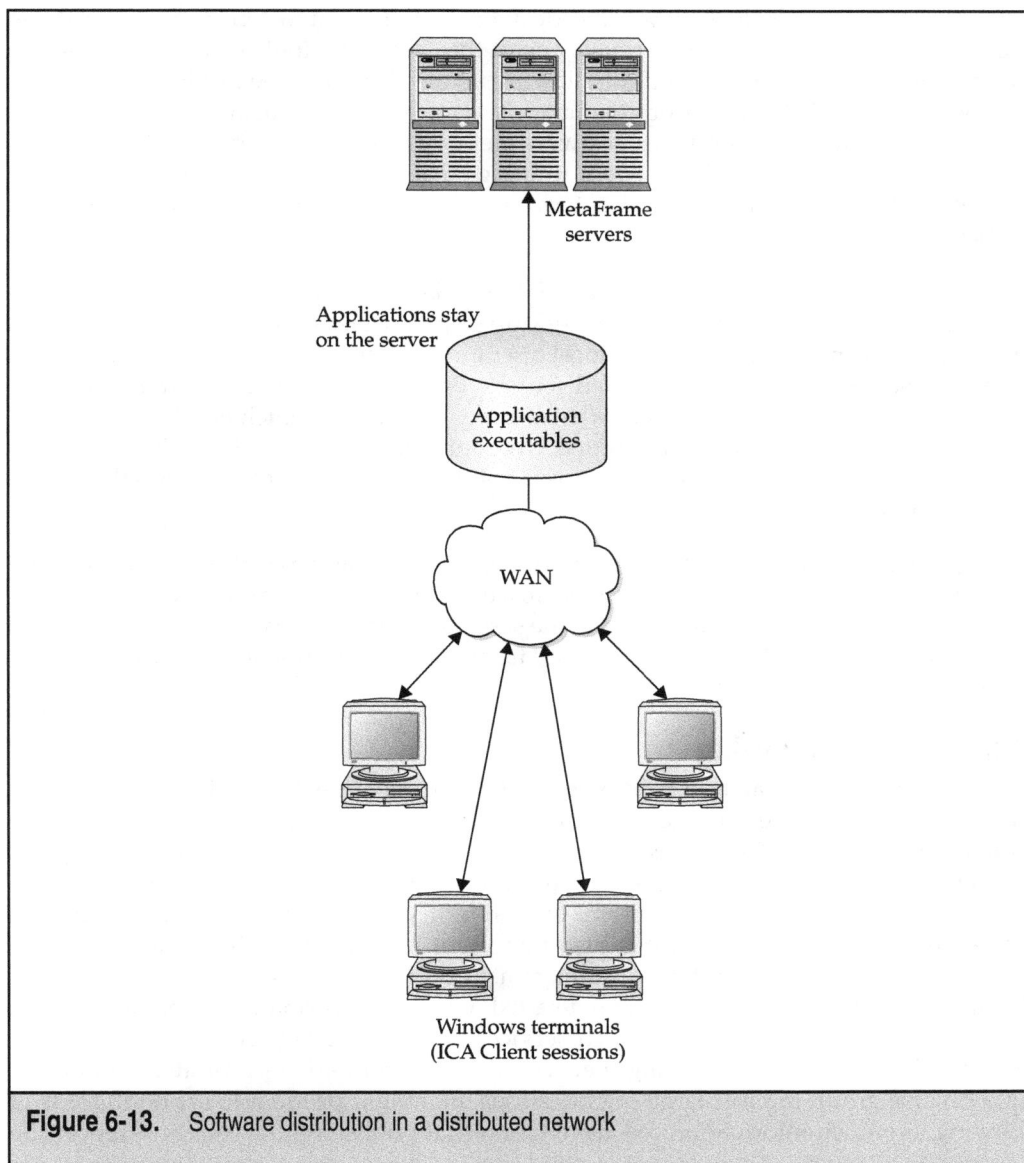

Figure 6-13. Software distribution in a distributed network

Range Solutions' Enteo and Microsoft Windows Software Update Service (WSUS), allow administrators to apply updates, patches, and security updates to Windows Server 2003, Windows Vista, and Windows XP.

Software Metering Similarly, software metering becomes far simpler in a centralized environment. All the applications are running centrally from the datacenter, and administrators can use Citrix EdgeSight to determine which users are running which applications. Furthermore, scripting techniques can be used to assign application access to user groups and to lock down the desktop to the point where users cannot run unauthorized applications. PowerFuse, one of the "security" tools mentioned earlier in this chapter, has an added benefit of allowing an application to be published to a large number of users while restricting concurrency to stay within licensing limitations.

In a distributed client network, software metering becomes much more complex and difficult to manage. Typically, an agent running locally on the desktop takes on the task of conversing with a manager and determining whether a user is authorized to run a particular application.

Desktop Lockdown   A common function of System Management Environment (SME) tools has historically been to lock down the desktop so that users cannot install unauthorized applications or make changes to the local operating system that would make it unstable or affect performance. Chapter 16 discusses desktop lockdown of XenApp using group policies and profiles as well as third-party applications such as RES PowerFuse, AppSense, and triCerat. In a distributed environment, these same tools, in addition to other major SME tools from Real Enterprise Solutions (RES), Microsoft, and HP provide this functionality for each desktop.

Desktop Remote Diagnostics   Although remote control tools such as GoToAssist from Citrix offer an excellent way to remotely connect to a user's desktop and allow an administrator to see what the user sees, with XenApp, the session shadowing feature built into the ICA session protocol provides this functionality from a central location in an efficient manner without added cost.

Management Reporting

The parts of the SME architecture presented so far have dealt mainly with collecting information and controlling the environment. Publishing and sharing the collected information and the results of those efforts for control are just as important. The value of management information increases the more it is shared. The IT staff should adopt a policy of "no secrets" and share information in terms of measured SLAs with users and management. That being said, it is also important to present the information formatted appropriately for the audience. Management typically is most interested in bottom-line information and would not find a detailed network performance graph very useful. A one- or two-page report listing each service level and the key metrics used to show whether that service level is being met would likely be more appropriate. Users make up a diverse group in most large organizations, making it prudent to err on the side of showing too much information. We have found that publishing the user SLA reports on a corporate intranet is a convenient method because it provides a central location for the information. If a more proactive method for distributing the information is desired, the URL for the intranet page can be e-mailed to the users.

NOTE: The format of your reports should *not* be determined by the capabilities of the measurement and reporting tools. The report should reflect the results of business-driven service-level agreements in order to be useful to their recipients.

Communication Plan   Part of effective reporting is establishing a communication plan. A communication plan can also be thought of in this context as a "reporting SLA." You must decide who is to receive the reports, at what frequency, and at what level of detail. If interaction between individuals or groups for review or approval is needed, define how this is going to happen and document it as part of the plan. For enterprises with an intranet built on Microsoft SharePoint, using Citrix Web Interface for Microsoft SharePoint may be the easiest way to create a one-stop-shop for internal access and information.

On the subject of what to publish, we have found the following reports to be very useful.

Daily Reports   The idea behind a daily report is to provide users and management with a concise view of performance against SLAs. The report should show only key indicators for each SLA. Sometimes called a *hot sheet*, this report should only be one or two pages in length. Figure 6-14 shows an example of such a report. The ideal delivery mechanism

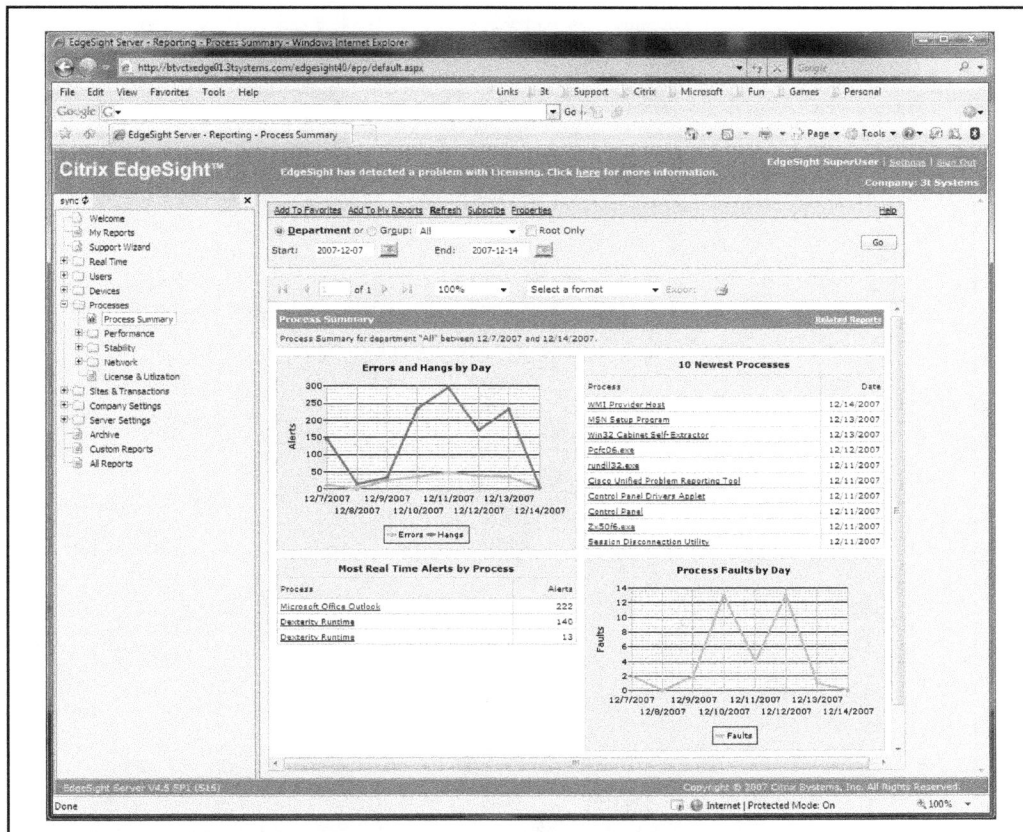

Figure 6-14.   A Citrix EdgeSight daily report

for such a report is on an intranet site (such as an MSAM site, as discussed earlier) or through e-mail. Enterprises often combine the hot sheet with other pertinent information that may affect user service over the next 24 to 72 hours, such as downtime or approved configuration changes from the configuration management process.

Periodic Reporting Periodic reports should have more detail than daily reports. At whatever interval is defined in the communication plan, detailed performance information should be published to users and management. This type of report should show *all* indicators used to measure SLA performance. The data used to generate this type of report is also used for predictive analysis or *trending*. For example, periodic views of disk space utilization will show how fast new disk space is consumed and when new storage should be put online. Trend reports allow you to stay ahead of demand and avoid resource-based outages.

CHAPTER 7

Building a Project Plan for Managing and Deploying Citrix XenApp Platinum Edition

After the project plan, architecture, and design are complete, the implementation begins. Project management is a key element in successful execution. This chapter, while not attempting an in-depth discussion of such a large topic, covers certain elements crucial to an application delivery system implementation, including preparing for organizational change, executive sponsorship, project manager authority, stakeholder buy-in, project reporting and tracking, task assignment, project change control, scope creep, and timeline management. We show examples of how tools such as service-level agreements and help desk software can help you manage changes to the environment to enhance benefits to management and end users. We also talk about the needs for the support environment both during and after the implementation.

This chapter also covers the transition methodology, from deploying applications to various endpoints, to delivering all applications and managing them centrally, regardless of where they physically run. First, we'll review the process of setting up a proof-of-concept pilot program. We next talk about expanding the pilot to a beta program in order to identify and resolve any issues that arise in a small-scale production environment. We then cover expanding the beta to an enterprisewide rollout of XenApp Platinum. Finally, we discuss postproduction processes of ongoing measurement and reporting, change control, upgrades, and changes to the environment.

NOTE: Although this book primarily focuses on XenApp, it is important to note that the fundamentals in this chapter are also applicable to a rollout of a XenDesktop infrastructure (a XenDesktop environment will typically include XenApp for both performance and organizational reasons).

PREPARING FOR ORGANIZATIONAL CHANGE

In most organizations, it is difficult to successfully migrate to an application delivery environment through mandate alone. An edict from top management is essential, but the planning team needs to supplement it with a strategy for internally selling the project as part of their overall change management plan. IT will probably have ultimate project ownership and an IT member will probably have to take the initiative in promoting an application delivery environment throughout the organization. For purposes of this chapter, we will assume that the IT person leading the initiative is the CIO.

TIP: IT people often underestimate the resistance that a paradigm shift to an enterprise application delivery system nearly always generates.

Implementing an enterprise application delivery environment does not involve a major alteration in an organization's mission statement or culture. It does, however, change to some extent the way in which employees accomplish their daily work. Planning for organizational change can address these concerns and help minimize project roadblocks. The steps for managing the change process are as follows:

1. Establish a need and sense of urgency for implementing centralized application delivery.

2. Create a compelling vision of the Application Delivery Center.

3. Recruit executive support.

4. Carefully plan the process.

5. Communicate to all stakeholders.

6. Build momentum and remove obstacles.

7. Monitor the progress.

8. Publicize early successes.

9. Expand the Application Delivery Center.

10. Prepare for future capabilities.

Establish a Need for the Application Delivery Center

A project definition document should include the justifications for an application delivery environment. A sense of urgency should now be included in order to generate support. A letter from the CEO, for example, can explain the financial benefits that will accrue from application delivery and consequently make it clear that this is a course of action that the organization is undertaking.

Create a Compelling Vision of the XenApp Environment

Although the CIO may have a vision for an organizationwide application delivery platform, the actual implementation often unfolds over various stages. It is important to develop a vision that can be shared with management and users alike of daily life using application delivery. The pilot and beta can be very useful in this regard. A particularly attractive advantage that can be demonstrated to both users and management alike is the ability to work seamlessly from any connection from anywhere. Users tend to get very excited by this capability because of the vastly increased flexibility it affords them. They no longer need to be constrained by physical location or device type. Management is naturally enthusiastic as well because the productivity of their employees can significantly rise because they are no longer unable to work due to bad weather or car troubles.

Recruit Executive Support

With any change in the organization or infrastructure, it is important to obtain executive sponsorship. Inevitably, conflicts will arise in terms of resource availability, and even outright opposition to the project can surface. The executive sponsor must be able to step in and resolve these issues in order to keep the project on track.

In order to better facilitate organizational change, promotion of the project should be expanded to enlist the support of other top managers. The CIO should meet with the appropriate executives either in a group or individually. She should take the time to explain the server-based computing philosophy to them, along with the financial and other benefits they can expect. She should also be realistic about the challenges they can expect to face during the project implementation and the results they will see upon its completion. Her team should customize an appropriate excerpt from the project plan to hand out to these executives.

IT Staff Assessment

Is the IT staff ready for an application delivery solution? They should be early adopters of the technology during the pilot phase and be convinced enough about the benefits so that they are advocates themselves.

If the IT staff is used to operating in the ad hoc manner normally associated with network administration, they need to understand that server-based computing requires the rigors of mainframe shop methodology, including controlled access, change control, and planning and procedures. Controls must be put into place to ensure that the IT staff will help, and not hinder, the application delivery implementation. If certain staff members are unwilling or unable to support the project, they should be reassigned to another support area.

Skill Levels   Does the IT staff have the necessary skills to install and manage an enterprise application delivery solution? They must have Windows Server expertise and experience, including an understanding of Active Directory, DNS, reporting, and Registry editing. Scripting capabilities are also a requirement for large implementations. A router and firewall expert must be available to manage large wide area networks and remote access. A skills assessment should be part of the initial project planning, and training or additional personnel should be obtained in order to cover the skill areas that are lacking. In addition, each of the individual components of XenApp Platinum Edition (Access Gateway, EdgeSight, Password Manager, Smart Auditor, and so on) will require specific expertise and individual focus. In larger organizations, we recommend delegating individuals specific areas of focus and ownership to ensure competency and depth.

IT Training   What training is appropriate for the IT staff prior to implementation? A thin client Terminal Services class and a Citrix XenApp class are strongly recommended. If most of the work will eventually be done internally, an advanced XenApp course is recommended as well.

Cultural Assessment

How will application delivery be received in the organization? The design plan should be modified, where necessary, in order to ensure that the organization's cultural norms will not be a roadblock to success.

Working Environment   In an environment such as a bank, where users commonly run similar applications and work as part of a unit, application delivery is likely to be very well accepted. Users will immediately appreciate the higher reliability and increased flexibility that Citrix XenApp enables. An engineering firm, on the other hand, with independent users accustomed to purchasing and loading their own software, will likely run into some resistance if they try to force employees to operate only in a XenApp environment. This type of environment may be better suited for a combination of XenDesktop and XenApp, depending on the desktop security needs of the organization.

Remote Users Remote users tend to be very enthusiastic toward application delivery because they receive access to the corporate resources they need in order to do their jobs more productively when away from the office. It is crucial to provide both adequate and redundant bandwidth to prevent problems with reliability and performance that can quickly turn remote users hostile toward a remote application delivery solution.

Managers Managers, in general, tend to resist the idea of application delivery until they actually use it; then they quickly become converts. They are usually impressed by the increased productivity they witness among their employees, as well as the capability for their employees to work remotely. The project management team can help foster enthusiasm among the managers for application delivery by showing them when the reduced corporate IT costs should be reflected on departmental bottom lines.

Political Assessment Politics usually comes down to allocation of resources, money, power, or all three. How will an application delivery solution impact the profit-and-loss statements of the different departments involved? What happens to a regional IT division when the computing model switches to a centralized application delivery architecture? It is important to be aware of these issues in order to take actions to minimize potential disruption to the project.

Communicate to All Stakeholders

Communication is perhaps the biggest key to successfully managing organizational change. In addition to the executive communications mentioned earlier, it is also important to educate and inform the internal IT staff, middle management, as well as the end users.

IT Staff

Migrating to an application delivery model invokes a fear on the part of IT that often significantly supersedes that of end users. PC fix-it technicians, for example, will likely see an application delivery solution as a threat to their job security. Regional IT staff will also be wary because the need for remote office support personnel usually is reduced. The CIO must come up with a strategy that presents the project's advantages, including fewer user complaints, elimination of the majority of help desk calls, much more efficient troubleshooting, and more time for IT staff to learn new and challenging technologies to help the organization move forward.

CAUTION: Do not oversell the enterprise application delivery solution. Set realistic expectations. Make sure users know the benefits, but also let them know about any problems or limitations they can expect to encounter, particularly in terms of performance and reliability, during the implementation period.

Build XenApp Momentum and Remove Obstacles

The ultimate goal of IT should be to create a buzz about the Application Deliver Center project. This can be accomplished by keeping the pilot program small and controlled, and by making sure that the pilot is a resounding success. Including capabilities either not possible or much more difficult to accomplish in the fat-client environment, such as effective logon from outside the LAN, document collaboration, rapid application delivery of new apps or new versions of existing apps, and single sign-on, helps make application delivery particularly attractive. Improved help desk support is another application delivery attribute often highly valued by users. It is important to limit the size and scope of the beta not only to ensure control, but also to help create an atmosphere of scarcity and exclusivity. The objective is to have users clamoring to be included as part of the XenApp project.

Users and department heads must buy into the goals of the XenApp project and understand its powerful positive implications for the organization.

Management Meetings

Hold group meetings with managers from different departments or divisions. Give them a chance to air their concerns and perspectives. Emphasize the benefits to the entire organization of implementing an application delivery solution. Stress that, although they may perceive that their employees have less control over their environment, managers actually now can devote their time to their business rather than to managing their computing infrastructure.

Although the goal for these meetings should be to provide a forum for managers to ask questions and air concerns, it should be clear that the project is going to take place. It is important to emphasize the positive benefits and to develop a spirit of cooperation and enthusiasm.

Entitlement Issues

Department staff may feel that because the money for the new system is coming out of their budget, they are entitled to their own servers. Employees may feel that they are entitled to their own PCs. These perceptions need to be changed. Users need to understand the benefits that a XenApp Platinum environment will provide to the organization as a whole. Some former capabilities, such as the ability to operate CD-ROMs, might be limited if they run in pure thin-client mode. On the other hand, users will gain computing advantages such as the ability to access their desktop from any PC or terminal. Another powerful user incentive is the potential for telecommuting. Many users discover that they prefer a XenApp environment because they experience increased reliability, flexibility, and performance. They also do not have to worry about causing problems by inadvertently changing their desktop. A properly configured XenApp environment will limit their ability to delete icons or INI files or create other mischief that can slow down productivity or impair their ability to do their jobs.

Problems with Perception of Central IT

If the corporate network has a history of performance or reliability problems, department managers are going to be very reluctant to put all of their eggs in the corporate data center basket. To reassure them, explain the elaborate steps that are being taken to upgrade the network infrastructure and describe the policies and procedures that will result in a far more reliable network environment. Explaining the redundancy and disaster recovery capabilities of the XenApp environment can help further mitigate any fears.

It is often productive to define an SLA in cooperation with the department managers in order to clarify expectations. If IT fails to meet the SLAs, the managers should have recourse, such as credits in a bill-back situation.

Budgetary Concerns

Application delivery, by definition, means centralized applications and resources. Individual computing fiefdoms will disappear. You may wish to implement a billing model that charges departments for actual resource usage in order to alleviate fears of arbitrary budgetary impacts.

Disposition Issues

If the project design plan calls for replacing certain PCs with terminals, department heads may not be happy about the impact on their budgets. During this preliminary stage, discuss disposition issues and how they will impact book value. If possible, incorporate charitable deductions in order to lower the burden. In some cases, it may not be necessary to replace all the PCs with thin-client terminals. Most PCs can be rebuilt and "dummied" down to make for excellent terminals for connecting to a XenApp environment. Refer to Chapter 5 for more details on client types and usage.

Monitor the Progress

Constantly solicit and measure user feedback. IT can then make any adjustments necessary in order to ensure user satisfaction. This will add a great deal to the process of building a very successful enterprise XenApp environment.

Publicize Early Successes

Internal success stories should be generated about the attributes of the XenApp environment. The idea is to create a buzz around the organization where people are excited about, rather than resistant to, the upcoming changes. At the VA Medical Center, for example, we had a doctor thank our implementation team for making his life better because he could now access so much more of the data he needed, and he could do it much more quickly and far more easily than he could in the previous distributed PC environment.

Expand the XenApp Environment

Most organizations choose to roll out an enterprise XenApp environment in phases. The original scope of the project is often less than a complete enterprise deployment. As phases are successfully implemented, and the user surveys show improved satisfaction with IT, the scope of the XenApp environment can be expanded. Providing feedback to management about the existing and expected financial savings can help to further promote XenApp expansion.

Prepare for Future XenApp-Enabled Opportunities

Once the XenApp environment has been expanded throughout the enterprise, the organization's IT department should run exceptionally well. Employees will have more computing capabilities than before at a much lower IT budget and with fewer IT personnel. The organization will also have opportunities that go beyond those that are realistic in a distributed PC environment. We discuss some of those opportunities in this book, such as business continuance, more efficient centralized storage devices, and greatly enhanced security and virus protection. However, other possibilities are now potentially available as well. For instance, a large janitorial organization might decide to have a thin-client terminal manufacturer make their terminals look like time clocks in order to enable janitors to enter data right into the ERP application. A construction company might outfit foreman and inspectors with wireless tablet devices in order to have real-time information flow back and forth from the job sites. An organization concerned about ramifications from the Sarbanes-Oxley Act might introduce third-party products such as KVS, which will enable them to track and categorize all e-mail documents for quick and simple discovery.

CAUSES OF PROJECT FAILURE

Examples of application delivery failures are, unfortunately, not in short supply. They often occur when an organization implements a XenApp pilot or beta with a goal toward enterprise expansion, but then forgoes the rollout. Many organizations approach a Terminal Services implementation from a PC networking perspective. Although it is sometimes possible to deploy a successful Windows 2003 Server or Novell network without extensive planning and piloting, this will rarely work in an application delivery solution. Both cultural and political aspects are added to the technical challenges to make unplanned deployment nearly a guarantee of failure.

Inadequate Preparation for Organizational Change

IT often underestimates the impact of an application delivery model on the cultural, political, and other aspects of the organization. Preparing for the organizational change as described earlier in this chapter is a key component to a successful enterprise deployment.

Skipping Project Planning Steps

Many organizations skip the pilot, project definition, and infrastructure assessment steps and go straight to project planning, or even a beta. This is bound to be troublesome if not an outright failure.

Lack of a Proof-of-Concept Pilot

The proof-of-concept pilot is essential for testing all applications under an application delivery model before implementation. Proceeding immediately to a production pilot or beta can leave users frustrated with application performance or reliability, or both. Even a small number of frustrated users can provide the type of negative feedback that will quell any further server-based computing expansion.

Lack of a Project Definition Document

Some internal evangelists might be sold on the idea of enterprise application delivery solution and persuade management to implement one without enough thought to the objectives, scope, roles, risks, and success criteria. Without a project definition document, the planning, project management, and implementation teams have no touchstone with which to keep the project on track.

Lack of an Infrastructure Assessment

Project design committees often like to skip the infrastructure assessment step and jump straight to planning. This tends to be the most enjoyable part of the project, when participants contribute their knowledge to build a solution. Unfortunately, it is virtually impossible to create an optimally effective plan without a detailed infrastructure assessment. Additionally, infrastructure flaws that are tolerated under distributed computing are likely to be amplified in an application delivery solution. When users become completely dependent on a central server farm for executing their applications, the infrastructure has to be extremely solid.

Inadequate Planning

Sometimes even large server-based computing implementations are performed without knowledge of basic tools and methodologies that can dramatically facilitate deployment. We once had lunch with the architects of a 5,000-seat Citrix XenApp project who were complaining about bandwidth issues. It turned out that they had never even heard of the bandwidth management tools provided with XenApp Platinum. Using bandwidth management from the start would have prevented their problems.

PROJECT MANAGEMENT

Incisive project management is key to a successful application delivery conversion. Here are the major steps in project-managing an enterprise application delivery implementation:

▼ Identify a project manager.

■ Put together a project management team.

■ Control project change.

■ Create a project implementation plan.

■ Prepare for implementation.

■ Start the project.

■ Provide user support.

▲ Measure success.

Identify a Project Manager

A dedicated and competent project manager is essential to a successful implementation. There should be only one manager for the overall project, and that person should have both the responsibility and the authority to keep it on track. Communication is key. The project manager needs to make sure that both good and bad news travel fast.

CAUTION: The larger the project, the less chance it has for success. Migrating to an application delivery environment is a major IT project. Give this project the full attention of your IT staff, and do not run it in parallel with other IT projects.

Put Together a Project Management Team

Although one project manager should have overall authority, it is often a good idea to appoint a team to assist with the project implementation plan. An IT manager and business manager are two key roles to help resolve problems and keep the project on track. Someone from procurement should be on the team along with experts in the various technologies that will be utilized. The executive sponsor should at least be associated with the team in order to lend their authority. It is important to include employees who are involved in the areas of the company that will be affected by the project. This provides two benefits: First, the team benefits from their expertise in the area in question. Second, the employees get to be involved in the change, and the hope is that they will be less resistant to it.

Control Project Change

Scope creep is highly likely in large deployments. Users will often insist on accessing applications that were never included in the plan. They may insist that the project's viability in terms of meeting established performance and uptime SLAs as well as projected ROI targets hinges on these additions. The ability to rapidly deploy an application in a XenApp environment is one of its strongest selling features, yet the application implementation is a detailed process requiring extensive preliminary testing. A change control process is essential for keeping the project on track.

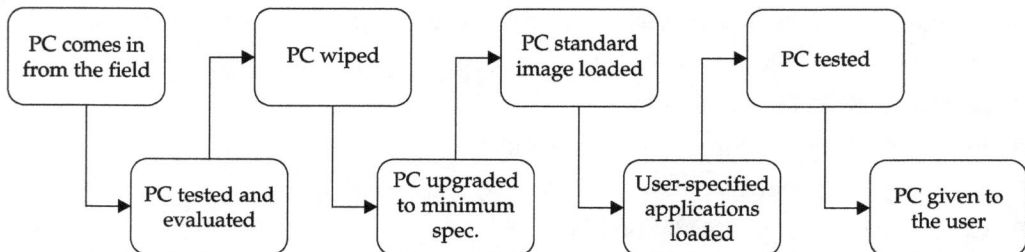

```
PC comes in          PC wiped          PC standard          PC tested
from the field                         image loaded

      PC tested and      PC upgraded       User-specified       PC given to
      evaluated          to minimum        applications         the user
                         spec.             loaded
```

Change Control Process

Change requests in server-based computing range from minor (such as a user's request to continue accessing their local C: drive) to major (such as a demand to host a DOS application that is known to have problems running under Windows Terminal Services). Because you are implementing a central processing environment, all changes to the design plan should be approved by the project manager and recorded. Changes that will affect the project budget or schedule may require additional approval.

Consider, for example, a request to add an application to the Terminal Services environment during the server farm rollout phase. This requires that the rollout be postponed while the new application is thoroughly tested in conjunction with the other hosted applications. All affected parties and stakeholders require notification of the rollout postponement. Once the new configuration proves stable, a new server image disk needs to be created, and the server rollout begins again. Because this seemingly innocuous change can have broad implications—not only for the project time and budget, but also for many users—it is probably appropriate to have the business manager and IT manager sign off on the change along with the project manager.

Change Control Guidelines

Changes should only be made when required by stakeholders or when circumstances cause a significant deviation from the project design plan. The reasons for all changes should be documented along with any changes to the schedule or budget that result. We provide suggestions for testing procedures and change control in Chapter 16.

Conflict Resolution

Conflicts are inevitable in a large project. An enterprise environment will demand IT resources that are already likely to be in short supply. Some users will be frustrated at a perceived loss of personal flexibility. Many users consider themselves IT experts and will disagree with the technology or the way it is deployed. Conflicts should be quickly referred to the project manager for resolution. Approaches to solving the problem include the following:

▼ **Ignoring the conflict**   Sometimes it is better for the project manager to simply ignore the conflict if it is not likely to have a big impact on the project or is likely to resolve itself.

■ **Breaking up the fight**   This approach is useful if both parties are stuck in an argument. The project manager can interfere in order to take the energy out of the argument.

■ **Compromising**   Compromise may be required at times, such as allowing a user who was scheduled to be entirely thin client to run in hybrid mode. Keep in mind, though, that any nonstandard implementations detract from overall project efficiency and organizational computing effectiveness.

■ **Confronting**   This approach involves getting all parties together to work out their problem in an environment promoting conflict resolution.

▲ **Forcing a resolution**   Sometimes the project manager must use their authority or the authority of the IT manager or the business manager to mandate a resolution. This method should be used as a last resort.

Create a Project Implementation Plan

An enterprise application delivery project starts with a project definition document that states the goals, scope, roles, risks, success criteria, and project milestones. The project design plan then lays out the specifics of the major components. A project implementation plan is the fourth step in this process. Whereas the project planning document provides a roadmap for implementation, the project implementation document covers the project management aspects of migrating to a application delivery environment.

Project Constraints

The project implementation plan must be created with regard to time, money, and people resources. Identifying these constraints will help determine how to apply corporate resources to the project. The following table indicates that management has decreed the application delivery implementation be done quickly:

	Most Constrained	Moderately Constrained	Least Constrained
Time	X		
Budget		X	
People			X

Time is the most important element, whereas human resources are less constrained. Because time has the least flexibility, internal resources need to be diverted to the application delivery project, while funds also should be used to bring in outside consultants and perhaps implementers.

Another constraint, often inevitable in an application delivery implementation, is user satisfaction. Users can make or break an implementation, and they are likely to resist the change if no preparatory work is done. It is therefore essential for the project manager to keep the users in mind when designing the project plan. The objective should be both to minimize disruption in user operations and to generate enthusiasm among users for the new paradigm.

Define Your Plan

Your plan will take shape as you define the major elements of implementation. Consider timing, key milestones, and budget, and then communicate the plan to everyone involved.

Project Timing   Time is invariably the most constrained resource, and it is often not the most visible to participants. Clearly communicating the timing of the project's phases will help to convey the appropriate level of urgency.

Key Milestones   Identifying key milestones enables participants to easily measure progress. Stakeholders should be involved in defining milestones. The milestones can provide a chance for the team to pause and ask, "Where are we and how far do we have to go?" They can also provide an opportunity for positive communication to the stakeholders and the company at large when they are reached on time and on budget.

Estimated Project Costs and Cash Flows   Defining the broad budget for the project conveys the significance of the resources being expended. It also enables appropriate stakeholders to measure expenditures against it.

Implementation Strategy   There are certainly many different ways to implement an application delivery solution. Providing a summary of your strategic approach will help eliminate confusion and uncertainty.

Upside and Downside Potentials   Any new IT project has risks as well as potential rewards. Upside potential in this environment can include many unexpected results, such as increased sharing of best practices among previously isolated corporate divisions.

Likely Points of Resistance with Strategies for Overcoming Them

Potential technical, financial, and political roadblocks should be listed along with approaches for resolving them. For instance, if employees in a particular remote office are determined to keep their own file server and LAN, a strategy for a phased implementation in their case might be appropriate.

Technical Challenges   Terminal Services is an evolving technology. Technical challenges will be present in every large enterprise rollout. Identify any problem areas that could jeopardize customer satisfaction with the project. Set action plans for resolving technical challenges. For instance, if a 16-bit application is quirky on Windows 2003 Server, it either should not be hosted or should be isolated on a separate server or server farm and accessed from the main production farm via pass-through.

Identify Unresolved Design Issues   Some design parameters will remain vague prior to the project implementation. These questionable areas should be referred to experts to help eliminate any confusion or uncertainty. For instance, when designing a network-attached storage (NAS) solution, we bring in the manufacturer in order to size the unit appropriately.

Define Project Roles

Define the roles and responsibilities of staff members during the project implementation. Some of the roles you might need to define include project management assistance, teams for implementing server-based computing migration, procurement, wide area network implementation, bandwidth management facilitation, and storage consolidation. If using an integrator or consultants, define their roles, responsibilities, and tasks as well. These may be limited to consulting, or they may include project management or hands-on implementation.

Manage the Tasks

Projects are broken down by tasks that can be defined as a unit of work that is important to the project completion. Tasks can also include related subtasks. Assign managers to each task and set performance SLAs. For instance, one task may be to order an ATM link to the data center by a certain date. The SLA may be to order all data lines and equipment on or before the due date.

Develop a Work Breakdown Structure (WBS)   Tasks need to be organized into logical milestones, sequenced, assigned, associated with necessary resources for their completion, and communicated to team members. The WBS is a standard method of organizing project tasks in one of two formats: either an organizational chart with each box listing tasks, as shown in Figure 7-1, or an outline WBS, as shown in Figure 7-2. The outline form tends to work better for projects with many layers of tasks. Both techniques show the different levels that are required and include subprojects or milestones, major tasks, subtasks, and minor tasks.

Develop a Project Schedule   The key is to find ways to schedule parallel activities in order to complete the project within the allotted timeframe. Building an enterprise application delivery architecture is somewhat akin to a construction project. The most common scheduling technique in this case is the critical path method (CPM), which uses historical data to estimate task durations.

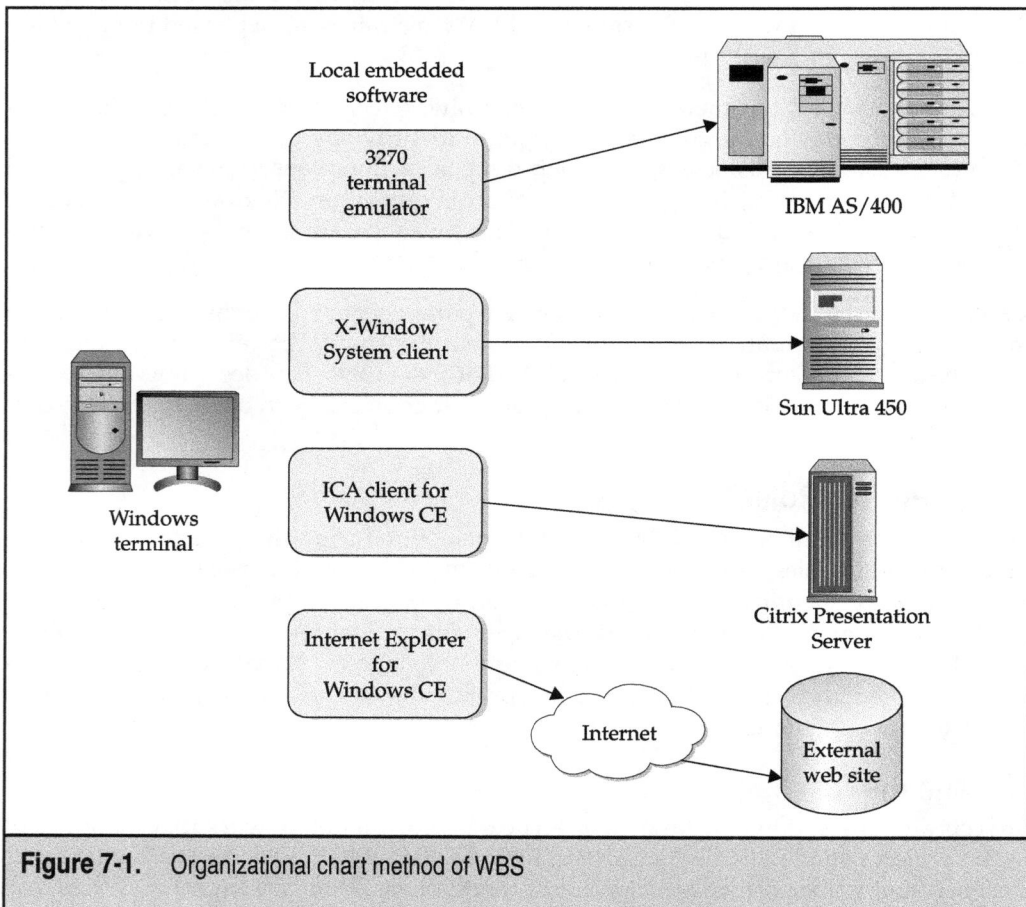

Figure 7-1.   Organizational chart method of WBS

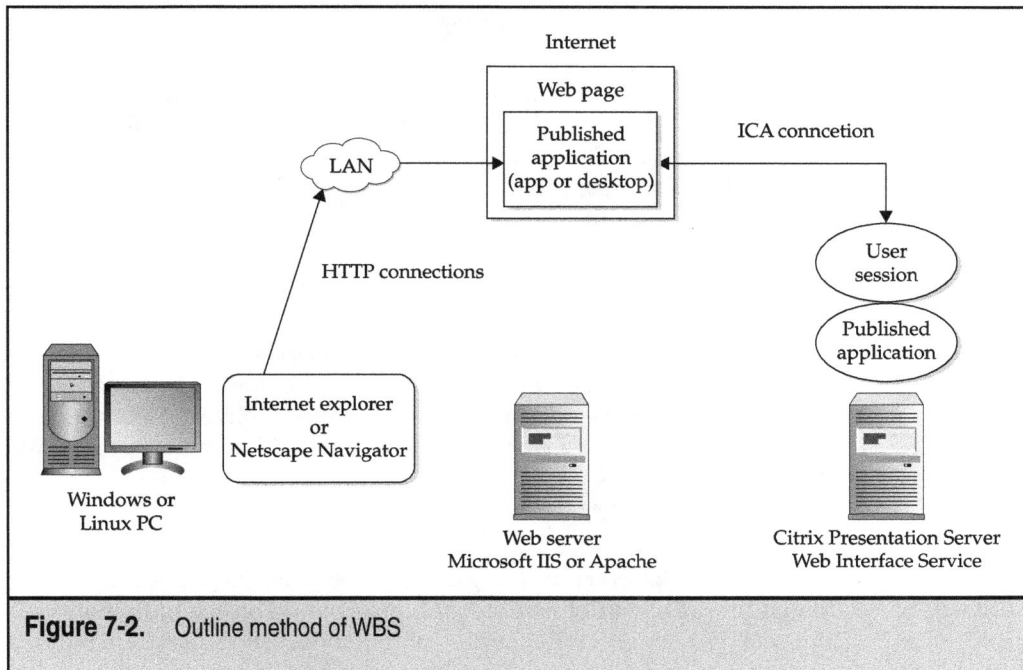

Figure 7-2. Outline method of WBS

Coordinate Tasks   In a large enterprise project, different elements of the organization will require coordination between them. Assign specific managers, as necessary, to ensure this coordination takes place. For each task it should be clear who has ultimate responsibility for its completion. Although several people may contribute, only one person can be responsible. This is the person whom the project manager will rely on for communication on the status of that task.

Define Project Documentation   Detail how the project will be documented for IT staff, managers, and end users. This documentation should conform to the communication plan described later in this chapter. It should include documentation about the data center configuration as well as about equipment and data lines at each remote office.

Establish an Internal Marketing Plan   Formulate an internal marketing plan. Identify points of resistance in the organization and establish action plans for overcoming them.

Prepare for Implementation

Organizational preparation for the project implementation should start with a word from the executive sponsor. Surveys can then be distributed in order to more precisely define the project tasks. Ordering lines and equipment is the next step in preparing for deployment of implementation teams.

Announce the Project to the Organization

Announcement of the project should incorporate sponsorship statements from key corporate executives and give all employees a clear vision of what is coming, what it will look like, what to expect, how it will benefit them and the organization, and how it will affect their daily work. At one East Coast company, the vice president of MIS created a "Back to Business" video that emphasized how XenApp eliminates much of the futzing around that PCs tend to foster. By mixing humor with a description of benefits, he created an extremely effective marketing tool.

Executive Mandate

Although we put a lot of emphasis on selling the project to users, an executive mandate is still required. A formal letter should go out from a high-ranking executive, preferably the CEO, telling all managers and users that a new application delivery infrastructure will be taking place. It should emphasize that this is an organizational initiative and that everyone is expected to make it work.

Surveys

The distributed nature of a PC-based computing environment means that many organizations, particularly larger ones, do not have a good grasp of the exact equipment and applications run by users. This is especially the case with remote offices or where managers have had the authority to purchase their own hardware and software. Creating surveys for both users and remote offices will enable the project manager to assess the true environmental condition and make appropriate ordering decisions. Even organizations with an existing network management system (NMS) in place often find that the inventory capabilities are not accurate enough to rely upon. In such cases, the inventory report from the NMS can be used as a basis for the survey, and then the user representative for the site can be asked to correct the report.

WAN Survey   If the existing WAN infrastructure does not provide adequate connectivity to all remote offices under Terminal Services, a site survey should be completed at least 60 days before the installation in order to allow for bandwidth upgrades. This timing is crucial due to the inevitable delays caused by the local and national exchange carriers. A user count and printer count (including types of printers) will help determine the type and size of bandwidth connection to each site. Including the address and ZIP Code helps the WAN team decide whether certain technologies, such as a DSL connection, are viable options.

LAN Survey   Make sure the LANs in the selected remote offices are ready for a transition to an application delivery solution. For example, daisy-chained hubs that might have worked in a PC-based computing environment can kill XenApp sessions. This is because users often have at least one more Ethernet hop to the data center server backbone, which may be enough to exceed the IEEE Ethernet standard. Another example is a poorly performing server that may have problems when the implementation team tries to copy data from it. Such problems can also give the field deployment teams a "heads up" for what equipment they might need in order to migrate local desktops and servers. For example, if the LAN backbone has problems, a field technician might plan on bringing their own hub to connect the server to the deployment PC with a CD-RW drive to pull the data from the server.

Application Survey   Despite the best efforts of the planning committee and despite any company policies that are created regarding an application delivery implementation, some users in remote offices will nearly always have local applications that they insist are required for them to do their job. It is far better to learn about these applications ahead of time in order to make appropriate accommodations for them as part of the implementation design process.

NOTE: We cannot stress enough about the importance of learning everything about an application before hosting it in a XenApp environment. This rule must still be followed even in the sometimes-unwieldy arena of remote office migration. We learned this the hard way. In one implementation, we came across many custom-written applications utilized in remote offices. Most were written in Microsoft Access and easily migrated to XenApp. At one site, however, we migrated an application to the corporate data center and were told it no longer worked. After extensive debugging, we asked the user for more information. The user replied, "The application never really worked, but I thought that it might work once you moved it."

Printer Survey   An accurate count of the number and types of printers and print servers will help determine the type and size of connection required to each remote site. It is also important to determine any printers required apart from users' default printers. Printers that are not going to be supported as part of the application delivery environment should be eliminated. Otherwise, they are bound to cause problems and may even lead to Terminal Services problems. The implementation team can bring new printers with them to replace the nonsupported units.

IP Address Survey   It is important that the IP addresses are managed across the enterprise. Whether this is done manually or by using management software, the point is that the lack of a workable scheme can cause a lot of system administration overhead and confusion. If such a system is not in place before the application delivery project, consider using the project as an excuse to put one in place.

PC Survey   Determining the condition of each user's PC may aid a decision about whether to replace it with a thin-client device. Create criteria for determining whether a PC will work in the new application delivery environment. This might include having an existing network interface card (NIC), having an existing desired local operating system, or being within a certain number of years old.

User Survey   Complete a user survey at least two weeks before installation to allow enough time to order and ship required equipment as well as to set up the user accounts. This survey should cover all relevant information about each user, including whether the user requires access to only XenApp-approved applications and whether the user's existing machine meets the new application delivery environment standards. The survey should also measure users' satisfaction with the existing computing environment in order to establish a baseline for judging the success of the application delivery environment once implemented.

Order Equipment

Equipment must be ordered for the application delivery implementation as well as for any upgrades to the existing infrastructure.

Equipment Purchase Lead Time   The surveys will show the existing type and condition of the equipment at headquarters and at remote offices. Order new equipment required for the installation a minimum of two weeks beforehand. This is necessary in order to stage the equipment prior to a large rollout. If you are rolling out 2,500 thin clients to remote offices, for example, the logistics become daunting in terms of delivery confirmation, asset tracking, and shipping. Nothing will throw up a red flag on a project like not having all the equipment in and configured.

Asset Tracking System   It is important to have some type of asset-tracking system in place in order to record the equipment ordered and where it is deployed. If your organization does not yet utilize one, the application delivery project is a good time to start one. Ideally, the system would be accessible by the field deployment technicians so that as they deploy each user, they can enter that user's equipment information directly into the system.

Remote Office LANs   Remote offices may have inadequate hubs, or even lack a network altogether. Order any hubs, switches, network interface cards, print servers, and cabling to be put in place ahead of the migration team. If you are ordering for many remote offices, order four weeks ahead of time to allow for staging and shipping.

Personnel Resources

Necessary personnel must be identified for both the upgrades and for the actual project implementation. For instance, later in this chapter we describe the composition of the implementation teams. Decisions need to be made about the number of technicians required to migrate users at headquarters and at all remote offices. Although the actual migration time for a user in a remote office can often be kept down to about an hour, travel and logistics make a four-hour average estimate more realistic. The time, money, and resource constraints will determine how many technicians are assigned to the project.

Infrastructure Upgrades

In Chapter 3, we discussed the importance of doing an in-depth infrastructure assessment. The project management team needs to review that assessment again, factoring in the results from the surveys. Deficiencies in the network infrastructure that were tolerated in a PC-based computing environment are likely to be disastrous once users depend on the corporate data center for all their processing. Any infrastructure deficiencies must be resolved prior to the migration to an application delivery solution. Both equipment and human resources must be secured for the upgrades and for the project implementation.

Data Center Upgrade   The data center often requires upgrades such as implementing a gigabit switching solution or a new firewall to enable secure Internet access. These projects require planning and implementation before the enterprise rollout.

Network Backbone Upgrade   One way to think of a Citrix XenApp server farm is as if it were actually hundreds or thousands of PCs. The backbone infrastructure, therefore, needs to be both very fast and reliable. Examine the existing backbone carefully using a network analysis tool, if necessary, in order to spot any deficiencies. Any problems must be fixed before the beta implementation.

Network Operating System Upgrades   Some organizations take the opportunity during an application delivery implementation to either upgrade or migrate their network operating systems. This should be treated as a separate subproject, and the migration or upgrade should be completed before the application delivery rollout—ideally, before the pilot. Attempting to do this project concurrently with an enterprise application delivery implementation leaves far too many variables to troubleshoot in the event of problems. It can have another undesirable side effect: Users who experience problems related to the change in operating system or infrastructure may think that the Terminal Services or XenApp software is responsible.

We have found that during migrations, Citrix can often be a magnet for blame when users experience problems after the initial cutover, even though issue may be unrelated to Citrix. Users notice that Citrix is a new piece in their day-to-day activities and because the problems did not exist prior to Citrix and Terminal Services, then they must be to blame. The only way to mitigate these kinds of issues is to try and not do other IT projects concurrent with a Citrix implementation.

Data Center Storage   The project design planning document will include the selected storage medium at the data center—whether NAS, SAN, or general-purpose file servers. The surveys will show the amount of hard drive storage currently required by users and by remote office servers, enabling ordering of the appropriate storage for the data center. Of course, user and remote office storage requirements for XenApp-hosted applications can be ignored. Significant economies of scale are obtained by centralizing all data storage instead of requiring a surplus for each user. As a result, the requirement for central storage will be less than the cumulative totals of existing distributed hard drives.

Wide Area Network Upgrades   The surveys will show the number of users per remote office, enabling decisions about how much bandwidth to supply. Some organizations will install their first WAN as part of an application delivery architecture. Others will upgrade their existing system, while still other organizations will add redundancy. In an ideal world, this implementation should be completed well before the application delivery infrastructure rollout, but in practice it is often not possible. Allow 60 days for ordering and installing data connectivity lines or upgrades, whether using a frame relay connection, a leased line, DSL, cable, or ISDN. Do not rely on your telecommunications company; follow up to make sure they are staying on schedule. Test the lines once they are in place before sending an implementation team to a remote office. Also test redundancy, even if this is just a dial-up to the data center.

Start the Project

Establish a regular meeting schedule to review milestones and budgets. Work on the exception principle. Focus on what is not going according to plan. Fix it fast. Be prepared to add resources in order to meet the schedule. Issue a weekly list of targets and key troubleshooting assignments.

Maintain Quality and Accountability

Make careful and informed decisions about key equipment purchases or leases. System reliability should be a prime consideration in any application delivery project. Unreliable system elements can jeopardize overall system performance. Monitor all subcontractors and vendors to ensure that they are staying on target with their assigned tasks. Move quickly to correct targets that aren't being met.

Project Budget

It will be difficult to accurately estimate the budget required for a large application delivery deployment because of the tremendous number of variables involved. Fortunately, application delivery solutions tend to save organizations so much money that even significant budget overruns would compare favorably with the PC-based computing alternative.

Budget Contingencies Management will want to see a budget and expect the project manager to hold to it. This is why it is important to build in contingencies for travel, cost overruns, and unexpected problems. It will sometimes be necessary to spend more than planned in order to achieve the desired results. It is also wiser to deviate from the budget in order to circumvent a problem before it becomes a crisis. Again, the vast savings enabled by the overall project should make this the wise alternative.

Budget Monitoring Tying the budget to the project milestones is a good method for monitoring progress and keeping expenditures on track. It also can provide stakeholders with a clearer example of benefits. For instance, a project milestone might be replacing 500 old PCs with new thin-client terminals. The thin-client terminals cost $1,000 each, while purchasing 500 new PCs would cost $1,500 to $2,000 each (including the extra installation PCs require). Offset the project budget at this point against the cost of purchasing new PCs and the cost of upgrading those new PCs in two or three years.

Communication Plan

It is essential to communicate about the project with users. We recommend over-communicating about the project migration parameters and expectations. Regular e-mails are certainly valuable. Prepare a list of frequently asked questions (FAQs) to help inform users about their new environment.

Issue Regular Project Updates Relay the key achievements since the last update. Talk about the project status and where the project is going in the next period. Discuss what is required to ensure success. Part of the established communication plan should be to report on the project's progress to key stakeholders.

Handling Complaints Enhance the help desk department as explained later in the chapter. Enlist the aid of regional managers, if necessary, to help set user expectations during the implementation. Managing user expectations is something that should be done continuously during the process. This will decrease the number of calls to the help desk.

Publish Deployment News Use e-mail or an intranet to publish ongoing news about the migration. Let users know of potential bottlenecks or other problems before they take place. Share the wins as well. Publish user testimonials about the migration.

Deployment Guide Creating a deployment guide for implementation teams is discussed later in this chapter. In some organizations, users will be doing their own client setup. In these cases, the deployment guide can be of great assistance to them as well.

Provide User Support

Providing adequate user support is essential to a successful enterprise application delivery implementation. Even though users may experience initial problems, they will have much better attitudes if they can receive prompt and competent help.

Enhance the Current Support Structure

Part of the infrastructure assessment described in Chapter 3 is an analysis of the organization's help desk methodology and escalation procedures. Once the enterprise application delivery solution is in place and stabilized, help desk requirements will dwindle. Not only does Citrix XenApp enable superior troubleshooting through shadowing capabilities, but also the number of problems will fall because the processing takes place centrally. During the implementation phase, however, the frequency of support requests will increase. In addition to the confusion and problems of implementing a new computing infrastructure, the help desk will, in effect, be supporting two environments during the transition. Be prepared to supplement the help desk with additional personnel during this period.

Establish Service-Level Agreements (SLAs) Establish and manage SLAs for the help desk during project implementation. Ensure that users receive the help they need to get them through the transition without frustration.

Support Processes Cover every shift and every time zone. A process should be in place, and the appropriate personnel identified, for escalating problems that are not resolved by the first-line support people in an acceptable timeframe.

Virtual Call Center Create a virtual call center whereby any member of the implementation team can assist if required. Use help desk software to enable this collaboration among different individuals from different areas working on the same user problem.

Triage Process Have a "S.W.A.T." team available to go onsite to handle particularly tricky problems that surface during the implementation. Consider using outside experts for the "S.W.A.T." team who have a high level of experience with Citrix XenApp, Windows, and networking.

Status Reporting

The help desk should work in conjunction with the project management team to give continuous status updates. These updates can take place through phone calls, e-mail, and an intranet. They should reflect user attitudes about the migration process in order for adjustments to be made.

Measure Success

Establish success metrics ahead of time and measure results against them. For instance, an SLA might be to enable users in remote offices to access their data within 24 hours of migrating to server-based computing. Measure and report the actual results of how long it takes users to gain access.

Use Measurement Tools at Milestones

Survey the users at project milestones to measure their perceptions versus expectations. For instance, a project milestone might be to have all small remote offices online as XenApp users. Surveying users can reveal any problems with performance or reliability, which will enable adjustments to the design plan before proceeding to the next milestone.

Project Success on a Macro Level

On a macro level, metrics should include project performance against budgeted costs, estimated timelines, and user satisfaction. Measuring success is discussed further in this chapter in the section "Postproduction Management."

PROOF-OF-CONCEPT PILOT PROGRAM

In Chapter 3, we discussed setting up a proof-of-concept pilot program as an important element in the design of an enterprise application delivery solution. The pilot is also the first step in an enterprise rollout. It serves as a basic test of application performance using Terminal Services and Citrix XenApp.

At first, the pilot program should be a nonproduction system designed to ensure that the desired applications perform together adequately over XenApp and Terminal Services. The next step is to expand the nonproduction pilot to a small production pilot or test group with carefully selected participants running specific applications.

Pilot Platform

The pilot hardware should be representative of the hardware that will eventually be used in the data center to support the enterprise rollout. The pilot program should not be constrained by any difficulties or limitations in the existing network infrastructure. For instance, if the network backbone is causing latency issues, the pilot should be set up on a separate backbone. If a data line to a remote office frequently fails, the remote office should not be part of the pilot program.

Application Selection

The objective is to load all applications to be hosted under XenApp as part of the proof-of-concept, nonproduction pilot program. That being said, most organizations have far too many applications to reasonably host together in a XenApp environment. During the infrastructure assessment and project plan design process, the appropriate applications are studied in great detail and are carefully selected for application delivery. Because the pilot takes place before this assessment begins, you can pare down the applications to be hosted in this environment by following a few suggestions:

▼ *Use representative samples.* Applications should be a representative sample of the production suite.

■ *Eliminate duplications.* Look over the list of all applications to eliminate obvious duplications. For instance, if 90 percent of projected XenApp users run Microsoft Office and 10 percent run Corel WordPerfect Office, you can reasonably assume that MS Office will win out as the new corporate standard under server-based computing.

▲ *Develop selection criteria.* Create a list with "must-have" and "should-have" features to help pare down the applications in the pilot program. For instance, a must-have feature would be that an application is stable under standard NT workstation. A should-have feature would be that the application is 32 bit.

Testing

The performance, stability, and interaction of the various applications individually and collectively under Terminal Services must be tested and evaluated. One way to do this is by using test lists.

The application information gathered during the infrastructure assessment can be used to prepare the test lists. The lists should include the attributes to be tested along with the expected outcomes. Record the actual outcome for each test and whether it passed or failed. In Chapter 13 we discuss application testing in some detail.

Expanding to a Production Pilot Program

Start with a pre-pilot survey geared toward recording the current state of user performance, reliability, and satisfaction in a fat-client environment. Use the survey results to set expectations for the users about the performance under Citrix XenApp. Be sure they are prepared for the inevitable problems that the new environment will precipitate, as well as for any differences they are likely to encounter by running their applications in a XenApp environment.

It is acceptable to ask "leading" questions in the survey to set expectations, but they should strive for quantifiable answers where practical. For example, instead of asking, "Does your PC crash on a daily basis?" you can ask, "How many times per day does your PC need to be rebooted?" The results should be tabulated and published to the users who participated.

Selecting Applications

The objective of the pilot program is to prove the value of application delivery by running crucial applications successfully in the XenApp environment. Misbehaving, but noncrucial applications should not be included as part of the production pilot, unless the pilot is about using the XenApp Streaming and Isolation features.

TIP: You can use batch files or WSH (Windows Scripting Host) to remove or move icons for applications that are currently run locally on a user's PC. This allows for a quick rollback in the event that the pilot program does not succeed.

The following are some minimum requirements for running an application in a production pilot program. These are suggestions to help get you started on your own list.

▼ Ensure the application is stable in the current distributed environment.

■ If it is a DOS application, ensure it does not extensively poll the keyboard. This can cause huge CPU utilization on the XenApp server. You should seriously consider replacing any DOS application with a 32-bit Windows version if possible.

■ If it is an older or custom application, make sure it doesn't use hard-coded pathnames for files. Because most paths need to be user specific in a multiuser environment, this can cause major headaches.

■ Ensure the application represents the most users possible. Using our previous example, we would want to test MS Office and not WordPerfect Office because the former represents 90 percent of the users.

▲ Ensure that applications with back-end integration requirements (such as database or terminal session connectivity) have upgraded to the latest version. We have found that many applications that fit this description, such as IBM Client Access and various reporting packages, work fine in a multiuser environment but only if you use the latest version.

Testing and Evaluation

Start with the test lists defined in the pilot program for component and system testing, and layer in tests aimed at the production environment. Such tests would include a larger number of users running the applications, competing network traffic, reconnection to a user session, use of shadowing to support an application, and the effect on applications of backing up and restoring data.

Determine what performance data needs to be collected and how to collect it. System management tools such as Citrix EdgeSight can be useful here, as well as user surveys. One of the best testing methods at this stage is simply saturation: Let the users pound away at the applications, and see what they come up with.

Selecting the Participants

The production pilot program should include a larger sample of users than the nonproduction pilot, but the number should remain relatively small. The exact number will be based on the size of your organization and the complexity of your application environment. Ideally, the users selected should be representative of the users who will participate in the application delivery environment, but they should also be friendly to the project. We have found that keeping the number of participants in the production pilot between five and ten users, and no more than 50 for large companies, seems to work best.

Choose which categories of users will participate in the pilot, keeping in mind that you are looking for a representative mix of the ultimate application delivery participants. A small pilot, therefore, might still include thin-client-only, mobile, and hybrid users. We recommend including at least one thin-client terminal as part of the pilot, if possible, in order to get across the point that there is more than one way to deliver applications. Of course, a thin-client terminal can only be used when all required applications for a user or group are accessible from a XenApp server.

The location of users is also important. If users in remote offices will be part of the pilot program, the network's wide-area infrastructure needs to be very sound. As discussed in Chapter 3, remote office users should be trained ahead of time not to engage in excessive bandwidth utilization practices such as copying data from a local hard drive back to the data center server, or downloading MP3 files from the Internet connection via the XenApp server farm. Alternatively, you should have a method to limit the bandwidth available to users. We've already discussed TCP rate control and custom queuing as two common methods. We've summarized these and other requirements as follows:

▼   Choose a small but representative mix of users. The users selected should access different groups of applications from different types of clients.

■   Use this opportunity to test key parts of your infrastructure with server-based computing. Choose users in major regional offices, telecommuters, and VPN users.

■   Choose users who are open to the thin-client concept. Demanding users are fine as long as their demands are reasonable, but avoid high-maintenance users.

▲   At this stage, choose users who are computer literate and can make the "paradigm shift" necessary to participate fully. We are not saying they have to be programmers or system administrators, just experienced users who have some command of their current desktop.

Customer Care During the Pilot

We discussed customer care in detail earlier in this chapter. It is crucial to alert the help desk and to put special mechanisms in place for expediting any problems users encounter. A sour experience during the pilot program, even among friendly users, could end up poisoning the entire application delivery project. On the other hand, if users receive fast and competent responses to issues that arise, they are more likely to start an early, strong, favorable buzz about the new technology. A good technique is to have a "triage" process in which the help desk can quickly categorize a pilot call from a normal production call and route it appropriately. After a call is identified and routed to the first tier of support, it should go directly to the pilot implementation team. This is an excellent method for keeping the team in tune with the users and making continuous, incremental improvements to the pilot environment.

Training Techniques

It is important for the ultimate success of the project to formulate a training plan for all employees involved, including users, help desk technicians (all levels), and administrators. Some suggestions are provided in the following list:

▼ **Users** If your organization, like many, is already using a Windows desktop environment, moving to an application delivery solution will not represent a large functional difference to users. Training a large number of users is also very expensive. We recommend integrating a short orientation, perhaps 15 to 30 minutes, into the user migration process. The user should be oriented, the data migrated, the client installed, and the client device configured all during the same visit by a deployment technician.

■ **Help desk** The people fielding technical support and administrative requests must not only understand the basics of application delivery, but they must also be trained in how to do whatever they do now in the new environment. Creating users, adding them to groups, and giving them access to file storage and applications are different tasks in Citrix XenApp and must be the subject of training. The deployment team is a good source of targeted information on these operations, so build time in the schedule to have them give input into the training plan.

▲ **System administrators** These individuals usually represent the smallest group and need the most training. They will eventually receive calls from other groups and are responsible for solving problems in production. You should build money into the budget for the training programs offered by Citrix and Microsoft. Specifically, the Citrix Certified Enterprise Administrator (CCEA) and Microsoft Certified System Engineer (MCSE) programs should be considered for administrators.

Controlling the Pilot Program

A carefully implemented pilot program is likely to be successful, but this very success leads to quick requests for enhancements. It is important not to cave into pressure from users to introduce new variables, such as additional applications, as part of the pilot. Do not stray from your pilot plan until after the initial testing is complete. If adjustments such as adding applications must be made before a pilot implementation, the initial proof-of-concept testing offline should be repeated and then the new server image introduced to the users. Don't assume that because the production pilot worked with ten applications that it is acceptable to add an eleventh. Everything must be tested before being deployed. Also realize that your deployment team is limited. If you are forced to spend a lot of time testing new applications or features at the last minute, this is likely to have an impact on the schedule.

Creating a Variance Process Define a variance process before the pilot that defines the handling of scope creep. You can publish this process as part of the user survey or other communication given to the pilot users. Decide who needs to approve requests for additional applications or pilot participants, and have a mechanism ready to handle this process. We've found such requests often come from management members who outrank the deployment team. If you must implement a change, be ready to clearly and concisely communicate the impact it will have on the deployment schedule, resources, and cost.

Handling Objections to an Application Delivery Model Despite careful pilot participant selection, some users may still object to the concept. Be prepared to do a quick sales presentation that shows them both the personal and corporate benefits of migrating to a application delivery environment. If you run into unreasonable or unfounded objections, be ready to pass them to the proper management members. The executive sponsor for the pilot is an excellent choice to help handle objections. Another important tool is to have the facts at hand regarding any objection. We've found that users sometimes couch objections in terms sympathetic to their case that do not always reflect the facts. For example, a user may go to his manager and say, "The pilot team says I can't have the printer on my desk anymore." In reality, the pilot team published a list of compatible printers, and this user's printer wasn't on it. Be ready to tell this user and his manager how they can get a compatible printer or what to do as a workaround.

Assessing Performance

Document your expectations of the pilot program before you begin. Decide up front on the success metrics for the pilot. Take measurements of application performance in the current distributed environment, and compare these to performance under an application delivery solution. For example, the time it takes to launch Microsoft Word can be measured in both environments. Other examples include the time it takes to print a certain document or to open a specific file.

In addition to the user-oriented metrics mentioned, include system and cost metrics. An example of a system metric is the time it currently takes to support a regional file server when it fails as compared to the time it takes to fix a file server in the data center. An example of a cost metric would be the cost of flying a technician to the site where a problem is occurring as opposed to having a technician handle the problem at the data center.

After the pilot, create a report on whether success metrics were met. Document any problems encountered along with their solutions. Document any open issues or new questions raised by the pilot, along with the actions being taken to resolve them.

ENTERPRISE ROLLOUT

All contingencies must be completed before the start of the enterprise rollout. Data centers and network upgrades should be complete. Equipment staging should be ready. Rollout teams should be ready to be deployed.

User Training During Rollout

Ensure high attendance for training sessions through management e-mails and user incentives. Be creative. Include project marketing along with the training sessions in order to reinforce initial project acceptance. Use rainbow packets, desk-side orientation, and videos. If your help desk charges users per incident, establish a grace period for free support during the conversion. As discussed previously, the amount of training necessary is likely to be limited to a short orientation to the new environment. Of much greater importance is effective marketing to get the users to embrace the change as something positive.

Expanding Service-Level Agreements

Pilot SLAs should be expanded to fit the conditions appropriate to a production rollout. For example, you may want to intentionally set the help desk response to a short period—say, one hour—for newly converted users, to make sure any initial problems are solved quickly.

Creating a Deployment Guide

For a large enterprise conversion to application delivery, creating a deployment guide can be very helpful in making the process go smoothly. This is particularly important if you have a large number of remote offices requiring multiple implementation teams. Though the audience for such a guide is technically proficient, it is important to have a guide for reasons of consistency. If deployment technicians are allowed to carry out the migration their own way, it will be that much more difficult to troubleshoot problems as they arise. The deployment guide should include the following sections:

▼ **User communication FAQ** Arm the deployment technician with answers to common questions encountered during the pilot and beta stages. This type of FAQ will help tremendously with conflict resolution and will help maintain a professional image for the technician.

■ **Contact information** List the appropriate contacts and phone extensions for IT staff to support specific issues, including desktop migration, printer setups, wide area network problems, and thin-client terminals. The escalation paths for different types of problems should be clear.

■ **Data migration procedure** Spell out the specific steps for migrating data.

■ **Client installations** The deployment guide should include detailed instructions for installing each type of ICA client you intend to deploy. Each installation method should include a checklist and any relevant screenshots to make the procedure clear.

> **TIP:** Using Citrix Web Interface to deliver applications or a published desktop will automatically deploy the ICA client and keep it current with the latest release.

■ **Desktop device configuration** Include a table showing all categories of users and their associated devices, such as hybrid PCs, laptops, and thin-client terminals. Include a list of the appropriate equipment for each category of user, such as a monitor or network card. Include IP and DNS setup as well as things such as how to set up LPD printing on thin-client terminals.

- **Shadowing users** Support personnel can use shadowing to take control of users' PCs or thin-client terminals for troubleshooting purposes. Show how to set up shadowing, including screen prints for each step.

- **VPN or Internet dial-up connectivity** If remote users are connecting to the data center through a WAN or VPN, explain how to set up the VPN client software on a PC, configure the thin-client terminal's Secure ICA functions, or whatever is appropriate to your environment.

- **Printing** Recap which printers are supported and which ones will work with bandwidth management devices, if appropriate. If printers are not supported, include instructions about the proper procedures to take when such a printer is encountered during deployment.

- **IP address scheme** A workable IP addressing scheme needs to be implemented if it hasn't been already. If DHCP is to be used, explain how to configure the clients to take advantage of it.

- ▲ **General migration issues** Include answers to problems that the implementation team may encounter, such as what to do if a user scheduled for migration is absent or if a user's PC is not operating properly under XenApp.

Creating Migration Databases

A large migration involves a large number of employees, all requiring current information. Developing databases to sort and track this information will significantly enhance the process. Making this database available in some ubiquitous fashion, such as web publishing, will help ensure its adoption and currency. Following are some ideas for different aspects of the deployment process that you should consider tracking in this way.

Locations Database

List every location and pertinent information, including current status, data connectivity status, number of users, type of users, and the implementation team assigned. The implementation, WAN, and procurement teams should update this database as part of their normal process. For example, after a user is installed, the deployment team member can connect to the locations database from the user's new client and enter the information that the user has been installed and any asset information on the equipment assigned to that user.

Change-Management Database

Track everything that changes at the data center, including new applications, printer drivers, and all unscheduled downtime. This enables much better troubleshooting of modifications causing problems. Significant changes in the field, such as large bandwidth increases, premise router changes, and the like, can also be entered here for all to see.

Survey Databases

User surveys taken at the various deployment stages can be entered and the results tracked here.

Migrating Headquarters

Converting users at headquarters to an application delivery environment is much easier than migrating remote offices. The planning design document should cover most of the contingencies you are likely to run up against when migrating headquarters. The close proximity of these users to IT and the lack of bandwidth variables make it relatively easy to identify and remedy problems. For these reasons, it is generally advisable to migrate headquarters before migrating users at remote offices, even though the latter may have the greater need. As always, new users should be added to the application delivery environment in layers in order to minimize disruptions caused by unexpected problems.

User Training for Headquarters Migration

If IT is unable to bring users to headquarters for training before migration, they will have to rely on videos and other media such as documentation for much of the application delivery orientation. A quick training procedure should be developed for the implementation team to use when they are at the site doing the conversion.

Client Operating System Upgrades

Although the Citrix ICA clients will operate with nearly any operating system—from DOS to Windows XP to Linux—some organizations prefer to standardize on one operating system platform to make administration easier. In this case, the operating system can be migrated as part of the implementation process. Because the result will be users accessing their applications from the corporate data center, individual PC issues are a minor concern in terms of project success.

User Data Migration

It is possible to write scripts to migrate data off users' local PCs and transfer it to a centralized file server. This can be accomplished through batch files or with WSH (Windows Scripting Host).

Desktop Application Migration

In the pilot program, we recommended leaving local applications in place and moving, or removing, icons. In a production environment, we recommend eliminating applications from local PCs altogether in order to ensure that users operate only in the intended application delivery environment. There are many methods for uninstalling applications. Microsoft SMS has this capability, or you can "roll your own," using scripting tools such as WSH and ADSI, as mentioned in Chapter 13.

Planning for Remote Office Migration

The project design document will almost certainly focus on the corporate data center and users at headquarters. Although remote offices and their users can be categorized in broad terms, the project plan is not likely to encompass specific implementation details if a large number of remote facilities are part of the project. In these cases, we recommend creating a separate implementation plan for rolling out the application delivery solution.

Assess Remote Office Infrastructure

Completing a detailed assessment of the remote office networks and environments enables much better planning and, consequently, a much smoother implementation. A good tool for this is a site survey. You can assess the infrastructure, the number of users, equipment, and any other special needs in the survey. As we will discuss later in the chapter, you will have several teams available for doing field deployments. During the inevitable periods when the team members are not in the field due to scheduling, have them perform the surveys.

> **NOTE:** You may already have a tool in place, such as Microsoft's SMS or Enteo's NetInstall Server, that is capable of doing hardware inventory across the WAN. This is useful but is not a substitute for a site survey. Use the polling results from these programs during the survey as part of the discussion with the people onsite, but don't treat these results as gospel. Not all hardware you are interested in will respond to a poll, and you need to be as accurate as possible.

Determine Time Constraints

Because implementing an application delivery solution is usually very economically advantageous, time is often the biggest project constraint. Establish guidelines to ensure that project timelines are met. Communicate these time limits to users before the implementation in order to help gain their support in making the migration successful. Make the time limits part of the SLA for the implementation team, and manage them. This means accurate collection of the data and publishing the results to the team. Then discuss what can be done to improve problem times.

Implementation Team Follow-Up   Create a way for the implementation teams to check on the status of each time-critical item remotely. One method to accomplish this follow-up is to create an intranet site that can be accessed once the user is online.

System Implementation Time Limit   Set a maximum amount of time that an implementation team member can spend on any single system to ensure that an office can be migrated in a reasonable amount of time. For instance, you may determine that converting a user to an application delivery environment should take no more than an hour. If a conversion runs over an hour, the user is given a thin-client terminal, and their existing data is not migrated to the data center. Though this is obviously not ideal, it will keep the project on track and only inconvenience the user in question.

PC Preparation Time Limit   Set a limit, tied to the conversion time limit, on how much time to spend preparing a PC for migration. For instance, if the conversion time limit for a PC is an hour, you may wish to set a 30-minute time limit on preparing the PC.

Communication Lines   If a new or upgraded WAN was put into place, confirm that the line was installed, and test connectivity before the implementation team's arrival at a remote office. Do not, under any circumstances, rely on the telecommunication provider's word that the line is in and working. Test it yourself.

User Accounts   Set up user accounts in NT a minimum of one day before the installation. The help desk, in cooperation with the field deployment teams, should do the setup.

Remote Office Data Migration

In a typical conversion from a PC-based to a centralized application delivery model, data will be migrated from PCs and remote office servers back to the corporate data center. Remember that the migration process can take longer than planned due to unexpected problems such as delays in the WAN implementations, conflicts in employee work schedules, and delayed shipments of hardware.

User Training for Remote Office Migration

Users should first be exposed to preliminary marketing materials and videos so that they know what to expect. The implementation team's responsibilities should include a brief user training session. Users should sign forms indicating that they have received training prior to the implementation team's departure.

In some organizations, the ability of application delivery to deliver computing capabilities inexpensively means that it will sometimes be a user's first experience with networking services, or even with using a computer. In these cases, extra thought needs to go into the training of using the PC, applications, and network in order to save the help desk from a deluge of calls.

Desktop Data Migration

There are many techniques for migrating data from PCs back to the data center, depending on the infrastructure and service-level agreements. It is important to come up with a universal method where possible. In a local area network environment, the bandwidth should be sufficient to copy the data directly to the servers. If a wide area network has sufficient bandwidth to copy files to the data center, this methodology will be the easiest to use. Your first impulse might be to copy the user data over the network to the data center. In a large, distributed organization with many offices, this could quickly cripple the network. Sometimes simple methods are the best ones. After trying many sophisticated methods, we've found the following works well:

1. Tell the users that they will have access to their current working files immediately, and the rest of the data on their hard disks in 48 hours, as part of the deployment SLA.

2. Make sure the users' accounts and login environment are ready.

3. From the users' desktops, copy their working files across the network to the data center. The data allowance for this copy should be small—perhaps 5MB to 10MB maximum. Most users will have far less data than this.

4. Using a prepared boot disk and a parallel-attached backup device, reboot the PC and copy the contents to the removable media.

NOTE: There are many options when deciding what to copy to the media in such an operation. If users have been using Windows for a while, most of their data is probably in the My Documents folder. Rather than guess, it is better to copy all data except the Windows directory. Program files, of course, should not be copied.

5. Send the removable media via overnight shipping to the data center.

6. Provide a brief orientation. When users log in, they should immediately have access to their working files and new applications.

7. Within 48 hours, load the removable media at the data center and copy the files into the users' directories.

NOTE: If minimal filtering was done when copying the data from the client, filtering should be done when restoring the media at the data center. Consider a simple script that copies files by extension (*.XLS, *.DOC, *.WRI, and so on) to the users' new home directories. It will catch most of the data they need. If anything is missed, you still have the removable media to refer to. Store this media long enough to be sure users won't be likely to need another restore.

Migration of Server Data

Data can be moved to the data center before the rollout via backup media, scripting, or replication. Anything that changes after that date can be moved over the WAN. Any modern backup program can do backups based on the "archive bit" of the file that is set each time a file is written to tape. A full backup of the server can be done and sent to the data center before the deployment team arrives. After all the users at that site have been converted, a differential backup (only changed files) is run and sent via overnight delivery to the data center. Those files are then restored as soon as possible. This scheme works because any file the user is currently working on is copied to the data center over the WAN for immediate access as part of that user's migration process.

Rogue Applications

Even the best planning often does not prepare implementation teams for what they face in the field. When unexpected applications are discovered, the project manager should be immediately notified, particularly if the users are scheduled to be converted to run in thin-client mode only. A decision can then be made about whether to allow access to the applications locally, or to halt the rollout and do the preparatory testing required to host the applications on XenApp. One technique is to migrate what you can at that office but leave one or two PCs and the local file server just for running the problem application. Establish a "sunset period" in which the equipment will be removed and the application will no longer be available or supported.

Remote Office Migration Teams

A project with many remote offices will likely require several teams to ensure a successful migration within a reasonable time period. These might include one or more implementation teams, a WAN team, and a procurement team.

Implementation Teams

Enough implementation teams should be chosen to meet the timelines for data migration. An implementation team completes the appropriate remote site surveys and submits them (online preferably) to the WAN team. The WAN team can then make sure that adequate communication lines are ordered and installed before the field team's arrival.

Choosing Team Members Desirable qualities for team members include both technical skills and training capabilities. Personality and training skills generally outweigh technical skills. Making the implementation process very simple can compensate for the lack of technical skills in implementers. On the other hand, superior technical skills do not compensate for the lack of interpersonal skills. When implementers do a good job explaining the server-based computing system, the users are more understanding when inevitable problems occur. The individual team member should be armed with skills for conflict resolution and must be familiar with the support and escalation process. Team members must also be people that the users will trust and want to work with.

Consultant/IT Staff Mix If using a consulting company to help with your migration, we recommend using a mix of internal and external consultants on each team. This provides expertise and objectivity combined with internal IT and organizational knowledge. It also provides a good, informal method of transferring knowledge from external experts to internal staff.

Facilitating Effective Teamwork It is important that the implementation teams work together and share their experiences in order to avoid making the same mistake twice. Facilitate this practice by giving each team member a cell phone and two-way radio, by giving each member access to the corporate e-mail system, and by having members of the project management team join each implementation team for part of their trips. Scheduling weekly teleconferences for all members can be particularly useful in helping to avoid making repetitive mistakes and for sharing ways to improve the implementation process among all teams and members. These conferences can also be a forum for sharing good news and quickly improving methods when problems occur.

The Road Kit The material that each deployment team member will carry makes up the road kit. It should be well stocked, and the procedures for replenishing it should be simple and understood by team members before they visit the first site. Using our sample methods described in this chapter, a road kit might contain a boot disk, CD-RW drive, laptop, overnight courier materials, Ethernet cables, cross-over cables, and an extra floppy drive.

WAN Team

The WAN team orders data connections and bandwidth upgrades. They confirm the installation of these lines. They order and ship any required routers or bandwidth management devices to remote sites before the implementation, or make sure the telecommunication provider does so.

Procurement Team

Responsible for the overall logistics of the project, the procurement team orders and ships the equipment. They should check to ensure receipt of the equipment at least one week before installation. The procurement team also updates the remote office surveys to reflect the new equipment and properly tracks the asset on the company's books after it has been installed. They should also process equipment returns, have the ability to quickly respond to mistakes, and make sure the deployment team and the site have the equipment they need.

Deployment Challenges

Every application delivery implementation will face unique challenges, depending on the existing environment, project scope, and technology utilized. Some issues will be impossible to anticipate. Others are fairly common and include travel, printing, local file sharing, CD-ROM sharing, and access to legacy systems from remote locations.

TIP: Do not make assumptions. When replacing a user's PC with a thin-client terminal for one of our clients, the implementation team encountered a particularly irate user. The implementation team member could not get the new terminal to communicate with the existing monitor despite hours of troubleshooting. After a second day of lost productivity, the team leader finally discovered that the monitor had never worked. The user neglected to tell the installer because he wanted to see if the new thin-client terminal could fix it.

Travel

Extensive remote office implementations require dealing with issues such as travel arrangements and scheduling. Covering large geographical regions may necessitate a great deal of travel, which may in turn limit the number of willing participants on implementation teams. In addition, last-minute scheduling changes can quickly eat up the travel budget. Careful planning and control are essential in managing this project cost.

Bad or Inconsistent Backups

It is best not to rely on any existing backups. The safest procedure is not to wipe out any hard drives or recycle existing PCs until you are sure that all required data is off the PCs, on the new servers, and the users have had the opportunity to confirm this and sign off on the operation.

Printing

Printing is such a major challenge that we devoted Chapter 17 to it. In general, try to standardize as much as possible on the printers used. In particular, try to limit the print drivers to those supported natively by Windows Server 2003 or use the Universal Print Driver wherever possible. Some older printers simply will not run well under Terminal Services. Replacing these printers before the migration will eliminate the added pressure on the implementation teams of ordering new ones onsite.

Data Line Procurement

Anticipate problems in getting WAN connectivity completed according to installation promises. Plan to do more work up front in order to ensure that the data connectivity is complete before installation. Even when a local exchange carrier (LEC) confirms that a data connection is complete, take the time to test it yourself. We've seen miscommunication between an LEC and a national telecommunication carrier cost a project weeks of time and thousands of dollars.

PCs

Use Web Interface to automatically deploy and keep the ICA client current. Otherwise, even the easy task of installing the Citrix ICA client can become arduous when migrating thousands of users. In this case, the easier migration may be to simply provide users with a thin-client terminal with a preconfigured connection to the XenApp server.

Inaccurate Site Surveys

Most organizations depend on user surveys to determine the type and state of equipment in remote offices. Impress upon the survey respondents how crucial it is for them to report this information accurately in order to avoid costly implementation delays and potential downtime. If your organization already has a tool in place that does hardware inventories, such as Microsoft SMS or HP OpenView, make sure the data is current. If possible, confirm critical items shown in the inventory, such as site routers or servers, with a phone call.

POSTPRODUCTION MANAGEMENT

You have now rolled out an application delivery solution across the enterprise. Your users are happy, and your IT staff has joined the swelling ranks of application delivery evangelists. Performance should be compared with both expectations and established success metrics. The results should be reported to both management and users.

Measure User Satisfaction

One method for measuring user satisfaction is to send out surveys asking users to grade the project on various criteria, including performance, reliability, how well it meets expectations, ease of use, training, and implementation. Compare the user satisfaction results with those obtained in surveys taken before the deployment. You can also use the surveys to find out what other attributes users would like.

Rate Project Milestones

Were project milestones reached on time? For instance, one milestone may have been to migrate all headquarters users within 60 days of the project start. Record and publish the results.

Update the Budget

Measure actual expenditures against the budget. Update the financial feasibility model with the project costs as well as with costs as they accrue going forward. This will enable a return on investment (ROI) to be calculated for the project over a three-to-five-year period.

Measure Application Delivery Center Benefits

During the beta and the production deployment, you established service levels for your new environment. These service levels represent an agreement between the IT staff and the user community. Part of the agreement is that the IT staff will manage the system to meet certain established metrics and goals. The data needed to establish whether these goals are being met needs to be collected diligently and continuously. For example, if part of the SLA is 99.99-percent system uptime, every blue screen or other server outage needs to be recorded, as well as major network disruptions for a given region or data center.

Publish Results

The collected data does no good unless the appropriate people review it. There should be a policy of no secrets between the IT staff and the user community. Establish a reporting cycle as part of the SLA. It may not be critical for a user to see a daily status, but it may be appropriate to display quarterly or monthly SLA results. This will depend on your corporate culture and what your internal reporting capabilities are.

Establish a Steering Committee

A technique for keeping IT staff and the user community focused on continuous improvement is to create a committee made up of both groups. The user representatives should be as diverse as the reach of the server-based computing project. If the new environment is multinational, a representative from each major region or country should participate. The exact scope and responsibility of the committee will depend on your corporate culture, but it should at least evaluate and recommend changes to the XenApp environment.

Provide a Forum for Feedback "Outside the Box"

The help desk will record user problems and outages. In addition, you should provide a way for any employee of the company to give suggestions or constructive criticism. This input should be reviewed and evaluated by the steering committee. We've found that brilliant suggestions sometimes come from the most unlikely places.

Make Facts-Based Decisions on the Future Direction of Your Application Delivery Environment

Collecting and reporting on established SLAs and keeping the users involved result in invaluable information for making decisions about the future of your company's application delivery initiative. Even after a successful rollout, there may be factions within the company that remain unconvinced as to the value of an application delivery solution. Having facts to back up a recommendation to expand the infrastructure or to add applications can mean the difference between the ultimate success or failure of the environment.

Establish a Server-Based Computing Lab

To maintain a high quality of service, it is necessary to maintain a lab environment where new versions of software and hardware can be evaluated and tested. This lab does not need to be onsite. In fact, manufacturers often allow their facilities to be used for this purpose, as long as you agree to share the results. Regularly check the websites of Microsoft and Citrix for the latest information on changes and upgrades. The Citrix knowledge base, in particular, is an excellent place to find this kind of information. Because your new environment is now tested and stable, any change must be rigorously evaluated and tested before deployment.

Share Your Experiences

After getting the proper clearance from management, seek out other companies that have undergone similar deployments, and offer to share information. Even if a non-disclosure agreement is necessary, the result will be an enrichment of the environment at each company. Participate in related forums and events from Citrix and Microsoft to keep up on the latest developments and share your experiences. Finally, seek out peers on the Internet, in discussion groups, chat rooms, e-forums, or other areas.

Application delivery on an enterprise level is an emerging technology. Manufacturers of hardware and software are eager to help you publicize your success by writing and publishing success stories. In this way, you can help contribute to the growing momentum behind this new and tremendously exciting industry.

CHAPTER 8

Disaster Recovery and Business Continuity

W hen you think of a disaster, what typically enters your mind? A hurricane, flood, or tornado? Those are the easy ones. What exactly constitutes a disaster? We sometimes think of a disaster as a huge, catastrophic event that wipes out the whole city. What about the not-so-obvious situations, such as confiscation of property, a virus outbreak, local power failure, structural problems?

One company suffered a major outage when their second-floor data center collapsed due to the weight of the equipment. Another company lost all their servers to a pornography raid by police when they discovered that an employee was hosting porn on one of the organization's severs.

Let's think about situations where the data center is up and running but employees cannot get to the building. Could this be a problem for your organization? In some cities, weather can prevent a workforce from getting to the office.

Another company's main business center is located in a city hosting a political convention this year. During the event their building must be evacuated and employees will not be able to get to the office or the data center.

It is not always a "smoking hole" in the ground that renders business offline or unable to access their primary resources. What they need is a plan for maintaining workflow and a method for providing application delivery for users during times of disruption.

This chapter focuses on how to utilize an application delivery model to provide full disaster recovery and business continuity within the realm of business possibility for large and small businesses alike.

It is important to note that even smaller organizations will benefit from the discussion in this chapter. Many small companies feel that they cannot afford server redundancy, let alone data center redundancy. Although this chapter focuses more on a mid-sized organization plan, these same best-practice approaches apply to even the smallest customers—just on a lesser scale. Even a home-based workstation with a large hard drive configured to mirror data from the main corporation, stationed next to a single Citrix XenApp server to handle remote access, will dramatically reduce the risk of severe business loss in most disaster scenarios.

THE ULTIMATE NACHO

What most companies need is a plan for both short-term and long-term situations. Organizations need to keep users productive at all levels of the data center—from a single server failure, short-term building power failure, long-term building power failure, prevented building access, and full data center interruption.

Figure 8-1 shows an example of the "ultimate nacho." Although this is a generic design, every organization has some components of this design already in place. There just needs to be a business driver to push things to the next level in order to achieve business continuity (BC) and disaster recovery (DR).

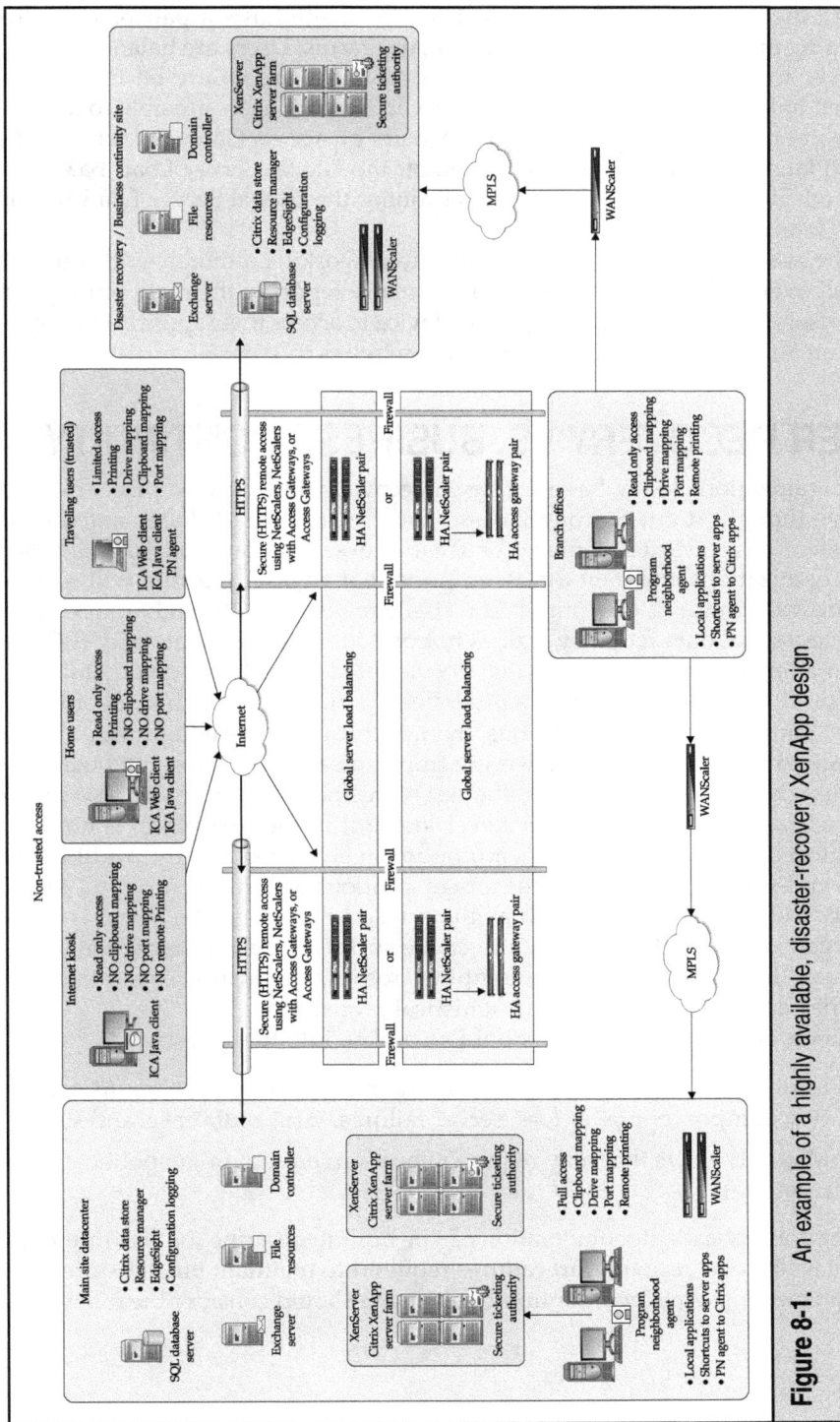

Figure 8-1. An example of a highly available, disaster-recovery XenApp design

From the diagram, you can see that the main site hosts a pair of virtualized servers running on XenServer and hosting XenApp farms. Users are balanced between each XenServer to even the load. In the event of a hardware failure on the XenServer, the users can balance over to the other XenServer. Remote users are able to access their resources in one of two ways: through HA pairs of Access Gateway Advanced Editions behind Platinum Edition NetScalers running the Global Server Load Balancing option or through Platinum Edition NetScalers running the Global Server Load Balancing and Access Gateway Enterprise options.

In the event of a failure at the main site, users working remotely will automatically be balanced over to the DR site. Users that normally report to the main office now become remote users and can use any computing device to access their applications and information, from anywhere, over any connection—wireless to Web.

DISASTER RECOVERY VS. BUSINESS CONTINUITY

Many organizations today have a disaster recovery (DR) plan in place—although very few have thought it out thoroughly, and even fewer have it documented or tested on a consistent basis. Most DR plans for smaller organizations consist of a tape backup. These organizations maintain the assumption that anything further will cost more than the statistical chance of downtime. The challenge is that although a tape backup does provide potential data recovery, it does not provide business continuity (BC). A *business continuity* plan is an all-encompassing, documented plan of how an organization will return to productive activity within a predefined period of time. This not only includes IT services, but also telecommunications, manufacturing, office equipment, and so on. It is important to understand that recovering from a disaster is a subset of business continuity. Although DR is the most important part of business continuity, just having the ability to recover mission-critical data (or never losing it in the first place) is not sufficient to return most organizations to even a minimum level of productivity. Additional concepts such as end-user access and offsite storage locations are critical for a full return to productivity. In the same light, though, without recovery of the data, access is a moot point. Most organizations today could not re-create such electronic information as accounting and e-mail data in the event that computer records are lost or corrupted, or recovery from tape backup fails (a significant statistical probability).

Business continuity planning should be broken into two phases:

▼ Minor disasters that do not involve a major facility problem (database corruption, temporary power loss, server failures, virus outbreaks, and so on)

▲ Major disasters that may require relocation (natural or geopolitical disasters, for example)

From these phases, documentation can be built to describe the risk mitigation procedures as well as the recovery procedures required to maintain business productivity.

When creating a business continuity plan, you should consider the following aspects:

▼   What defines a minor and major disaster, and what are the critical points at which a BC plan will be enacted?

■   Which applications, key business systems (including non-IT-based systems), and employees are defined as critical?

■   Where will employees be housed if their main location is unavailable?

■   What time period is acceptable for mission-critical systems to be down, and what is an acceptable time to enact the BC plan?

■   How will access to critical data, business systems, and applications be provided within the predefined time period following a disaster?

▲   Who will be responsible for enacting and maintaining the BC plan?

From the preceding list, it is clear that BC planning focuses primarily on two objectives: *recovery time* and *recovery point*. Put simply, an organization must ask the questions "How long can we be down?" and "What do we need to have available after that time?" When initiating a DR/BC study, many companies start out with an attitude that the entire IT infrastructure has to be continuously available, or at least recoverable, in a very short time window, such as four hours. Without the help of Citrix technologies, though, few companies can afford this kind of high availability for the entire IT infrastructure. And even with a data center delivery solution in place, an effort should be made to prioritize what must be recovered and how long it can take.

Recovery Time Objectives

When examining the disaster recovery needs of your organization, you will likely find differing service-level requirements for the different parts of your system. For example, it may be imperative that your billing and accounting system come back online within two hours in the event of a disaster. Although inconvenient, it may still be acceptable for the manufacturing database to recover in 24 hours, and it may be acceptable for engineering data to come back online in two weeks (since it may be useless until new facilities are in place anyway). A key to a successful BC plan is knowing what your recovery time objectives are for the various pieces of your infrastructure. Short recovery times translate directly into high costs, due to the requirements of technology such as real-time data replication, redundant server farms, and high-bandwidth WAN links. Fortunately, with Citrix XenApp and Terminal Services, you don't have to hunt down PCs across the enterprise to recover their applications; all of your application servers will be located in the data center. We recommend using a tiered approach when applications and users must be restored.

NOTE: A continuity plan requires an ongoing process of review, testing, and reassessment, because most organizations will change significantly over the course of a year, thus making a two-year-old DR/BC plan useless.

The Data Center Delivery Solution to Disaster Recovery and Business Continuity

A major theme throughout this book has been building robustness into application delivery. Redundancy of the network, server, application, and the entire data center has been discussed. We also made the assumption that onsite and offsite tape backups are performed nightly. Most minor disasters can be mitigated by simply following the best practices in this book. It is impossible, though, to guarantee uptime for a single location, due to the large number of both internal and external risks. Additionally, the data center is not the only thing requiring redundancy—a workstation with access to the mission-critical applications and data for an employee to work from is also required.

A delivery approach to business continuity decouples the desktop from the workstation. A disaster may preclude employees from accessing their normal workstations, but with access to a browser, the employees can still securely access the virtualized applications and desktops. This access remains whether the "desktop" is running in the normal data center or at the disaster recovery site. If employees are prevented from entering their office due to a natural disaster, they can still continue working from another office, from home, or even from an Internet café.

Some of the more typical problems with a distributed environment that are solved with an application delivery solution are listed here:

▼ Foreseeable disasters often entail evacuation of large numbers of workers, thus leading to the need to have total flexibility for where knowledge-based workers work, what device they are working from, and when they work.

■ Even if the workers are not displaced, if the data center is displaced, it is highly unlikely in a distributed environment that users will still have sufficient bandwidth to access the data at a new location. In an application delivery environment, the bandwidth requirements are much lower and more flexible (we show later in this chapter that Internet bandwidth from any source is sufficient if the application delivery environment is built properly).

■ The availability of specific replacement PCs on a moment's notice cannot be guaranteed, thus making it difficult in a distributed environment to guarantee that users will have the necessary processing power to run their applications. In an application delivery environment, a user's desktop CPU power and operating system environment are largely irrelevant, allowing the use of whatever hardware might be available.

▲ The manpower required to quickly install and configure ten or more applications for hundreds or thousands of users is enormous in a distributed environment. With an application delivery infrastructure in place, the applications don't need to be installed or configured, because they are already on the server farm (or backup server farm).

With this clear advantage, many organizations today are embracing an application delivery solution as the only possible solution to IT business continuity.

Application Delivery Business Continuity Design

Conceptually, there are two simple approaches to fulfill immediate resumption failover requirements in an application delivery environment: failover of the data center and failover of the client environment. If both are in place, under major disaster circumstances, an organization will simply switch the data center to another location (DR site) and then have users connect to the new data center from wherever they can get an Internet connection. Of course the larger an organization is, and the more dispersed its users are, the more complex this task will be. Additionally, for small organizations, this solution may appear to be overkill, because the cost of the redundant data center may exceed the value of the data. Approaches to reducing the cost of business continuity include the following.

▼ Defining only a subset of users and applications that need access following a disaster, thus reducing the amount of redundant infrastructure.

■ Placing lower expectations when defining what is acceptable downtime, thus allowing the use of a cold backup rather than a hot backup.

▲ Increasing the acceptable amount of data loss. For example, if a full day of data loss is acceptable, then the main and redundant data centers require less bandwidth than if all data must be current to within 30 minutes.

From this list, it is clear that prior to implementing a business continuity plan, we must answer the questions from the first section of this chapter regarding how long we can be down and who needs to have access. In order to provide guidance in this process, we will use our ever-faithful company, CME Corporation, from our previous books as a guide. As you may remember, Clinical Medical Equipment (CME) is a fictitious company that designs, manufactures, sells, and supports a proprietary diagnostic and treatment module for the health care industry worldwide. In this example, CME has a single, central data center located at corporate headquarters in Denver, Colorado hosting up to 3,000 users at any given time.

The CME Business Continuity Plan

CME's infrastructure is similar to many mid-sized and enterprise organizations. CME has multiple branches, a large number of mission-critical applications, and the perceived need for immediate recovery from business interruption.

The apparent downside to CME's current approach to service delivery is that all of CME's eggs are in one basket—at the CME Denver Corporate headquarters data center. Should a natural, accidental, or geopolitical disaster occur on or near this site, all 3,000 users will lose access, potentially forever. To resolve this problem, CME is building a remote backup site, CME Omaha (go Huskers), as the hot backup site. In order to minimize costs, CME will only replicate a subset of the corporate data center hardware to permit rapid recovery of mission-critical services and applications and allow managers to make an informed decision regarding permanent rebuilding of the entire corporate data center at the alternate site. In order to achieve this objective, CME has defined a prepositioned hot backup at CME Omaha for initial reconstitution (8- to 24-hour survivable), which provides immediate access for a subset of users while the corporate staff is moved to CME Omaha.

CME's IT staff have met with CME's executives and answered the questions posed earlier in this chapter. Table 8-1 shows the results.

With the business-continuity requirements documented and defined, CME's IT group is now able to create the technical portion of the document to ensure that the requirements will be met.

Business Continuity Question	CME's Answer
What applications are defined as critical, and what is acceptable downtime for them?	CME has determined that not all applications and users have the same requirement for access and availability in the case of a major disaster. Accordingly, CME has defined three tiers of availability: Tiers 1, 2, and 3.
	Tier 1 requires application availability and user access within two hours, regardless of cause, Tier 2 requires application availability and user access within 24 hours, and Tier 3 requires application availability and user access within two weeks.
	The Tier 1 applications include Microsoft Exchange e-mail and Microsoft Great Plains accounting software (including payroll, human resources, and accounts receivable/payable functions). Tier 2 applications include the Oracle-based Manufacturing (including production schedules, bill of materials, supply chain information, and inventory). Tier 3 includes all remaining applications. (Note that this timeline has been set at two weeks to allow for a temporary facility move.)
Who are the key personnel requiring access at each tier?	Tier 1 key personnel who require access include all top-level managers/directors, critical IT staff, and a limited number of predefined support staff (about 50 people total). It is important to note that some of these key users must be located at CME Omaha to provide skill set redundancy in the case of a major disaster in Denver.
	The key personnel to which access must be guaranteed grows in Tier 2 to include a larger set of personnel (about 500 people total) across all CME locations required to operate these key systems. These additional personnel include accountants, human resource managers, remaining IT staff, key manufacturing and development engineers, and lower-level managers.
	Tier three includes all remaining personnel.

Table 8-1. CME's Business-Continuity Definitions

Business Continuity Question	CME's Answer
What defines a major disaster and what are the critical points at which a business-continuity plan will be enacted? (Note that the CME Corporation data center has internal data redundancy, including redundant network core components, bandwidth, servers, HVAC, and power. Therefore, the business-continuity plan calls for a data center failover only in the event of a major disaster in which the determination that more than eight hours of localized downtime will occur. This may be a guess or a well-known fact, depending on the type of disaster and available information.)	Any event that will cause a minimum of eight hours of downtime at the Denver data center will enact the data center failover. Here are examples: ■ A major server hardware or network infrastructure failure occurs, which, due to delays in getting replacement equipment, causes an outage at the data center for more than eight hours ■ A malicious ex-employee sabotages the infrastructure ■ A government organization confiscates servers and data due to illegal employee activity Examples of less common disasters might include the following: ■ A severe snowstorm that renders major utilities offline or causes structural damage to the building ■ A train derailment at the nearby depot that forces evacuation due to a hazardous spill ■ A localized geopolitical disaster that renders the facility unusable
How long is acceptable before enacting the business-continuity plan and who is responsible for enacting the BC plan?	Once notification of a major outage has been issued, a decision will be made by the BC team (which consists of the CIO, CTO, CEO, CFO, and their support personnel) within one hour regarding whether to fail over to the CME Omaha data center. Note, though, that this provides only one hour of time to accomplish the actual failover of the data center within the specified two-hour window.
How will access to critical data and applications be provided within the predefined time period following a disaster, and where will employees be housed if their corporate headquarters location is unavailable?	Employees required for Tier 1 and Tier 2 continuity must have broadband or dial-up Internet connectivity from home and must complete the BC training and maintain the accompanying BC documentation at their residences. CME will provide the broadband connectivity and a thin-client or corporate laptop for the 50 Tier 1–designated employees. Tier 2 employees will use existing employee-provided hardware and Internet connectivity to connect from their residences or other CME branches. These Internet connections will provide full access to the Tier 1 and Tier 2 applications. Tier 3 will utilize a makeshift facility, if required, in addition to any home-based access.

Table 8-1. CME's Business-Continuity Definitions (continued)

AN INFORMATION TECHNOLOGY PLAN TO MEET BUSINESS CONTINUITY REQUIREMENTS

CME's centralized application delivery environment makes the implementation of these requirements possible. CME Omaha, as the recovery site for Tier 1 and Tier 2, will need to have hot support for 500 users. These users will require the defined Tier 1 data, applications, and access through the Internet. Tier 3 will be implemented back at the Denver facility or a temporary facility (which could be CME Omaha) will be used. During the two-week window between Tier 2 and Tier 3, CME IT will have to work feverishly to acquire all of the required hardware to replace any hardware lost in the disaster.

Hot Backup Data Center Design

A *hot backup data center* is a backup data center with real-time servers, ready to be used at a moment's notice. The advantage of a hot backup data center is that it provides a fast resumption plan. The disadvantage is that it requires redundant hardware that generally remains idle except to receive updates and periodic testing.

The most important element of the data center design is geographical location. In order for the backup data center to truly provide resumption, the data center must be located a significant distance from the main data center, and it should not be subject to the same disasters as the main data center (for example, both data centers should not be close enough that a single hurricane could render them both useless).

The rest of the data center design components should mimic the main design center. In the case of CME, the backup data center only needs to support 500 users, so the data center will be much smaller than the corporate data center, which supports 3,000 users. Additionally, there is no need replicate the testing and training environment, or some of the redundancy that exists at the main data center. Therefore, the CME Omaha hot backup data center will be about ten percent of the size and cost of the main data center.

Backup Data Center Components

Although the backup data center is much smaller than the main data center, defining the critical components is still an important part of the business-continuity plan to ensure that everything will work upon failover. Although the list of required hardware and software for most organizations will differ, studying the components required at the CME data center and comparing these to the headquarters' data center will allow you to extrapolate what is needed for your organization.

CME's backup data center will require the following components:

▼ Ten Citrix XenApp servers imaged from the CME headquarters data center to support the 500 possible users required upon failover

■ A DMZ-based NetScaler Enterprise/Access Gateway Enterprise appliance and an internal Web Interface

■ One Oracle Database server

■ One Microsoft SQL server

■ One Microsoft Exchange server

■ LAN and WAN networking components to support the DR site

■ Internet connectivity utilizing a separate ISP than what is used at the Denver data center

■ A firewall with DMZ and VPN hardware

■ An Internet-based secondary mail server to queue mail in case the Exchange server is offline

■ Internal and Internet DNS servers

■ Storage area network solution (SANS)

■ Appropriate tape backup units to facilitate the recovery of archived data and any information not located on the SAN

▲ Backup power for the data center

Hot Site Data and Database Resumption

The most critical part of the business-continuity plan is the ability to recover the file and database data (the disaster-recovery section of business continuity). Even if the full business-continuity plan is not enacted, the recovery of data is critical. For example, if the Oracle data becomes corrupt or the Oracle cluster should completely fail, even though this does not constitute a disaster, it is critical that the data be recovered quickly and easily. Worse yet, if a government seizure should happen, there must be a plan to restore the data to nonseized hardware in a timely manner. In order to service this, all databases, files, and e-mail data must be copied to the backup data center nightly at a minimum. Although this is easy to accomplish with file data, doing this with database and e-mail data is more difficult. The larger SANS vendors (HP, EMC, and LeftHand Networks) all support a snapshot technology to effectively copy Exchange and database data across a WAN to another similar SANS device. Also, some non-hardware-based technologies (such as NSI Software's Double Take) mirror Microsoft Exchange and other database software. Note that in the CME scenario, they are only copying the data at night. Therefore, if a disaster happens late in the day, requiring failover to CME Omaha, all data created in the course of the day will be lost. If your organization requires less data loss risk than this, the solutions from LeftHand, EMC, HP, and NSI can provide up-to-the-second transaction redundancy (typically called "double-commit"), but the dedicated bandwidth requirements and associated costs increase dramatically. Figure 8-2 shows an example of how database server(s) can be set up for replication to a DR site.

Restoration of the Applications and User Access

For any environment that wishes to have a robust, fast resumption plan, all applications requiring immediate availability and flexible user access following a disaster must be installed in a server-based computing environment at the backup data center. In CME's case, all applications required for Tier 1 and Tier 2 business continuity are installed on the on-demand access server farm at CME Omaha. Thus, the applications will fail over automatically from CME Denver data center to the CME Omaha data center using the Global Server Load Balancing (GSLB) configuration on the NetScalers. The Web Interface server and Citrix XenApp server farm will be configured identically to the larger farm at CME Denver. All applications, load-balancing services, and user services supported

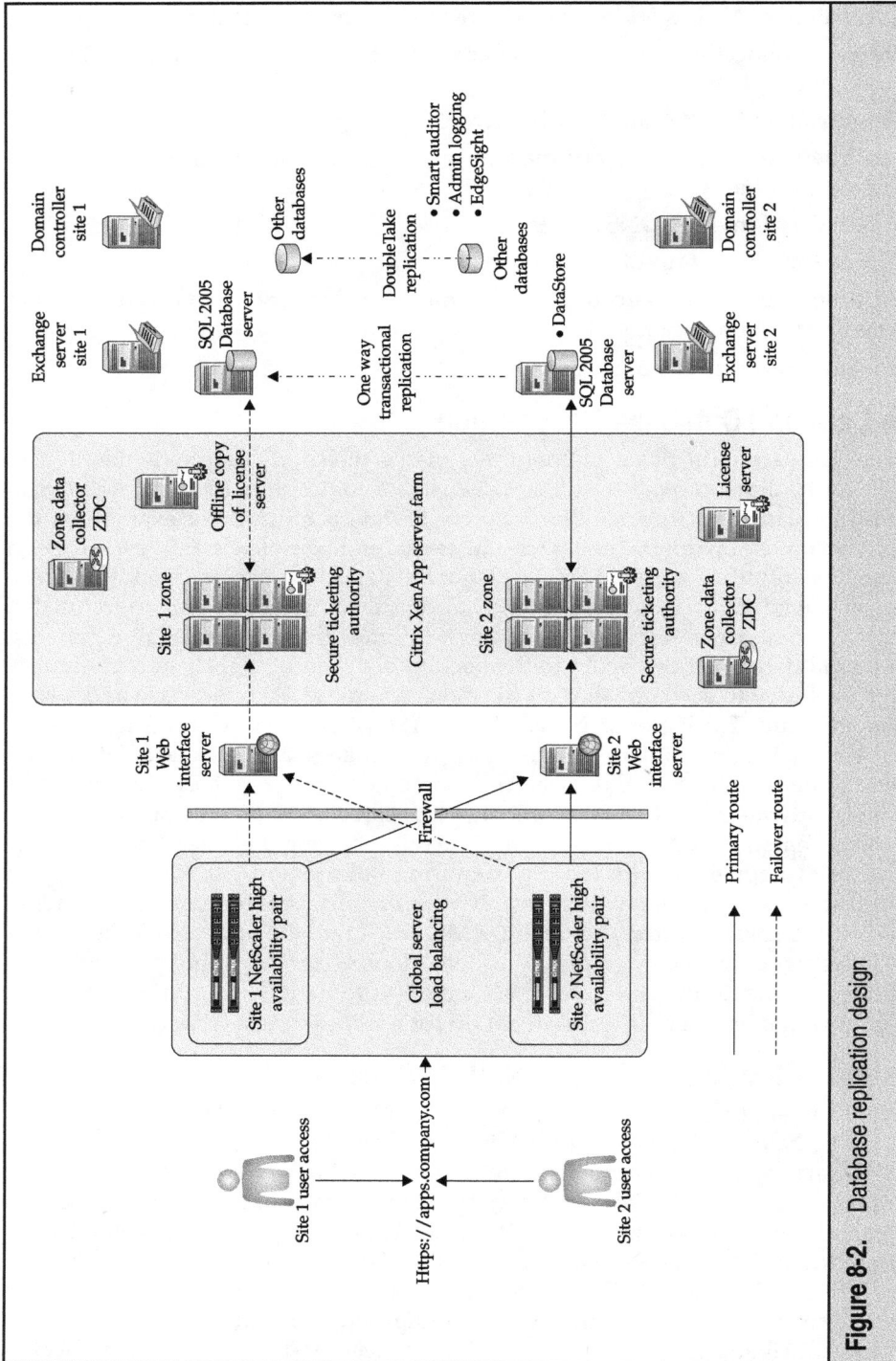

Figure 8-2.   Database replication design

from the corporate Citrix XenApp server farm will be fully supported from the CME Omaha farm, with no additional configuration or work following the failover.

User access to these applications becomes the remaining hurdle. All CME branch offices have Internet (MPLS) connections into the CME Denver data center. CME has also defined that all of the Denver Tier 1 and Tier 2 users who may have been displaced from the disaster will have access from their home Internet connections (assuming, of course, that Denver's Telco infrastructure has not been rendered unavailable by the disaster). Thus, all users will have full access to the CME Omaha backup data center through the Internet.

Because CME decided to front-end all their Internet-facing sites with Citrix NetScalers, users will not have to worry about how they access the backup resources at CME Omaha. NetScaler provides site-to-site load balancing using the GSLB feature. This provides for immediate access and negates the problem of propagation delays in "repointing" both public DNS resources and BGP routing tables to claim the corporate identity at CME Omaha. Within seconds, the BGP and DNS changes will have gone into effect, allowing remote users access through the standard Internet-accessible URL.

In addition to remote user access, some employees will need co-located office space. CME Omaha was designed with sufficient capacity in the form of WLAN hardware and prepositioned access switches to support temporary users from other locations.

Full Restoration Plan

Following a major disaster and an accompanying failover to CME Omaha, if the disaster necessitates a new facility, there is a risk that restoration of the original Denver location may not happen within two weeks—or ever. Accordingly, the Tier 3 plan may require either enhancing the temporary infrastructure at CME Omaha and salvaging the Denver site (to make CME Omaha the new corporate home) or rebuilding a new CME corporate data center in Denver or some other location to house and support all the CME corporate users long term.

Again, if the CME corporate facility is rebuilt and the server and network infrastructure is restored and tested, a period of downtime (usually 24 hours) must be planned to manually fail back the BGP and DNS to point back to the primary location and to return users to that facility.

Documentation

Now that CME's plan is falling into place, an all-inclusive document needs to be created. This document should, at a minimum, include the following items:

▼ Emergency phone numbers for all manufacturers and support vendors

■ Names and contact information for the 50 Tier 1 people

■ Specifics on how the plan will be implemented, and who will implement it

■ Network diagrams

■ Security policies

▲ Emergency IT response information

This document should be reviewed and updated twice per year by the BC committee. Additionally, the 50 Tier 1 employees should receive formal training annually to keep them updated with policies and procedures. Tier 2 employees should receive a yearly e-mail or other document to keep them updated on the procedures.

Maintenance of the Hot Backup Data Center

Although the hot backup data center will not be used for general day-to-day activity (other than the storage area network, which will receive the backups every night), in order to guarantee two-hour failover, the backup data center must be maintained. The same maintenance items that are logged to the main data center must also be replicated to the backup site. Items such as service packs, hotfixes, application updates, security updates, and so on must all be kept up to date. A simple approach to keeping XenApp and Windows 2003 servers up to date is to use the procedures discussed in Chapters 9, 13, and 18 to keep servers at both sites updated anytime changes are made. Additionally, the SANS should be checked weekly to ensure that the data being copied over every night is indeed current and usable.

Test of the Business-Continuity Plan

Twice a year (for example, once during a summer break and once during a winter break), the business-continuity plan should be tested. It is imperative that all Tier 1 personnel be included in this test. The test should ensure successful connectivity, availability, and data integrity, as well as confirm that everyone knows how and when to set procedures in motion.

DISASTER-RECOVERY SERVICE PROVIDERS

It is important to note that everything discussed in this chapter can be outsourced to myriad providers, although your organization will still have to set the parameters of Table 8-1 and follow through with yearly testing and updating. It is important that whoever is chosen understands your organization's environment and can accommodate the on-demand access portion of the solution.

PART III

Installation and Configuration

CHAPTER 9

Citrix XenApp with Application Streaming

In Chapter 2 we discussed Citrix XenApp 4.5, its functions, and its purposes in detail. As a reminder, Citrix XenApp 4.5 is available for Windows Server 2003 (Standard, Enterprise, and Datacenter) and comes in three tailored editions (Platinum, Enterprise, and Advanced).

In this chapter, and over the next few, we discuss the installation and configuration of XenApp Platinum Edition and all its components. As mentioned before, XenApp Platinum Edition includes everything in XenApp Enterprise Edition, plus functionality found only in Platinum, such as SmartAuditor and EasyCall powered by the Communication Gateway. Other components featured in Platinum Edition include Citrix EdgeSight (which provides performance monitoring for applications), Secure Remote Access provided by Citrix Access Gateway and SmartAccess, single sign-on, self-service password reset, and Hot Desktop provided by Citrix Password Manager.

Citrix XenApp Platinum Edition requires the following servers to fully provide an end-to-end application-delivery solution for your organization:

▼ XenApp Server(s)

■ A Password Manager server

■ A SmartAuditor server

■ A large centralized storage location for Application Streaming profiles and Installation Manager packages

■ A server or workstation for profiling applications to be streamed to servers and desktops

■ An Installation Manager packaging server for creating IM packages

■ One or more Microsoft SQL 2005 server(s) to house the data store, Resource Manager Summary database, Configuration Logging database, EdgeSight database, and the new SmartAuditor database (a Feature Pack 1 addition)

■ Microsoft Exchange Server for notifications and alerts from the XenApp components

■ A web server for Web Interface, Advanced Access Controls (a.k.a. Access Gateway Advanced Edition), and EdgeSight

▲ And last but not least, a central licensing server

Each of these products should be installed on Windows Server 2003 with SP2, including all relevant hotfixes and patches, and should include appropriate components to support each of the different products. Refer to your organization's written policies and procedures for your specific build requirements.

Besides the list of servers mentioned are a few appliances that need to be included in the list, such as the Access Gateway for the remote access piece and the Communications Gateway for the EasyCall feature.

Whew! That's a lot of servers and components. The dollars are already stacking up in your head about now. However, don't panic and throw this book out the window quite yet. Some of these servers and services can be consolidated onto fewer servers to help simplify the rollout and save some money, which never hurts in the eyes of the CFO. Our recommendation is to use virtualization technology to help reduce the number of physical servers required and to get the most functionality out of the less-demanding servers roles.

By no means do these next few chapters map out the only way for configuring XenApp 4.5 and its components, or the order for building the components. Instead, they offer a solid guideline for implementation, with tips and tricks along the way to help you make the most of your deployment. The ultimate goal is to provide your users with the best experience in application delivery across a large variety of devices and connections.

CITRIX XENAPP 4.5 WITH FEATURE PACK 1

For the purposes of this chapter and the installations that follow we will be using Citrix XenApp Platinum Edition. Citrix XenApp Platinum Edition is designed for single-point control of servers, licenses, and resources in large organizations and multinational corporations. The Platinum edition enables all of the features available with the previous edition, such as system monitoring and analysis using Resource Manager, application packaging and delivery using Installation Manger, systems management capabilities using Network Manager along with integration with third-party SNMP management consoles, and performance monitoring of servers in the Microsoft Operations Manager 2000 and 2005 environments using the Citrix XenApp Provider and the Citrix XenApp Management Pack.

With the release of Platinum Edition 4.5 and the newly released Feature Pack 1, you now have access to new features such as Application Streaming, Configuration Logging, Health Monitoring and Recovery, SpeedScreen Progressive Display, Trusted Server Configuration, and Non-Administrator Client Installations. Further enhancements in this release include Alerts Storage and Reporting, Monitoring Profiles, PN Agent backup URL support, and a multilingual user interface. We will cover all these in greater detail in this and the following chapters.

Let's get to the meat of what you came to this chapter for—the installation and configuration of Citrix XenApp Platinum Edition.

Citrix XenApp Licensing Overview

Software licensing, just like software, continues to evolve. Both Microsoft and Citrix licensing is required for all Citrix environments. As discussed in Chapter 2, Microsoft licensing with Windows Server 2003 offers both per-user and per-seat (that is, per-computer) implementations. Citrix licensing is offered on a concurrent user (CCU) basis. With both Microsoft and Citrix licensing, the license is not only an agreement describing the cost to the user and revenue to the vendor, it is also a technical implementation in which licenses are managed by the servers, and user access and feature function is disallowed if insufficient licenses are available. Although most companies today look at software licensing as purely an ethical and legal concern, for many applications, including Citrix and Microsoft, it is also a technical concern. On more than one occasion we have received calls from customers in a panic because users couldn't get logged in as a result of too few licenses or a configuration mistake with the licensing.

The technical implementation of XenApp Platinum (or any individual component, such as EdgeSight or Password Manager) licensing requires that one license be available for each concurrent user ICA connection to a XenApp farm. The ICA client software is essentially free—it can be installed on any device at no cost. Of course, when it is used to connect to a server, it will use up a concurrent license on the server farm. The Platinum licensing is intelligent enough to recognize when a single user is running more than one session into the farm, and thus only takes one license for that user. More interesting here is that the same holds true of connections to multiple farms if both farms are sharing the same licensing server. Because Citrix connection licenses are edition specific (that is, they understand the difference between an Advanced server, an Enterprise server, and a Platinum server), we highly recommend that all environments use a consistent Citrix edition. This will avoid the problem of Citrix checking out two licenses to a single user because that user is connecting to both an Enterprise Edition server and a Platinum Edition server.

Once the first Citrix product is purchased, software can be installed on as many servers as desired. The license code provides for concurrent connections, regardless of how many servers those connections are spread across, as long as all the servers are of the same edition. Obviously, each additional server does require a new license of Windows Server 2003, but from a Citrix standpoint, the number of servers has little bearing on the number of concurrent licenses. This provides a great deal of flexibility for Citrix administrators, allowing them to add servers when more power or flexibility is needed within the farm, without having to purchase more Citrix licensing.

TIP: Possibly the most significant gain from this licensing model is that it allows an administrator to build nonproduction test servers within their farm without having to purchase additional Citrix licenses.

Purchasing Citrix Licensing

Citrix sells their software licenses through a worldwide group of resellers who purchase the licenses through several large distributors or, in some cases, from Citrix directly.

The XenApp license is more than an agreement describing the cost to the user and revenue to the vendor. It is a technical licensing implementation in which licenses are pooled by the XenApp servers themselves and used to calculate the authorized use of the product. In short, if the license provides for 20 users connecting to a XenApp server, user number 21 will be denied access to the resources on the server.

Citrix Licensing Programs

Citrix offers XenApp licenses via the following programs:

▼ **Citrix EASY Licensing Program**   EASY allows you to buy only what you need, simply and easily. EASY Licensing provides customers with greater flexibility in purchasing Citrix solutions and maintaining licenses by enabling them to benefit from the ease of electronic delivery. EASY Licensing is best suited to small business customers and departments with one to 499 users.

- **Citrix OPEN Licensing Program**   Designed for customers making volume purchases, OPEN Licensing is based on a large initial purchase, offering four corporate levels of discounts. The larger your initial purchase, the higher the discount level. Ideal for medium to large companies that plan to make a significant investment in Citrix access products, OPEN Licensing is easy to administer and grows with the company. It is suited for companies with 500 to 4,999 users.

- **Citrix Academic Licensing Program**   Academic Licensing is a single discount level of OPEN Licensing available exclusively for nonprofit and educational customers, providing a volume discount off the suggested retail price of qualified Citrix products. Academic Licensing offers significant discounts at only a fraction of the minimum purchase requirements to nonprofits, K-12 schools, universities, and colleges.

- ▲ **Citrix FLEX Licensing Program**   FLEX Licensing is recommended for large national/multinational customers (5,000+ users) deploying a significant amount of Citrix product. This qualifies the customer for a greater cost savings. FLEX Licensing customers forecast purchases over a two-year buying period, and are required to make a minimum initial purchase based on a percentage of this forecast. Designed for the largest customers, FLEX Licensing offers several levels of discounts that vary by purchase commitment.

Prior to purchasing your Citrix products, you must register the specific licensing program for which your company qualifies. After you complete the registration process for EASY and OPEN programs, you will receive a customer ID that allows you access to the personalized license management portal on the Citrix website at http://www.mycitrix.com. Once the online registration process has been verified, your order will be placed by your Solutions Advisor. You will then receive an e-mail with instructions for obtaining your license file(s) from the fulfillment area of MyCitrix.com.

For the Academic and FLEX programs, contact your Citrix authorized reseller for assistance.

Citrix License Server

The first step for setting up a Citrix environment is to install the licensing server. Citrix licensing offers a centralized license model, meaning that multiple Windows-based server farms can use the same license server and pool licenses among them.

Every time the Independent Management Architecture (IMA) service is started and every time a user logs onto a XenApp Server, the IMA service checks with the license server to make sure a license is available. In larger environments or environments with multiple zones or sites, the network traffic generated from the license server can be significant and therefore should be taken into consideration when planning a XenApp environment.

Platinum licensing can be installed on either a dedicated stand-alone server or a server that is running other services or applications such as a web server or a file server. The number of servers making connections to the license server will determine whether a dedicated license server or a shared license server should be used.

Environments with fewer than 200 continuous connections (a connection that starts up and checks out a startup license, then forms a connection—such as a XenApp or Access Gateway connection), or an agent connection (such as a Password Manager Agent connection that connects to the license server during startup and ends the connection after it has completely started) can typically utilize a shared license server (shared with other applications). This shared server resource should be stable and highly available.

If there are between 200 and 5,000 continuous connections or agent connections to the license server, a server should be dedicated to running the Citrix licensing software. In large enterprise environments, multiple dedicated license servers may be required (approximately one for every 500 connections). If the environment is larger than 5,000 continuous connections or agent connections, a license server should be dedicated to each Citrix product. Here are some other guidelines for multiple license servers:

▼ When you have geographically dispersed sites that each need a local license server

■ When you have multiple Citrix products across a WAN and one of those products, such as Password Manager, requires a local license server

■ When you want to segment departments by license server for ownership or security purposes

▲ When you have one product (of several) that requires licensing customizations to communicate across a firewall and there are a lot of license files on the license server

NOTE: When deploying multiple license servers in your environment, plan your deployment so that you can share licenses as much as possible. Deploying multiple license servers can limit your ability to share licenses among products. To share licenses among products on your network, the products must communicate with the same license server.

Some additional points to consider when deploying multiple license servers:

▼ License servers do not communicate with each other. As a result, one license server cannot access or use licenses stored on another license server.

■ Users connecting to product servers that are pointing to different license servers take a license from each license server.

■ If you are deploying multiple license servers and you want to maximize your license-sharing capabilities, Citrix recommends you group licenses for the same types of products on the same license server. That is, consider keeping all XenApp licenses on one server, all Password Manager licenses on a different server, and so on. Otherwise, your ability to share licenses within a product may be limited.

▲ You cannot run two Citrix license servers on a single computer. Multiple license servers must be installed on separate computers.

The hot topic these days is disaster recovery and business continuity (DR/BC). So, what do we do about licensing recovery when a disaster occurs? All license files are bound to the NetBIOS name of the license server and are case sensitive. Obviously having more than one server with the same name on the network cannot happen. Do not panic—Citrix was nice enough to give us some flexibility when licensing is down.

If the license server is unavailable, the XenApp Servers will continue to log users into the farm and allow application functionality. The XenApp Servers at this point have entered a grace period. The licensing grace period for XenApp 4.5 is 30 days. The XenApp servers maintain a copy of the licensing information in the LHC (local host cache) for just this reason. The servers will continue to seek a "heartbeat" from the license server every five minutes until the grace period ends. The event logs contain entries that document when the servers went into the grace period and when the grace period will expire.

One thing to note is that in order for a XenApp Server to enter a licensing grace period, the server must have contacted the license server at least once prior to the license server failure.

Although you have 30 days to bring up a new license server in the event of a catastrophe, which should be plenty of time, some IT administrators must have the "ace in the hole" when it comes to DR/BC (a backup and recovery plan for every component in the data center). So, if you fit this category, we have three recommendations for maintaining DR/BC for the license server:

▼ **Clustering using MS Clustering Services** This version of the Citrix License Service can be installed on Microsoft Clustering Services. To accomplish this configuration, you need at least two nodes available in the active-passive configuration (this is the only cluster type supported by Microsoft Clustering Services).

■ **Cold standby solution** Install the server, completely configured, including the imported license file(s). When your default server fails, just turn the cold standby on and connect it to the LAN. Because the hostname of the cold spare is the same as that of the production server, no additional configuration is needed. This is a good solution for virtualization. Keep a virtual image of the license server on hand for a fast and easy licenses recovery. The key to success, of course, is that if you add additional licenses to your production (active) license server, you must replicate these additions to the cold spare as well.

▲ **Transferring the license to another IIS server** Within MyCitrix.com it is possible to return licenses for reallocation. Return your licenses first and then reallocate them using the hostname of the new IIS server.

Citrix License Server Requirements

The following minimum requirements are recommended for running Citrix Licensing (license server and License Management Console):

▼ Windows Server 2003.

■ Minimum PIII 1GHz, 512MB RAM.

- Java JRE 1.5.0_06 or higher (included in the License Management Console installation).

- Tomcat 4.1.24 (included in the License Management Console installation).

▲ IIS 6.0 or Apache HTTP Server 2.0.49 for the License Management Console. (Apache HTTP Server is available from http://httpd.apache.org.)

Citrix License Server Installation and Configuration

To install a license server with a license file, follow these steps:

1. Install the license server and the License Management Console.

2. Gather licensing information.

3. Connect to http://www.mycitrix.com/ to download the license files.

4. Add the downloaded license files to the licensing server.

Installing the License Server and the License Management Console

To install the Citrix Licensing component, perform the following tasks:

1. Build and configure a Windows 2003 server with Internet Information Services (IIS) according to your company's written policies and procedures.

2. Log onto the computer where Citrix licensing will be installed, with an account that is a member of the local Administrators group. This can be a domain administrator or a local administrator account.

3. Select the Autorun.exe file from the root of the product installations CD.

4. Choose Product Installations and Updates | Install Citrix Licensing.

5. Accept the license agreement (do not forget to scroll all the way to the bottom of the agreement), review the installation prerequisites, and verify that the Citrix Licensing option is the only one selected.

6. Setup will automatically install the necessary versions of Microsoft .NET Framework, Java Runtime Environment (JRE), and Visual J# .NET, if these were not previously installed.

7. Choose the destination folder where the licensing components should be installed. By default, the licensing components are installed in C:\Program Files\Citrix\Licensing on a 32-bit system and C:\Program Files (x86)\Citrix\Licensing on a 64-bit system.

8. Install both the License Management Console (LMC) and the License Server software (IIS or Apache is required for the LMC).

NOTE: Running licensing setup requires temporarily stopping a Web Service (IIS or Apache), which affects any dependent services. Run Setup when it is not disruptive to shut down this service.

9. Accept the default license file location. License files must be stored on the same drive as the license server software. By default, the license files are stored in C:\ Program Files\Citrix\Licensing\MyFiles on a 32-bit system and C:\Program Files (x86)\Citrix\Licensing\MyFiles on a 64-bit system.

> **NOTE:**   License files cannot be stored at the root directory level. They must be stored in a folder or a subfolder.

10. Select the web server—in our case, Microsoft Internet Information Server (IIS).

11. Select OK to restart the Microsoft IIS server.

12. Click Next to install the licensing components, review the installation summary, and then click Finish.

> **NOTE:**   A citrix_startup.lic file should exist on all license servers upon installation. This file should never be deleted or renamed because it is a Citrix system file that allows product servers to maintain open connections to the license server, tracks which product servers are connected to the license server, and stores licensing system information.

Gathering Licensing Information

Before installing the software, gather your Citrix license information to avoid any interruptions during the installation:

▼ License code (e-mailed from a reseller or received directly from Citrix)

■ User ID and password for MyCitrix.com

> **NOTE:**   A MyCitrix user ID and password will be e-mailed to your organization's official contact following the purchase of a Citrix product. If the contact did not receive an e-mail or if a new logon is needed, contact your reseller or Citrix Customer Care.

▲ The exact, case-sensitive spelling of the name of the server or cluster (hostname) where the license server software is installed.

> **NOTE:**   The best way to get this information is by typing hostname at a Windows command prompt.

Downloading and Adding the License Files to the License Server

The license file has to be added to the server and then the server configuration reread in order for it to take effect. All licenses do not have to be allocated and downloaded at once. Different numbers of licenses can be dedicated to specific environments or geographic locations. Here's one of the two most common methods for adding the file to the license server and forcing a reread:

1. Open Start | Programs | Citrix | Management Consoles | License Management Console.

2. Select Configure License Server.

3. Select Download License File from MyCitrix.com.

4. Connect to http://www.mycitrix.com, sign into your MyCitrix account, and follow the directions to allocate or activate licenses to get a license file.

5. Download the appropriate license file(s).

6. Save the files to a location that is accessible from the license server or directly to the License Server in the C:\Program Files\Citrix\Licensing\MyFiles directory.

7. Complete the licensing inventory.

8. Verify the correct licenses are installed.

And here's the other method:

1. Copy the license file to your license server's C:\Program Files\Citrix\Licensing\MyFiles folder.

2. Update the license data stored on the license server. Open a command prompt, navigate to C:\Program Files\Citrix\Licensing\LS on a 32-bit system and C:\Program Files (x86)\Citrix\Licensing\LS on a 64-bit system, and then execute the following command:

```
lmreread -c @localhost.
```

Preparing the IMA Data Store Environment

Citrix provides several choices for database storage of the data store, including the following:

▼   **Microsoft Access**   Access is a lightweight database that is included with Windows Server operating systems. The Access database is created on the first server in a new farm. It is most appropriate for small to mid-sized farms.

■   **Microsoft SQL Server 2005 Express Edition SP1**   This type of database is most appropriate for small to medium-sized farms and can be administered using standard Microsoft SQL Server tools.

▲   **Microsoft SQL Server, Oracle database, and IBM DB2**   These are all true client/server databases that offer robust and scalable support for multiple-server data access. They are suited for use in farms of any size.

Because this text focuses on enterprise environments, we will look at using SQL Server 2005 for our data store. Although Oracle and DB2 are also excellent enterprise database choices, SQL Server, according to Citrix customer information, has been the most deployed database of enterprises for the purpose of IMA data store collection. SQL supports all current Citrix features, including database replication, direct-mode access, and the Resource Manager Summary database. For readers interested in running the IMA data store on Oracle, we highly recommend you refer to *Citrix Access Suite 4 Advanced Concepts: The Official Guide, Second Edition.*

Data Store Connection Type

An additional task when planning the data store is deciding on a direct (direct to the database) or indirect (through an intermediary server) communication model. This is determined by the type of database you choose for the data store and the size of your environment. Here are some points to keep in mind:

▼ If you are in a large-farm environment, have a mission-critical farm, or are using Oracle, SQL, or DB2 as the database for your data store, Citrix recommends accessing the data store *directly*.

▲ If you are in small to medium-sized environment and you are using SQL Server 2005 Express or Microsoft Access as the database for your data store, each server in the farm must access the data store *indirectly*.

You specify whether you want servers to communicate directly or indirectly with the data store when you run Setup to install XenApp on the subsequent servers in your farm. Keep the following points in mind:

▼ **Direct access** To make a direct access to the data store, a server must have the appropriate ODBC drivers installed and configured correctly. The server then connects directly to the server on which the database is running.

▲ **Indirect access** For indirect access, a server connects to an intermediary server (running Citrix XenApp) that connects to the data store directly. If you are using SQL Server 2005 Express and Microsoft Access as the database for your data store, during setup select to join the farm indirectly. SQL Server Express and Microsoft Access can only access the data store indirectly. We do not recommend that you use indirect access for mission-critical farms because the XenApp Server running the intermediary connection is a single point of failure. Instead, configure an Oracle or SQL database and use a *direct* connection.

Sizing for the Data Store

Although each environment differs in size and complexity, here are some general guidelines when choosing the database type for the storage of the data store. If your environment does not fit a specific area, err on the side of caution and round up! Murphy and his laws are right around the corner.

	Small	Medium	Large	Enterprise
Servers	1–50	25–100	50–100	>100
Named Users	<150	<3000	<5000	>5000
Applications	1–50	50–100	100–500	>500

Generally speaking, the small and medium-sized environments that have one location are a good fit for Microsoft Access and SQL Express. The large and enterprise environments are better suited for SQL, Oracle, and IBM DB2 databases. However, best practices dictate the use of the latter databases for all Citrix data store deployments. These database types offer performance and redundancy options when scaling up your environments and they play a significant part in DR/BC scenarios.

Installation and Preparation of Microsoft SQL Server

If your enterprise already has a server running SQL Server 2005 with available capacity, simply connect to it according to the following Citrix installation instructions. If a SQL server with capacity is not readily available, it will need to be installed and configured on another dedicated Windows 2003 server (hardware or virtual, the choice is yours). Obviously, the management of a SQL server can be a full-time activity all by itself, but for the purposes of an IMA data store, a general default installation (with some minor adjustments) running on a dedicated hardware box or virtual machine will suffice. For the sake of security, stability, and functionality, it is imperative to keep current with the latest service pack level.

To download the latest service pack for Microsoft SQL Server 2005, visit http://www .microsoft.com/downloads. At the time of this writing, we are using Service Pack 2 for SQL Server 2005.

NOTE: If you installed Microsoft SQL Server 2000 using the Typical installation option or via unattended installation procedures (sqlins.iss file), you will need to set the default SQL authentication mode. By default, Windows Authentication is the security model. Therefore, when you try to connect a Citrix server to the newly created data store by using a standard SQL login such as system administrator (SA), you will receive the following error message:

```
Unable to connect to server SERVER_NAME:
Server: Msg 18452, Level 16, State 1[Microsoft][ODBC SQL Server
Driver][SQL Server]
Login failed for user 'sa'. Reason: Not associated with a trusted SQL
Server connection.
```

To prevent this behavior, install the SQL instance using Mixed Mode Authentication.

TIP: When building a database server (such as SQL for our deployment), set it up with two RAID configurations: one with RAID 1 (a two-drive mirror) for the operating system and the other with three or more drives using RAID 5 (striping with parity) for the database. This allows the OS and the SQL database to run on separate disk spindles, thus providing optimal performance, maximum uptime, and recovery capabilities.

Citrix XenApp supports the following versions of Microsoft SQL Server for the farm's data store:

▼ SQL Server 2000 with Service Pack 3a: MDAC 2.8, Windows Server 2003 with Service Pack 1

■ SQL Server 2005: MDAC 2.8, Windows Server 2003 with Service Pack 1

▲ SQL Server 2005: MDAC 2.8, Windows Server 2003 x64

Creating the IMA Data Store on SQL Server 2005

Once the SQL server is running, the data store can be created on the SQL Server. Here are step-by-step instructions for creating the data store:

1. Choose Start | Programs | Microsoft SQL Server 2005 | SQL Server Management Studio.

2. In Management Studio's left pane, expand *<SQL Instance Name>* | Databases.

3. Right-click the Databases folder and choose New Database.

4. A dialog box appears. In the Name box, enter a name and click OK.

NOTE: When choosing a database name for the Citrix products, make sure you use a name that is representative of the database type. We recommend conventions such as CitrixDS for the data store, CitrixRM for Resource Manager, CitrixES for the EdgeSight database, and so on. This is strictly a guide—the actual name will not affect the farm in any way.

5. Expand the Security | Logins folder and right-click and choose New Login.

6. A dialog box appears with the General tab displayed. In the Login Name box, enter a name. Make note of the name because you will need it during the XenApp installation.

7. For the Authentication method, choose SQL Server Authentication and then enter a password. Remember the password; you must enter it during the XenApp installation.

8. For the Default database, change the database to the name you specified in step 4 and select the appropriate default language.

9. Click Server Roles in the left pane and choose sysadmin for the server role for this database.

NOTE: Microsoft SQL Server supports Windows and Microsoft SQL Server authentication. For high-security environments, we recommend using Windows authentication only. The user account used for installing, upgrading, or applying hotfixes to the data store must have database owner (db_owner) rights to the database. When you finish installing the database with database owner rights, set the user permissions to read/write only. Doing this increases the security of the database.

10. Click OK. Database creation is complete.

Citrix XenApp Installation

Citrix XenApp 4.5 with Feature Pack 1 and its components can be installed on computers running the Microsoft Windows Server 2003 family (with SP1 or SP2): Standard Edition, Enterprise Edition, and Datacenter Edition. XenApp is supported on both 32-bit and 64-bit systems. If you use a method for installing XenApp other than the Autorun program, take the time to understand the prerequisites for each of the components and make sure they are met prior to the component installation.

CAUTION: Make sure that Terminal Services is installed and configured prior to installing Citrix XenApp; otherwise, the installation will fail. Also, make sure you remove the Internet Explorer Enhanced Security Configuration from Windows components before installing Citrix XenApp. Leaving this configuration enabled can cause some undesirable effects in the user profiles.

For a new Citrix XenApp installation, the following are required:

▼ The Microsoft Windows Server 2003 operating system

■ 400MB of disk space for Citrix XenApp, Enterprise Edition

■ 50MB of disk space for the XenApp Console

■ 25MB of disk space for Access Management Console

■ 35MB of disk space for Document Center

■ Terminal Services in application mode

■ Microsoft .NET Framework, version 2.0 (will be installed during the Autorun part of the XenApp setup)

■ Java Runtime Environment, version 1.5.0_09 (will be installed during the Autorun part of the XenApp setup)

▲ Visual J# .NET, version 2.0 (will be installed during the Autorun part of the XenApp setup)

Preinstallation Tasks

Prior to installation, the following tasks should be performed:

1. Choose the server farm name to be used.
2. Install and configure the licensing server per the instructions given previously in this chapter.
3. Configure the data store per the instructions given previously in this chapter.
4. Determine what XML port is going to be used.
5. Determine whether or not server drives will be remapped.

Installation Instructions for Citrix XenApp

These step-by-step instructions for installing Citrix XenApp 4.5 FP1 are not intended to be all-inclusive, but they will provide a good basis for installation in most organizations.

To install Citrix XenApp 4.5 FP1, do the following:

1. Place the Citrix XenApp CD into the CD drive and let it Autorun.
2. Click the option Product installations and updates | Install Presentation Server 4.5 and its components.

3. Scroll to the bottom of the license agreement. (If you don't, you will become a member of an elite list of IT administrators who didn't either and then will be reminded by the software that you *have* to.) Select the radio button for I Accept the License Agreement and then click Next.

4. Click Next on the Prerequisites Installation screen.

NOTE: If the prerequisites are not already installed, they will be installed automatically.

5. Select the components desired for the installation. If Licensing is installed elsewhere, just accepts the defaults.

6. Select the radio button "I already have a license server, or will use the product CD to install one later." Click Next to begin the prerequisites installations.

7. Click Next to begin the installation of the Citrix Access Management Console.

8. Click Next on the Select Destination Folder screen or change the destination folder and then click Next again.

9. Select the components desired and click Next. We recommend that you choose all the components except Web Interface. You may not need all of them right away, but when you need them you will not want to wait for the installs.

10. Click Next on the Ready to Install the Application screen to confirm and begin the installation.

11. Click Finish to complete the installation of the Access Management Console and to begin the XenApp setup.

12. Click Next to begin installation of Citrix XenApp.

13. Select the components desired and click Next.

NOTE: We recommend that if you're using Installation Manager, only install the Installation Manager Installer Service on the application servers. Additionally, deselect Program Neighborhood Agent. This feature is primarily used on client devices.

14. Select the desired option for the pass-through authentication behavior and click Next. If No is selected at this screen, a reinstall of XenApp must be done in order to change the setting.

15. If this is the first server in the farm, select Create New Farm. If this is a subsequent server in the farm, select Join an Existing Farm (the steps for this are about the same).

    a. Assign a name for the new farm.

    b. Choose your database type for the Citrix data store. For this example, we are using a SQL Server data store. Click Next to start the Data Source Wizard.

c. Enter a data source description. We choose "Citrix database connection - CitrixDS" for this example.

d. Enter the name of the SQL server your database resides on (created earlier). We choose TOYS-SQL-01 for this example. Click Next.

e. Choose SQL Server Authentication and enter the credentials created during the SQL server and data store creation. (See, I told you that you were going to need it. You should have paid more attention.)

f. Verify that the correct database name is listed in the Change the Default Database To: field. It is not necessary to check the box and enable the field if the correct database is already listed. If it is not listed correctly, check the box, choose the correct database (in our example it is CitrixDS), and then proceed with the next step.

g. Accept the defaults for languages and locations and click Finish.

h. Verify the settings and click Test Data Source. If the test is successful, click OK to continue.

i. Enter the credentials for the initial farm administrator account and click Next. The wizard defaults to the account being used to do the installation (local administrator or domain administrator), but you may choose another account with administrator privileges. After the installation is complete, you may add other accounts for farm administration, as needed.

NOTE: It is important to use a domain administrator account and to add a local administrator account following installation. If this is not done and the domain settings are changed, the Access Management Console will become inaccessible, requiring a reinstallation of the software.

j. Decide on whether or not to enable IMA encryption and then click Next.

NOTE: The IMA encryption feature provides a more robust AES encryption algorithm to help protect data in the data store. You must install identical encryption keys on all servers in the farm in order to use this feature. If you are not sure how to proceed, skip this step. You can always enable this feature at a later time.

k. Enter the hostname of your server hosting Citrix Licenses and click Next.

l. Keep the default option of allowing shadowing and then select the check box "Force a shadow acceptance popup."

CAUTION: Although this setting is not required, for most environments it can be a mandatory policy for user interaction. If you choose the option to prohibit shadowing of the ICA and RDP sessions on this server, a full reinstall of XenApp will have to be performed to reverse this decision. On the other hand, if shadowing is enabled during installation, it can later be disabled using the Citrix Connection Configuration Utility without a reinstall. Check with your organization's written policies and procedures for the requirements for this setting.

m. Choose a port for XML communication. The default port is port 80.

TIP: We strongly recommend changing this to another port (we chose 8090 for our installation). When you implement a remote access solution using the Access Gateway and Web Interface, using port 80 for XML communication will add complexity to secure access configurations.

n. Select the desired user options to be added to the Remote Desktop Users group in Windows 2003 and click Next. For our needs, the Add the Authenticated Users Now option made the most sense.

NOTE: If the Conference Manager or guest users are not going to be used, it is best to leave the Anonymous users out of the Remote Desktop Users group.

o. Review the installation selections to verify they are correct and then click Finish.

16. After installation is complete, click Close and proceed to the XenApp Console installation.

17. Click Next, Next, and then Finish to complete the Citrix XenApp Console install.

18. Click Next to begin the installation of the Document Center.

19. Click Next to accept the default installation location.

20. Click Finish to complete the installation of the Document Center.

21. Examine the installation summary to make sure everything installed correctly and then click Finish. Take note in the summary screen about the other installations from the components CD that are a complement to the Platinum product. These add-ons include SmartAuditor, the latest ICA client version (10.1 at the time of this writing), Streaming Client 1.1, Streaming Profiler, and EdgeSight for XenApp.

22. Click Yes to reboot the server.

Installation is now complete. Now the configuration of XenApp and the installation of additional components and applications can be done.

DELIVERING APPLICATIONS WITH APPLICATION STREAMING

One of the new and exciting features of XenApp 4.5 is Application Streaming. The Application Streaming feature changes the way we think about delivering applications to end users. Application Streaming allows Citrix administrators to install and configure applications on one file server and then deliver those applications to desktops and XenApp

Servers on demand. Another added bonus about Application Streaming is that updates, upgrades, and patches can be installed one time on the file server instead of across all servers and workstations.

The Application Streaming feature offers the following benefits to enterprises:

▼ Cost-effective, scalable application delivery to end users and servers

■ Lower cost of installing and maintaining applications and servers in large farms

▲ Access to any application, anywhere, anytime, regardless of connection

There are added benefits when streamed applications are run on client desktops:

▼ Optimal utilization of computing resources

■ Elimination of application compatibility issues

▲ Elimination of peripherals-access issues

With Application Streaming, organizations can take advantage of the following features:

▼ **Install once, deliver anywhere**   Deliver an application to any client requesting it but install it once on the Profiler workstations and replicate it to multiple file servers within the organization.

■ **Seamless updates**   Update your application like normal without having to redo the application profile. The update is run once on the Profiler workstations and updates are delivered to the users just like the original program.

■ **Application isolation**   Applications run within isolation environments that keep them from interfering with others running on the same client. An application's specific data files (such as INI files) and Registry keys are all isolated and maintained centrally for the streamed application.

■ **Application caching**   To increase performance, applications can be cached on the client to allow faster access to the application a second time.

■ **Dual-mode streaming**   Stream applications to the client or virtually from the XenApp Server. If an application streamed to the client desktop fails, it can run streamed from the XenApp Server.

■ **Simplify deployment of applications to the farm**   Instead of installing applications to every server on the farm, stream the applications to the server from the central file share.

■ **Offline access**   Once delivered, applications are available to the user while disconnected from the network.

▲ **Disaster recovery**   On-demand application delivery is a powerful model for disaster-recovery situations because the application and data are not lost when the streamed application profiles are backed up, and desktops and servers are easily replaced.

Application Streaming Components

Figure 9-1 shows the components that make up each of the four functional areas of Application Streaming and a general summary of the types of tasks administrators must perform.

▼ **Licensing**   Consists of the License Server and the License Management Console. Use the License Management Console to manage licensing.

■ **Administration (server farm)**   Consists of the following:

- ■ Farm servers
- ■ IMA database
- ■ Web Interface
- ■ Access Management Console (used to configure and manage the server deployment and to publish streamed applications)

■ **Streaming Profiler**   Use the profiler to create streaming application profiles.

▲ **Streaming Client and optional Program Neighborhood Agent**   Program Neighborhood Agent enumerates available applications for the user and the Streaming Client finds the correct application for the client workstation, sets up an isolation environment in which the application runs, and streams application files on demand.

If streaming to the client desktop fails, the Streaming Client running on the server can stream the application to the server for presentation on the client workstation. Alternatively, you can opt to stream applications to servers instead of desktops and have the servers present the applications to devices that have XenApp clients installed. This eases deployment of applications to servers in your farm.

Licensing

Licensing behaves much in the same way as all the rest of the Citrix products. You need a central Citrix licensing server that holds the license files for the specific products (for more information on licensing, refer to the section titled "Citrix XenApp Licensing Overview" earlier in this chapter). The one thing to consider when thinking about streaming applications to the servers and the desktops is that if you decide to stream applications to the desktops, you will use one of your XenApp connection licenses. For example, let's say you are licensed for 50 concurrent users (CCUs) of XenApp Enterprise or Platinum. From those 50 CCUs, you have 30 users connected to your XenApp Servers hosting applications, and you have also streamed applications to 20 workstations. Therefore, you will have used up all of your 50 licenses and no more users will be able to connect to the XenApp Servers for applications. If you are only interested in streaming applications to a subset of user desktops and those users will not connect to XenApp–hosted applications, you should consider purchasing the standalone Streaming to Client licenses for those users. This is a separate license file used for streaming applications to the desktops that is priced a bit lower for only this purpose.

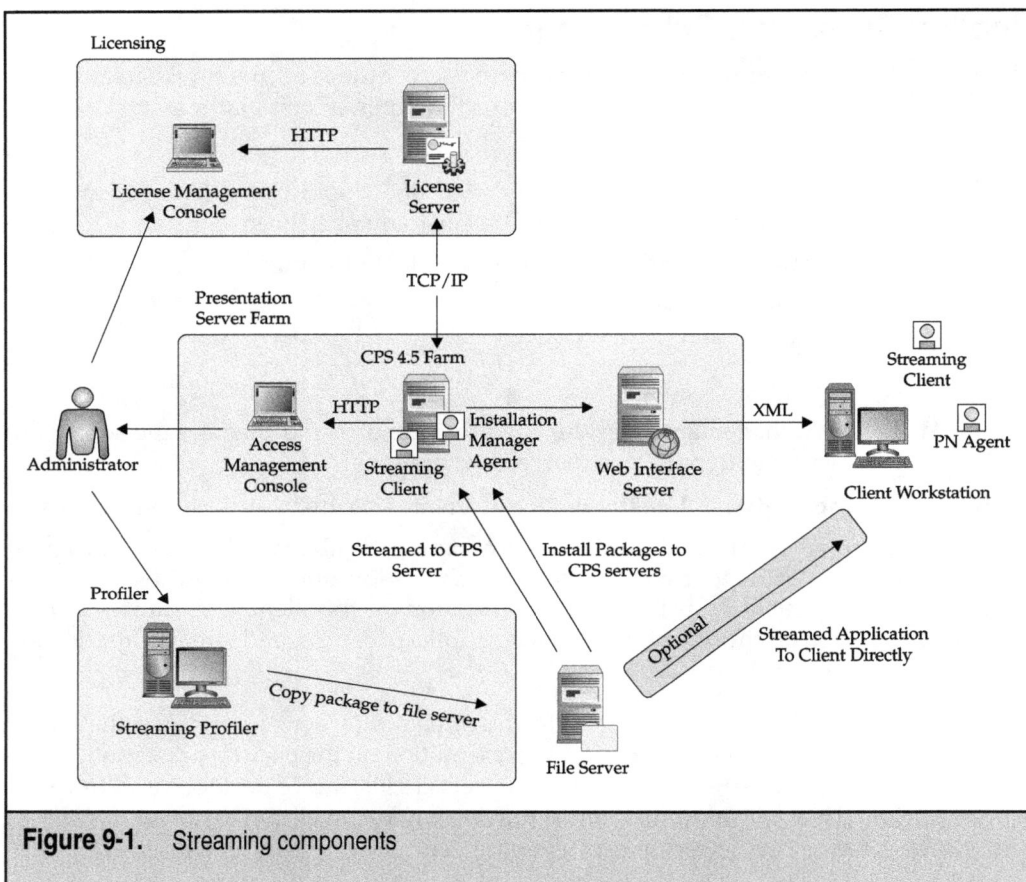

Figure 9-1. Streaming components

The Streaming Profiler

The Citrix Streaming Profiler is used to create application *profiles* to deliver applications to your users by streaming them to their desktops or the XenApp Servers. With the Profiler, administrators can build an application that includes several operating system *targets* to match the variety of user environments.

The Profiler is an application that enables you to prepare Windows applications, web applications, browser plug-ins, files, folders, and Registry settings in order to stream them to users' workstations. The Profiler machine should be one that closely represents the environment your end users will be using to run the streamed applications. The Profiler must be installed on one of the following servers or workstation types:

▼ Windows 2000 Professional, Service Packs 3 and 4

■ Windows XP Professional, Service Packs 1 and 2

■ Windows XP Professional 64-bit Edition, Service Pack 1

- Windows 2003 Server, Service Pack 1 or 2
- Windows 2003 Server, R2
- Windows 2003 Server 64-bit Edition with Service Pack 1 or 2
- Windows Vista
▲ Windows Vista, 64-bit Edition

CAUTION: You must install the Streaming Profiler on a separate, newly installed computer with an operating system that matches the typical operating system of your end users' client computers or the XenApp Servers.

We recommend using virtualization technology to build both a server that matches your XenApp farm and a workstation (or workstations) that matches your client environment. This extends to drive letters and languages. For example, if the target system has a main drive letter of G:\, the Profiler should also contain a main drive letter G:\. This will help minimize application profiling problems. The key to the Profiler is that it is on a machine that does not have any other roles on the network. It is solely used for creating application profiles. We will discuss this in more detail later in this chapter.

The Streaming Client

When a user runs an application enumerated by Program Neighborhood Agent or through a Web Interface site, the Streaming Client finds the correct application in the profile on the file server, sets up the isolation environment on the client, and then streams the application from the file server to the safety of the isolation environment set up on the client. For more information on this, refer to the next few sections.

Profiles: Not Just for Users Anymore

This section describes how to install and configure the Streaming Profiler and how to create an application profile for use on your servers and workstations. Once a Profiler is installed and configured, you can begin creating profiles for delivering applications to the server as published applications or stream them to workstations for both online and offline use.

We will be using Office 2007 to stream to the XenApp Server and workstations for access. We will demonstrate how to configure the application for access from the Web Interface and Program Neighborhood Agent and configure failover when streaming to the desktop is unavailable.

The Profiler—Installation and Configuration

After you determine which client and server target types you will be building profiles for, build a simple and clean replica of those environments. Ensure that all the drive letter mappings, language settings, service packs, and hotfix levels are as close to the targets as possible.

> **TIP:**   Even though multiple operating systems are available when building an application profile on a single Profiler, it is a good idea to try to match the Profiler's operating system to the target's operating system when at all possible. This will offer the best success rate of the profiled application.

To install the Profiler, follow these steps:

1. Insert the XenApp Components CD into the workstation you want to use to profile resources.

2. To install the Profiler, in the Autorun window, choose Presentation Server Utilities | Install Citrix Streaming Profiler for Windows.

3. Choose a language for the installer interface.

4. Accept the licensing agreement.

5. Take the defaults and finish the installation.

6. After installation, restart the workstation.

Initialize a New Profile and Target

Launch the Profiler for the first time and build the Office 2007 profile resource. You have two methods for creating a profile: a quick install and an advanced install. A quick install is designed for packaging a standard application in a target, whereas an advanced install is for packaging multiple applications or resources in a target. We are going to profile Office 2007 in the following steps:

1. Open Start | Programs | Citrix | Streaming Profiler | Streaming Profiler.

2. Click New Profile to start the wizard.

3. Enter a profile name (we used "Office 2007" for this example).

4. Decide on the User Profile Security setting (for this example, we chose Enhanced):

   ■ **Enhanced**   Does not permit any executable files to run other than those included in the target. For example, if the client is running an Internet Explorer plug-in included in the target, the Enhanced security setting prevents the client from running any other plug-ins the user might download.

   ■ **Relaxed**   Permits executable files to run that are accessed through the profiled resource.

> **TIP:**   When running the wizard for creating profiles, you'll see a check box at the bottom of some of the screens that reads "Save these settings and skip this screen in the future." If you know that you will always be using a setting, check this box and you will not be prompted again. If you decide later that you wish to undo that setting, open Edit | Preferences from the menu bar and uncheck the setting from the appropriate tab.

5. Choose a target operating system and target language for the profile. (We chose Windows XP Professional and English.)

NOTE: Make sure you do not choose a target operating system that is older than the profiling system. For example, on a Windows XP Professional Profiler, do not pick Windows 2000 Professional as the target.

TIP: When choosing a target operating system, you may also specify the service pack level by choosing the Set Service Pack button. Type the number representing the service pack level in the applicable field for Minimum Level, Maximum Level, Exact Level, or, for a range, Minimum Level and Maximum Level.

6. Choose an install option (we chose Quick Install for the Office 2007 suite):

   ■ **Quick Install** Use this option if the application you are installing has an installation program, such as Setup.exe (recommended for normal installations).

   ■ **Advanced Install** Use this option if you are installing Internet Explorer plug-ins, editing Registry settings, installing an application manually, or installing from multiple installers. Advanced Install provides the opportunity to repeat the installation procedure as many times as you need, so you can add a variety of multiple resources to a target. The advanced options include Run install program or command line script, Install IE plug-ins, Select files and folders, and Edit registry. For more information on these options, refer to the following sections.

7. Click Browse to choose an executable file or a script you run to install the application in the current target. In this step, you are only choosing the installer, not running it. If needed, enter the required command-line arguments and then click Next.

8. In the Run Installer dialog box, ensure the installation program and command-line parameters are correct, and then click Launch Installer. After you launch the installer, the Back button is disabled. Do not click Exit until the installer finishes. In our example, we browsed to the location of Setup.exe on the Office 2007 media.

9. After the application installer finishes, if the application you are installing requires restarting, the Profiler detects it and performs a virtual restart.

10. When the installer is done, click Next to proceed.

11. On the Run Application dialog box, you can choose to run an application in order to complete the application install. This allows you to enter a serial number, accept a license agreement, or complete product activation as a part of the install process.

12. On the Select Applications screen, you can choose which applications to list on the target machine and executables you wish to make available for publishing. You can add new ones or modify existing ones to customize the profile. We chose to modify the name of the Microsoft Word application to read "Word 2007" and remove the "Digital Certificate for VBA Projects" from our list.

13. Choose whether or not to sign the profile using a trusted Certificate Authority.

14. On the Build Profile dialog box, click Finish to complete the profile build.

Update an Existing Profile and Target

Next, let's install Office 2007 hotfixes into the Office 2007 package we just created:

1. Open the Office 2007 package (if you closed it after the previous steps) and right-click on the target (Windows XP Professional in our environment) and select Update/Install Application. This will unpack the profile into an isolation environment on the Profiler's computer so that you can make changes.

2. Select Advanced Install and click Next.

3. Select Install IE Plugins...or Online Updates and then click Next.

4. Click the button to launch IE.

5. An instance of IE will launch within the isolation environment.

6. From that instance of IE, go to the Office Update website and run the update.

7. After you finish and close IE, click Next in the wizard.

8. Finish the wizard as you did when you created the profile.

9. The profile will be packed up again into CAB files in the local temp directory.

10. Save the profile. This will copy the CAB files back to the file share.

11. After installing all the resources you want to include, choose Continue with none of the above, which enables you to finish creating the target.

Internet Explorer Plug-Ins

Here's how to install Internet Explorer and its plug-ins:

1. If you have Internet Explorer running, close it.

2. From the Select Install Method window of the wizard, choose Install IE Plug-ins.

3. Click Launch Microsoft Internet Explorer. This command runs Internet Explorer in an isolation environment.

4. Using Internet Explorer, install all the plug-ins to be made available to your users.

Including Files and Folders

You may need to include specific files and folders that are not installed by an application installer but are required for the application to run. To include files and folders in a target, follow these steps:

1. From the Select Install Method window of the wizard, choose Select Files and Folders.

2. Select the files and folders you want to include.

   a. To select files and folders for inclusion in the target, use the Look In pull-down menu to choose a folder.

   b. In the Selected Files list, select the files you want to include in the target and click the arrow between the Select Files list and the Current Files list.

   c. To create new folders, rename files and folders, or delete files and folders in the Current Files list, use the buttons at the bottom of the list.

   d. After you include all the files and folders the application requires, you can simulate a system restart by checking Perform Virtual Restart.

Including Registry Settings

You may need to include Registry settings in the isolation environment on the client machine. The following describes the steps for adding Registry settings.

CAUTION: Always be careful when making changes in the Registry. As most of you know, messing around in the Registry can cause problems for your machines. If you did not know this was the case, you may want to reconsider your decision to perform this step, get some assistance, or make sure that you have a good backup plan.

Here's how to include customized Registry settings:

1. If you have Windows Registry Editor open, close it before proceeding.

2. From the Select Install Method window of the wizard, choose Edit Registry.

3. Click Launch Windows Registry Editor.

4. Use Windows Registry Editor to make the Registry changes you want to include in the target. Note that the Registry changes made here are included in the isolation environment of the target, not the Registry on the Profiler workstation.

5. After saving the Registry settings, you can simulate a system restart in the target by checking Perform Virtual Restart.

Saving to a Profile Share

When saving a profile to a file share, you must type the UNC path to the network file share where you want to store the profile. Note that Save To displays the location where you are saving the profile based on what you provide for the UNC path and the name you provide for the profile. Here is an example of what might be entered for the UNC path:

```
\\citrixserver\profiles
```

Here is the actual storage location based on the values of UNC Path and Profile Name:

```
\\citrixserver\profiles\Profile Name\Profile Name.profile
```

At this point, you can also change the name of the profile. After you save your profile to a file share, you can use other workstations to add unique targets to the profile.

The previous sections describe the basics for creating a Streamed Application profile. There are many options and configurations, many of which we did not cover in this section. Therefore, consult the admin guide for more details on advanced configurations and profiling techniques.

Storing Profiles on a File Server

When the profile creation is complete, it must be stored on a file server. Each profile consists of directories and subdirectories filled with files. Do not modify these files directly; only use the Profiler to modify these files. This section describes the structure of the profile directories and the files within them.

A profile folder on a file share contains the following:

▼ Profile manifest file (.profile), which is an XML file that defines the profile

■ Target CAB files providing isolation environment contents for applications in the targets

■ Hash key file (Hashes.txt) for digital signatures and signing profiles

■ Icons repository (Icondata.bin)

▲ Scripts folder for pre-launch and post-exit scripts

For example, if you create a profile called PDF Viewer with a single target, the profile (a folder called PDF Viewer) has contents similar to the following on the file share:

▼ PDF Viewer.profile (the manifest file)

■ 720edd68-0972-49e6-aa00-80974eb81d5b_1.cab (the target CAB, first version)

■ Hashes.txt

■ Icondata.bin

▲ Scripts folder

The next section describes the details of each of the profile components.

Manifest File

The manifest file is the top file in the data structure that defines a profile. It is an XML-formatted text file that describes the profile. Manifest files have the extension .profile.

The information in a manifest file includes the following items:

▼ Description

■ Create date

■ Modify date

■ User profile security (Boolean)

■ Scripts

■ File type association

■ Internet Explorer application (Boolean)

■ Applications

▲ Targets

Targets

Each time a target is created, it is assigned a GUID so it can be uniquely identified and independently cached on the user client workstation. The GUID is used to identify the isolation environment so that no two different installations of the same named target occupy the same location in the execution system cache. The GUID and version are used to determine the target CAB filename, which is a compressed subdirectory structure within the profile structure.

Once the client is streamed the application, the directory structure on the workstation includes a version number. This is used to detect when updates to the application are available on the file share and ensures that the clients are always running the latest version.

Digital Signatures

You have the option of digitally signing the contents of a profile. The manifest file indicates whether the profile is digitally signed. When this option is enabled, the manifest file will digitally sign the entire profile. The hashes for all files in a target are stored in a single file, hashes.txt.

Icons

Icons for the applications are stored in a separate file called icondata.bin to help keep the manifest file size small. These icons can be changed when publishing the application. You can choose your own icons or pick from the other icons that come with the application.

Scripts

The Streaming Client can execute scripts associated with a profile or target according to the following:

▼ Before the client executes the first application from a profile

▲ After the client terminates the last application from a profile

After creating a script, use the Profiler to add the script to a target. When you add a script to a target, the Profiler copies the script file to the profile. The Profiler also retains the original filename of the script. Scripts can be used in pre-launch and post-launch and are independent of the Profiler. Scripts consist of the following:

▼ A disk file that is executed

■ Arguments for the executable

▲ A Boolean value indicating whether or not the script is enabled

Publishing a Streamed Application

At this point we have created an application profile, updated it, and pushed it to a file server for safekeeping. Now it is time to publish the application for use on the servers and workstations. The steps and options in the wizard vary depending on the application type you select. This procedure describes the basic options available for streamed applications.

To publish an application using the wizard, follow these steps:

1. Under the Presentation Server node of the Access Management Console, expand the farm to which you want to stream an application. Select the Applications node. Then, from Common Tasks, select New | Create Folder. Create a folder for the application(s) you are publishing. We created one labeled "Microsoft Office."

2. Select the folder you created and from the Common Tasks pane choose New | Published Application.

3. In the Publish Application wizard, click Next.

4. On the Name page, provide a display name and application description. We chose "Word 2007" and "Office 2007 Application," respectively.

5. Choose the type of application to publish (we chose Application). Then choose the application type or delivery method (in our case, Streamed to client).

   The three types of application delivery methods are

   ■ Accessed from a server

   ■ Streamed if possible, otherwise accessed from a server

   ■ Streamed to client

   We discuss these methods more in detail later in the chapter, so keep reading.

6. Specify the application location. Select the application profile containing the application you want to publish. To select the profile, click Browse and or type the UNC path to the manifest, which is a .profile file (for example, \\file server\file location\Office 2007\Office 2007.profile).

7. After you select a profile, the application drop-down list is populated with the applications in the profile. From the drop-down list, select the application you want to publish. We chose Word 2007.

8. On the Offline Access page, specify whether or not you want the published application to be available offline to configured users. For more information about this option, see "Offline Access to Applications Streamed to Desktops," later in this chapter.

9. On the Users page, create the Configured Users list for users or groups who have access to the application.

10. On the Shortcut Presentation page, you can change the icon for the application and choose how the application is enumerated on the user's workstation.

11. On the Publish Immediately page, choose whether or not to make the published application immediately available to your users. By default, the published application is available when you click Finish.

12. Decide on whether you would like to configure advanced application options. If so, check the box and click Next. Otherwise click Finish.

Advanced configuration options include Access Control, Content Redirection, Alternate Profiles, and User Privileges. These options are exactly the same as they are with regular published applications.

Delivery Method for Streamed Applications

You have to choose a delivery method for each application you publish from the servers. When using Application Streaming, you have some options to stream the application to the server or a user's workstation or desktop. In the Publish Application Wizard, you have three options for delivering an application to the users:

▼ Accessed from a server

■ Stream if possible, otherwise accessed from a server (a.k.a. "dual-mode streaming")

▲ Streamed to client

Accessed from a server   We are all used to this option from days of old with Presentation Server. This is a traditional published application, and the type of delivery method enables users to use ICA to launch an application from the server. This option has three types of applications that users can access:

▼ **Installed application**   Launches applications installed on the server

- **Installation Manager packaged application** Schedules Installation Manager to install the application on the server and then allows users access
▲ **Streamed to server** Streams the application up to the server from the file share and then allows access

Stream if possible, otherwise accessed from a server This option tries to first launch the application for the user locally, unless the client does not meet the requirements. Then it will fall back to launching the application from the server, either streamed or locally installed on the server.

If the client cannot launch the application locally, it falls back to one of these previously mentioned alternative delivery methods.

Streamed to client This option allows users to stream the application to their desktop for local access using the Streaming Client and either Program Neighborhood Agent or Web Interface. This option, if selected, is available only to users who meet all the requirements to have applications streamed to their desktops. Those users who do not meet these requirements will not be able to access the application.

Offline Access to Applications Streamed to Desktops

Offline access to streamed applications is exactly what it sounds like: the ability to use applications that are streamed to the desktops when you leave the comfort and serenity of the office LAN. When administrators decide to make applications available to users while disconnected from the network, the Citrix Streaming Client caches each streamed application on the hard drive of the client workstation. After the application is cached, the user can disconnect from the network or server and continue to run the application in offline mode for the period of time specified in the license. Pretty cool, huh?

NOTE: Offline access is only available with the "Stream if possible, otherwise accessed from a server" and "Streamed to client" delivery options.

First things first: Before we can perform this gift from the gods, we need to set up offline access permissions, make sure we meet the licensing requirements, set up offline licensing, and enable offline access to applications. Currently this feature is only available through the Program Neighborhood Agent.

Configuring Offline Access Permissions Follow these steps to configure offline access permissions:

1. From the Access Management Console, select the farm.
2. Under Common Tasks, select Modify Farm Property | Modify All Properties.
3. From the Farm Properties dialog box, select Offline Access | Users.
4. To choose the user accounts that can have offline access, use the Select Directory Type drop-down box to select either Citrix User Selector or Operating System User Selector.

5. Click Add to open the Select Users or Groups dialog box:

6. If you selected Citrix User Selector (default selection), complete the following in the Select Users and Groups dialog box:

    a. Select your account authority from the Look In drop-down list. The drop-down list contains all trusted account authorities configured on the servers in the farm.

    b. Select Show Users to display all user names in the selected domain.

7. If you selected Operating System User Selector, use the standard Windows dialog box to select your user or group.

8. Click OK.

9. The list of user accounts is added to the Configured Accounts list.

Offline Licensing In order to use offline streamed applications, you must obtain the correct license file from Citrix or your reseller. For more information see the "Citrix XenApp Licensing Overview" section earlier in this chapter.

Once the proper licensing is in place, you can configure the time period for which the applications can be used offline. Under Offline Access | Offline License Setting, you can set the range from 2 to 365 days (the default is 21 days). This is the number of days the application can be used both online and offline before it needs to "check in" with the server and renew the lease.

If the license is near expiration while offline, the user receives a notice to log back into Program Neighborhood Agent to renew the license or lease. If the user does not comply, the police will be dispatched to the user's location and they will be arrested. (Just kidding. I wanted to make sure you were still with us.) Seriously, if the license is not renewed, the user will not be able to use the application—either offline or online. Therefore, your offline settings need to align with the user behavior and LAN access; otherwise, productivity could be affected.

Enabling Application Offline Access In the application properties, under the offline access setting, you can enable offline use. Offline applications use fully cached copies of the application on the user's workstation. While the user is connected to the local area network (LAN), the Streaming Server will download (transfer) a copy of the application profile to the workstation using two caching methods:

▼ **Pre-cache application at login** The default option when installed. Very handy but may increase the login times and cause network delays.

▲ **Cache application at launch time** Another handy option. This is a better option for networks where a lot of users log in at the same time.

With either method, the users will log into the environment using Program Neighborhood Agent and will check out an offline license (or renew one currently held) and possibly start downloading applications, depending on the configuration chosen.

If you are using the "Pre-cache application at login" option (the default option), the user is notified when the download begins and ends. Once it is complete, the user may disconnect from the network and continue to use the application offline until the lease expires or is renewed.

If "Cache application at launch time" is chosen, the user launches the application and must remain connected until the application completes before they can disconnect. During the downloading time, the user may begin to run and use the application while the download occurs. The main parts of the applications are streamed first, and then the "not so popular" pieces follow, such as help, mail merge, and references. This allows the users to begin working in the application right away while the downloading continues.

The best option for working with offline access to applications is to predeploy them. In the Program Files | Citrix directory is a utility called RadeDeploy.exe that pushes new or updated applications to workstations overnight to help minimize network overload during business hours. This is perfect for delivering applications that are used more frequently in the organization.

Follow these steps to run RadeDeploy:

1. On the client desktop that has the Streaming Client installed, open a command prompt. Enter the command line with the UNC path to locate the manifest file (.profile) on the network file share using the following example:

```
radedeploy /deploy: \\file server\file location\Office 2007\
Office 2007.profile
```

To enumerate applications, use the following:

```
radedeploy /enum
```

To add applications, use

```
radedeploy [-m] /deploy:filename
```

where *filename* can be a .profile file. Filenames with embedded spaces should be quoted. Also, [-m] means to monitor deployment until complete.

Use the following to delete applications:

```
radedeploy /delete:BrowserName
```

2. The utility selects the target and automatically deploys the best fit to bring the necessary files to the client

Once you have completed these steps, you can open up the properties of the application from Access Management Console | Presentation Server | Application. Select an application and under Common Tasks choose Modify Application Properties | Modify All Properties. From here, you can configure application properties such as its name and description, whether or not the application is enabled or disabled, offline availability, icons, connection types in which the application can be accessed, and so on. These options vary with each environment, so we will not cover each of them in detail here. Refer to the administration guide for more information.

The Streaming Clients

There are two ways to get applications streamed to the desktops using the Streaming Client: with the Program Neighborhood Agent (PN Agent) or with the Web Interface (WI) in a web browser.

With Program Neighborhood Agent and the Streaming Client, you can enable application icons in the Start menu or on the desktop and you can enable offline applications. This method allows the full streaming feature set to be used. You configure a PN Agent site on a Web Interface server and set up access just like a normal site. Published resources are enumerated on the client in the Start menu. Also, it allows users to configure options on their desktops for the agent interaction, and PN Agent runs in the background keeping tabs on the applications and configurations. Because the PN Agent site is centrally managed, administrators are able to dynamically control the client population from a single location and in real time. This method is supported over HTTP (port 80) and HTTPS (port 443) for ease of communications through firewalls.

Users can access streamed applications through the Web Interface using the locally installed Streaming Client. Offline applications cannot be used with this method. Users will connect to a Web Interface site and click an available application. Then the streamed application will launch off the local client using the Streaming Client installed on the client machine.

Installing the Streaming Client

Follow these steps to install the Streaming Client:

1. From the XenApp Components CD, run Autorun.exe. Choose Citrix Presentation Server Clients | Install Citrix Streaming Clients for Windows.

2. Choose the language in which you want the client installer to run. (In this step, you are only choosing the language for the installer, not the language of the client.)

3. On the Welcome screen, click Next and then accept the license agreement.

4. On the Select Client screen, take one of the following actions:

    a. If you want to make offline applications available to your users, install Program Neighborhood Agent along with the Streaming Client (see the next section for more details on installing the PN Agent).

    b. If you do not want to install Program Neighborhood Agent, choose Entire feature will be unavailable. If you intend to provide access to applications through a web page only, Program Neighborhood Agent is not required.

    Click Next.

5. On the Client Name screen, choose a unique name to represent the client to the server. It is recommended that you use the computer name as the client name (selected by default).

6. On the Use Local Name and Password screen, choose whether or not to pass your local user name and password to the server. If you are using single sign-on, choose Yes. Click Next.

7. Review the list of clients you chose to install. The applicable client for these installation instructions is Citrix Streaming Client. To begin the installation of the Streaming Client, click Install.

8. After installation is complete, click Finish and restart the workstation.

9. After installing the Streaming Client and restarting your workstation, the Citrix Streaming Service starts automatically on the client computer and runs as the user Ctx_StreamingSvc.

After the Streaming Client is installed, you can set the default location for the application cache. The Streaming Client will evaluate the available space at this location to make sure there is enough space for the applications requested as well as evaluate whether the requested applications will reach the maximum cache size limit (1,000MB by default). If this location will not support the space requested, application files will be removed, starting with the one that was used the least, until there is enough room to allow the new application to run. The default location is

```
%Program Files%\Citrix\RadeCache
```

If you wish change the default location, run clientcache.exe from the %Program Files\Citrix\Streaming Client folder. This program will allow you to change the location for the cache as well as the size.

NOTE: When changing the cache size, use an integer that represents the size in MB. For example, for a 2GB cache size, enter 2000MB.

Installing Program Neighborhood Agent

Follow these steps to install the Program Neighborhood Agent:

1. From the Streaming Server Components CD, run Autorun.exe. Click Product Installations and Updates | Install Citrix Streaming Clients for Windows.

2. Choose the language in which you want the client installer to run. (In this step, you are only choosing the language for the installer, not the language of the client.)

3. On the Welcome screen, click Next and then accept the license agreement.

4. On the Select Client screen, ensure Program Neighborhood Agent is selected for installation. Then click Next.

5. To configure Program Neighborhood Agent, enter the URL to the server on which you created your Program Neighborhood Agent site through the Access Management Console. Here is an example:

```
http://server_name.domain.com
```

For more information about creating a Program Neighborhood Agent site on your server, see the *Web Interface Administrator's Guide*, which is available from the Document Center.

6. On the Select Folder Name screen, choose a folder name that Program Neighborhood Agent creates in the Start menu of the client workstation. This menu contains an enumeration of applications published on the server.

7. On the Client Name screen, choose a unique name to represent the client to the server. It is recommended that you use the computer name as the client name.

8. On the Use Local Name and Password screen, choose whether or not to pass your local user name and password to the server. If you are using single sign-on, choose Yes. Click Next.

9. To begin the installation of selected clients, click Install.

10. After installation, click Finish and restart the workstation.

11. After you install the Program Neighborhood Agent and restart the computer, the Program Neighborhood Agent icon appears in the notification area of the client desktop.

Both the PN Agent and the Streaming Client can be installed using the command line. This installation method requires the use of a TRANSFORMS file. For more information, refer to the *Citrix Application Streaming Guide* for a list of command-line switches and parameters.

CHAPTER 10

Password Manager

PASSWORD MANAGER OVERVIEW

Citrix Password Manager provides password security and single sign-on access to Windows, web, proprietary, and host-based applications running in the Citrix environment as well as local applications on the desktop. Users authenticate one time with their primary login and Password Manager takes over, automatically logging onto password-protected information systems, enforcing password policies, monitoring all password-related events, and even automating user tasks, including password changes.

The primary components of Password Manager are

▼ The central store

■ The Password Manager Console

■ Password Manager Agent software

▲ The Password Manager Service (Optional)

The Central Store

Password Manager uses a repository known as the central store to store and retrieve information about your users and environment. Password Manager relies on the data in the central store to perform all default and configured single sign-on functions.

The central store contains user data and administrative data:

▼ **User data** in the central store includes user secondary credentials, security questions and answers, service-related data (for example, provisioned data, question-based authentication data, key recovery enrollment, and so on), and user Windows Registry data associated with Password Manager.

▲ **Administrative data** in the central store includes application definitions, password policies, security questions, and other settings made through the console for Password Manager features and components. The central store enables the agent software running on a user PC or computer running Citrix XenApp to communicate with the central store and services, and to provide user credentials to applications to which the user has been granted access.

The agent maintains a local store on the user PC. The local store contains only the user's secondary credentials, key recovery information, and security questions and answers (if applicable). It synchronizes with the central store to allow users to roam throughout the enterprise and always have access to saved user credentials.

The Password Manager Console

The Password Manager Console is the administration center for Password Manager. It is responsible for the user experience, how Password Manager functions, which features are enabled, the security configuration, and other password-related functions.

The console is divided up into four major sections:

▼ **User Configurations**   These configurations allow administrators to tailor particular settings for the users based on their geographic locations or business roles. The settings of the other three nodes are used to create user configurations.

■ **Application Definitions**   These definitions provide the information necessary for the agent software to supply user credentials to applications, and to detect error conditions if they occur. Application definition templates are supplied with Password Manager to speed this process. Customized definitions can be created for applications that cannot use these templates.

■ **Password Policies**   Password policies control password length and the type and variety of characters used in both user-defined and automatically generated passwords. From here, character exclusions, password history, and password complexity rules can be set. Typically these settings are mirrored with company security policies regarding passwords.

▲ **Identity Verification**   Security questions provide an added layer of security to the agent software by protecting against user impersonation, unauthorized password changes, and unauthorized account unlocking. Users who enroll and answer these security questions can later answer those questions to verify their identity and perform self-service tasks in their account, such as resetting their primary password or unlocking their user account.

The Password Manager Agent Software

The Password Manager Agent is the software that allows devices to interact with applications that require authentication on behalf of the users. The Password Manager Agent is designed to run on client devices: desktop and laptop computers, handheld computers, and other devices. The agent software in this case provides credentials and access to applications running locally on the client device.

You can also publish the agent software on a computer running Citrix XenApp. The agent software in this case provides credentials and access to published applications. Users can use the agent software to access local applications even when they are not connected to a network. User credentials are synchronized when users reconnect to your enterprise network.

When you install the agent software using the Autorun option provided on the Password Manager CD, the installation software detects your operating system (32- or 64-bit) and installs the appropriate agent.

When a user tries to access an application that requires authentication, the agent software intercepts the application's request for authentication, finds the correct credentials, and submits them to the application.

In addition, the Password Manager Agent provides support for remote and mobile users. Remote and mobile users can obtain a license from the license server before disconnecting from the network and continue to use the functions of Password Manager while off the corporate network. A user's secondary credentials are stored locally—so even a fully disconnected user can access them.

The Password Manager Service

The Password Manager Service runs on a web server that provides the foundation for optional features included in this release. Install the Password Manager Service if you plan to implement at least one of the following modules:

▼ **Account Self-Service module** Allows users to reset their Windows passwords and unlock their Windows accounts

■ **Data Integrity module** Protects data from being compromised while in transit from the central store to the agent

■ **Provisioning module** Allows you to use the console to add, remove, or update credential information for your users

▲ **Credential Synchronization module** Synchronizes user credentials using a web service

Password Manager Editions

Password Manager comes in two editions: Advanced and Enterprise. Each edition offers user, security, and administration features. Tables 10-1, 10-2, and 10-3 summarize each of the different features, respectively.

User Features	Advanced Edition	Enterprise Edition
Single sign-on to Windows applications	X	X
Single sign-on to web applications	X	X
Single sign-on to host-based terminal emulator applications	X	X
Citrix Access Client	X	X
Localized user interface	X	X
Support for SAPGUI, Internet Explorer 7 (32-bit, 64-bit)	X	X
Self-service password reset		X
Self-service account unlock		X

Table 10-1. User Feature Comparison

User Features	Advanced Edition	Enterprise Edition
Self-service feature integration with Web Interface		X
Hot Desktop fast user switching		X
Hot Desktop/SmoothRoaming integration		X
Account association		X

Table 10-1.   User Feature Comparison *(continued)*

Security Features	Advanced Edition	Enterprise Edition
Automated password change	X	X
Transparent password change	X	X
Encrypted passwords in memory, storage, during transmission	X	X
Password policy enforcement—automatic password changes	X	X
Password policy enforcement—manual password changes	X	X
Password expiration	X	X
Password token and biometric support	X	X
Basic support for smart cards	X	X
Smart card support		X
Cryptographic data integrity assurance	X	X
Kerberos and Federated Environment Support (ADFS, SAML)		X

Table 10-2.   Security Feature Comparison

Administrator Features	Advanced Edition	Enterprise Edition
Batch credential provisioning	X	X
Integration with user provisioning products	X	X
Windows NT file share support	X	X
Microsoft Active Directory support	X	X
Novell NetWare network share support	X	X
LDAP directory support	X	X
Administration by Active Directory groups	X	X
Citrix Streaming Server support	X	X
Citrix Access Management Console	X	X
Suite-integrated licensing	X	X
Windows Server 2003 64-bit compatibility	X	X
Named user licensing	X	X
Concurrent user licensing (Citrix Password Manager for XenApp only)		X

Table 10-3.   Administrator Feature Comparison

Planning a Deployment

This section helps guide you in determining which Password Manager components to choose in your deployment. Even a basic plan will help you structure your deployment and get the most out of the installation while minimizing user problems.

The following steps provide a basic template for starting a Password Manager installation:

1. Research features that might be implemented in your environment.
2. Choose the devices in the environment where Password Manager will be installed.
3. Prepare devices for the installation.
4. Obtain proper licenses for the product installation.
5. Create a central store and install the Password Manager components with optional features.

6. Create, edit, or review password policies.
7. Create or edit application definitions.
8. Create user configurations based on corporate requirements.
9. Install the agent software on users' desktops or XenApp Servers.
10. Notify users that Password Manager is available to help manage application credentials.

Component Locations

You can install the service, console, and agent software in any of the following allowed combinations or scenarios:

▼ You can install the service and console on the same computer.

NOTE: Do *not* install the service and the agent on the same computer.

■ You can install the agent on any computer or client device in your environment for access to locally installed SSO-enabled applications.

■ You can install the console and Application Definition Tool on any computer in your environment.

■ For testing purposes, you can install the console and the agent on the same computer so that you can verify that changes you make at the console are reflected on the agent.

▲ You can deploy the agent software in a Citrix XenApp environment. In this case, the agent submits or provides credentials for XenApp–published applications only (not applications installed locally on the user workstation or client device).

NOTE: Do *not* install Password Manager or any of the components on a Domain Controller.

Choosing a Central Store Type

The central store can be one of the following:

▼ **Active Directory**   The central store uses the Active Directory environment and objects to store and update Password Manager data.

■ **NTFS network share**   The central store uses a Windows network file share to store the Password Manager data.

▲ **Novell shared folder**   The central store uses a Novell NetWare shared folder to store the Password Manager data.

NOTE: Citrix Password Manager allows you to migrate users from one central store type to another if you later decide that one type is more suitable than the current one used in your environment.

To keep from getting overly verbose, we will focus on the two most popular store type choices: Active Directory and NTFS network share.

Active Directory

An Active Directory central store leverages the benefits of Active Directory user authentication and object administration. For example, you can apply user-specific settings to any level in a domain, organizational unit, group, or user.

In general, you should choose Active Directory as your central store if the following apply:

▼ You already implement Active Directory backup and restore best practices as recommended by Microsoft (although this is not a requirement).

▲ You prefer the high availability that is built into Active Directory to be extended to the central store data.

Advantages

Some of the advantages to using the Active Directory Central Store are:

▼ Active Directory includes built-in failover and redundancy, so additional measures for disaster recovery are not needed.

■ Active Directory replication helps to distribute central store administrative and user data across your enterprise.

▲ No additional hardware is needed when using an Active Directory central store.

Considerations You must extend your schema when using an Active Directory central store, which requires careful planning and implementation. Extending the schema affects the entire forest. You might want to extend the schema and create your Active Directory central store during non–peak usage hours. Your Active Directory replication cycle latency affects how quickly these changes are copied to all domain controllers in the forest. Intersite replication of central store data across large enterprises using WANs requires you to configure replication correctly to reduce latency. (However, intrasite replication typically introduces less latency.)

NTFS Network Share

With an NTFS file share central store, Password Manager creates a shared folder named CITRIXSYNC$ with two subfolders, named People and CentralStoreRoot. The People folder contains a subfolder for each user and includes the appropriate read and write permission properties for the user. The CentralStoreRoot folder contains administrative data.

NTFS Central Store Advantages   The advantages of the NTFS file share for the Central Store are:

▼   You can emulate the look and feel of an Active Directory central store without having to extend your Active Directory schema. Yet, you can take advantage of your existing Active Directory hierarchy or groups.

> **NOTE:**   Associating user configurations to groups is supported only in Active Directory domains that use Active Directory authentication.

■   User data is always up to date because it is stored in a central location to avoid any data replication latency associated with Active Directory.

■   You can load-balance your shares among multiple computers that can each host an NTFS network share for higher availability.

▲   Helps reduce the authentication task workload from your Active Directory environment.

Considerations   When using the NTFS file share for a Central Store, consider the following:

▼   You might need additional hardware to host the central store.

■   You need to back up central store files and folders (including their related permissions) regularly. You also must maintain and implement disaster recovery plans where you replicate files and folders for site recovery.

▲   Your enterprise network topology might require users (and the Password Manager Agent) to transfer user data across one or more WAN links. In this case, consider implementing the Distributed File System technology included as part of Microsoft Windows Server. The Microsoft website http://support.microsoft.com describes the Distributed File System technology in more detail.

Create an Active Directory Central Store

Before creating the AD central store, ensure that the current server is a part of the AD domain and that the user account being used for the configuration is a member of the Schema Administrators and Domain Administrators security groups. Also make sure the AD Schema Master is set to allow updates.

To create the central store, follow these steps:

1.   Open Windows Explorer and select the CD-ROM drive or downloaded install file.

2.   Click Autorun.exe.

3.   Click Step 2: Create your central store (see Figure 10-1).

4.   Click Create your central store in your Active Directory domain (see Figure 10-2).

5. Click Step 1: Extend your Active Directory schema for the new directory objects (see Figure 10-3).

6. Click Yes in the confirmation dialog box. A command window appears.

7. After the schema is extended successfully, press any key to close the command window.

NOTE:　Before you complete the next step, ensure that the schema extension propagated to all domain controllers throughout your Active Directory environment.

---

8. Click Step 2: Create your central store in the extended schema.

9. Click Yes in the confirmation dialog box. A command window appears.

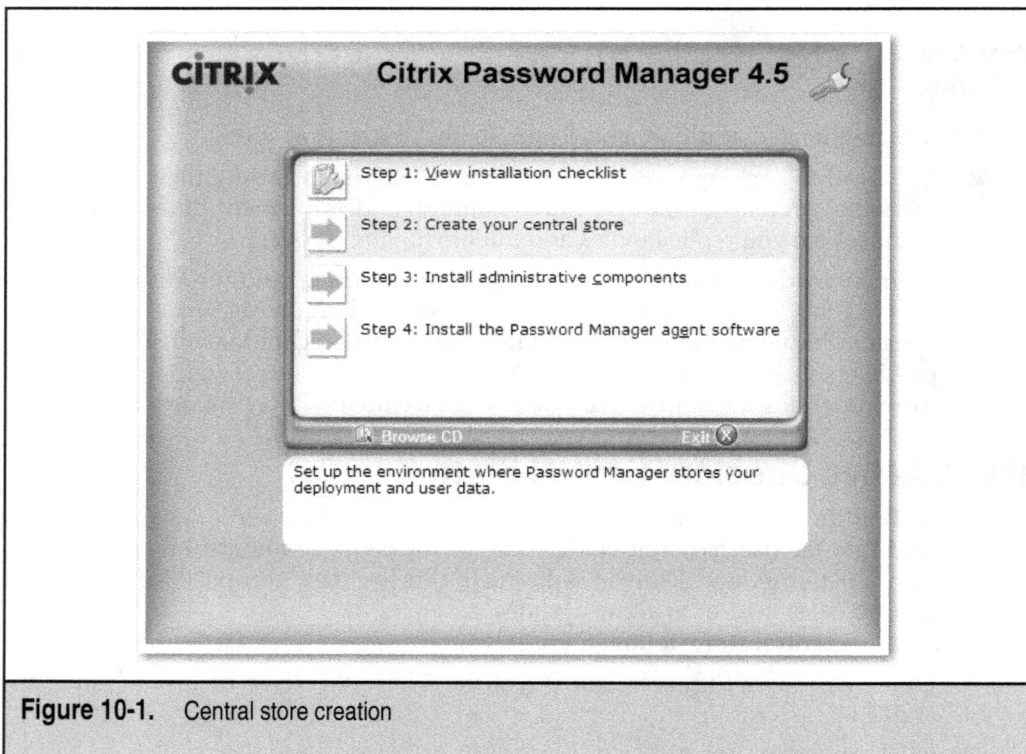

Figure 10-1.　Central store creation

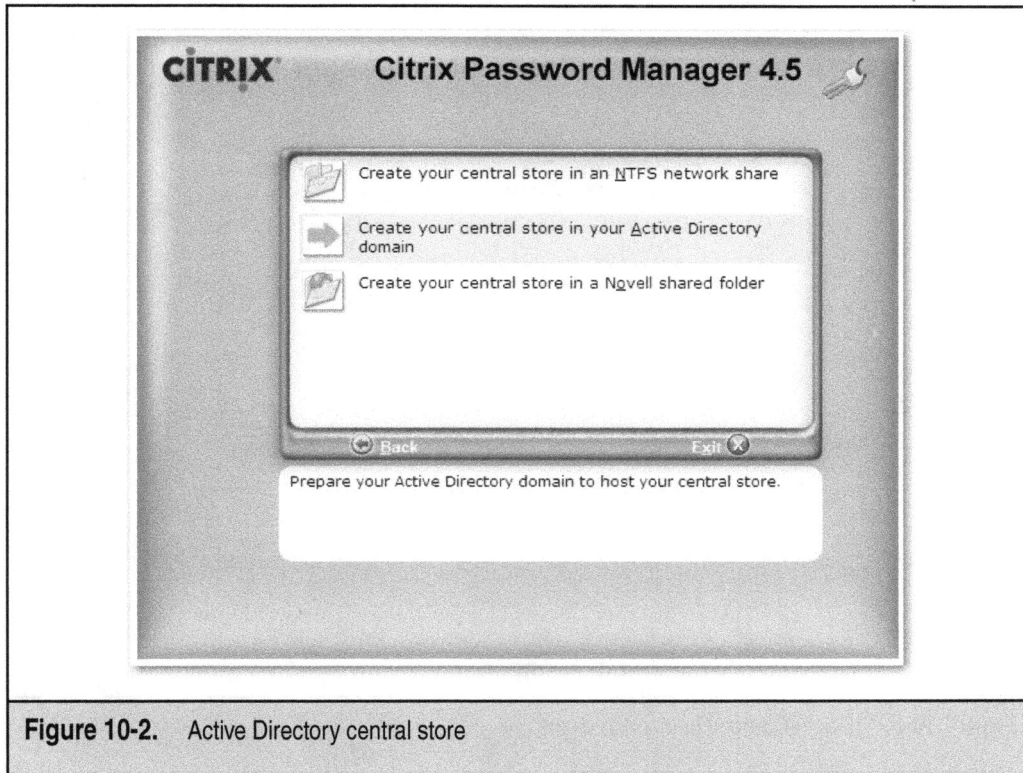

Figure 10-2. Active Directory central store

10. After the schema is extended successfully, press any key to close the command window.

11. The Active Directory central store is now created.

Optionally, the central store can be created using the command line. This allows administrators to customize the installation by passing parameters to the executable. For the Active Directory install, two files must be executed:

▼ **CtxSchemaPrep.exe**   Extends your Active Directory schema for use with Password Manager

▲ **CtxDomainPrep.exe**   Updates the permissions of the Active Directory domain root to allow users to create Password Manager objects under their User object.

For information on creating the other central store types, refer to the *Password Manager Installation Guide*.

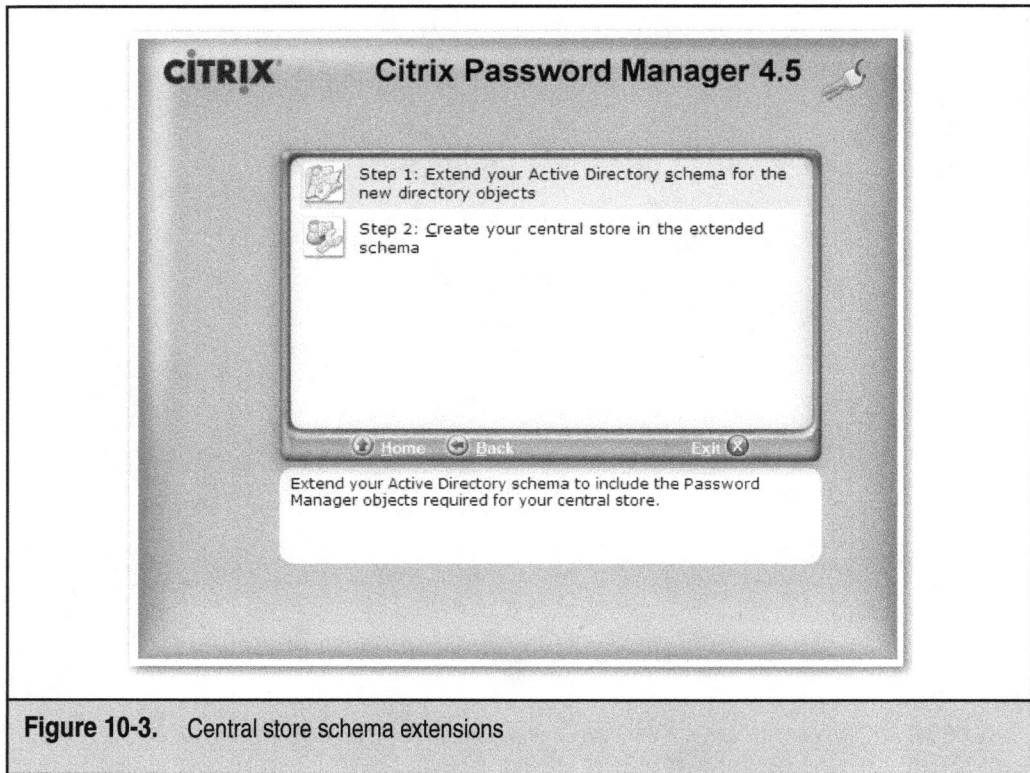

Figure 10-3. Central store schema extensions

Installing and Configuring the Password Manager Service

The Password Manager Service is a web service that uses Secure Sockets Layer (SSL) to encrypt the data shared by the Password Manager Service, the console, and the agent. It uses a dedicated web server to host the *optional* features (modules) included in Password Manager.

The Password Manager Service requires a server authentication certificate from a Certificate Authority (CA) or from a Public Key Infrastructure (PKI) in your organization. An SSL certificate is necessary to ensure secure communication from the service to the agent and console and to verify that the agent and the console are communicating to the correct service.

The certificate must have a common name that matches the server's fully qualified domain name (FQDN) and must be a minimum key length of 1,024. The certificate needs to be installed in the server's local computer certificate store, and this certificate must be installed on the service, console, and agent's workstations.

The Password Manager Service can require up to three service accounts for the various modules of the service.

▼ **Service account** (Required for all services except Credential Synchronization.) Use the existing Network Service or Local Service accounts.

NOTE: If you choose to create a domain account as the service account, you must register a service principal name for this domain account and the service computer in Active Directory by using the setspn.exe utility. A local user account may not be used as the service account. Only the built-in local accounts may be used.

■ **Data proxy account**   Requires read/write access to the central store, and must be a member of the service server's local administrator's group.

▲ **Self-service account**   Required account for the Self-Service Password Reset and Self-Service Account Unlock features.

Installing the Service Modules

Perform a standard default install of the service module.

Configuring the Service Modules

After you have successfully completed the modules install, the Configuration Wizard should launch. The wizard can be run at any time by clicking Start | Programs | Citrix | Password Manager | Service Configuration. The Welcome screen lists any service modules that were installed. Follow these steps:

1. Click Next in the Service Configuration Welcome screen.

2. In the Configure Service screen, specify the following:

   ■ **Connection Setting**   Specify the port number for the service connection (the default port is 443).

   ■ **SSL Certificate**   Select the SSL certificate installed on the service computer to use for communication with client devices. Select the Display Long Name check box to show the LDAP information contained in the certificate.

   ■ **Virtual Host Name**   Use Default Value is selected by default if the SSL certificate name and virtual host name match. The virtual host name must match the SSL certificate name. The virtual host is the machine name visible to users when the certificate was created and might not be the actual machine name. For example, the certificate name might include a wildcard (asterisk character) or an upper- or lowercase domain name that does not match the certificate domain name case.

   ■ **Account Credentials**   Select the local computer account to use for the service.

3. Click Next. The Create Signing Certificate screen appears.

4. Perform one of the following:

   ■ If the wizard detects a signing certificate, click **Next**.

   ■ If the signing certificate does not exist, specify a signing certificate expiration time, in months. The default expiration time is 12 months. Click **Next**.

5. Select the central store you created earlier.

6. Type the user name, password, and domain of the data proxy account used to communicate with the central store and then click Next.

7. Choose from one of the following options:

    ■ **I do not plan to use the Data Integrity module in this environment**   Select this option if you do not require your central store data to be digitally signed and written securely. Select this option also if you did not install the Data Integrity module.

    ■ **I plan to use the Data Integrity module in this environment**   Select this option if you do require your central store data to be digitally signed and written securely and you selected this service module to be installed. Enter the name of the computer hosting the Data Integrity module and the port for the service (the default is 443).

8. Perform one of the following:

    ■ If you installed the Self-Service module, the account credentials screen appears. Type the credentials for this feature and click Next.

    ■ If you did not install the Self-Service module, click Next.

9. Click Finish to commit the service configuration information. Click Finish again to close the Applying Settings dialog boxes.

Installing the Password Manager Console

The Password Manager Console can be installed on any computer on the network. Here are the steps to follow:

1. Open Windows Explorer and select the CD-ROM drive.

2. Click Autorun.exe.

3. Click Step 3: Install administrative components.

4. Click Step 3: Install Password Manager Console.

5. Click Next, accept the license agreement, and click Next again. The Install Type screen appears.

6. Select one or more of the following components to install and click Next:

    ■ **Console**   Select this option to install the console, required to create and manage policies, application definitions, user configurations, and so on.

    ■ **Application Definition Tool**   Select this option to install the tool that enables you to create application definitions without needing to start or use the full console.

NOTE: The Application Definition Tool can be installed directly from the Password Manager Console, or it can be run as a standalone module. You can run the standalone mode of the Application Definition Tool without having to install a console; however, the Application Definition Tool is installed automatically with the Password Manager Console.

- **Citrix Access Suite Console Licensing**   Select this option to help manage your licensing from the console.
- **Citrix Access Suite Console Diagnostics**   Select this option to help Citrix support/troubleshoot console issues.

7. Click Next and then click Finish when the installation is complete.

8. Click Start | Programs | Citrix | Management Consoles | Access Management Console. The Configure and Run Discovery screen appears.

9. Click Next. The Select Products or Components screen appears.

10. Click Citrix Resources to select Configuration Tools and Password Manager and then click Next.

11. Select the central store type that you previously created and click Next.

NOTE: If you created an NTFS network share or Novell shared folder central store, type the UNC path to the share. If you are running discovery as part of an upgrade to Version 4.5 and your central store type is an NTFS network share, you will be prompted to upgrade the central store. Click OK to upgrade or Cancel to exit. If you do not upgrade your central store at this time, you can use previous versions (4.0 and 4.1) only of the console to work with the central store.

12. Perform one of the following:

- If you installed the Data Integrity module and enabled it during the service configuration, select the check box, type the server name and port number in the text fields, and click Next.

- If you installed the Data Integrity module and do not want to enable it, leave the check box cleared and click Next. Make sure you first disabled it through the Service Configuration Wizard on the service computer. The Preview Discovery screen with the configuration summary appears.

13. Click Next to start discovery.

14. When discovery is successful, click Finish.

Installing and Configuring the Agent Software

To obtain credentials and access to local applications, users must run the agent software on their client devices. The agent is designed to run on desktops, laptops, handheld computers, and other devices. For example, mobile users should install the agent on their laptops so that they can use the agent features even when they are not connected to the network (offline mode). Synchronization of user credentials occurs when mobile users reconnect to the network.

When the agent software is installed using the Autorun.exe option provided on the Password Manager CD, the agent software appropriate to the local operating system (32- or 64-bit) is installed. If the agent software is installed manually, the appropriate agent software MSI file for the machine operating system should be used. The 32-bit agent software is on the Password Manager CD in the Agent folder. The 64-bit agent software is in the x64 folder within the Agent folder.

▼ *NOTE:* Before the agent software can be installed, there must be a central store, management console installation, and user configurations.

For testing purposes, both the console and the agent can be installed on the same machine (note that this is not supported on a Windows Vista machine). This provides an efficient way to verify that changes made at the console are reflected on the agent.

▼ *NOTE:* Agent software installed on a client or XenApp device displays a notification icon of a key on a blue background.

An image of the agent software can be installed on a network share using a utility available on the product CD. Go to Autorun | Step 4: Install the Password Manager agent software | Create Password Manager agent installation image. Then follow the wizard prompts. The utility creates an installation image of the Password Manager Agent that contains custom parameters.

Agent Considerations

If you are performing a fresh installation of XenApp Platinum Edition that includes Password Manager, install the Password Manager Agent last.

When you configure or change the location of the license server or any other parameter related to licensing, the changes are not applied to any agent software that is in use within your environment. You must shut down and restart the agent software to apply the changes.

If you plan to use Hot Desktop in your environment as part of your agent installation, see the section "Password Manager's Hot Desktop Feature" later in this chapter.

For all operating systems other than Windows Vista, you will need to restart the device after you install the agent software so that the GINA DLL can be registered and installed. The agent software will not run until the workstation is restarted.

▼ *NOTE:* Graphical Identification and Authentication (GINA) is the Windows component that controls the dialog box that users see when they press the key combination CTRL-ALT-DEL. Installing software that uses a custom GINA DLL might require a certain order to be followed. To ensure that Password Manager is called first during the logon process, make sure that the Password Manager Agent is installed last.

PASSWORD MANAGER OPTIONAL FEATURES

Password Manager has several optional, unique, and powerful features that provide administrative automation, additional security, user automation, and usability. The features we will cover at a high level in this section include the Hot Desktop feature, Account Self-Service, Data Integrity (encryption), and credential provisioning.

Account Self-Service

If you are deploying Password Manager in an Active Directory environment, the Account Self-Service feature is available to allow users to reset their primary password or unlock their Windows domain accounts without the help of administration or help desk personnel.

Self-Service Password Reset allows users who forget their primary password to reset their password and unlock their own accounts. Account Unlock allows users to unlock their domain accounts when a lockout event occurs.

During the enrollment process, users are required to answer a series of security questions created and selected by the administrator. When the users need to reset their password (or if they wish to unlock their password), they must provide correct answers to each of the security questions to be allowed to do so.

Administrators have the flexibility to make certain questions required or optional, but all of the required security questions must be answered correctly in order to proceed with unlocking accounts or resetting password.

Data Integrity

The Data Integrity module ensures that administrative data that passes between the Password Manager Agent and central store is trusted and authorized. The console signs the data using a public and private key with RSA public key cryptography. After the console signs the data, it sends both the data and the signature to the central store. The agent receives the data and signature from the central store during synchronization. The agent then contacts the Password Manager service to obtain a copy of the public key it needs to verify the signature it received from the central store.

NOTE: If you already implement a security framework that protects data in transit, such as IPSec (Internet Protocol Security) or SMB (Server Message Block) signing, you do not need to install the Data Integrity module.

Once the agent has been configured to use Data Integrity to authorize data from the central store, it will never accept data that has failed the data integrity check. If the data does not pass the check, an error is logged in the event logs and the user is notified to contact their administrator.

Provisioning

Credential provisioning is a tool for the automation of the initial credential setup process intended to aid in the setup of multiple users. It uses information about your environment to create a template that you can use to add, remove, or change credential information in your central store. For example, if you have a significant number of users and applications that you need to set up, simply create an application definition for the application and use credential provisioning to add the credentials for all users who will use the application.

Whether you are rolling out a new installation of Password Manager, adding several hundred new users and new applications, or simply clearing out unneeded information, credential provisioning gives you the ability to complete these tasks quickly.

Summary of Provisioning Tasks

To manipulate credential information in your central store for SSO-enabled applications contained in user configurations, you must perform the following tasks:

1. Install the Provisioning module of the Password Manager service.
2. Create a user configuration that uses the provisioning service.
3. Generate a credential provisioning template.
4. Populate the template with user credential data and select a command to run.
5. Process your provisioning data.

CAUTION: The XML file you use to provision credentials contains highly sensitive user-related information. Citrix recommends that you delete the file or move the file to a secure location when credential provisioning is completed.

After the credentials are added, removed, or modified in the central store, they are ready for use in your environment. When users start the agent software, the credentials are recognized by SSO-enabled applications and made available to your users. First-time users of the agent software do not need to perform initial credential setup if you added all credential information to the central store by the process of credential provisioning. If you need to manipulate the credentials of many users, consider using the Credential Provisioning Software Development Kit (SDK) located in the \Support\Provisioning folder on your product CD.

NOTE: Adding, changing, or removing credentials from the central store can consume a large amount of system resources. Citrix recommends that you perform credential provisioning during off-peak hours.

Generating a Credential Provisioning Template

A provisioning template is an XML document that contains information about the applications included in your selected user configuration:

▼ Application group
■ Application definition name and globally unique identifier number (GUID)
▲ User information such as user name and password

It also includes add, remove, and modify commands that you use when you import the edited template into Password Manager.

To generate a credential provisioning template, perform the following tasks:

1. Click Start | Programs | Citrix | Management Consoles | Access Management Console.

2. Expand the Password Manager node and select User Configurations.

3. Select a user configuration.

4. In the Common Tasks area, click Generate Provisioning Template.

5. In the Generate Provisioning Template dialog box, type a name for the template and click Save.

6. Click OK to confirm that a template in XML file format was created.

The resulting template includes sample command information and specific information about the selected user configuration.

Credential Synchronization (Account Association)

In most cases, each user has one Windows account allowing them to access the domain and applications. Password Manager binds their credential store to that account. However, sometimes users may have more than one account that they use to access applications. In these cases, Password Manager can use Account Association to automatically synchronize credentials between both accounts.

Password Manager's Hot Desktop Feature

What do hospitals, warehouses, banks, schools, and training facilities all have in common? All of them share the same type of user base. Many medical, financial, and educational facilities have an access scenario that supports many users sharing one piece of hardware for daily workloads. The problem with this access method is that it does not support fast user switching. That is to say, it takes too long for one user to log out of a machine and the next user to log into that same machine in order to get some work done.

Password Manager's Hot Desktop feature provides a unique solution to this problem. Hot Desktop provides users a fast, secure, and efficient means to rapidly log in and out of a common workstation by allowing the user to quickly authenticate to the workstation using a familiar Windows GINA login dialog box, use SSO-enabled applications through Password Manager credentials, and securely log out of their session, thus allowing the next user the same access and speed.

Hot Desktop Shared Account

The purpose of Hot Desktop is simple—create a common or shared account for the workstation to act as the primary account. This account will have all the applications and settings in common with all the users sharing this machine. For instance, we can create an account that will log onto the workstation at bootup. Within this account's login we can configure all the applications that are shared by all the users working on this machine, such as Microsoft Office 2007, CRM, and an Enterprise Resource Management (ERP) package. We will set the ERP package to auto-start.

Next, the user logs into this machine and their session will "run on top" of the already running session. Hot Desktop simply manages the login differences between the already running session and the new user's session, and then it combines the two for a seamless interface for this user. Once the first user is finished working, their settings are logged out of the machine and the "common" session is restored to the "startup" state, awaiting the next user's login. Because each user only has to load the session differences between the shared account and their own, login and logout time are dramatically reduced.

Here are some guidelines for creating the shared account:

▼ Ensure that the account does not belong to the local or domain administrators group.

■ The shared account can be a local or domain account. Any privileges available to the shared account are available to the Hot Desktop user only for those applications you specify.

■ The Hot Desktop installation process verifies the logon name and domain of the shared account. When you create this account, ensure that you select the Password Never Expires option. Do not use expired credentials.

■ Ensure that the account has limited privileges. Limit permissions to Hot Desktop use only.

■ Specify the domain name to which the workstation belongs using the domain's NetBIOS name and not the fully qualified domain name (FQDN). If you are using a local account, specify the host name of the device.

▲ As a best practice, name the shared account "Hot Desktop." This ensures that users see the message "Logoff Hot Desktop" when they log off from a Windows environment. If you have more than one group of Hot Desktop users, you can name each shared account accordingly (for example, "Hot Desktop Marketing," "Hot Desktop Accounting," and so on).

Applications that are used in a Hot Desktop environment must meet the following requirements:

▼ Applications that require user credentials must be defined for use with Password Manager in application definitions and user configurations.

■ Applications that are launched by the shared account must be able to run in the Windows interactive environment. In this scenario, the applications (and the Hot Desktop users) must have access to the user profiles, network shares, and other resources associated with the shared account.

■ Applications must shut down cleanly when sent the request to do so. Hot Desktop terminates applications using procedures similar to a logoff from a Windows interactive session. Graceful application termination is particularly important in a Hot Desktop environment because the application might be used many times before the workstation or client device is shut down.

▲ Any application that must save sensitive data in the user's profile or needs access to the user's profile for settings should run as the Hot Desktop User account. Applications that can share "community" configuration information can run as a shared account.

CHAPTER 11

Citrix Access Gateway Enterprise

As discussed in previous chapters, users are moving further and further away from applications and corporate resources. More and more users are working remotely from home, hotels, branch offices, and the local coffee shop. With a new movement to gain mobility and stay operational, companies are faced with the challenge of delivering applications to their employees no matter the location or the device of access. Some delivery methods are easier to accommodate than others. These days you can find signs in shops advertising high-speed Internet almost anywhere, but what about at the beach or in the mountains? Sure, if you have high-speed Internet access and a portable powerhouse capable of sending a person to Mars, this should be a no-brainer, right? But what if the employee is in a really, really remote and secluded vacation spot with minimal Internet access and a small form factor device such as a Treo or other mobile operating system device? How do we deliver applications to it? How do we keep it safe and secure and ensure that proprietary company information does not end up on a printer at the hotel for all to see?

There are many ways to provide on-demand application delivery to the remote workforce. Choosing which method depends on many factors—connection speed, location of the users, the type of device the user is connecting with, and whether the device is a corporate asset or a public kiosk. In the past the most important factor used to be the location of the end users. Now with today's demand for remote connectivity, *all* of these factors must be considered and controlled. IT administrators now have complex sets of requirements for allowing users access to corporate information safely and securely over the public wire.

This chapter focuses on the state-of-the-art delivery of applications and corporate resources using the Citrix Access Gateway Enterprise Edition.

THE CITRIX ACCESS GATEWAY ENTERPRISE SOLUTION

As the designated replacement for the legacy Secure Gateway/Web Interface (SG/WI) solution and the Standard and Advanced editions, the Citrix Access Gateway Enterprise (AG-E) is a quantum leap in secure access technology, combining the benefits of an SSL proxy for Citrix ICA traffic with universal SSL VPN technology to provide secure access to Citrix services, internal file shares, and internal web resources. The AG-E is a hardened network appliance that delivers secure applications and access to corporate data over the public Internet or private SSL VPN using Citrix's policy-based access control called SmartAccess.

Different connection methods make configuration and management difficult for the administrator and users. The Access Gateway Enterprise does not have this problem because it supports most applications and protocols through a single method—a much simpler and more cost-effective approach.

For internal LAN/WAN users, securing access to the servers (above and beyond native ICA encryption) is often not needed; thus a simple deployment of Web Interface for Citrix XenApp (WI) or Web Interface for PN Agent with the appropriate ICA client provides a full solution. However, for home-based or traveling users (external users accessing the network via the public Internet), Citrix has three Access Gateway editions that enable delivery of applications and resources through a familiar web interface with Standard edition, the new NAVUI portal page of the Advanced edition, and the built-in portal pages of the Enterprise edition.

A secure application delivery solution, for the purpose of this book, can refer to any of the aforementioned methods available for creating a web-based application delivery solution: the Access Gateway Standard Edition, Model 2010 (a simple built-in portal-like page working with or without Web Interface); the Citrix Access Gateway Advanced, Model 2010 (the Access Gateway appliance with Advanced Access Controls [AAC]); or the Access Gateway Enterprise Edition, Model 7000 or higher (an appliance based on the NetScaler platform with integrated components of the Advanced Access Control built into the OS). The Secure Gateway/Web Interface (SG/WI) configuration is a "no-cost" (no additional licensing) feature available for Citrix XenApp. It has only minor changes since the Presentation Server 3.0 version and is still supported in the Platinum edition at the time of this writing.

Key Features, Benefits, and Capabilities

The following is a list of some of the key features of the Access Gateway Enterprise Edition:

▼ Provides remote access for the most demanding and complex environments that require increased scalability and/or performance.

■ Offers high availability for uninterrupted access to critical applications and resources.

■ The tightest level of integration and control of remotely delivered Citrix XenApp applications and data through SmartAccess. Citrix XenApp–published applications are accessible from within the NAVUI's page, allowing users to quickly access and launch published applications.

■ The natural replacement for existing Citrix XenApp customers who leverage the Secure Gateway.

■ Enterprise-class SSL VPN features include client-side cache clean-up, detailed auditing, and policy-based access control for web and server applications.

■ Remote users can work with files on shared network drives, access e-mail and intranet sites, and run applications just as if they are working inside of your organization's firewall.

■ Certified to meet government and commercial security standards such as Federal Information Processing Standard (FIPS) 140-2 and ICSA.

■ Supports the Access Gateway universal license (included in XenApp Platinum Edition) Access Gateway architecture.

■ Supports most applications and protocols, including Voice Over IP.

■ Industry-standard encryption that secures and protects information with SSL/TLS encryption.

■ Desk-like access provides users with the same network and application access as if they are physically connected to the network.

■ Advanced XenApp integration using endpoint analysis and client location to control which published applications are available to the user. This feature extends

SmartAccess to XenApp, including the use of Access Control filters to control local client drive mapping, clipboard operations, and local printer mapping.

■ Multiple logon points are available through a single gateway appliance, which allows for different authentication methods, different branding, and a different user base through various logon points.

■ Network resources enable direct SSL virtual private network (VPN) connectivity to servers, services, and networks within the corporate LAN.

■ Browser-only access with any web browser on any device to websites, files, and e-mail.

▲ Secure corporate e-mail access over the Internet through a web-based user interface. Allows users to securely access Microsoft Outlook and Lotus Notes in real time and synchronize information for offline use. Enables secure access to corporate network file shares over the Internet through a web-based user interface.

Topology

The Access Gateway Enterprise can run in three modes when providing users access to the data center:

▼ **Pure Secure Gateway**   VPN authentication is off and the users access the applications through Web Interface in direct mode.

■ **Secure Gateway with Single Sign-On**   VPN authentication is on and the users access applications through Web Interface in indirect mode with their credentials passed through to Web Interface for access to applications.

▲ **Secure Gateway with SmartAccess**   VPN authentication is on, both pre-authorization and post-authorization End Point Analysis (EPA) scans are enabled and configured, users access applications through Web Interface in indirect mode with the Access Gateway Enterprise mode enabled, and XenApp is configured for filters and access policies (see Figure 11-1).

Architecture

The following are the core components of the Access Gateway:

▼ VPN virtual servers

■ Authentication, Authorization, and Accounting servers

■ Client plug-ins or the Secure Access Client

▲ Internal resources to be accessed

Virtual Servers

The Access Gateway virtual server is an internal entity that is a representative of all the configured services available to clients. The virtual server is also the access point through which clients access these services.

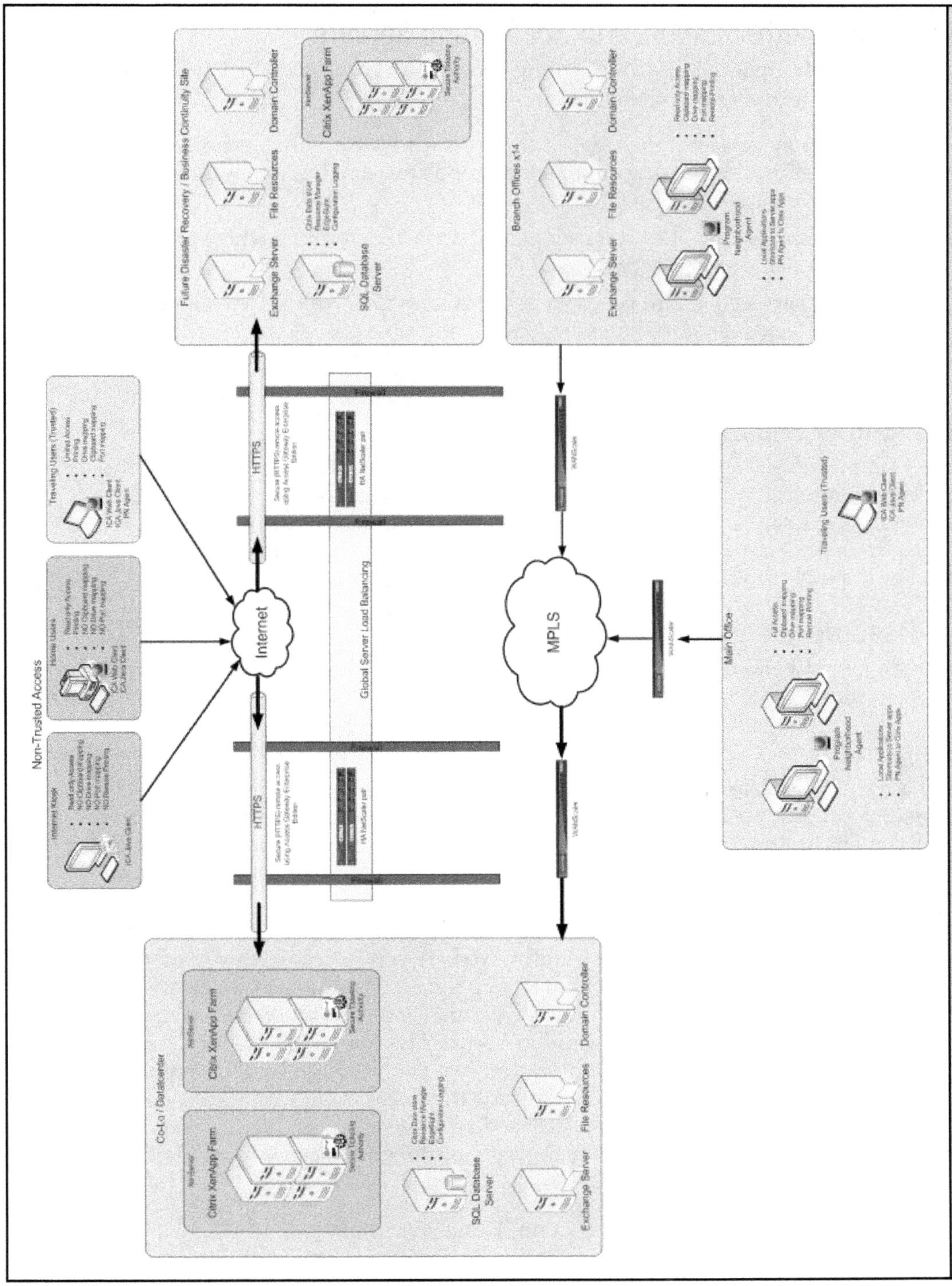

Figure 11-1. Access Gateway Enterprise topology with Smart Access

Authentication, Authorization, and Accounting Servers

Authentication, Authorization, and Accounting services are processes that the Access Gateway uses to perform various client tasks:

▼ **Authentication service**   Provides the Access Gateway with user name and password verification—using either a local repository on the Access Gateway or externally using LDAP or RADIUS.

■ **Authorization service**   Defines user permissions to determine which resources a given user is allowed to access.

▲ **Accounting service**   Maintains data about Access Gateway activity, including user logon events, resource access instances, and operational errors. This information can be stored on the Access Gateway or an external server.

Client Plug-in or Secure Access Client

The Access Gateway uses a plug-in or the Secure Access Client to connect users to resources. Depending on the client's operating system or the Access Gateway configuration, the client's browser can use one of two types of plug-in. For Windows clients, the default plug-in is an ActiveX plug-in. For other clients, such as Macintosh OS X and Linux (and optionally for Windows users), there is a Java applet plug-in.

Internal Resources

These include all networked services to be accessed using the Access Gateway, such as file servers, applications, and websites.

Licensing

All three Citrix Access Gateway editions are now licensed together in the new Universal License file. The Access Gateway Universal license is a version-less and edition-less license entitlement for the Access Gateway product line. It can be applied to any edition of Access Gateway or any model of Access Gateway appliance to enable a relevant functionality scheme based on the number of concurrent users of XenApp Platinum Edition. The Access Gateway Universal license allows customers to simply purchase the needed number of concurrent remote access users and move between Access Gateway editions as their needs change simply by purchasing new appliances. The license files for the Access Gateway Standard and Enterprise Editions are installed directly on the appliance, whereas the Access Gateway Advanced Edition license files are stored on the Citrix license server along with the XenApp Platinum licenses. Even though the Platinum edition includes the concurrent connection licenses for the Access Gateway scenarios, the Access Gateway appliance itself must be purchased separately.

When you receive your Access Gateway Enterprise appliance, licensing occurs in the following order:

1. Receive the License Authorization Code (LAC) via e-mail.

2.   Configure the Access Gateway with the host name.

3.   Allocate the Access Gateway licenses from MyCitrix.com. Use the host name to bind the licenses to the appliance during the allocation process.

4.   Generate the license entitlement and download the license file.

5.   Install the license file on the Access Gateway.

The license is installed on the Access Gateway in the /nsconfig/license directory. This license defines the maximum number of concurrent users that can log onto the appliance. User licenses are locked to the appliance host name or FQDN. The host name needs to be changed in three places:

▼   On the Access Gateway using the command-line interface

■   In the rc.conf file

▲   In the hosts file

The rc.conf and hosts files must always be in the /nsconfig directory. If these two files are not in the directory, they must be created using a text editor, such as Vi.

SECURE APPLICATION DELIVERY—SMARTACCESS

Of all the trends leading organizations to on-demand computing, one of the most significant is the dependency on IT staff to make everything easy to deploy and intuitive for end users. This dependency leads to the necessity of making any software deployment obvious and void of any required end-user instructions. Therefore, the largest cost savings of on-demand access is in the actual delivery of the application. Although Citrix allows a user to manually configure an ICA session, and even allows an administrator to automatically push an ICA application icon to users' desktops, the most recognized interface for users today is still a browser-based interface. The web browser has become the ubiquitous access center—even the not-so-savvy end user has seen a web interface, and a significant number of the working population spends some portion of their day clicking web icons or blue hyperlinks as well as typing URL addresses.

Although Citrix provides several automated ways to deliver application and corporate resources to end users, the combination of the Web Interface and Secure Gateway, and their successor, the Citrix Access Gateway appliance, provide a secure web-based deployment that continues to revolutionize application delivery.

INSTALLING ACCESS GATEWAY ENTERPRISE EDITION

The installation procedures in the following sections are presented as a high-level sequence of events. They are neither all inclusive nor intended to accurately detail configuration processes and procedures for Access Gateway Enterprise Edition (AG-E) with SmartAccess. Implementation of AG-E in a production environment requires extensive planning and a full understanding the business's access strategy and needs, particularly when the full capabilities of the Citrix Access Gateway are to be effectively leveraged.

Capabilities such as endpoint analysis and policy-based access based on identity, endpoint scan results, roles, and similar variables should never be undertaken without a carefully planned process and specific requirements and goals. Administrators are encouraged to read the complete design and implementation guidance for AG-E available on Citrix's Web site or from a trusted advisor before proceeding with any CAG implementation. Once a full understanding is achieved, administrators should work to define a corporate access strategy.

Component Systems Requirements

The Citrix Access Gateway Enterprise Edition (AG-E) architecture requires a few basic building blocks: an Access Gateway Enterprise Appliance, Model 7000 or higher (AG-E); a Web Interface (WI) server, and a XenApp server farm running the Secure Ticketing Authority (STA) component of a XenApp server.

Citrix Access Gateway

This is a Citrix Access Gateway Enterprise 7000 series (or higher) appliance running version 8.0 or higher of the OS.

Citrix XenApp with Secure Ticketing Authority (STA)

At least one XenApp farm server (preferably the infrastructure server) must be designated as the STA. It is a good idea to have more than one server listed in case that server is down for maintenance and no one will be able to log in. However, do not list *all* the servers in your farm because this can cause an unnecessary increase in traffic and slow down application enumeration.

Web Interface

Web Interface (WI) integration requires Web Interface version 4.5 and higher as well as the corresponding Access Management Console. With the Access Gateway solution, Web Interface servers are no longer required in the DMZ to provide remote allocation delivery for the organization. The only requirement for a WI server is Windows Server 2003, Internet Information Services 6.0, .NET Framework 2.0, Visual J# .NET 2.0, and ASP.NET.

Domain Services (LDAP)

Even though there are a number of ways to authenticate a user to the AG-E, for the example that follows, we will be using LDAP. In order to use LDAP, you will need a domain account with admin rights to communicate to the domain for authentication.

Clients

The purpose of the Access Gateway is to provide remote users with access to applications and internal resources.

Basic connectivity to the Citrix Access Gateway requires only the familiar ICA clients and two types of plug-ins: an ActiveX plug-in, which transparently intercepts traffic to be tunneled to the internal network, and a Java applet plug-in, which listens on pre-configured application ports using the client's loopback interface to manage the client's connections.

Supported versions of the ICA client are Citrix XenApp Client version 9.2 and greater (current version as of this writing is 10.2) and the Client for Java version 9.3 and greater (current version as of this writing is 9.5). This allows logon and enumeration of the resources provided by the Access Gateway Enterprise and to applications served up through the Access Gateway Enterprise via Web Interface and a XenApp farm. The following are the system requirements for the ActiveX and Java client plug-ins.

The ActiveX plug-in supports the following Windows operating systems:

▼ Windows 2000

■ Windows XP Home Edition

■ Windows XP Professional

▲ Windows Server 2003

The ActiveX plug-in also requires the following:

▼ Java Runtime Environment (JRE) 1.4.2_05 or later

▲ Internet Explorer 5.5 or higher

The Java client plug-in requires the following:

▼ Macintosh OS X and Java Runtime Environment (JRE) 1.4.2 with Safari 1.2 (v125) browser

■ Linux distributions that have JRE 1.3 and above with Mozilla 1.2.1+ or Netscape 7.1 browsers

■ Windows 2000

■ Windows XP

▲ Windows Server 2003

JRE 1.3.1_01+ is required when using the following browsers:

▼ Internet Explorer

■ Netscape

▲ Firefox 1.5 (only)

The Secure Access Client

This client is required to support true VPN access to IP networks. The Secure Access Client acts as a proxy between the client computer and the Access Gateway appliance. The Secure Access Client can be distributed as a desktop application for Microsoft Windows or Linux operating systems, or it can be downloaded and installed automatically when users enter the secure web address of the Access Gateway appliance and a logon point in a web browser. In addition to the administrative rights previously stipulated for Windows 2000 and XP users, Linux users must have the TCL and TK packages installed to use the Secure Access Client.

Citrix Access Gateway

Configuring the AG-E is a multistep process. The CAG must be set up for basic management and connectivity via the serial console, and then additional settings are configured via the Administration Portal. The AG-E can be installed on the network infrastructure and works with other products such as load balancers, firewalls, and routers.

We recommend installing the AG-E in a DMZ (demilitarized zone) in between two networks—a public network and a private network. It can also be used to partition two LAN segments to provide access and security for instance between a wired network and wireless network or a data network and voice network.

Prior to configuring the AG-E, make sure the appliance is installed on the network and has access to all the network segments involved. Also, ensure the external servers that will be used for authentication, authorization, and accounting are configured; the network has a DNS server for name resolution to provide correct Access Gateway client functionality; and the AG-E has a certificate that is signed by a trusted Certificate Authority (CA).

Let's Get Physical

Here are the steps to physically install and prepare the Access Gateway for configuration:

1. Secure your Access Gateway appliance in the server rack.
2. Connect the Ethernet cables.
   a. Connect one cable to a port labeled 1/1, 1/2, 1/3, 1/4, 1/5, or 1/6.
   b. Connect another cable to an available port labeled 1/1, 1/2, 1/3, 1/4, 1/5, or 1/6.

NOTE: If your configuration requires fewer than eight ports, any of the eight available ports can be used. We recommend disabling the unused ports. Disabling unused ports is mandatory in a high-availability configuration. To disable network interfaces, at a command prompt type **disable interface <idl**, where **id** is the interface label, such as 1/2.

3. Connect a computer to the serial console on the front of the appliance. The terminal emulation application must have a baud rate and character format configured to 9600 baud, 8 data bits, 1 stop bit, and no parity.
4. Turn on the appliance.
5. Connect a computer to the Access Gateway using the serial console cable.

6. Start a terminal emulation application (such as HyperTerminal) and set the following:

   a. The port to which you connected the serial cable (usually COM1).

   b. 9600 bits per second (bps).

   c. 8 data bits.

   d. Parity set to None.

   e. Stop bits set to 1.

   f. Flow control set to None.

7. Change the root password by typing

   ```
   set system user nsroot <newpasswd1>
   ```

   where *newpasswd1* is the new password for the Access Gateway.

8. Add a mapped IP address by typing

   ```
   add ns ip <mappedIP> <mappedIPSubnet> -type mip
   ```

   where *mappedIP* is the IP address you have assigned for the mapped IP address, and *mappedIPSubnet* is the subnet mask.

9. Set the default gateway by typing the following:

   ```
   add network route 0.0.0.0 0.0.0.0 <defaultGatewayIPaddress>
   ```

   This command tells the Access Gateway to route packets sent to the host at 0.0.0.0, which is not directly reachable, to the default gateway IP address.

10. Set the Access Gateway IP address by typing the following:

    ```
    set ns config -ipaddress <AccessGatewayIPaddress>
    -netmask <AccessGatewaySubnetMask>
    ```

11. Save your configuration by typing the following:

    ```
    save ns config
    ```

12. Restart the Access Gateway by typing the following:

    ```
    reboot
    ```

You have now successfully physically installed your Access Gateway appliance and performed the basic setup. The Access Gateway Enterprise can be configured using both the Configuration Utility and a command-line interface. For the remainder of this chapter, we will be using the Configuration Utility and point out key command-line references.

The Access Gateway Configuration Utility

To set up the Access Gateway to use the Configuration Utility, you need a computer on the same network as the appliance. You must be an administrator or part of the administrators' group on the computer to configure the Access Gateway.

Once the basic setup is complete on console, plug in a network cable between you and the AG-E. Give your machine an IP address in the same subnet as the AG-E's IP address. Open up a web browser and browse to the IP address of the Access Gateway previously configured using the HTTPS protocol, as shown next. For example, if the IP address of the AG-E is set to 172.20.1.2, type the following in a browser:

```
https://172.20.1.2
```

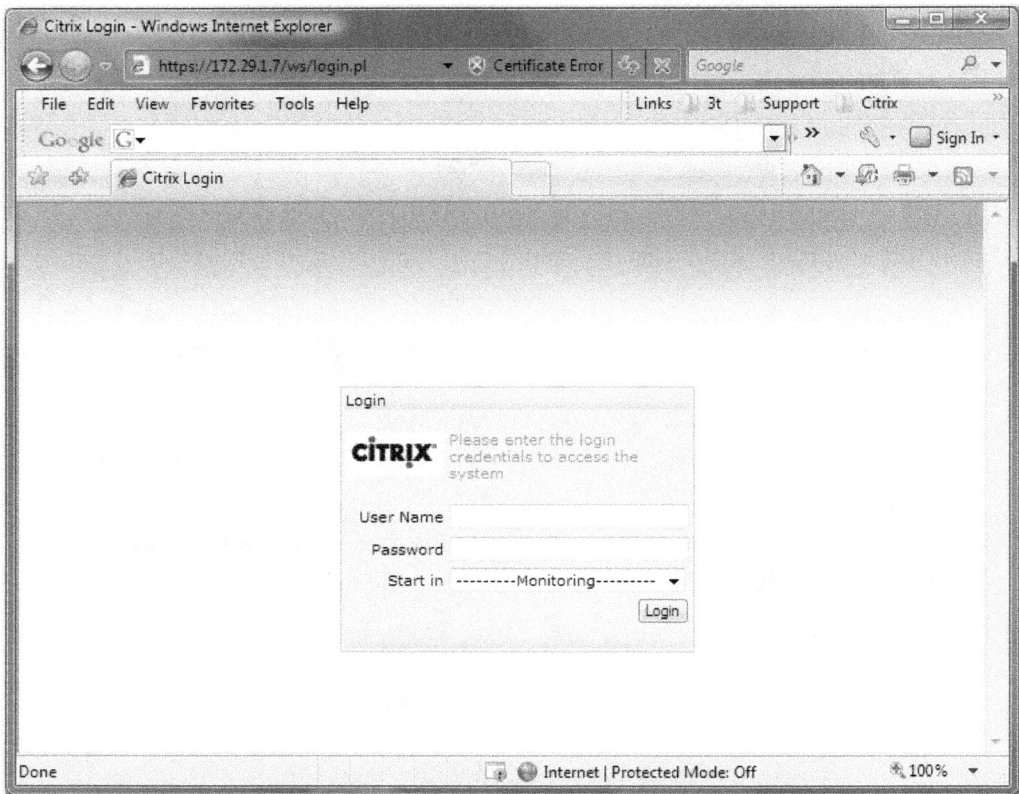

Log in using the username nsroot and the password you assigned earlier. By default you will start at the monitoring page of the utility. The Configuration Utility home page is the central location for quick access to the system documentation and management utilities. From this location, you can launch the Configuration Utility to configure the system and the Statistical Utility to monitor the system.

When you click the System Configuration Utility, you are presented with two choices: the Applet Client and the Web Start Client. In order to avoid this screen in the future, at the login prompt simply use the pull-down menu to chose to log in directly to the Configuration Utility, as shown next. This will get you right into where you need to be to begin building virtual servers for remote access.

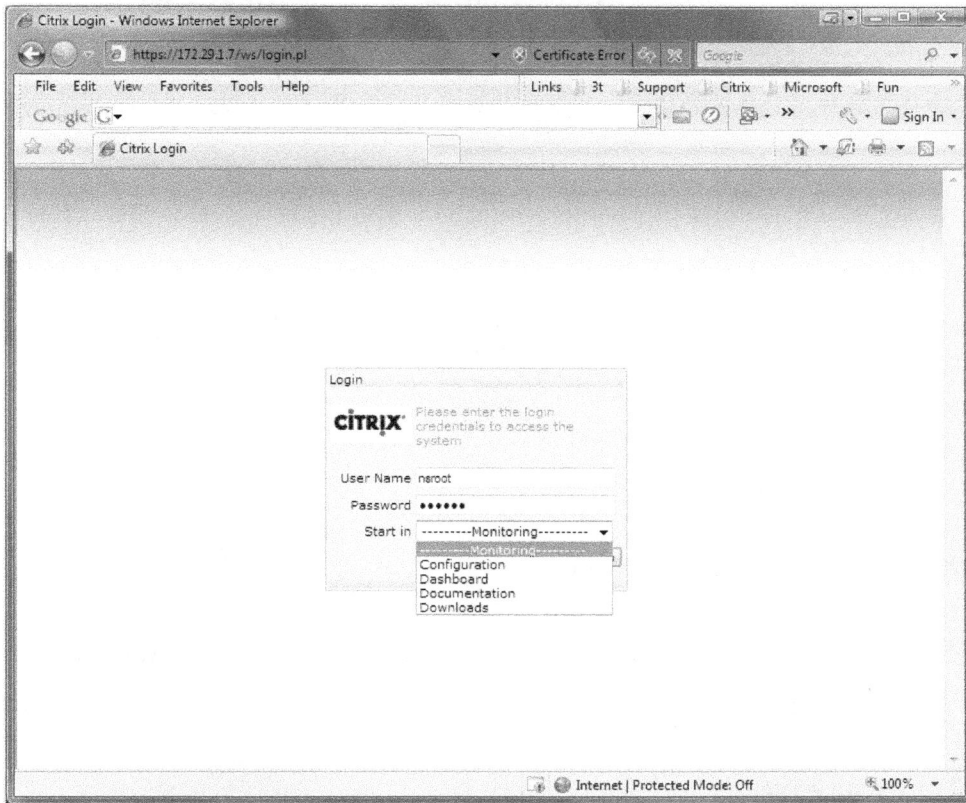

The Access Gateway Enterprise Configuration Utility, shown next, opens up and allows you to make configuration changes, perform maintenance, and view system information.

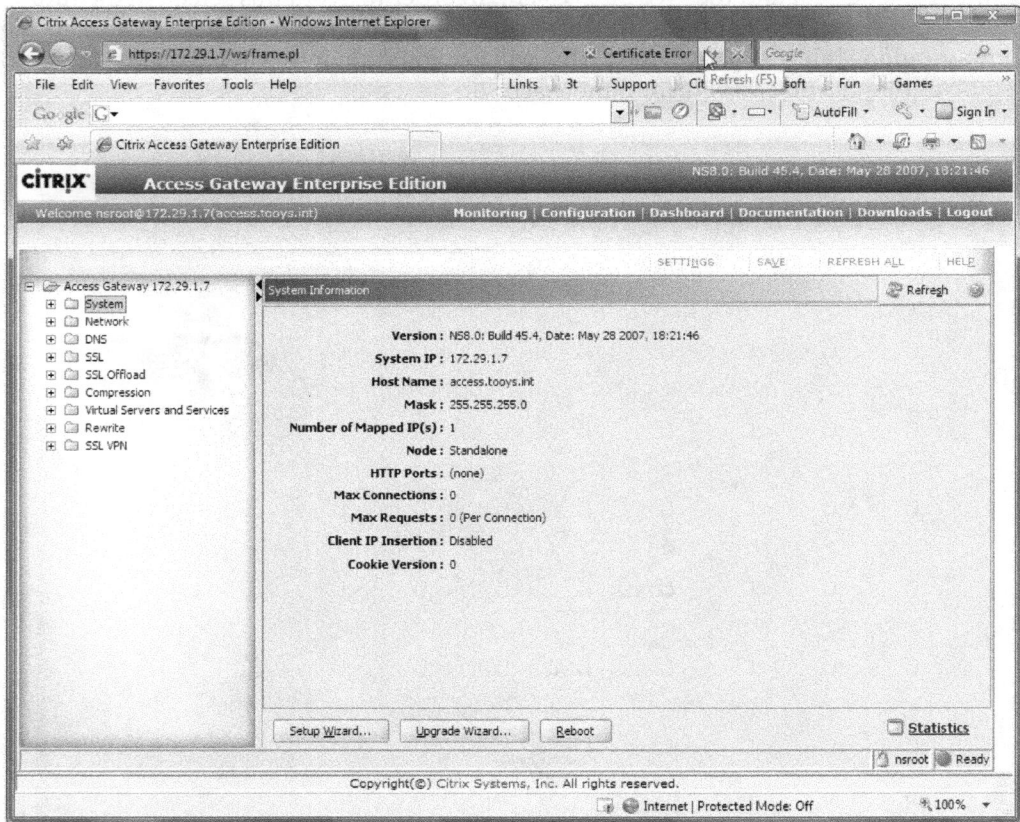

Once you are logged in, use the SSL VPN Policy Wizard to configure the following items:

▼ Virtual servers

■ Certificates

■ DNS and WINS servers

▲ Authentication

Licensing

Before users can access resources through the Access Gateway, a valid license file must be installed. Unlike the other editions of the Access Gateway, the Enterprise edition requires two licenses: a platform license and concurrent user license (CCU). Both must be installed on the appliance.

The platform license is freely available from MyCitrix.com and enables the SSL VPN functionality of the appliance. The platform license is already installed on the appliance for versions 8.0 and higher.

NOTE: If you are upgrading from versions prior to 8.0, you will need to install the platform license immediately after the upgrade to 8.0 or above.

The concurrent user license or Access Gateway Universal License is obtained through license fulfillment and activation using the Citrix Activation System at MyCitrix.com. This license enables the appliance to support a specified number of users through the SSL VPN or XenApp applications.

Access Gateway Universal Licenses can be obtained as a standalone license file purchase or are included with a XenApp Platinum purchase.

Once you have obtained the required license files, in the Access Gateway Configuration Utility, select System | Licenses and click the Update License button at the bottom of the screen. Browse to locate the platform license file and click OK. When prompted to restart, choose No. Next, click Browse again and locate the license file you obtained from Citrix Activation System on MyCitrix.com. Click OK. This time when prompted to restart, choose Yes.

After the reboot, under the System | Licenses node, you should now see the SSL VPN field with a green checkmark and the Maximum SSL VPN Users Allowed field equal to the number of users that were allocated on the MyCitrix site.

Obtaining an SSL Certificate for the Citrix Access Gateway Enterprise

In order to obtain a certificate for the AG-E, you must complete the Certificate Signing Request (CSR) and send that off to a third-party Certificate Authority (CA) and get a signed certificate for use on the AG-E for securing communications through the Access Gateway. This secure communication is for the SSL VPN connections as well as the SSL relay for the published applications and resources through the AG-E's portal.

To create a CSR on the Access Gateway, follow these steps:

1. Launch the Configuration Utility and log in (out of the box, the default user name and password are nsroot and nsroot, respectively)

2. Navigate to CA Tools and in the right pane under Create Certificate/Keys, click Create RSA Key and enter the following information:

   ■ **Key Filename** *FQDNSiteName*.key
   ■ **Key Size** 1024
   ■ **PEM Algorithm Encoding** DES3
   ■ **PEM Passphrase** *SitePEMPassPhrase*

Verify the passphrase. Then click Create and click Close.

3. Click Create Certificate Request (CSR) and enter the following information:

- **Request File Name**   *FQDNSiteName*.csr.
- **Key File Name**   *FQDNSiteName*.key. (Click browse and select it from the list.)
- **PEM Passphrase**: *SitePEMPassPhrase.* (Do this only if the certificate is in PEM format.)

4. Under Distinguished Name Fields, type the information:

   - **Common Name**   The fully qualified domain name (FQDN) of the Access Gateway

   - **Organization Name**   Your company name

   - **State/Province Name**   Your state or province

   - **Country Name**   The country in which you reside

   - **Email Address**   The address to which the Certificate Authority returns the signed certificate

5. Click **Create** and then click **Close**.

   A digital ID, also known as a *digital certificate* or *SSL certificate*, is the electronic equivalent of a passport or business license. It is a credential issued by a trusted authority that individuals or organizations can present electronically to prove their identity or their right to access information.

   When a Certification Authority (such as VeriSign, Thawte, or GEOTrust) issues digital IDs, the CA verifies that the owner is who they say they are. Just as when a government issues a passport and officially vouches for the identity of the holder, when a CA gives your business a digital certificate, it is putting its name behind your right to use your company name and web address.

   The processes for obtaining a certificate may differ slightly between CAs, but the steps are basically the same. Most CAs will include a variety of services and extras with their certificate offerings. These services may include 40- or 128-bit SSL (Global Server) IDs; business authentication; and protection against loss resulting from the theft, corruption, impersonation, or loss of a certificate. Be sure to check with each potential CA for details on its individual services and choose the options that best meet the needs of your organization.

   In order to complete the certificate request, organizations may need to provide the following documentation to the Certificate Authority:

   - **Proof of organization**   Before a Secure Server ID can be issued, the CA will need to verify that your company or organization has the legal right to conduct business under the name you specify in your enrollment request. Documentation may include a business license, the registration of a trade name, or a Dun & Bradstreet number. If you have a Dun & Bradstreet D-U-N-S Number registered for your organization, it may help expedite the verification process and issuance of your Secure Server ID.

NOTE: Your organization's legal name must match the organization name in your enrollment request. Otherwise, the CA will be unable to authenticate your organization.

   - **Proof of domain name**   To issue your certificate, your domain name registration must be verified against the organization name provided during enrollment. CAs can only issue a Secure Server ID to the organization that has the legal right to use the domain name. The Common Name (domain name) for the server that will use the Server ID must be the fully qualified domain name. For example, the 3t Systems FQDN for the Access Gateway would be cag.3tsystems.com, where **3tsystems.com** is the domain name and **cag** is the host name.

Once the signed certificate is returned to you, pair it with the private key. This may take a few days to get back from the third-party CA.

6. Open the Configuration Utility and in the left pane click SSL and then CA Tools.

7. Under Create Certificate/Keys, click Create Certificate.

8. In Certificate File Name, click Browse and select the certificate.

9. In Certificate Format, select the format of the certificate. The default is PEM.

10. In Certificate Type, select Server (if you are installing a certificate signed by a CA).

11. In Certificate Request File Name, click Browse, select the file, and click Select.

12. In Validity Period (Number of Days), type the number of days for the expiration notice.

13. In CA Certificate File Name, click Browse, select the file, and click Select.

14. In CA Certificate File Format, select the format of the certificate. The default is PEM.

15. In CA Key File Name, click Browse, select the private key, and click Select.

16. In CA Key File Format, select the format of the certificate. The default is PEM.

17. In PEM Passphrase, type the password for the private key.

18. In CA Serial Number File, click Browse, select the file, and click Create.

Here's how to install the CA-signed certificate and private key on the Access Gateway:

1. In the Configuration Utility, in the left pane click SSL and then click Certificates.

2. In the right pane, click Add.

3. In Certificate-Key Pair Name, type the name of the certificate.

4. Under Details, select either Local System or Remote System.

   ▪ If you select Local System, the certificate is located on your computer. Click Browse, navigate to the certificate, and click Select and then Install.

- If you select Remote System, the certificate is installed on the Access Gateway. Click Browse, select the file, and click Select.

5. In Key Filename, click Browse, click the file, and click Select.

6. If the certificate is in PEM format, in the Password field type the password for the private key.

7. If you want to configure notification for when the certificate expires, in Expiry Monitor, click Enable. In Notification Period, type the number of days, click Install, and click Close.

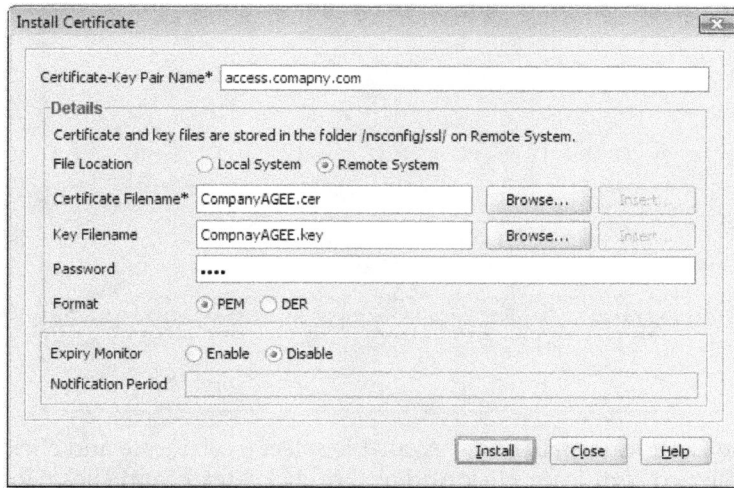

Creating a SSL VPN Virtual Server

The next step in the configuration is to create an SSL VPN virtual server for users to connect to. Use the SSL VPN Wizard to guide you through the process or follow these steps:

1. In the Configuration Utility, in the left pane click SSL VPN.

2. In the right pane, click SSL VPN Policy Manager.

3. Under Configured Policies/Resources, click Virtual Servers.

4. Under Related Tasks, click Create new virtual server.

5. Type the name of the virtual server (for example, SmartAccess).

6. Enter the IP address.

7. Enter the port number (the default is 443).

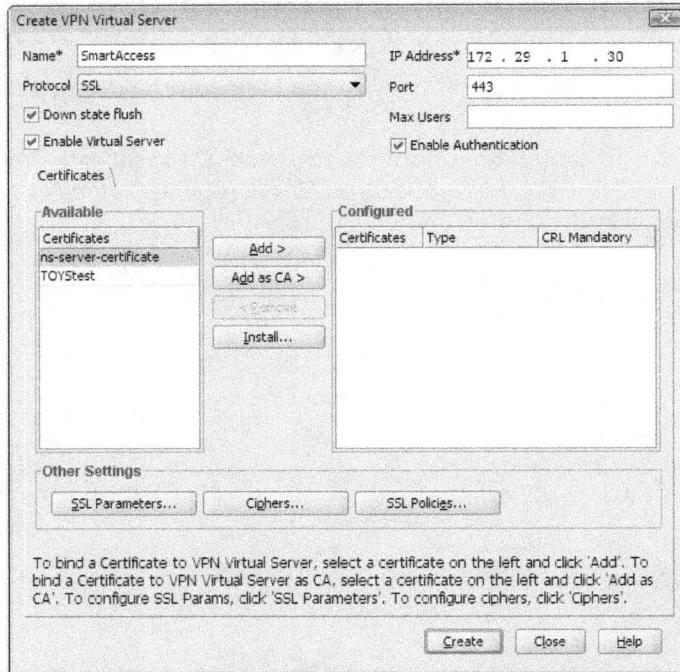

8. On the Certificates tab, under Available select a certificate and click Add. If it is a CA-signed certificate, click Add as CA, click Create, and click Close.

9. In the Configuration Utility, click Save at the top of the page.

To configure a virtual server using the command-line interface, type the following at a command prompt:

```
add vpn vserver <name> ssl <ipAddress> <port>
```

Here, *name* is the name of the virtual server, *ipAddress* is the primary IP address for users to connect to the Access Gateway, and *port* is the port number on which the virtual server listens. This is usually port 443.

DNS and WINS

In order for clients to properly connect through the Access Gateway, a valid DNS server must be configured. WINS is needed only if client access to a Windows host is needed. To add a Domain Name Server to the Access Gateway, follow these steps:

1. In the Configuration Utility, in the left pane under SSL VPN, click Global.

2. In the right pane, under General click Configure SSL VPN global settings.

3. Under DNS Server Addresses, click Add.

4. In the Enter the Name Server IP Address field, type the IP address of the DNS server.

5. Click Create, click Close, and then click OK.

6. Click Save in the Configuration Utility.

To add a name server using the command-line interface, type the following at a command prompt:

```
add dns nameserver (<dnsVserverName> | <IPaddress>)
```

Here, *dnsVserverName* is the name of the DNS server and *IPaddress* is the IP address. You must specify one or the other, but not both.

To configure a WINS server, type the following at a command prompt:

```
set vpn parameter winsIP <IPaddress> dnsVserverName <dns_vserver>
```

Here, *IPaddress* is the IP address of the WINS server and *dns_vserver* is the name of your DNS server.

Authentication

The Access Gateway uses an authentication design that incorporates industry-standard authentication servers such as RADUIS, LDAP, TACACS+, and others to allow administrators the flexibility to customize the authentication types used for user access.

Administrators can also use local users and groups to connect users to resources. The design centers on the use of policies to control the authentication procedures you create and can be applied at the global or virtual server level, as shown next. These policies can be prioritized to allow multiple authentication servers to help create levels of authentication.

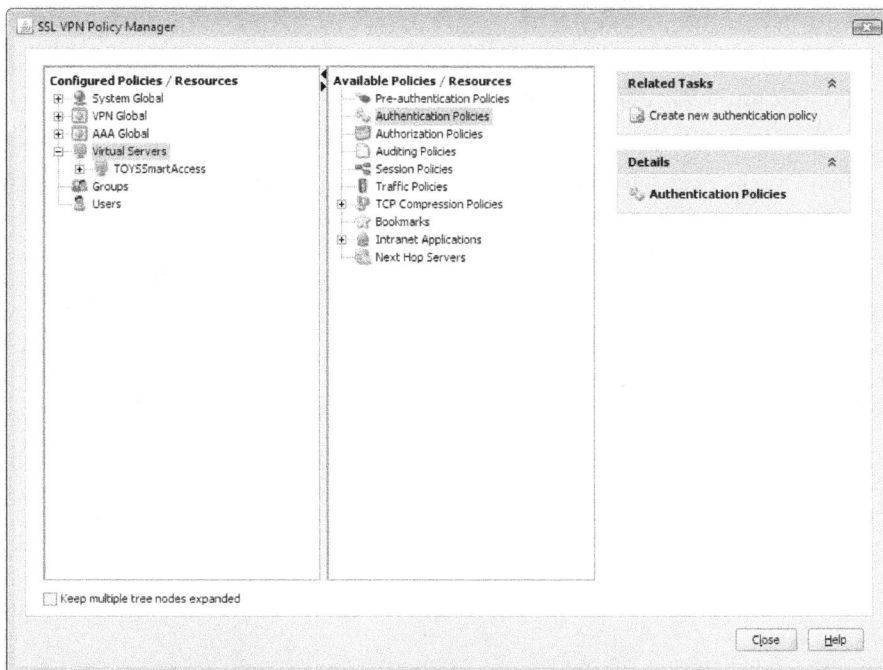

Creating Local Users and Groups   Administrators can use local users and groups to apply authorization and session policies, create bookmarks, specify applications, and allow users to access file shares and servers.

To create local users, follow these steps:

1. In the SSL VPN Policy Manager, under Configured Policies/Resources, click Users.

2. Under Related Tasks, click Create new user.

3. In the User Name field, type the user name. The total length of a user name cannot exceed 128 characters. The total length of all user names together cannot exceed 1,400 characters.

4. Select External Authentication to have users authenticate against an external authentication server, such as LDAP or RADIUS. Clear the check box to have the Access Gateway authenticate against the local user database.

5. In Password and Confirm Password, type the password for the user.

6. Click Create, click Close. Close the SSL VPN Policy Manager, and in the Configuration Utility click Save.

Follow these steps to create a group:

1. In the SSL VPN Policy Manager, under Configured Resources/Policies, click Groups.

2. Under Related Tasks, click Create new group. The total length of any single group name cannot exceed 128 characters. The total length of all group names together cannot exceed 1,400 characters.

3. In the Group Name field, type a name for the group.

4. On the Users tab, select the users who belong to the group and then click Add.

5. Click Create, click Close. Close the SSL VPN Policy Manager, and in the Configuration Utility click Save.

RADIUS Authentication   When you use the Access Gateway with a RADIUS server, the AG will act like a RADIUS client when it communicates with the RADIUS server. Depending on the configuration of your RADIUS server, you may need to configure a network access server IP address or a network access server identifier.

When using RADIUS, keep in mind the following points:

▼   If you enable the use of the network access server IP address, the appliance sends its configured IP address to the RADIUS server, rather than the source IP address used in establishing the RADIUS connection.

■ If you configure the network access server identifier, the appliance sends the identifier to the RADIUS server. If you omit the network access server identifier, the appliance sends its host name to the RADIUS server.

▲ When the network access server IP address is enabled, the appliance ignores any network access server identifier that is configured, using the network access server IP address to communicate with the RADIUS server instead.

To add a RADIUS server, follow these steps:

1. In the left pane of the Configuration Utility, click SSL VPN.

2. In the right pane, click Global.

3. Under Authentication, click Authentication Settings.

4. In the Maximum Number of Users field, type the number of users who can be authenticated using RADIUS.

5. In Default Authentication Type, select RADIUS.

6. Complete the settings as they are configured on your RADIUS server and click OK.

After you complete the configuration, the policy must be bound to the global or virtual server level to make it active. Refer to the upcoming section on how to bind the authentication policy.

LDAP In order to bind the Access Gateway to one or more LDAP servers, you will need to provide the following information:

▼ Base DN

■ Bind DN

■ Bind DN password

▲ Logon name

To configure an LDAP server, follow these steps:

1. In the left pane of the Configuration Utility, click SSL VPN.

2. In the right pane, click Global.

3. Under Authentication, click authentication settings.

4. In the Maximum Number of Users field, type the number of users who can be authenticated using LDAP.

5. In Default Authentication Type, select LDAP.

6. Complete the settings as they are configured on your LDAP server and click OK.

After you complete the configuration, the policy must be bound to the global or virtual server level to make it active. Refer to the upcoming section on how to bind the authentication policy.

TACACS+ Authentication   To configure the Access Gateway to use a TACACS+ server, provide the server IP address and the TACACS+ secret. The port needs to be specified only when the server port number in use is something other than the default port number of 49.

To configure a TACACS+ server, follow these steps:

1. In the left pane of the Configuration Utility, click SSL VPN.

2. In the right pane, click Global.

3. Under Authentication, click Authentication Settings.

4. In the Maximum Number of Users field, type the number of users who can be authenticated using TACACS+.

5. In Default Authentication Type, select TACACS.

6. Complete the settings as they are configured on your TACACS server and click OK.

After you complete the configuration, the policy must be bound to the global or virtual server level to make it active. Refer to the upcoming section on how to bind the authentication policy.

Client Certificate Authentication Along with the normal username and password for the user's authentication, a user can be authenticated using attributes from a client SSL certificate that is presented to the Access Gateway's virtual server. In order to authenticate users based on a client-side certificate, you need to enable client authentication on the virtual server and request the certificate.

To enable client certificate authentication using the Configuration Utility, follow these steps:

1. In the left pane of the Configuration Utility, click SSL VPN.

2. In the left pane, click Global.

3. Under Authentication, click Authentication Settings.

4. In the Maximum Number of Users field, type the number of users who can be authenticated using the client certificate.

5. In Default Authentication Type, select Cert.

6. In User Name Field, type the name of the certificate field that holds the user names.

7. In Group Name Field, type the name of the certificate field that holds the group name. Then click OK.

When the certificate is installed on the Access Gateway, enable client certificate authentication. You can do this using the command-line interface or the SSL VPN Policy Manager.

To enable client authentication using the command-line interface, at a command prompt type the following:

```
set ssl vserver <vServerName> -clientAuth ENABLED clientCert
[(MANDATORY|OPTIONAL)]
```

After you complete the configuration, the policy must be bound to the global or virtual server level to make it active. Refer to the upcoming section on how to bind the authentication policy.

To configure client certificate authentication using the SSL VPN Policy Manager, follow these steps:

1. In the Configuration Utility, in the left pane click SSL VPN.

2. In the right pane, click SSL VPN Policy Manager.

3. Under Configured Policies/Resources, expand the virtual server node and then click a virtual server.

4. Under Related Tasks, click Modify virtual server.

5. On the Certificates tab, click the certificate, click Add, click OK, and then click Close.

If SSL client certificate-based authentication is enabled on the Access Gateway, users are authenticated based on certain attributes of the client-side certificate. After authentication is completed successfully, the user name or the user and group name of the user are extracted from the certificate and any policies specified for that user are applied.

Binding Authentication Policies   After you configure authentication on the Access Gateway, you need to bind the policy on the global or virtual server level.

To bind an authentication policy, follow these steps:

1. In the left pane of the Configuration Utility, click SSL VPN.

2. In the right pane, under SSL VPN Policy Manager, click SSL VPN policy manager.

3. Under Available Policies/Resources, click an authentication policy and drag it to one, some, or all of the following locations under Configured Policies/Resources:

   ■ System Global | Authentication Policies

   ■ VPN Global | Authentication Policies

   ■ Virtual Servers | *Server Name* | Authentication Policies, where *Server Name* is the name of the virtual server

Citrix XenApp and the Secure Ticketing Authority (STA)

Unlike previous versions, Citrix Presentation Server 4.0 and XenApp 4.5 install the STA service on every server in the farm by default. Because this communication takes place over the XML port, best practices recommend changing this port from the default of TCP 80 to an alternative port, such as TCP 8081 or 8090. This provides a more secure communication port from the Access Gateway to the XenApp servers and helps avoid conflicts with IIS. Every XenApp farm server runs the STA service; however, we recommend using XenApp farm infrastructure servers as the logical target for STA connectivity from the Web Interface, Access Gateway, and associated access center components. Infrastructure servers are otherwise normal XenApp farm members but do not deliver applications. These servers are reserved for tasks such as Zone Data Collectors, STA services, Farm Metric Services, and the like. Keeping the infrastructure maintenance workload insulated from the application delivery workload ensures anomalies related to application delivery workload (such as a misbehaving application or server resource issue) cannot degrade infrastructure service or availability.

To configure the STA, follow these steps:

1. In the SSL VPN Policy Manager, under Configured Policies/Resources, expand the Virtual Servers node, select your virtual server, and select the STA Servers node. Right-click and select Add. For the URL, type the HTTP URL that corresponds to the XenApp XML Service, as shown next. The path to the STA (/Scripts/CtxSta.dll) can be omitted.

2. Click Create and then Close.

```
Configure STA Server                    [×]

   URL  http://192.168.1.200:8081/|

            Create      Close      Help
```

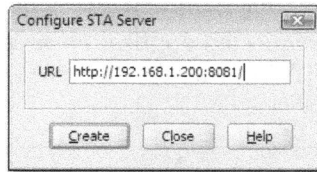

NOTE: If the XML Service is running on a port other than 80, enter the port number after the server address, such as **http://192.168.1.200:8081/** or **http://server.company.com:8090/**.

Web Interface

To use the Web Interface (WI) to deliver XenApp farm applications to the AG-E, the Web Interface Version 4.5 or greater must be installed in accordance with Citrix's *Web Interface Administrators Guide*. In order for this to happen, the Access Gateway must work with Web Interface to provide secure access to resources on the LAN.

Typical steps in this process are as follows:

1. A user types the web address of the Access Gateway in the address field of a web browser.

2. The Access Gateway receives the request and relays it to the Web Interface. If the Web Interface is behind the Access Gateway in the DMZ or in the secure network, Citrix recommends that users be authenticated using the Access Gateway.

3. The Web Interface responds by sending a logon page to the client browser.

4. The user enters and submits valid user credentials that are sent to the Web Interface through the Access Gateway.

5. The Web Interface sends the user credentials to the Citrix XML Service available from the server farm and obtains a list of applications that the user is authorized to use.

6. The Web Interface populates the web page with the list of published resources that the user is authorized to access.

7. When the user clicks a published application link, the Web Interface sends the IP address and port for the requested computer running XenApp to the STA and requests a session ticket for the user. The STA saves the IP address and issues the requested ticket to the Web Interface.

8. The Web Interface generates an ICA file containing the ticket issued by the STA and sends it to the client browser.

9. The client web browser uses the ICA file to launch the XenApp client. The client connects to the Access Gateway using the FQDN in the ICA file. Initial SSL/TLS handshaking is performed to establish the identity of the Access Gateway.

10. The Access Gateway receives the session ticket from the client and contacts the STA for ticket validation.

11. If the ticket is valid, the STA returns the IP address of the computer running XenApp on which the requested application resides. If the session ticket is invalid or expired, the STA informs the Access Gateway and an error message appears on the client device.

IMPORTANT: The ICA file generated by the Web Interface contains the fully qualified domain name (FQDN) or IP address of the Access Gateway. The address of the server(s) running XenApp is never revealed to the XenApp client.

12. On receipt of the IP address for the computer running XenApp, the Access Gateway establishes a secure connection to the client device. When the ICA connection is established, the Access Gateway encrypts and decrypts data flowing through the connection.

To create the Web Interface site to be used with the Access Gateway, follow these steps:

1. Open the Access Management Console. Configure and run discovery if prompted to do so.

2. Select Citrix Resources | Configuration Tools | Web Interface and then click Create site.

3. For the site type, choose Access Platform site and click Next.

4. Keep the default IIS site and path selected (/Citrix/AccessPlatform/) and click Next.

5. Choose Local File for the configuration source and click Next.

6. Choose Use Built-in Authentication or Advanced Access Control for the authentication settings and click Next.

7. Click Next and then Finish. The Specify Initial Configuration Wizard launches. Click Next.

8. Enter the XML Service information for your XenApp farm and click Next.

9. Select an application type and click Next.

10. On the Specify Access Method panel, select Using the Advanced Access Control and enter your SSL VPN URL for the server portion of the Authentication Service address. For example, enter the following:

```
https://access.company.com/CitrixAuthService/AuthService.asmx
```

11. Click Next and Finish. Select the site in the left pane of the Access Management Console.

12. In the center pane, select Manage Secure Client Access | Edit Gateway Settings.

13. Under Gateway Server, in the Address (FQDN) field, type the Access Gateway FQDN. This must be the same name used on the Access Gateway certificate.

14. In the Port field, type the port number. The default is 443.
15. To enable session reliability, click Enable Session Reliability.

NOTE: In order to use Session Reliability during a connection through Web Interface, it must be enabled in the properties of the XenApp farm.

16. Under Secure Ticket Authority, click Add.
17. In the Enter the Secure Ticket Authority URL field, type the name of the computer running XenApp and then click OK.

NOTE: If the XML Service is running on a port other than 80, enter the port number after the server address, such as **http://192.168.1.200:8081/Scripts/CtxSta.dll** or **http://server.company. com:8090/Scripts/CtxSta.dll**. Make sure you include the colon.

18. In the center pane, click Manage Secure Client Access | Edit DMZ Settings.
19. In the Client Address Table, select the Default entry and then click Edit.
20. In Access Method, select Gateway Direct and click OK twice.
21. Select Manage Secure Client Access | Edit DMZ Settings. Change the Default access method from Direct to Gateway Direct. Click OK.

Client Access

Now that you have an Access Gateway appliance up and running on the network, it might seem like a good idea to get some users connected to it and to the resources on the network. The two types of access we address here are the SSL VPN and remote access to XenApp applications using the SSL Proxy. We also look at the SmartAccess function in a little more detail.

SSL VPN

As with normal VPN appliances, the Access Gateway can terminate an SSL VPN connection and allow users access to the resources on the network. One of the outstanding features about the Access Gateway is that the VPN client—the Secure Access Client (SAC)—includes all the configurations for a VPN connection in the file that is downloaded to the user during the initial install. When there is an update to the configuration, the next time a user launches the Access Gateway client, a new configuration will be downloaded to the user's machine with all the updated information.

Clientless Access to XenApp

Another method for gaining access to resources, particularly XenApp applications, is through clientless access to XenApp. Before diving in too deeply, let's clear some things up. There is really no such thing as true "clientless" access to anything. There is always a client—whether it is a plug-in to IE in the form of an applet, a Java-based application, or whatever. There is always a client-side requirement for accessing resources.

The clientless access for the Citrix Access Gateway is no exception. The "clientless" access we are referring to is access without the VPN client running. This would be access through a web browser using the ICA web client or Java client.

In order to gain access to XenApp applications using clientless access, follow these steps:

1. In the Access Gateway configuration utility, select the SSL VPN node and click SSL VPN Policy Manager.

2. Select Session Policies in the right pane and then click Create New Session Policy.

3. For Request Profile, click New to create a new session profile.

4. In the Create Session Profile window, enable the check box to override the Client Experience | Home Page setting. Set it to your Web Interface site URL. For example, use http://*ServerIPAddress*/Citrix/AccessPlatform/ as the URL for the home page.

5. For the Secure Gateway and SmartAccess settings at the bottom of the window, set the ICA Proxy mode to ON and enter your Active Directory domain name as the SmartAccess NT Domain. The SmartAccess NT Domain should match the domain of your XenApp farm.

6. Click Create to finish creating the new session profile. You are returned to the session policy window.

7. The policy needs an expression to determine under which conditions it should be enabled. In order to enable this session policy regardless of the connection, add the named expression ns_true as the condition. From the named expressions, choose ns_true, click Add Expression, click Create, and click Close.

8. In the left pane of the Policy Manager, expand the VPN Global node. Drag the session policy icon onto the VPN Global | Session Policies node. Close the SSL VPN Policy Manager.

SmartAccess

In the Advanced version of the Access Gateway, the Advanced Access Control server was used to determine what endpoint security requirements would be evaluated in order to obtain access to the corporate applications. In the Access Gateway Enterprise Edition, the SmartAccess components of Advanced Access Controls are built into the appliance and are configured as session policies.

Like with the Advanced edition, carefully plan the rules and the endpoint analysis scan you implement. Adding too much complexity can make access difficult and make troubleshooting failed attempts complicated.

For this example we will be configuring a scan for a company.txt file. If the file exists, access to the Notepad.exe program will be available. If the file does not exist, access to Notepad will not be made available and we will close down the drive mapping and clipboard virtual channels so that they may not be used.

Here are steps that outline the configuration just mentioned. These steps configure the SmartAccess policies and link them to the XenApp farm:

1. In the Access Gateway Configuration Utility, open the SSL VPN Policy Manager.

2. Under Available Policies/Resources, click Session Policies. Under Related Tasks, click Create New Session Policy.

3. For the policy name, type **CompanyEPA**.

4. Next to Request Profile, click New. As shown next, name the profile **SmartAccess-Filter** and click Create. You are returned to the Create Session Policy window.

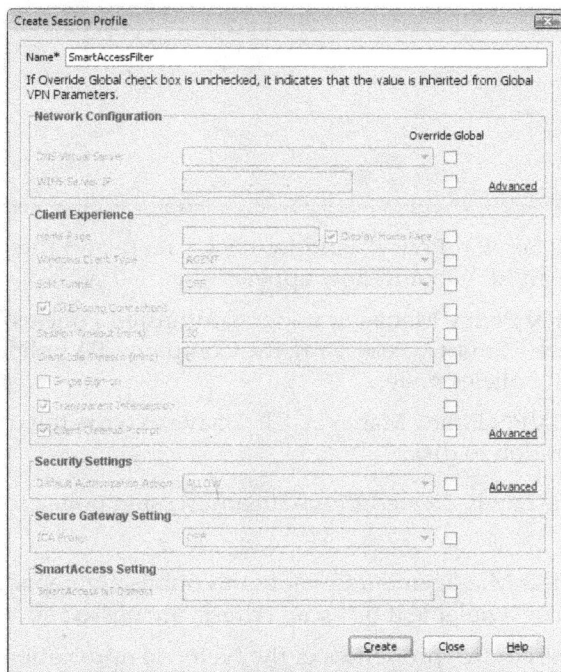

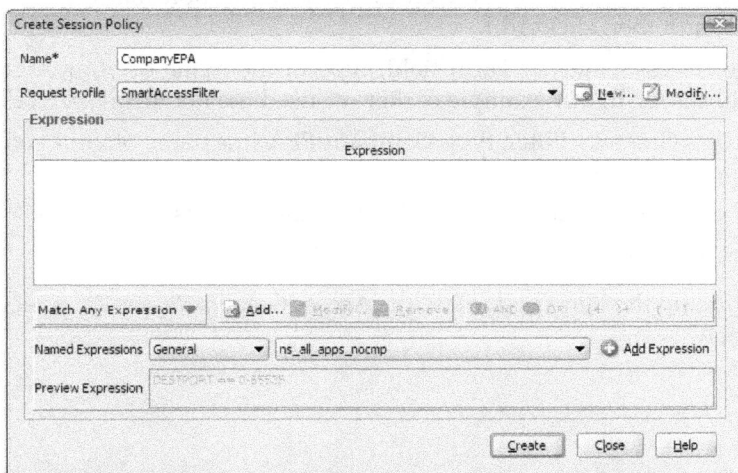

5. Beneath the Expression editor, click **Add**. The Add Expression window appears.

6. As shown next, in Expression Type, select Client Security. In Component, select File. In the Name field, type **C:\\\\company.txt**. Click OK and then Close. You are returned to the Create Session Policy window.

7. At the Create Session Policy window, click Create and then Close. The session policy CompanyEPA should now appear.

8. In the SSL VPN Policy Manager, under Configured Policies/Resources, expand Virtual Servers | SmartAccess. Drag the CompanyEPA policy onto the SmartAccess | Session Policies node.

9. Close the SSL VPN Policy Manager. Click Save to write the running Access Gateway configuration to disk.

In order to link the newly created EPA scan and session policy to XenApp, complete the following steps:

1. Open the Access Management Console and publish Notepad.exe for the application that is to be available if our scan criteria are passed successfully.

2. Edit the access control properties of the Notepad application.

3. Change the connections allowed to "Any connection that meets the following filters" and then click Add.

4. In the Access Gateway Farm field, type in the name of your Access Gateway virtual server. In our example earlier we used the name SmartAccess.

5. In Access Gateway Filter, type **CompanyEPA** (the name of your conditional session policy).

6. Click OK. Click to clear Allow All Other Connections.

7. Click OK to finish the configuration.

This will link up the XenApp farm to the Access Gateway's session policy. Now what do we do with it?

XenApp Policies and Filters

The next step is to create a couple of XenApp policies that will enforce our user access scenarios to the clipboard and drive mappings while the users are connecting to applications. To do this we will need to create two policies: one for allowing access to the clipboard and drive mappings (AllowClipDrive) and the other to deny access to them (NoClipDrive) . Here are the steps to follow:

1. Open the Presentation Server Console by clicking Start | All Programs | Citrix | Management Consoles | Presentation Server Console.

2. Right-click the Policies node and click Create Policy. Create a policy called No-ClipDrive and a policy called AllowClipDrive and then click OK.

TIP: The filtered AllowClipDrive policy must be given a higher priority than the NoClipDrive policy so that when it applies to a user, it overrides the policy that disables client device mapping.

3. Edit the properties of the NoClipDrive policy and configure it to *disable* client drive mapping, client clipboard mapping, and client printer mapping.

4. Edit the properties of the AllowClipDrive policy and click Enabled for client drive mapping, client clipboard mapping, and client printer mapping.

5. Right-click the NoClipDrive policy and select Apply this policy to. Click Access Control in the left pane, check the box next to Filter Based on Access Control, check the box next to Apply to connections made through Access Gateway, and keep the setting applied to Any Connection. Click OK.

6. Right-click the AllowClipDrive policy and select Apply this policy to. Click Access Control in the left pane, check the box next to Filter Based on Access Control, and check the box next to Any connection that meets any of the following filters.

7. Click Add. Type **SmartAccess** for the farm name and type **CompanyEPA** for the Access Gateway filter name. Click OK.

Testing Enumeration and Access

At this stage, users should be able to access the gateway through the URL, sign on, and receive a published application list. From there you should be able to verify that, with the Company.txt file present on the client device, users can gain access to the new application Notepad.exe and that clipboard use and drive access should be available for this and other applications. At the same time verify that without the Company.txt file, users should not have access to Notepad.exe and that for other applications, no clipboard and drive mapping is allowed.

> **NOTE:** The clipboard and drive mapping test assumes that in your test environment other applications are available through the Access Gateway from which you are testing.

To test application enumeration and launch, follow these steps:

1. Point your web browser to the URL of your Access Gateway (for example, https://access.company.com).

> **TIP:** Make sure the client you are testing from contains the root CA for the certificate you are using for the Access Gateway. If it does not have the root installed, the connection will fail.

2. Log in using domain credentials. You should see a list of published applications that are assigned to the user account that's logged in.

3. Log out and create a file on the root of the local C drive named Company.txt.

4. Log into the Access Gateway again. The Notepad application should now be in the list of applications. When you launch the application, you should have access to local drives and the clipboard function should work.

5. Log off, close all browser windows, and delete the Company.txt file.

6. Log back in again. This time the Notepad application should *not* be in the list of applications. When you launch other applications, you should *not* have access to local drives and the clipboard function should be disabled.

Congratulations, you made it. This should give you a great foundation for the endless possibilities of configuring remote application delivery for your XenApp environment. This is merely the beginning. With careful planning and testing, you can develop a secure and reliable environment for your users to access corporate resources while traveling away from the office, working from home, or working from a different branch location using any device over any connection.

CHAPTER 12

Citrix EdgeSight
for XenApp

Citrix administrators, IT consultants, network engineers, and anyone who uses applications hosted on a Terminal Server are all too aware of the many calls received from users blaming Citrix farms for the likes of application slowness, delays, and even occasional network disconnections. To date there has not been a useful and intuitive way of tracking these types of issues or a detailed reporting source to help determine the real cause behind these types of calls. When Citrix announced the EdgeSight product line in October of 2006, Citrix administrators were heard rejoicing in data centers around the world. Since then, Citrix extended the EdgeSight product line to include EdgeSight for XenApp, EdgeSight for Endpoints, EdgeSight for NetScaler, and EdgeSight for Load Testing. Citrix has invested in the EdgeSight product line, and Citrix administrators now have a full set of tools to help monitor, test, and report on all performance aspects of their Citrix environments.

Citrix EdgeSight is included with Citrix XenApp Platinum Edition. This chapter will focus on the EdgeSight for XenApp component and discuss the architecture, installation, configuration, and usage.

EdgeSight for XenApp provides real-time and historical visibility into all user sessions, application processes, and server performance across the Citrix XenApp farm. Resource Manager has been a trusted and loyal friend for some time, but even with the Summary Database enabled, administrators have a hard time making good use of the performance data collected to help with real-time troubleshooting or overall farm performance analysis. EdgeSight for XenApp provides an abundant and immediate wealth of information that will be spoken about for years to come.

CITRIX EDGESIGHT FOR XENAPP ARCHITECTURE

EdgeSight for XenApp has a unique architecture in that it uses a multitier database design. Each EdgeSight for XenApp server agent maintains its own local database on the XenApp server. The agent databases utilize what Citrix calls the "15/5/60 model" for data sampling intervals. This model refers to a 15-second sampling level for the most recent four hours. After this time the agent aggregates the level up to five-minute sampling levels, and finally prior to uploading the agent database to the EdgeSight database server the agent further aggregates the level into one-hour samplings. The agents by default are scheduled to upload their individual data to the EdgeSight database server twice a day, at the default times 05:00 and 19:00. The power of this distributed database model is that the performance impact on the network is very low and predictable. The other benefit in the design is the dual use of the EdgeSight Console to allow Citrix administrators to access real-time user, process, and device data directly from the agent databases as well as detailed historical data from the EdgeSight Server database.

Figure 12-1 illustrates the components that make up an EdgeSight for XenApp environment. We will discuss each of these in detail.

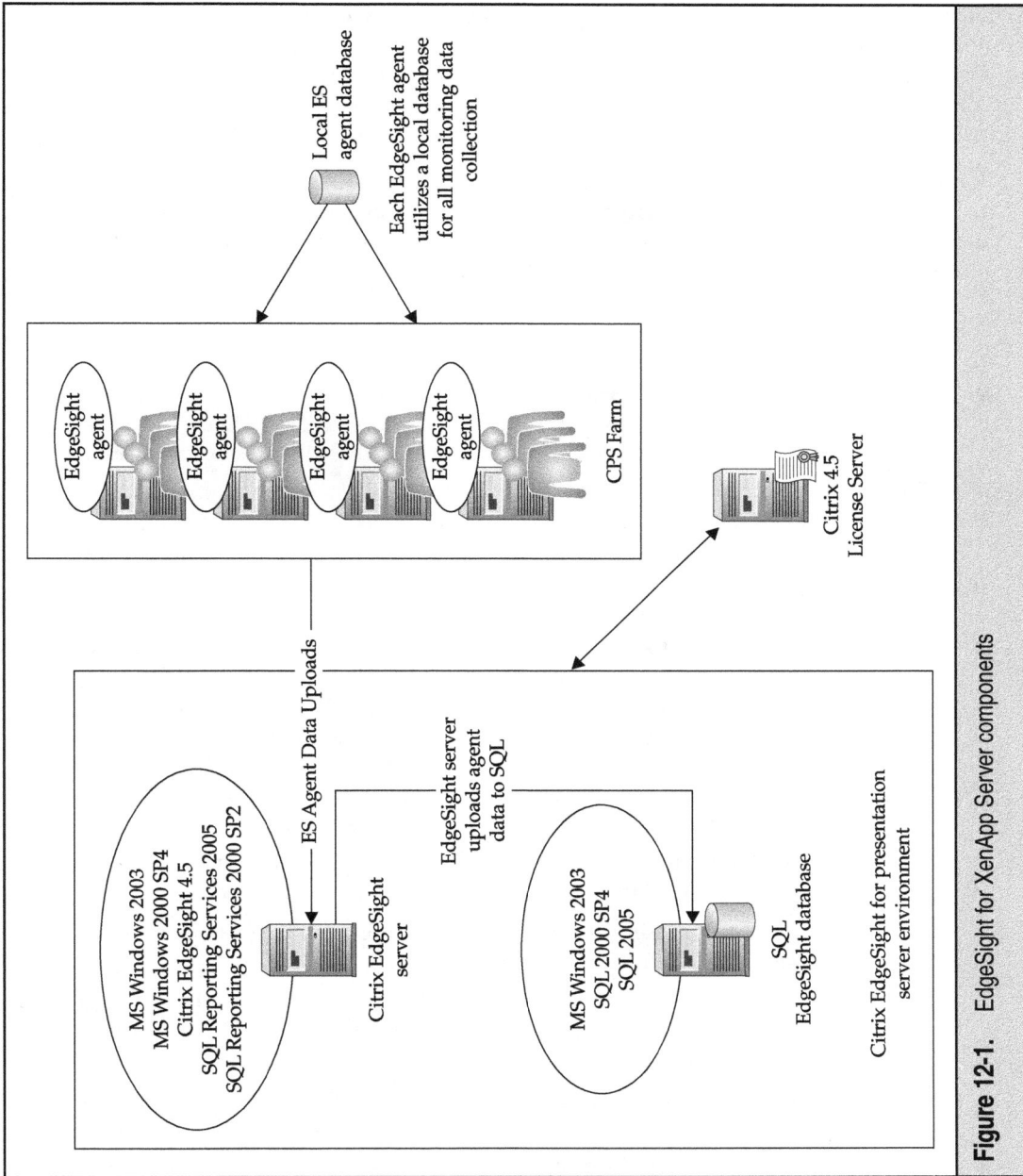

Figure 12-1.   EdgeSight for XenApp Server components

Citrix EdgeSight Server components provide the primary interface for Citrix administrators to display both real-time agent data and historical aggregated data for the entire environment. EdgeSight Server also allows Citrix administrators to set up real-time alerts for notification of critical system events and it's the primary point for all configuration tasks and changes. The following components make up Citrix EdgeSight Server:

▼ **Database Server** Stores the data uploaded from the XenApp server agents. On a daily basis, the server performs aggregation operations on the data to produce information for reports. This component requires Microsoft SQL Server 2000 SP4 or Microsoft SQL Server 2005. This component can be installed on a single hardware platform or, as shown in Figure 12-1, can be installed on a separate hardware platform for improved performance and to make use of an existing Microsoft SQL environment.

■ **Web Server** Displays performance and availability information using a dynamic and graphical reporting interface called the EdgeSight Server Console. The default install provides access to over 300 standard reports and provides the ability to create additional custom reports.

■ **Report Server** Generates and displays performance and availability information in the form of reports. The Report Server uses Microsoft SQL Reporting Services 2000 SP2 or Microsoft SQL Reporting Services 2005. This component is installed on the hardware platform with the EdgeSight Web Server.

■ **Citrix EdgeSight for XenApp Server Agent** This software installs on each XenApp server. The agent components consist of a Windows service called Citrix System Monitoring Agent and a local database called RSDATR.FDB (stored in C:\Documents and Settings\All Users\Application Data\Citrix\System Monitoring\Data). The EdgeSight for XenApp Agent collects and records information about user sessions, server performance, application usage, and network connections. Key features of the agent include the following:

■ Support for MetaFrame Presentation Server 3.0 and later running on 32-bit and 64-bit versions of Windows Server 2003.

■ Local database ranging in size from 50MB to 250MB of disk space (depends on the Agent Data Retention Settings defined).

■ Uses the standard HTTP protocol to upload the local database to the EdgeSight Server. Optionally, the agent can be configured to use HTTPS if required for additional security.

■ Network traffic generated during agent data uploads ranges between 30KB and 100KB, and real-time alerts are approximately 200KB.

▲ **Citrix License Server** The Citrix License Server for Windows provides license management. EdgeSight for XenApp requires version 4.5 of the Citrix License Server. The EdgeSight Server obtains licenses on behalf of the EdgeSight for XenApp server agents.

EdgeSight for XenApp Design Considerations

At this point a quick design discussion is in order. When planning your installation, you can install the required server components on separate physical machines. In all cases, ensure that the machines have sufficient memory and processor capabilities and that the machines are in the same domain. In Figure 12-1 we elected to separate the EdgeSight Server components onto separate hardware. This decision is based on two factors:

▼ In many environments, a well-established Microsoft SQL Server deployment is already in place to support other corporate applications. In some cases, we recommend making use of this environment for the EdgeSight Database component. Many well-established corporate Microsoft SQL Server deployments incorporate a number of enhancements such as clustering, managed backups, and monitoring, all of which will also benefit the EdgeSight deployment.

▲ By separating the EdgeSight Web Server component from the EdgeSight Database Server, we will see increased performance in the EdgeSight Reporting Server because of the use of dedicated hardware.

Citrix supports installing all EdgeSight Server components on a single hardware platform (for example, Web Server, Database Server, and Reporting Services). This design saves on hardware costs and simplifies the installation process. This design can impact the performance of the server components in a large environment. It does not lend itself to some of the advanced features of Microsoft SQL Server as discussed earlier.

Citrix EdgeSight Licensing Overview

The implementation of EdgeSight for XenApp as part of the XenApp Platinum Edition deployment takes advantage of Citrix's new simplified licensing model. The release of Feature Pack 1 for XenApp Platinum Edition uses a single license file, which contains valid usage data for each of the components contained in the Platinum edition, including EdgeSight for XenApp. With the Platinum licensing model, the checkout request process is not used. Once the EdgeSight for XenApp agent detects the presence of a Platinum license, the license is considered valid and the request and return process is not completed.

Citrix EdgeSight for XenApp requires version 4.5 of the Citrix License Server. The Citrix License Server can be installed directly on the EdgeSight Server, or an existing Citrix License Server 4.5 in the environment can be used. A Citrix XenApp Platinum Edition deployment will already have the License Server in production and the correct license files already installed, so it is best to use this one.

▼ **NOTE:** EdgeSight for XenApp will only upload data for servers that are using a valid XenApp Platinum license or EdgeSight for XenApp standalone license. If you would like to monitor performance of XenApp server users beyond the number of Platinum licenses owned, you can purchase additional Platinum licenses or separate EdgeSight for XenApp licenses to cover the concurrency of your farm.

Citrix EdgeSight SQL Licensing

Due to the architecture of EdgeSight for XenApp, valid Microsoft SQL licenses are required. The amount and type of Microsoft SQL licenses depend on the architecture design; in the example in Figure 12-1 we have divided the SQL Reporting Services component from the SQL Database component on different pieces of hardware. This design requires a full processor-level Microsoft SQL license for both the EdgeSight Server and the EdgeSight Database Server. Alternatively, in a per-device model we would need a valid SQL CAL for each Citrix XenApp server agent installed.

CITRIX EDGESIGHT FOR XENAPP

This section provides a detailed review of the preparation and installation tasks for Citrix EdgeSight for XenApp. In our example we elected to use Microsoft SQL Reporting Services 2005 and dual-server deployment architecture. The two-server platforms will have the following components installed and the recommended hardware specifications:

▼   Web Server

   ■ Windows Server 2003 SP1 or R2

   ■ Microsoft updates and patches for installed components

   ■ CPU: 2GHz, Core™ 2 Duo Processor

   ■ Memory: 1GB of RAM

■   Database Server

   ■ Windows Server 2003 SP1 or R2

   ■ Microsoft updates and patches for installed components

   ■ CPU: 2GHz, Core™ 2 Duo Processor

   ■ Memory: 2GB of RAM

■   Citrix License Server

   ■ CPU: 1GHz or faster CPU

▲   Memory: 512MB of RAM

For the remainder of this section, all preparation and installation tasks will be focused on this design. Other supported options will be listed when applicable.

Citrix EdgeSight for XenApp Server Installation Overview

We will start with a high-level installation roadmap to follow when planning and building an EdgeSight environment. Each item listed should be completed in the listed order to ensure a successful deployment.

Create Required Accounts

EdgeSight for XenApp has the following service, user, and database account requirements:

▼ **RSUSER**   This account should be a domain-level account with general domain user rights. This account will be used for Reporting Services access to the Reporting Services database in SQL. It will also require local admin rights on both the EdgeSight Server and EdgeSight Database server. In addition, the account will need to be a Security Administrator and Database Creator within Microsoft SQL 2005. This account should be treated as a service account, and its password should be a strong password set to never expire (if the password is set to expire, the service will quit working the day the password expires).

■ **EdgeSight SuperUser**   This account is used within the EdgeSight Web Server Console for all configuration and initial reporting access. It must be a domain-level account with a valid email address. This account will not be used for any related services and should fall under the normal domain-wide password security restrictions.

▲ **SpectUser**   This account is created during the EdgeSight Server installation and is given Connection rights to the EdgeSight database within SQL. It is created as a part of the installation, but a password will need to be defined. This account is a SQL security account only.

Determine the SQL Version and Platform

It is very important to make this determination early in the installation process and decide if a single- or dual-server architecture will be used. If an existing Microsoft SQL Server installation will be used, verify and note the SQL version, including service packs. Also ensure that enough disk space for the creation and storage of the EdgeSight database and logs is available.

The default file group size for the EdgeSight database files is 500MB, and the log file group size is also 500MB. The EdgeSight database is made up of one primary database file and seven additional database files, labeled FG1–FG7. Each of these database files will be 500MB in size per a default configuration.

Obtain Required Media

Often this step is overlooked and can cause delays during the actual installation process when everything comes to a grinding halt because the installation media is nowhere to be found or the prerequisite software has not been downloaded. The following list details the media and supporting software downloads required:

▼ Microsoft SQL Server 2005 or Microsoft SQL Server 2000 SP4 media.

■ Microsoft SQL Reporting Services 2005 or Microsoft SQL Reporting Services 2000 SP2.

(SQL Reporting Services 2005 is part of the base SQL Server 2005 media, and SQL Reporting Services 2000 SP4 is a separate download from Microsoft.)

NOTE: Ensure that the service pack level of the Microsoft SQL Server install corresponds to the service pack level of Reporting Services.

■ NET 2.0 Framework (available from Microsoft's website, or the installer is located on the Citrix XenApp Platinum media under the Support folder).

■ Microsoft Windows Script 5.6 or higher.

■ Microsoft XML Parser 3.0.

▲ The most recent copy of the EdgeSight Agent installers (available from the Citrix website).

TIP: The media kits do not always contain the most recent versions of software and components. Always check the Citrix support site under the EdgeSight section for the most recent service packs and installers.

Prepare Servers for Installation

Prior to installing the EdgeSight Server components, you should install all prerequisites on each server along with the necessary Windows components needed for the installation. The installation and configuration requirements for each of the EdgeSight components are listed next.

EdgeSight Server Prerequisites and IIS components:

▼ Microsoft Windows Server 2003 STD SP1 or higher.

■ IIS.

■ ASP.NET.

■ Microsoft Message Queuing (MSMQ).

■ Microsoft Distributed Transaction Coordinator (MSDTC).

■ Enable Network COM+ access.

■ Enable Network DTC access.

■ Ensure ASP.NET is allowed in IIS.

■ .NET Framework 2.0.

■ Windows Script 5.6 (only for a dual-server install).

■ Microsoft XML Parser 3.0 (only for a dual-server install).

■ Microsoft SQL Client Connectivity components (if using SQL Reporting Services 2005).

■ Microsoft SQL Client add-on tools and SQL-DMO objects (if using SQL Reporting Services 2000).

▲ Microsoft Excel (used to display real-time reports).

EdgeSight Database Server prerequisites:

▼ Microsoft Windows Server 2003 STD SP1 or higher.

■ Microsoft SQL Server 2005 (recommended) or Microsoft SQL Server 2000 SP4 Standard Edition.

▲ SQL configured for mixed-mode authentication.

Microsoft SQL Reporting Services

In a dual-server architecture such as our example, SQL Reporting Services 2005 will be installed on the EdgeSight Server. The following tasks need to be completed:

▼ Create ReportServer virtual directory.

■ Create ReportServer database.

■ Assign RSUSER account permission to the ReportServer database.

■ Initialize ReportServer database (not required for Microsoft SQL Standard Edition).

▲ Configure e-mail settings.

EdgeSight Licensing

Under the new Citrix simplified licensing model, EdgeSight for XenApp utilizes the Citrix XenApp Platinum Edition license. Ensure the current Citrix Licensing server is configured to use the 4.5 version and that a valid Citrix XenApp Platinum Edition license has been allocated and installed on the Citrix License Server.

EdgeSight Server

During installation and configuration, the following tasks will be accomplished:

▼ The EdgeSight Web Server will be installed.

■ The EdgeSight Console will be installed.

▲ The EdgeSight Database will be created on the EdgeSight Database server.

After installation, provide the following information for the configuration of the EdgeSight server:

▼ Company name

■ Time zone

■ EdgeSight SuperUser account

■ E-mail settings, including SMTP server address, e-mail address for EdgeSight event messages to be sent to, and the display name and e-mail address for the From field of any sent e-mails

■ Licensing type

■ Reporting Services ReportServer URL

■ RSUSER account information

■ Department names

▲ Group names

EdgeSight Agent

The final step in the installation roadmap is to deploy the EdgeSight agents to each XenApp server. The EdgeSight agent can be installed using System Management tools such as Microsoft SMS, Enteo's NetInstall Server, or Citrix Installation Manager. The MSI file supports full unattended installations using standard MSIEXEC commands.

During an EdgeSight agent install, you will need to provide the following information:

▼ Company name

■ Department name

▲ EdgeSight Server name and port number (80/443)

Additionally, some of the components will require some minor configuration, which will be covered in the installation section. Whew! That is one long roadmap—good luck getting it folded and back in the glove compartment. All kidding aside, by now you can see what we mean by our earlier statement with regard to Citrix upping the ante with the installation challenges for Citrix EdgeSight for XenApp.

Citrix EdgeSight for XenApp Installation

This section provides an installation walkthrough of EdgeSight for XenApp. This material assumes a Windows server has been built according to company policies and procedures.

Install the Server Prerequisites

1. Install the required Windows components (Control Panel | Add/Remove Windows Components):

   ■ IIS 6.0.

   ■ Microsoft Message Queuing (MSMQ | Message Queuing | Application Server).

   ■ Microsoft XML Parser 3.0 or higher (only on a standalone machine or a machine without Web Interface).

   ■ Windows Script 5.6 or higher (only on a standalone machine or a machine without Web Interface).

   ■ Microsoft .NET Framework 2.0. (At the time of this writing, .NET Framework 3.0 is not supported.)

2. Visit Microsoft's website for updates and patches for installed components.

3. Reboot.

4. Ensure that an e-mail-enabled domain account is created for the EdgeSight SuperUser.

5. Ensure that a SQL database connection account has been created.

NOTE: For the initial database creation, the SQL account used to install the database components must have Security Administrators (sysadmin) and Database Creators (dbcreator) permissions.

6. Ensure that a domain service account is created for the EdgeSight service.

7. Install SQL Database Services, Client Connectivity Components, and Reporting Services (SQL 2005) if Web Server and SQL Server are on different machines. Follow these steps:

CAUTION: Do not create the EdgeSight database prior to installation. The database will be created with proper access during the installation.

---

a. Launch \\<path to SQL2005 CD>\Setup.exe.

b. Accept the license agreement.

c. Confirm installation of the Microsoft SQL native client and the Microsoft SQL Server 2005 setup support files.

d. Click Next to begin the installation wizard.

e. Click Next after the Systems Configuration Check and begin the installation.

f. Enter registration information and the license key.

g. Select the following check boxes: SQL Server Database Services, Reporting Services, and Workstation components, Books Online and development tools.

h. Click Advanced and choose not to install Documentation, Samples, and Sample Databases.

i. Accept the default instance and click Next twice.

j. Select the option Use the Built-in System Account/Local System. Select the SQL Server and SQL Server Agent check boxes under Start services at the end of setup. Click Next.

k. Choose Mixed Mode for the Authentication setting.

l. Set the SQL SA password.

m. Accept the defaults and click Install.

n. Once the setup process is complete, click Next and then Finish.

o. Verify the following configuration requirements are installed and configured:

- Network COM+ access is enabled.
- The default website is running.
- ASP.NET is allowed in IIS.
- IWAM and IUSR users are active and enabled.
- The IIS_WPG group is enabled and the AS-PNET user is enabled (if using Windows Server 2003).

Install EdgeSight Server

To Install the EdgeSight server component:

1. Launch the option EdgeSight Server and Components Installers | Citrix EdgeSight Server from the EdgeSight CD.

2. For Setup type, choose Custom.

3. Select EdgeSight Server Website and Database.

NOTE: Ignore the warning "A valid SSL Certificate was not detected. The secure logins setting will be disabled for the EdgeSight Website. This could present a dangerous security risk." This is for encrypting the EdgeSight web server front end.

4. Choose the SQL server and authentication account with SA privileges and then test the connection.

NOTE: This account is used for database creation only and will not be used for client connections.

5. For Database selection, provide a name or choose an existing database for an upgrade.

6. Assign a password to the SpectUser account.

7. If desired, change File Group Location and Log File Location to a separate partition (optional).

8. Configure the database properties as follows:

   ■ **File Group Location** Accept the default file group location or click the Browse button to select a different location.

   ■ **File Group Size** Accept the default file size or enter a new file size. Each of the eight files in the file group is created using the specified size. The default value is sufficient space for most installations.

   ■ **Log File Location** Accept the default log file location or click the Browse button to select a different location.

   ■ **Log File Size** Accept the default log file initial size or enter a new file size. The default value is sufficient space for most installations.

   ■ **Recovery Model Options** Select a database recovery model (Simple, Bulk-logged, or Full) from the drop-down menu. The default recovery model is Simple.

9. Click Next. The Server Location screen is displayed.

10. Choose Install and Finish and perform post-installation setup.

Setup Initial Company

Once EdgeSight is installed, setup will prompt you to setup and configure the Initial Company. To create the Initial Company, follow these steps:

1. To set up the initial EdgeSight company, point your browser to http://*<server name>*/edgesight40/setup (should launch automatically from setup).

2. Create the initial company.

3. Choose the time zone.

4. Configure the EdgeSight super user account (a universal login ID to be used by the Citrix EdgeSight administrators).

5. Add the SMTP server to route e-mail.

6. Add the event e-mail address (the person who will be notified of important events occurring on the website).

7. In the From field, type in the Display name / e-mail address that the report will show as sent from.

8. Select which types of agents for which uploads are supported on the server from the EdgeSight Server Mode drop-down menu. You can change the server mode at any time after installation using the EdgeSight Server Console.

9. Click Finish.

10. To test the login point a browser to http://*<servername>*/edgesight40/app/ suilogin.aspx.

Creating a Reporting Services User

Create a local server account called RUSER for Reporting Services Communications.

> **TIP:** You can substitute a domain account for security purposes. Use Domain\Service Account as a substitute for the RSUSER account.

Configuring Reporting Services Databases

To configure the Reporting Services database:

1. Launch the Reporting Services Configuration Manager (Start I Programs I Microsoft SQL Server 2005 I Configuration Tools I Reporting Services Configuration).

2. Accept the defaults and click Connect. Verify that the Service Status is running.

3. Select Report Server Virtual Directory from the navigation pane at the left of the window. Select the New button next to the Name field.

4. Create a new virtual directory. Accept the defaults.

5. Select Report Manager Virtual Directory from the navigation pane at the left of the window. Select the New button next to the Name field. In the Create a New Virtual Directory dialog box, accept the defaults by clicking OK.

6. Select Windows Service Identity. Select the Built-in Account radio button and select Network Service from the drop-down menu. Click Apply to update the configuration file.

7. Select Web Service Identity. Verify that the ASP.NET Service account is set to NT Authority\NetworkService account.

8. Create a new application pool associated with Reporting Services.

9. Select the New button next to the Report Server drop-down menu.

10. Enter **'ReportServer'** in the Application Pool Name field. Select the Built-in Account radio button and select Network Service from the drop-down menu. Click OK to create the application pool.

11. Verify that the application pool for Report Server is now displayed as "'ReportServer'."

12. In the Report Manager drop-down menu, select 'ReportServer' to use the new application pool. Click Apply to update the configuration. Verify that the web service identity settings were correctly applied.

13. Select Database Setup from the navigation pane. Select <EdgeSight Server> from the Server Name pull-down field.

14. Select New next to the Database Name field to create the Reporting Services database.

15. In the SQL Server Connection dialog box, select SQL Server Account from the Credential Type drop-down menu and enter your system SQL connection user name (SQL SA account) and password. Use the default setting for the database name and language.

NOTE: This account must have the' '"master" database as the default database in SQL for this step to work.

---

16. For Credential Type, use the Reporting Services user account created under the Creating a Reporting Services User section and click Apply. Select Windows Credentials from the Credentials Type drop-down menu. Enter the account name in the Account Name field and the password in the Password field (refer to documentation for account info). Click Apply.

17. A SQL Connection dialog box will appear. Verify SQL Server Account is chosen and enter the user name and password for the SQL connection.

18. The Encryption Keys step is not required for this installation and therefore will be skipped.

19. Select Initialization from the navigation pane. Verify that the current machine and instance are listed. Verify that the check box is checked and then click the Initialize button. Verify that the initialization process completed correctly.

NOTE: If you are using the Standard edition of Reporting Services, the initialization pane is grayed out in Reporting Services Configuration Manager. You should still see the check mark. This is grayed out because scale out to a web farm is not available in this edition. If the Report Server Windows service is running, it is already initialized.

20. Click on Email Settings in the navigation pane. Enter the sender address (From field) and the actual SMTP server to be used to deliver mail generated by Reporting Services. Apply the e-mail settings.

21. Skip the Execution account page.

22. Click Exit.

Configuring Reporting Services Website

To configure the Reporting Services Website:

1. Verify the Reporting Services installation. Open the IIS Manager and validate that the application pools and websites are set up correctly.

2. Open the SQL Server Management Studio and verify that the ReportServer and the ReportServer TempDB were both created.

3. Configure security for the new Reporting Services user by following these steps:

   a. Display the report server home page in a browser (for example, http://*myserver*/reports)

   b. Click Site Settings. The Site Settings page is displayed.

   c. Locate the Security settings and click Configure site-wide security. The System Role Assignments page is displayed.

   d. Click New Role Assignment. The New System Role Assignment page is displayed.

   e. Assign the System Administrator role to the new user by entering the user name (Database Connection account) in the Group or User Name field and selecting the System Administrator check box. Click OK to complete the assignment. The new user is now displayed on the System Role Assignments page.

   f. Click Home to return to the Home page.

   g. Click the Properties tab. Site users and roles are displayed.

   h. Click New Role Assignment. The New Role Assignment page is displayed.

   i. Assign all roles to the new user by entering the user name (Database Connection account) in the Group or User Name field and selecting all role check boxes. Click OK to complete the assignment. The new user is now displayed on the Properties tab.

   j. Close the browser.

4. Configure access to Reporting Services from EdgeSight using the Server Console for your specific EdgeSight software. Follow these steps:

a. Log into the EdgeSight Server Console (http://EdgeSight Server/edgesight40/ app/suilogin.aspx) and go to Server Settings | Reporting Services | Server.

b. Enter the URL for the server running SQL Server Reporting Services: http:// EdgeSight Server/ReportServer.

c. Enter the user name (Database Connection account), password, and domain name (Domain) associated with the account used to access the report server.

d. Click the check boxes to select the actions listed next. It is recommended that you select all available actions in order to facilitate your use of Reporting Services capabilities.

   ■ **Load Default Reports**   Enable this action to load the default set of standard reports. If this action is disabled, the default reports are not loaded from the report server.

   ■ **Generate Report List Mappings**   Enable this action to display the default reports under an associated node in the navigation tree. This option is automatically selected if the Load Default Reports option is selected.

   ■ **Create Default Schedules**   Enable this action to create a set of default report-generation schedules for use when creating subscriptions. If this action is disabled, no default schedules are created.

e. Click OK–Update Report Server Settings. The Reporting Services Configuration dialog box is displayed, showing the configuration status. Errors are displayed in red text. If you encounter an error, close the dialog box and correct the settings, or contact the system administrator for your report server.

NOTE: Reports will take some time to load. Be patient.

f. When the configuration is complete, click Close to close the dialog box.

Post-installation Tasks

Once you complete the Reporting Services portion of the setup, you need to complete some post-installation steps.

1. Install the latest version of Flash for the website report viewer.

2. Install Microsoft Excel (for viewing real-time reports).

3. Install the EdgeSight service pack or updates (Service Pack 2 at the time of this writing).

4. Update Reporting Services as follows:

   a. Log into the EdgeSight Server Console (http://EdgeSight Server/edgesight40/ app/suilogin.aspx) and go to Server Settings | Reporting Services | Server.

   b. Enter the URL for the server running SQL Server Reporting Services: http:// EdgeSight Server/ReportServer.

   c. Enter the user name (Database Connection account), password, and domain name (Domain) associated with the account used to access the report server.

   d. There are three options to select when updating Reporting Services:

      ■ **Load Default Reports**   Enable this action to load the default set of standard reports. If this action is disabled, the default reports are not loaded from the report server.

      ■ **Generate Report List Mappings**   Enable this action to display the default reports under an associated node in the navigation tree. This option is automatically selected if the Load Default Reports option is selected.

      ■ **Create Default Schedules**   Enable this action to create a set of default report-generation schedules for use when creating subscriptions. If this action is disabled, no default schedules are created.

   e. Click OK–Update Report Server Settings. The Reporting Services Configuration dialog box is displayed, showing configuration status. Errors are displayed in red text. If you encounter an error, close the dialog box and correct the settings, or contact the system administrator for your report server.

5. Configure the departments. For a XenApp server–only install, the common use of department definitions is to define a department for each unique XenApp farm. Other typical department definitions would be production and disaster-recovery farm definitions.

   a. In the EdgeSight Server Console, navigate to Company Settings | Server | Device Management | Departments.

   b. Select New Department from the right pane.

   c. Type the department name and click OK–Create a Department.

6. Configure the groups. For a XenApp server–only install, the common use of group definitions is to define a group for silo sets of farm servers. Other typical group definitions would be for virtual and physical servers.

   a. In the EdgeSight Server Console, navigate to Company Settings | Server | Device Management | Groups.

   b. Select New Group from the right pane.

   c. Type the department name and click OK–Create a Group.

7. Configure the alerts. Alerts allow the monitoring of specific events as they occur on the agent devices.

    a. Navigate to Company Settings | Server | Alerts | Rules.

    b. Click New Rule, select the rule, and configure it as required.

    c. Navigate to Company Settings | Server | Device Management | Groups.

    d. Click the yellow star below the Alert Rules column.

    e. Click Associate New Rule in the bottom window.

    f. Select the rule from the Select an Unassigned Alert Rule drop-down menu.

    g. Click OK to return to the Device Management window. Repeat these steps for all alerts.

    The following are the recommend alerts for a XenApp-only deployment:

    ■ Process Hung Alert, Process Fault Alert, and Application Error Alert for the critical applications.

    ■ For XenApp environments you should monitor the core XenApp functions, such as the XTE Service (xte.exe), IMA Service (imasrv.exe), License Server (lmgrd.exe and citrix.exe), Winlogon (winlogon.exe), and print subsystems (spoolsrv.exe and cpsvc.exe).

    ■ Set alerts for High Resource Utilization 90%, Process Hung, and Process Terminated for each of the core components.

8. Configure the antivirus software. If the antivirus software is not correctly configured, the performance of the agent device will suffer, resulting in poorer end-user performance. Complete the following steps on each XenApp server device if running antivirus software. Configure the antivirus software to *not* scan the EdgeSight data folder or processes as follows:

    a. Exclude the agent folder: \Documents and Settings\All Users\Application Data\Citrix\System Monitoring\Data.

    b. Exclude the agent processes from being scanned: \Program Files\Citrix\System Monitoring\Agent\Core\rscorsvc.exe and \Program Files\Citrix\System Monitoring\Agent\Core\Firebird\bin\fbserver.exe.

9. Confirm port 9035 is open between the EdgeSight Server and each XenApp Server EdgeSight agent. This port is required for remote EdgeSight Console access to the agent database.

10. Update the RemoteSecurity Registry. By default the EdgeSight Agent database is only accessible from the EdgeSight Console if the user account used from the console is a local administrator on the XenApp server. This can be addressed using one of two methods:

- Update the Registry key HKEY_LOCAL_MACHINE\Software\Citrix\System Monitoring\Agent\Core\4.00 values on each XenApp server and change the RemoteSecurity value to 0.

- Provide an additional value to the same Registry key called RemoteSecurityGroup and assign a valid Active Directory group name to this value.

EdgeSight Agent for XenApp Install

Install the EdgeSight for XenApp agent. For each server in a XenApp farm, complete the following steps:

1. Execute the EdgeSightEPAgent.msi file.
2. Accept the license agreement.
3. Enter the company name and department name. (These must match the names set up on the EdgeSight Server).
4. Accept the default file locations.
5. Enter the EdgeSight Server name and leave the port as 80. (If your deployment requires the use of SSL encryption between the EdgeSight agents and EdgeSight Server, then update the entries on the dialog box to reflect this.)
6. Click Install to begin the installation.
7. Click Finish at the completion screen.
8. Select the appropriate option at the Server Reset dialog box.

TIP: A server reset will be required, although you will be able to manually start the Citrix System Monitoring service without a reset to allow the EdgeSight agent to check into the EdgeSight Server and complete the initial upload. The initial check-in and data upload should occur within 15 to 20 minutes from starting the Citrix System Monitoring service.

Go ahead and give yourself a pat on the back—or if someone is with you, have them pat you on the back. You have finished an EdgeSight for XenApp installation. Pretty easy, right? Okay, maybe you missed lunch or are late for dinner. Soon, however, you will reap the fruits of your hard work when we dig into the EdgeSight Server Console in the next section and start using this great new tool.

Citrix EdgeSight for XenApp Console

In this section we provide a review of the EdgeSight Server Console. The EdgeSight Server Console is the primary interface for accessing both real-time EdgeSight agent data and historical EdgeSight database data. The EdgeSight Server Console is a very powerful tool; the dynamic nature of the interface eases troubleshooting and also lends itself to unexpected correlation with other key metric data. We will start by getting our bearings with relation to the EdgeSight Server Console layout, shown in Figure 12-2.

Citrix administrators will access the EdgeSight Server through the EdgeSight Server Console that is installed on the EdgeSight Web Server. The EdgeSight Server Console is accessible from any web browser on the LAN and is governed by a local user database. The web server requires a local installation of Microsoft Excel for viewing remote reporting. When you are using the console, you browse pages supplied by the web server that display reports based on the data stored in the Citrix EdgeSight database. The console is broken into the various components described next:

▼ **Navigation tree items**   These items can be further separated into five content types.

■ **Reports**   This item displays reports using default parameters. These reports are often summary reports.

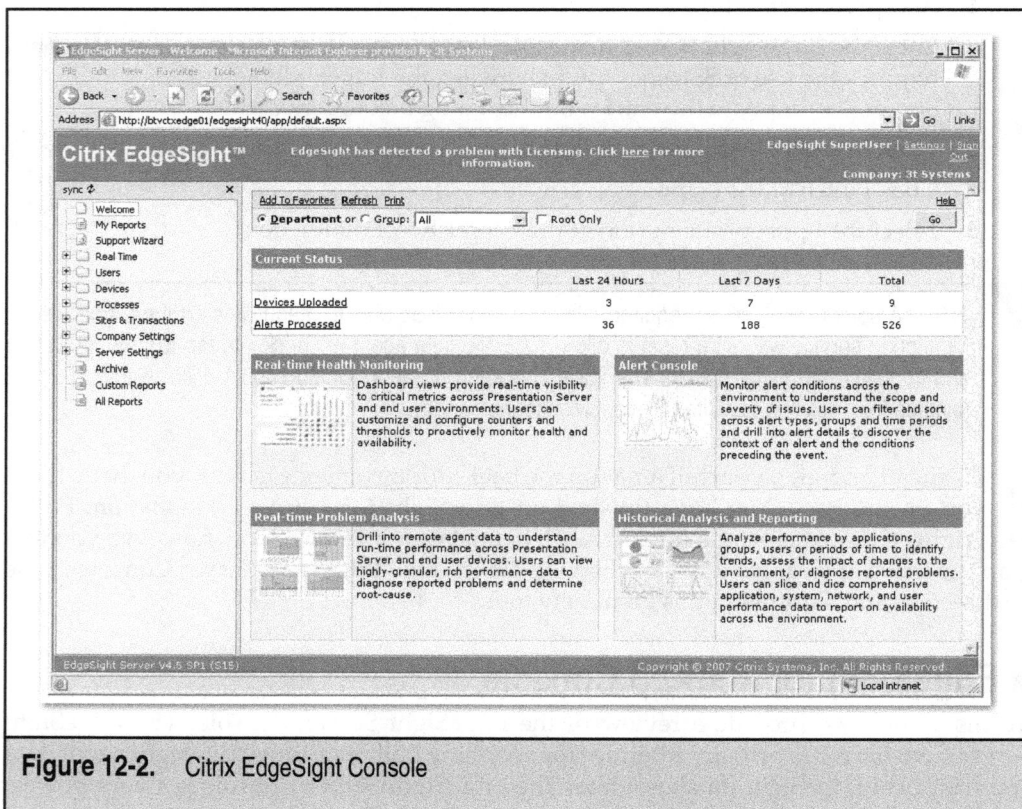

Figure 12-2.   Citrix EdgeSight Console

- **Report List**   This item displays a console page with a listing of reports that you can display.

- **Remote Reports**   This item displays reports based on data from a specific agent database. You must specify a device name to display these reports.

- **Wizards**   A wizard helps step you through a procedure, such as finding reports related to a specific problem.

- **Pages**   This item displays a static console page rather than a report. These pages are used to specify company settings, upload reports, set user preferences, and configure the EdgeSight Server.

- **Navigation tree functions**   The navigation tree can be separated into three functions, which give you a better sense of the depth of EdgeSight reporting:

  - **Remote Reporting**   This includes all items within the Real-time folder. These items are used to provide access to the wealth of real-time data within each device's agent database. This function also provides access to the real-time alerts.

  - **Historical Reporting**   This includes all items within the Users, Devices, Processes, and Sites & Transactions folders. These reports are further divided into performance, stability, and network data within each folder.

  - **Configuration**   This includes all items within the Company Settings and Server Settings folders. These folders provide access to all required EdgeSight Server configuration tasks.

- **Menu bar**   Use the menu bar to perform common operations on the current page, such as adding pages to your favorites, refreshing page data, and printing pages.

- **Filter bar**   The filter bar allows you to refine a list of reports displayed. After selecting a report, you can use the filter bar to further filter the data displayed. The filtering options include department, group, time period, process, device, user, site, and other data types.

- ▲ **Report display**   This is where all report data is displayed; this is also used for listing reports when a report list is selected.

Citrix EdgeSight for XenApp Console—Dynamic Reports

Let's focus on the dynamic nature of the graphical reports displayed within the EdgeSight Server Console. Figure 12-3 shows an example of a historical report for XenApp Summary; the EdgeSight Console allows us to click on any data point in the graphs and dynamically drill down into the supporting data.

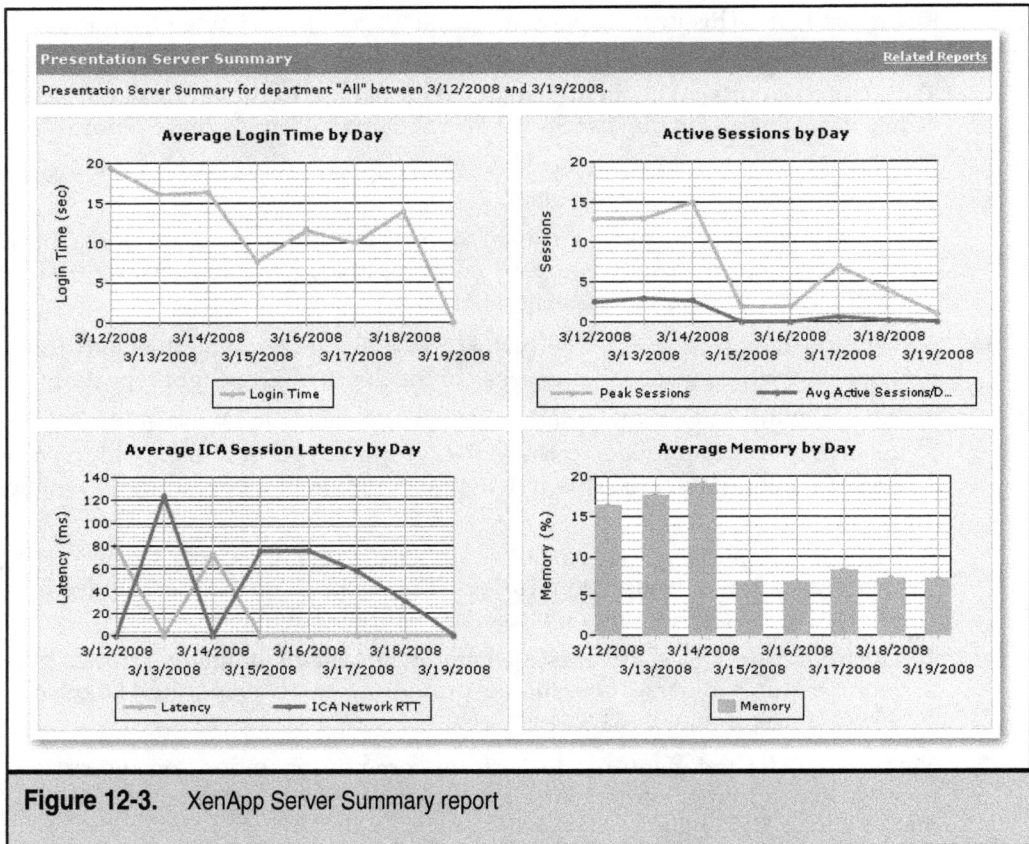

Figure 12-3. XenApp Server Summary report

Here we have clicked through one of the Login Time data points on the Average Login Time by Day report. This report displays the supporting data showing the aggregated login times on each of the XenApp servers. Each report is a listing for each XenApp server with the ability to drill down into the individual user login information that supports the server-level report. At the user level, the report displays username, session start data/time, client IP address, client name, session duration, and individual login time in seconds (see Figure 12-4).

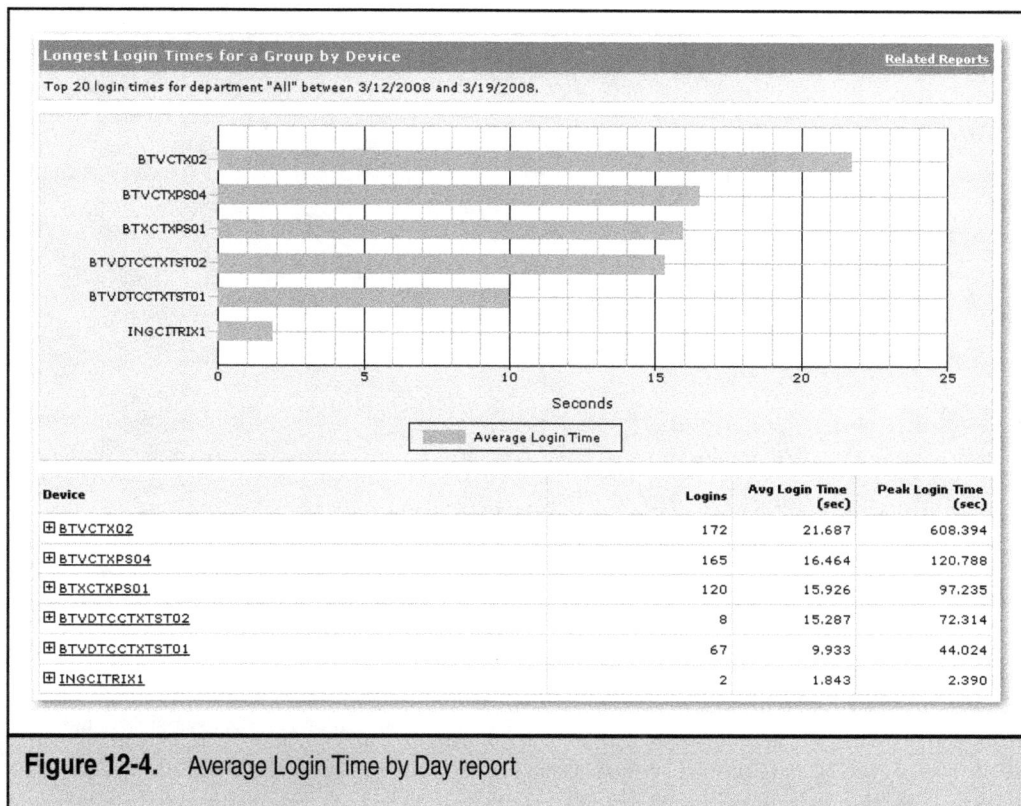

| Longest Login Times for a Group by Device | | | Related Reports |
| Top 20 login times for department "All" between 3/12/2008 and 3/19/2008. | | | |

Device	Logins	Avg Login Time (sec)	Peak Login Time (sec)
⊞ BTVCTX02	172	21.687	608.394
⊞ BTVCTXPS04	165	16.464	120.788
⊞ BTXCTXPS01	120	15.926	97.235
⊞ BTVDTCCTXTST02	8	15.287	72.314
⊞ BTVDTCCTXTST01	67	9.933	44.024
⊞ INGCITRIX1	2	1.843	2.390

Figure 12-4.   Average Login Time by Day report

In the next example, we see the Real-time Alert Console displayed. It is used to aggregate all the alerts we defined within the EdgeSight Console into one easy-to-view report (see Figure 12-5). This report has the same dynamic ability to drill into the data as shown in the previous examples.

You should be getting an idea of the power of EdgeSight and the EdgeSight Console. The ability to dynamically drill down into reports to expose more and more detail helps you quickly begin to piece together a complete picture for troubleshooting.

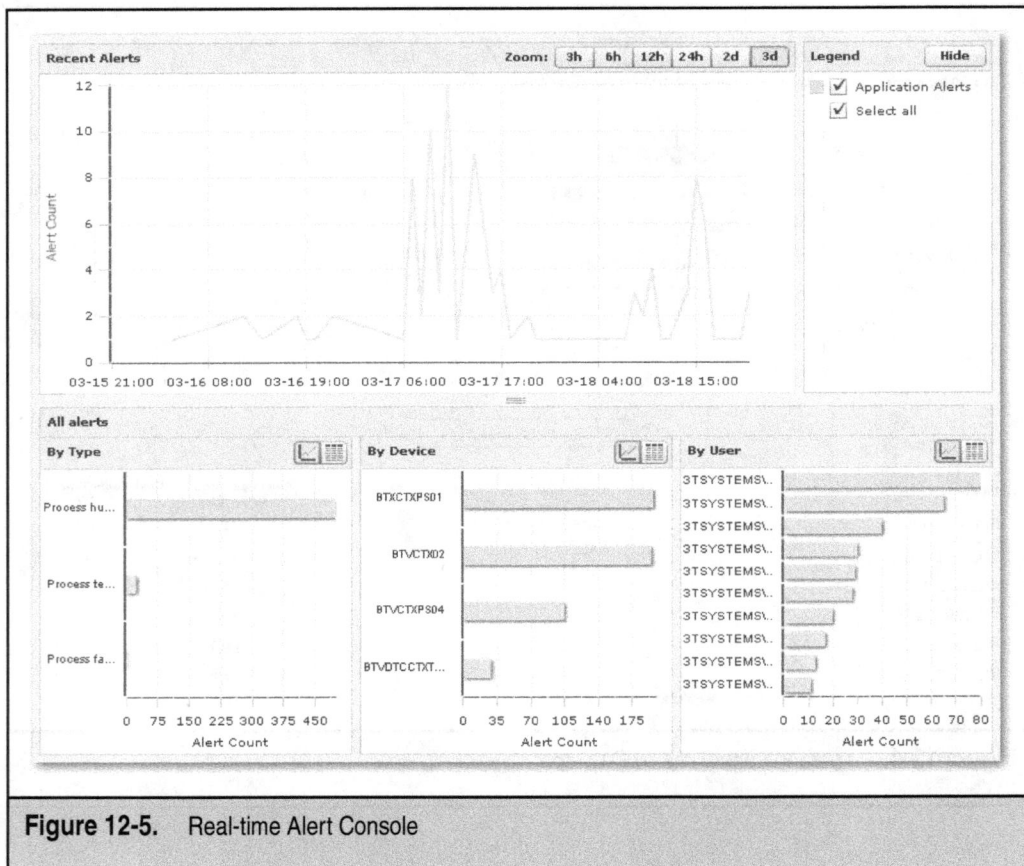

Figure 12-5. Real-time Alert Console

Citrix EdgeSight for XenApp Console—Security, Configuration, and Maintenance

The EdgeSight Server Console also provides a complete set of tools to manage all aspects of security, configuration, and maintenance for the EdgeSight Server.

Security One of the first areas you as an administrator will need to address is providing additional user access to the EdgeSight Server Console. EdgeSight can define additional authentication providers beyond the default e-mail provider. Listed next are the supported authentication providers:

▼ **E-mail authentication provider** This is the default authentication provider set up during the installation of the EdgeSight Server. It uses an e-mail address format for each user name. After you create a new user account and select the e-mail authentication provider, the EdgeSight Server will e-mail the address and provide instructions on how to access the EdgeSight Server Console and a temporary password.

▲ **Active Directory authentication provider**   This provider enables integration with Active Directory, allowing you to assign existing domain-level user accounts for access to the EdgeSight Server. To set up this provider, you will need to know the following information:

   ■ The LDAP path for the search base of your Active Directory forest. This should be entered in the following format: LDAP://*yourdomain*.com.

   You can also elect to use an existing Global Catalog server in place of the LDAP server entry. The format is similar: GC://yourdomain.com.

   ■ The user name and password for the account used to query Active Directory for users and groups.

Next, you need to assign the new users to a specified role. EdgeSight Server has two built-in roles: Administrator and Report Viewer. You can also create custom roles with very granular access to the EdgeSight Console.

Configuration   Other key configuration tasks within the Company Settings and Server Settings sections include Device Management, Application Categories, Application Vendors, Reporting, Agent Workers, Agent Schedules, Companies, Licensing, Farm Authentication, and Report Server settings. As you can see, this list is quite extensive. We will focus on Agent Workers and Agent Schedules in a later section, so let's take a look at a few of the other configuration settings:

▼ **Application Categories**   EdgeSight Server has a built-in list of 34 application categories. The categories cover standard applications such as Microsoft Office versions, e-mail applications, and database tools, as well as nonstandard categories such as instant messengers, spyware programs, malware programs and Trojan horse programs. Each new process captured during the default grace period of seven days is immediately categorized and tracked. This information is available from the Company Settings | Server | Categories | Edit item under the Details section for each category.

■ **Application Vendors**   EdgeSight Server has a built-in list of 131 application vendors. Similar to Application Categories, each process captured during the default grace period is tracked by vendor. If a process does not match a default vendor, the process will be listed as "uncategorized."

▲ **Reporting**   EdgeSight Server has the ability to allow users to subscribe to and receive specific reports. The subscription process is driven by an EdgeSight Server Console user, but the reports can be delivered to non-EdgeSight users. The reports can be delivered via e-mail or to a file share. The report format options are XML, CSV, TIFF, PDF, Web Archive, and Excel. The subscriptions must be assigned to a configured Reporting Services schedule. The schedule defines the time range for the report data, the interval for reporting, and the time for report execution.

Maintenance   Administrators know that the more database applications they deploy in their environments, the more headaches they have over time trying to keep on top of database growth and archiving. Citrix EdgeSight for XenApp has taken this worry away.

The EdgeSight Server Console has a fully integrated database-grooming interface. The EdgeSight database has 18 SQL tables that store data for the historical reports and real-time alert settings. The grooming interface allows you to edit the Groom Days setting per table to control how long data will be held in the database. Table 12-1 lists each table, with report data type, table name, and the default Groom Days setting.

The EdgeSight agent database and configurations are managed through the EdgeSight Server Console. The EdgeSight agent checks in with the EdgeSight Server once per day

Data Type	Table Name	Default Setting
Company Devices	instance	30 days
CPS Client Start Performance	ctrx_client_start_perf	30 days
CPS Environmental Usage	e image_event	30 days
CPS ICA Roundtrip Performance	ctrx_ica_rt_perf	30 days
CPS Server Start Performance	ctrx_server_start_perf	30 days
Application Performance	image_perf	30 days
Application Usage	usage	90 days
Citrix Session Performance Data	ctrx_session_perf	30 days
Citrix System Performance Data	ctrx_system_perf	30 days
Device Asset Changes	asset_change	90 days
Disk Usage	drive_space	30 days
Stability	alert	30 days
Real-time Alerts	alert_incoming	15 days
Light Trace Performance Data	ltrace_event	30 days
Messages	message	30 days
Network Statistics	core_net_stat	10 days
Network Transactions	core_net_trans	10 days
System Performance Data	system_perf	30 days

Table 12-1. Default Database Grooming Schedule

for configuration changes. The default scheduled time is 06:30. The EdgeSight agent has three types of settings, as listed next:

▼ **Agent Configuration**   The Agent Configuration settings determine how long the local agent database will keep the collected data as well as the default collection times and days. Here are the configuration options with their default settings:

■ Days to Keep in DB: 3 days

■ Max Days to Keep in DB: 5 days

■ Data Collection Start Date: Sunday

■ Data Collection End Date: Saturday

■ Data Collection Start Hour: 00:00

■ Data Collection End Hour: 00:00

■ Maximum Database Size: 350MB

■ **Agent Worker Schedules**   The Agent Worker Schedules settings determine the agent data upload days and times to the EdgeSight Server:

■ CPS Default Data Upload (1): Once a day at 05:00

■ CPS Default Data Upload (2): Once a day at 19:00

▲ **Agent Worker Configuration**   The Agent Worker Configuration settings determine what type of data will be collected by the agent. The following options should be enabled:

■ Asset History (collects all asset history)

■ Configuration Check (checks for configuration changes)

■ Database Maintenance (performs scheduled database maintenance)

■ Drive Space Calculation (calculates drive space)

■ Fault Report Cleanup (cleans up files created for fault and snapshot reports)

■ Performance Upload (uploads agent data to the EdgeSight server)

Citrix EdgeSight for XenApp Usage

We have walked you through the EdgeSight for XenApp architecture, provided a lengthy installation roadmap, detailed the installation process, and given you an overview of the EdgeSight Server Console environment. So now you're probably saying to yourself, "How do I really use this tool?" That is a great question, and it deserves a great answer. In this final section we outline some of the common ways EdgeSight for XenApp can be used within your environment.

Application Issues

Applications are the most important part of a XenApp environment. Before EdgeSight, administrators had to rely on users contacting the help desk to report application crashes. Many times the users did not provide complete crash information or they would wait until multiple failures before reporting the problem.

In addition, administrators are often charged with trying to re-create an error or crash so they can forward the appropriate information to either a developer or a vendor.

With EdgeSight for XenApp, the EdgeSight agent is always running on the Citrix XenApp server. It captures a standard mini-dump file for any published application that crashes. These mini-dump files contain a complete set of information that can be used by an application developer to address issues. The complete text of an application error is captured along with the exact time it occurred.

After the deployment of EdgeSight for XenApp, administrators no longer need users to report these issues or hope they can re-create them. Here are the key reports for this area:

▼ **Process Faults for a Process by Day** This report, located in the EdgeSight Server Console under Processes | Stability | Faults, lets the administrator select a particular process and view each crash that has occurred over a specified timeframe. Expanding any of the dates where there are crashes will display the details surrounding the event. Clicking on the Info button opens a dialog box where the crash files collected can be downloaded.

■ **Process Errors by Day** This report, located in the EdgeSight Server Console under Processes | Stability | Errors, lets the administrator select a particular process and view each error that has occurred over a specified timeframe.

Expanding any of the dates where there are errors will display the details surrounding the event, including the exact error message.

■ **Most Process Faults for a Group by Process** This report, located in the EdgeSight Server Console under Processes | Stability | Faults, shows the administrator which applications have crashed the most in their environment. Expanding any of the applications in the display table will detail additional information surrounding the event. Clicking on the Info button opens a dialog box where the crash files collected can be downloaded.

▲ **Most Process Errors for a Group by Process** This report, located in the EdgeSight Server Console under Processes | Stability | Errors, shows the administrator which applications have had the most errors in their environment. Expanding any of the applications in the display table provides additional information surrounding the event, including the exact error message.

Citrix Farm Health

Often administrators are asked to provide a set of high-level reports reflecting the overall health of a particular enterprise application or for the entire Citrix XenApp farm. In addition, many times they are asked to provide a comparative analysis of the end-user experience across the Citrix XenApp farm by silo group, hardware type, or application version.

Gathering sets of information from various sources, including the help desk, network operations, and resource managers, and correlating them together can be very time consuming. It may also not be possible to slice this information into the various groupings mentioned previously.

With EdgeSight for XenApp, administrators can pull this data with one report—which can be sent as an e-mail subscription—that provides a complete picture of ICA latency, login times, session counts, and system utilization across the entire farm or for a subset of servers, application, or users.

From this report, administrators can drill into any peaks of the dataset to determine which users or servers were contributing to the data. A key report for this is the XenApp Server Summary. This report, located in the EdgeSight Server Console at Devices | Presentation Server Summary, gives the administrator a complete picture of the metrics listed previously for any group of Citrix servers. Departments and/or groups can be created so that the data can be displayed for the entire farm, for a silo of application servers, or for any other group of servers.

ICA Login Times

We all know that ICA login times are one of our most visible issues; add to this the fact that troubleshooting ICA login time delays—which may happen all the time, sporadically, or for only certain sets of users—can be very difficult. Administrators often look at profile sizes to see if they are larger than normal for some users. They also may have to visit user sites to get an idea of the actual experience the users are having. Gathering and correlating network logs from various sources may be difficult and time intensive.

With Citrix XenApp Server 4.5 and EdgeSight for XenApp, we can quickly show which points in the login process are slowest for any user accessing a XenApp server. If the bottleneck occurs during the XenApp server authentication process, or while mapping client drives, mapping client printers, executing logon scripts, or executing user GPOs, administrators can see this information within one report. Here are the key reports for this area:

▼ **Startup Time Detail for a User by Session**   This report, located in the EdgeSight Server Console under Users | Performance | Sessions, allows the administrator to select a particular user and view the startup time on both the client and the server for the user's session. Furthermore, the data is broken down into the individual pieces of the login process to help determine which part is taking the longest.

▲ **Longest Login Times for a Group by Device**   This report, located in the EdgeSight Server Console under Devices | Performance | Login Time, allows the administrator to see which servers have historically had the highest login times. Expanding any of the server names in the display table will detail the users contributing to that data.

Client/Server Application Health

Application owners want to understand how a certain application is performing in a XenApp environment. They also may be releasing a new version shortly and want to understand how the end-user experience will be impacted. Currently, administrators may rely on user feedback to see how an application is running or whether an upgrade went smoothly. Often the new version is released to a small set of "test users," and if there are no reports of performance problems or application issues, the new application is released to the entire environment.

Because EdgeSight captures error messages, system resource utilization, and network performance data for any process running where the EdgeSight agent is installed, reports can show this information for a specific version of the application. Administrators can then compare these metrics to see if the end-user experience is better or worse. EdgeSight provides a complete view of the health of the application and can quickly help administrators quantify its impact on the environment. Here are the key reports:

▼ **Stability Summary for a Process** This report, located in the EdgeSight Server Console at Processes | Stability | Stability Summary for a Process, allows the administrator to select a specific application and view the amount of errors, crashes, and "not responding" alerts that have occurred over a specified timeframe.

■ **Network Summary for a Process** This report, located in the EdgeSight Server Console at Processes | Network | Network Summary for a Process, allows the administrator to select a specific application and view the average network delay, volume, roundtrip time, and transaction or web errors that have occurred over a specified timeframe.

▲ **Performance Summary for a Process** This report, located in the EdgeSight Server Console at Processes | Performance | Performance Summary for a Process, allows the administrator to select a specific application and view the average system resources being utilized over a specified timeframe.

Capacity Planning

In today's business world, companies are constantly changing, and IT has to be flexible enough to change at the same pace as the business side of the company. Many times, administrators are asked to forecast the number of new servers needed to handle increased capacity. New applications are also constantly being introduced into our Citrix farms, and we need a way to understand what resource load these applications will consume before we commit to purchasing new hardware.

EdgeSight for XenApp can easily show administrators the average system resource utilization and average number of sessions over time. Many times, the increase in users can be handled sufficiently with the current infrastructure if we understand our current usage. This results in shifting the organizational budget to higher-priority areas. When new resources are required, administrators, by using EdgeSight, will have sufficient data to detail the increased requirements. Here are the key reports in this area:

▼   **XenApp Server Summary**   This report, located in the EdgeSight Server Console at Devices | Presentation Server Summary, gives the administrator a complete picture of the memory utilization and average session count for any group of Citrix servers. Departments and/or groups can be created so that the data can be displayed for the entire farm, for a silo of application servers, or for any other group of servers.

■   **Memory Summary**   This report, located in the EdgeSight Server Console in Devices | Performance | Memory, gives the administrator a complete picture of the memory utilization by class of server across any group of Citrix servers. Departments and/or groups can be created so that the data can be displayed for the entire farm, for a silo of application servers, or for any other group of servers.

▲   **CPU Summary**   This report, located in the EdgeSight Server Console in Devices | Performance | CPU, gives the administrator a complete picture of the CPU utilization by class of server across any group of Citrix servers. Departments and/or groups can be created so that the data can be displayed for the entire farm, for a silo of application servers, or for any other group of servers.

These are just a few of the many usage scenarios for EdgeSight for XenApp. We hope that in reading this chapter you have been able to see the great value of implementing EdgeSight within your Citrix farm. With EdgeSight, you will be able to provide a more proactive approach to managing your Citrix farm, and your time spent troubleshooting application and user issues will be more focused and productive.

CHAPTER 13

Application Installation and Configuration

The purpose of the infrastructure discussed so far in this book is to provide software applications to users. Whether these applications automate the organization (say, using ERP, MRP, or CAD/CAM), provide recordkeeping and documentation for the organization (with such things as accounting applications, word processors, spreadsheets, document management, and so on), or allow the organization to communicate effectively (through e-mail, printing, file sharing, or presentation software), applications have become critical to a vast majority of organizations and their users. Without applications, there is no need for IT infrastructure of any kind.

Because all enterprise organizations (as well as a large majority of small and mid-sized businesses) today have applications that fill these needs, the debate comes down to how to most effectively and cost-efficiently build an IT infrastructure that provides these applications to users that need them. Additionally, many organizations, as they have grown and become more diverse, desire to deploy these applications to a wider set of users with fewer constraints.

At the core of the access platform value statement is providing these applications to users anytime, anyplace, from any device. Of course it goes without saying that the users must be able to run the applications without delay, slowness, or problems, and with the latest base of available features. We have made the argument throughout this book that the Citrix Application Delivery System succeeds at all of these far more efficiently than standard client/server computing. There is one large caveat though—the applications have to work in the XenApp environment. If the applications do not run as well, or better, in a XenApp environment as they do from a desktop PC, then the Citrix Application Delivery projects will fail. With this said, it is obvious that application installation and configuration is the fulcrum upon which any access platform project will swing from success to failure.

Several times we have discussed building a pilot or test environment prior to making any significant investment in a Terminal Services/XenApp infrastructure. The most significant reason for the test environment is to ensure that an organization's applications run effectively. Chances are good that most, if not all, of your applications will run in a Terminal Server/XenApp environment. However, there are still older applications, or poorly written ones, that remain at the core of many organizations. The success of any application delivery platform project depends largely on whether these applications can be fixed, upgraded or replaced, run in hybrid mode (run locally on some users' machines while all other applications are run from the Terminal Servers) for a period of time, or relegated to a kiosk where users access them as needed. If none of these are an option, the project simply can't go forward. Probably the single most significant reason to consider Citrix XenApp 4.5 is the improved Application Isolation Environment (AIE) feature with Application Streaming, which provides the necessary tools to "fix" many of the rogue and poorly written applications. It is this new feature set that allows many organizations that previously could not utilize XenApp effectively to now move forward with a full enterprise strategy.

This chapter focuses on how applications are installed in a XenApp environment, the use of the Application Isolation features of Citrix XenApp 4.5, the applications' requirements, some tricks to making nonconforming applications work, application optimization, specific tips and checklists for common applications, and an application testing methodology. It also introduces the Application Streaming feature of XenApp. Refer to Chapter 9 for a more detailed explanation of how to install and configure applications for the streaming environment.

The installation and testing methodology presented in this chapter is critical not only at implementation, but throughout the life of the on-demand application delivery environment. All application installations and updates, even minor hotfixes, must be subjected to a strict systematic installation and testing methodology.

APPLICATION STRATEGIES

The idea behind building an *application delivery system* is to provide a means of distributing common applications to users that is low in cost and complexity, but high in functionality and performance. It is important to keep this "end state" in mind when selecting or writing applications to be run in a Citrix XenApp environment. An application that is not stable in a traditional distributed computing network isn't likely to work any better under XenApp. In fact, it may exhibit new problems. It is also critical to take the client environment into account. In the days of old there were just a couple of scenarios for the client environment: PCs and thin clients. With current trends in lower-cost laptops and desktop PCs, and the mobility requirements of the users, the capabilities and user experience of each can be quite different and will affect application functionality and availability.

All application installations and updates, even minor hotfixes, must be subjected to a strict systematic installation and testing methodology. From a high level, we suggest the following methodology:

1. Identify and confirm the requirement for the installation, update, or hotfix.

2. Research the manufacturer instructions and warnings for the software to be installed.

3. Install the application in the test environment.

   a. Decide whether to install it normally, utilize the isolation environment, or stream the application.

   b. Configure the application.

4. Perform the recommended testing algorithm according to company policies and make any necessary fixes, Registry changes, or optimizations to verify application functionality.

5. Following full testing, install the application to one production server.

6. Perform the testing algorithm again.

7. Publish to the remaining required production servers.

Application Features and Requirements

We have created the following list of features and requirements to aid you in the application selection process:

▼ The application should be stable and perform well in a traditional, distributed computing environment.

■ The application should have stated support from the manufacturer. In the early days of on-demand access technology, application support was hit or miss (more miss than hit). With Windows Server 2003, however, in order for a software package to gain the Microsoft Windows Certification, the application must also support execution under Terminal Services. As such, multiuser support has become the norm rather than the exception.

■ Ideally, an application should execute in multithreaded fashion and make efficient use of memory and CPU resources when running in a multiuser environment.

■ The use of multimedia in applications should be kept to an absolute minimum. Sound, graphics, or video should be limited to mission-critical features only, because the complexity and cost of the extra network bandwidth consumed by these features must be justified.

▲ The application should make the most use of the Windows printing system and be as efficient as possible in the creation and distribution of print jobs. Here again, we issue a warning regarding graphic-intensive programs: They typically generate enormous print files that then travel over the LAN or WAN to the printer. This must be taken into account when planning for the management of the available bandwidth.

INSTALLING AND CONFIGURING APPLICATIONS

Because the operating system needs to allow multiple users to run and access applications (and thus application Registry settings) simultaneously, a program must be installed in such a fashion that the Registry changes are replicated for all users. There are two basic methods for installing an application on a Citrix XenApp server to cause this replication to take place. The recommended method is to use the Control Panel and run the Add/Remove Programs application. The other is to run the "change user /install" and "change user /execute" commands from a command prompt.

Using Add/Remove Programs

The advantage to installing an application using Add/Remove Programs from the Control Panel is that it creates the "shadow key" properly in all cases. The Add/Remove Programs application monitors changes to the HKEY_CURRENT_USER key and saves them in the shadow key. This key is then propagated to each user, as shown in Figure 13-1, so that they may have unique settings for that application.

NOTE: Do not allow the system to reboot until after you click Finish in the Add/Remove Programs application. Doing so will ensure that the shadow key information is safely written.

Using Change User /Install

For certain types of applications and when installing updates, hotfixes, and patches, it is sometimes necessary to use the change user/install command from a command prompt. Under normal circumstances this procedure works well, but in some cases the shadow key information is missing. For example, there is a known problem installing Internet Explorer in this manner, but it works perfectly well using the Add/Remove Programs application. This method involves opening a command prompt, typing change user /install, installing the application, and then typing change user /execute.

NOTE: If you use this method, make sure you do not allow the system to reboot without first issuing the change user /execute command. If you do not issue the command, the system may not properly record the changes to the Registry.

When you're installing an application in Windows 2003 Server editions with Terminal Services enabled (either by inserting the CD for the application or launching the executable), Windows usually detects that it is not in "install" mode and will prompt you to run the program through Add/Remove Programs. Some applications are known

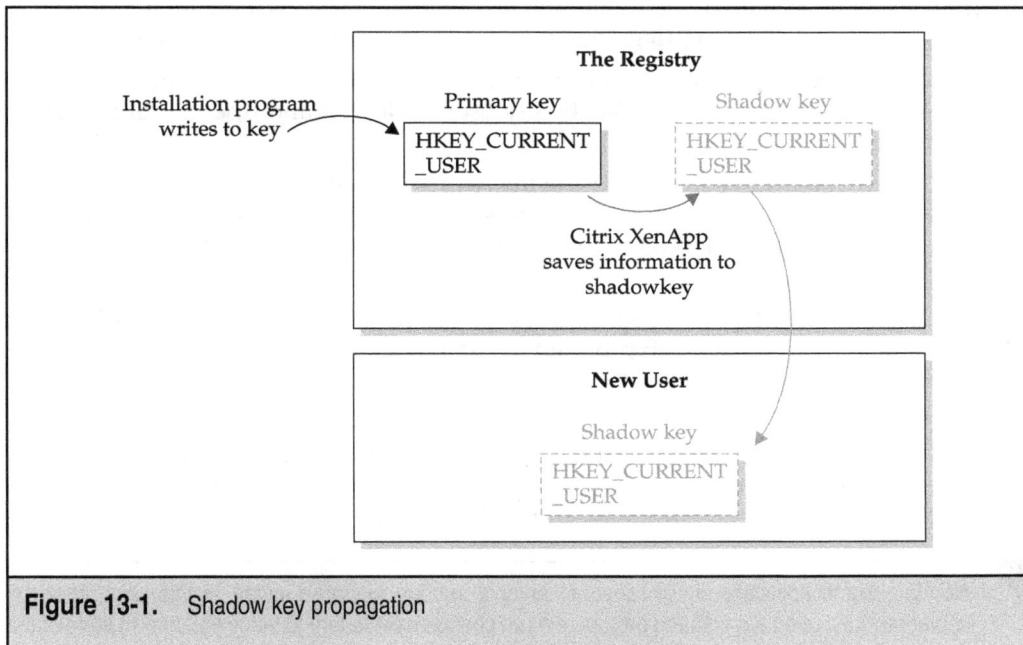

Figure 13-1.   Shadow key propagation

to be "terminal server aware," such as Microsoft Office, and will install properly into the "all users" keys without running in install mode. It is a good practice to always use the Add/Remove Programs application in Control Panel first to install the application; then, if that fails, use the command prompt with change user /install command.

What about updates, hotfixes, and service packs? A good rule of thumb is that if the update is a full download and it is launched using an .exe or .msi file, use Add/Remove Programs. If the update is done through a web browser, such as a patch for Internet Explorer or an Adobe Reader update, use the command line to change into install mode and then browse for the update and run it.

Keep in mind when you're installing applications and updates on a Terminal Server that all users should be logged off the server and that the server should be rebooted prior to the installation or update. Again, *all users must be logged off* prior to the installation or update. Failure to do so may result in some serious undesirables on the servers. Keep in mind that when a Terminal Server is placed into install mode, all changes made on the server are written to the "All Users" Registry hive. Therefore, any user's personal settings and changes could be made available to all users logging into the machine.

The Application Installation Checklist

The basic procedure for installing applications on a Windows Server 2003 running Citrix XenApp is as follows:

1. Verify that the Terminal Server is a domain member and that DNS and WINS are properly configured.

2. Make sure you are logged onto the test server console as a member of the local Administrators group (logging on as a domain administrator is preferred).

3. Verify all users are logged off the server and all sessions are cleared out of the Access Management Console. Notify users to log off and reset all disconnected sessions.

4. Disable logons to the server using the Access Management Console (select Server | Properties | Presentation Server settings; then uncheck the Enable Logons to This Server check box) to prevent users from logging on during the application installation.

5. Run the Add/Remove Programs application from the Control Panel and browse to the application's setup program to begin installation. This will put the server into install mode, similar to running `change user /install` from a command prompt.

6. Click Finish after the application has completed installation and before the server reboots. This will put the server back into execute mode, similar to running change user /execute from a command prompt.

NOTE: Some applications will cause a server to reboot during an install. In this case, after the server reboots, open a command prompt and run change user /query to verify the current state of the server before proceeding to the next application.

7. If an application compatibility script exists, run it. Review the notes in the script and any "read me" notes on application compatibility and then perform any other necessary steps.

8. If the product has service packs or online updates, such as one of the Microsoft Office products, place the server into install mode using the command line and run the updates or patches. If the patch or service pack is an EXE or MSI, go through the Add/Remove Programs application.

9. At this point, the application is installed and testing can begin.

NOTE: Although you can install and uninstall applications with Add/Remove Programs, we don't recommend it. We recommend using the imaging process (Ghost), automation software (RES Wisdom, Microsoft SMS, or Altiris), or using Citrix Installation Manager (discussed later in this chapter) to create standard server images, including packaged applications. If an application needs to be removed, simply restore the image that was current before the application package was installed. Alternatively, you can unpublish the application within Installation Manager. Other methods can leave remnants of the application in the form of leftover Registry changes or library files—which can cause problems with the system or with other applications.

XenApp's Application Isolation Environment

In the Citrix Presentation Server 4 release, the Application Isolation Environment (AIE) was introduced. As mentioned earlier in this chapter, this feature has fundamentally changed the face of Presentation Server, allowing many organizations to consolidate farms and minimize the number of application silo servers present in each farm. An application silo is a group of servers dedicated to serving up applications that do not "play well" together on the same server. It is also used to run more than one version of the same application on the same server (for example, Office 2003 and Office 2007), where in the past these two programs would step on one another during the install and more than likely not work. In some cases, applications that previously would not be compatible with Terminal Services could be installed. This feature set essentially allows an administrator to install applications on a XenApp server as if each is the only application on the server, virtualizing the file space and Registry space. This virtualization effectively "fixes" applications that weren't written to understand Terminal Services multiuser mode or that conflict with other applications installed on the server.

How AIE Works

An isolation environment is a virtual environment that can be created on a Citrix XenApp server. To understand the concept of an isolation environment, think of it is as an isolation bubble into which applications that previously caused problems in a Terminal Services/XenApp environment can be installed and executed. One or more "misbehaving" applications can be run in this isolation bubble without affecting the rest of the system. A "misbehaving" application in the context of an isolation environment is one that exhibits incompatible or unsociable behaviors relative to other applications or the system in general when installed on a XenApp server.

An isolation environment is created by virtualizing specific operating system resources so that an incompatible or unsociable application can be safely installed and published on a XenApp server. The isolation environment provides a virtual mapping from an application's view of system resources to the physical operating system resources. The mapping is accomplished through the use of rules. Rules specify how an application behaves within an isolation environment. Applications that are run in isolation are known by the Management Console, but the physical Windows operating system is unaware that the application exists or is installed.

NOTE: Typical candidates for application isolation are legacy applications not designed for use with Terminal Server, applications that exhibit compatibility issues in a multiuser environment, or any applications that cannot coexist on a single server. Applications that install Windows services or drivers will not function correctly and, therefore, are not candidates for isolation environments.

When to Use Application Isolation

Application compatibility or sociability problems that application isolation attempts to resolve or mitigate typically involve file, Registry, or system objects on a XenApp server. The following are some behaviors that help identify application compatibility or sociability issues on XenApp:

▼ **When you cannot open multiple instances of an application** A single user is unable to open more than one instance of an application, or two users attempting to launch a published application experience application launch failure. This occurs when an application is designed to lock certain system resources upon execution.

■ **When you cannot install different versions of the same application on a single server** Multiple versions of some applications cannot be installed or executed on a single XenApp server. This is because the two versions of the application share the same resources or overwrite existing files from a previous installation. Usually, the application installer simply does not allow installations of multiple versions to continue. In some cases, one version of the application stops working after two versions of the application are installed.

■ **When applications share a system resource or resources** There are instances when two or more applications share specific system files (DLL, INI, and so on), resulting in conflicting versions of the file being present. For example, applications that use the Java Runtime Environment (JRE) can cause conflicts of this type.

■ **When applications use hard-coded file paths or settings** If an application uses hard-coded file paths or settings, you may be unable to publish different versions of that application on XenApp. Typically such applications do not allow per-user settings and paths. An application may use hard-coded file paths or settings if multiple users are unable to launch individual instances of the application.

▲ **When an application does not integrate well with XenApp** Some applications are not designed to run on Terminal Services and do not work well on XenApp. Such applications are typically not designed for multiuser environments and hence don't perform as expected on XenApp. Other applications that are problematic to install on XenApp use hard-coded path and key names (HKEY_LOCAL_MACHINE) and do not differentiate between individual users that run the application. This results in conflicts such as the inability to launch multiple instances of an application, multiple users being unable to launch the same application, and so on.

Using Isolation Environments

Isolation environments can be created, configured, and used in conjunction with application publishing on a server farm by following the minimum steps described in this section. The isolation environment must be enabled prior to configuration. To enable/disable isolation at the farm level, follow these steps:

1. In the scope pane of the Access Management Console, select the farm, select Action | Modify Farm Properties | Modify All Properties.

2. Select the Server Default | Isolation Environment page in the farm's Properties list.

3. Use the Application Isolation check box to enable/disable isolation environments for the farm.

When you first enable the isolation environment for the farm, all the servers are also enabled by default. Some situations may not require all servers be enabled across the entire farm. For this situation, administrators may choose to disable the isolation environment on the each server that does not require it. To enable/disable isolation at the server level, follow these steps:

1. In the Access Management Console, choose Modify Server Properties | Modify All Properties.

2. Select the Isolation Environment page in the server's Properties list.

3. Clear the Use Farm Settings check box and use the Application Isolation check box to enable/disable isolation environments for the farm.

Creating Isolation Environments

1. Create an isolation environment from the Presentation Server Console.

2. From the Actions menu, select New | Isolation Environment.

3. Enter a name for the new isolation environment and click OK. The new isolation environment appears in the Contents pane for the Isolation Environments node.

Isolation Environment Properties

New isolation environments created in the Presentation Server Console have default settings designed to address most compatibility issues that may cause problems. Optionally you may choose to configure custom settings for the isolation environments. When tweaking these settings to match your server farm, consider the following associated property variables:

▼ **Applications** Specifies which applications are associated with or installed in this particular isolation environment.

■ **Roots** Specifies the virtual directories and Registry locations in which files modified by users (user profile root) and applications (installation root) reside.

■ **Rules** Specifies policies that prescribe how an isolated application accesses system resources, such as files, the Registry, and named objects.

▲ **Security** Specifies the security policy to apply to this isolation environment. Isolation environment security can be "enhanced" or "relaxed."

Applications An isolation environment can contain a published application that is associated with an isolation environment or an application that is installed into the isolation environment. Each is further defined here:

▼ **Associated applications** Applications are installed directly onto the operating system on one or more servers running XenApp and are configured to launch within the confines of an isolation environment. The isolation environment forces the application to launch in the isolation environment and access a virtualized version of system resources. This prevents direct access of key system resources by the application, which in turn prevents the occurrence of application conflicts and incompatibilities. These applications can also be accessed from outside the isolation environment. Deleting an isolation environment has no effect on the application; however, user-specific files created within the isolation environment are deleted. To associate a published application with an isolation environment, follow these steps:

1. In the Access Management Console, select the Applications node.

2. Select Action | New | Published Application.

3. Use the Application Publishing Wizard to publish the application. On the Location page, select the Isolate Application check box and click the Settings button to select the isolation environment to use.

4. Complete the wizard by specifying the other properties for the published and isolated application. For more information, see the Access Management Console Help.

▲ **Installed applications** By installing an application into an isolation environment, it becomes completely isolated. Application shortcuts, Registry settings, paths, and so on, reside within the confines of the isolation environment. If an isolation environment is deleted, paths to applications installed into the isolation environment are deleted as well. These are applications installed into an isolation environment using the aiesetup command. To use aiesetup to install an application into an isolation environment, follow these steps:

1. Ensure the application is not already installed on the server. If it is, uninstall the application.

2. Designate and configure the isolation environment you plan to use.

3. Use the command *aiesetup* to install the application in an isolation environment in your farm. The aiesetup command must be run at the command prompt of the server on which you wish to install the application. To run aiesetup, type

```
aiesetup Isolation_Environment_Name Setup_application [parameters]
```

at the command prompt, where *Isolation_Environment_Name* is the name of the target isolation environment, *Setup_application* is the installation file (MSI or EXE) for the application to be installed, and *[parameters]* is the commands the installer executes at run time.

NOTE: When using a remote session into the server for installing applications in the isolation environment, make sure you use the /console switch. A regular RDP connection will cause an error with the Windows Installer Service.

4. On the server, use the Application Publishing Wizard in the Access Management Console and on the Location page, complete the following settings:

   a. Check the Isolate Application check box (disabled by default) and click Settings.

   b. In the Isolation Settings dialog box, from the list of available isolation environments, select the isolation environment into which you installed the application.

   c. Click the "Application was installed into the isolation environment" check box (this is disabled by default).

   d. Select the application from the Choose Installed Application list.

   e. If applicable, enter application parameters in the Command Line Arguments field.

5. Click OK and then continue with the steps in the wizard to publish the application.

Roots   The roots specify the virtual directories and Registry locations in which files modified by users and applications reside. The following root locations are administrator-defined for an isolation environment:

▼   **User profile root (user-specific location)**   Specifies the location in which the files or Registries modified or added by the user reside. The user profile root is a unique folder created for each user profile. This setting enables the isolation environment to create and maintain profile-specific copies of files modified by a user.

Files created or saved by the current user are located in the folder called C:\ Documents and Settings\[User_profile]\Application Data\Citrix\AIE\[AIE_name]\Device\[Drive_letter]\, where:

- *[User_profile]* is the logon name for the current user.
- *[AIE_name]* is the name of the isolation environment in which the application is running.
- *[Drive_letter]* is the physical drive where this folder resides.

NOTE: If you set the Security property for this isolation environment as Enhanced Security, users are prevented from executing files located in C:\Documents and Settings\[User_profile]\Application Data\Citrix\AIE\[AIE_name]\Device\[Drive_letter]\.

▲ **Installation root (application-specific location)** Specifies the per–isolation environment location of a directory/Registry key hierarchy for applications installed into an isolation environment. Installation root is unique for each isolation environment. This setting enables applications that normally conflict with each other to coexist. Make sure you specify an explicit address, such as "c:\" (with a trailing slash).

NOTE: Do not set the installation root to a mapped drive or a network drive specified through a Universal Naming Convention (UNC). Citrix does not support network shared locations for installation roots. You can, however, set the user profile root to a mapped network drive or UNC path.

Rules Isolation environments are constructed by defining a set of rules that specify how the application behaves within the confines of an isolation environment. XenApp server administrators can define and use rules to exert control over application interactions with operating system resources. This section describes the general types of rules that can be created and best-practice information for such rules. The rules engine is a powerful way to control how isolation environments interact with the systems resources of the operating system. Rules can be of the following types:

▼ **Isolation rule** An isolation rule forces isolated applications to search for a resource in the user profile root, followed by the installation root, and finally in the virtual location requested by the application. An isolation rule can be per user or per isolation environment. In the case of the former, a copy of system resources is created in the user profile root for each user. If the isolation rule is per isolation environment, a single copy of the required system resource is created in the installation root location and shared by all users accessing that particular isolation environment. Create per-isolation-environment rules for resources that can be shared. For an installation of Office 2003, for example, you can create a rule that isolates the Registry hive HKEY_LOCAL_MACHINE\SOFTWARE\classes. Because each user does not require a separate version of this hive, you can create a rule that isolates this particular Registry hive for the isolation environment.

NOTE: Create per-user-isolation rules if you need to ensure that each user gets a personal copy of the requested resource.

■ **Ignore rule** An ignore rule does not modify the request made by the application but is passed through the isolation environment unmodified so that an application can write to the underlying system. Basically ignore rules allow access outside of the isolation environment to the location requested by the application. The ignore rule is essentially a special redirection rule, where redirection occurs to the *actual* location requested by the application. Ignore rules were created because there are instances when an application inside an isolation environment needs to share data with an application outside the isolation environment.

For example, users can print to network printers available within an ICA session. These printers are automatically created when the user connects to a published application on a XenApp server. If the published application is running within an isolation environment, called My_AIE, which has an isolation rule applied to it, auto-creation of network printers fails because a copy of the Registry hive HKEY_CURRENT_USER\Printers is created for each user. You can ensure printer auto-creation occurs by creating a rule for My_AIE, which ignores the Registry hive HKEY_CURRENT_USER\Printers.

■ **Redirection rule** A redirection rule modifies a request for a resource to reference another physical location. No search is made in the user profile root, installation root, or original location requested by the application. Redirection rules are used to allow an application to access files, Registry keys, and objects in a specific location without first searching the user profile root and installation root locations.

For example, if an application creates the file C:\temp\data.txt for users regardless of which user it is, then it might make sense to redirect those files to C:\aietemp\ %USERNAME%. This means if user A runs the application in an isolation environment, then C:\temp\data.txt is created in C:\aietemp\UserA\data.txt. Redirect rules allow administrators to punch holes through an isolation environment to the real system while preserving isolation among applications.

▲ **Prioritization of rules** A rule for an isolation environment is based on a specific location—either a file path or a Registry key path. Rules are matched by the most specific path to the resource being accessed. A rule applies to the object (file, Registry, or named object) specified and all the children of the specified path, unless a more specific rule exists.

As an example, you could create an ignore rule for the file path C:\Documents and Settings\%USERNAME%. This means that every file and directory created under C:\Documents and Settings\%USERNAME% is created in the real system location. Because of the specified ignore rule, this directory location is not isolated. Now add a per-user-isolation rule for C:\Documents and Settings\ %USERNAME%\Windows. This isolates the per-user Windows directory, C:\ Documents and Settings\%USERNAME%\Windows.

Using the most-specific-match concept, the following occurs when an application attempts to open these files:

■ If an application opens the file C:\Documents and Settings\%USERNAME%\ Application Data\CompanyA\foo.txt, then the ignore rule for C:\Documents and Settings\%USERNAME% applies.

■ If an application attempts to open C:\Documents and Settings\ %USERNAME%\Windows\Win.ini, then the isolate-per-user rule for C:\ Documents and Settings\Windows applies.

Restrictions and Limitations to Rules   Do not modify or delete the available default rules. If the default rules are modified, the isolation environment may be unable to run applications correctly.

You can use an asterisk (*) as a wildcard character only at the end of an "ignore named object" rule. For example, the rule "ignore object*" ignores all named objects with a name starting with "object." Use of an asterisk (*) is not allowed in isolate or redirect object rules.

File system rules can apply to either files or directories. A rule can be created to alter the behavior of individual files or of directories and all of the files within them. For example, you may have a redirect rule for "C:\temp\fileA.txt" as well as one for "C:\ temp\subdir1."

Rules that specify a Registry object apply only to Registry keys. They do not apply to Registry values.

Rules are interpreted at run time; therefore, any modifications to existing rules are interpreted the next time an application associated with or installed into an isolation environment is launched. If a modification takes place during a launch of an isolated application, these changes will not affect running applications. The modified rules will be interpreted and take effect the next time the application is executed. It is important to keep in mind that changing rules for installed applications may have adverse effects on application behavior.

Uninstalling Isolated Applications

Prior to the introduction of isolation environments, an administrator could remove applications from a server by running the appropriate uninstall program using the Windows Add/Remove Programs functionality. However, uninstall programs do not necessarily delete everything that was installed into isolation, resulting in an incomplete uninstall.

An application installed within an isolation environment can be efficiently removed by running the uninstall routine for the application. Then, using the Access Management Console and the Presentation Server Console, you can remove all links for the application previously removed. This deletes all the files that reside in the installation root location of the isolation environment (typically, C:\Program Files\Citrix\AIE\<aiename>) and also deletes the Registry entries under installation root (typically, HKLM\Software\ Citrix\AIE\<aiename>).

Because an application's file system and Registry are isolated, this approach provides a clean uninstall of the application from the server.

User-specific files resident in the user profile root of the isolation environment folder are also deleted; therefore, we recommend that you follow whatever process your company policy dictates with regard to backing up user-specific files before you delete the isolation environment folder.

Deleting Isolation Environments

To delete an isolation environment, simply select it in the Presentation Server Console and delete it. Deleting an isolation environment does not remove application- or user-specific files resident in the deleted isolation environment folder on-disk. Because applications installed into isolation environments may not function correctly when the isolation environment is deleted, it is a good practice to delete the contents of the isolation environment folder when deleting an isolation environment.

Publishing the Isolated Application

After you install an application into an isolation environment, it must be published on the server farm so that users can access the application. To publish an application installed into an isolation environment, use the Application Publishing Wizard.

The Application Publishing Wizard provides a guide through the process of publishing an application and allows the selection of application isolation settings for the application to be published. Follow these steps to publish the application:

1. In the Access Management Console under Presentation Server | Applications, choose New under Common Tasks to start the Application Publishing Wizard.

2. Enter a display name for the application and the application description.

3. In the Choose the Type of Application to Publish dialog box, select Application as the Application Type and keep the default setting of Accessed from a Server.

4. On the Location screen, place a check mark next to Isolate Application and click Settings. The Isolation Settings dialog box appears.

5. In the Isolation Settings dialog box, from the list of available isolation environments, select the isolation environment into which you installed the application.

6. Check the Application Was Installed into Environment check box.

7. Select the application you need from the Choose Installed Application drop-down list. Enter application parameters, if applicable, in the Command Line Arguments field.

8. Click OK to save the configuration and return to the Application Publishing Wizard.

9. The command line and working directory should now be populated with the isolation path.

10. Continue with the application-publishing steps as normal.

▼

NOTE: Do not modify rules once an application is installed and in use. If you do so, the effect is similar to that experienced when you rename directories or keys into which an application is installed. It can cause unpredictable results because the resources used by the application have effectively been moved or relocated by the modified rules.

APPLICATION ISOLATION 2.0—APPLICATION STREAMING

This is the latest addition for XenApp 4.5 Enterprise and Platinum Editions. The Application Streaming feature simplifies application deployment to end users. With the Application Streaming feature, you can install and configure an application on one file server and deliver it to any desktop or server on demand. Upgrading or patching an application is simple, because you are required only to update or patch an application stored in one place: on the file server.

Here are some of the key benefits to utilizing the Application Streaming feature:

▼ Cost effective, scalable application delivery to end users and servers

■ Lower cost of installing and maintaining applications and servers in large farms

▲ Access to any application, anywhere, anytime, regardless of connection

There are additional benefits when streamed applications are run on client desktops:

▼ Optimal utilization of computing resources

■ Elimination of application-compatibility issues

▲ Elimination of peripherals-access issues

Organizations can profit from these benefits by taking advantage of the many streaming features included with this release of XenApp server. Application Streaming offers the following features:

▼ **Install once, deliver anywhere** Install the application once into a central file share using a profiler machine and deliver an on-demand application to workstations and servers with consistency and accuracy.

■ **Seamless updates** No need to re-create a new program share on the central server; just run the manufacturer's recommended update program from the profiler machine and the program is ready for delivery to the end users just as simply as the original install.

■ **Application isolation** Keep conflicting applications running seamlessly on the clients without risk of creating inconsistent DLLs and data files, thus causing fewer problems on the workstations and servers.

- **Application caching** Although not a requirement for applications to run, application caching can help increase performance the next time the application is launched. Each time the application is run, it is checked for the latest updates and all the files available to execute the application properly are verified.

- **Wide range of target environments** Nearly all current Win32 execution platforms can host streamed applications. The streaming client operating systems are Windows XP Professional, Vista, and Windows 2000 Professional. With dual-mode streaming, target environments are increased to include all supported XenApp clients.

- **Dual-mode streaming** If launching a streamed application fails on the client device, the XenApp Application Streaming feature seamlessly streams the application to the server, which then presents the application to the client device through an ICA connection.

- **Easy deployment of applications to farm servers** Instead of installing all applications across all the servers in the farm, you can profile an application from the central file share and distribute it to the users on-demand when requested. You can stream the application to the servers in the farm to avoid conflicts with core applications. You can also update the application one time at the central source instead of several times across all the servers. This guarantees the same application delivery to all the servers in the farm.

- **Consistent end-user experience** Icons for streamed applications appear next to the other application icons in the Web Interface, the Program Neighborhood Agent, or on the desktop for seamless integration with the user's existing environment. The user does not have to know where and how the application is running.

- **Offline access** Streamed applications can be made available to the users while away from the local area network. A "time-to-live" configuration setting can be made to render the offline application unusable once expiration has occurred. In the event of a lost or stolen corporate resource, such as a laptop, the licenses attached to the applications installed on that resource would not be lost or stolen as well.

▲ **Easy disaster recovery** On-demand application delivery is a powerful concept for disaster-recovery situations. Once the application profiles are backed up, replacing servers and desktops becomes an easy task.

For more detailed information on installing and configuring applications into the streaming environment in XenApp 4.5, refer to Chapter 9.

APPLICATION-TESTING PROCEDURE

Each application should go through two phases of testing—component testing and system testing—in order to assess how it functions running by itself and as part of a fully configured server. The strategy is to have as much breadth and depth of testing coverage as is practical, given the realities of most fast-paced corporate IT departments. The effort of creating and refining an application-testing process is worthwhile. Over time, the IT staff will become fast, proficient, and confident at running the tests.

Component Testing

This phase of testing is designed to exercise an application running by itself in a multiuser environment. This can be especially important with applications that were not written specifically for this environment, do not have application-compatibility scripts, or are older DOS or 16-bit applications.

Generic Functions

The generic functions of the component test phase are functions that are common to most applications. Examples of generic functions are Execute (run the program), Exit, File-Print, File-Open, and Cut and Paste. Coverage of generic functions is important to ensure the application works as expected in a multiuser environment. One test list can be created that will cover every application slated for deployment, or at least broad categories of applications. Not every test on the list will apply, but running the test list is important nonetheless.

Specific Functions

As the name implies, these are functions that are specific to each application. At least one test list should be created for each application to cover specific functions. Examples are running a custom macro in Microsoft Excel, creating a new project in Visual J++, and changing the color saturation in Adobe Photoshop.

System Testing

The system-testing phase is designed to ensure that an application behaves predictably on a server loaded with other applications. This is also typically the phase that includes some load testing for performance. A system test involves the following steps:

▼ *Run the component tests again on a fully configured server.* Such a server has all the applications slated for production deployment loaded; has the network connected; and is participating in a domain, a server farm, and load balancing. The idea is to set up an environment that is as close to the production environment as possible.

■ *Test the necessary application-integration functions.* Examples include database access through Microsoft Excel, cutting and pasting between applications, running a mail-merge macro in Microsoft Word, or running a custom client application that provides a front-end user interface to a legacy system.

■ *Load-test the application.* Establish as many user sessions as are likely to be used in production. This can be done either literally, through scripting, or via commercial testing applications such as Citrix EdgeSight for Load Testing. Have several people run test lists on the application simultaneously.

▲ *Test the application using all targeted client environments.* This includes not only desktop PCs, laptops, and Windows terminals, but also different points in the enterprise network and other different types of network connections.

Test Lists

There is no secret to creating good test lists, but there is an art to it that can only be mastered with practice. The most important thing to remember is not to let "best get in the way of better." In other words, it is better to start with a basic test list and improve it over time than to delay the test process until the perfect test list is completed. The perfect test list will never be realized without experience in the process.

We have provided the following example of a test list as a starting point. Feel free to adapt it to other programs or even modify its structure to fit your needs. Table 13-1 shows a test list of generic functions that can be applied to most applications. In addition

Step	Test	Description	Expected Result	Result	Pass/Fail	Notes
1	Launch Method #1	Click the application icon on the desktop.	The application executes.	Application is executed.	P	
2	Launch Method #2	Click Start | Programs, the program group, and the application name.	The application executes.	Application is executed.	P	
3	Open a document	Choose File | Open from the menu.	The default or last data directory is displayed.	The default directory was displayed.	P	Might want to run this test two more times to see which directory is displayed.
4	Print a document	Choose File | Print from the menu.	Current document prints in full.	Document printed.	P	
...						
24	Exit Method #1	Choose File | Exit from the menu.	The application exits.	Application is exited.	P	
25	Exit Method #2	Click the X in the upper-right corner of the main application window.	The application exits.	Application is exited.	P	This method is faster.

Table 13-1.   Generic Functions Test List

to this generic list, a more specific list should also be developed to ensure that a particular application's functionality has been fully tested.

Pass or Fail Status

Once a test list has been run, a report of the application, test lists, tests run, and the status can be generated. It is not unreasonable to expect an application to pass all tests before being considered for production deployment.

Test Cycles

All test lists run on a particular application are considered one test cycle. Keep in mind that all tests may not pass. Following the test cycle, and after any fixes or corrections have been made, all test lists with failed tests should be run again. Once all the failed tests have passed, a final run of the entire suite of test lists is advisable to make sure nothing new was "broken" during this phase. This is often referred to as "regression testing." The cycle repeats until all tests pass or until the pass percentage meets a predetermined acceptance level. Once all tests have passed or met the goal, the application can be considered a candidate for production deployment.

THE PRODUCTION DEPLOYMENT PROCESS

Once an application has completed the testing process, it is time to manage its deployment into the production environment. Unless extensive load testing was done before deployment, we recommend publishing or streaming the application to one or two servers to begin with to allow users to begin using the application(s). If you are using published applications through Web Interface, PN Agent, or Program Neighborhood, this is an easy way of seamlessly getting the new application to users for use, as shown in Figure 13-2. If you are running a full desktop, you should consider using the ICA Passthrough capability to direct users to the new application from the existing full desktop, as shown in Figure 13-3. You should also consider having an "early adopter" user group that can begin employing the application before it is deployed throughout the enterprise. A week or two of running the application in this manner can reveal any last-minute issues not discovered in testing, without unduly burdening the user community with problems.

▼

NEW FEATURE: When you are integrating new applications into an existing production environment, Application Streaming really shows off its capabilities. Because the application is not actually being installed on the production server, testing and integration into the existing environment is significantly simplified and less obtrusive for the users and servers.

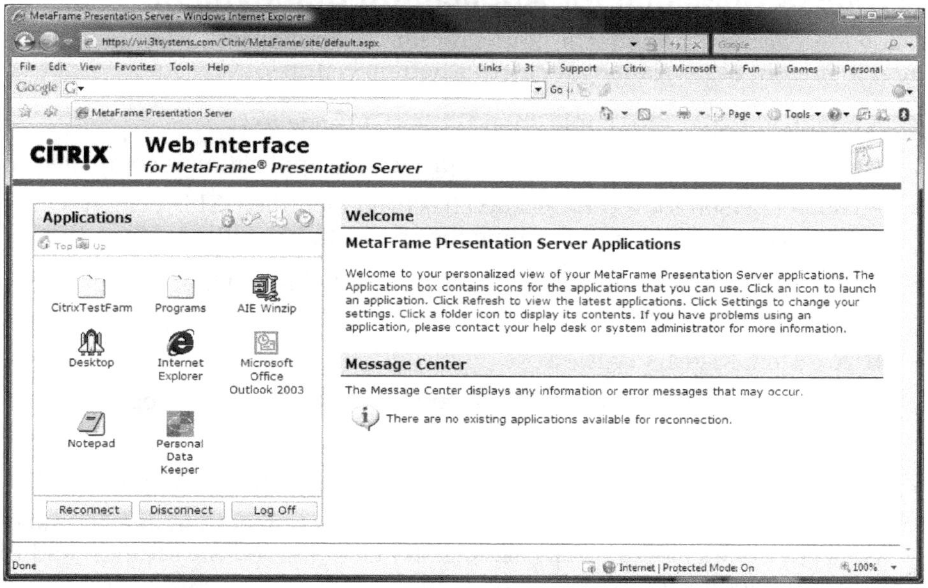

Figure 13-2. Deploying new applications using published applications through Web Interface

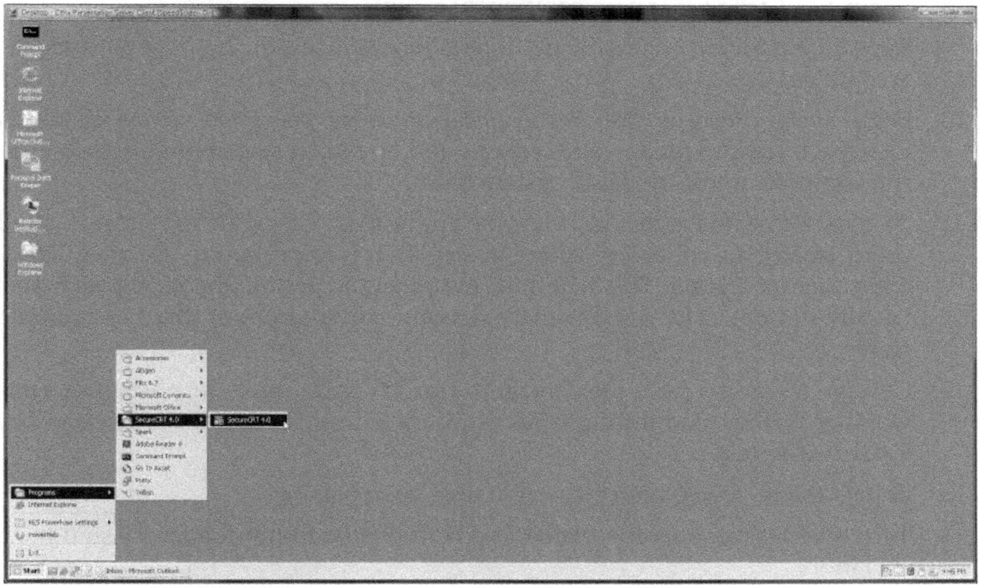

Figure 13-3. Deploying a new application using full desktops

Sample Process Checklist for Application Deployment

The following checklist provides a guideline for an application-deployment process. Modify it to fit your organization and established procedures.

1. A qualified request for application support is made to IT.

2. Verification that management has approved the application is completed.

3. A contact person for the application has been identified. This person will be the point of contact for communicating the application's status.

4. A review of the application's specifications and requirements is done.

   ■ Is the software 32-bit?

   ■ Are there Registry entries?

   ■ If the app is internally developed, are network paths hard-coded?

   ■ Are there any system library dependencies?

5. Install the application on the test server. Document all steps of the install.

6. Perform any necessary software configurations for operation in a Terminal Services environment—for example, Registry changes, INI file settings, and file or directory modifications.

7. Create specific function test lists. Determine the suitability of generic function test lists and modify them as appropriate. Create test lists for both component and system test phases.

8. Begin Test Cycle 1. Perform component testing.

9. Repeat component testing until all tests have passed or the pass percentage is acceptable.

10. Begin system testing. Add the application to the last good server image that includes other production applications and operating system modifications. Re-run component tests and add system tests.

11. As part of system testing, load-test the application. Test with a single non-admin user (usually the contact specified in step 3). It is important to use a regular domain user for testing. This will flush out potential permission problems that are usually not detected when using a domain admin account that has unlimited rights.

12. Get five test users from the contact to run selected system test lists. Determine whether further load testing is necessary or if results can be extrapolated from the five-user test.

13. Repeat the test cycle until all system tests have passed.

14. Turn over testing documentation and certification to production IT staff for installation.

15. Install the application on one or two production servers and make the application available to the appropriate users. Monitor the server's performance to ensure that there are no utilization spikes or any other irregularities.

16. Survey users to see if the application is performing properly.

17. Schedule production deployment using a chosen distribution method (for instance, streaming, imaging, or packaging).

18. Deploy the application.

19. After one week of production, survey a sample of users to see if the application is performing properly.

Mass Deployment

Once an application has gone through the preceding installation and testing procedure, step 17 calls for production deployment across the farm to all users who need the application. Obviously, in smaller organizations, the installation of an application on two or three servers is often less time-consuming than the time it would take to automate and implement the process. But in larger enterprises the installation of an application across 100 servers can be a daunting task. In this case, the investment in developing the automation and deploying it pays off very quickly. We have seen large enterprises deploy full suites of applications overnight across thousands of servers to thousands of users by utilizing one of the automation procedures we detail here.

Imaging Software

As detailed in our previous book, *Citrix Access Suite 4 for Windows Server 2003: The Official Guide*, there are multiple ways to build servers for use with Citrix and Terminal Services. Building a standard server installation image and cloning that image to multiple servers can save time, but this has also shown to produce inconsistencies among the applications and the server operating systems. Although free utilities are available for changing the SID of a server image after it is cloned, is it certain that the server is truly unique and that all the applications installed will take the change to the server's name and SID properly? As the previous book states, this method is extremely useful for the initial builds of the servers, and for major rebuilds, but can be tedious for minor application upgrades and maintenance as well as operating system hotfixes and patches. For the purposes of server and application maintenance and singular application installs, it is a recommend practice to use packaging software such as Citrix Installation Manager.

Other software vendors also have effective enterprise-wide software deployment and packaging suites, such as NetInstall Server from enteo. These product suites not only offer application packaging and deployment to the XenApp server but can also deploy applications packages and updates—and some offer operating system deployments to other server types, desktops, workstations, and laptops. These methods of using packages to build servers and deploy applications, updates, and patches to them promise the best opportunity to build the Citrix XenApp farm with the upmost accuracy, and they guarantee a consistent delivery framework to the users.

For more information about enteo's NetInstall Server and the benefits of enterprise management software, visit www.enteo.com.

Installation Manager for Citrix XenApp Server

Installation Manager (IM) is designed to automate the application-installation process and facilitate consistent application replication across the XenApp farm(s) throughout the enterprise. IM can also be used for software updates, patches, and service packs, both attended and unattended across all XenApp servers in the farm regardless of location, hardware, and network connection. Although IM does not facilitate the initial server building and configuration process, it is quite handy for software installation and maintenance. Through the use of IM, applications can be distributed across multiple servers in minutes rather than days or weeks. Installation Manager for Citrix XenApp server is bundled with the Enterprise and Platinum editions of XenApp 4.5 and cannot be purchased separately.

Installation Manager creates a central repository for software application packaging and distribution. Having a central repository that packages, distributes, and inventories applications aids administrators in the following ways:

▼ Allows for rapid and consistent application deployment

■ Allows all software to be deployed and managed from a single location

■ Allows scheduling of application deployment/distribution during low server load times

■ Allows retention/tracking of all applications/versions contained in each server in the server farm

▲ Allows quick replacement of damaged or corrupt applications

What's New?

In the XenApp 4.5 release, administrators can now install and publish applications into the isolation environment that follow the same rules and confinements stated earlier. Different versions of the same application as well as incompatible applications can be rapidly deployed safely on multiple servers without fear of file and data corruption, possibly reducing the number of application silos and lowering administrative overhead.

Also new in this release is Windows Server 2003 x64 Edition awareness. If the farm is running Presentation Server 4.0 or XenApp 4.5, Installation Manager will now accept a 64-bit server into the server groups for deploying applications.

NOTE: As of this version, Windows Server 2003 x64 cannot be used to package applications for use with IM, but once a package is built using the 32-bit version of Window Server 2003, the application can be installed on a 64-bit system.

Installation Manager Components

When implementing Installation Manager for your XenApp farm(s), you need to be aware of four main areas or components. Some of the components can be shared on a single server, keeping in mind that a large environment may demand that the roles be split out for performance purposes.

▼ **Package Management server** XenApp server running the Access Management Console, used to manage and schedule application installation and deployments. This can be any server in the farm and does not need to be a standalone server. As discussed in previous sections, a "tools" server is a good candidate for this function.

■ **Network share point server** A Windows server with a file share containing the Installation Manager packages used for application deployment. This role can be shared with the Package Management server. There can be more than one of these servers in an environment for separated geographical locations to aid with region-based deployments.

■ **Packager server** A server running XenApp Enterprise Edition dedicated to creating Application Deployment File (ADF) packages. This server must be a pristine server build and *cannot* be used to deliver applications to users. This server will be used to record application installations and later have the applications rolled back to maintain the server's integrity. This server is discussed in more detail later in this chapter.

▲ **Target server(s)** Servers with XenApp Enterprise Edition running the Installer Service component of Installation Manager that applications will be deployed to.

Deploying Application Packages

Using Installation Manager to deploy applications across the farm is done using a basic four-step process. This section provides an outline and more detail into each step:

▼ Identify and configure the four server roles explained earlier in this chapter.

■ Identify the package and format to deploy.

■ Store packages to the network file share.

▲ Deploy packages to the target servers using Citrix Installation Manager.

Identify and Configure the Server Roles As a part of implementing IM for deploying packages to the XenApp servers, server roles for IM must be assigned to server hardware and configured. Here are the server roles to identify:

▼ The target server(s) on which software is to be installed

■ The server that will be the Package Management server

■ A network share point location to store packages

▲ A Packager server for Application Deployment Files (ADF) if packages will be created and used

Identify the Package and Format to Deploy IM can deploy several types of software, including applications, service packs, upgrades, hotfixes, and patches, as well as other types of files. These files are bundled up in packages. Packages may include one or more software bundles or components. For example, a package may include an application and the update for the application together in one source file.

Within the Console, several packages can be added to a package group. Package groups contain multiple packages with various types of applications for deployment to a department or office location. They make it easier to track and organize the packages.

The next step is to decide on the format type of the package that will be created. There are three format types:

▼ **MSI** These are installation packages based on the Microsoft Windows Installer Service. MSI packages are created by software manufacturers using specialized software. These files are useful when the application has multiple components within the package. MSI packages sometimes require "transforms" files to help with the installation of MSI packages by applying installation "rules" for how the MSI packages should behave. An example of this would be installing versions of Microsoft Office on a Terminal Server.

■ **MSP** MSP packages act like MSI packages, but are primarily used for patches and updates to applications rather than for installing the applications.

NOTE: The nice part about using MSI and MSP packages is that they simply need to be incorporated into the deployment schedules and stored on the file share. This makes these packages the best choice to keep application deployments simple and quick.

▲ **ADF** The third option for creating application packages is Application Deployment Files, or ADF. ADF packages are created using the Packager server component of Installation Manager. ADF packages are great for use with applications that require user intervention and customization during the install because these changes can be captured as a part of the package build. ADF packages can be used to deploy applications, updates, or upgrades to existing applications or other files as required by the user base. A more detailed explanation on building ADF packages appears later in this chapter.

Store Packages to the Network File Share(s) All packages must be copied to a share point (or points) on the network in order to deploy them to the target servers from the Console. When deploying packages to multiple sites across the WAN, set up multiple file shares or replicate them using DFS or a third-party product such as DoubleTake. You can replicate packages across the WAN during off hours for scheduled deployments the next day.

This will prevent heavy loads on the network during working hours and speed up the package deployment times.

Deploy Packages to the Target Servers Using the Console, you add the package to the Installation Manager database and then schedule when you want to install the software on your target servers. You can also use the Console to publish an application to make it available to your client users. All packages must be scheduled for deployment to target XenApp servers from the Console.

Citrix Installation Manager Installation and Configuration

There are as many ways to set up application deployment in IM as there are applications to deploy. For the purposes of keeping this section shorter than an encyclopedia collection, we simply cover the basic requirements, provide installation tips, and include a brief example of packaging an application for deployment. We chose to install Office 2003 across a XenApp farm of 100 Windows Server 2003 Terminal Servers running Citrix XenApp 4.5.

The following tasks were completed prior to the installation of other components:

▼ Windows Server 2003 with Terminal Services was installed and fully configured according to written policies and procedures.

▲ The fully qualified domain names (FQDNs) of all the servers in the farm were registered in DNS.

To install Installation Manager on a Terminal Server, follow these steps:

1. Make sure all users are logged off the server and then disable logins.
2. Close all applications on the server, including the Console.
3. Insert the Citrix XenApp CD-ROM in your CD-ROM drive:

NOTE: If your CD-ROM drive supports the Autorun feature, the installation splash screen appears. If the splash screen does not display, click Run from the Start menu and type *D:***Autorun.exe**, where *d* is the letter of your CD-ROM drive.

4. Click the Product Installations and Updates icon.
5. Click the Install Citrix Presentation Server 4.5 and Its Components icon. The Setup Wizard starts. Follow the instructions onscreen.
6. When the Component Selection page appears, ensure the Installation Manager component is selected.
7. Finish the wizard.

For the current example, our environment consists of four servers, as shown in Figure 13-4.

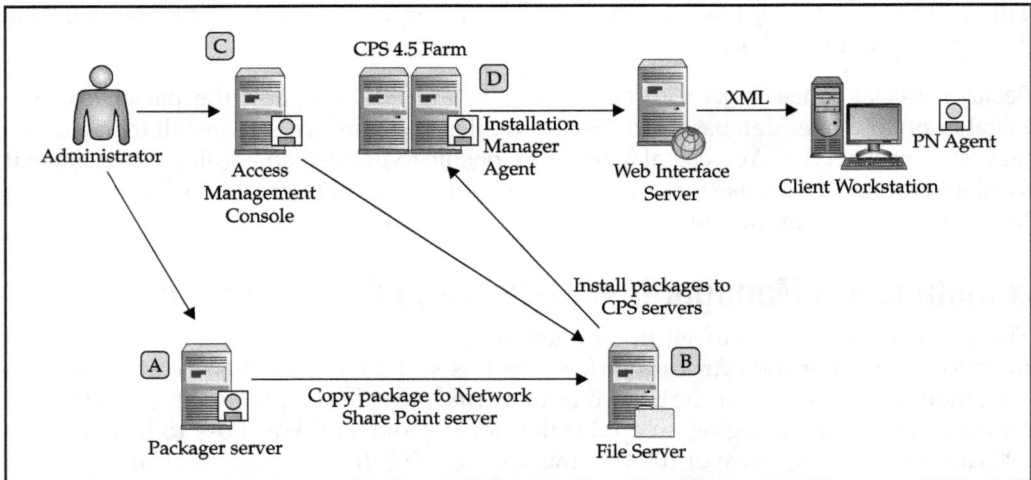

Figure 13-4. Installation Manager server configurations

The configurations of the servers in Figure 13-4 are listed in Table 13-2.

This environment operates by creating packages (server A) and storing them on a network server file share (server B). After the packages are created, they are deployed (server C) to all the target servers (server farm D). Although some of these functions can be combined on a couple of servers, in a large environment, the machines serving these roles should be dedicated to provide the flexibility and bandwidth necessary. The

Server Name	Function	Operating System (OS)
Server A	IM Packager server	Windows Server 2003 with XenApp 4.5. This is a pristine installation dedicated to creating packages.
Server B	Network share point server	Any accessible network file share.
Server C	Packager Management server	Windows Server 2003 hosting Citrix XenApp running the Console.
Server Farm D	Target servers (IM installer service and IM subsystem)	Windows Server 2003 with XenApp 4.5 hosting applications.

Table 13-2. Server Configurations for Installation Manager

Packager server should not share a role with any other servers. This will help maintain a "clean" environment for creating application packages.

The Application-Packaging Process

When creating application packages, you are presented with three options:

- **Package Installation Recording**   Packager captures the procedures to install an application.

- **Package an Unattended Program**   Packager prompts for the application and associated command-line parameters. This is for applications that can be installed without a user interface.

- **Package Selected Files**   Packager prompts for files and/or folders.

If the option Package Installation Recording is selected, the Packager prompts you to choose to add application compatibility scripts and/or additional files. It then records the installation of an application and builds the package, which is stored in the network file share.

If the Package an Unattended Program option is selected, the Packager requests you for the application executable, optional command-line parameters, and any additional files. The executable, command-line parameters, and additional files are then compiled into a package and stored in the network file share.

If the option Package Selected Files is selected, the Packager prompts you for the files and/or folders. These files and/or folders are collected and created as a package that is stored in the network file share. Figure 13-5 provides a conceptual design of the package-building process.

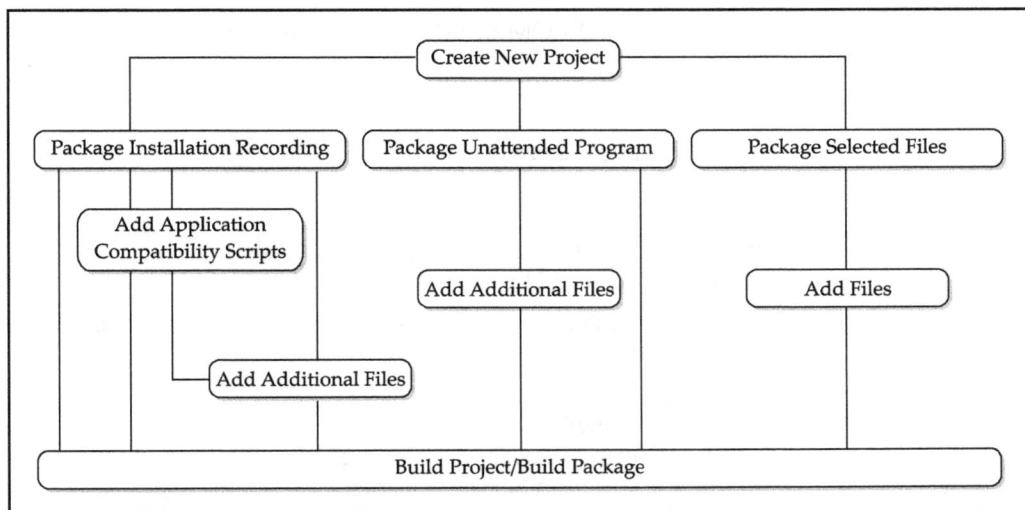

Figure 13-5.   The conceptual design of a package-building process

The Job Process

A job is a package that has been scheduled for installation or uninstallation on target servers. The process for creating a job is displayed in Figure 13-5. To create a job, select a package to be installed or uninstalled. The Job window prompts you for the target servers to process the job, the name of the job, and a schedule for the job. If you choose to execute the job immediately, it is saved to IM and then immediately executed. If you choose to schedule the job later, it is saved to IM and executed at the scheduled time.

Packaging Office 2003 for IM Deployment

Before you can create and manage packages, a network account must be created in Active Directory that has permission to interact with the file systems and XenApp server to install packaged applications. In the Presentation Server Console, right-click the Installation Manager Node and select Properties. In the left pane, select Network Account and enter the account created earlier.

Microsoft Office 2003 uses a Microsoft Installer (MSI) package for unattended installation. The MSI file for Microsoft Office 2003 is PROPLUS.msi. For this example, we use a custom transforms file we created prior to this process. This same procedure should work for any MSI file.

For more information on creating a custom transforms file, refer to Microsoft's documentation and procedures.

To create a Installation Manager package for Office 2003, perform the following steps:

1. Create a folder for Office 2003 on the IM network share server (server B).

2. Insert the Microsoft Office 2003 CD-ROM or connect to a network share with Office 2003.

3. Open a command prompt or run the command on server A.

4. Change drives to either the CD-ROM drive or the network share with Microsoft Office 2003.

5. Type the following:

   ```
   msiexec /a \\<Path>\ PROPLUS.msi
   ```

6. Enter the product code.

7. Enter the IM network share path (\\Server B\Office 2003 share). The Office 2003 administrator installation files will be copied.

8. Copy the Termsrvr.mst file created prior to the IM network share path (\\Server B\ Office 2003 share) on server B.

Creating the Office 2003 Package

The following steps should be performed in order to add the Office 2003 MSI package (or any other MSI package) to the Presentation Server Console:

1. Open the Presentation Server Console.

2.   Expand the Installation Manager node.

3.   Right-click the Packages node.

4.   Select Add Package.

5.   Enter the package name.

6.   Choose Yes to add transforms or command-line parameters.

7.   Add the Termsrvr.mst file.

Scheduling a Microsoft Office 2003 Package for Target Servers

The following steps detail the procedure required for scheduling and installing the Microsoft Office 2003 package on target servers:

1.   Open the Presentation Server Console.

2.   Expand the Installation Manager node.

3.   Expand the Packages node.

4.   Right-click the Office 2003 package.

5.   Select Install Package.

6.   Select the target servers on which the package will be installed.

7.   Click Next.

8.   Schedule a time to execute the package or execute the package immediately.

CAUTION: Executing a package is bandwidth intensive. Start by testing a small package targeted to a limited number of servers to get a feel for the load that will be put on the network. For larger server farms, schedule the execution for off-hours, and spread the executions over time to ensure the network can support the additional load. Executions over a WAN will require even greater planning and testing to ensure that the package will be fully executed prior to users resuming use of the WAN.

9.   Click Finish.

10. Click OK.

After these steps are completed, in the Package Properties view of the Presentation Server Console, a job entry for the Office 2003 package is displayed. The job entry states the job name, status, and scheduled time, as well as the success of the installed package. For additional information on manually creating packages and recordings, consult the administrator's guide for Installation Manager.

Packaging Applications Using the Packager

When the Packager records the changes made when software is installed, it creates an Application Deployment File (ADF). This is a script file in human-readable format that contains information about the environment, resources, and files required to install and run the software on a server.

An ADF package is built by the Packager. The ADF package houses the ADF file and the folders containing the software installation files. The ADF package stores all the information that Installation Manager needs to re-create the software installation on target servers.

Before you begin using the Packager, ensure the following:

▼ The Packager server is a clean server that closely matches the target server environment.

■ No other applications or background processes are running on the Packager server. Also, make sure you disable all sessions before you begin a recording.

■ The applications and software components you want to package are accessible. You need the CD-ROM or other media containing the software you want to package, or make sure the installation files are available on the Packager server or on a file share you can access.

■ A directory exists in which to save the project. The default directory is Drive:\ Program Files\Citrix\IM\Packager\Projects.

▲ The appropriate accounts and permissions required are configured to run the Packager and copy packages to the network share point.

To use the Installation Manager Packager to build an ADF package via an Installation Recording, follow these steps:

1. Click Start | Programs | Citrix | Administration Tools | Installation Manager Packager.

2. The New Project Wizard should start; otherwise, go to File | Project Wizard.

3. Choose Package an Installation Recording and click Next.

4. Name the project and browse to the network file share for package locations. Create a folder for your project, select that folder, and click Next.

5. Browse to the installation program's EXE file. Add any command-line parameters for the program and click Next.

6. Choose whether or not you wish to include compatibility scripts and then click Next.

7. Choose a build location and click Finish to begin the recording.

▼

NOTE: Recording will stop automatically when the install program and all the programs it starts exit. In the list of install programs running, if the programs you are installing are not listed, you can click the Stop Recording button.

8. Install the application as you would normally.

9. When the application install is complete, Installation Manager will finish the project.

NOTE: If you are packaging an installation recording, the recording does not continue if a restart is required during the application installation, unless your application supports an unattended installation. If you do not want your application to restart the server (which stops the recording process), choose No when the application prompts you to restart. If there is no prompt, press ALT-TAB to display the dialog box, click Done, and save the project. Click OK at the request to restart.

APPLICATION LICENSING

One of the most common questions we hear when discussing on-demand access computing is, How will it change the licensing requirements of our organization's applications? The answer is simple: It won't—but it will make it easier to manage, track, and add/delete licenses. Most application manufacturers license their applications on either a concurrent-user basis, a per-computer basis, or a per-user basis. By having the applications and any application-metering software centralized, the managing and reporting of application software is dramatically simplified. Although neither Windows Server 2003 nor Citrix XenApp inherently tracks application usage or access, Citrix Resource Manager (included with the Enterprise edition of XenApp 4.5) and Citrix EdgeSight provide a variety of tools and reports regarding user and application usage. Additionally, tools from Real Enterprise Solutions (RES), triCerat, and AppSense provide robust application usage, metering, and reporting.

APPLICATION ACCESS AND SECURITY

Following the installation of applications, you should configure the security to only allow specific group access to applications. Some applications (for example, Office 2003) will be provided to a large majority of users, whereas other applications, such as accounting and payroll software, should be tightly locked down. Locking down file permissions based on group access is an obvious way to lock down an application, but this method is usually time consuming, because most applications have multiple components such as Registry entries, shared DLLs, and executable files. Additionally, many applications can be accessed through operating system holes or other applications such as web browsers. We highly recommend the use of RES, enteo, or AppSense utilities to provide a cleaner and more automated approach to locking down applications and their usage, while logging any unauthorized attempts at accessing the applications.

CHAPTER 14

Extending the Power of Platinum—Feature Pack 1

In this chapter we examine the new features available in Feature Pack 1 for XenApp Server 4.5. As with almost all minor software releases, Feature Pack 1 includes both patches to repair existing issues as well as new functionality created based on user feedback. We begin by discussing the added components and features offered in the new release, and then discuss some of the specific details covered with the hotfix rollup pack. We conclude the chapter by discussing the methods and processes required to transition your existing environment to Feature Pack 1 as well as some important items to consider.

SmartAuditor

In today's environment, everyone is concerned with compliance. Whether you are regulated by HIPAA, GLBA, PCI, or any of the other industry regulations, it is extremely important to have an audit trail to demonstrate compliance. SmartAuditor is a new feature available in Feature Pack 1 that not only assists with compliance and security issues, but can be used as a very powerful troubleshooting tool.

SmartAuditor allows you to monitor and record a user's ICA session. This can be done manually, or it can be configured to "trigger" when certain events take place. For example, if you have a specific user who keeps getting virus alerts, you can launch SmartAuditor when they open their web browser and view the sites they visit. This will allow you to determine where the malicious content comes from—and potentially what use policies are being violated. This type of monitoring will also help enforce proper use policies and ensure compliance.

Another possible use of SmartAuditor is to protect highly sensitive data and to monitor who is accessing specific applications for compliance purposes. Your organization may be concerned about tracking what financial information is released to the public, and by whom. By using SmartAuditor to monitor the financial application, you would have a visual record of who accessed the data and when. This type of forensic trail is extremely valuable when creating and enforcing acceptable use policies.

The SmartAuditor feature consists of five components:

▼ **SmartAuditor agent**　This component is installed on each XenApp server.

■ **SmartAuditor server**　This component is an IIS 6.0 web server that handles two specific functions. First, the SmartAuditor Server acts as a broker and is responsible for directing and triggering the interactions with the other SmartAuditor components. Second, it manages the recorded session files.

■ **Policy Console**　This component is an MMC plug-in that allows you to specify which sessions are recorded and when.

■ **SmartAuditor database**　This component is a SQL server database schema that interacts with the storage manager to record the metadata and queries required for session recording.

▲ **SmartAuditor player**　This component is the interface for actively monitoring or playing back your recorded sessions.

Each of these components (with the exception of the SmartAuditor player) can be installed on a single farm server; however, for larger deployments, a dispersed deployment is recommended. Although a SmartAuditor agent can only communicate with one SmartAuditor server, it is possible to install and manage multiple SmartAuditor servers. This scenario also applies if you are recording a large number of sessions or using applications with high graphic requirements such as a medical imaging package.

The installation process for SmartAuditor is divided into three separate parts: administration, agents, and the player. The administration portion involves setting up the database, server, and Policy Console. Once these components are created, the agents can be installed on the XenApp farm servers. It is possible to install the agents on an individual server in the farm rather than on all the servers; however, keep in mind that you will only be able to record sessions on a server where the agent is present. Finally, the player will need to be set up on a separate workstation. Because the player is a graphic-intensive application, it should not be installed as a published application, but rather run locally on a separate, physically secure PC.

NOTE: We recommend installing Playback Protection on the SmartAuditor player. This will encrypt the recorded session files before they are downloaded to the player.

SmartAuditor Administrative Components

The first step in installing SmartAuditor is to install the administrative components. Here are the steps to follow:

1. On the server designated for the SmartAuditor administration components, use one of the following methods to launch autorun.exe:

   ■ Use the XenApp Server 4.5 with Feature Pack 1 Components CD.

   ■ Download the software from the Citrix website using your My Citrix account.

TIP: The media kits do not always contain the most recent versions of software and components. Always check the Citrix support site for the most recent service packs and installers.

2. Choose Platinum Edition Components | SmartAuditor.

3. Choose SmartAuditor Administration.

4. Ensure that only the check boxes for the components you want to install are selected.

5. Click Determine SmartAuditor Administration Prerequisites to confirm that you have the required software installed. Then click Install Citrix SmartAuditor Administration.

6. Follow the wizard's instructions to complete the installation of the selected components and then click Finish.

> **TIP:** If you are installing all the administration components on the same server, ensure that SQL Server 2005 is installed on the same server as well. When you reach the Database Configuration screen, accept localhost in the Accessing User Account for Computer or Localhost field. Otherwise, if you are installing the SmartAuditor server and the SmartAuditor database on different servers, type the name of the SmartAuditor server in the following format: **domain\machine-name$**. Ensure that the dollar symbol ($) follows the name.

SmartAuditor Server Agents

The next step in the installation procedure is to install the SmartAuditor agents. Follow these steps on each XenApp server in the farm on which you want install the SmartAuditor Server agent:

1. On the servers in which the SmartAuditor agents will be installed, use one of the following methods to launch autorun.exe:

   ■ Use the XenApp Server 4.5 with Feature Pack 1 Components CD.

   ■ Download the software from the Citrix website using your My Citrix account.

> **TIP:** The media kits do not always contain the most recent versions of software and components. Always check the Citrix support site for the most recent service packs and installers.

2. Choose Platinum Edition Components | SmartAuditor.

3. Choose SmartAuditor Agent for Presentation Server.

4. Verify that a check mark appears next to the required software. Then click Install Citrix SmartAuditor Agent.

5. Follow the wizard's instructions to complete the installation of the selected component and click Finish to complete the installation.

> **NOTE:** If you are installing the SmartAuditor agent on the same server as the administrative components, accept the default entry, localhost, when you reach the SmartAuditor Agent Configuration screen that displays the Enter the Name of the SmartAuditor Server field. Otherwise, if you installed the SmartAuditor Agent on a different server, type the name or the FQDN of the SmartAuditor server.

SmartAuditor Player

The final component of the SmartAuditor installation is the player. To install the SmartAuditor player, follow these steps:

1. On the workstation in which the SmartAuditor player will be installed, use one of the following methods to launch autorun.exe:

   ■ Use the XenApp 4.5 with Feature Pack 1 Components CD.

   ■ Download the software from the Citrix website using your My Citrix account.

TIP: The media kits do not always contain the most recent versions of software and components. Always check the Citrix support site for the most recent service packs and installers.

2. Choose Platinum Edition Components | SmartAuditor.

3. Choose SmartAuditor Player.

4. Verify that a check mark appears next to the required software. Then click Install Citrix SmartAuditor Player.

5. Follow the wizard's instructions to complete the installation of the selected component and then click Finish to complete the installation.

EasyCall

Included in the Platinum Edition licenses are EasyCall (Communication Gateway) connection licenses. These licenses can be used in conjunction with a Communication Gateway appliance (sold separately). The number of connection licenses available is equal to the number of concurrent users of XenApp Platinum purchased. Simply put, EasyCall gives the user the ability to hover over a phone number in any published, streamed, or installed Windows application and dial that number with a single mouse click. In order to take advantage of this bundled feature, a Citrix EasyCall gateway appliance must be installed and integrated with the existing phone system.

When the user clicks on a phone number in any application, the EasyCall gateway first dials the user's telephone. Once the user picks up the handset, EasyCall will dial the destination number and connect the calls.

In addition to the click-to-call feature, EasyCall can be configured to connect users regardless of their location. Profiles can be created for a home phone, a mobile phone, or any other location where the functionality may be required. These profiles will integrate with the existing PBX system via the gateway and utilize toll-bypass/least-cost routing features. Finally, a Web Services API is available that allows you to build click-to-call and directory functions into your applications.

The installation and configuration of the Communication Gateway is outside the scope of this book. For more information, see the associated administrator's guide or contact your local Citrix reseller.

Streaming Client and Profiler 1.1

As discussed in Chapter 9, XenApp Platinum and Enterprise Editions allow you to profile applications so they can be streamed to your users on demand. Prior to Feature Pack 1, the Streaming Client and Profiler 1.1 encountered difficulties with certain applications (including Microsoft Office 2007). In Feature Pack 1, Citrix provides new code that not only functions easily with Microsoft Office 2007, but allows applications larger than 2GB to be profiled and streamed. This is accomplished by creating multiple .cab files and configuring them in a contiguous sequence.

Health Assistant

XenApp 4.5 includes the new Health Assistant, formally known as the Health Monitoring and Recovery feature. The Health Assistant allows administrators to run various tests against XenApp servers that can provide metrics for expansion purposes, or even simple health checks. The Health Assistant allows you to run two basic types of tests: prepackaged and custom.

The original release of XenApp Platinum 4.5 included four prepackaged tests:

▼ **Terminal Services** This test enumerates the list of sessions running on the server and the session user information.

■ **XML Service** This test requests and creates a ticket from the XML service.

■ **IMA Service** This test queries IMA to ensure it is running correctly.

▲ **Logon Monitor** This test monitors logon/logoff cycles and compares them to customizable timeframes.

These basic tests allow you to check the status of any server in your farm with just a few clicks. However, these tests are not the only option.

In addition to the preinstalled tests, Health Assistant allows you to create and implement your own custom test modules. The Health, Monitoring, and Recovery SDK package can be downloaded from the Citrix Developer Network (http://community.citrix.com/cdn/). It includes a readme file with detailed implementation and security information, as well as various sample scripts that can be used as the foundation for building custom tests. Feature Pack 1 contains no new additions to the SDK package; however, several new prepackaged tests are available for you to use.

In Feature Pack 1, Citrix introduced several new prepackaged tests to monitor and maintain the health of the server farm. These new tests allow you to monitor aspects of your server farm that are key to running a smooth operation, without the time-consuming task of creating custom test scripts. The new tests are Printing, Local Host Cache, DNS, XML Thread, and ICA Listener. As most administrators are aware, these key areas are critical to maintaining a healthy server farm and network.

The following list describes what each test checks:

▼ **Check DNS (Checkdns.exe)** This test consists of a forward DNS lookup that uses the local hostname to query the IP address from the local DNS in the computer's environment.

■ **Check Local Host Cache (CheckLHC.exe)** This test ensures that the data stored in the LHC is not corrupted, whereas the consistency check ensures no duplicate LHC entries exist.

■ **Check XML Threads (Checkxmlthreads.exe)** This test checks the current value of the number of worker threads running in the Citrix XML Service and compares that number with a number you specify to determine whether a pass (value is lower) or fail (value is greater) situation has occurred.

- ■ **Citrix Print Manager Service Test (Cpsvctest.exe)**   This test determines whether or not session printers can be enumerated.

- ■ **MS Print Spooler Test (Spoolertest.exe)**   This test attempts to enumerate printer drivers, printer processors, and printers using the Windows print spooler.

- ▲ **ICA Listener (ICAListener.exe)**   This test determines whether the ICA listener can accept ICA connections by detecting the default ICA port, connecting to the port, and trying to send data.

Web Interface 4.6

XenApp with Feature Pack 1 also includes several enhancements for Web Interface. In addition to improved compatibility with Windows Vista, Web Interface 4.6 now offers a new client detection and deployment process. This feature examines a user's local environment and determines which method is optimal for connecting to the published or streaming applications. It then guides the user through a series of simple steps to help them configure their local environment to conform to these settings, including any changes required in the web browser. By assisting with these settings, the feature gives the user the ability to optimize their performance as well as reconnect to lost sessions, where they may not have been able to before.

Workspace control allows for the reconnection of previously disconnected applications or applications currently being delivered to the user on some other client device. Certain default settings in Internet Explorer 7 can block file transfers if they appear to have been initiated by someone other than the current user. In order to eliminate this issue, Web Interface 4.6 has changed the way it launches and reconnects to user sessions so that Internet Explorer 7 and other browsers can now recognize the Citrix traffic and allow it to pass. In situations where reconnection is no longer possible, Web Interface 4.6 will tell the user which specific browser settings to change to prevent the connection issues in the future. This level of self-support will decrease help-desk calls and allow users to make changes as needed without assistance.

The new Program Neighborhood Agent Services take this self-service concept one step further. A new feature allows users who use explicitly supplied domain credentials to change their Windows password if it expires. This change can be made regardless of whether the user is in the domain to which they are attempting to authenticate. Therefore, you can deploy the Program Neighborhood Agents in workgroup configurations and change expired passwords by authenticating to the domain in which applications are published.

Finally, Citrix has included integration between Web Interface 4.6 and SharePoint 2007. This means users can launch published or streamed applications directly from a Microsoft SharePoint site rather than using a separate Web Interface site. This level of integration helps avoid the confusion associated with retrieving information from multiple sources.

Hotfix Rollups

XenApp 4.5 with Feature Pack 1 includes two hotfix rollup packs. These rollups are consolidated sets of code, designed to make it easy to apply all previous patches, updates, and hotfixes in a single implementation. Currently, Hotfix Rollup Pack 1 is available in both 32-bit and 64-bit versions. Hotfix Rollup Pack 2 is only available in a 32-bit environment. It should also be noted that in order to take advantage of the enhanced functions in either of these releases, the XenApp Client must be version 10.1 or higher.

Many of the issues addressed in the hotfix rollups are known issues with specific Microsoft programs, and although they are not considered "mission-critical" functions, they can cause problems for people who are used to using them. These types of user problems can escalate rapidly, turning a potentially minor functionality problem into a skewed perception of the success or failure of a XenApp installation.

One of the new features in Office 2007 that has proven to be a difficult change for people to adapt to is Live Preview. The Live Preview feature allows users to view formatting changes in whatever application they are working, without actually applying those changes to the document itself. Prior to the current hotfix rollup, Live Preview was enabled by default, and there was no way to change that setting on a global scale. This hotfix rollup will allow you edit the Registry and set the default value to "disabled."

▼

NOTE: When editing the specific Registry key, you can set the flag value to any number between 0 and 6. If you choose to use any settings other than 0 (disabled) or 6 (enabled), the server may become unstable.

Another concern for PowerPoint users will be familiar to people who have used earlier versions of the Citrix software. Prior to Feature Pack 1, anyone using PowerPoint was unable to highlight a graphical object (such as a .bmp file) in a local text editor and then paste it into a published PowerPoint presentation. This is now possible once the hotfix rollup packs have been installed.

Also, certain features within Microsoft OneNote function incorrectly in a XenApp environment. Many OneNote users have grown fond of the notification area icon, which gives rapid access to certain OneNote features. After OneNote is launched the first time, the notification icon is placed in a separate startup folder and is launched by the Explorer shell. Because seamless sessions do not launch the Explorer shell, this icon is not launched automatically. The hotfix rollup packs address these specific Microsoft concerns, as well as several general issues in the XenApp environment.

Most XenApp administrators have used the Application Isolation environment. By creating completely separate silos for specific applications, with their own copies of certain DLLs and other components, you can publish many applications on the same server that would otherwise need separate systems. As a basic example, you can run and publish different versions of Microsoft Office from the same XenApp server. Hotfix Rollups 1 and 2 have resolved some of the problems with the Application Isolation environment. Specifically, the Microsoft Office 2007 suite has been fully tested and is ready to be deployed in this fashion.

Prior to Hotfix Rollups 1 and 2, users may have encountered issues when attempting to copy files to mapped network drives. Specifically, data-consistency checks would occasionally fail because the buffering mechanism reported false data and generated an error message. As a result, the copy failed. This has been corrected, and the error messages no longer occur.

Several other minor functionality problems are addressed by these hotfix rollups. For a complete list, visit the Citrix Knowledge Base (#CTX116289). An important thing to note regarding hotfixes and patches is that most of the code changes released by Citrix are discussed on the Citrix support forums. If you encounter repeated problems or need technical assistance, the support forums are an excellent venue for interacting directly with Citrix and working on specific solutions in the rare event that there is a problem with the actual code.

UPGRADE VERSUS MIGRATION

One of the most important decisions you will have to make concerning the upgrade to Feature Pack 1 is the method you will use to complete the installation. The transition can be divided into two basic paths: an upgrade and a migration. An upgrade involves installing the new software onto your existing servers, whereas a migration is the process of installing a completely new farm and then cutting over. You need to consider several factors when deciding which path is best for your environment, and the decision criteria may surprise you.

The main goal of IT has always been to become more efficient. As time passes, the mounting pressures to do things faster, better, and with less time and effort are a constant driver. When you examine your possible paths to any upgrade, the future returns on time spent today can become exponential. So, as you attempt to decide which path to follow, there are some basic questions you should ask regarding your existing processes. Do you have a methodology for building and deploying XenApp servers? Is there a documented process that will map the technical requirements to the business goals? Have you developed implementation and testing plans to avoid downtime during a cutover? If the answer to any of these questions is "no," this may be a very good opportunity to invest some extra time and prevent a host of issues in the future.

Migration

Like most IT projects, the first task in any large undertaking is to define your requirements. This is your opportunity to sit down with line-of-business managers, financial people, and regular end users and determine what their needs are. This will be the CFO's opportunity to tell you if he is interested in total cost of ownership, return on investment, or simply the bottom line. Your line-of-business managers will be able to offer suggestions on how the new system might improve productivity or workflow, or perhaps inform you of an upcoming initiative to encourage employees to work from home. End users will most likely offer you a litany of difficulties they have had in using the system, and what portions of the technology are confusing to them. Gather all of this information diligently, so you can incorporate it into your own decision-making process as you move through the migration. Remember, if you adhere to this process, you will be creating a template that can be used for future projects, regardless of the application or function you are implementing.

The next step in the migration process will be to create and document your design. You can build on the feedback from your peers as you proceed. For example, if the bottom line is the main financial driver may be inexpensive, disposable servers are the best route to take. If ROI is more important, maybe it is time to investigate blade servers and virtualization to save time and money as you grow. Line-of-business managers may be more interested in maintaining the same look and feel of the existing environment rather than supporting remote users, which will help determine which access method to use. All these factors go into creating your design, which should act as a "blueprint" for the migration process.

Once your design is complete, it is time to begin testing. For implementations of any size, it is recommended that you create a small-scale test farm that mimics the production environment as closely as possible. During this phase you will discover potential obstacles and adjust your plan accordingly. You can determine if new versions of your existing productivity apps will function properly in server-based computing environment, as well as test the "human factor" by allowing certain end users to work in the new environment and gauge their reactions. During this phase it is extremely important to document any issues that may arise so you can incorporate feedback into the overall plan.

Citrix offers some very helpful advice in their knowledge base to assist you with the migration plan as well as your implementation. The basic recommended template for implementation includes the following steps:

▼ Server build process

■ Configuration of settings

■ Application installation

■ Help desk training

■ User training

■ Staged rollout

▲ Rollback

By creating and following a set methodology, you will increase the chances of the transition being a success and meeting as many of the business goals as possible. Not only will this further your own career potential, but you will have created a template for future projects, whether they involve application delivery or other technologies.

Upgrade

There are certainly times in any environment when moving to the next patch or release needs to be as simple as possible. This is especially true if you already have the processes in place that were mentioned earlier in the migration section. However, there are a few things to keep in mind as you move forward with the upgrade process.

The upgrade of any server in a farm will automatically place the entire farm into mixed mode. This happens regardless of which zone the upgraded server resides in. Something to consider prior to upgrading your first server is that XenApp 4.5 requires the latest version of the licensing server to function. Therefore, the license server is the logical place to start. Timing is also very important as you examine which components to upgrade and when.

If your farm is small enough, or you have available planned downtime, it is best to upgrade all your servers when you are not in production because problems may arise when you are running multiple versions on the same farm. Administration of the farm can rapidly become more complex because different consoles must be used to manage different servers. Also, certain IMA functions cannot be enabled in a mixed environment such as IMA encryption and configuration logging. Potentially, users may be directed to servers running different versions at different times, and although the disparities between the two may be small, users can become frustrated as their experience becomes less consistent.

Although many of these issues may prevent the business from following the upgrade path, it is still a viable and supported option. Even more so than during a migration, it is critical to follow documented plans and published guidelines. In an upgrade scenario, it might also be beneficial to bring in a Citrix partner who has had experience performing upgrades and can help you through the process.

PART IV

Delivery, Management, and Administration

CHAPTER 15

Citrix XenApp Client Configuration and Deployment

As discussed throughout this book, on-demand access moves the vast majority of IT work and expertise from the client to the server environment. It also simplifies the client environment to the thinnest form possible. Delivery of on-demand computing requires that the client software installation and configuration be instant and invisible to end users. The advances made by both Microsoft and Citrix over the last three years continue the trend of reducing desktop configuration—in many cases to no configuration at all. Chapter 5 detailed the client choices and discussed which client devices to use and when. This chapter, building on Chapter 5, discusses the configuration and installation of the clients.

ICA CLIENT OPTIONS FOR APPLICATION ACCESS

Windows Terminal Server with Citrix XenApp 4.5 accepts connections from the following types of clients:

▼ A device running a web browser (Internet Explorer, Mozilla, Netscape, and so on)

■ A thin client running ICA or RDP clients

■ A PC running any Windows operating system with an ICA or RDP client installed

■ A PowerPC Macintosh, a 68K Macintosh (for ICA), or a Macintosh running OS X for ICA and RDP

■ A PC running a Linux operating system with a windowing system and an ICA client installed

■ An IBM, HP, or Sun UNIX desktop running a windowing system with an ICA client installed

■ Any number of tablet and handheld devices running Windows CE, Pocket PC, or CE.NET with an RDP or ICA client installed

▲ A Java-enabled device (anything from a cell phone to a Linux appliance) running the ICA Java client

The decision as to which of these client types an organization will use depends on their current network, client environment, security requirements, and whether or not the organization will be running all or just a few applications from the XenApp environment (the "hybrid" environment is discussed in Chapter 5). Table 15-1 compares the features and options of some of the more common ICA clients. The latest and most detailed version of this table can be found at http://download2.citrix.com/FILES/en/products/ClientFeatMatrix/Citrix_ClientFeatureMatrix.pdf.

As you can see there are a lot of choices to pick from, but for the scope of this book we discuss the Windows clients only.

	Win32 10.x	CE WBT 10.x	CE HPC 10.x	Java 9.x	Mac OS X 10	Linux X86 10.x	Solaris SPARC 8.x	HP-UX 6.30	AIX 6.30	SGI 6.0	OS/2 6.01
Display + Graphics											
Core Functionality*	X	X	X	X	X	X	X	X	X	X	X
Seamless Windows	X	X		X		X	X	X	X	X	
Text Entry Prediction	X	X	X	X	X	X	X	X	X	X	
Panning	X			X	X	X	X	X	X	X	
Scaling	X		X								
Browser Acceleration	X	X	X	X	xx	X	X				
Multimedia Acceleration	X	X									
Image Acceleration	X	X	X	X		X	X				
Flash Acceleration (Server feature)	X	X	X	X	X	X	X	X	X	X	X
Dynamic Session Resizing	X	X	X	X		X	xx				
Client Device Mapping											
Drives	X	X	X	X	X	X	X	X	X	X	X
Printers	X	X	X	X	X	X	X	X	X	X	X
COM Ports	X	X	X		X	X	X	X	X		X
Audio (Server to Client)	X	X	X	X	X	X	X	X	X		X
Audio (Client to Server)	X	X	X			X	X				
Clipboard	X	X	X	Text only	X	X	X	X	X	X	Text only
USB PDA Sync	X	§	§			X					
TWAIN Support	xx	§	§								
Connectivity											
PN Agent Interface	X	X	X	N/A		X	X				
Multifarm Support	X	X	X	N/A		X	xx				
Password Expiration Support	X			N/A							
Roaming Smartcard Support	X										
Backup URL	xx	xx	xx		xx						

Table 15-1.   XenApp ICA Client Comparison

	Win32 10.x	CE WBT 10.x	CE HPC 10.x	Java 9.x	Mac OS X 10	Linux X86 10.x	Solaris SPARC 8.x	HP-UX 6.30	AIX 6.30	SGI 6.0	OS/2 6.01
Support Through Access Gateway	xx										
Auto Client Reconnect	X	X	X	X	xx	X	X	X	X		
Roaming User Reconnect	X	X	X	X		X	X	X	X		
Extended Parameter Passing	X	X	X	X	X	X	X	X	X		
Content Publishing	X	X	X	X		X	X				
Content Redir. Client-Svr	PN Agent	X	X		Manual	Manual	Manual	Manual	Manual		
Content Redir. Svr-Client	X	X	X	X		X	X	X	X		
Auto Printer Detection	X	X	X	X	X	X	X	X	X		X
Universal Printing	X			X	xx(v2)	X	X				
UPDv3	X	§	§		N/A	N/A					
Windows Key Passthrough	X	X				X					
Workspace Control	X	X	X			X	xx				
Session Reliability	X	X	X	xx							
Security/ Authentication											
Smart Card	X	X	xx		xx	X	X		X		
NDS Credentials	X	X	X	X	X	X	X	X	X		
SSL (Including DNS Resolution)	X	X	X	xx	X	X	X	X	X		
TLS	X	X	X	X	X	X	X	X	X		
AES Support	xx				xx	xx					
SOCKS 4 and 5 Support	X	X	X	X	X	X	X	X	X	X	
Auto Proxy Discovery	X	xx	xx	X	X	X	X	X	X		
Secure Proxy	X	X	X	X	X	X	X	X	X		
NTLM Proxy Authentication	X	X	X	xx		X					
Passthrough Authentication	X			xx							
Signed Packages	X			X							

Table 15-1. XenApp ICA Client Comparison *(continued)*

	Win32 10.x	CE WBT 10.x	CE HPC 10.x	Java 9.x	Mac OS X 10	Linux X86 10.x	Solaris SPARC 8.x	HP-UX 6.30	AIX 6.30	SGI 6.0	OS/2 6.01
Enhanced Proxy Detection	xx	§	§			xx					
Non-Administrator Client Installation	xx	N/A	N/A			X					
Trusted Server Configuration	xx	xx	xx			xx					
International											
Time Zone Support	X	X	X	xx****	X	X	X	X	X		
Enh Unicode Keyboard Support***	X		X	X		X	xx				
Virtual Channel SDK	X	X	X	X		X	xx (SPARC only)	X	X		

*Core Functionality — 1280×1024 resolution, 24-bit color depth, memory and persistent cache, international keyboard support, TCP/HTTP browsing, disconnect/reconnect, up to 128-bit encryption

§ Not implemented due to platform restrictions.

*** Enhanced Unicode keyboard support provides more versatile double-byte character entry using the local IME and/or handwriting recognition functions.

**** Some limitations (details in readme).

xx = Denotes change from previous version.

Table 15-1. XenApp ICA Client Comparison *(continued)*

Which Client Do I Use?

As the needs of users change, the ways in which users access resources change. As organizations continue their current growth rates, Citrix provides three options for delivering applications to your user base: Program Neighborhood Agent, Program Neighborhood, and Web Client. Also, within the Web Interface realm is Web Interface for SharePoint Services (WISP), which we also cover.

NOTE: For information about clients for other client devices and operating systems, see the documentation included on the Citrix XenApp Components CD or visit the Citrix website at http://www.citrix.com.

Each of these client options has a different method for delivering applications to users: on a desktop, through a web browser, and via a user interface. Also, different client features are available with each one. Refer to Table 15-1 for a full list of features offered with each client.

To decide which client best fits your needs, consider the way users access published resources, the way you want to manage this access, and the feature set your users will need. The following sections summarize these considerations.

Program Neighborhood Agent

The Program Neighborhood Agent supports the full Citrix XenApp feature set (refer to Table 15-1). Using the Program Neighborhood Agent in conjunction with Web Interface, you can integrate published resources with users' desktops. It is centrally administered and configured in the Access Management Console using a Program Neighborhood Agent site created in association with a site for the server running Web Interface. It is also one of the clients that use the Application Streaming feature of XenApp 4.5 FP1 to provide applications streamed to the user desktops.

The PN Agent runs in the Windows notification area and generates icons in the Start menu, the notification area, or both for the users to work with. Users can double-click, move, and copy icons, as well as create shortcuts in their locations of choice. The Program Neighborhood Agent works in the background. Except for a shortcut menu available from the notification area, it does not have a user interface.

Because the PN Agent is tied into a Web Interface site, it is dynamically managed from a central point and changes are represented in real time. This is the preferred method of delivering applications to your LAN-based or VPN users. Users connecting through an Access Gateway Enterprise appliance or NetScaler appliance can use the PN Agent to access their applications just like they were at the office.

Web Client

The next choice for connecting users to applications and resources is the Web Client and Web Interface site. The Web Client is a smaller client that can be installed from a .cab file or from the main .msi file and either distributed through your environment using existing deployment products (SMS, Enteo's NetInstall Server, or Altiris) or by having users download and install it from the Web Interface site.

The Web client is perfect for internal use because of its small file size and because it runs in a web browser. Another bonus for the Web client is that no end-user configuration is required—there's not even a user interface. All configurations are handled by the Web Interface site and pushed to the client during connections to the applications. This client requires the presence of the following on client devices: Microsoft Internet Explorer 5.0 through 7.0; Netscape Navigator 4.78 and 6.2 through 7.1; Mozilla Firefox 1.0 through 1.5.

Program Neighborhood

The last of the three clients is the full Program Neighborhood client. Program Neighborhood supports the full Citrix XenApp feature set and requires user configuration and maintenance. Use Program Neighborhood if you are not using the Web Interface to deliver resources. Program Neighborhood does not use Web Interface sites in any way. It is a full-featured Windows 32-bit client.

If you want users to access your published resources from within a user interface, use Program Neighborhood. Via Program Neighborhood's own user interface—the Program Neighborhood window—users can browse for groups of published resources (referred to as "application sets") or create custom connections to individual published resources or to computers running Citrix XenApp. Just like with PN Agent, users can double-click, move, and create desktop shortcuts in their locations of choice.

One of the things to keep in mind if you are thinking about using Program Neighborhood is that the configurations are held on the client device. If you make changes to your farm or server topology, you will have to update each client with the new information. There is no central configuration point for this client. Not to worry: You can use scripts and third-party products such as SMS, RES Wisdom, Enteo's NetInstall Server, and Altiris to distribute these changes. In future releases of XenApp, the full feature set of the Program Neighborhood Client will begin to be phased out and administrators should consider using the XenApp Web Client or Program Neighborhood Agent for their Application Delivery solutions.

In case you missed all that, Table 15-2 provides a summary.

The Push or Pull Client Debate

Although the device choice for running the ICA client is nearly limitless, the way in which we provide visibility of the applications to these devices is limited to four choices:

▼ Citrix Web Interface

■ Citrix Program Neighborhood and Program Neighborhood Agent clients

Client	Access Method	User Involvement	Client Features
PN Agent	Transparent integration of published resources into user's desktop	Central administration of user settings	Supports the full feature set of Citrix XenApp
Web Client	Web browser–based access to published resources	Central administration of user settings	Supports the full feature set of Citrix XenApp
Program Neighborhood	An interface users access from their desktops	Requires initial user configuration	Supports the full feature set of Citrix XenApp except for zone preference and failover

Table 15-2.   Client Summary

- ■ A Microsoft Remote Desktop web connection
- ▲ A manually configured ICA or RDP client connection

The first three of these choices are "push based," meaning they provide a user with the icon, configuration, client software, and updates to the client software without the user having to understand the configuration, perform it, or step through an installation. The last choice requires that a user (or administrator) perform an installation, configure the client software, and then configure a connection. In this chapter, we focus on the first two options and the changes, the improvements in these methods of client deployment, and what is required for each. For the other two options, consult the previous edition of this book or the appropriate administration guides.

All the latest Citrix ICA clients are available from the Citrix website (http://www.citrix.com/English/SS/downloads/downloads.asp?dID=2755). The Citrix XenApp Client Packager is an all-in-one client for users of either 64-bit or 32-bit Windows devices (Windows Vista, XP, 2003, and 2000). It wraps the following clients into a single package:

- ▼ Web client
- ■ Program Neighborhood Agent
- ▲ Program Neighborhood

You can customize the Client Packager to deploy and maintain any number and combination of clients networkwide. Based on Windows Installer technology (MSI), the Client Packager lets you install, uninstall, modify, and repair clients as well as perform controlled client upgrades. An easy-to-use wizard guides you through the configuration steps.

Citrix Web Clients

When applications (or full desktops) are published through Web Interface, users access them via a web browser. This method is very easy for end users because they only have to know a URL address (or have it bookmarked or linked to) to connect and run a XenApp–published application. Users only see the applications that have been published to them by the administrator (using the Citrix Management Console as well as users and groups from Active Directory, Novell NDS, or Novell eDirectory). No client configuration is required by the end user. Web Interface supports Macintosh, UNIX, and Windows client types, as well as Netscape Navigator and Internet Explorer web browsers. Figure 15-1 shows a typical Citrix Web Interface access site.

This client requires the presence of the following on client devices: Microsoft Internet Explorer 5.0 through 7.0; Netscape Navigator 4.78 and 6.2 through 7.1; Mozilla Firefox 1.0 through 1.5.

In many organizations, home-based and traveling users need remote access that must also support remote users from all departments who may need to work from home on nights and weekends. These remote users are usually road-warrior salespeople and company executives. Home users have a large variety of client and operating system configurations, including Macintosh, Windows 2000, Windows XP, and Windows Vista machines. Remote users need access to Outlook e-mail and their Microsoft Office applications and files. In addition to these applications, sales groups need access to their

Customer Relationship Management software package (Microsoft CRM), and executives need access to their financial reporting and analysis tools (Microsoft Excel spreadsheets, FRx, and Crystal Reports applications, with links to the SQL server accounting databases). For the purposes of this chapter, we discuss what client they should use and how to deploy it in the simplest, lowest-cost model, with the smallest amount of ongoing support. For these types of users, we recommend using the Citrix Web Client.

Deploying the Web Client

Citrix Web Interface provides users with four choices of client software that will be pushed to them as a web client. The administrator can either force the use of a given client software choice or leave it to the user to choose which one to use.

The Universal Win32/64 Web Client This client software is identical to the Program Neighborhood Win32 client, except that it does not include the Program Neighborhood files and does not install an icon on the desktop or in the Start menu. The full web client is available as a self-extracting executable and as a .cab file. At approximately 1.8MB in size, this package is significantly smaller than the other ICA Win32 clients. The smaller size allows users to more quickly download and install the client software. You can configure the ICA Win32 Web client for silent user installation.

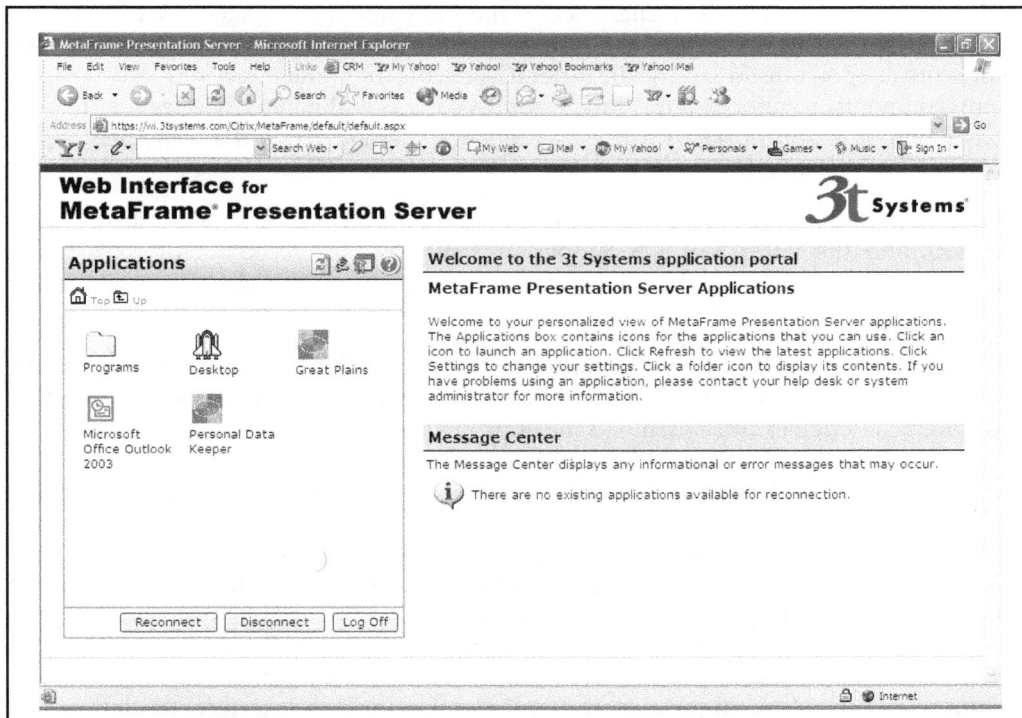

Figure 15-1. The Web Interface site

The Java ICA Client   The Java ICA client was updated significantly with the release of XenApp 4.5 to include more features and run faster. The Java client enhancements include the following:

▼   Support for SSL communication.

■   Certificate Revocation List (CRL) checking.

■   Kerberos authentication when the client is running on Windows 2000, XP, or Vista. (A trust relationship must exist between the client and an Active Directory Domain member server.)

■   Windows NT LAN Manager (NTLM) proxy authentication.

■   Session reliability.

■   User interface improvements with a more compact connection center and enhancements to the look and feel.

▲   Increased performance with better graphics, audio, and drive-mapping capabilities.

The Java client is the smallest and most unobtrusive of the ICA clients, intended for use on machines that are heavily locked down or that don't allow software installation (such as a kiosk). The ICA Java client will run on any operating system that is running a web browser with Java 2 Standard Edition (J2SE), version 1.5.x and higher. The Java client is not as speed-optimized as the other ICA clients for high latency or highly graphical environments, so although it is much improved, it is still generally relegated to situations where it is appropriate for use as a fallback method when the web client is not available or not installed.

The Macintosh Client   Citrix has ICA client software for both the older Macintosh clients (Mac OS) and the latest Mac OS X operating systems. In December of 2007, Citrix introduced version 10.x of the clients for computers running Mac OS X operating systems.

The UNIX ICA Client   UNIX users who connect to the Citrix Web Interface site must use the appropriate UNIX ICA or Java client. Administrators may configure Citrix Web Interface to automatically detect and download the appropriate UNIX client.

If your remote users are on Windows laptops and home PCs, we recommend that you configure Web Interface to detect and push to the users the appropriate ICA client (or ICA client update) for their machine. In order to support users from hotels, trade shows, and airport kiosks, we recommend you allow users to customize their Web Interface login session to select the Java client and only those modules required to improve load speeds. Whenever possible, use the full installation of the Win32 Web client (ica32t) in order to take advantage of the additional features and performance.

The Web client does not require any user or client-side configuration. There is a fair amount of server-side configuration and optimization for Web Interface, though, which is covered more throughout this chapter. ICA client-side optimization settings are covered later in this chapter.

A larger question should be raised at this point: Why not use this client for all your users? Although the web client is simple and sufficiently powerful for use throughout the organization, for cases where the client machine type is fully known and controlled, there are some advantages to fully integrating the Program Neighborhood client discussed next—for instance, it needs fewer clicks from the user because it doesn't require opening a web browser and going to a URL. Meanwhile, it allows for more user configuration. A more obvious point for thin-client users, though, is that many thin clients do not have a web browser, as discussed in Chapter 5.

Program Neighborhood Agent Client

PN Agent is a Windows 32 desktop client that utilizes a Web Interface server for its configuration. For local PCs, this ICA client provides a best-of-both-worlds solution, including a robust set of desktop-integrated features, yet requires little to no client-side configuration.

NOTE: PN Agent is only supported for use with Web Interface servers located inside the firewall. Clients external to the firewall cannot utilize PN Agent unless they are accessing the corporate network through a VPN solution such as the Access Gateway Enterprise, NetScaler, or another corporate solution.

The Program Neighborhood Agent handles the following functions:

▼ **User authentication** The client provides user credentials to the Web Interface when users try to connect and every time they launch published resources.

■ **Application and content enumeration** The client presents users with their individual set of published resources.

■ **Application launching** The client is the local engine used to launch published applications.

■ **Desktop integration** The client integrates the user's set of published resources with the user's desktop.

▲ **User preferences** The client validates and implements local user preferences.

For a complete list of Program Neighborhood Agent features, refer to the Client Feature Matrix available from the Client Download page of the Citrix website (http://www.citrix .com/).

One of the "cool factor" features of PN Agent is the support of client-to-server content redirection. This feature utilizes the content redirection function of XenApp and MIME type association. The PN Agent running on the client device recognizes launched applications and automatically updates a user's MIME type associations to call ICA applications from the XenApp rather than local applications. For example, if a user clicks a Microsoft Word file from their local system files, the Microsoft Word published application from the XenApp farm will be called rather than a local copy of Microsoft Word. When a user disconnects from the XenApp farm, the MIME types are returned to their original associations.

Program Neighborhood Agent employs a simplified user interface (compared with the full PN client) that removes complexity and features. For example, because all connection information is pushed down from a Web Interface site, the Program Neighborhood Agent does not require (or allow) a user to specify a farm to connect to, or to create a custom ICA connection.

Program Neighborhood Agent is a separate Win32 client downloadable from the Citrix website and is only available for Windows 32-bit clients. PN Agent is also available for WinCE WBT, WinCE HPC, Linux, and Solaris clients (see the Client Feature Matrix for the list of clients that support PN Agent Interface). It is installed using ica32a.exe or ica32a.msi.

Program Neighborhood Agent can be accessed from icons placed directly on the user's Windows desktop, Start menu, or system tray by the user, or done remotely by the administrator.

Installing the ICA Win32 Program Neighborhood Agent with the Windows Installer Package

The PN Agent Windows Installer package (ica32a.msi) can be distributed with Microsoft Systems Management Server (SMS), Windows 2003 Active Directory Services, or third-party software distribution products. This package can be downloaded as a part of the Citrix Access Client package.

NOTE: To install the ICA client software using the Windows Installer package, you must first install the Windows Installer Service on the client device. This service is present by default on Windows 2000 and Windows XP systems. To install ICA clients on client devices running earlier versions of the Windows operating system, you must use the self-extracting executable or install the Windows Installer 2.0 Redistributable for Windows, available at http://www.microsoft.com/.

Configuring the Windows Installer Package for Silent User Installation

The PN Agent Windows Installer package can be configured for "silent" user installation to ensure users don't see the installation options or attempt to interrupt or make the wrong installation option choices. Windows Installer informs the user when the client software is successfully installed. The user must clear the Windows Installer message box.

There are two options for creating a silent install package of the Citrix 32-bit ICA clients. You can create a new MSI package with your specific changes made to it, or you can create a TRANSFORMS file (.mst) and apply it to the original MSI package.

Creating a New MSI Package To configure the Program Neighborhood Agent Windows Installer package for silent user installation, follow these steps:

1. Create a temporary directory on your system and copy the desired 32-bit ICA client into it. For example, create the directory C:\MST and copy ICA32A.MSI into it.

2. Open the Orca editor (Microsoft's MSI file editor). It is available at http://msdn2 .microsoft.com/en-us/library/aa370557.aspx and is a part of the Windows SDK Components kit.

3. Open the ICA32A.MSI file in the Orca editor. The left pane of the editor (labeled TABLES) will now be populated with entries.

4. Look for the table entry labeled PROPERTIES and select it. The right pane will be populated with all the details or sub-properties of the PROPERTIES table.

5. In the right pane, select the Property column header to sort the column into alphabetical order. Locate the SERVER_LOCATOR object.

6. By default, the value of this object is PN Agent. Change this value to the name or IP address of a server that is hosting the Citrix XML service. Make sure to preface this server name or address with **http://** or **https://**.

7. Save the file. We recommend that you save it to a new filename (for example, newICA32a.msi). This will remind you that the file was modified from the original.

8. You can now deploy this new MSI file as you would normally.

Creating a TRANSFORMS File for the Existing MSI File   The process of creating a TRANSFORMS file is an extension of the process just listed for creating a new MSI package. The Windows Installer SDK includes a utility called MSITRAN. MSITRAN compares two MSI files and writes the differences to a new file. This file is used as the TRANSFORMS file. Here are the steps:

1. Follow the steps in the preceding section, "Creating a New MSI Package."

2. From a command prompt, run the MSITRAN utility using the syntax MSITRAN -g {base db} {new db} {transform} [{error/validation conditions}]. Here's an example:

```
MSITRAN -g ica32a.msi NewICA32A.msi ICA32A.MST X
```

NOTE: There is only a single space between each entry.

3. When you run this utility, you will see something similar to the following:

```
C:\ >msitran -g c:\mst\ica32a.msi c:\mst\newica32a.msi c:\mst\ica32a.mst xDone
```

4. The new MST file can now be used as the TRANSFORMS file for the original ICA32A.MSI file.

Central Configuration of the Program Neighborhood Agent Client

The advantage of PN Agent (and the ICA Web client) over the full Program Neighborhood client is that it is configured centrally via the Program Neighborhood Agent Web Interface site (refer to Figure 15-2) which changes a config.xml file on the Web Interface server rather than configuration files located on the local devices.

Users' logon methods, shortcuts, and access to the user interface are determined by the options set using the Program Neighborhood Agent site. Users' ability to determine their own logon method, audio settings, shortcut placement, and display settings can all be allowed or denied, depending on the organization's needs.

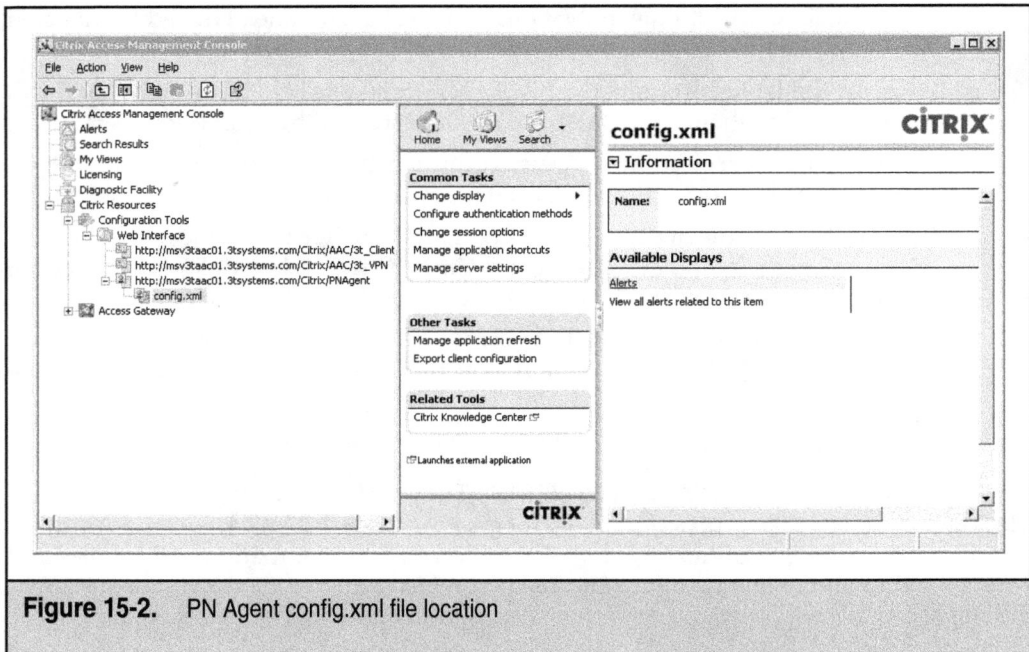

Figure 15-2. PN Agent config.xml file location

The custom options for all users running the Program Neighborhood Agent on a network are defined in a configuration file stored on the server running Citrix Web Interface. The client reads the configuration data from the server when a user launches the PN Agent, and updates the configuration data automatically at specified intervals. This allows the client to dynamically display the options the administrator wants the user to see based on the data received. The settings configured using the Web Interface site affect all users who read from this configuration file.

A default configuration file, config.xml, is installed with default settings and is ready for use without modification in most network environments. However, you can edit this file, or create multiple configuration files, using the Program Neighborhood Web Interface site. This allows you to add or remove a particular option for users quickly and to easily manage and control users' displays from a single location.

The default configuration file, config.xml, is placed in the \Inetpub\wwwroot\Citrix\PNAgent\conf directory on the server running the Web Interface during the installation process. New and backup configuration files created using the PN Agent Admin tool are stored in the same folder as the default configuration file. The data configuration files serve two purposes:

- To point clients to the servers that run users' published resources
- To control the properties on users' local desktops, thereby defining what tabs and options users can customize

A configuration file controls the range of parameters that appear as options in the user's Properties dialog box. Users can choose from available options to set preferences for their ICA sessions, including logon mode, screen size, audio quality, and the locations of links to published resources.

Multiple configuration files can be created to fill all of an organization's needs using the Web Interface site. After creating a configuration file and saving it on the server running the Web Interface, you will need to give users the new server URL that points to the new file.

NOTE: SSL/TLS–secured communications between the client and the server running Web Interface and smart card logon are not enabled by default. These features can be activated in the Configure Authentication Methods and Manage Server Settings sections of the config.xml file. In addition, SSL must be enabled on the XenApp Server to utilize SSL/TLS–secured communications (see Figures 15-3 and 15-4).

As discussed at length in Chapter 13, it is important to test all enterprisewide applications in the test environment prior to full deployment. The PN Agent deployment is no different and should be tested by installing a copy of the client on a single client device, then on five devices (preferably with different Windows operating systems and environments). The test installations allow a full evaluation of the default settings and determine whether or not adjustments are required to fit your particular network needs. Comparing between the configuration file and the client, you can monitor the effects of your changes on the client behavior.

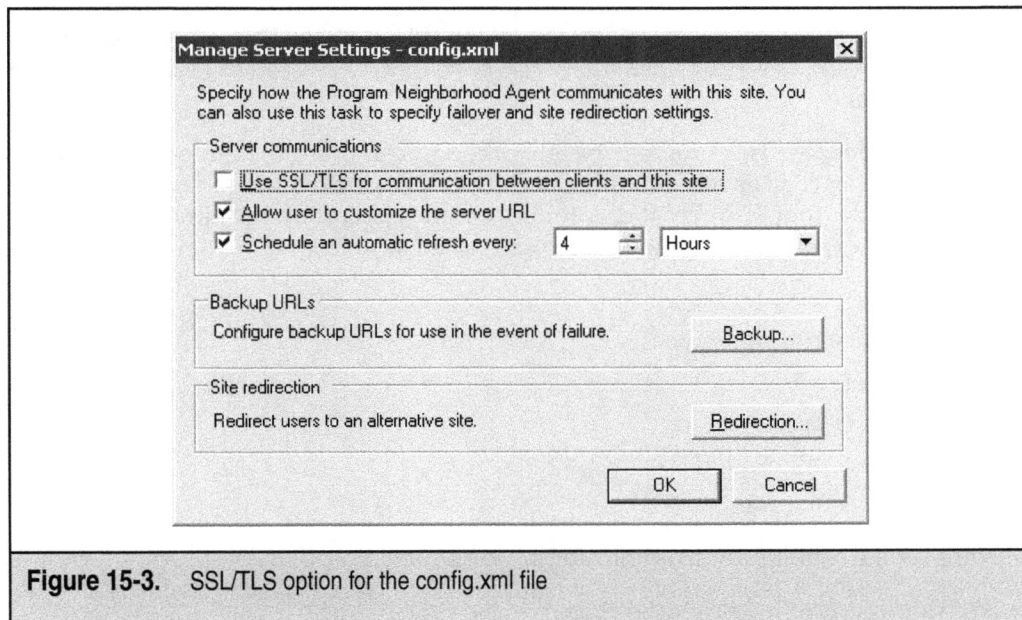

Figure 15-3.   SSL/TLS option for the config.xml file

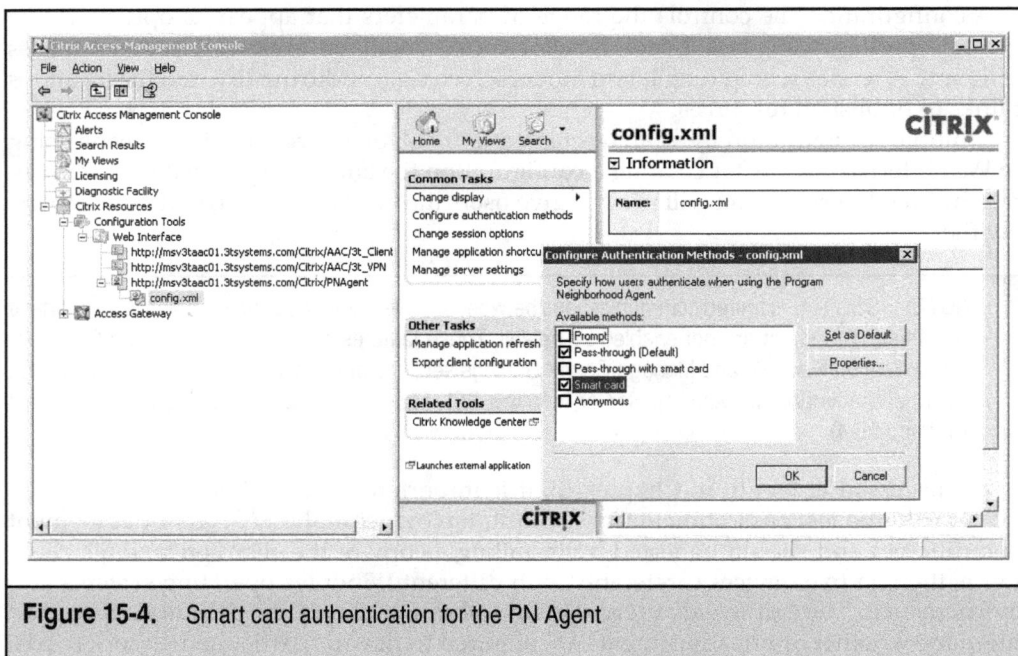

Figure 15-4.   Smart card authentication for the PN Agent

CAUTION: The settings in the configuration file are global, thus affecting all users connecting to that instance of the file. Make sure you export a backup of the config.xml file prior to making changes. The export client configuration option is located in the Other Tasks section of the PN Agent Web Interface site.

Configuration Settings   The Program Neighborhood Agent site is divided into several sections, allowing control and definition of different aspects of the user experience. The configurations for the PN Agent Web Interface site are similar to a Web Interface site that serves up applications. The configuration options are as follows:

- ▼   Manage server farms
- ■   Manage application types
- ■   Client-side proxy
- ■   Local site tasks
- ■   Import configuration
- ▲   Export configuration

Here are the configuration options for the config.xml file:

- ▼   Configure authentication methods
- ■   Change session options

- Manage applications shortcuts
- Manage server settings
- Manage application refresh
▲ Export client configuration

Administrators can define what users see in the Options dialog box of the Program Neighborhood Agent and also what options they can and cannot customize. Each setting as well as the settings that can be customized are detailed next.

By default, users can access the Program Neighborhood Agent Options dialog box from the Windows system tray. Administrators may choose to hide or display certain sections in the Options dialog box of the Program Neighborhood Agent system tray icon, including the Server Options, Application Display, Application Refresh, Session Options, and Reconnect Options.

NOTE: Changing these parameters directly affects the contents of the Options dialog box for all users affected by the configuration file you are modifying. If you remove an option from the Options dialog box, users cannot customize any options in those areas.

Enabling and Disabling User-Customizable Options   This section contains an overview of the options available in the Options dialog box, which are presented in the order in which they appear.

▼ Server Options   The Server Options configuration includes two options to configure: the server URL and the logon mode. The server URL can be changed by right-clicking the PN Agent icon in the system tray and selecting Change Server. This option can be toggled on or off in the Manage Server Settings dialog box (refer to Figure 15-3).

Providing users a choice of different authentication methods, or *logon modes*, may be necessary in environments where multiple users employ the same client device but require different authentication modes (see Figure 15-5). This allows you to determine what authentication methods are available to users, to force a default authentication method, and to allow a user to save their password. The definable authentication methods include User Prompt, Pass-Through, Pass-Through with Smart Card, Smart Card, and Anonymous Authentication. If multiple authentication methods are selected, users can choose their preferred authentication method from the Logon Mode drop-down list in the options of the PN Agent. If you do not want users to have access to any of these options, use the Configure Authentication Methods section of the Program Neighborhood Agent Web Interface site to hide the logon modes you do not want available (refer to Figure 15-4).

NOTE: If you enable the prompt for credentials logon mode, by default users can save their password. To disable this function, clear the **Allow User To Save Password** check box in the **Prompt | Password Settings** section in the properties of the **Configure Authentication Methods** dialog box.

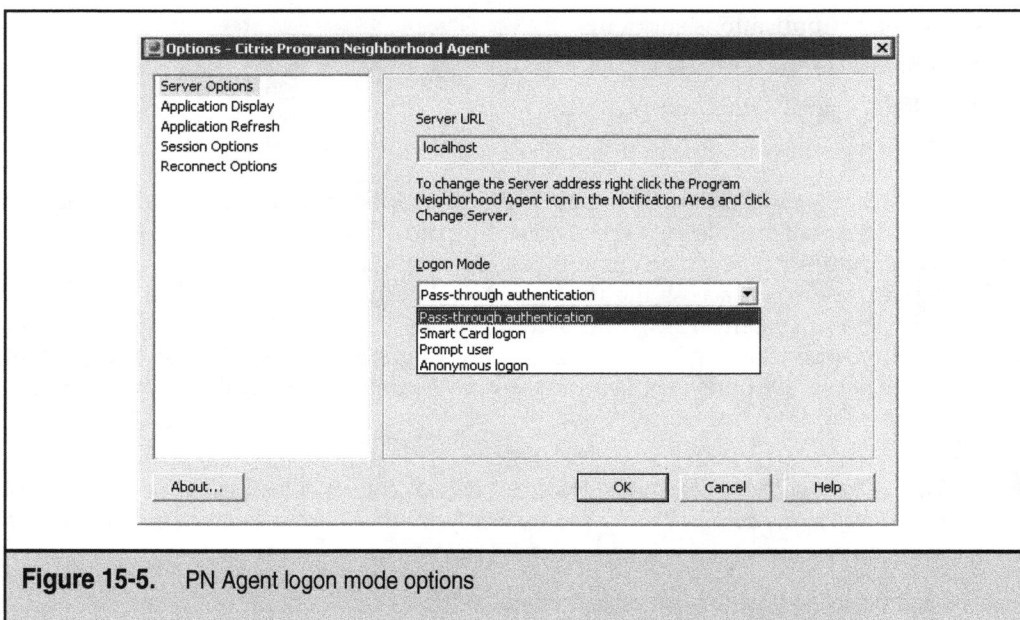

Figure 15-5. PN Agent logon mode options

NOTE: If you did not enable the Pass-Through Authentication feature when you first installed the Program Neighborhood Agent, you must reinstall the client software before you can use the Pass-Through Authentication logon mode.

■ **Application Display** The options available on the Application Display configuration let users place shortcuts to published resources in various locations on the client device, including the Windows desktop, the Start menu, the Windows system tray, and any combination thereof. Using the Manage Application Shortcuts option of the config.xml file in the Program Neighborhood Agent site, you can define which settings users are allowed to use and customize. Here, you can choose other suboptions for each of these three areas. Suboptions include using the Web Interface site configurations for shortcuts (defined in this dialog box), server farm settings (defined in the published application), or a combination of both; setting shortcut creation on the Desktop or Start menu to Always, Never, or Allow User to Specify; and configuring the folder structure and location where the icons will reside on the client.

New to this version of the PN Agent configuration is the ability to control shortcut removal. After a user logs off the PN Agent or closes it, the shortcuts assigned to the Start menu and Desktop can be removed. You can also remove shortcuts based on ones created by the PN Agent, or both the PN Agent and the user. The client queries the configuration file at connection time to validate each user preference against its controlling element in the file.

- **Application Refresh**   The options on the Application Refresh configuration let users customize the rate at which the ICA client queries the server running Web Interface to obtain an up-to-date list of their published resources. If you want to give users control over the refresh rate, you need to enable Application Refresh options first. Enabling the Application Refresh option makes all options on it user-customizable, unless you modify each option in the Manage Application Refresh section of the config.xml file on the PN Agent Web Interface site (see Figure 15-6).

- **Session Options**   The options available on the Session Options configuration let users set preferences for the window size, color depth, Windows key combinations (Alt-Tab), and audio quality of ICA sessions. Using the Change Session Options section of the config.xml file on the PN Agent Web Interface site, you can define what settings are available to the users. Users can choose each available option from a list. The preferences users set for color depth and sound quality affect the amount of bandwidth the ICA session consumes. To limit bandwidth consumption, you can force the server default for some or all of the options.

- **Reconnect Options**   The last option for user configuration in the Options dialog box for the PN Agent is the Reconnect Option. This configuration is also located in Change Session Options section of the config.xml file on the PN Agent Web Interface site in the section labeled "Workspace Control." Just like in the other Web Interface model, you can configure how an existing session is handled during a user logon or after the user logs in.

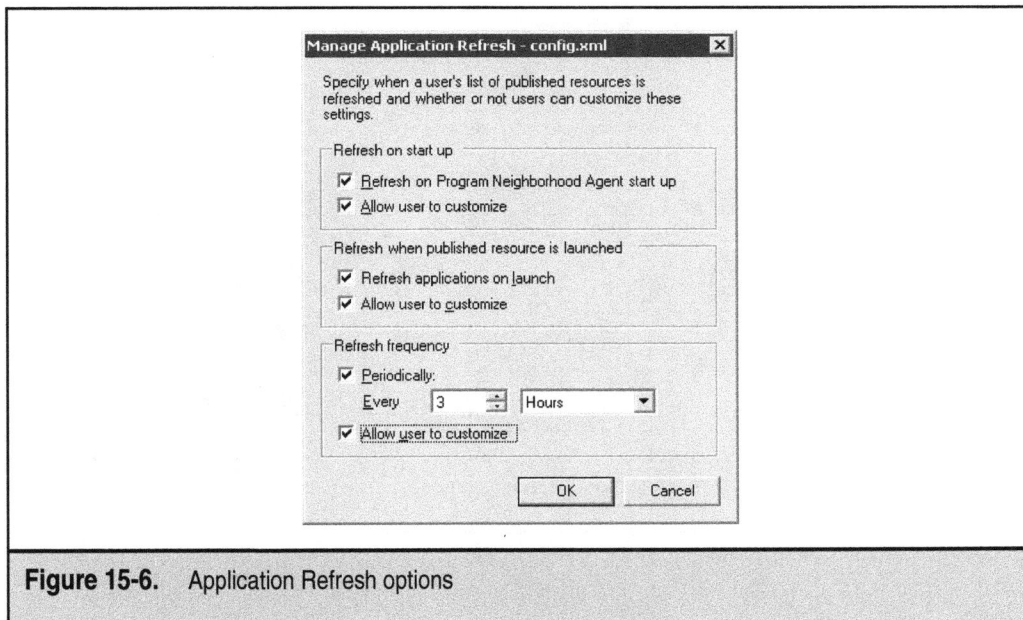

Figure 15-6.   Application Refresh options

NOTE: A quick note about Workspace Control. Before enabling this feature for XenApp connections—either through PN Agent, Web Interface, or the Program Neighborhood—carefully consider how your users work and their understanding of Smooth Roaming. There are two sections for configuring Workspace Control: Automatic reconnection during login and Enable Reconnect button after user logs in. Both sections have the same options on the server side and the agent side (see Figures 15-7 and 15-8) that are stated differently but represent the same thing.

The first section, "Automatically reconnect to sessions when users log in – All sessions," will "move" any active session or reconnect any disconnected session to the computer from which the new connection is being launched when a successful login happens. "Automatically reconnect to sessions when users log in – Disconnected sessions only" will reconnect any disconnected sessions to the computer from which the new connection is being launched upon a successful login. This selection will not affect active sessions. In the second section after a successful login, a button or option will appear for reconnecting your session based on the same rules as before.

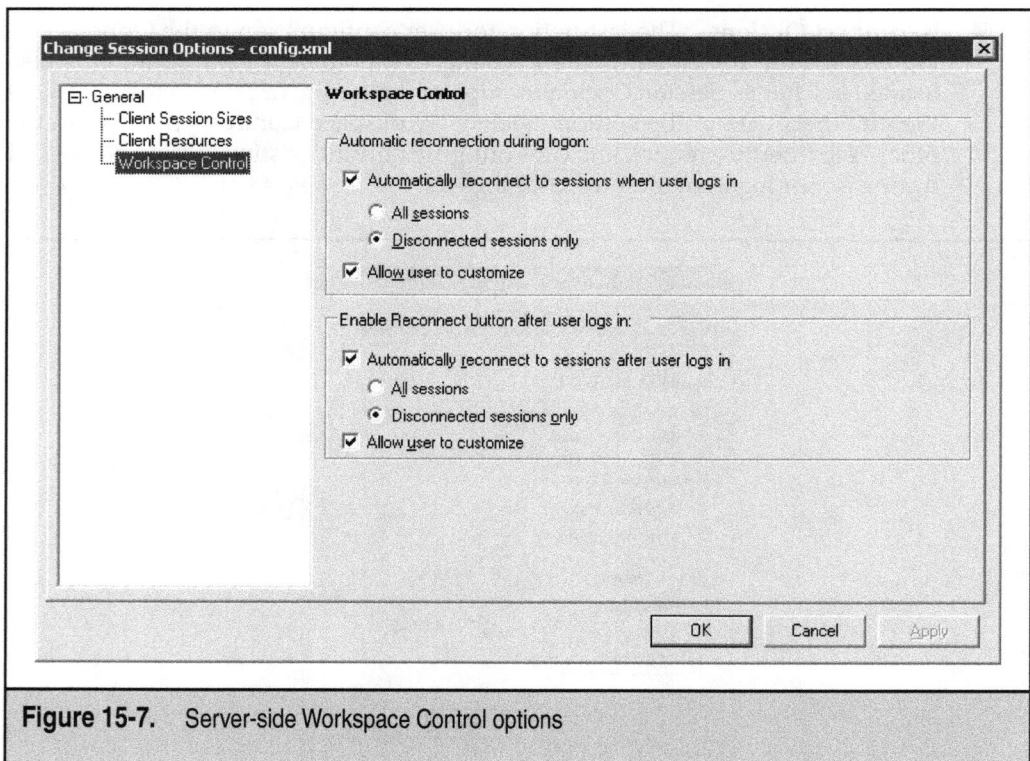

Figure 15-7. Server-side Workspace Control options

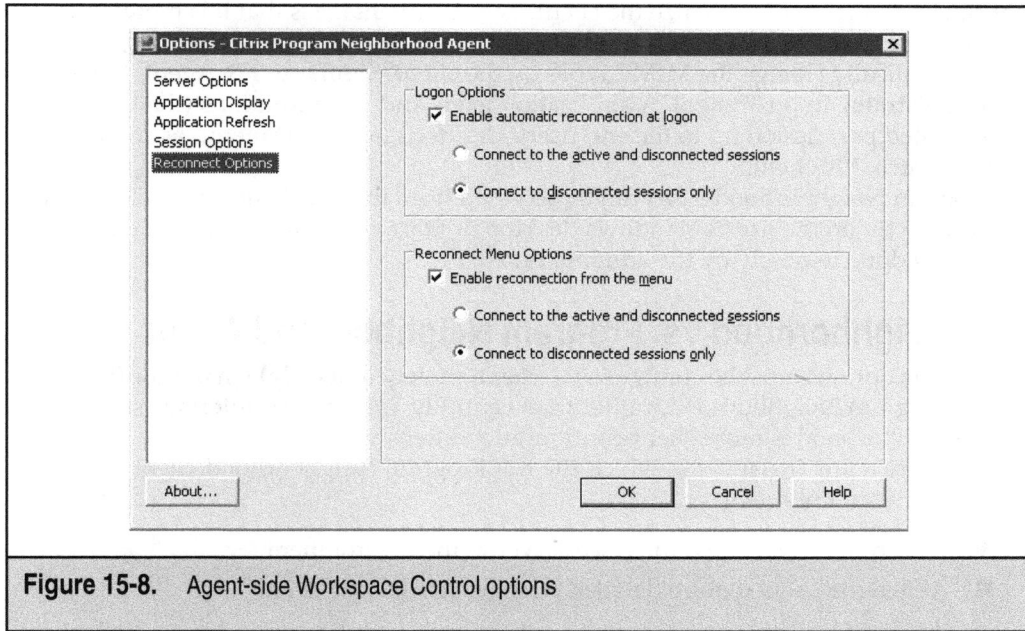

Figure 15-8.   Agent-side Workspace Control options

▲   **Manage Server Settings**   This option does not have a corresponding agent-side feature. It allows you to specify how the PN Agent communicates with the Web Interface site hosting the config.xml file. The two options worth noting here are Backup URLs and Site Redirection. With Backup URLs, you can specify backup servers for the Program Neighborhood Agent to contact if the primary Web Interface server is not available. In the event of a server failure, users are automatically connected to the backup server specified first in the Backup URL list. You may define a maximum of five backup URLs. Site Redirection is used to define when to redirect users to a new site running the Web Interface configured for PN Agent. You may choose from three options: Do not redirect, Redirect immediately, and Redirect the next time PN Agent starts. This is useful in situations where you create a new site for your users and want to redirect all of them from the old site to the new site without them having to enter the new URL manually.

Program Neighborhood Client

The big brother to the Program Neighborhood Agent client is the Win32/64 Program Neighborhood (PN) client, which provides users access to server farms, application sets, and published applications. The primary benefit of Program Neighborhood over the web client or the PN Agent client is that the user has a nearly infinite number of settings that can be changed to customize the client. The disadvantage is that it is more complex, must be configured at the client (rather than through the Web Interface server), and does not automatically change the MIME types on the client. Similar to PN Agent, PN allows an administrator to push the ICA application icons and configurations (that a user has been granted permission to) to the end users' desktops (and Start menu) as soon as they start the Citrix PN client.

Program Neighborhood icons can be accessed from the PN client, or the icons can be placed directly on the user's Windows desktop or Start menu by the user. Alternatively, this can be done remotely by the administrator.

Program Neighborhood vs. Program Neighborhood Agent

Because the options must be configured (either remotely or locally) via the configuration files of Program Neighborhood, rather than centrally via the Web Interface server, Program Neighborhood is more client-configuration intensive.

There are a few instances in which the full Program Neighborhood client should be used rather than PN Agent:

▼ When there is no Web Interface server in the environment

■ When the users require detailed configuration of the client

▲ In disparate user environments, where each user has very different client settings requirements, thus making the central administration and configuration of the client software of little value

UNIX and Linux ICA Clients

Earlier in this chapter, Table 15-1 showed how the UNIX and Linux ICA clients stack up to the Win32 ICA clients. The Linux 10.x client is comparable in features and speed to the Win32 clients, with the exception of image and multimedia acceleration. The only significant missing feature of the Linux 10.x client is the Program Neighborhood feature set, which isn't applicable to Linux. The UNIX clients remain one or more versions behind the Linux and Win32 clients but are still mature, fast, and feature-rich.

Although the normal deployment methods used in a Windows environment are not applicable (for instance, Active Directory, SMS, and so on), a Citrix Web Interface site can still be utilized to deploy the UNIX/Linux ICA client. Another option is a centrally run (and stored) script. Many UNIX and Linux environments utilize centrally stored and executed scripts for most applications in the environment, and the ICA client will deploy effectively using this method.

It is outside the scope of this book to cover the UNIX- and Linux-based clients in detail, so here are just some of the new features in the 10.x release of the UNIX client:

▼ **Automatic diagnostics** Users can automatically generate a file containing diagnostic information to help with support queries.

■ **Automatic color depth selection** This feature allows the client to use the best available color depth for a connection, instead of using a specific value for this setting.

- **Enhanced proxy detection support**   A proxy server can be automatically detected so users do not have to configure the proxy server manually. In larger environments, this feature also means administrators do not have to spend time supporting incorrect or dynamic configurations.

- **Advanced Encryption Standard support**   The client now supports the Advanced Encryption Standard (AES) cipher for connections using Transport Layer Security (TLS). This feature is only available when connecting to XenApp 4.5.

- **Program Neighborhood Agent backup URL support**   Administrators can specify backup URLs for Program Neighborhood Agent in their Web Interface configuration. If there is a failure, Program Neighborhood Agent is automatically redirected to one of the specified sites.

- **32-bit color icon support**   The client now supports high-color icons and automatically selects the color depth for applications visible in the PN Agent view and in the notification area provided for seamless applications.

- **Trusted server configuration**   Settings in configuration files are used to identify and enforce trust relationships involved in client connections. These trust relationships increase the confidence of client administrators and users concerning the integrity of data on client devices and prevents the malicious use of client connections. When this feature is enabled, clients can specify the requirements for trust and determine whether or not they trust a connection to the server. For more information, see the configuration files in $ICAROOT/config.

- **Internationalization support**   Users can now use Russian, Korean, Chinese, Arabic, Hebrew, and Thai locales for their client connections. This support includes keyboard input, display of published application names, and cutting and pasting text for published resources; however, local input method editors are not supported.

- **Philips SpeechMike support**   Users can now use Philips SpeechMike speech-processing devices to record dictations using applications running on the server.

- **Server history in Program Neighborhood Agent**   Users can now click the down arrow in the PNA Configuration dialog box to view and select from a list of previously entered server URLs instead of retyping server URLs to which the client connected in the past.

- **Smart card library support**   The client now supports the Linux smart card library pcsclite.so.1.

- **Seamless taskbar integration**   If you run a published application seamlessly and use a Linux window manager that supports this feature, the application can now add icons to the Linux taskbar.

- ▲ **General performance improvements**   Thinwire improvements result in enhanced graphics performance, and auto-client-reconnect now detects disconnected sessions more quickly.

For more information on the UNIX client, refer to the "Clients for UNIX Administrator's Guide."

Macintosh Clients

ICA and RDP clients are available for Macintosh OS X users, both of which are fast and full-featured. The configuration is very similar to the Win32 configuration (without the Program Neighborhood features). As Table 15-1 earlier showed, features such as local drive and printer mapping are fully supported on the Macintosh ICA clients.

Here are some of the new features for the OS X version 10.X client for the Mac:

▼ **Improved printing**   Users can now use the local Macintosh Print dialog box to control output and use any printer to which they can connect.

■ **Kerberos support**   Users can now connect to servers and applications using the Kerberos authentication protocol, and thus avoid entering their credentials whenever they try to connect.

■ **Improved graphics performance**   Via Citrix's SpeedScreen Image Acceleration technology, the connection now uses less bandwidth when displaying graphics.

■ **Session reliability**   If the connection to a server is lost, the user can continue to see the session while the client tries to reconnect.

■ **Encryption**   This release offers Citrix's SecureICA technology as an alternative means of encryption.

■ **Automatic reconnection**   If the client disconnects from a server unexpectedly, it attempts to reconnect automatically.

■ **Multiple session support**   Users can run multiple connections concurrently.

■ **File type association**   You can map file extensions to published applications so that ICA sessions are launched automatically using the correct application when a file is opened.

■ **Per-connection browsing**   Users can specify a server for a particular connection in order to define specific network protocols and servers or to change security settings for each connection.

■ **Support for high-resolution and color printing**   A print driver specifically for high-resolution and color printing is available when printing from published applications.

■ **Support for smart cards**   You can use smart cards to provide authenticating credentials when logging onto a server.

■ **SpeedScreen browser acceleration**   SpeedScreen browser acceleration, available to users running Internet Explorer 5.5 or 6.0 within a session, increases the rate at which images are downloaded and displayed.

■ **Dock and menu bar auto-hide**   When a session is running in full-screen mode, you can keep the menu bar and dock out of the way and only show them when you move your mouse to the top of the screen or to the edge where the dock is located.

▲   **Recent items option**   To enable users to find connection files more easily, a list of recently used items is available in both the client and ICA Client Editor File menus.

For more information, refer to the "Client for Macintosh Administrator's Guide."

What's New in Windows Client 10.x?

Version 10.x of the clients ships with Citrix XenApp 4.5 for Windows and runs on Windows 2003, Windows XP, and Windows Vista. It introduces a wide range of new features and performance improvements and is fully backward compatible with earlier versions of Windows and MetaFrame XP feature releases. The Clients for Windows now supports Windows XP (x64 edition), Windows XP Embedded, and Windows Fundamentals for Legacy PCs.

The highlights of version 10.x of the clients include the following:

▼   Program Neighborhood Agent now operates with the Citrix Streaming Client to provide application streaming to the user desktop as well as access to offline applications.

■   Non-administrator-modified web client installation for users who do not have administrator privileges on a "locked-down" computer, such as an Internet cafe or kiosk.

■   Trusted server configuration is designed to identify and enforce trust relationships involved in client connections. These trust relationships increase the confidence of client administrators and users concerning the integrity of data on client devices and prevents the malicious use of client connections. When this feature is enabled, clients can specify the requirements for trust and determine whether or not they trust a connection to the server. For example, a client connecting to a certain address (such as https://*.citrix.com) with a specific connection type (such as SSL) will be directed to a trusted zone on the server.

NOTE: When trusted server configuration is enabled, computers running Citrix XenApp Server must be added to a Windows Trusted Sites zone.

■   The Windows Installer package includes a Multilingual User Interface, meaning it automatically installs the clients in all supported languages. Beginning with Version 10.0 of the Windows clients, language-specific installation packages are no longer available.

■   32-bit color icon support. This feature supports high color icons and automatically selects the color depth for applications visible in the Program Neighborhood Connection Center dialog box and Windows notification area and task bar to provide for seamless applications.

- Administrators can specify backup URLs for Program Neighborhood Agent in their Web Interface configuration; in case the Program Neighborhood Agent cannot connect to the Web Interface site, it can failover to another specified site.

- Extends the SpeedScreen Multimedia Acceleration feature on the server to support additional media types on the client.

- Automatically detects a proxy server so users do not have to configure the proxy server manually. In larger environments, this feature is especially useful because it prevents administrators from spending time supporting incorrect or dynamic configurations.

- Program Neighborhood Agent can now use pass-through authentication to connect through the Access Gateway to computers running Citrix XenApp.

▲ The Clients for Windows now supports the Advanced Encryption (AES) cipher for connections using TLS.

That pretty much covers the new stuff—but there is some bad news. As of the 10.x client, you no longer have the option to use InstallShield client packages or the Client Auto Update feature to update the InstallShield packages. In order to update the clients, users can access a Web Interface site and administrators can use a third-party product such as SMS, Enteo, or Altiris.

Additionally, support for the IPX and SPX protocols is no longer available for client connections, and the ICA dial-in connections to XenApp are no more. Dial-in connections must go through a service such as Microsoft's Remote Access Service (RAS).

PERFORMANCE OPTIMIZATION OF THE ICA CLIENTS

Many optimization settings can be used to improve the ICA client user experience. Although most of these settings only make a difference (and are only necessary) with slow or highly latent connections, some of these features can improve the user experience even when bandwidth is not limited.

SpeedScreen Technologies

The SpeedScreen technologies that are present in XenApp 4.5 allow you to configure several features to improve connection speed and responsiveness. These features are detailed in the following sections.

SpeedScreen Latency Reduction Manager (SLR)

SpeedScreen Latency Reduction Manager provides mouse click feedback and local text echo, both of which reduce a user's perception of latency when typing and clicking. By default, mouse click feedback is enabled and local text echo is not enabled. You can enable and disable mouse click feedback at the server level and local text echo both at the server and application levels.

To change the server default settings for mouse click feedback and local text echo, follow these steps:

1. Start the SpeedScreen Latency Reduction Manager by clicking Start | All Programs | Citrix | Administration Tools | SpeedScreen Latency Reduction Manager.

2. Highlight a server in the list and from the Application menu choose Server Properties.

3. Choose each setting for the following:

   ■ Enable local text echo as default for all applications on this server

   ■ Enable mouse click feedback as default for all applications on this server

You can also configure local text echo for an individual application on a server as follows:

1. Start the SpeedScreen Latency Reduction Manager by clicking Start | All Programs | Citrix | Administration Tools | SpeedScreen Latency Reduction Manager.

2. Highlight a server in the list and from the Application menu choose New.

3. Run through the Add New Application Wizard for each application you wish to enable local text echo for.

> **NOTE:** Single instance or all instances of an application? When you apply SpeedScreen settings for an application, you have two options for the configuration: Apply settings to all installations of the selected application and Apply settings only to the installation that I selected previously. The first option registers only the executable name and applies SpeedScreen settings to all occurrences of this executable. For example, you can publish Word 2003 and Word 2007 on the same server. The second option registers the entire path to the application executable.

Local text echo can be set for individual input fields within an application. To view SpeedScreen settings for an application, right-click the application executable name in the SpeedScreen Latency Reduction Manager window and select Application Properties (or from the Application menu, select Properties).

The Application Properties dialog box containing existing SpeedScreen properties for the selected application appears. It shows the details of the application and allows you to configure the different application settings, such as "Disable local text echo for this application" and "Limit local text echo for this application," where you can echo the text in place or have it displayed in a floating bubble (personally, I like the bubble).

Click the Advanced button to force SpeedScreen into handling all input fields in this application in Native (Safe) mode. This option enables minimal SpeedScreen functionality for all the input fields in the configured application.

On the Input Field Configuration tab of the Application Properties dialog box, you can choose and configure a specific input field within an application to decide when SpeedScreen is active. Follow the wizard for the configuration of each application.

Another option for enabling and disabling these settings is on the Program Neighborhood client (see Figure 15-9) under Application Set Settings | Default Options.

Here are some rules of thumb:

▼ If latency is greater than 250 milliseconds, set SLR to On.

■ If latency is between 150 and 250 milliseconds, set SLR to Auto.

▲ If latency is between 50 and 80 milliseconds, set SLR to Off.

For known slower connections (for example, over a wireless WAN or dial-in connection), set the client mode to On to force the feature on, regardless of the latency detected by the server. To set the client mode to On via the Web Interface server, edit the template. ica file and add the following entries:

```
ZLMouseMode 1 (0-disabled, 1-enabled, 2-auto)
ZLKeyboardMode 1
```

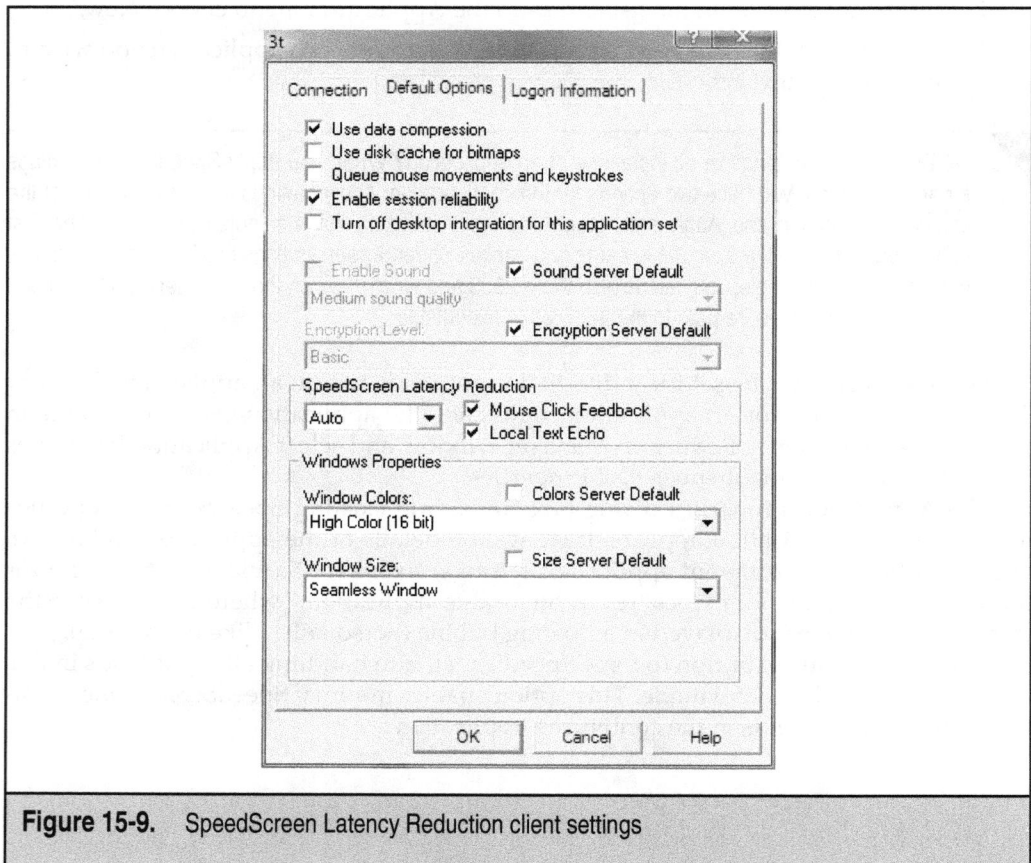

Figure 15-9. SpeedScreen Latency Reduction client settings

SpeedScreen Browser Acceleration

SpeedScreen Browser Acceleration optimizes the responsiveness of graphics-rich HTML pages in published versions of Microsoft Outlook, Outlook Express, and Internet Explorer. By default, SpeedScreen Browser Acceleration is enabled at the server farm level. You can customize the settings for this feature at the farm level and for individual servers. This feature is probably the most widely used SpeedScreen feature given that all of us use IE and Outlook on a daily basis. Enabling this feature will show immediate improvements in the areas mentioned previously (see Figure 15-10). This feature can be set at the farm and server levels.

SpeedScreen Multimedia Acceleration

SpeedScreen Multimedia Acceleration controls and optimizes the way Citrix XenApp passes streaming audio and video to users through published applications like Internet Explorer, Windows Media Player, or Real Audio Player. As a best-practice recommendation, we rarely allow multimedia to be played on the XenApp servers. However, today with podcasts and CBT courses and such, multimedia is the "wave of the future," so to speak. Therefore, it is becoming necessary to think about using multimedia on the servers. With this feature turned on, the server leaves the multimedia file in its original

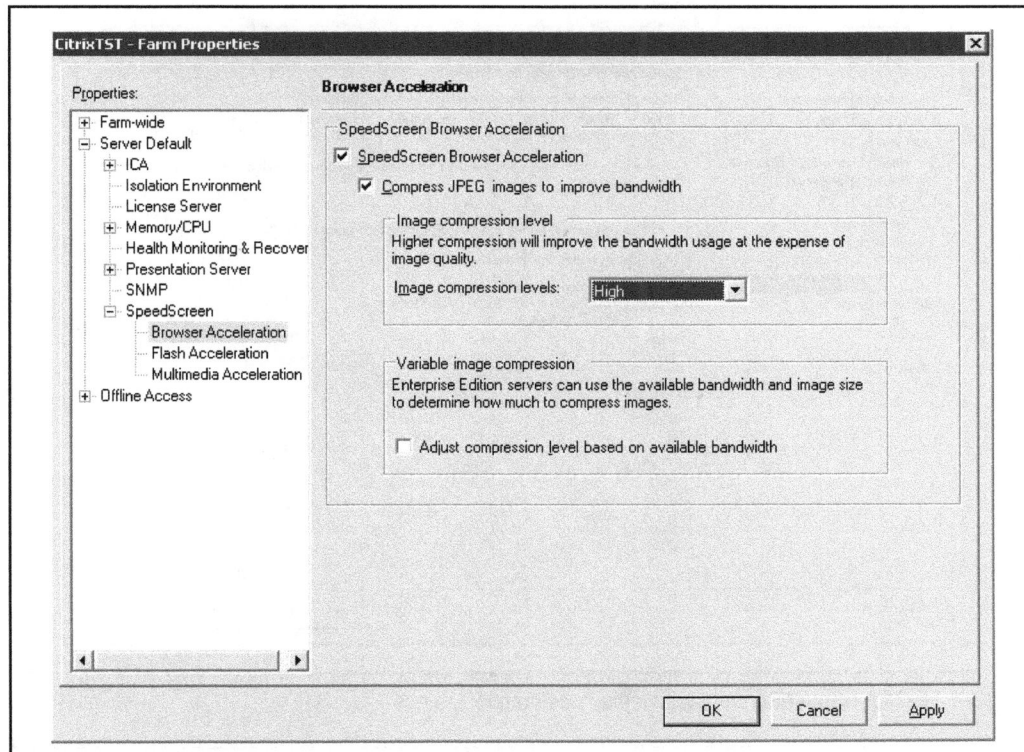

Figure 15-10. SpeedScreen Browser Acceleration settings

compressed format and sends it through the session to the user. This keeps the file small (thus saving bandwidth). The client device will decompress and render the file on the client (thus freeing up server CPU), and enhances the user experience. By default, Speed-Screen Multimedia Acceleration is enabled at the farm level; however, you can override the farm settings by changing this setting at the server level for a more customized configuration across the XenApp farm (see Figure 15-11).

SpeedScreen Flash Acceleration

SpeedScreen Flash Acceleration controls and optimizes the way Citrix XenApp passes Macromedia Flash animations to users. Macromedia Flash animations are a common component of many websites and web applications. This feature forces the Flash Player to start in a low-quality mode instead of the default high-quality mode, thus reducing the bandwidth consumption. By default, SpeedScreen Flash Acceleration is enabled at the server farm level; however, you can override the farm settings by changing this setting at the server level for a more customized configuration across the XenApp farm (See Figure 15-12).

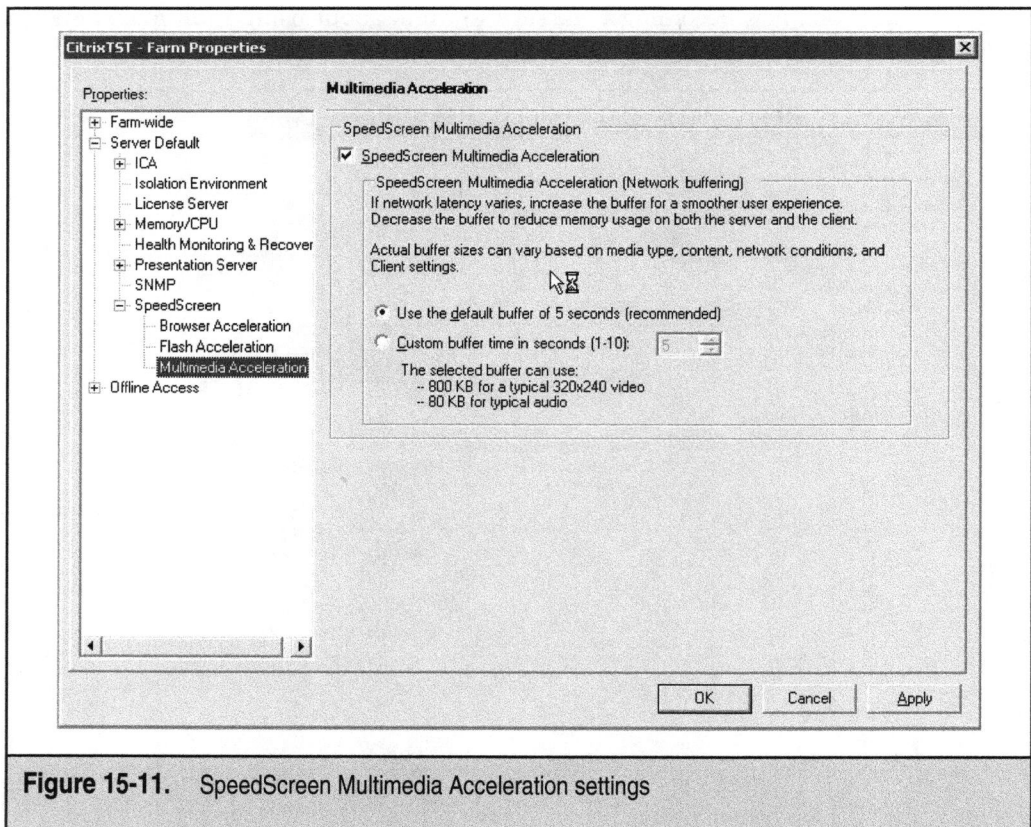

Figure 15-11.   SpeedScreen Multimedia Acceleration settings

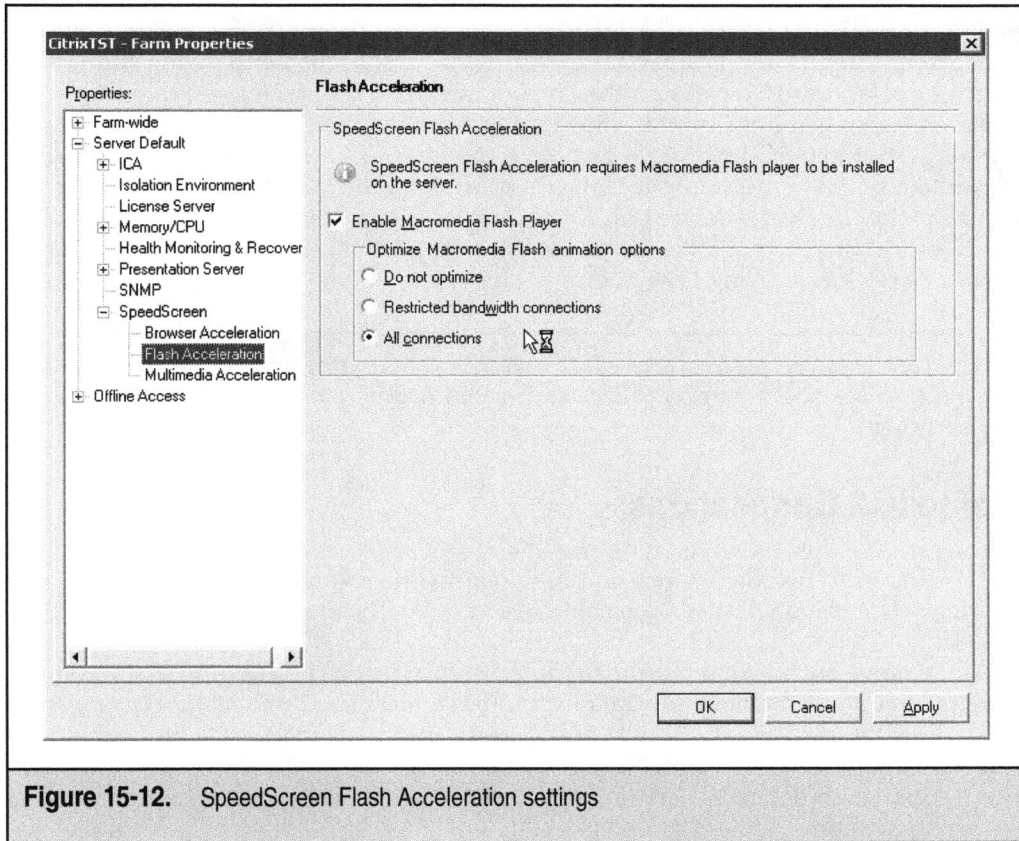

Figure 15-12. SpeedScreen Flash Acceleration settings

SpeedScreen Image Acceleration

SpeedScreen Image Acceleration offers a tradeoff between the quality of photographic image files as they appear on client devices and the amount of bandwidth the files consume on their way from the server to the client. SpeedScreen Image Acceleration attempts to remove the unnecessary and extraneous data that is usually associated with image files before transmission while trying to minimize the loss of image information. Use caution when applying this feature in situations where the quality of the image is important, such as X-rays and cardiograms. This feature is enabled by default but is not controlled in the Access Management Console. Use Citrix policy rules in the Presentation Server Console to override the default settings and accommodate different user needs by applying different levels of image compression to different connections (see Table 15-3 for policy rule settings).

SpeedScreen Progressive Display

SpeedScreen Progressive Display improves interactivity when displaying high-detail images by temporarily increasing the level of compression (decreasing the quality) of such an image when it is first transmitted over a limited-bandwidth connection to provide a fast (but low-quality) initial display. If the image is not immediately changed or overwritten by the application, it is then improved in the background to produce the normal quality image, as defined by the normal lossy compression level. This feature is controlled by Citrix policy rules and is configured under the Bandwidth | SpeedScreen | Image Acceleration Using Lossy Compression section.

> **NOTE:** Lossy compression is a method in which compressing the data and then decompressing it causes the data to possibly be different from the original, but close enough to be useful in some way.

Optimizing ICA Connections

Millions of XenApp users today access their applications over a local area network (LAN). Thanks to the low latency and high bandwidth afforded by the LAN, the user experience is normally indistinguishable from having the applications running locally on a PC.

As we move outside of the LAN, though, the connection choices for users to connect to their Citrix applications in several geographies are slim, and the relatively new solutions offered by wireless WAN (wWAN) carriers such as DirecPC satellite and mobile wireless carriers such as Sprint/Nextel, T-Mobile, Verizon, and others, offer a tremendous solution in the Citrix environment. By providing truly anytime/anywhere access to the Citrix environment, these solutions enable even traveling laptop carriers to stay connected everywhere (Boeing is even working to provide satellite connectivity on planes as well).

Wireless WANs, however, present the challenge of lower bandwidth and higher latency, as well as jitter (variable latency). These issues can be so pronounced in wWANs that the user experience is degraded to the point of being unacceptable.

Lossy Compression Level	Image Quality	Bandwidth Requirements
High compression	Low	Lowest
Medium compression	Good	Lower
Low compression	High	Higher
No compression	Same as original	Highest

Table 15-3.   Image Acceleration Policy Settings

TIP: Throughput and latency are the two elements that define the speed of a network. *Throughput* is the quantity of data that can pass from source to destination in a specific time. *Roundtrip latency* is the time it takes for a single data transaction to occur (that is, the time between requesting data and receiving it). Although most literature from wWAN providers focuses on throughput, the latency is far more important to XenApp usability. When shopping for a wWAN carrier, check on their latency.

The underlying wireless networks are based on circuit-switched voice architectures, which do not contain efficient mechanisms for sending data-link layer acknowledgments. To improve data efficiency, the networks typically wait for multiple frames to arrive before replying with an acknowledgment. This delay is directly reflected in the packet latency.

Latency has a critical impact on the XenApp user experience, because every user action must travel across the network from the client to the server, and the server response must return to the client before the user sees an update. On a LAN, latency is typically very low—less than 10 ms. Latencies on wired WANs, however, are typically in the 50–200 ms range, whereas wireless WANs are usually in the 300–3,000 ms range.

Latency normally increases with a corresponding increase in the size of the TCP packet. On a LAN, this increase is barely noticeable, because ample bandwidth is generally available. On a wired WAN, it typically has a minor impact. On a wWAN, for example, the latency for a 32-byte packet may be 400 ms, whereas the latency for a 1,460-byte packet may be significantly more, at 1,800 ms. This high (and variable) latency on a wWAN can significantly interfere with a XenApp session to the point where the user may find the experience unacceptable.

Citrix provides a variety of features and settings that can be configured to improve the user experience with wWANs. It is important to note that these changes do not raise the user experience to the level of a wired WAN connection, but they do take the user experience from unbearable to bearable. It is also important to note that these features are not available with the Microsoft Remote Desktop client.

Because our recommendation for all remote users is to utilize the Citrix Web Interface client, the client settings discussed will be implemented on the Web Interface server. With the newer versions of Web Interface there is an option to turn on bandwidth control and allow the users to choose to disable features to lighten the load across the network and improve their connection speed. Some of the settings remove features that users on LANs and wired WANs will want to maintain, such as drive mapping and printer mapping. Shutting down these virtual channels will give the ICA channel more room for video, keyboard, and mouse clicks, thus improving the session for the users. If users are using a custom-configured Program Neighborhood client, the settings referenced can be performed on the client.

The settings and features that can be set and optimized include the following:

▼ Enable SpeedScreen Technologies (see the previous section)

■ Enable Maximum Data Compression

■ Enable Mouse Movement and Keystroke Queuing

■ Enable Persistent Cache

▲ Optimize IIS to Cache Images and Utilize the Cache-Control HTTP Header

Enabling Data Compression

Clicking the Use Data Compression check box in the Program Neighborhood client settings improves the user experience for low-bandwidth connections. The ICA client compresses the data on the client side, and the XenApp Server decompresses the data on the server side. This compression and decompression inflicts a processor performance penalty on both the server and the client, but with the current processor power available on both sides, this penalty is negligible. Citrix's internal test statistics show that ICA compression produces an average ratio of 2-to-1, and higher ratios when highly graphical pages and print jobs are employed.

It is important to note that if ICA compression is enabled, a network compression tool such as Packeteer's Xpress, Expand's ACCELERATOR, or Verizon Wireless's Venturi Software Technologies will not improve performance. In fact, these tools often slow performance and cause other problems when ICA compression is enabled.

To enable maximum compression via Web Interface access, edit the template.ica file and add the following entries:

```
Compress On
MaximumCompression On
```

Use Disk Cache for Bitmaps

Clicking the Use Disk Cache for Bitmaps check box in the Program Neighborhood client settings causes commonly used bitmaps (images) to be stored locally on your client so that they do not have to be transferred over the ICA connection every time they are needed.

Queuing Mouse Movements and Keystrokes

Clicking the Queue Mouse Movements and Keystrokes check box in the Program Neighborhood client settings causes the client to send mouse and keyboard updates less frequently to the XenApp Server. Check this option to reduce the number of network packets sent from Program Neighborhood to the XenApp Server. Intermediate mouse packets are discarded, and the number of keystroke packets is coalesced into a single larger packet. Enabling this option improves performance only if you are using a low-bandwidth connection.

To set the mouse movement and keystroke queuing settings on the Web Interface server, edit the template.ica file and add the following entries:

```
MouseTimer 200
```

(This setting can be varied, but increasing this value too much could degrade interactive response.)

```
KeyboardTimer 50
```

(This setting can be varied as well, but again, increasing this value too much could degrade interactive response.)

SECURITY ON THE ICA CLIENT

Citrix ICA clients all support integration with enterprise security standards. Here are some of the more typical standards supported:

▼ Connecting through a SOCKS proxy server or secure proxy server (also known as security proxy server, HTTPS proxy server, or SSL tunneling proxy server)

■ Integrating the ICA Win32 clients with the Access Gateway or Secure Gateway with Secure Sockets Layer (SSL) and Transport Layer Security (TLS) protocols

▲ Connecting to a server through a firewall

Connecting to a Server Through a Proxy Server

Proxy servers are used to limit access into and out of a network, and to handle connections between ICA clients and XenApp Servers. The ICA Win32 clients support SOCKS and secure proxy protocols, and they can automate the detection and configuration of the ICA protocol to work with the client connection.

In communicating with the XenApp Server, the Win32 Program Neighborhood Agent and the ICA Win32 web client use proxy server settings that are configured remotely on the Web Interface server. Web Interface is configured by default to auto-detect the client's web browser settings and pass these to the client's ICA session.

In communicating with the web server, the ICA Win32 web client uses the proxy server settings configured through the Internet settings of the default web browser on the client device. Obviously, the local settings of the default web browser on the client device need to be set for the appropriate proxy settings.

Enabling Auto-Client Proxy Detection

If you are deploying the client in an organization with multiple proxy servers, consider using auto-client proxy detection. Auto-client proxy detection communicates with the local web browser to discover the details of the proxy server.

Follow these steps to enable auto-client proxy detection:

1. Start Program Neighborhood and then take one of the following actions:

   ■ If you are configuring an application set, right-click the application set you want to configure and select Application Set Settings. A Settings dialog box for the application set appears.

   ■ If you are configuring an existing custom ICA connection, right-click the custom ICA connection you want to configure and select Properties. The Properties dialog box for the custom connection appears.

   ■ If you are configuring all future custom ICA connections, right-click in a blank area of the Custom ICA Connections window and select Custom Connections Settings. The Custom ICA Connections dialog box appears.

2. On the Connection tab, click Firewalls.

3. Select Use Web Browser Proxy Settings.

4. Click OK twice.

Using the ICA Win32/64 Clients with Citrix Secure Gateway and Citrix Access Gateway

For external users (and some highly secure internal users), the ICA Win32/64 clients can be configured to use the Secure Gateway or Access Gateway. The clients support both SSL and TLS protocols. Although the Secure Gateway is still supported, we recommend that you always use the Access Gateway for remote access. It is a more secure method for delivering applications over the Internet to users. For information on configuring the ICA client for use with Secure Gateway, refer to *Citrix Access Suite 4 for Windows Server 2003: The Official Guide*. We discuss the Access Gateway ICA client configurations at length in Chapter 11.

Configuring and Enabling ICA Clients for SSL and TLS

SSL and TLS are configured in the same way, use the same certificates, and are enabled simultaneously. Here are some points to keep in mind:

▼ SSL provides strong encryption to increase the privacy of ICA connections and certificate-based server authentication to ensure the server you are connecting to is a genuine server.

▲ TLS (Transport Layer Security) is the latest standardized version of the SSL protocol. The Internet Engineering Taskforce (IETF) renamed it TLS when they took over responsibility for the development of SSL as an open standard. TLS secures data communications by providing server authentication, encryption of the data stream, and message integrity checks. Because there are only minor technical differences between SSL version 3.0 and TLS version 1.0, the certificates you use for SSL in your XenApp installation will also work with TLS. Some organizations, including those in the U.S. government, require the use of TLS to secure data communications. These organizations may also require the use of validated cryptography, such as FIPS 140 (Federal Information Processing Standard). FIPS 140 is a standard for cryptography.

When SSL and TLS are enabled, each time a connection is initiated the client attempts to use TLS first and then tries SSL. If it cannot connect with SSL, the connection fails and an error message appears.

System Requirements for SSL/TLS

In addition to the system requirements listed for each ICA client, the following must be met for SSL/TLS support:

▼ The client device must support 128-bit encryption.

- The client device must have a root certificate installed that can verify the signature of the Certificate Authority on the server certificate.

▲ The ICA client must be configured to be aware of the TCP listening port number used by the SSL Relay service on the XenApp Server.

Verifying Cipher Strength/128-Bit Encryption

You can determine the encryption level of your system by starting Internet Explorer and selecting About Internet Explorer in the Help menu.

From here, check the Cipher Strength value. If it is less than 128 bits, you need to obtain and install a high-encryption upgrade from the Microsoft website. Go to http://www.microsoft.com/ and search for "128-bit" or "strong encryption."

Download and install the upgrade. If you do not have Internet Explorer installed, or if you are not certain about the encryption level of your system, visit Microsoft's website at http://www.microsoft.com/ to install a service pack that provides 128-bit encryption.

NOTE: The ICA Win32 clients support certificate key lengths of up to 4,096 bits. Ensure that the bit lengths of your Certificate Authority root and intermediate certificates and those of your server certificates do not exceed the bit length your ICA clients support. Otherwise, your connection may fail.

Forcing TLS Connections for All ICA Win32/64 Clients

To force the ICA Win32 clients (including the ICA Win32/64 web client) to connect with TLS, you need to specify TLS in the configuration of the Secure Gateway server or SSL Relay service.

To configure the ICA Win32/64 Program Neighborhood client to use SSL/TLS, follow these steps:

1. Open the Program Neighborhood client and then take one of the following actions:

   - If you are configuring an application set to use SSL/TLS, right-click the application set you want to configure and select Application Set Settings. The Application Set dialog box appears.

   - If you are configuring an *existing* custom ICA connection to use SSL/TLS, right-click the custom ICA connection you want to configure and select Properties. The Connection Properties dialog box appears.

   - If you are configuring *all future* custom ICA connections to use SSL/TLS, right-click in a blank area of the Custom ICA Connections window and select Custom Connection Settings. The Custom ICA Connections dialog box appears.

   - If you are configuring an application set or an *existing* custom ICA connection, from the Network Protocol menu, select SSL/TLS + HTTPS. If you are configuring all future custom ICA connections, from the Network Protocol menu, select HTTP/HTTPS.

2. Add the fully qualified domain name of the SSL/TLS-enabled XenApp Server(s) to the Address List.

3. Click OK.

Configuring the ICA Win32 Program Neighborhood Agent to Use SSL/TLS

To use SSL/TLS to encrypt application enumeration and launch data passed between the Program Neighborhood Agent and the Web Interface server, configure the appropriate settings in the configuration file on the web server. The configuration file must also include the machine name of the Citrix server hosting the SSL certificate.

To use secure HTTP (HTTPS) to encrypt the configuration information passed between the Program Neighborhood Agent and the Web Interface server, enter the URL of the server hosting the configuration file in the format **https://** *<servername>* on the Server tab of the Program Neighborhood Agent Properties dialog box.

Configure the Web Interface to use SSL/TLS when communicating with the PN Agent:

1. Select Server Settings from the Configuration settings menu.

2. Select Use SSL/TLS for communications between clients and the Web server.

3. Save your changes.

NOTE: Selecting SSL/TLS changes all URLs to use HTTPS protocol.

Configuring Citrix XenApp to Use SSL/TLS when Communicating with the Client

Follow these steps to configure Citrix XenApp Server to use SSL/TLS when communicating with the client:

1. In the Citrix Access Management Console, open the Properties dialog box for the application you want to secure.

2. Select Advanced | Client Options and ensure that you select Enable SSL and TLS Protocols.

3. Repeat these steps for each application you want to secure.

Configuring the Appsrv.ini file to use TLS

Follow these steps to configure the Appsrv.ini file to use TLS:

1. Exit the Program Neighborhood Agent if it is running. Make sure all Program Neighborhood components, including the Connection Center, are closed.

2. Open the individual's user-level Appsrv.ini file (the default directory is %User Profile%\Application Data\ICAClient) in a text editor.

3. Locate the section named [WFClient]. Set the values of the following two parameters as shown next:

```
SSLCIPHERS={GOV | All}
SECURECHANNELPROTOCOL={TLS | Detect}
```

Set the value to TLS or Detect to enable TLS. If Detect is selected, the Program Neighborhood Agent tries to connect using TLS encryption. If a connection using TLS fails, the client tries to connect using SSL.

4. Save your changes.

Installing Root Certificates on the ICA Win32/64 Clients

To use SSL/TLS to secure communications between SSL/TLS-enabled ICA clients and the XenApp Server, a root certificate is needed on the client device that can verify the signature of the Certificate Authority on the server certificate.

The Citrix ICA Win32 clients support the Certificate Authorities supported by the Windows operating system. The root certificates for these Certificate Authorities are installed with Windows and managed using Windows utilities. They are the same root certificates used by Microsoft Internet Explorer. One exception to this is the Java client. Because this is a server-deployed client, the administrator of the Web Interface server must update the Java configuration files to include the Certificate Authority information and path.

If you use your own Certificate Authority, you must obtain a root certificate path from that Certificate Authority and install it on each client device. This root certificate path is then used and trusted by both Microsoft Internet Explorer and the Citrix ICA Win32 client.

Depending on the organization's policies and procedures, the administrator may prefer to install the root certificate on each client device instead of directing users to install it. In most cases, if an organization is using Windows 2000 Server or Windows Server 2003 with Active Directory, the root certificate can be deployed and installed using Windows 2000 Group Profiles.

NOTE: The following steps assume that your organization has a procedure in place that allows users to check the root certificate as they install it. It is important to verify the authenticity of a root certificate before installing it.

To install a root certificate on the Win32 client device, follow these steps:

1. Double-click the root certificate file. The root certificate file has the extension .cer, .crt, or .der.

2. Verify that you are installing the correct root certificate.

3. Click Install Certificate.

4. The Certificate Import Wizard starts. Click Next.

5. Choose the Place All Certificates in the Following Store option and then click Browse.

6. On the Select Certificate Store screen, select Show Physical Stores.

7. Expand the Trusted Root Certification Authorities store and then select Local Computer. Click OK.

8. Click Next and then click Finish. The root certificate is installed in the store you selected.

Certificate Revocation List Checking

When certificate revocation list checking is enabled, the ICA Win32 clients check whether or not the server's certificate has been revoked. This feature improves the cryptographic authentication of the XenApp Server and improves the overall security of the SSL/TLS connections between an ICA Win32 client and a XenApp Server.

Several levels of certificate revocation list checking can be enabled. For example, the client can be configured to check only its local certificate list or to check the local and network certificate lists. In addition, the certificate can be configured for certificate checking to allow users to log on only if all certificate revocation lists are verified.

To enable certificate revocation list checking, open the default.ica file and configure the SSLCertificateRevocationCheckPolicy setting to one of the following options:

▼ **NoCheck** No certificate revocation list checking is performed.

■ **CheckWithNoNetworkAccess** The local list is checked.

■ **FullAccessCheck** The local list and any network lists are checked.

▲ **FullAccessCheckAndCRLRequired** The local list and any network lists are checked; users can log on if all lists are verified.

NOTE: If you do not set SSLCertificationRevocationCheckPolicy, it defaults to NoCheck for Windows NT 4.0. For Windows XP and Windows Server 2003, the default setting is CheckWithNo NetworkAccess.

Meeting FIPS 140 Security Requirements

To meet FIPS 140 security requirements, the parameters listed in the following subsections must be included in the Template.ica file on the Web Interface server or in the user-level Appsrv.ini file of the local client device.

To configure the Appsrv.ini file to meet FIPS 140 security requirements, follow these steps:

1. Exit the Program Neighborhood Agent if it is running. Make sure all Program Neighborhood components, including the Connection Center, are closed.

2. Open the individual's user-level Appsrv.ini file (the default directory is %User Profile%\Application Data\ICAClient) in a text editor.

3. Locate the section named [WFClient].

4. Set the values of these three parameters as follows:

```
SSLENABLE=On
SSLCIPHER=GOV
SECURECHANNELPROTOCOL=TLS
```

5. Save your changes.

Enabling Smart Card Support

You can use smart cards in your Citrix XenApp environment. Smart cards are small plastic cards with embedded computer chips. Support for smart cards in XenApp Server is based on the Microsoft Personal Computer/Smart Card (PC/SC) standard. This section assumes that the smart card software (PC/SC software) and cryptographic service provider (CSP) software are already installed on the XenApp Server(s) and that the PC/SC software, smart card reader software drivers, and the smart card reader are installed on the client device. Refer to the documentation that came with your smart cards for detailed instructions for installation.

NOTE: XenApp supports only smart cards and smart card devices that are, themselves, supported by the underlying Windows operating system.

In a XenApp environment, smart cards can be used to do the following:

▼ Authenticate users to networks and computers.
■ Secure channel communications over a network.
▲ Use digital signatures for signing content.

If you are using smart cards for secure network authentication, your users can authenticate to applications and content published on servers. In addition, smart card functionality within these published applications is also supported. For example, a published Microsoft Outlook application can be configured to require that users insert a smart card into a smart card reader attached to the client device to log onto the server. After users are authenticated to the application, they can digitally sign e-mail using certificates stored on their smart cards.

Smart cards are supported for authenticating users to published applications or for use within published applications that offer smart card functionality. Only the former is enabled by default upon installation of Citrix XenApp.

Smart cards are supported on the following clients:

- ▼ Citrix XenApp clients for Windows
- ■ Clients for Linux
- ▲ Clients for Windows-based terminals

Enabling Smart Card–Based Login Through Program Neighborhood

Enabling smart card logon with pass-through authentication requires a smart card to be present or inserted in the smart card reader at logon time. With this logon mode selected, Program Neighborhood prompts the user for a smart card personal identification number (PIN) when it starts up. Pass-through authentication then caches the PIN and passes it to the server every time the user requests a published resource. The user does not have to subsequently reenter a PIN to access published resources. If authentication based on the cached PIN fails or if a published resource itself requires user authentication, the user continues to be prompted for a PIN.

Perform the following to enable smart card–based logon (Program Neighborhood):

1. For an application set, select the application set and click Properties on the Program Neighborhood toolbar.
2. For a custom ICA connection, select the custom ICA connection and click Settings on the Program Neighborhood toolbar.
3. From the Logon Information tab, select Smart Card.
4. Select Pass-Through Authentication to cache the PIN and pass it to the server every time the user requests a published resource.

Enabling Smart Card–Based Login Through Program Neighborhood Agent

First, install the Clients for Windows on your users' client devices using an administrator account. The pass-through authentication feature is available only in the Clients for Windows on the Components CD-ROM. For security reasons, the web client does not include this feature.

Second, enable pass-through authentication on the client. You can do this in one of two ways. Either configure a Group Policy to enable pass-through for all clients or edit the Appsrv.ini file.

To enable pass-through authentication for all clients, follow these steps:

1. Open the MMC Group Policy Object Editor snap-in.
2. Select the Group Policy Object you want to edit.
3. Right-click the Administrative Templates folder and choose Add/Remove Templates.

4. Click Add and browse to the icaclient template on the Components CD-ROM.

5. Click Open to add the template and then click Close to return to the Group Policy Object Editor.

6. In the console tree, expand the Administrative Templates folder.

7. Select Citrix Components | Presentation Server | Client User Authentication.

8. Select Local User Name and Password.

9. On the Action menu, click Properties.

10. Click the Settings tab.

11. In the Local User Name and Password area, select Enabled.

12. Select the Enable Pass-Through Authentication check box and click OK.

To enable pass-through authentication for a single client, follow these steps:

1. Open the Appsrv.ini file using a text editor such as Notepad.

2. In the [WFClient] section, add the following entries:

```
EnableSSOnThruICAFile=On
SSOnUserSetting=On
```

3. Save the updated file.

Third, ensure the Windows Directory Service Mapper is enabled on the server running the Web Interface. Web Interface authentication uses Windows domain accounts—that is, user name and password credentials. However, certificates are stored on smart cards. The Directory Service Mapper uses Windows Active Directory to map a certificate to a Windows domain account.

To enable the Windows Directory Service Mapper on IIS 6.0, follow these steps:

1. Open the Internet Information Services (IIS) Manager on the server running the Web Interface.

2. Right-click the Web Sites directory located under the server running the Web Interface and then click **Properties**.

3. From the Directory Security tab, select Enable the Windows Directory Service Mapper in the Secure Communications section.

4. Click **OK** to enable the Directory Service Mapper.

5. On the server hosting the PN Agent Web Interface site, enable Smart Card Authentication using the Access Management Console.

6. Click the Configure Authentication Methods task.

7. Select the Smart Card check box.

8. Click Properties.

9. Select Roaming under the Smart Card section.

10. Select the Enable Roaming check box and choose from one of the following options:

- **Disconnect sessions on removal**   This option disconnects a user's session when a smart card is removed.

- **Log off sessions on removal**   This option logs off a user's session when a smart card is removed.

   In the PN Agent options on the client and the server are two options for smart card authentication: Smart Card Logon and Smart Card with Pass-Through Authentication. Choose the one that fits your environment.

- **Smart card logon**   Prompts you for a smart card PIN when you log onto the Program Neighborhood Agent and every time you open published applications or content. A smart card needs to be present or inserted in the smart card reader at logon time.

- **Smart card with pass-through authentication**   Prompts you for a smart card PIN when you log onto the Program Neighborhood Agent. A smart card needs to be present or inserted in the smart card reader at logon time. After you log onto the Program Neighborhood Agent, you can access your set of published applications and content without further logon prompts.

Locking Down the ICA Client

As discussed in Chapters 5, 13, and 16, the lockdown of the desktop device, regardless of the device, is an important aspect to maintaining a minimal maintenance client environment. If a configuration can be changed on the client machine, there is a risk that it can be broken—and, of course, if the device fails, any configurations will have to be input again. Therefore, if the device can be fully locked such that user configurations and software (including client access software) cannot be changed, the environment will require significantly less support.

We recommend three applications for this purpose: RES PowerFuse, AppSense, and triCerat, each of which does a good job of efficiently and effectively locking down the desktop.

ICA and RDP Client Drive, Printer, and COM Port Mapping

Both ICA and RDP clients now support local drive, printer, and COM port mapping. Local mapping allows the client to force the server to map a local device so that a user is able to employ the local device from within the remote server session.

Although local mapping can be very useful for remote, home, and traveling users, it is important to selectively apply local mappings in remote office and LAN environments because the data stream created from sending data back and forth from the server to the client can be very intensive and cause other ICA/RDP sessions to fail.

All three items can be enabled or disabled from the server in the Citrix Management Console (for ICA) or the Terminal Services Configuration utility (for RDP). The server can also be configured to default to the client settings. The client local mapping settings can be configured for the RDP client from the Local Resources tab.

CHAPTER 16

Profiles, Policies, and Procedures

This chapter examines the different types of profiles available to assist in controlling and optimizing the server-based computing environment. The chapter also covers general deployment tips and guidelines for using Windows Group Policies to implement standard computing environments, and it evaluates some advanced Windows Server 2003 policy settings as well as the Group Policy Management Console (GPMC), along with account creation for your users and the service accounts needed for installing and configuring all the components of the Platinum edition of XenApp.

The last section of this chapter covers recommended best practices for utilizing all these pieces in your farm. So let's stop beating around the bush, so to speak, and get to it!

USER PROFILES

A user profile is simply a Registry hive in file format (NTuser.dat) and a set of profile folders (stored in *%systemdrive%*\Documents and Settings) that contains information about a specific user's environment and preference settings. Profiles include printer connections, background wallpaper, ODBC settings, MAPI settings, color schemes, shortcuts, Start menu items, desktop icons, mouse settings, folder settings, and shell folders such as My Documents. Profiles are automatically created the first time a user logs into any NT-based machine, including a Terminal Server.

NTuser.dat (the file that stores the user's Registry-based preferences and configurations) is loaded by the system during logon and is mapped into the Registry under the hive HKEY_CURRENT_USER. This file can be found at the root of the user's profile location, such as C:\Documents and Settings*username*\NTuser.dat. The set of profile folders, such as Application Data, Cookies, Desktop, and Start Menu, is also located at the root of a profile, such as C:\Documents and Settings*username*\Application Data. The Application Data profile folder is where applications and other system components store user data, settings, and configuration files. You can use three types of profiles with Terminal Services: Terminal Server–specific profiles, Windows Server mandatory roaming profiles, and Windows Server local profiles.

When a user logs onto a server running Terminal Server, the server first searches for the Terminal Server–specific profile. If Terminal Server cannot locate this profile, it attempts to load the user's Windows Server 2003 roaming profile or the Windows Server 2003 local profile. We cover the three types in detail in this chapter.

We recommend that you use either Terminal Server–specific profiles or roaming user profiles for your environment, rather than local profiles. These types help manage the size of the profiles and optimize the user experience. Terminal Server–specific profiles are recommended in most cases; however, you should consider the following situations when choosing which type of user profile to use with Terminal Server:

▼   If you are planning to keep the environment for your Terminal Server users standardized and under tight control, you can use mandatory roaming user profiles to restrict access to certain applications. You can also use mandatory roaming user profiles to assign users profiles that cannot be changed.

- If you assign roaming user profiles to users who tend to access the Terminal Server from different computers (for example, IT administrators, users who access the application from a kiosk, or users who work in certain task-worker environments), those users can retain their settings regardless of where they log on.

▲   If you are using Terminal Server in a load-balanced farm, you should plan to use roaming user profiles.

Windows Server Local Profiles

As the name implies, a *local profile* is a user profile that exists on a single machine. By default, a user will employ a local profile and may have several local profiles on different machines. This type of profile is not very useful for the average user because it cannot traverse a load-balanced server farm. Local profiles lead to end-user confusion because applications and environment changes do not follow the users when they log into different servers in the farm. For example, a user may change their background setting to green on one Terminal Server, log out, and then log back into a different terminal server to find that the background is not green. This is caused by having two separate local profiles, with one on each server. Local profiles are useful for administrators or service accounts that do not need their settings to roam from one server to another.

Terminal Server–Specific Profiles

Terminal Server–specific profiles are what we all know as the classic "roaming" profiles. You use Terminal Server–specific profiles to present a session to the user that is different from the user's workstation desktop or to create user profiles that are optimized to the Terminal Services environment. Here are some situations that might require Terminal Server-specific profiles:

▼   When you need to provide users who are accessing Terminal Server with an environment that is different from the environment on their local computers.

▲   When you need to provide a different look and feel for users with different roles and duties who are accessing the same terminal server.

A Terminal Server–specific profile is a centrally stored version of a local profile. The profile is "roaming" in that it is copied to every server that the user logs onto as their "local" profile. There, it is utilized as a locally cached copy until the user logs out, at which point it is saved back to the network shared directory. This is the primary type of profile employed in a server-based computing network due to the necessity of having user settings "roam" with the user. The corresponding files have an extension specific to the type (for example, NTuser.dat for a roaming profile).

Roaming profiles allow users to make changes and customizations to their "personal" environment. These changes are then recorded in the locally stored copy of the roaming profile. Once a user logs off, the profile changes are copied back to the network share from which it was originally loaded. This profile is then used the next time the user logs into the environment. Another item to remember with roaming profiles is that the last write wins. An example of this can be seen when a user logs into two different machines simultaneously. They may change something in their profile in one session (such as the background color to green) and proceed to log out. They then change the background color to blue in the other session and log out. As a result, the user will end up having a blue background the next time they log into a machine. This is due to the fact that the last logout causes the profile to be written back to the profile storage location, which overwrites any previous writes.

Terminal Server–specific profiles have the following advantages:

▼ User-specific application settings, such as default file locations, file history, and fonts, are saved to the profile.

▲ Users can customize the desktop environment. They can change colors, fonts, backgrounds, desktop icons, and the Start menu.

Default limitations of Terminal Server–specific profiles include the following:

▼ Profiles have no restriction on file size, which can lead to rapidly increasing disk space and network bandwidth consumption. This becomes a problem particularly when users drag large documents onto their desktop for easy access.

▲ Users are not prevented from making changes that might render their environment unstable or unusable.

Although Terminal Server–specific profiles were designed to allow users to make changes, these profiles can be locked down to reduce the number and kinds of changes a user can make to their environment. A review of how to implement Terminal Server–specific profiles with Group Policy is presented later in this chapter. This will help achieve a balance between giving users sufficient rights to change what they need while maintaining control and manageability of the profiles.

You can configure Terminal Server–specific profile settings for each user by following this procedure:

1. Open Active Directory Users and Computers.

2. Right-click the user for which you want to create profile settings and then click Properties.

3. Click the Terminal Services Profile tab.

4. In the Terminal Services User Profile Path dialog box, choose a location on the network to store users' Terminal Services profiles. This should be located on a network share.

TIP: We recommend that you set this property using Group Policy Objects (GPOs) under Computer Configuration\Administrative Templates\Windows Components\Terminal Services. Create a new Organizational Unit (OU) for Terminal Servers and apply this policy to the new OU. Do not use the GPO and the user account properties to set the profile and home directory path. Use one or the other. Using both configurations will create dual entries in the profile and home directories, thus causing sporadic behavior for the users during connections.

5. For the Terminal Services home folder, specify a path to a home folder for use with Terminal Server sessions. This directory can be either a local folder or a network share.

NOTE: Do not make the profile folder location and the home folder location the same path. This will cause all the files saved in the home folder to load along with the profile.

Windows Server Mandatory Roaming Profiles

A mandatory roaming profile is a specific type of roaming profile that is preconfigured by an administrator and cannot be changed by the user. This type of profile has the advantage of enforcing a common interface and a standard configuration. A user can still make modifications to the desktop, Start menu, or other elements, but the changes are lost when the user logs out because the locally stored profile is not saved back to the network share.

NOTE: If your users roam between computers that are running Windows XP Professional, Windows XP 64-bit Edition, and Windows Server 2003, you can use the "Prevent Roaming Profile changes from being propagated to the server" Group Policy setting to be sure that each client computer receives only the profile that applies to the particular platform the user is logged onto. For more information, see "Group Policy in multiplatform networks" in the Help and Support Center for Windows Server 2003. To find this topic, click Index in the Help and Support Center, type the keywords **Group Policy**, and then select the topic Multiplatform Networks.

Mandatory roaming profiles are created by renaming the NTuser.dat file in the roaming profile to NTuser.man. Mandatory profiles should be used for kiosk environments or where users cannot be trusted to change settings related to their profiles.

Mandatory roaming profiles have the following advantages:

▼ The profile size is fixed and typically small. This alleviates disk storage problems and potential network congestion.

■ The profile network traffic is cut in half because the locally cached profile is never copied back to the profile server.

▲ No user settings are saved. This eliminates some help-desk calls and prevents users from inadvertently destroying their environments. If the user has made inappropriate changes to the environment, logging out and logging back in will reset them to an original configuration.

The following are the disadvantages of mandatory roaming profiles:

▼ No user settings are saved. This lack of flexibility may lead to the need to create various "standard" mandatory roaming profiles to accommodate different needs.

▲ User-specific application settings, such as Microsoft Outlook profile settings, are not saved with the profile. Mailbox settings need to be set each time a user logs onto the system.

Many of the same beneficial restrictions of mandatory roaming profiles can be accomplished using a Terminal Server–specific profile without compromising flexibility. For this reason, mandatory profiles are not often utilized in organizations today.

Profile Mechanics

Two separate roaming profile locations can be specified in an Active Directory domain. Both are configured from within the Active Directory Users and Computers administration program:

▼ **Terminal Server Profile Path** The profile in this specified path is used when a user logs into a server with Terminal Services running. It is configured from the Active Directory Users and Computers administration program on the Terminal Services Profile tab, as shown in Figure 16-1. This setting is strongly recommended in an Application Delivery environment to keep users' Terminal Server profiles separate from their standard client OS profile.

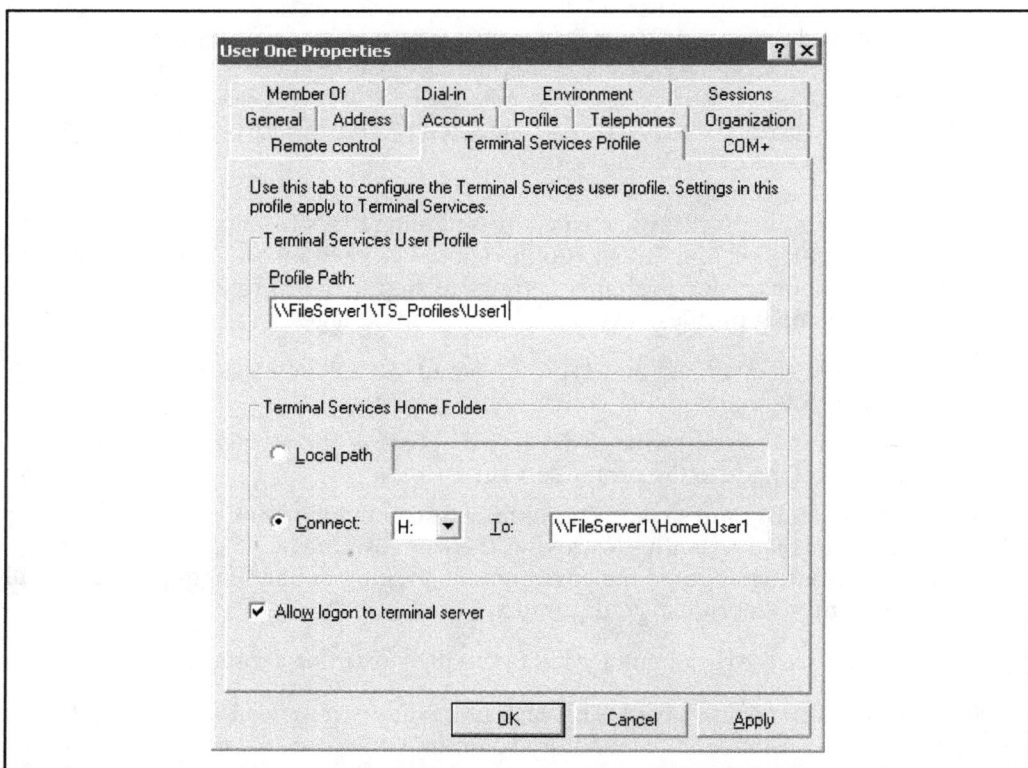

Figure 16-1. The Terminal Server profile path

> **NOTE:** Windows Server 2003 Active Directory environments can use Group Policy to set the Terminal Server profile path (see Figure 16-2).

▲ **User Profile Path**   The profile in this specified path is used when a user logs into a computer without Terminal Services running (such as a local workstation or laptop). This profile path is configured from the Active Directory Users and Computers administration program on the Profile tab, as shown in Figure 16-3.

The importance of these two profile paths is critical in setting up an optimized environment and is illustrated in the following example. Users located at a remote office in Colorado Springs, Colorado log into a Windows XP Professional desktop when they arrive at work. They have a value for User Profile Path populated for their user accounts that points to a local file server (\\COS-file-01\profiles\%*username*%). This keeps the profiles for their local workstation close to their workstation for optimal retrieval. The same users log into Citrix XenApp servers located back at the main office in Denver. The Terminal Services profile path for these users points to a server located in the corporate network in Denver (Den-file-01\profiles\%*username*%). This is done to avoid having profiles copied from the Colorado Springs server over the WAN links to the Citrix XenApp Servers in Denver and prevents user confusion that may arise from having a common profile for both their local workstation and Citrix XenApp Servers sessions.

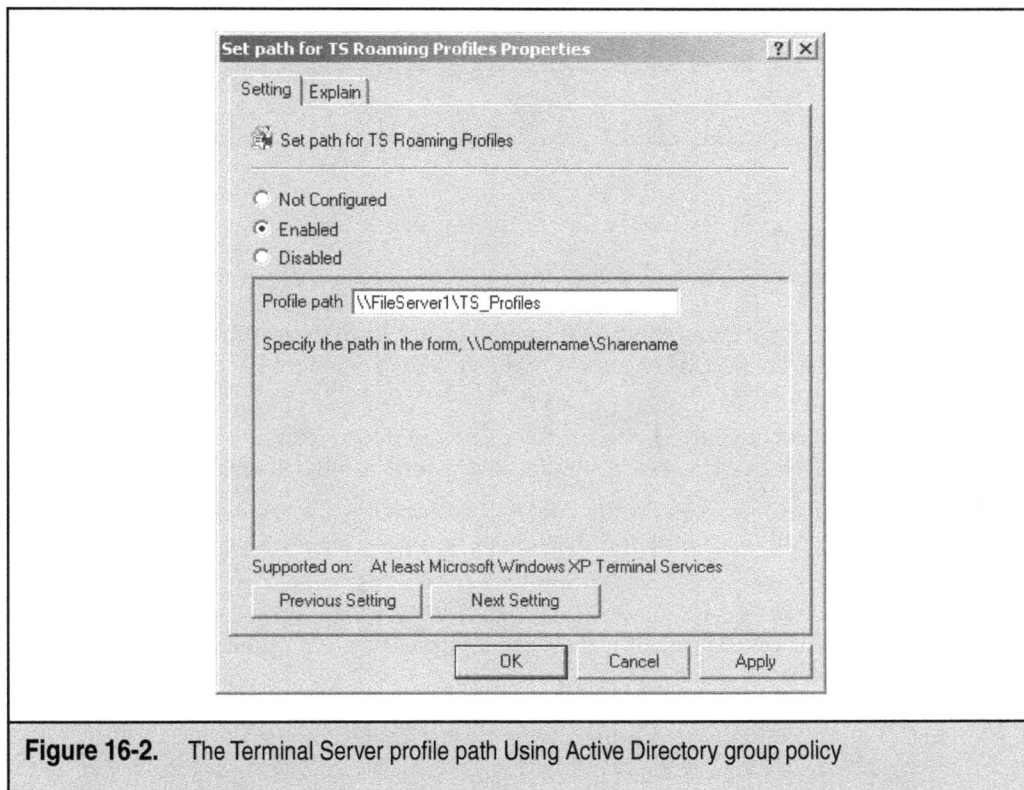

Figure 16-2.   The Terminal Server profile path Using Active Directory group policy

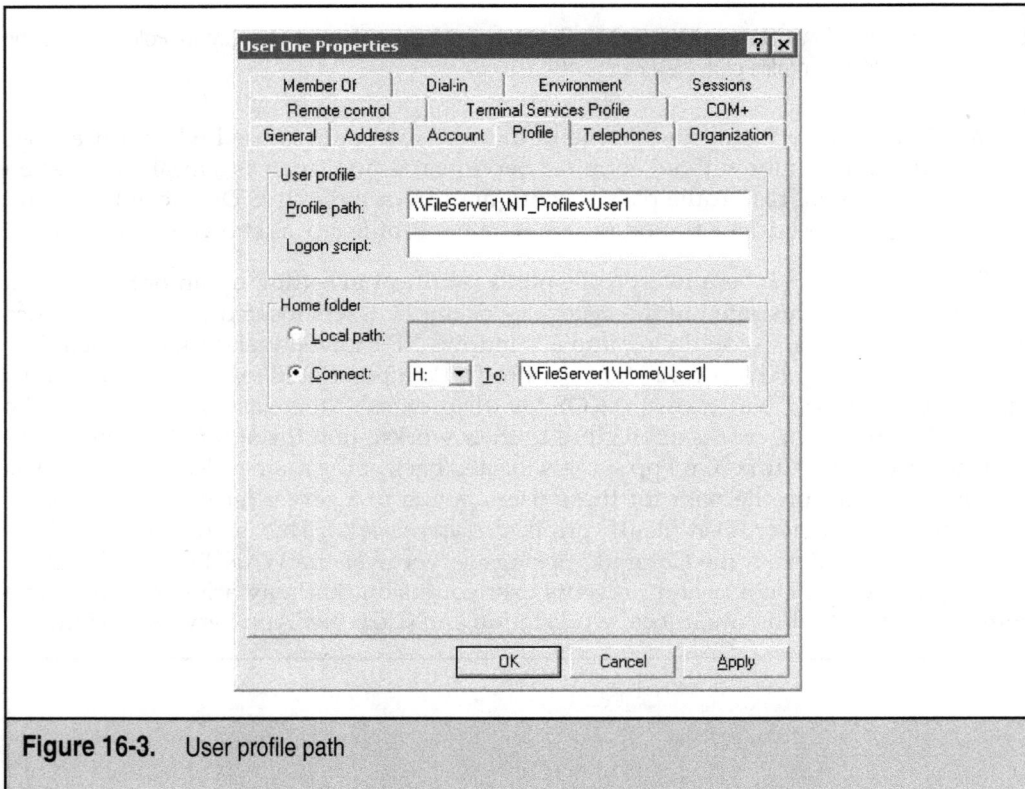

Figure 16-3. User profile path

Profile Processing

The process that occurs when a user logs into a Terminal Server is as follows:

▼ The Terminal Server contacts a domain controller to determine where the roaming profile is located, as specified in the Terminal Services Profile text field in the user's account.

■ If this field is configured, the profile is copied down from the specified network location to a locally cached version of the profile on the Terminal Server.

■ If the Terminal Services Profile field is left blank, the Terminal Server will look at the Profile Path text field and download that profile if it exists.

▲ If both fields are blank, the Terminal Server will use a local profile (if one already exists) or create one (if it does not exist) by copying settings from the default user's profile on the machine they are logging into. This process is illustrated in Figure 16-4.

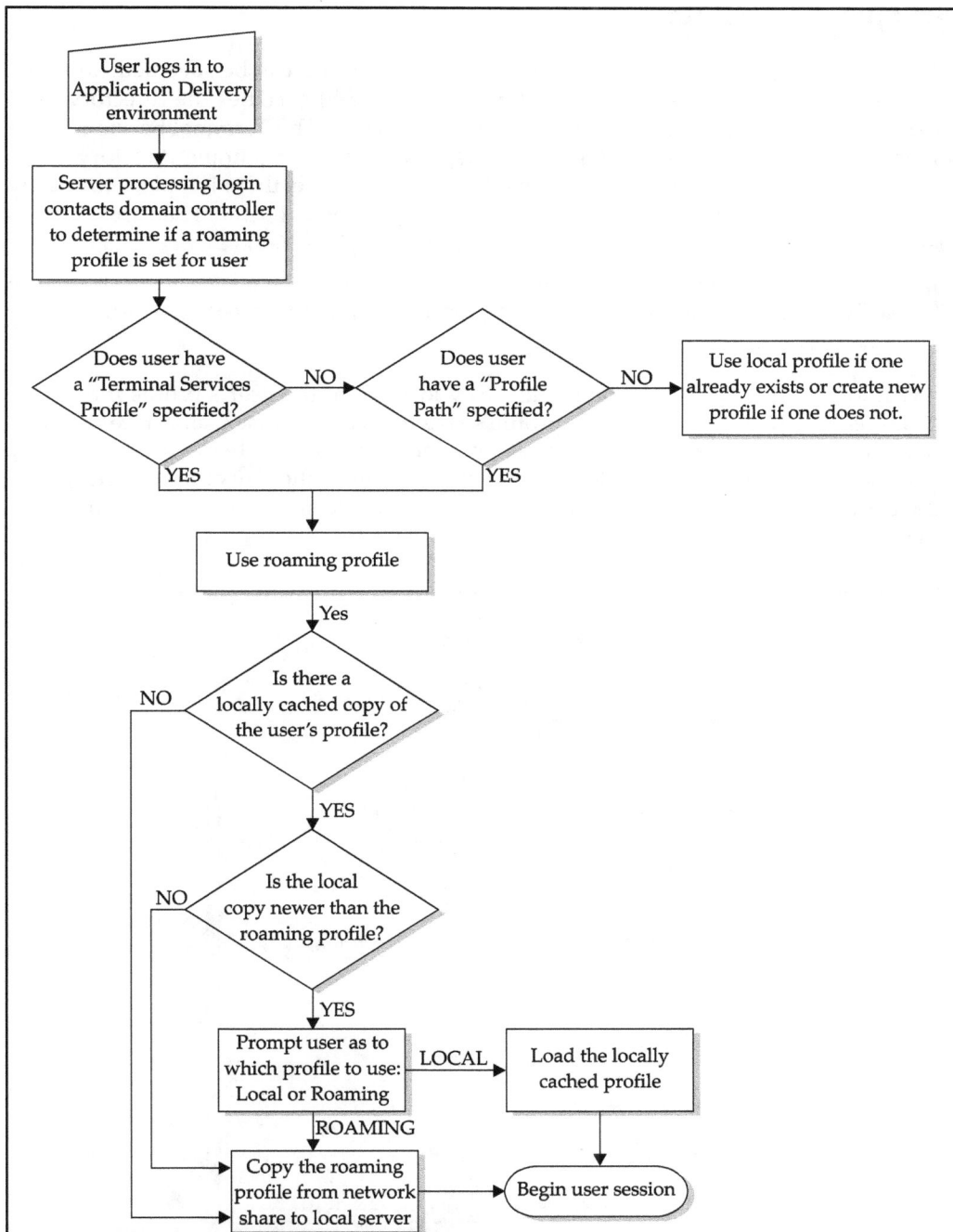

Figure 16-4. Profile processing

HOME DIRECTORIES

Like the profile path settings, two different home directories can be specified. Terminal Services home directory (shown at the top of Figure 16-5) specifies the directory used when a user logs into a server running Terminal Services. The Terminal Services home folder (shown at the bottom of Figure 16-5) specifies the user's home directory when they are utilizing a machine with Terminal Services. Likewise, there is a place to specify the user's home folder to use when they are not logging onto Terminal Services, such as their workstation or desktop (shown at the bottom of Figure 16-5).

NOTE: The Terminal Services home directory can be specified with Group Policy as described later in this chapter.

Windows 2003 defaults the home directory location to the user's profile if no other location is specified, thus causing a profile's size to swell because users store information at this location. Because a user's profile is copied across the network every time they log into or out of another computer, the goal is to minimize the size of the profile. Home directories accomplish this by giving the users a location to store their personal information outside of the profile.

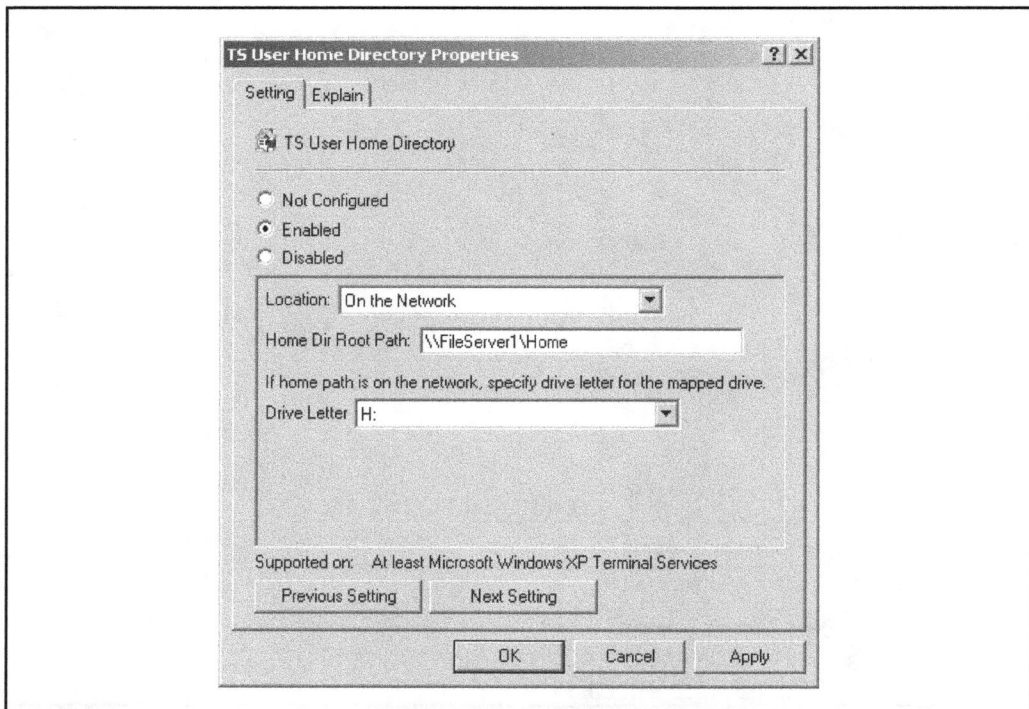

Figure 16-5.   The Terminal Server home folder path using Active Directory Group Policy

NOTE: Support for legacy applications that were not designed appropriately still may require the use of application compatibility scripts. The data from the application compatibility scripts is stored in the home directory.

Home directories should be placed on network file servers that are co-located with the Terminal Servers in order to facilitate the efficient transfer of files. We recommend creating a home directory share called "TSHomes$" (hidden share) on the local enterprise file server closest to the Terminal Servers and storing the home directories in this share.

GROUP POLICIES

Group Policies are used in Windows Server 2003 to define change and configuration management. They are used to define user and computer configurations for groups of users and computers. Configuration of Group Policy is done through the Group Policy Object Editor from within the Microsoft Management Console (MMC) snap-in or the Group Policy Management Console (GPMC), which can be downloaded from Microsoft's website. The Group Policy settings are contained in a Group Policy Object, which is associated with selected Active Directory objects such as Sites, Domains, and Organizational Units. There is also an option for local policy creation to assist in controlling specific computers.

Using Group Policy, an administrator is able to control the policy settings for the following:

▼ **Registry-based policies**   This includes Group Policy for the Windows 2003 operating systems and their components, as well as for applications. To manage these settings, use the Administrative Templates node of the Group Policy snap-in.

■ **Security options**   These include local computer, domain, and network security settings.

■ **Software installation and maintenance options**   These include centralized management of application installation, updates, and removal.

■ **Scripts options**   These include scripts for computer startup and shutdown as well as user logon and logoff.

▲ **Folder redirection options**   These options allow administrators to redirect users' special folders to network storage locations.

Implementing Windows Group Policies for Registry-based policies, security options, and folder redirection is essential in a well-managed environment. Administrators should use Group Policy to ensure users have what they need to perform their jobs, but do not have the ability to corrupt or incorrectly configure their environment. Many common user lockdown settings are contained in the Windows Explorer component under the User Configuration section. A new Terminal Server configuration section is available in Windows Server 2003 Group Policy that did not exist in prior versions. The new settings are contained in the Terminal Services component under Computer Configuration.

The Terminal Services component of the Computer Configuration Group Policy provides a place to set several important configurations, including the following:

▼ Keep-alive settings

■ The path for the Terminal Services roaming profile location

■ The path for the Terminal Services home directory

▲ Idle, disconnected, and broken connection timeouts

Machines that are a member of an Active Directory domain process Group Policies in a very systematic way. The processing order is as follows:

1. Local Group Policy Object

2. Site

3. Domain

4. Organizational Unit (OU)

Exceptions to the default order are due to Group Policies being set to No Override, Disabled, Block Policy Inheritance, or Loopback Processing. The key things to remember are the order in which policies are applied and that a Domain setting will override a Site setting. Understanding this will help in troubleshooting problems with policy settings not being implemented. For example, if the same settings are applied at both the Site and OU levels, the OU policy will still be implemented unless special settings (such as No Override) have been configured.

The Group Policy Management Console

Windows Server 2003 introduced a new tool to manage Group Policy called the Group Policy Management Console (GPMC). The GPMC, now with Service Pack 1, is a separate installation and can only be used in conjunction with Windows Server 2003 machines. The installation files can be found at http://www.microsoft.com/windowsserver2003/gpmc. The Management Console can be installed on either Windows Server 2003 or Windows XP Professional with SP1.

Some of the key enhancements of the Group Policy Management Console include the following:

▼ A unified graphical interface that makes Group Policy easier to administer

■ The ability to back up and restore Group Policy Objects

■ The ability to import/export and copy/paste Group Policy Objects and Windows Management Instrumentation filters

■   Simplified management of Group Policy–related security and delegation

■   HTML reporting for GPO settings and the Resultant Set of Policy (RSOP) data

▲   Scripting of Group Policy–related tasks exposed within this tool

The Group Policy Management Console allows an administrator to view the scope of created policies, as shown in Figure 16-6. It also enables an administrator to view the RSOP applied to users or computers, as you can see in Figure 16-7. This is very handy in situations where settings are not behaving as expected, because the administrator can see which policy is overriding the other and make the appropriate changes.

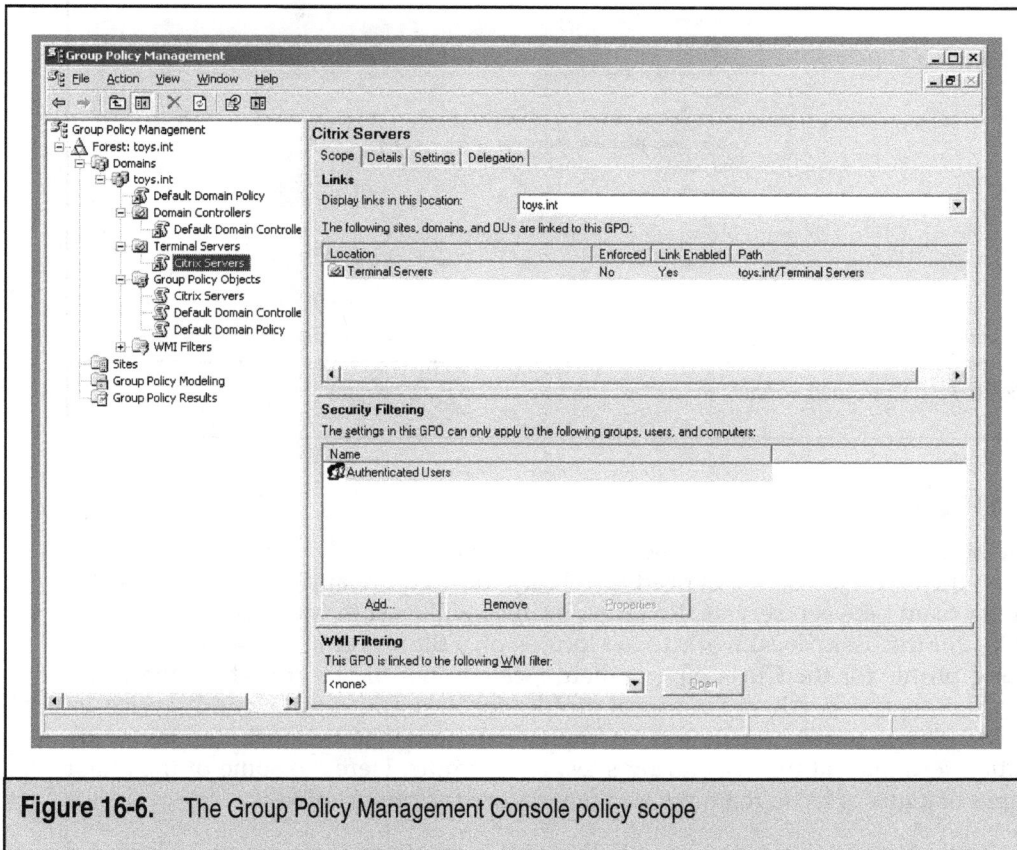

Figure 16-6.   The Group Policy Management Console policy scope

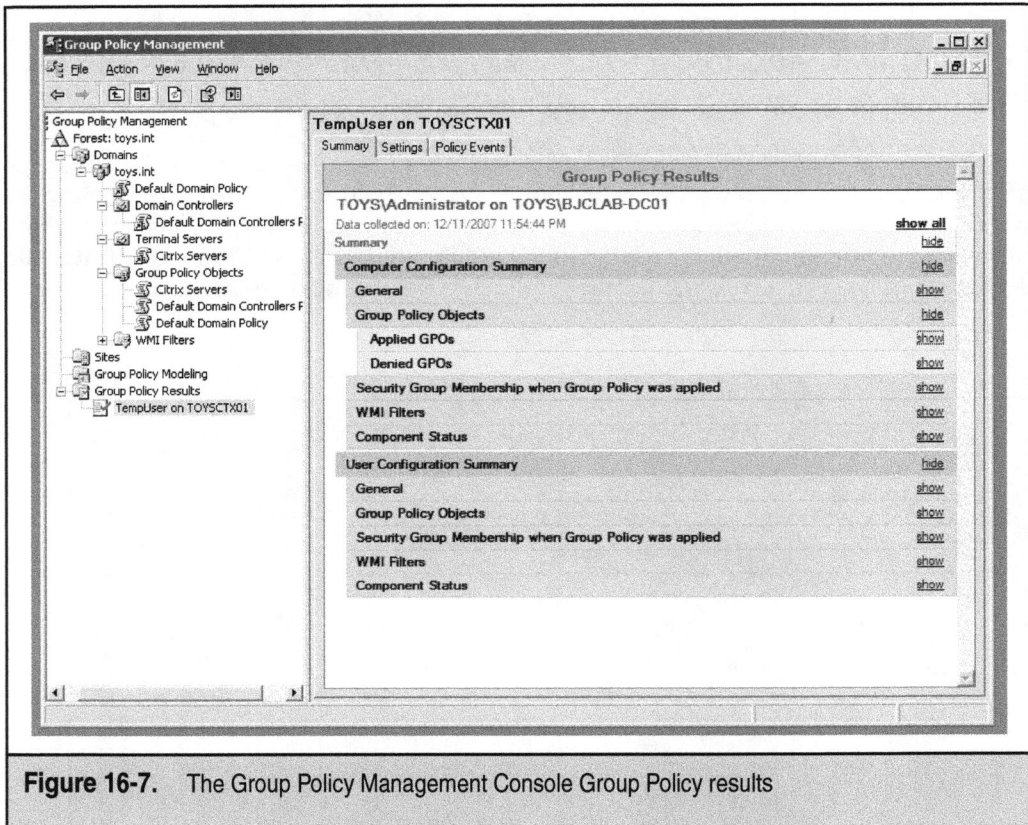

Figure 16-7.   The Group Policy Management Console Group Policy results

BEST PRACTICES

In most situations, administrators should choose roaming profiles for all standard users due to the fact that users will need the ability to configure application settings and have them roam between servers. Roaming profiles will exist in two locations: a roaming profile for the users' local workstation located on a file server at the same office, and a roaming profile for the Citrix environment located on a file server where the Citrix XenApp Servers reside. Always use local profiles for the administrators and service accounts. Mandatory profiles are perfect for implementations that use kiosk stations for job application terminals at manufacturing sites, for example. Here are some of the major challenges of a mix of local, roaming, and mandatory roaming profiles:

▼   Implementing different Group Policies for users when they log into a Terminal Server

- Limiting the profile file size
- Locking down the desktop
- Eliminating inappropriate application features
- Limiting access to local resources
- ▲ Controlling application availability

In order to overcome these challenges, use Group Policy to redirect appropriate folders to minimize profile size, lock down the desktop environment, and eliminate inappropriate application features. Citrix user policies and published applications will be used to limit access to local resources, define shadow permissions, and control application availability. This can also be addressed using third-party products such as RES Power-Fuse.

Implementing Different Group Policies for Users when They Log into a Terminal Server

Because the Terminal Servers are special-use computers within the environment, users should have different settings and configurations applied to their environment when they log into the Citrix XenApp Servers versus logging into a local workstation or laptop. The processes for achieving this are listed next:

- ▼ Create a separate OU in Active Directory for the Citrix XenApp Servers.
- Move the Citrix XenApp Servers to the newly created OU.
- Create and apply a new Group Policy to the Citrix XenApp Server OU.
- Assign appropriate permissions to the Group Policy.
- ▲ Enable loopback processing within the Group Policy Object.

Create a Separate OU in Active Directory for the Citrix XenApp Servers

We recommend installing the Group Policy Management Console (GPMC) to build and manage your OU and GPO structure. Follow these steps, as illustrated in Figure 16-8, to create a separate OU in Active Directory:

1. Choose Start | Programs | Administrative Tools | Group Policy Management.
2. Select the top-level domain and right-click to select New Organizational Unit.
3. Enter the name for the OU that will house the Citrix XenApp Servers. Click OK. We used Terminal Servers for our example.

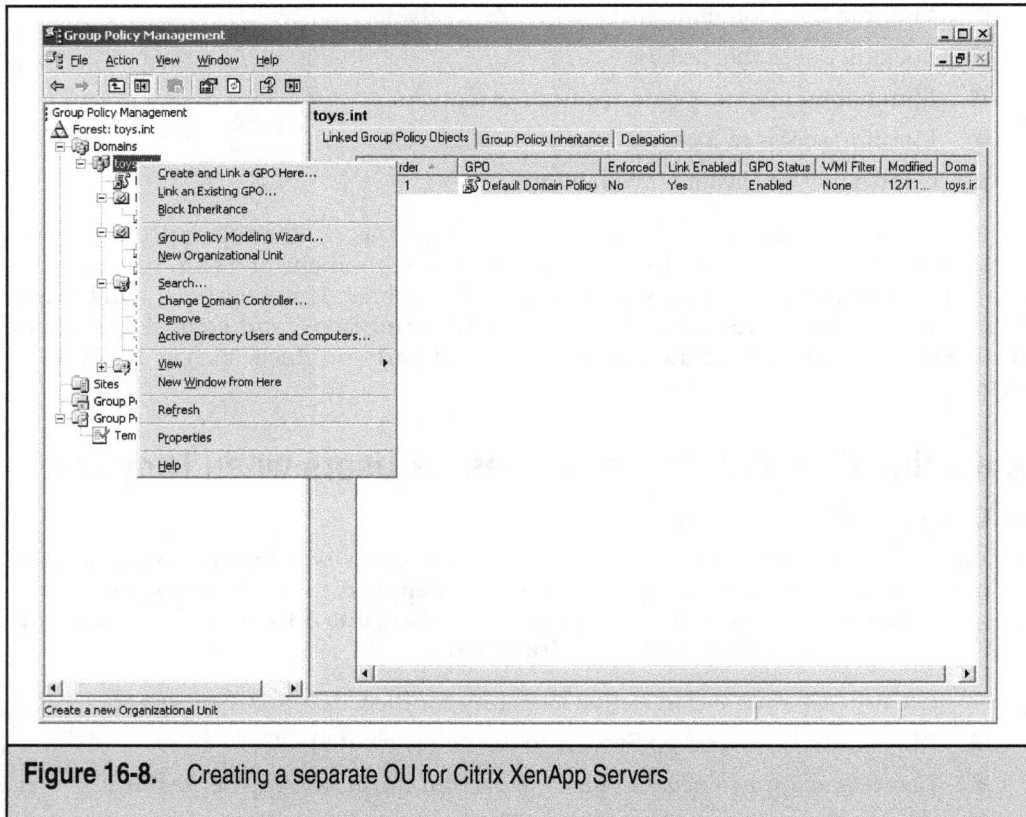

Figure 16-8. Creating a separate OU for Citrix XenApp Servers

Move the Citrix XenApp Servers to the Newly Created OU

Perform the following steps to move the Citrix XenApp Servers to the newly created OU:

1. Locate the Citrix server (found in the Servers or Computers OU), right-click it, and choose Move.
2. Select the newly created OU dedicated for Citrix XenApp Servers and then click OK.
3. Repeat this process for all Citrix XenApp Servers.

Create and Apply a New Group Policy to the Terminal Servers OU

Figure 16-9 shows the creation of a new Group Policy. Follow these steps to create a new Group Policy:

1. Right-click the new OU and select Create and Link a GPO Here.

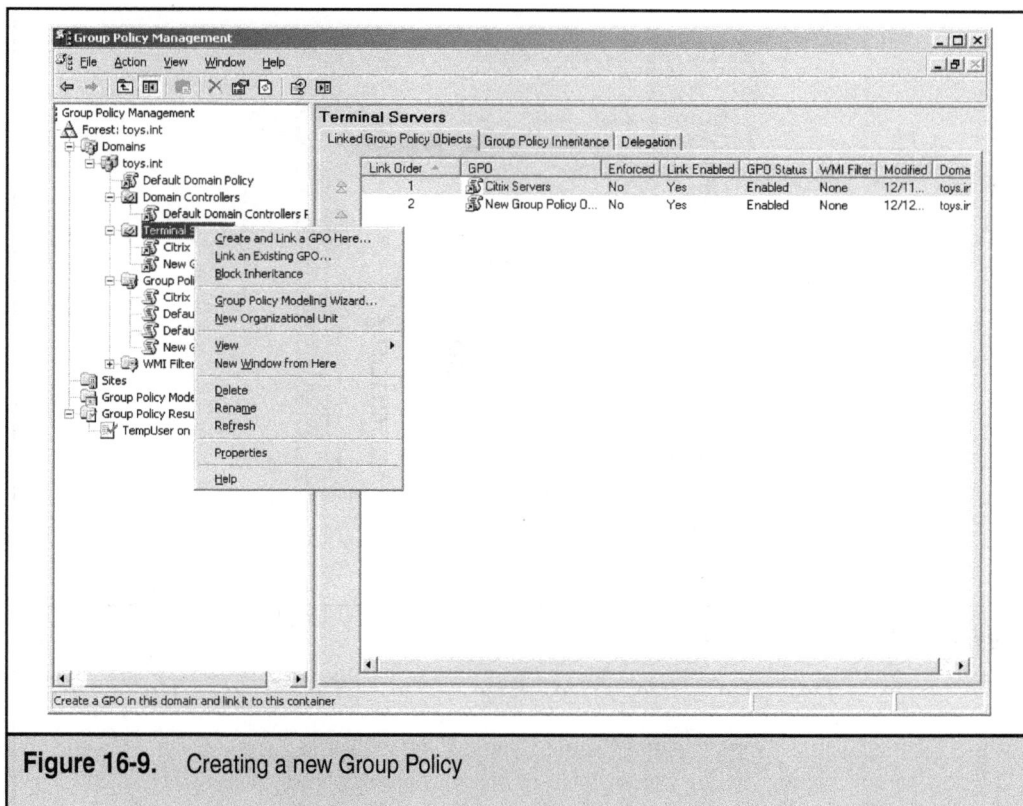

Figure 16-9.   Creating a new Group Policy

2. Choose a name. We used Citrix Servers.
3. Select the new Group Policy to see the details.

Assigning Appropriate Permissions to the Group Policy

Figures 16-10 and 16-11 show the application and denial of Group Policies by group. The steps to apply or remove a Group Policy are as follows:

1. Select the Group Policy Object and in the right pane select the Delegation tab.
2. Toward the bottom-right select the Advanced button.
3. You should now be viewing the Security tab.
4. Add and remove the appropriate users and groups (deny the Apply Group Policy attribute to any user or group to which the Group Policies should not apply), as shown in Figure 16-11.

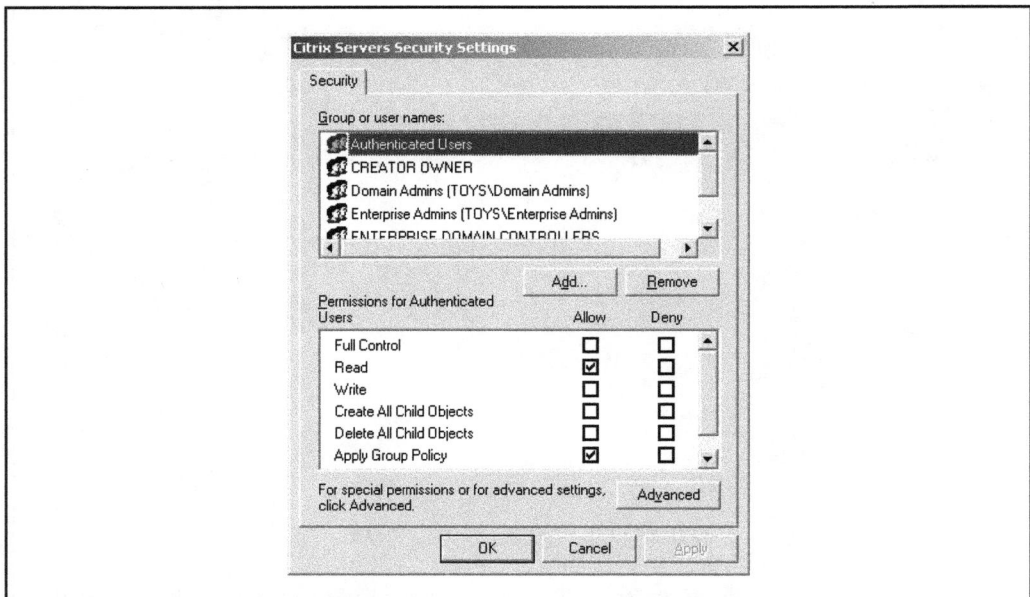

Figure 16-10. Applying the Group Policy to the Citrix users group

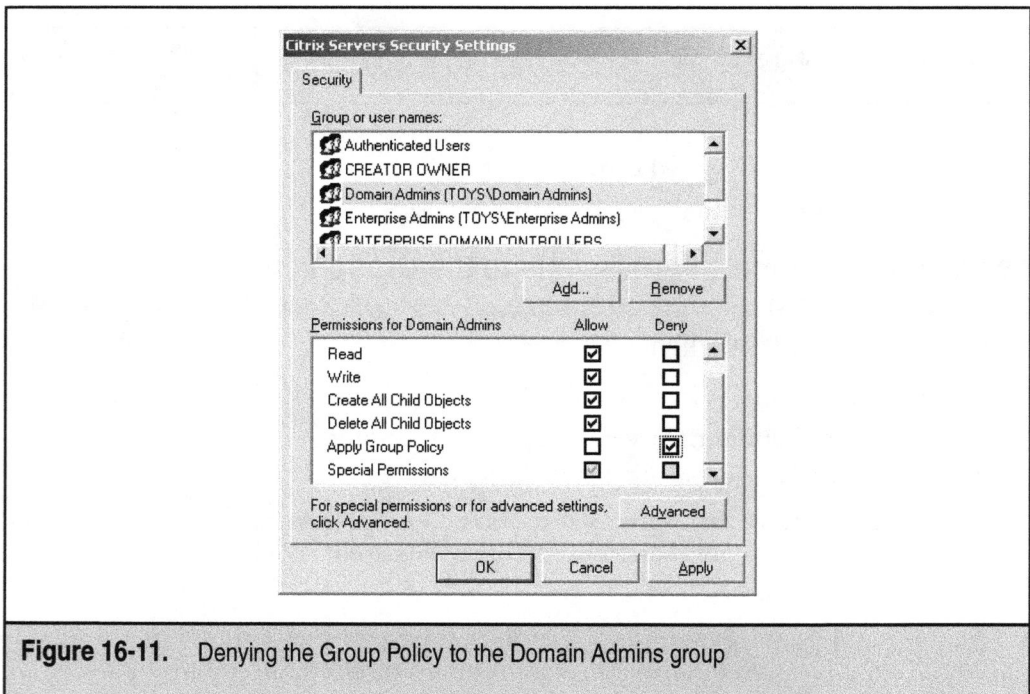

Figure 16-11. Denying the Group Policy to the Domain Admins group

Enabling Loopback Processing Within the Group Policy Object

Figures 16-12 and 16-13 show the Group Policy Enabling process and how to change the loopback mode setting to Replace. The steps are as follows:

1. Select the Group Policy Object (Citrix Servers in our example) and click Edit.

2. Choose Computer Configuration | Administrative Templates | System | Group Policy folder and then double-click to select the User Group Policy loopback processing mode (see Figure 16-12).

3. Check the radio button next to Enabled.

4. Set the mode to Replace or Merge based on the user environment (see Figure 16-13).

NOTE: *Replace* means that the user settings defined in the computer's Group Policy Objects replace the user settings normally applied to the user through Group Policy. *Merge*, on the other hand, means that the user settings defined in the computer's Group Policy Objects and the user settings normally applied to the user are combined. If the settings conflict, the user settings in the computer's Group Policy Objects take precedence over the user's normal settings.

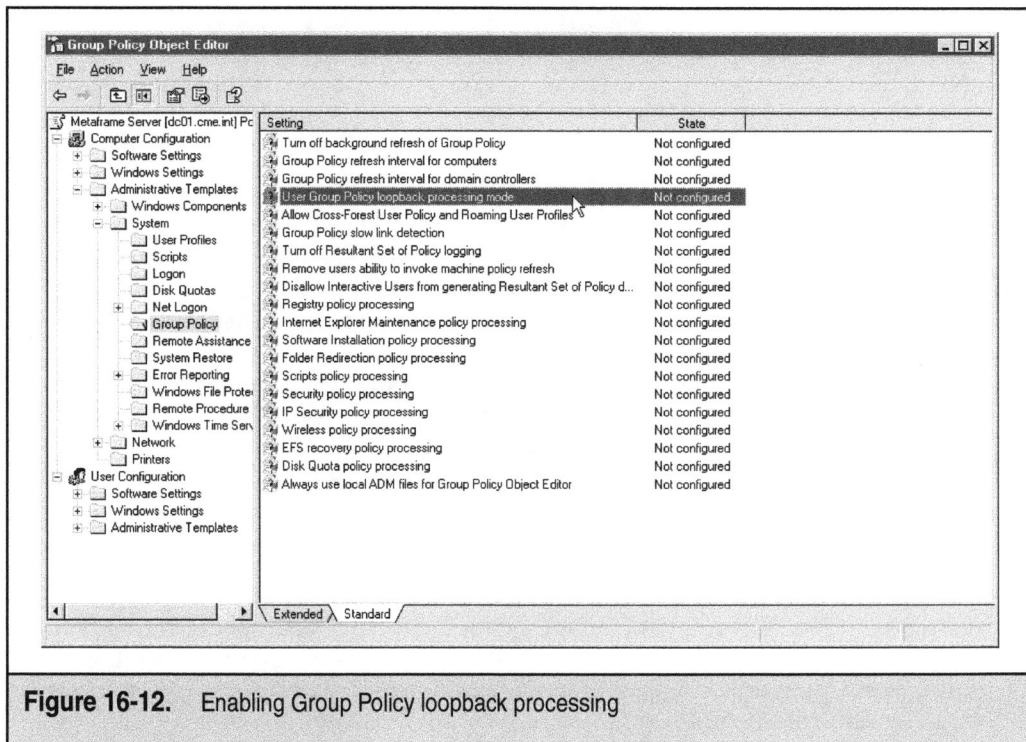

Figure 16-12. Enabling Group Policy loopback processing

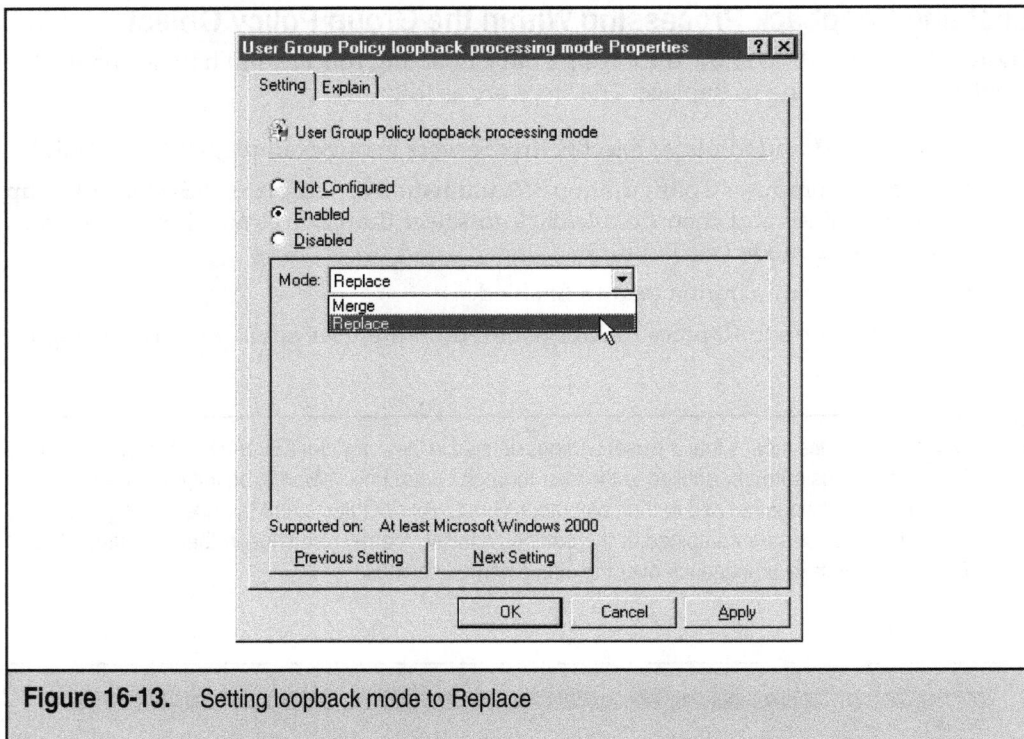

Figure 16-13. Setting loopback mode to Replace

Limiting the Profile File Size

Profiles tend to grow in size over time. This is largely due to users saving documents in their My Documents folder, dragging items onto their desktop, or saving information into the Application Data folders contained in the profile. To keep the profile sizes minimized, configure network shares to store profiles and then configure the preceding folders for redirection to the user's home directory using Group Policy. As mentioned earlier, to store Terminal Server profiles in a central network share, we use TSProfiles$ (hidden share). This helps to distinguish them from normal profiles used on client operating systems. "Normal" profiles can be stored in a share called NTProfiles$ (hidden share).

TIP: Use hidden shares for the folder locations. This will keep "curious" users from seeing the folders when they are browsing the network looking for shares to access. It will not prevent them from accessing these folders if they type the path in the Explorer address bar manually, but it will help keep honest users honest. This also helps keep the network browser traffic to a minimum.

The redirection of Application Data, Desktop, and My Document folders is configured within the existing Group Policy assigned to the XenApp Server's OU. Figure 16-14 shows an example of the Application Data folder redirection settings. To configure redirection, follow these steps:

1. Edit the existing XenApp Servers policy from within the Group Policy Object Editor.

2. Open User Configuration | Windows Settings | Folder Redirection.

3. Right-click Application Data and select Properties.

4. The setting field option should be set to "Basic – Redirect everyone's folder to the same location."

5. The Target Folder Location option should be set to "Create a folder for each user under the root path."

6. Set the root path to the location of the user's home directory (\\FileServer\ TSHomes$).

7. Follow steps 3 through 6 for Desktop and My Documents.

NOTE: Folder redirection through Group Policy is only available with Active Directory domains.

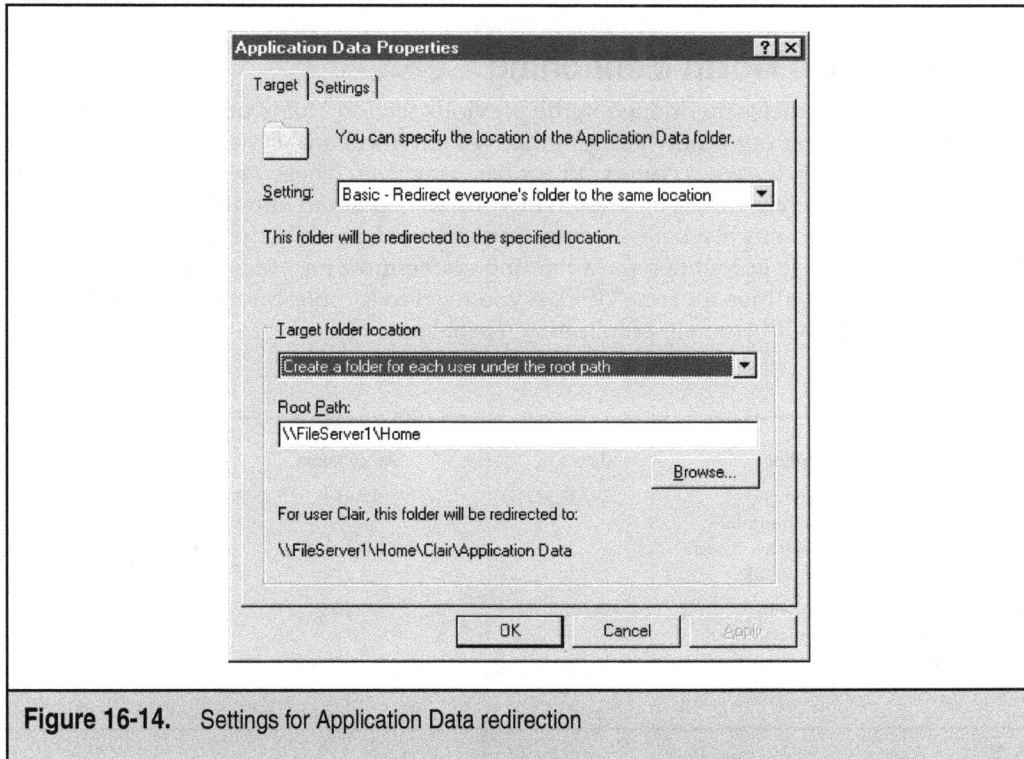

Figure 16-14. Settings for Application Data redirection

Locking Down the Desktop

The amount of control that users are given over their desktop environments varies from organization to organization. Securing the desktop can be accomplished in many ways, including the following:

▼   Using Group Policy to redirect the Desktop and Start menu folders to a common read-only folder on a network share and to limit the functionality of the Windows Explorer shell.

■   Using a third-party utility such as RES PowerFuse or triCerat's Simplify Lockdown.

▲   Using Group Policy to completely remove Desktop, Start menu, and Windows Explorer shell functionality and use the Citrix Program Neighborhood Agent client executed from the XenApp Server's desktop.

We strongly recommend using one of the third-party utilities to assist with implementing a locked-down desktop environment and use Group Policy to assist with redirecting critical folders (such as My Documents, Application Data, and Desktop) to the user's home directory. This will save you loads of time when building a desktop for user access.

Additional Policies Worth Mentioning

In addition to the policies mentioned in the previous section, many other policies should be used when rolling out a new Terminal Server environment. Listed in Table 16-1 are some of the key policies we recommend for best practices. These are just recommendations, and each policy setting you enable in your environment should be evaluated for need and tested thoroughly before being implemented in a production environment. The policy names are guidelines for a naming convention for your GPOs. You should not group all your settings into one GPO. If you need to troubleshoot problems, you can disable parts of the GPO to help eliminate the problems.

Policy Name	Location	State	Policy Name	Remarks/Settings
Delete cached copies of roaming profiles	Computer\ Administrative Templates\System\ User Profile	ENABLED	TSProfiles	
Add the Administrators security group to roaming user profiles	Computer\ Administrative Templates\System\ User Profile	ENABLED	TSProfiles	

Table 16-1.   Recommended Group Policy Settings for Terminal Servers

Policy Name	Location	State	Policy Name	Remarks/Settings
Wait for remote user profile	Computer\ Administrative Templates\System\ User Profile	ENABLED	TSProfiles	
Log users off when roaming profile fails	Computer\ Administrative Templates\System\ User Profile	ENABLED	TSProfiles	
Do not detect slow network connections	Computer\ Administrative Templates\System\ User Profile	ENABLED	TSProfiles	
Timeout for dialog boxes	Computer\ Administrative Templates\System\ User Profile	ENABLED	TSProfiles	Value=0
Hide these specified drives in My Computer	User\Administrative Templates\Windows components\Windows Explorer	ENABLED	HideABCDDrives	
Do not display Manage Your Server page at logon	Computer\ Administrative Templates\System	ENABLED	TSPerformanceSettings	
Run logon scripts synchronously	User\Administrative Templates\System\ Scripts	ENABLED	TSPerformanceSettings	
Don't display the Getting Started welcome screen at logon	Computer\ Administrative Templates\System\ Logon	ENABLED	TSPerformanceSettings	
User Group Policy loopback processing mode	Computer\ Administrative Templates\System\ Group Policy	REPLACE	TSGeneralSettings	User Settings defined under this policy *replace* any previously applied.
Remove Windows Security item from Start menu	Computer\ Administrative Templates\Windows Components\Terminal Services	ENABLED	TSGeneralSettings	For published desktops only.
Remove Disconnect option from Shut Down dialog	Computer\ Administrative Templates\Windows Components\Terminal Services	ENABLED	TSGeneralSettings	For published desktops only.

Table 16-1.   Recommended Group Policy Settings for Terminal Servers *(continued)*

Policy Name	Location	State	Policy Name	Remarks/Settings
Remove and prevent access to the Shut Down command	User\Administrative Templates\Start Menu and Taskbar	ENABLED	TSGeneralSettings	For published desktops only.
Set path for TS Roaming Profiles	Computer\ Administrative Templates\Windows Components\Terminal Services	ENABLED - CUSTOM	TSProfiles	\\ServerName\ TSPROF$
Use the specified Terminal Server license servers	Computer\ Administrative Templates\Windows Components\Terminal Services	ENABLED - CUSTOM	TSGeneralSettings	Optional, unless you have to specify different LIC SRV for different TS servers.
TS User Home Directory	Computer\ Administrative Templates\Windows Components\Terminal Services	ENABLED - CUSTOM	TSProfiles	<DRIVELTR>:\ = \\ServerName\ TSHOME$
Time Limit for Disconnected Sessions	Computer\ Administrative Templates\Windows Components\Terminal Services\Sessions	ENABLED	TSGeneralSettings	1 hour
Set a time limit for active but idle Terminal Services sessions	Computer\ Administrative Templates\Windows Components\Terminal Services\Sessions	ENABLED	TSGeneralSettings	4 hours
Folder Redirection	User\Windows Settings	BASIC	TSGeneralSettings	Redirect all users to the Same Location (\\ServerName\ TSHOME$\ %USERNAME%). My Pictures follows My Documents. Users are *not* granted exclusive access.
Add Logoff to the Start Menu	User\Administrative Templates\Start Menu and Taskbar	ENABLED	TSGeneralSettings	
Turn off personalized menus	User\Administrative Templates\Start Menu and Taskbar	ENABLED	TSGeneralSettings	
Remove Clock from the system notification area	User\Administrative Templates\Start Menu and Taskbar	ENABLED	TSGeneralSettings	

Table 16-1.   Recommended Group Policy Settings for Terminal Servers *(continued)*

Policy Name	Location	State	Policy Name	Remarks/Settings
Remove Balloon tips on Start Menu Items	User\Administrative Templates\Start Menu and Taskbar	ENABLED	TSGeneralSettings	
Prohibit user from changing My Documents path		ENABLED	TSGeneralSettings	System-level redirection policy cannot be reverted by user.
Screen Saver		ENABLED	TSGeneralSettings	
Screen Saver executable name		(TBD)	TSGeneralSettings	Optional.
Password protect the screen saver		(TBD)	TSGeneralSettings	Optional.
Screen Saver timeout		(TBD)	TSGeneralSettings	Optional.
Prohibit user configuration of Offline Files		NOT CONFIGURED	TSGeneralSettings	
Exclude directories in roaming profile	User\Administrative Templates\System\ User Profiles	ENABLED	TSPerformanceSettings	Default (History, Local Settings, Temp, and Temporary Internet Files), Add Desktop.
Run legacy logon scripts hidden		ENABLED	TSPerformanceSettings	
Turn off automatic update of ADM files		ENABLED	TSPerformanceSettings	

Table 16-1. Recommended Group Policy Settings for Terminal Servers *(continued)*

Eliminating Inappropriate Application Features

Many common applications, such as the Microsoft Office Suite, have features that are not appropriate for an Application Delivery environment. An example of this type of feature is the Office Assistant that represents the help interface in the Office product line. The Office Assistant utilizes unnecessary resources and, because of the animated graphics, does not perform well in XenApp environments. Many common applications have compatible template files for Group Policy. The Office 2003 template file is office11.adm, and for Office 2007 you can download and use the Office System Administrative Template files (ADM, ADMX, ADML) and Office Customization Tool, version 2.0 from Microsoft's website. You can add these template files to the Group Policy by right-clicking one of the Administrative Template areas in the Group Policy Management Console and then clicking Add/Remove Templates. By clicking the Add button, you can browse to the appropriate template file and add it to the Group Policy Management Console. The template files are located in the %systemroot%\inf directory if the application has been installed on that server; otherwise, they can be copied from the product media.

Another common area of concern is applications that display splash screens at initialization. Many of these, such as NetMeeting and Internet Explorer, can be controlled via Group Policies. Several other applications have command-line switches that enable you to publish them to users with their graphics suppressed.

Custom .adm files can be created to add more policies as well as custom Registry settings through the Group Policy interface. For more information on writing custom .adm files, refer to http://support.microsoft.com/kb/225087.

Change Control

We recommend testing all changes and tracking any modifications to policies and profiles through a revision control system. This can be as simple as keeping a written change log or as complex as using revision control software such as Component Software's CS-RCS (http://www.componentsoftware.com/products/rcs/) or Serena's Change Request Management software (http://www.serena.com/products/change-request-management/index.html). Whatever the case, the important thing is that all personnel involved with administering the system or making changes follow the same change-control procedure and have easy access to tracking systems.

CHAPTER 17

Citrix Policies
and Printing

Since the inception of networking, printing has been a primary concern during the design and implementation phases of building networks. Whether the issue is quality of the print job, bandwidth needs, performance requirements, paper tray demystification, or simply determining where a print job went, administrators have struggled with providing secure, fast, and simple printing solutions to their users. This chapter explains the Windows printing environment, shows the options available to administrators within Citrix XenApp, defines terminology unique to printing within XenApp, and provides a troubleshooting section for systematic resolution of the most common problems. Third-party print driver utilities are also discussed as alternatives for managing the XenApp Server print environment beyond the tools inherent in Citrix XenApp.

WINDOWS PRINTING EXPLAINED

From the perspective of most users, printing is a very simple process. Type some text into an application, click the printer icon in the toolbar, and pick up the pages from the printer. Unfortunately, things aren't so simple for a system administrator. Devoting just a bit of thought to the difficulties of printing in complex environments is enough to give the average administrator a headache. In a less complex printing environment, the client computer, print server, and printer (or "print device" if you are fluent in Microsoft speak) are typically all located in a single well-connected LAN environment. When printer problems occur, an administrator is able to walk to all the devices involved in the print process to investigate and troubleshoot problems. As companies grow, expanded LANs and WANs complicate printing. The print server, client, and printer may all be on different segments of the network, with some components located at different physical sites.

In a Terminal Server/XenApp environment, these three key components (client, print server, and printer) are often located across WAN links. New concepts and new terms also exist in a XenApp environment that must be considered in order to effectively design, implement, and maintain that environment. Printing problems cause end-user frustration and, in turn, cause users to reject the new technology. With proper planning, testing, consideration, and a good troubleshooting methodology, however, XenApp printing can be managed and work properly.

The Windows Print Process

The Windows environment effectively shields the end user from the complexities of the print process. However, to appreciate the difficulty of developing and maintaining a complex and robust print environment, an administrator must understand the fundamentals of the print process.

When a Windows user clicks the print icon, the following occurs:

1. The application generates an output file, including document formatting, called an enhanced metafile (EMF).

2. The EMF is sent to the local print spooler.

3. From the EMF file, the local print spooler generates a spool file using a print driver. The spool file includes printer-specific information needed by the printer to create the final document.

4. The print job is queued by the print spooler in the local spool folder and forwarded to the printer or print server, where it is transformed from print commands to hard output.

In Citrix Server farm environments, the XenApp Server acts like a regular client workstation during printing. The application running from the Terminal Server generates the EMF, the EMF file is sent to the local print spooler, and a spool file is generated. The spool file may then be sent directly to the printer, to the print server that holds the queue for that printer, or to a client connected to the XenApp Server, where it is re-spooled to the printer or print server.

THE CITRIX XENAPP SERVER PRINT ARCHITECTURE

No two printing environments are the same. What we do know about printing, however, is that every environment will have one or more of three printing options:

▼   **Option A**   Clients have a local printer attached physically to the PC via an LPT or USB port.

■   **Option B**   Clients have a network printer connected to the PC via the LAN.

▲   **Option C**   Clients have neither Option A nor Option B configured on the PC.

Which type of options you have in your environment or the deployment you choose depends greatly on your server farm and the user's requirements. This section describes the types of printer connections available to you and helps you decide on the best one to use.

When planning your printing environment, think about the types of printer configurations you already have in the organization, whether you have any network or bandwidth limitations, how you want to manage the printing environment, the requirements of your users, and the policies you need to implement to control printing.

There are three basic printer configurations to consider when using Citrix Xenapp:

▼   **Redirected client printers**   Any printer that is set up in a Windows OS (these printers appear in the Printers folder on the client device) is a client printer. Locally connected printers, printers that are connected on a network, and virtual printers are all considered client printers. These are usually created on and managed by the local client operating system. During logon to a server running XenApp Server, redirected client printers are auto-created for the new session based on the printing policy settings. This includes printers created on the client device by software installations such as Adobe Writers and the Office Document Image Writer.

- **Auto-created network printers**   Printers that are connected to print servers and shared on a Windows network. In Windows network environments, users can set up a network printer on their computer if they have permission to connect to the print server. In a XenApp environment, administrators can import network printers and assign them to users based on group membership and Citrix policies. When a network printer is set up for use on an individual Windows computer, the printer is a client printer on the client device. This configuration uses printer drivers installed on print servers, as well as print devices configured and accessible through these print servers. These printers are imported into XenApp and can be assigned to users through policies.

▲ **Server local printers**   Printers physically attached to and network printers configured on each server running XenApp. These are usually created by an administrator on the Citrix XenApp using the Add Printer Wizard from within the Printers applet in the Control Panel. If the printer is added to the XenApp Server with the port pointed to a share such as *printserver**sharename*, the print job is sent to the print server before heading to the printer. If the printer is added to the server and the port specifies the actual printer itself (such as an LPR queue to the printer's IP address), the XenApp Server is essentially the print server, and the job is sent directly to the printer.

Local printers are not typically utilized in an enterprise XenApp environment because of the need for the administrator to set up and maintain every printer in the environment on each XenApp Server. Additionally, if the XenApp Server is acting as the print server for print jobs, it is using precious resources to serve up printing and not applications. However, local printers can be utilized successfully in smaller XenApp farms (three or fewer servers).

> **TIP:**   Ideally, XenApp Servers should be dedicated to serving up published applications. If the servers have other roles, such as print server, Zone Data Collector, or housing the Data Store, they cannot hold as many users running applications, thus increasing the number of Terminal Servers needed in the farm. We recommend building up a separate server (either physical or virtual) for these other roles. We call such a server a "Tools" server. This server will not serve up published applications but is a member of the server farm.

Redirected Client Printers

Redirecting client printers allows a user to access their locally installed printers from within a XenApp session. Client printers are mapped into the XenApp Server session upon login and are sometimes referred to as "auto-created printers." They are automatically removed from the server upon session termination. Published applications often rely on auto-created printers to provide access to a printer, because print management utilities may not be available from the application itself. Client printers are supported in different ways, depending on the operating system of the client machine. XenApp Servers are able to automatically map all printers that are installed locally on Windows 32-bit clients, provided a suitable driver is installed on the server or the universal print driver is used.

By default, in Citrix Presentation Server 4.0 and XenApp 4.5, auto-created client printers are named according to standard Windows conventions. The Citrix XenAPP Server naming convention for client printers and the client printer ports they connect to include the session ID as part of the name. This ensures no name collisions, thereby enhancing security. These printers will show up in the user's session as follows:

printer_name **on** *server_name* (**from** *client_name*) **in** *session_ID*

If legacy printer names are being used or forced via Citrix policies, they will show up as this:

Client*user_name#name_on_remote*

> *TIP:*   Many legacy applications don't rely solely on the native Windows print features; instead, the applications read from the available Windows printers and store the selected printer in an INI file, configuration file, or similar structure. Because these files are part of the user's profile, the application expects the printer name to be identical from session to session. With the new naming convention ("in *session_ID*"), the name changes every session and the application is unable to "reset" the previously stored printer name—it no longer exists. To overcome this behavior, use the legacy printer naming policy.

Policies control client printer mapping and naming, which printers connect by default, which drivers to use, and how printer properties associated with these printers are managed. Printing policies are evaluated during initial logon and remain in force throughout the session. After evaluating these policies, printers are enumerated from the client and, depending on the policies in effect for the session, are auto-created.

After the required printers are auto-created, any retained printer properties are applied to restore the printer state. On logoff or a session reset, all auto-created client printers for the session are deleted. Before these client printers are deleted, printer properties modified during the course of the session are saved for future reference. Depending on the client and printer properties retention policies in force, these retained properties come from the client itself or the server-side user profile.

At the time of a disconnect, client printers are put into an offline state that remains in force until the original client reconnects to the session if workspace control is invoked or the printer is deleted by reconnecting from another client or logging off. When a client reconnects to a session, existing printers are enabled if the reconnection is from the same client. If not, client printers associated with the previous client are removed and new client printers are constructed within the session based on the policies that were in force at the time of logon.

Client Printer Security

Because client printers auto-created in a XenApp session are actually local printers managed by the local print provider and Citrix spooler extensions, the local print provider maintains a single shared namespace for all local printers on a server. This means that a user's client printers may be visible and potentially accessible to users from other sessions on the server.

To solve this problem, in Presentation Server 4.0 and above, the default security descriptor applied to client printers restricts access to the following:

▼ The account the print manager service runs in (default: Ctx_cpsvcuser)

■ Processes running in the SYSTEM account, such as the spooler

▲ Processes running in the user's session

Access to the printer from all other processes on the system is blocked by Windows security. Furthermore, requests for services directed to the print manager must originate from a process in the correct session. This prevents the possibility of bypassing the spooler and talking to the remote printing interfaces of CpSvc.exe directly.

Sometimes administrators need to manage other users' print queues in their sessions. By default, even administrators are denied access to those print queues. Any attempt to access them gets the following response:

You do not have access to this printer. Only the security tab will be displayed.

It doesn't matter who you are connected as or even if you attempt to take ownership.

During logon, the actual session settings for printing are derived from a combination of policies, base Terminal Services defaults, and an optional "DefaultPrnFlags" value in the server's Registry. In the absence of a configured policy or modifications to base Terminal Services defaults, default values for all bit flags listed are initially 0. Setting a bit to 1 enables one of the documented functions. Enabling the bit flag is often used to disable or turn off default behavior.

For administrator access to auto-created printer sessions, on each server navigate to HKEY_LOCAL_MACHINE\SOFTWARE\Citrix\Print (if the "Print" key is not present, add this as well) and follow these steps:

1. Add a REG_DWORD value named DefaultPrnFlags to the Registry key.

   Key   HKEY_LOCAL_MACHINE\SOFTWARE\Citrix\Print.
   Name   DefaultPrnFlags.
   Type   REG_DWORD.
   Data   *value* in hexadecimal. (The default is zero unless one or more bit values are added.)

2. Add the hexadecimal bit value for the CTXPRN_ADMINS_CAN_MANAGE flag (0x00004000).

▼

NOTE: If more than one flag is needed, add the bit values together for each of the flags and then add the combined value into the DefaultPrnFlags entry. For example, if you need both CTXPRN_ADMINS_CAN_MANAGE (0x00004000) and CTXPRN_DONT_LOG_AUTOCREATE_FAILURE (0x08000000), the entry for DefaultPrnFlags would be 0x00004000 + 0x08000000 = 0x08004000.

Turning Off Client Printer Auto-Creation

In some situations, you may want to turn off auto-created printing altogether. To do this, configure a policy so that no client printers are auto-created. This means that only network printers or local printers (printers attached directly to a server) can be used. Here are the steps to follow:

1. In the Presentation Server Console, select the Policies node.

2. On the Contents tab, choose the policy for which you want to configure printing rules or create a new one.

3. From the Actions menu, choose Properties.

4. In the policy's Properties dialog box, expand Printing and then Client Printers.

5. Under Client Printers, enable the Auto-creation rule.

6. Select "Do not auto-create client printers."

7. Save and enable the policy.

> **TIP:** In previous versions of Presentation Server (3.0 and earlier), the properties of auto-created client printers were retained in the server-side user profile. During logoff, user printing preferences, printer device settings, and other data were written into the HKEY_CURRENT_USER\ Printers\Citrix key. During logon, retained properties in the profile were applied to the created client printers, effectively re-creating the printer exactly as it was the last time the user logged on. In Citrix Presentation Server 4.0 and higher, printer-retained properties are streamed to the client so that they are retained for roaming profiles. Not all clients support the new protocol extensions required to service this functionality, so properties are still retained in the server-side user profile as needed. If you are experiencing problems with auto-created printers for a user, open the user's profile (NTUSER. DAT) in a Registry editor, browse to the \Printers\Citrix key, and remove all the printer retention entries. This should give the user a "clean slate" for the next logon. This can be set and forced using Citrix policies. Refer to the "Citrix Policies" section later in this chapter for more detail.

Auto-created Network Printers

Auto-created network printers allow an administrator to import available printers from network print servers. The import process will install (if it is not already installed) the print driver from the network print server onto the XenApp Server when a user logs on. Once the printers are imported, an administrator can have those printers auto-created automatically for users according to a XenApp policy. Additionally, it is possible to set basic default print properties for these printers. Users can then be given the ability to change those print settings, or the administrator can push those settings back down to the user at each user logon.

Here are the advantages of auto-created network printers:

▼ Printers can be auto-created for users according to a XenApp policy.

■ Printer settings can be established for the user.

■ XenApp integration with network print servers is seamless.

▲ Network traffic is minimized by taking the client out of the print process.

Here are the disadvantages of auto-created network printers:

▼ Users cannot utilize local printers unless client auto-creation is also used.

▲ The XenApp Servers must have direct IP connectivity to the print device *outside* the ICA channel.

Importing the Network Print Server

The importing of network print servers is rather simple:

1. Select Printer Management in the Presentation Server Console.

2. From the Network Print Servers tab, choose Actions | Printer Management | Import Network Print Server.

3. Specify the network print server to import. You can import all the printers on the selected server, or select individual printers from the list displayed.

4. Click OK.

When the operation finishes, the print server appears on the Network Print Servers tab in the Presentation Server Console.

Assigning Network Printers to Users Through Policies

By configuring session printer rules in policies, you can assign default printers and connect users to printers according to specific attributes of users' sessions (filtering). Follow these steps:

1. In the Console, select the Policies node.

2. On the Contents tab, choose the policy for which you want to configure printing rules.

3. From the Actions menu, choose Properties.

4. In the policy's Properties dialog box, expand Printing and then select Session Printers.

When configuring session printers for a policy, follow these steps:

1. Identify network printers to which you want the applicable sessions to connect by adding printers to the list.

2. Use the drop-down list to choose the default printer for all sessions to which the policy is applied.

3. Use a filter to apply the policy.

When multiple policies are applied to a user session, printer rules are merged.

Server Local Printers

In smaller environments (fewer than three XenApp Server servers) local printers can provide a robust printing environment without requiring a large amount of administration to maintain them. All XenApp Servers are also print servers and need individual print queues to each network printer used by clients. In larger farms, this process becomes very time intensive. When a new printer is introduced to the environment, the administrator needs to configure the printer on each Terminal Server in the environment.

Here are the advantages of local printers on a XenApp Server:

▼ Excellent LAN printing performance.

■ Reliability.

▲ Printer setup per user is very controlled.

Here are the disadvantages of local printers on a XenApp Server:

▼ Additional overhead needed for XenApp Servers to process print jobs.

■ Poor WAN printing performance.

■ Users must browse the network for printers they need that are not configured.

▲ Printers must be configured for each user.

Network Considerations

Before configuring printing and policies for your environment, carefully consider where the print jobs will be routed across the network. All print jobs that are initiated by the server-hosted application are delivered to the XenApp client by the ICA protocol. Whether the next step of the print job is compressed through the ICA protocol or traverses the network uncompressed depends on the type of printers configured and the print job policy.

The impact of print job routing on the network is as follows:

▼ **Auto-created printers** By default, all print jobs route from the client to the server, back through the client, and then to the print device. The print job traffic from the server and back through the client is compressed by means of the ICA protocol.

■ **Network printers** By default, all print jobs route from the server and directly to the print server. The print job traffic from the server to the print server is not compressed and is treated as regular network traffic.

▲ **Print job routing policy** This policy stipulates the routing of the print job traffic and changes the default, if configured. Although it may at first seem counterintuitive to designate that network print jobs should be routed through the client device, the reduction in network traffic is generally greater than the resource cost on the client device.

When print jobs must traverse a network where bandwidth is limited, such as a heavily used WAN link, it is advantageous to route the print job through the client device so that the ICA protocol compresses the print job. Also, by doing so, printer bandwidth can be controlled.

MANAGING AND MAINTAINING PRINT DRIVERS

Driver selection is a critical decision for XenApp printing. It is important to have a print driver that will be compatible with the multiuser environment but at the same time will provide the printing functionality required by the users. Although things have come a long way from the Windows NT 4.0 Terminal Server Edition's "blue screen of death" and limited support from third-party providers, drivers are still a paramount concern of printing in the XenApp environment. The following driver selection topics are explained and their advantages and disadvantages discussed: the printer manufacturer native driver, the Microsoft operating system native driver, and the Citrix universal print driver.

The Printer Manufacturer Native Driver

The printer manufacturer native driver is a print driver included with the printer or downloaded from the printer manufacturer's website.

Advantages of printer manufacturer native drivers include the following:

▼ All features of the printer are included with the driver (printing to mailboxes, two-sided printing, collating, stapling, and so on).

▲ They are usually more current than the drivers included with Microsoft Windows.

The disadvantages of printer manufacturer native drivers are as follows:

▼ The drivers are often not written for a multiuser environment and may cause the spooler service to crash any time a user prints with that driver.

■ Although they may be certified as multiuser compliant, some advanced features still may not function properly (graphics printing, landscape, duplex, watermarks, and so forth).

▲ Drivers are not designed for a network environment and often have additional components that are not desirable (control panels, print monitors, and others).

Printer manufacturer native drivers have become better over time in terms of supporting the Terminal Services structure, but there are still many inherent problems. Windows Server 2003 drivers have improved due to more multiuser compatibility requirements by Microsoft. There will always be issues with drivers written by third parties due to the complexities involved in the print subsystem and the reluctance of some third-party providers to correctly code and test drivers for Terminal Services.

Microsoft Operating System Native Driver

Microsoft operating system native drivers are the built-in drivers that ship with the Windows operating system. Windows Server 2003 natively supports over 3,800 devices.

The advantages of Microsoft native drivers include the following:

▼   Drivers are included with the operating system.

■   Drivers are written as a part of the operating system, so there will be fewer incompatibility problems.

▲   Many driver features are still available.

The disadvantages of Microsoft native drivers are as follows:

▼   Advanced printer features are not always supported (printing to mailboxes, stapling, and so on).

▲   Printers that are newer than the operating system do not have drivers.

This driver option is usually preferred because it is specifically written for compatibility with Terminal Services and still has many of the required printer features.

> *CAUTION:*   It is possible to install—directly via Add Drivers or indirectly via an imported network print server—a legacy driver (one not certified for Windows Server 2003/Windows XP). In Windows Server 2003, Microsoft changed the print driver mode from "kernel mode" to "user mode." Kernel-mode drivers were responsible for the majority of spooler crashes in Windows NT and Windows 2000 when a "bad" driver was invoked in a multiuser environment. Many of these legacy drivers were never certified for Terminal Services. "Bad" user-mode drivers will normally only impact printing functionality in the user's session, not globally (all users on the server). Ensure only user-mode drivers are allowed to propagate to the Citrix printing environment.

The Citrix Universal Print Driver

Citrix XenApp now includes three iterations of universal print drivers. The following table details the drivers included in the three distinct universal print driver sets:

Driver	Description	Presentation Server Release
PCL4/LaserJet Series II driver	Monochrome 300 dpi	MetaFrame XP FR2
PCL5c/Color LaserJet 4500 driver	Color, 600 dpi, and duplexing	MetaFrame XP FR3
Color LaserJet PS	Color and 300 dpi	MetaFrame XP FR3
Citrix Universal Driver (Enhanced MetaFile)	Unique new driver developed by Citrix based on enhanced metafile technology	Presentation Server 4

Whereas previous versions of Citrix Presentation Server supported the PCL4 and PCL5c universal print drivers that were based on Hewlett-Packard LaserJet II (300 dpi monochrome) and 4500 (600 dpi color and duplex) drivers, the new enhanced metafile-based driver can support all common printer capabilities and forms, as well as discover underlying client printer capabilities.

To take advantage of any version of the universal print driver, the corresponding XenApp client must be installed on the client device. For example, Version 9.*x* of the XenApp client corresponds to Presentation Server 4. See the ICA Client Feature Matrix at http://www.citrix.com/English/SS/downloads/downloads.asp?dID=2755 and click the ICA Client Feature Matrix link under Related Articles to determine which client versions support the various versions of the universal print drivers.

To disallow any specific version(s) of the universal print driver, you should delete them by following the instructions within Knowledge Base Article CTX089874. For example, in some environments, only monochrome 300 dpi printing is required, so the other universal print drivers that are automatically installed during a XenApp deployment can be removed.

With the newest version of the universal print driver, users can select from various printing options, including paper size and stapling. From the user perspective, in most cases it will not be evident that the native driver is not being used.

The advantages of the universal print driver include the following:

▼ There are no additional print drivers to install on XenApp Server.

■ It is a very stable print driver.

▲ It reduces print job size, which increases print speeds, especially over low-speed connections.

The disadvantages of the universal print driver are as follows:

▼ It is only supported on Win32, Mac OS X, Solaris, and Linux clients.

▲ It is limited to 600 dpi.

Universal Printing

The Universal Printer feature (not to be confused with the Citrix universal print drivers) available with Citrix Presentation Server 4.0 and higher is designed to relieve the burden of administering a multitude of print drivers and to avoid problems with driver maintenance, replication, and other client printing issues.

The universal print solution employs a Citrix-developed universal driver along with the underlying network infrastructure, which allows this driver to remotely manipulate most of the settings of a client-side printer. The universal print driver capability is automatically installed on all computers running XenApp Server, where it acts like a proxy for print drivers operating on the Windows client. For example, actual printer capabilities and validated printer document settings are retrieved directly from the client (with intelligent caching) as required by applications on the server.

The universal printer facilitates the exchange of capabilities and document settings with the remote client. When a print request is sent, all document settings (including the device-dependent settings) are placed in the spool file. The spool file is then sent to the client for processing.

As well as increased speed and better handling functionality, the universal printer provides a Preview option that allows a user to preview the print job on the client before printing. You have the option of using the advanced universal printer feature to create a single generic universal printer that is not bound to any specific client printer. When enabled, this can be used to drive any client printer. This effectively limits the number of auto-creations of printers, thereby limiting the impact on system resources.

Installing the Universal Printer

For administrator access to auto-created printer sessions, on each server navigate to HKEY_LOCAL_MACHINE\SOFTWARE\Citrix\Print (if the "Print" key is not present, add this as well) and then follow these steps:

1. Add a REG_DWORD value named DefaultPrnFlags to the Registry key.

   Key   HKEY_LOCAL_MACHINE\SOFTWARE\Citrix\Print.
   Name   DefaultPrnFlags.
   Type   REG_DWORD.
   Data   *value* in hexadecimal. (The default is zero unless one or more bit values are added.)

2. Add the hexadecimal bit value for the CTXPRN_AUTO_CREATE_GENERIC_ UPD_PRINTER flag (0x00000020).

▼

NOTE: If more than one flag is needed, add the bit values together for each of the flags and then add the combined value into the DefaultPrnFlags entry. For example, if you need both CTXPRN_ ADMINS_CAN_MANAGE (0x00004000) and CTXPRN_AUTO_CREATE_GENERIC_UPD_PRINTER (0x00000020), the entry for DefaultPrnFlags would be 0x00004000 + 0x00000020 = 0x00004020.

The latest 32-bit Windows clients are capable of receiving and displaying print jobs in a viewer application on the client. For such a client, it is possible to create a single, generic universal printer that is not bound to any of the underlying client printers. This printer is generic in the sense that it does not know about or manage any device-specific settings. As such, it is also more efficient to use because there is no need for capabilities or document settings exchanges with the client when printing. Because creating an additional printer within a session incurs overhead, by default, the creation of the generic universal print driver printer is turned off.

If the CTXPRN_AUTO_CREATE_GENERIC_UPD_PRINTER flag is set, the system auto-creates the generic "Citrix universal printer" in addition to the other printers dictated by other auto-creation flags. For users who do not require special printer capabilities, creating only a single generic universal print driver printer within the session instead of one printer for each underlying client printer can provide a scalability savings. To see this savings, this flag must be enabled and default auto-creation polices also must be overridden or assigned through policies.

Printer Driver Installation

The proper way to install print drivers is to use the Print Server Properties dialog box. It can be found by going to Start | Settings | Printers. In the Printers window, select File and then choose Server Properties. On the Drivers tab, administrators can see all the print drivers installed on the server. They can also add, remove, and update drivers, as shown in Figure 17-1.

Drivers can also be installed using the Add Printer Wizard. The Add Printer Wizard method installs the printer as on a normal workstation. An unused local port is selected during the installation of the printer. The printer is then deleted manually, leaving the print drivers behind for use in auto-creation. The preferred method for adding print drivers is the Print Server Properties dialog box. A few quick tips for driver installation:

▼ Only install print drivers for printers that will be used by ICA clients in the farm.

■ Always install print drivers on the same XenApp Server and then replicate the drivers to the other servers in the farm.

▲ If possible, install print drivers that work for multiple printer types. This limits the number of required print drivers in the environment.

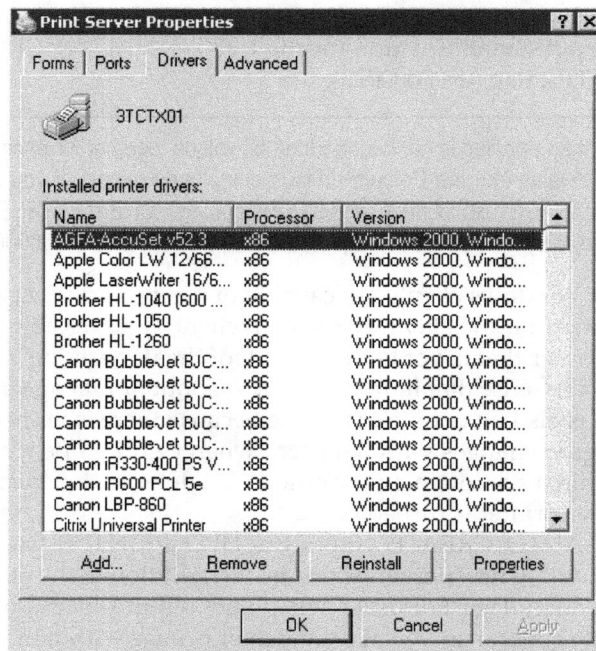

Figure 17-1. The Drivers tab in the Print Server Properties dialog box

Driver Removal

Print drivers can be removed from the server operating system much as they are installed. The Driver section of the Server Properties dialog box (shown earlier in Figure 17-1) has a Remove button for the removal of print drivers. It is best to remove any unneeded print drivers. Print drivers causing printer spooler instability should be removed immediately.

Driver Replication

Driver replication allows for print driver installation on multiple servers without having to visit each server and manually install the driver. It is important to only replicate Windows 2003 drivers to Windows 2003 servers. There are two built-in ways to handle driver replication in a XenApp environment:

▼ XenApp server manual driver replication

▲ XenApp server auto-replication

XenApp Server Print Driver Manual Replication

Manual replication requires administrator input to invoke the process, which then runs without further user intervention.

Manual replication is started via the following steps:

1. Log onto the Presentation Server Console.

2. Open Printer Management.

3. Click Drivers.

4. In the right pane, in the server pull-down at the top, select the server that has all the drivers installed and have been tested and contain known-good drivers.

▼

TIP: Always use one server in the farm to replicate drivers from. This server should have all the drivers that have been tested and are compatible for your farm. This will ensure that all the drivers replicated across the farm are consistent.

5. Select the driver or drivers to be installed on the right side. (Hold down the CTRL key for multiple-selection.)

6. Right-click a selected driver and click Replicate Drivers.

7. Select whether you want to replicate to all same-platform servers or select the servers. You can also choose whether to overwrite any existing drivers if you are performing updates to existing drivers (as shown in Figure 17-2).

XenApp Server Print Driver Auto-Replication

The automatic replication process is designed for drivers that frequently change in the environment. Automatic replication requires no user intervention to start the replication process, but it can cause longer IMA service start times as well as increased CPU and network traffic loads.

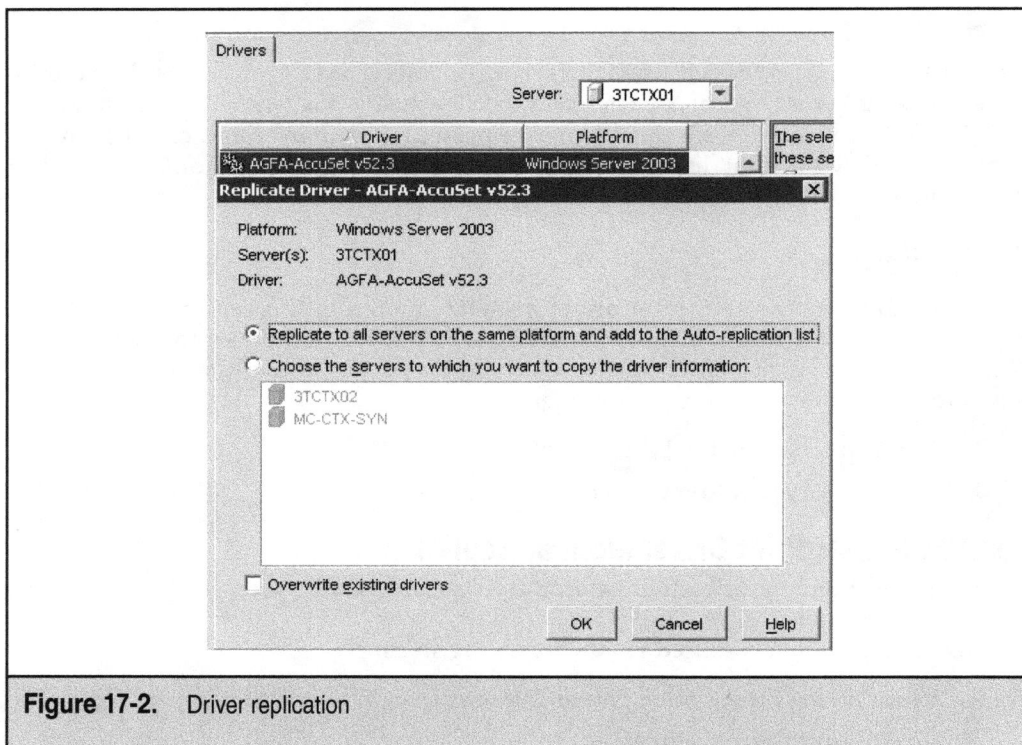

Figure 17-2.   Driver replication

Auto-replication is configured using the following steps:

1. Log onto the Presentation Server Console.

2. Open Printer Management.

3. Right-click Drivers and click Auto-Replication.

4. Choose the operating system platform of the drivers to be configured and then click the Add button to add the drivers that should be auto-replicated.

Client Printer Driver Compatibility

Driver compatibility is a configurable option from within XenApp Server that allows administrators to specify either a list of acceptable (Allowable) drivers for printer auto-creation or a list of incompatible drivers that are not to be mapped when presented to the XenApp by the client (Never Create). Incompatible drivers would typically be ones such as fax drivers, Adobe distillers, and so on. The interface for entering and managing these lists is accessed in this way:

1. Log onto the Presentation Server Console.

2. Open the Printer Management section.

3. Right-click Drivers and select Compatibility.

The server platform for the drivers can be selected. The primary choice is Allow Only Drivers In The List (Allowable) or Allow All Drivers Except Those In The List (Never Create). Drivers are then added to or removed from the list with the Add and Remove buttons. The driver name can be either typed in manually or selected from a list of drivers already installed on the XenApp Servers.

Client Print Driver Mappings

Print driver mappings are integral to a successful implementation of client auto-created printers. By using print driver mappings, an administrator can create mappings between known compatible drivers on the server and client-side drivers that are not compatible or do not exist on the server. The Driver Mapping console provides a graphical interface to map client printer drivers to server print drivers. The list of mappings is held in the data store so that it is available to all servers in the farm. To access the Driver Mapping console, follow these steps:

1. Log onto the Presentation Server Console.

2. Open the Printer Management section.

3. Right-click Drivers and then click Mapping.

The Driver Mapping console allows you to enter, remove, or edit driver mappings. A driver mapping is created by clicking Add and then typing the exact client-side print driver.

TIP: To find the exact driver requested by the client, open the event viewer on the server and look for the failed auto-created printer entries (see the following code). In the details of the error the exact driver will be listed. In the code listed next, look at the line Printer: (hp LaserJet 3030 PCL 6. Simply copy and paste **hp LaserJet 3030 PCL 6** into the mapping creation dialog box.

```
Client printer auto-creation failed. The driver could not be
installed. Possible reasons for the failure: The driver is not in
the list of drivers on the server. The driver cannot be located.
The driver has not been mapped. Client name:
(WI_wjVjgPokMIp92q9uB) Printer: (hp LaserJet 3030 PCL 6 (from
WI_wjVjgPokMIp92q9uB) in session 3) Printer driver: (hp LaserJet
3030 PCL 6)
```

Afterward, choose an existing server driver from the drop-down box. It is important to test the mapping to make sure the print driver prints properly to the client printer. You could, for example, map a client dot-matrix printer to a server color laser driver, but print output would not be usable. Some printer manufacturers, such as Hewlett-Packard, provide lists of drivers that are Terminal Server–compatible and which driver to use for printers whose driver is not supported.

Print Driver Maintenance

The proper installation and removal of print drivers is an important part of managing the printing environment. If the driver is not installed or removed properly, it can cause printing system instability in the XenApp environment. It is also important to make sure the print drivers are consistent throughout the environment.

PRINTER BANDWIDTH MANAGEMENT

XenApp has built-in functionality to manage printer bandwidth within a XenApp client session. When a print job is transmitted through the ICA channel, it leads to increased bandwidth consumption. Failure to control printer bandwidth leads to slow or unresponsive sessions during printing. If the bandwidth is managed, the print jobs take longer to complete, but the user's session is not adversely affected. The bandwidth that print jobs are allowed to consume in the ICA channel can be configured either on the per-server level or as a XenApp Server policy. The following formula is a guideline for using printer bandwidth management:

$$BandwidthLimit = \frac{BandwidthAllocatedforICA-(AveragePerSessionBandwidth)(NumberofConcurrentUsers)}{NumberofConcurrentUsers}$$

- ▼ **BandwidthAllocatedforICA** This value is the bandwidth size allocated for ICA traffic across a specific WAN link.
- ■ **AveragePerSessionBandwidth** This is the average bandwidth used per ICA session.
- ▲ **NumberofConcurrentUsers** This value is the number of concurrent users that access the Citrix servers through the connection link.

NOTE: If this equation results in a negative number, set the bandwidth available for printing to 5Kb.

For example, if there is a T1 line from site to site with a 500Kb allocated partition for ICA and ten concurrent users who use 30Kb per session, we would limit the user printing bandwidth per session to 20Kb, as shown here:

$$20Kb = \frac{500Kb - (30Kb)(10)}{10}$$

As mentioned earlier, the settings for printer bandwidth management can be configured on a per-server basis or a policy basis.

Server-Level Bandwidth Setting

The server-level setting can be configured in the properties of the individual server, or it can be done in the Printer Management section of the Presentation Server Console. The following steps are used to configure the bandwidth setting for an individual server:

1. Log onto the Citrix Presentation Console.

2. Click Printer Management.

3. Click the Bandwidth tab in the right pane.

4. Right-click the server to be configured and then click Edit.

5. Select the radio button next to Limited and enter the number of Kbps that is appropriate for that server. Click OK.

> **NOTE:**   You can copy the setting for a server to other servers in the environment by right-clicking the server and then selecting the servers in the dialog box that would be appropriate for that setting.

Limiting Printing Bandwidth Through Policies

The best practice for limiting printing bandwidth is to configure policies to do it. You can set a policy rule to limit bandwidth in sessions to which the policy is applied. You apply such a policy to sessions that have slow connection speeds. To configure a printing bandwidth policy, follow these steps:

1. Log onto the Presentation Server Console.

2. In the left pane of the console, select the Policies node.

3. In the right pane of the console, select a policy that you apply to sessions with low connection speeds.

4. From the Actions menu, choose Properties.

5. In the policy's Properties page, open Bandwidth | Session Limits and then choose Printer.

6. Use the Printer rule to enable and disable the printing bandwidth session limit. When enabling the printing bandwidth session limit, provide a bandwidth limit in kilobits per second.

7. Click OK.

After configuring a printing bandwidth limit in a policy, consequent sessions to which it is applied adhere to the limit. You must apply a policy through a filter for the policy to affect sessions.

TROUBLESHOOTING

Troubleshooting printing problems in the XenApp environment can be complex and exasperating. This section outlines a methodology to solve the most common printing problems. Most printing problems can be avoided or fixed by investigating a number of basic areas, such as service state, printer settings configuration, client-side printer drivers, server-side printer drivers, printing permissions, printer driver names, and client name.

Service State

Two basic services must be running for printing to work properly: the Print Spooler and the Citrix Print Manager Service.

The Print Spooler can typically just be restarted if it is not running. If it will not restart or immediately stops, more troubleshooting must be done. Many times these types of problems are caused by a corrupt print job that must be manually deleted from the spool directory or a bad print driver. If neither of these options resolves the issue, research current hotfixes for Citrix that address Print Spooler issues. There are many other possibilities, but these are typically a good place to start.

The Citrix Print Manager Service was introduced with Presentation Server 4 to aid in the printer creation and management processes, but it has many other possible issues of its own.

The Citrix Print Manager Service utilizes the ctx_cpsvcuser account. The user account must have at least Power User permissions on the XenApp Server. It also must have at least Query Information and Virtual Channels permissions on the ICA-tcp listener. In many government environments, departmental and federal mandates preclude any user account from being a member of the "Power Users" group, and standard Windows Group Policy Objects will remove all accounts from this group, resulting in printing failures. In these cases, the ctx_cpsvcuser account must be given equivalent (or greater) permissions.

NOTE: By default, the XenApp Server Setup creates a local account for the purpose of running the Citrix Print Manager Service. If the domain policies on your system prohibit the use of local accounts, the account for this service cannot be created during setup. To be able to use the Citrix Print Manager Service in this case, prior to the installation of XenApp you must create a substitute domain account with Windows privileges that are equivalent to the privileges for this local account. To substitute your newly created domain account for the local account, during a scripted or unattended installation of Citrix XenApp, run the CTX_SERV_PRINTER_LOGON property and provide the new domain account name as a parameter.

Citrix Policy Problems

Client printers and session printers will not be created if a policy is not configured properly or if it is overridden by a higher priority policy. Verify the printer settings in each policy and that they are applied to the appropriate users and groups. Verify that the priority of the policy is working in the appropriate order. A good way to verify the settings for a user, group, or IP range is to use the search function in the Policy section of the Management Console. An administrator can search on various users, group, and other properties to see exactly what policies are applied to a specific user and in what order.

Event Log Events

Errors in the Windows Event Viewer can give a lot of valuable information about potential printing issues. You may see service events about Print Spooler or Citrix Print

Manager stoppages. The Security log can show issues with printer or driver security. The Application log can contain Citrix events that show errors in printer creation and driver installations. The Citrix events will typically report both the client-provided driver name (as installed on the client) and the server-side driver being used for printer creation.

Client Machine Issues

Many of these steps can also pertain to issues that may originate on the client machine. If the print spooler on the local machine is not running, the print jobs will not be able to print to a client printer. If the client machine is secured to a point that the ICA virtual channel is not allowed to access the spool directory, the print job will not be delivered to the local spooler. If a user is not able to print a test page from Notepad or some other application on the local machine, the Citrix printing will certainly also fail. In these cases and in many of the server-side issues, normal printing troubleshooting applies.

Driver Issues

Even with improved technologies, drivers (including the UPD) can cause erratic behavior. "Knowing the rules" will allow administrators to effectively troubleshoot driver-related issues.

Native Drivers

Common problems with native drivers are usually the result of selecting the wrong driver, lack of driver availability, or driver incompatibility. Check the following:

▼ Verify that native drivers are certified user-mode drivers.

■ Avoid monolithic drivers. Many "all-in-one" printers use drivers intended for installation on a PC directly attached to the target printer. These drivers include multipurpose features such as scanning and copying that cannot be "hooked" through the appropriate ICA channel. Most vendors (notably Hewlett-Packard) provide a current compatibility listing of alternative drivers suitable for the print engine but without the multifunction support. For example, HP recommends the DeskJet 970 driver as an alternative driver for its all-in-one Office Jet printers in a Citrix environment.

■ Avoid drivers that poll for printer status. Drivers for modern USB-connected printers typically include job monitors and status monitors that communicate continually with the target printer. Although the driver component usually works on XenApp, the USB port is not directly attached to the server and cannot be polled. Uninstall or disable status features or use an alternative driver.

▲ Driver names reported by the client don't match (character for character) the native driver on the server. This issue has existed through all versions of Citrix. Track the problem via Event Log entries and create the appropriate client-to-server driver mapping.

UPD Drivers

UPD-based printing is heavily dependent on correct configuration on the client. Check the following:

▼ Ensure a local print driver is installed and functional.

■ Verify that the client-side driver does not exceed the page limits of the UPD driver. The UPD driver enforces a one-quarter-inch margin. Therefore, client printers that expect to produce full-bleed pages will not print correctly.

■ The Windows 2000 PCL5c driver causes corruption in some document types. Ensure the Windows Server 2003 driver is used instead.

■ Applications that inject custom PCL formatting (PCL form overlay functions) into the print job may fail with the UPD. These applications must be configured to use GDI rendering instead of PCL EscapePassThrough.

▲ Full functionality requires ICA client version 9 or greater.

CITRIX POLICIES

Citrix user policies are similar in nature to Group Policies but are restricted to controlling only Citrix XenApp–related settings. Citrix policies are configured from within the Presentation Server Console under the Policies node. Once a policy is configured, a conditional filter needs to be specified to determine how the policy is applied. All conditional filters must be met for the policy to apply to a Citrix connection. Filters are based on the following criteria:

▼ Access control
■ Client IP address
■ Client name
■ Server(s) connecting to
▲ Users or groups

Policies are particularly useful in configuring settings, such as locking down the number of sessions a user or group of users can have, printing requirements, or shadowing permissions. Citrix policies allow an administrator to turn on and off (per group or user) the options discussed in the following sections.

To Limit Bandwidth Used for the Following:	Use This Policy Rule:
Desktop wallpaper	Visual Effects I Turn off desktop wallpaper
Menu and window animations	Visual Effects I Turn off menu animations
Window contents while a window is dragged	Visual Effects I Turn off window contents while dragging
Compression level for image acceleration and image acceleration for dynamic graphics	SpeedScreen I Image acceleration using lossy compression
Client audio mapping	Session Limits I Audio
Devices connected to a local COM port	Session Limits I COM ports
Cut-and-paste using local clipboard	Session Limits I Clipboard
Printers connected to the client LPT port	Session Limits I LPT Ports
Custom devices connected to the client through OEM virtual channels	Session Limits I OEM Virtual Channels
Client session	Session Limits I Overall Session
Printing	Session Limits I Printer
TWAIN device (such as a camera or scanner)	Session Limits I TWAIN Redirection

Table 17-1.   Bandwidth Policy Rules

Policy Rules

Tables 17-1 through 17-5 present rules you can configure within a policy. Policies can contain multiple rules. Table 17-1 presents rules related to bandwidth usage.

Table 17-2 presents rules related to mapping various functions to client devices.

To ...	Use This Policy Rule:
Control whether or not to allow audio input from client microphones	Resources | Audio | Microphones
Control client audio quality	Resources | Audio | Sound quality
Control audio mapping to client speakers	Resources | Audio | Turn off speakers
Control whether or not client drives are connected when users log on to the server	Resources | Drives | Connection
Control how drives map from the client device	Resources | Drives | Mappings
Improve the speed of writing and copying files to a client disk over a WAN	Resources | Drives | Optimize | Asynchronous writes
Prevent client devices attached to local COM ports from being available in a session	Resources | Ports | Turn off COM ports
Prevent client printers attached to local LPT ports from being made available in a session	Resources | Ports | Turn off LPT ports
Allow the use of USB-tethered, Windows CE–based PDA devices	Resources | PDA Devices | Turn on automatic virtual COM port mapping
Configure resources for the use of TWAIN devices, such as scanners and cameras	Resources | Other | Configure TWAIN redirection
Prevent cut-and-paste data transfer between the server and the local clipboard	Resources | Other | Turn off clipboard mapping
Prevent use of custom devices, such as an electronic pen (stylus)	Resources | Other | Turn off OEM virtual channels
Turn off auto client update	Maintenance | Turn off auto client update

Table 17-2. Client Device Policy Rules

Table 17-3 presents rules related to printing.

To ...	Use This Policy Rule:
Control the creation of client printers on the client device	Client Printers	Auto-creation
Allow the use of legacy printer names and preserve backward compatibility with prior versions of the server	Client Printers	Legacy client printers
Control the location where printer properties are stored	Client Printers	Printer properties retention
Control whether print requests are processed by the client or the server	Client Printers	Print job routing
Prevent users from using printers connected to their client devices	Client Printers	Turn off client printer mapping
Control the installation of native Windows drivers when automatically creating client and network printers	Drivers	Native printer driver auto-install
Control when to use the universal print driver	Drivers	Universal driver
Choose a printer based on a roaming user's session information	Session printers

Table 17-3. Printing Policy Rules

Table 17-4 presents rules related to the user workspace.

To ...	Use This Policy Rule:
Limit the number of sessions a user can run at the same time	Connections	Limit total concurrent sessions
Direct connections to preferred zones and fail over to backup zones	Connections	Zone preference and failover
Control whether or not to use content redirection from the server to the client device	Content Redirection	Server to client

Table 17-4. User Workspace Policy Rules

To ...	Use This Policy Rule:
Control whether or not shadowing is allowed	Shadowing | Configuration
Allow or deny permission for users to shadow connections	Shadowing | Permissions
Use the server's time zone instead of the client's estimated local time zone	Time Zones | Do not estimate local time for legacy clients
Use the server's time zone instead of the client's time zone	Time Zones | Do not use Clients' local time
Identify which credential repository to use when using Citrix Password Manager	Citrix Password Manager | Central Credential Store
Prevent the use of Citrix Password Manager	Citrix Password Manager | Do not use Citrix Password Manager
Override the delivery protocol for applications streamed to client	Streamed Applications | Configure delivery protocol

Table 17-4.   User Workspace Policy Rules *(continued)*

Finally, Table 17-5 presents the rule related to security.

Limiting Access to Local Resources

Local resources are the resources located on the machine establishing the connection to the XenApp Server or Terminal Server. These are resources such as local machine drives, locally installed print queues, the clipboard, as well as LPT and COM ports. Local resource access can be controlled through two methods. In previous versions of Presentation Server this was done through the Citrix Connection Configuration Console and by editing the properties of the ICA-tcp or RDP-tcp connection. With XenApp 4.5, this tool has been removed from the toolset and now the configuration is done in the Terminal Services Configuration Console (Start | Programs | Administrative Tools | Terminal Services Configuration). The problem with this tool is that it has to be configured on each

To ...	Use This Policy Rule:
Require that connections use a specified encryption level	Encryption | SecureICA encryption

Table 17-5.   Security Policy Rule

server individually and applies to all users logging into the server. The better method is to use Citrix policies. An example of denying access to local drives follows. A policy is configured for denying drive access as well as any other custom settings needed for different local LPT or COM port access. The following steps are required to set up different local drive access rules per user or group:

1. Open the Citrix Presentation Server Console and log in as a full Citrix administrator.

2. Right-click Policies and select Create Policy, as shown in Figure 17-3.

3. Enter a descriptive policy name and click OK.

4. Double-click the new policy to display the properties.

5. Open the Client Devices section.

6. Open the Resources section.

7. Open the Drives section.

8. Click Connection.

9. Select the radio button for Enabled.

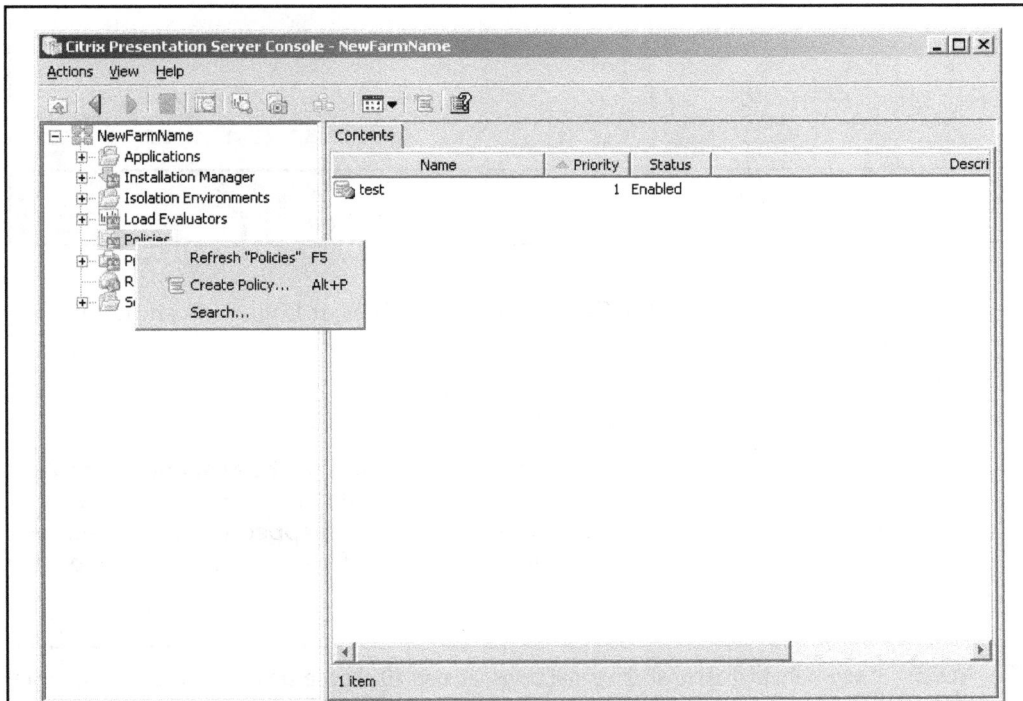

Figure 17-3.   Citrix Presentation Server Console – Create New Policy

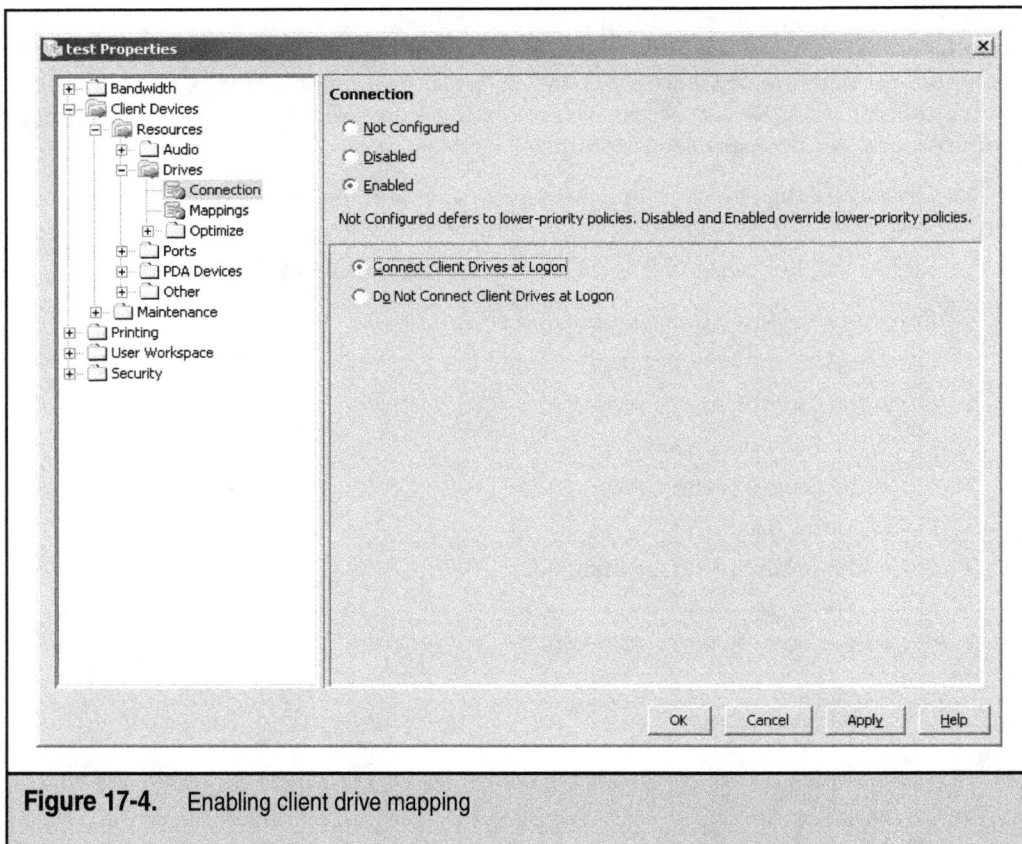

Figure 17-4. Enabling client drive mapping

10. Select the radio button for Connect Client Drives at Logon, as shown in Figure 17-4.

11. Click Mappings.

12. Select the radio button for Enabled.

13. Click the selection box next to the drives that should not be available to the user or group, as shown in Figure 17-5. (By default, all drives are mapped when a user logs on. If you want to stop drives from being mapped when the user logs on, use this setting to prevent users from saving files to their local drives, for example.)

NOTE: If you want to disable all drive mappings, at step 10 choose Do Not Connect Client Drives at Logon and then skip steps 11–13.

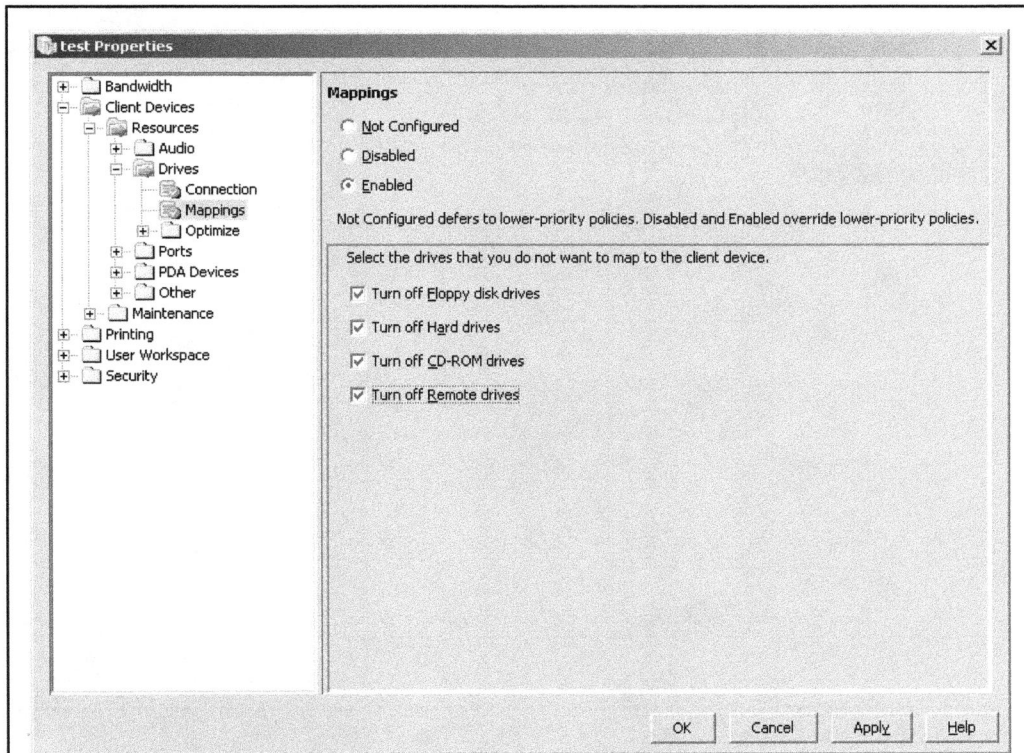

Figure 17-5.   Deny local drive mapping

14. Click OK to close and save the policy's Properties dialog box.

15. Right-click the policy and select Apply this policy to....

16. Choose Users from the left pane.

17. In the right pane, check the box for Filter based on users, as shown in Figure 17-6.

18. Add the users and groups to which you would like this policy to apply.

19. Click OK to close the dialog box and apply the policy to those users.

Every environment has different requirements for which policies to enable and enforce. There are far too many combinations to mention them all here. This is simply an example of how to use Citrix policies to help control access to your environment on a user-by-user or group-by-group basis. Keep in mind that other methods are available for filtering the policy.

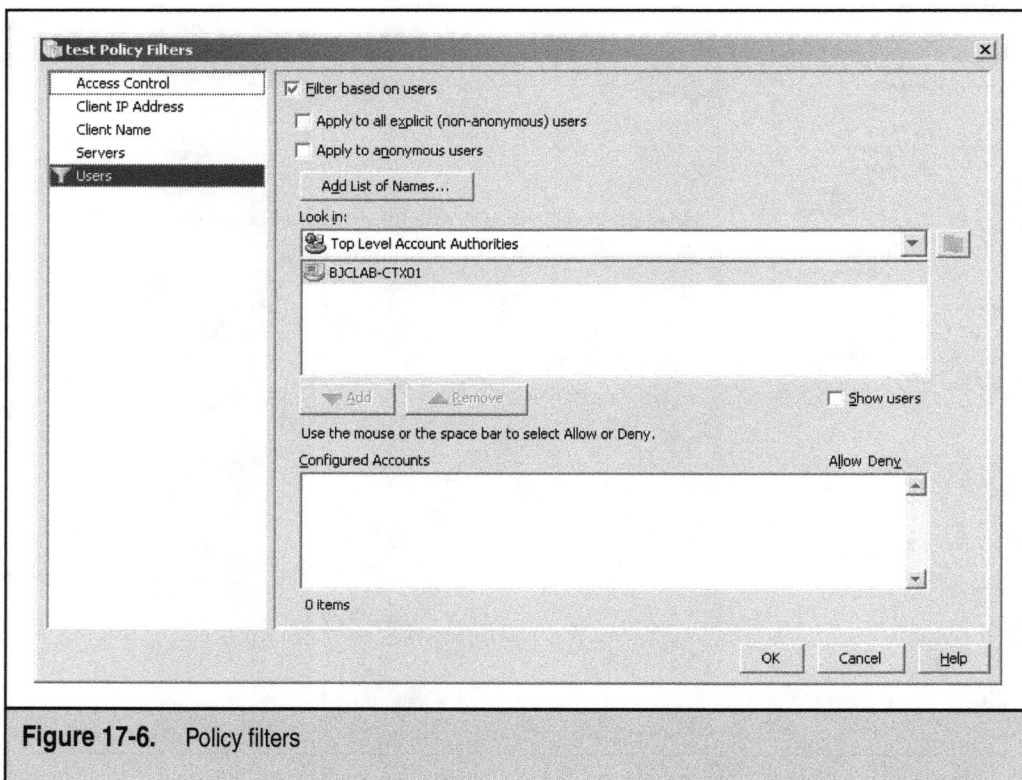

Figure 17-6. Policy filters

In the previous example, you might have chosen to filter this policy based on the servers that the users access. Let's say you have a silo of servers running the Office suite and a silo of servers running your accounting program. When your users connect to the server running Office, it is acceptable to allow users to save files to their local computers, so there are no restrictions for local resources on those servers. However, when the users launch the accounting application, you do not want to allow them to save these files anywhere but to the local area network.

In this case, you can create a policy that denies access to all local ports and drives using the same method as before. This time, on the Apply this policy to... selection, choose Servers from the left pane and enable the Filter Based on Servers check box. In the window below this, place checkmarks next to the server running the accounting application only. Pretty slick, huh?

It gets even slicker. You can even use both files from the preceding example and restrict a user or group of users when they connect to only certain servers. For instance, you can restrict the users Brian, Alan, and Tim from having access to their local drives only when they connect to servers TS01 and TS02. For everyone else on those servers, local drives are still available.

Magic, you say? Not quite, but close. This type of configuration is where the power of policies really shines.

Controlling Application Availability

Application availability is controlled using Citrix published applications. When published applications are created via the Access Management Console (AMC), the administrator grants access to selected groups or users. Users will get their applications based on published application group membership.

> *TIP:* We recommend creating a security group for each of your applications in Active Directory Users and Computers. We typically use the naming convention *CTX_AppName*. For example, for the Office suite, use CTX_Office2007 or CTX_Word07. Then publish the application to this group. This way, you control access to applications using AD groups and do not have to open each application every time you need to add a new user. This saves you a lot of administration time.

Citrix Policy Best Practice

It's really up to you! There is no right or wrong way to set up and configure Citrix policies. Unlike Windows GPOs, Citrix policies are very specific to the environment in which they are installed. What we can tell you is to look closely at the power of the policies and make sure there is a policy—either Windows or Citrix—that can make farm administration more consistent and easier to maintain. The more configurations you can enforce in GPOs and Citrix policies, the better the user experience will be—and the better your life will be maintaining the farm.

CHAPTER 18

Ongoing Administration

The goal of ongoing administration is to ensure that IT services are delivered according to service-level requirements agreed to by IT management and other relevant decision makers within a company. The day-to-day operations of an IT department should be proactive, which requires that the proper products, services, and infrastructure are in place to identify and prevent potential problems. This chapter provides guidance on how to manage and troubleshoot the on-demand application delivery infrastructure. Using these methodologies, you can achieve reliable, available, supportable, and manageable solutions built on Microsoft and Citrix products and technologies.

This chapter also examines the need to develop dedicated support systems to track and facilitate the resolution of end-user problems, perform maintenance on infrastructure, track service-level agreements, and assist in communicating IT progress to the end-user community. In some companies this may be any combination of help desk, service desk, operations, or call center services. Regardless of what it is called or how items are combined, the function of these critical components must be analyzed for successful management and operation of the on-demand access environment.

SCHEDULED MAINTENANCE ACTIVITIES

Specific tasks should be performed at daily, weekly, monthly, and quarterly intervals to ensure service levels are being met. General tasks are outlined in this section to provide a guide for XenApp Server administrators. It is very important to schedule time at defined intervals to ensure maintenance activities happen and any administrative actions are documented for reference later. Daily issues and maintenance should be tracked and reviewed so that persistent problems can be identified and a timeline can be created for resolving them.

On a quarterly basis, a baseline comparison should be conducted against the information monitored and gathered throughout the period. This will identify any inconsistencies that may need to be addressed. Performing a user-load trend analysis will help administrators determine proper use of server resources. If trending indicates degradation of server performance due to overloaded servers, expansion of the Citrix environment (such as adding more load-balanced servers) may be necessary. A project, which includes analysis of infrastructure and design, should be initiated and subsequent requisition of hardware, software, and resources scheduled.

Daily Maintenance Activities

Daily maintenance activities are centered on the essential tasks to ensure the Citrix farm is highly available and servicing end-user needs. These tasks should include, but not be limited to, the following:

▼ **Backing up the data store** A Microsoft Access–based data store (DS) can be backed up either by using the dsmaint backup command utility or by copying the backup data store file (mf20.bak) that is created every time the IMA service is stopped to a network share. This task is most commonly executed daily with a scheduled script. Third-party data stores (SQL or Oracle) require additional configurations from within SQL or Oracle management software to ensure proper backup of the data store. The sample reboot script that follows copies the backup data store file to a network share:

```
Change logon /disable
msg - Please log off and save your work. The server is going down in 5 mins.
sleep.exe 300
net stop "Print Spooler" /Y
net stop "Citrix Print Manager Service" /Y
sleep.exe 30
del c:\WINNT\System32\spool\PRINTERS\*.* /q
REM ** unremark the next line for a Microsoft Access as the IMA data store
REM copy C:\Program Files\Citrix\Independent Management Architecture\mf20.bak
\\backupserver\share
sleep.exe 30
Change logon /enable
tsshutdn.exe /REBOOT
```

NOTE: Sleep.exe is part of the Windows Server 2003 resource kit.

■ **Rebooting servers** Servers should be rebooted frequently to eliminate any "hung" processes or memory leaks. A simple reboot script like the one just shown can be used as a scheduled task to reboot servers running Advanced, Enterprise, or Platinum editions of XenApp Server. Alternatively, servers running XenApp Server Enterprise or Platinum have reboot functionality included and can be scheduled from the server properties in the Presentation Server Console, as shown in Figures 18-1 and 18-2.

CAUTION: Do not reboot all your servers at the same time on the same day. We recommend that you reboot a few servers each day, alternating them in sets. For example, if you have 12 servers in your farm, reboot four of them on Monday, the next four on Tuesday, the last four on Wednesday, and then repeat. With this pattern or something similar, if a patch or an update installed on a server prevents it from rebooting properly, only a subset of your farm is inoperable. This will still allow users to log in and work while you debug the reboot problems and address the issue before the next reboot cycle. Also, rebooting a whole farm of servers (more than ten) at one time can cause a severe load on the data store, prompting delays in IMA service start times.

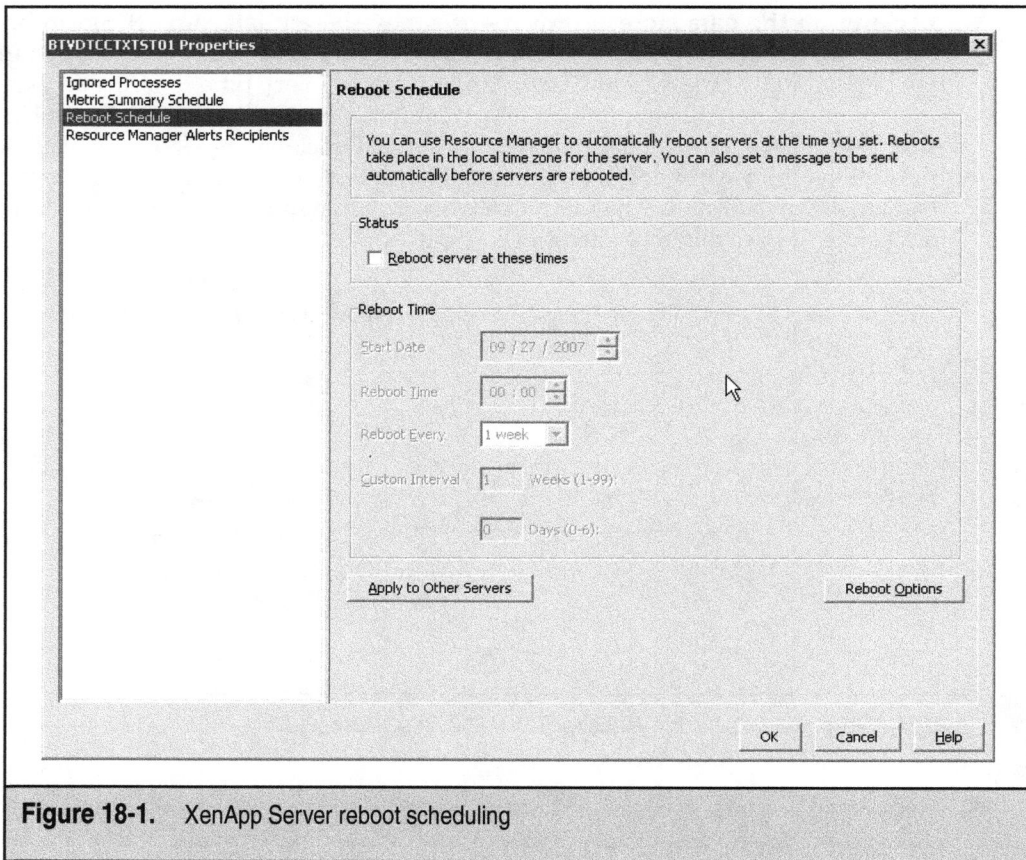

Figure 18-1. XenApp Server reboot scheduling

■ **Verifying that all servers are communicating properly with the data store** This can be done either by running qfarm from the command line with the /app and / load extensions (to make sure all servers are showing up and load values are appropriate) or by viewing the status of the server from the Presentation Server Console. qfarm with the /app switch details which servers are providing which applications, checking to make sure all servers and appropriate applications are listed to verify communication. qfarm with the /load switch details all servers and their associated load levels. Load levels should be within 0 to 9999 at all times. A load level of 10000 indicates a server is reporting maximum load on a particular load evaluator. If the load level is above 10000, it indicates a problem with load balancing or the data store. qfarm used with the /online or /offline switch displays which servers are currently online or offline in the farm. See Table 18-1 for Load Manager values.

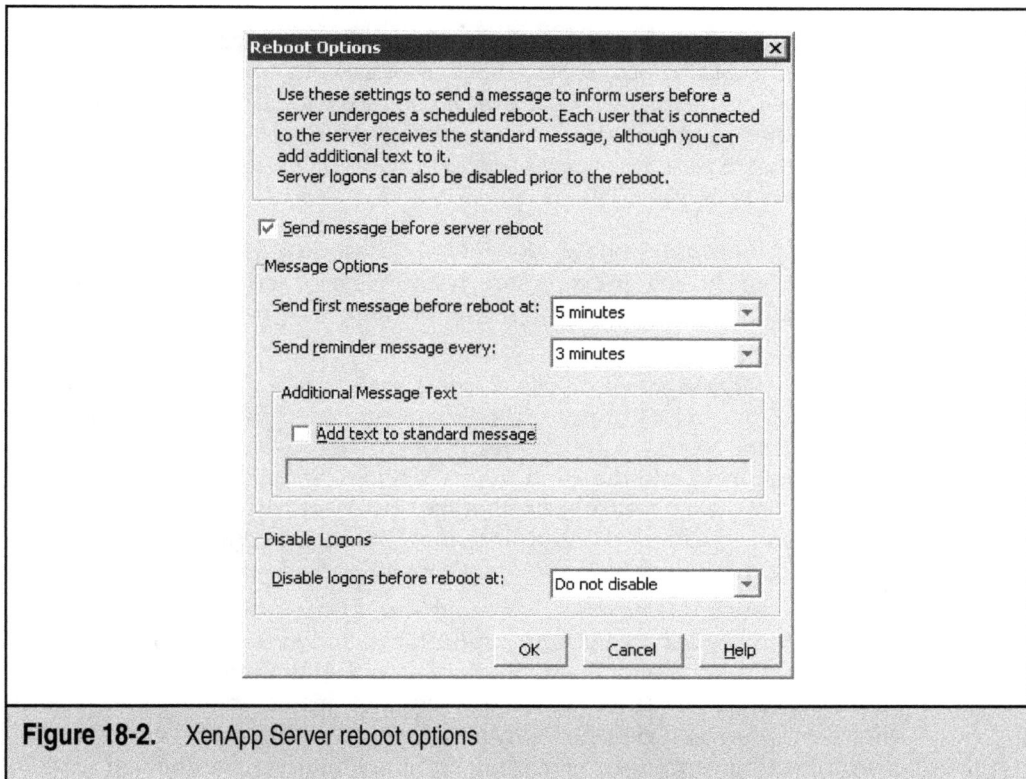

Figure 18-2. XenApp Server reboot options

Value	Description
0–9998	This is the normal range for Load Manager.
99999	No load evaluator is configured.
10000	Load is at 100 percent (full load).
20000	The Presentation Server Console contains an incorrect server edition or a license mismatch.
99990	Results when a custom administrator with restricted rights runs the qfarm command.

Table 18-1. Load Manager Values

NOTE: In order for Load Manager to reflect correct values, you must configure load evaluators that accurately represent your farm. If you use the *default* load evaluator, the maximum load for a server is 100 users. If 30 users are logged onto this server in the farm, the load on that server will show 3000 (or 30% load). However, your machine might be at full capacity with 30 users. In this situation, copy the default load evaluator and make your maximum load 30. This will show a more accurate figure when the qfarm /load command is run.

- **Performing a thorough review**   Review any Resource Manager Performance alerts, virus notifications, and data store backup logs or scripts for proper execution. Notifications should be configured for these whether they are e-mail or SNMP traps.

- **Logging into EdgeSight**   EdgeSight offers a unique view into the XenApp server farm, so take a look around. The EdgeSight Web Console should be a part of a daily routine for checking the health of the XenApp server farm. It offers real-time monitoring into the applications, devices, and network activity of the XenApp server, allowing administrators the opportunity to proactively prevent problems. Refer to Chapter 12 for more information on configuring and using Citrix EdgeSight to monitor and troubleshoot a XenApp server farm.

- **Assessing event viewer errors**   Event logs should be checked daily on all servers to ensure the operating system, applications, and system security are functioning normally. EdgeSight is a great place to look at the centralized log files of the Citrix server (see Chapter 12). Other event log consolidation tools exist, such as Microsoft Operation Manager, which can dramatically simplify the daily task of checking each event log by providing a unified interface for viewing logs.

- **Troubleshooting problems**   Troubleshoot daily user problems and handle emergency hardware issues such as failed hard drives, network cards, and so on.

- ▲ **Checking for session states using Access Management Console (AMC)**   Reset lengthy disconnected sessions if disconnect times are not enforced. Record and trend the number of disconnected, idle, and active sessions to help refine session disconnect settings.

Weekly Maintenance Activities

Weekly maintenance activities focus on proactive actions aimed at keeping both the farm and servers healthy. These tasks should include, but are not limited to, the following:

- ▼ **Verifying concurrent user need does not exceed current purchased licensing**   The License Management Console (LMC) provides one-stop access to all licensing information. Use the LMC to validate the number and types of licenses installed and to generate historical reports on license consumption. Access the LMC via a web browser at http://<server name>/lmc/index.jsp as shown in Figure 18-3. Note that LMC access is controlled from within the LMC itself, and it allows the administrator to grant different levels of user access to LMC functions. Look for a low number of available licenses to determine when there is need for additional licensing. Also, check the status on Subscription Advantage expiration or if license usage has exceeded the number allowed.

■ **Checking free space** Check free space on all servers to ensure sufficient space is available for proper operation. Once a server gets below 10 percent of the total disk space available, the performance of the server will be affected.

■ **Ensuring antivirus definitions are up to date** XenApp servers typically process the same types of traffic and applications as a desktop PC, and as such are subject to malware. A malware infection on a XenApp server could disrupt service to dozens of users.

■ **Generating reports** Create reports on downtime/uptime, performance problems, and lingering issues to understand and react to problems in the environment. Update the user community on current problem resolution and uptime of the environment through e-mail, an intranet, or other means.

▲ **Reviewing and applying any critical Windows, application, or Citrix updates/ hotfixes** Stay up to date with the latest patches or fixes to prevent unnecessary problems. The changes should be applied to a test server first to verify operability before rollout to production servers.

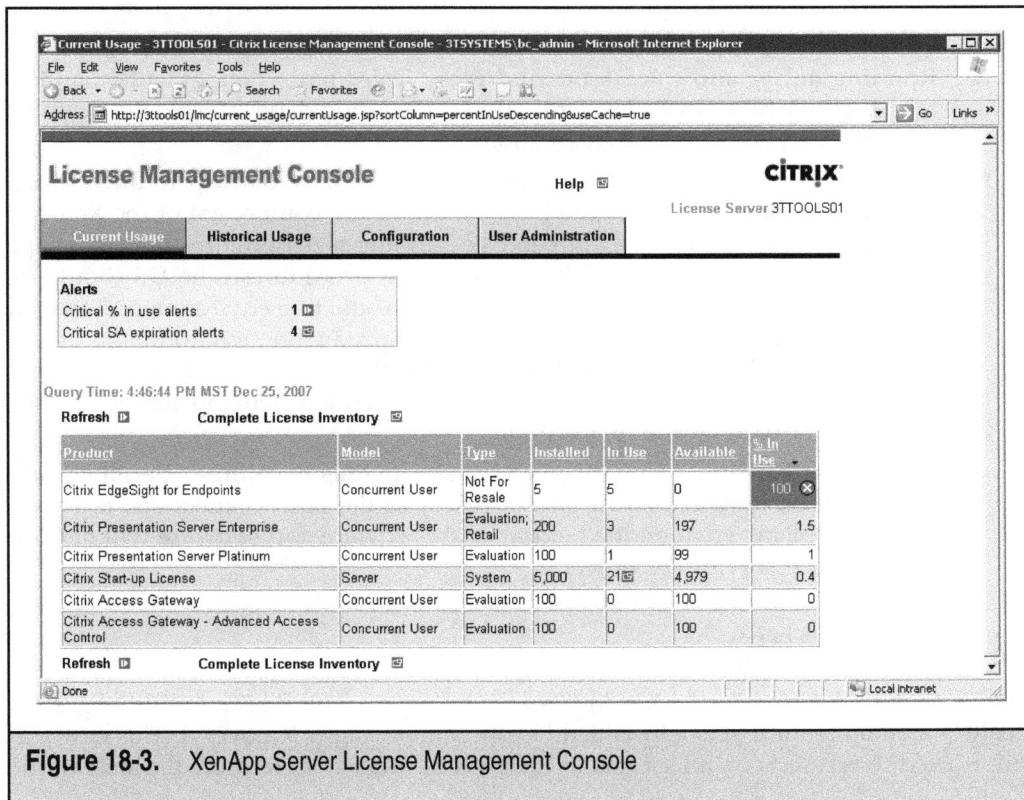

Figure 18-3. XenApp Server License Management Console

Monthly

Monthly maintenance activities focus on high-level farm administration and housekeeping. These tasks should include, but are not limited to, the following:

▼ **Monitoring bandwidth utilization for ICA sessions**   Review the current bandwidth versus the bandwidth needed to support printing, session responsiveness, and potential growth.

▲ **Updating printer drivers and driver mappings and removing unused drivers**   The latest versions of the drivers should be used, all servers should contain the same drivers, unused drivers should be removed, and driver mappings and compatibility lists should be updated. Many problems with print driver inconsistency can be overcome by relying on the universal print driver (UPD).

Quarterly

Quarterly maintenance activities focus on reviewing current farm design and monitoring performance levels. These tasks should include, but are not limited to, the following:

▼ **Analyzing usage and growth patterns**   Analyze farm usage and future growth patterns to estimate requirements for the expansion of the XenApp Server environment, then perform budgetary and growth planning.

■ **Running defrag and chkdsk on all drives**   Third-party defragmentation utilities, such as Executive Software's Diskeeper, should be utilized to facilitate scheduled and robust defragmentation.

■ **Performing test restores of the data store from tape backup to an isolated testing environment**   Since the DS is an important component of the XenApp Server environment, we recommend performing a periodic restore from tape backup. This restore should follow established procedures. The DS should be restored onto equipment similar to that in the production environment. To avoid network conflicts and the risk of affecting the production environment, the restored DS should be in an isolated test network. Administrators should check the operability of the restored data store by adding a XenApp server into the farm and connecting to an application.

▲ **Performing baseline comparisons against previous baselines**   Baseline comparisons indicate whether the current sizing of the farm is adequate. If performance problems are identified, additional hardware and software will need to be purchased and implemented.

FARM MONITORING

New with the 4.5 release of the XenApp Server Enterprise and Platinum Editions is the Health Assistant feature (formally called Health Monitoring & Recovery). This new feature is used to run tests on all servers in the farm in order to determine the state of the servers as well as any health risks, such as the status of Terminal Services, the XML service, the IMA service, and logon/logoff cycles.

When you enable Health Assistant on the farm, by default, the tests will run on all the servers in the farm. If you wish to disable a specific server from running the tests (the data collector, for instance, because it does not serve up applications), this can be done manually through the Access Management Console. An example of the use of Health Assistant is when a server's IMA service is down. Most monitoring software can detect that the service is unavailable and can e-mail you, but cannot take action to prevent user issues. Citrix, however, prevents the downed service from interfering with user productivity by detecting the failed service and redirecting users to another server using server load-balancing.

Each server in the farm has the Health Check Agent (HCA), which runs the preconfigured tests and reviews the health of the server. When a test fails, the server can take action to correct the problem and log the event in the server's event logs.

Accessing Tests

Follow these steps to access the Health Assistant tests:

1. Take one of the following actions in the Access Management Console:

   - To access the tests by server, in the scope pane expand the Presentation Server and Servers nodes and then select a server. Next, select **Action | Modify Server Properties | Modify All Properties**.

   - To access the tests by farm, in the scope pane expand the Presentation Server node and select a farm. Then select **Action | Modify Farm Properties | Modify All Properties**. In the **Farm Properties** dialog box, expand the Server Default node.

2. Select the Health Assistant. The Health Assistant page that appears allows you to view the following standard tests and any custom tests you import. Out of the box, XenApp Server 4.5 comes with four tests.

   - **Terminal Services**   This test enumerates the list of sessions running on the server and the session user information, such as user name.

   - **Citrix XML Service**   This test checks the health of the XML service by ensuring it is able to process XML ticket requests.

   - **Citrix IMA Service**   This test queries the service to ensure it is running by enumerating the applications available on the server.

   - **Logon Monitor**   This test monitors session logon/logoff cycles to determine whether there is a problem with session initialization. If there are numerous logon/logoff cycles within a short time period, the threshold for the session is exceeded and a failure occurs. The session time, interval, and threshold can be configured by modifying the parameters in the Test file field. These parameters are listed and described in Table 18-2.

Logon Monitor Test Parameter	Description
SessionTime	Defines the maximum session time for a short logon/logoff cycle. The default is five seconds.
SessionInterval	The time period designated to monitor logon/logoff cycles. The default is 600 seconds.
SessionThreshold	The number of logon/logoff cycles that must occur within the session interval for the test to fail. The default is 50 cycles.

Table 18-2. Logon Test Monitor Parameters

With the release of Feature Pack 1, six new tests are included in the update to the Access Management Console. This update is called the Web Interface 4.6 Extension and Health, Monitoring & Recovery (HMR) Test Pack. Once the update is installed, you will have access to the following new tests:

▼ **Check DNS (Checkdns.exe)**   This test ensures DNS health on the local server. The test consists of a forward DNS lookup that uses the local hostname to query the IP address from the local DNS in the computer's environment. The test passes successfully if the returned IP address matches the IP address that is registered locally with the NIC. By default, only a forward DNS lookup is performed. The /rl flag can be applied to run both forward and reverse DNS lookups.

■ **Check Local Host Cache (CheckLHC.exe)**   This test performs integrity and consistency checks on the local XenApp server's local host cache (LHC). The integrity check ensures the data stored in the LHC is not corrupted, whereas the consistency check ensures no duplicate LHC entries. These operations are similar to those in other XenApp Server utilities found in DSCheck and DSVerify.

NOTE: Because this test can be CPU intensive, it is recommended that you use a longer test interval of 24 hours (86400 seconds) while keeping default values for the test threshold and timeout.

■ **Check XML Threads (Checkxmlthreads.exe)**   This test performs a threshold check on the current number of worker threads running in the Citrix XML service. Run this test with a single integer parameter to set the maximum allowable threshold value. The test checks the current value on the system and compares that to the input value. If the value found on the system is greater than the input value, the test fails; otherwise, the test passes.

- **Citrix Print Manager Service Test (Cpsvctest.exe)** This test determines the health of the Citrix Print Manager service by enumerating session printers. In cases where the test cannot enumerate session printers, such as service hangs or crashes, the test fails.

- **MS Print Spooler Test (Spoolertest.exe)** This test checks whether the print spooler installed with Windows is healthy and ready for use. This test also helps determine whether system printer issues exist that you must address. The test attempts to enumerate printer drivers, printer processors, and printers.

- ▲ **ICA Listener (ICAListener.exe)** This test detects whether the server is able to accept ICA connections. The test detects the default ICA port, connects to the port, and sends it some data. If it gets the appropriate data back, the test succeeds.

Modifying Test Settings

You can modify the settings of Health Assistant tests by server or across all servers in a farm by opening the Access Management Console and modifying the properties of the farm or of each server.

NOTE: If you are making changes at the farm level, there are two places to adjust. Under Farm-wide | Health Monitoring & Recovery, you can adjust the maximum percentage of servers that HMR can exclude from the load balancing. The other location is a bit lower in the left pane under Server Default | Health Monitoring & Recovery. Here you can adjust the settings for the tests that are run on the entire farm.

For this discussion, we are modifying the tests at the farm level. Open the Health Assistant section in the AMC, select the test you wish to change, and click Modify. Each test will have different values, but the settings are the same:

- ▼ **Interval** The amount of time to wait before running the test.
- **Threshold** The number of times this test will fail before triggering an action.
- **Time-out** If a test does not return within this specified amount of time, the test will time out.
- ▲ **Recovery Action** You can choose different actions to be taken if a server fails a test; these include restarting the server and preventing user connections from being initiated on it until the problem is fixed. If a server fails a test, an alert appears in the Access Management Console. Through the Health Assistant page, you can configure one of the following actions to be taken automatically if a test fails:
  - **Alert Only** Sends an error message to the event log, but takes no other action. The test continues to run, and if it subsequently successfully passes, an event is sent to the system log. This recovery action is the default for all tests except the Citrix XML Service test.

- **Remove Server from Load Balancing**   Excludes the server from load balancing. Clients do not attempt to make new connections to this server through Load Manager. To restore one or more servers to load balancing, use the **enablelb** command-line utility.

- **Shut Down IMA**   Shuts down the Citrix IMA Service. After this happens, tests continue to run but failures will not trigger events to be sent to the event log until the Citrix IMA Service is up and running again.

- **Restart IMA**   Shuts down and then restarts the Citrix IMA Service. After this happens, tests will run but failures will not trigger events to be sent to the event log until the Citrix IMA Service is up and running again.

- **Reboot Server**   Restarts the server. An alert will be triggered before the server is restarted. After the system is restarted, the tests will resume.

Developing Custom Tests

If you want to perform particular tests not included in the Health Assistant, you can develop custom tests using the Health Assistant SDK package. This package includes a Readme file with information you will need to use the SDK, including security requirements and return values. In addition, the SDK contains various sample test scripts you can use to develop custom tests that can be run on a server farm or on individual servers in a farm. The Health Assistant SDK package is available for download from the Citrix Developer Network.

MONITORING PERFORMANCE

As with earlier releases of Presentation Server, once Citrix is installed on a Terminal Server, new performance monitoring counters are added to the default Terminal Server counters (see Figure 18-4). These can be accessed from Start | All Programs | Administrative Tools | Performance.

NOTE: The entire ICA counter list is exposed only on a server running the Platinum or Enterprise edition of XenApp Server. On a server running the Advanced Edition, only latency-related counters are available.

Performance monitoring counters that directly relate to the performance of ICA sessions, networking, and security are installed with XenApp Server. We recommend you use performance monitoring to get accurate accounts of system performance and the effects of configuration changes on system throughput. You can add and then view the following categories of XenApp Server–related counters (called *"performance objects"*) in Performance Monitor:

▼ Citrix CPU Utilization Mgmt User

■ Citrix IMA Networking

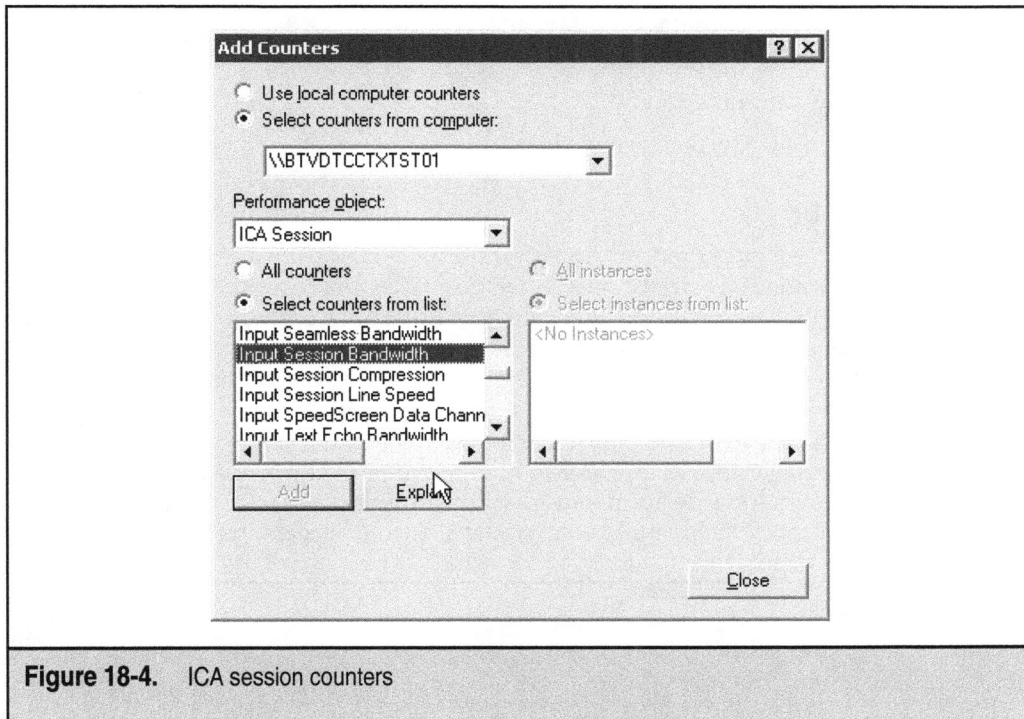

Figure 18-4. ICA session counters

- Citrix Licensing
- Citrix XenApp Server
- ICA Session
- ▲ Secure Ticket Authority

Resource Manager and Monitoring Tools

Another method of monitoring the resources and data on the XenApp server farm is to use the monitoring tools that come with XenApp Server. These tools are Resource Manager and the Access Management Console snap-ins. Administrators can use these tools to help collect, display, store, and report data about performance, user activity, and application or process use. Here are some common uses for these tools:

- ▼ Monitoring servers
- Monitoring the server farm
- Identifying, diagnosing, and solving problems
- Gauging and justifying future resources

- ■ Planning and scaling the server farm
- ■ Billing users for resource usage
- ■ Delegating administration
- ▲ Reporting on performance and activity

Resource Manager

Resource Manager is configured in the Presentation Server Console, and it tracks and stores information about a variety of activity that takes place on the server farm. Resource Manager is included with the Platinum and Enterprise editions of XenApp Server and is installed as a component of the installation. When installed, it automatically creates a set of default metrics and assigns limits to define the normal operation of each one. Each of these metrics can be customized to more closely match the details and capabilities of your servers and farm (see Figure 18-5).

Because Windows Performance Monitor utilizes pieces of Citrix, Resource Manager is able to track most Windows Performance Monitor counters as server metrics. Therefore, administrators can check the overall health of the farm and servers from one location.

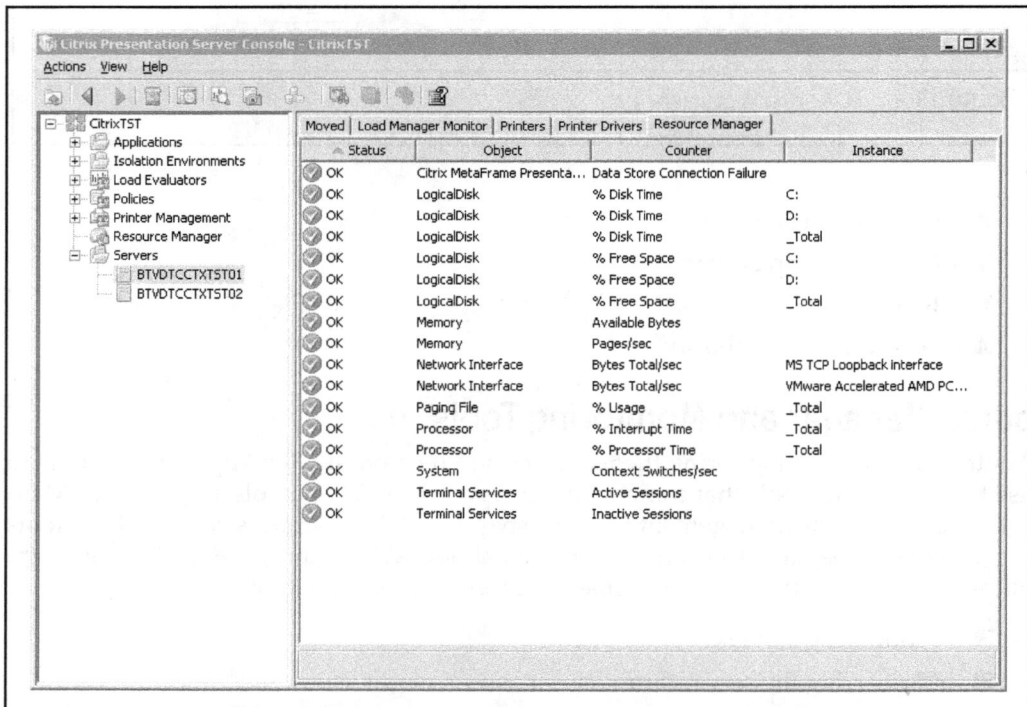

Figure 18-5. Resource Manager Default Metrics

Installation and the Summary Database

In order to run Resource Manager, you will need XenApp Server 4.5 Enterprise or Platinum edition. If you wish to keep historical data beyond the four-hour real-time view, you must configure a Summary Database using a SQL 2000/2005 or Oracle 9i/10g database server. Resource Manager is installed as a component of the XenApp Server installation.

You need to decide on at least one server to act as the farm metric server. The farm metric server interprets metrics that apply to the entire farm and sends alerts if configured to do so.

Before you can begin using the Summary Database, you need to install and configure a database in either SQL or Oracle. For this example, we are using SQL Server. Create a new database and ensure that the database server has enough room to store a month's worth of data. From there, we will create a system data source name (DSN) and finally configure the server to connect to the database server.

Setting a System Data Source Name To set a system data source name for the Microsoft SQL Server DBMS, follow these steps:

1. Choose a server to be your Database Connection Server.
2. Open the ODBC Data Source Administrator dialog box on this server.
   a. If your Database Connection Server is a 32-bit server, select Start | Control Panel | Administrative Tools | Data Sources (ODBC).
   b. If your Database Connection Server is a 64-bit server, select Start | Run, type **%SystemRoot%\SysWow64\odbcad32.exe**, and then press Enter.
3. Select the System DSN tab. Click Add.
4. In the Create New Data Source dialog box, select SQL Server. Click Finish.
5. In the Microsoft SQL Server DSN Configuration dialog box, type **rmsummarydatabase** in the Name box. Type a description (optional) and then select the server with the DBMS installed on it from the Server list. Click Next.

NOTE: You must type **rmsummarydatabase** exactly. Any spaces or spelling errors will make the database unrecognizable to the Database Connection Server. However, the field is not case-sensitive.

6. Select how Microsoft SQL Server authenticates your identification; you can set up the system DSN in one of two ways:
   - Click "With Windows NT authentication using the network login ID" to use Windows NT authentication.
   - Click "With SQL Server authentication using a login ID and password entered by the user." Then select the "Connect to SQL Server to obtain default settings for the additional configuration options" check box and type a user name and password in the Login ID and Password boxes, respectively.

7. Click Client Configuration.

8. In the Edit Network Library Configuration dialog box, select TCP/IP under Network Libraries. Click OK and then click Next.

9. Select the "Change the default database to" check box and then select the database you created on the DBMS server from the list. Click Next and then Finish.

10. In the ODBC Setup dialog box, you can click Test Data Source to confirm the DSN configuration. Click OK twice to close the dialog box.

11. Click OK to close the ODBC Data Source Administrator dialog box.

Configuring the Database Connection Server   To configure a server to act as the Database Connection Server, follow these steps:

1. In the left pane of the console, click Resource Manager.

2. In the right pane, click the Summary Database tab. Click Configure.

3. In the Summary Database Configuration dialog box, select your Database Connection Server from the Server list. Only servers running Resource Manager appear in the list.

NOTE: If a server name appears dimmed, the server is running an older version of Resource Manager and should not be selected.

4. Enter the database server access credentials in the User and Password boxes. These must match valid credentials defined within the supporting database server (that is, the Oracle or Microsoft SQL Server database you are using).

5. Click Test to check the connection to the database.

Enabling the Summary Database   Once the database is built and the connection server is configured, the only thing left to do is turn on the Summary Database. To do this, follow these steps:

1. In the left pane of the Presentation Server Console, click Resource Manager.

2. In the right pane, click the Summary Database tab. Click Configure.

NOTE: The first icon in the Status panel is Not Configured and shows a red circle with a slash when the Summary Database is off or a Database Connection Server is not configured. In this state, Resource Manager servers are not creating or storing information in the Summary Database.

3. In the Summary Database Configuration dialog box, select the Summary Database Enabled check box.

4. Click OK twice.

NOTE: The first icon in the Status panel is OK (represented by a green circle with a checkmark in it), meaning the Summary Database is on and a Database Connection Server is correctly configured and in use. In this state, Resource Manager servers are collecting information for the database.

Access Management Console Snap-Ins

In addition to Resource Manager, the Access Management Console has several snap-ins to aid in monitoring your server and farm health:

▼ **Dashboard** Gives the administrators a display (in tabular or graphical format) of the metric data to help diagnose and monitor server performance across the farm. The Dashboard view allows admins to configure groups of metrics, called "monitoring profiles," and assign them to a server in the farm. Monitoring profiles are used to define a complete monitoring configuration for one or more servers to monitor all the metrics the profile defines. Admins can view real-time and historical performance metrics as well as metrics from the Resource Manager database.

NOTE: Servers running versions of XenApp Server older than 4.5 cannot be associated with a monitoring profile. However, you can still use the Presentation Server Console to configure custom performance metrics for these servers.

■ **Report Center** Enables admins to analyze and report on various aspects of deployments using records of system activity. Admins can also create reports about current activities or past activities using the Summary Database. For example, they can compare quarterly data for server uptime, CPU utilization, or application availability with agreed-upon figures in a service-level agreement (SLA).

▲ **My Knowledge** Makes available the alerts for Suite Monitoring and Alerting and context-sensitive information about them, which helps you understand their meaning and impact so that you can take appropriate actions. The two types of context-sensitive information are knowledge articles provided by Citrix and articles provided by your company.

Monitoring with Citrix EdgeSight

Even though Performance Monitor and Resource Manager are great tools to aid you in keeping tabs on the server farm, the real gem is the new product Citrix EdgeSight. Citrix EdgeSight for XenApp Server is an end-to-end performance management solution for XenApp servers. It monitors user sessions and server performance in real time, allowing you to quickly analyze, resolve, and proactively prevent problems.

Citrix EdgeSight for XenApp Server provides the following benefits:

▼ It provides complete user-session data, identifying which server is supporting individual end users and delivering highly detailed session-level data, allowing you to quickly isolate and resolve application performance problems.

▲ It enables effective resource management and capacity planning through the ability to view resource consumption based on the number of active user sessions as well as the effects of new applications on a server.

We covered EdgeSight in Chapter 12, but as a refresher of how good EdgeSight really is, imagine Resource Manager going to the gym for 12 hours a day for two years, all the time working with the best personal trainers and taking advantage of all the technological advances available—and then double it. That would about cover it.

FARM MANAGEMENT

Farm management is required to verify that the farm continues to meet the needs of the business environment. Servers should be monitored to verify that the load is appropriate. Too many users, runaway processes, memory leaks, and poor applications on a server can lead to poor performance.

Citrix has graciously provided administrators with a nice collection of tools for managing servers, server farms, published resources, and connections. The two main consoles are the Access Management Console and the Presentation Server Console. Both consoles are installed by default when you install XenApp Server. Either console may be installed on the XenApp servers (Typical install). Alternatively, to make things a bit easier, you can install either or both on your workstation. For performance reasons it is preferred that the Access Management Console be installed on the XenApp server. Only users in the Citrix Administrators group are authorized to use the AMC.

The Access Management Console (AMC) for XenApp Server

The Access Management Console (AMC) is a snap-in for the Microsoft Management Console (MMC) that enables Citrix administrators to perform a number of management functions, such as setting up and monitoring servers, server farms, published resources, and sessions. The first time you launch the console, the Configure and Run Discovery Wizard runs. Discovery is an important Access Management Console operation that checks for items (such as devices or applications) that were added to or removed from your Citrix environment. Appropriate changes are then made to the console tree. After the initial discovery is performed, use the wizard to locate newly installed products or snap-ins and to update the console if items are added or removed from your deployment.

The AMC allows XenApp Server administrators to do the following:

▼ Configure servers and farm settings from any connected workstation.

■ Manage applications and servers, and view zones in multiple farms.

■ Manage client sessions and server processes.

■ Publish applications to isolation environments.

■ Create Citrix administrators and modify their privileges.

■ Monitor the performance of servers and server farms.

■ Troubleshoot alerts using information in My Knowledge articles.

■ Create reports with Report Center.

■ Configure access to published applications using Web Interface.

■ Create trace logs to assist Citrix Technical Support with problem analysis.

▲ View hotfix information for Citrix products.

The main user interface of the console consists of three panes:

▼ The *scope pane* contains the console tree.

■ The *task pane* (in the middle) displays administrative tasks and tools. This pane is typically not present in other MMC snap-ins.

▲ The *details pane* (on the right) displays items and information associated with the selected node in the console tree.

Typically, you move around in the console as follows: Selecting a node in the left pane updates the items and information displayed in the details pane. The **Change Display** menu in the task pane allows you to view different items and information associated with the node. To modify or otherwise administer an item, you select it and click a task in the task pane or details pane.

The AMC queries the Zone Data Collector (or a server you select) for information such as running processes, connected users, and server loads. Depending on the size of the server farm, the console might affect performance in the server farm. It is best to only open one copy of the AMC at a time and connect to the Zone Data Collector (ZDC) so that the console can query data directly. Auto-refresh of the AMC should not be used in most situations due to the additional load it places on the ZDC server.

Controlling Access to the Management Console

The AMC uses standard Windows logon and user account authentication to grant access to designated farm administrators. Access to the AMC must be granted through the AMC interface by adding a user or group to the Administrators section. To add a new administrator, the current administrator must have the privilege type "Full Admin."

NOTE: By default, the first administrator account in the Administrators group is the account that was logged into the server during the install of XenApp Server.

To add a new Citrix administrator, follow these steps:

1. Open the Access Management Console and browse to Citrix Resources | Presentation Server | *Farm Name* | Administrators.

2. Highlight the Administrators group and select New | Add Administrator in the middle section.

3. In the dialog box that appears, add the user or group account and click Next.

4. Configure the alert contact details for Resource Manager alerts or SMS messages and click Next.

5. The Privileges dialog box now appears. Select the appropriate privilege type for the new administrator and click Next.

The access granted to an administrator is fully customizable. There are options for View Only, Full Administration, and Custom as well as the ability to disable the account. Custom permissions can be used to create level-one help desk personnel access, which only allows for administration of user sessions. All levels of the AMC have their own access rights, so it is possible to create administrator logons for managers such that they have access only to the areas they need to perform their job, but little else beyond that.

Using Server and Application Folders within AMC

The AMC provides the ability to group servers and applications into folders. There is no correlation between AMC folders and Program Neighborhood, Web Interface, or Program Neighborhood Agent folders displayed within application sets. The AMC folders help to manage a large number of servers and increase the performance of the AMC because the AMC queries data only for the servers or applications in the current folder view. One way to increase the response time of the AMC is to divide the list of servers into folders based on their zones or location (see Figure 18-6).

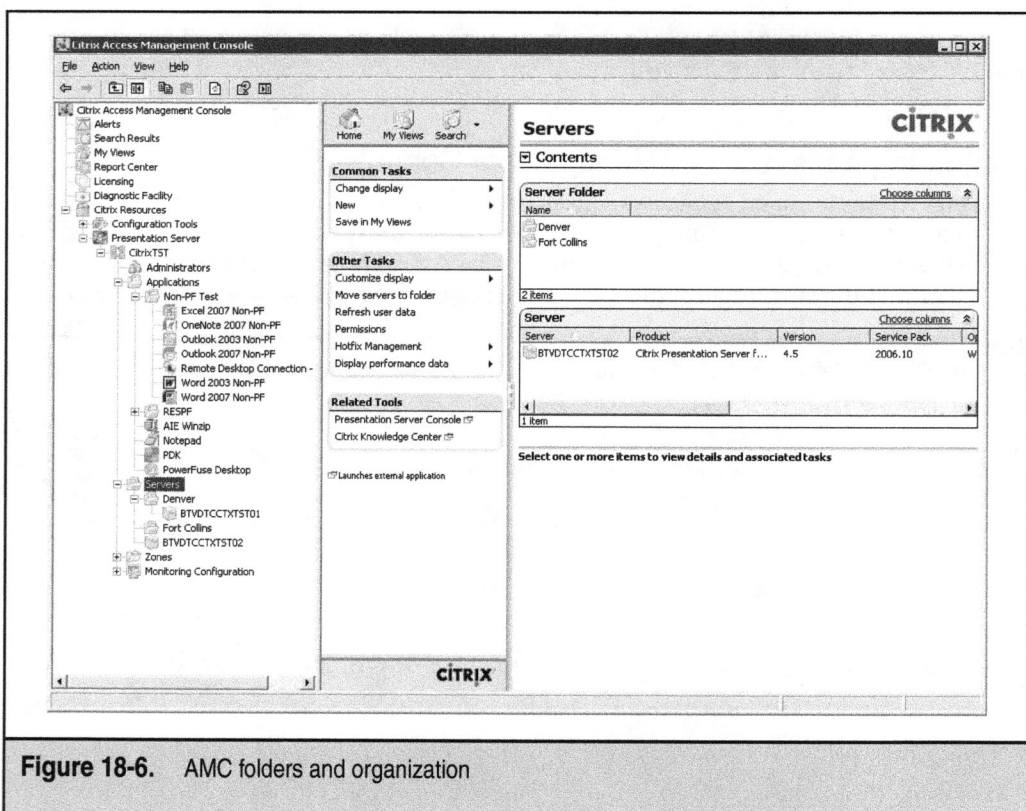

Figure 18-6. AMC folders and organization

Managing Users and ICA Sessions

Some of the main tasks of a Citrix administrator revolve around management of users and sessions. If a server has a problem or needs to be taken down for maintenance, logons must be disabled and later reenabled. Sessions will also need to be reset, logged out, or disconnected for users so that they can get back into the system with a clean start.

Current users with sessions on a server can be viewed from several locations in the AMC: by selecting the Farm node in the scope pane, by selecting the Server node in the scope pane, by selecting an individual server from the server list, or by selecting from an individual published application from the application list. Each option's display choice differs depending on the option chosen. For example, if the Farm node is selected, the Change Display option offers information on both Users and Offline Session (see Figure 18-7). If a server is chosen from the list of servers, the Change Display option offers information on Users and Sessions (see Figure 18-8). From a published application the display can be Connected Users or Configured Users.

Once a user's session is chosen from any of these methods, several options are available to manage the user's session.

To display information about users or sessions in the scope pane, choose from each method mentioned previously. Then in the task pane under Common Tasks, select

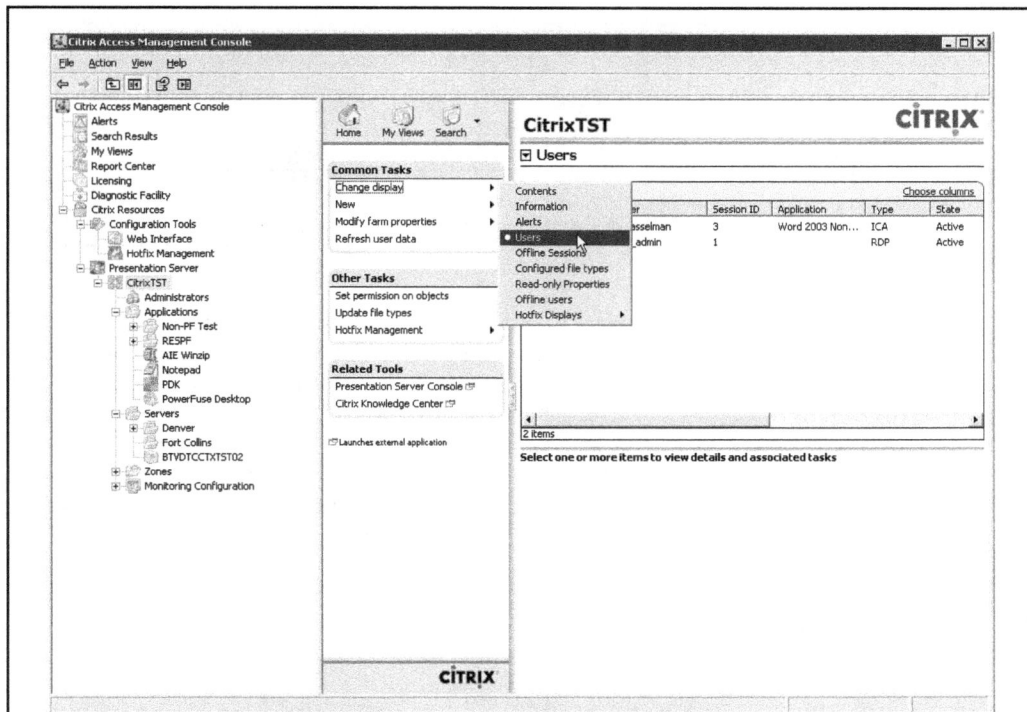

Figure 18-7.   Managing users from the Farm node

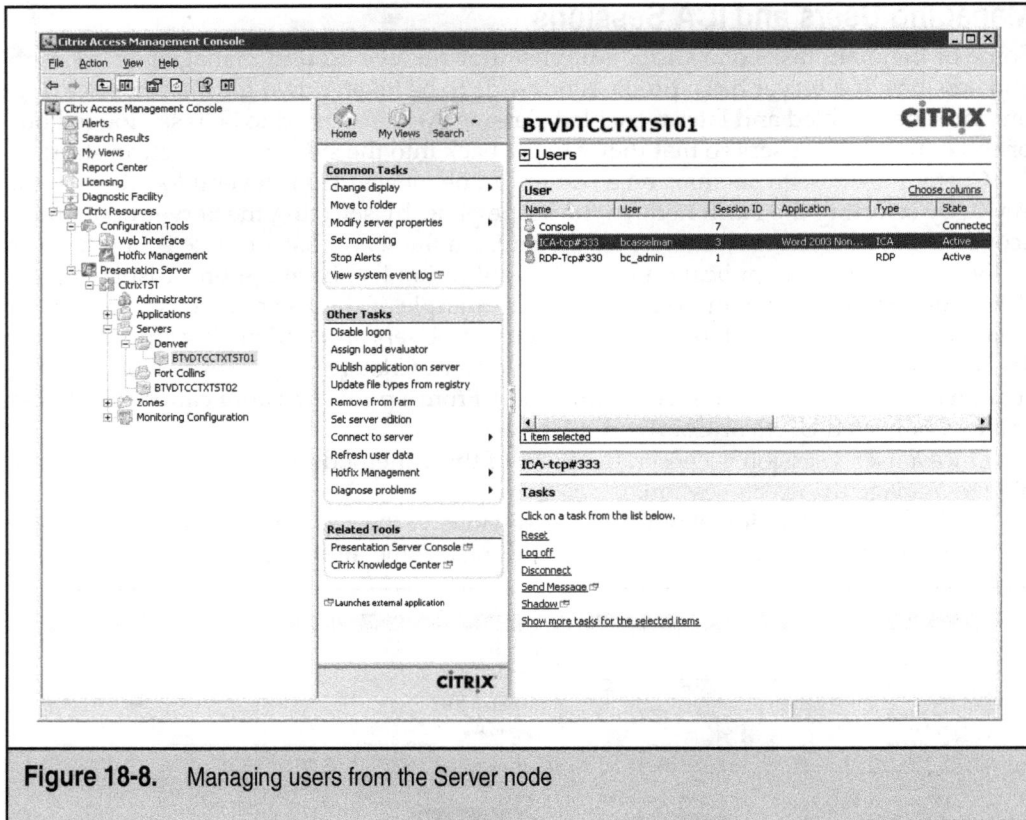

Figure 18-8.   Managing users from the Server node

Change Display and choose from the choice of views (see Figure 18-9). For example, to log off a user's session, from the scope pane select the Applications node and choose an application that users are connected to. Then under Common Tasks choose Change Display | Users and highlight the user's session in the details pane and from the Tasks list select Log Off.

From this view in the AMC, administrators can perform specific administrative tasks for the user's sessions. When selecting a user's session in the details pane, you can see the following tasks toward the bottom of the pane to manage that user's session:

▼ **Reset** Terminates all processes that are running in a user's session. Resetting effectively deletes the session and results in loss of data for the user. Only reset a session when it is not responding or malfunctions. This can be performed on a single user or a group of users.

■ **Log Off** Forces one or more user sessions to end. Logging off a user's session can result in the loss of data. It is recommended that a message be sent to the user, allowing them to safely exit all applications.

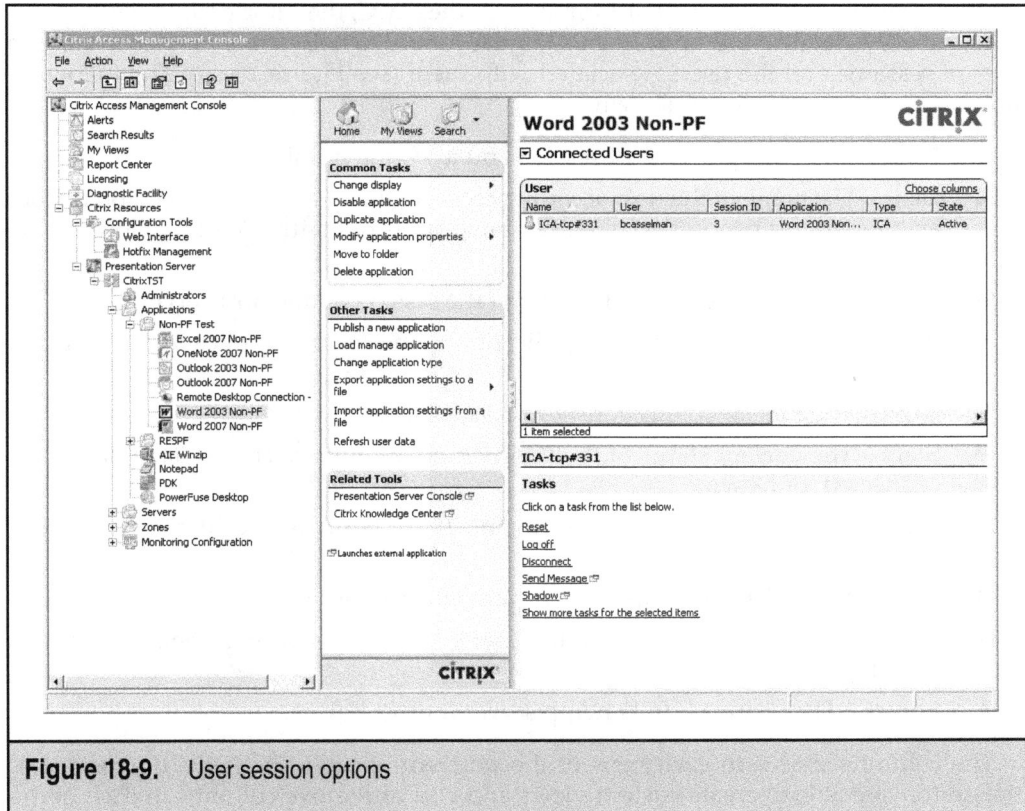

Figure 18-9. User session options

- **Disconnect** Closes one or more sessions between the client and server. This does not terminate the session; therefore, all programs and processes will continue to run on the server until the session is logged off or reset.

- **Send Message** Sends administrative messages to one or more users logged into the servers.

- **Shadow** Monitors a user session, similar to watching the screen of the client that initiated the session. While shadowing a session, you can also use your keyboard and mouse to remotely control the user's keyboard and mouse in the shadowed session (if configured to do so). For more information on shadowing, refer to the next section.

▲ **Show More Tasks for the Selected User** Used to view detailed information about the client cache, session information client modules, and processes associated with a user's session.

NOTE: When you select a Remote Desktop session (RDP), the Shadow option becomes a Status option.

While you're viewing session information in the AMC, the information that appears in the console's details pane appears in a tabular format to help you identify the various types of sessions and the users associated with them (see Figure 18-10). The following information for each session is shown:

▼ **Name** Displays the type of session and a session number.

■ **User** The name of the user account accessing the system. (If the session is from an anonymous connection, the user name starts out with "Anon" followed by a session number.)

■ **Session ID** The numeric identifier of the session on the host server.

■ **Application** The published application name for the application running in the session.

■ **Type** The type of connection—Console, RDP, or ICA.

■ **State** The current status of the ICA session, as either Active, Listen, Idle, Disconnected, or Down.

■ **Client Name** The name given to the ICA client device in the ICA client software.

■ **Logon Time** The time the user logged onto the server.

■ **Idle Time** Displays how long the user's session has been in the Idle state (no activity).

▲ **Server** The name of the XenApp server for the session.

The columns shown in each view at the different areas in the AMC by view. Administrators are able to create custom views and add or remove columns in each of the default views.

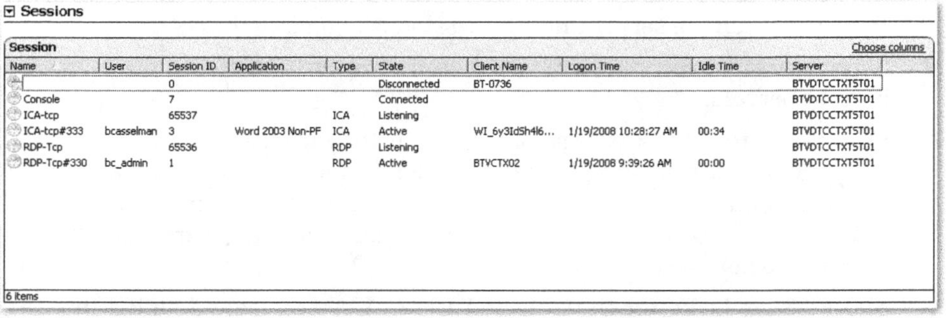

Name	User	Session ID	Application	Type	State	Client Name	Logon Time	Idle Time	Server
		0			Disconnected	BT-0736			BTVDTCCTXTST01
Console		7			Connected				BTVDTCCTXTST01
ICA-tcp		65537		ICA	Listening				BTVDTCCTXTST01
ICA-tcp#333	bcasselman	3	Word 2003 Non-PF	ICA	Active	WI_6y3Id5h4l6...	1/19/2008 10:28:27 AM	00:34	BTVDTCCTXTST01
RDP-Tcp		65536		RDP	Listening				BTVDTCCTXTST01
RDP-Tcp#330	bc_admin	1		RDP	Active	BTVCTX02	1/19/2008 9:39:26 AM	00:00	BTVDTCCTXTST01

Figure 18-10. Session information

Command-Line Management

Information about server farms, processes, servers, sessions, Terminal Servers, and users within the network session can also be viewed using the command-line tool QUERY, with the appropriate parameters. The QUERY tool only shows information on the currently logged-in server, unless another server is specified with the following parameter:

`/server :<servername>`

We highlight some of the more frequently used commands in this section. Refer to the administrator's guide for a full list of commands and parameters.

▼   **Query Farm (qfarm)**   Returns information for IMA-based servers within a server farm.

   /disc   Displays disconnected session data for the farm.

   /load   Displays server-load information for all servers within the farm or for a specific server.

   /zone   Displays all data collectors in all zones.

■   **Query Server (qserver)**   Displays data about the servers present on a network within a server farm running in interoperability mode. qfarm is the recommended command for this information.

   /addr   Displays address information for the specified server.

   /app   Displays application names and the server load for the specified server.

   /disc   Displays disconnected session data on the current server.

   /load   Displays local data on the specified server.

▲   **Query User (quser)**   Displays all user sessions on the current server.

Enabling or Disabling Logons

To enable or disable logons from the AMC, select the server in the scope pane of the Access Management Console and select **Action | All Tasks | Disable Logon**.

   Logons can also be disabled from the command prompt using the change logon command. This command has three options: enable logons, disable logons, and query the current logon state of the server.

Managing Zones

In a XenApp server farm, a *zone* is a grouping of XenApp servers that share a common data collector, which is a XenApp server that receives information from all the servers in the zone. A zone in a XenApp server farm elects a Zone Data Collector (ZDC) for that zone if a new server joins the zone, a member server restarts, or the current ZDC becomes unavailable. A ZDC becomes unavailable if the server goes down or is disconnected from the network, or if you move the server to another zone.

When a zone elects a new ZDC, it uses a preference ranking of the servers in the zone. You can set the preference ranking for the servers in a zone on the Zones tab in the server farm's Properties dialog box. As shown in Figure 18-11, each zone has four levels of preference for election of a ZDC. This order, from highest to lowest preference, is as follows:

- Most Preferred
- Preferred
- Default Preference
- Not Preferred

All servers in a zone are assigned to one of the four election preference levels. When the zone elects a new ZDC, it tries to select a server from the first preference level. If no servers at this level are available, the zone selects a server from the second level, and so on.

When you create a farm, the election preference for all servers is Default Preference, except for the first server added to the zone, which is set to Most Preferred and is the initial ZDC.

On the Zones tab in the console, a colored symbol appears next to each server name to indicate the election preference setting. You can change the default election preference to designate a specific server as the ZDC. To do this, set the election preference for the server to Most Preferred. If you do not want some servers to be the ZDC, set the election preference for those servers to Not Preferred.

Managing Application Access

Before you publish resources, consider how the configuration of your users' accounts can affect their access. You publish resources for specific users and user groups. The Application Publishing Wizard allows you to set up two types of application access: anonymous access and explicit (configured) user account access.

Adding and Removing Users or Groups from a Published Application   Users are granted access to the applications via the Published Application Wizard. In some situations it might be desirable to create all the applications and then go back and provide user access once a plan for user access is developed.

To give a user access to a published application, open the AMC and do the following:

1. In the scope pane, browse to the Applications node and select the published application to add users to.

2. Right-click the published application and select Modify Application Properties | Modify Users.

3. Select either Allow Anonymous Users or Allow Only Configured Users.

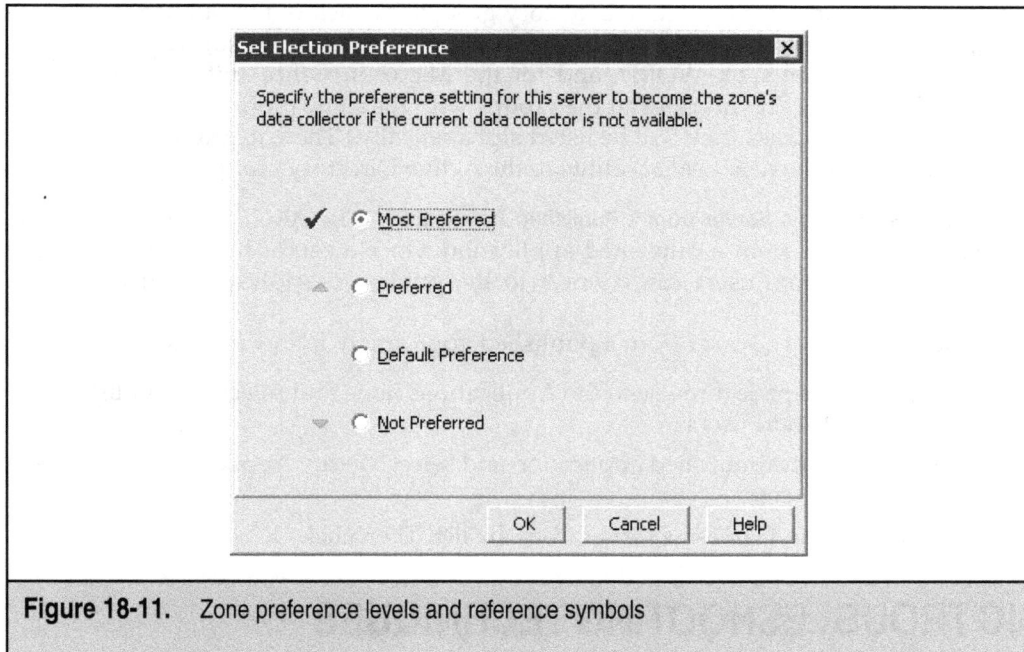

Figure 18-11.   Zone preference levels and reference symbols

NOTE: During XenApp Server installation, Setup creates a special user group named Anonymous. By default, anonymous users have guest permissions. Publishing applications for this special Anonymous user group lets you completely eliminate the need for user authentication for those applications. The anonymous user accounts XenApp Server creates during installation do not require additional configuration. If you want to modify their properties, you can do so with the standard Windows user account management tools.

4. For configured users, choose a directory type from the pull-down list. Choose either Citrix User Selector or Operating System User Selector. The Citrix User Selector option displays accounts that are available to the farm. The Operating System User Selector option displays accounts available from the local machine.

CAUTION: Choosing accounts from the operating system selector may allow user accounts to be chosen that might not be valid to the farm. Such accounts can be removed from the list when the selector type is closed.

5. Click Add and select the users or groups to grant access to the published application and then click OK.

To remove a user, from the same dialog box simply highlight the user account and click the Remove button.

We recommend creating Active Directory groups for each of the published applications and assigning these groups to the applications. For example, for Microsoft Word create a group called CTX_WORD, and for the Microsoft Office suite create a group called CTX_OFFICE. (If you label all the groups with the same prefix, it will be easier to find them in AD because they will be listed alphabetically.) Then, to grant access to new users, simply add the new user accounts to the Active Directory group.

Adding and Removing a Server from a Published Application   The AMC can be used to add and remove servers from a published application. Once a server has been added to a published application, users can connect to the published application on the newly added server.

To add or remove a server from a published application, follow these steps:

1. In the scope pane, browse to the Applications node and select the published application to add users to.

2. Right-click the published application and select Modify Application Properties | Modify Servers.

3. Click Add and choose a server from the list. Then click OK.

BASIC TROUBLESHOOTING TECHNIQUES

Although troubleshooting any distributed system can be challenging and time-consuming, applying a structured methodology to troubleshooting can help sort through possible causes and reveal the root of most problems.

This section includes troubleshooting procedures for some of the more common problems found in a XenApp Server environment.

Connections

One of the most common problems in the XenApp Server environment that requires troubleshooting involves connectivity. When users cannot connect to the XenApp server, numerous possibilities need to be considered:

▼ **The ICA client is not configured properly.** This is often the problem if only one user cannot connect to the farm. If the user is using Program Neighborhood, check the server location address by selecting the connection, right-clicking, and selecting the Properties option. You can enter the proper server location address in the Address List box by clicking the Add button. Note that if TCP/IP + HTTP is used, the appropriate XML port must be entered when adding the server location. If the Program Neighborhood Agent is being used, make sure the Web Interface URL is correct.

■ **The XenApp Server is not accepting any more connections.** Check to make sure logons have not been disabled by launching the AMC, highlighting the server(s) in question, right-clicking, and selecting Properties. Next, click the Meta Frame Settings option and make sure in the Control Options section that the Enable Logons To This Server check box is selected.

- **The XenApp Server's load level is too high.** If the load level of a server is too high, new sessions will not be directed to the server. Check the load on the server from within the AMC. Highlight the server(s) in question and click the Load Manager Monitor tab. If the server is reporting a full load, check the load evaluators to make sure they are appropriate. This can also be checked by running qfarm/load from a command prompt. A server at maximum load will report the load as 10000.

- **The listeners are down.** Listeners (both ICA and RDP) are the control mechanism by which new sessions are established to a XenApp server. The state of the listeners can be checked from the AMC. Click the server(s) in question and select the Sessions tab. The listeners for both ICA (ICA-tcp) and RDP (RDP-Tcp) will be shown and should be in a listen state. If either is in a down state, new connections cannot be established to the server, and the listener should be reset by right-clicking the listener and selecting Reset. If this does not bring the listener back to a listen state, reboot the XenApp server. Also verify that nothing else is using port 1494. A common way to check connectivity to the XenApp server is to run the following from a command prompt:

```
telnet <insert server name> 1494
```

  For example, telnet us-den-ctx01 1494. The response should be ICAICAICA, which is an ICA banner from the Citrix server. This output will continue until the Telnet session is broken or times out. If this does not appear, there may be a problem with the listeners.

- **Not enough idle sessions are available.** By default, two idle sessions are available for logons. If more than two connections are made before one of the idle sessions frees up, an error is received on the client when trying to connect. Typically, if the user attempts to connect again, they will be able to log on. If errors of this nature occur during peak login times, increase the number of idle sessions by editing the following Registry key: HKLM\System\ CurrentControlSet\ Control\Terminal Server\IdleWinStationPoolCount.

- **Network issues are present.** This could be on the server or client side of the network. The main items to verify include, Are the server's network cards functioning properly? Are routers and switches between the client and server configured correctly? Are firewall settings blocking ICA traffic? Are client network cards configured and functioning properly? As mentioned earlier, one of the best ways to establish connectivity to the XenApp server is to run the following from a command prompt:

```
telnet <insert server name> 1494
```

  The response should be ICAICAICA, which is an ICA banner from the XenApp server. If this does not appear and the ICA listener is up and running, then something is blocking communication from the client to the server.

- ▲ **Core services are not functional.** At a minimum, both the Independent Management Architecture (IMA) and Citrix XML services must be running for a XenApp server to function properly. Check both these service states by selecting Control Panel | Administrative Tools | Services to ensure they are both in a Started state. If their status shows blank, right-click the service and select the Start option. A way to test and see whether the XML port is responding is to run the following from a command prompt:

```
telnet <insert server name> <xml port>
```

For example, telnet us-den-ctx01 8090. The response should be a blank command window.

Shadowing Users

Many end-user problems can be resolved without physically visiting the user by utilizing the shadowing technology included with XenApp Server. Permissions for shadowing are best set up in a Citrix policy and only granted to administrators and managers within the company. Shadowing rights enable the control of a user session to instruct the user on how to perform a certain function, troubleshoot client-side problems, or promote general education about applications, printing, and system orientation.

Shadowing can be initiated in a couple ways. For one, it can be started from within the AMC by right-clicking the user sessions to be shadowed and selecting the Shadow option. Another method is to use the Shadow task bar found on the ICA Administrator toolbar. A popular way to give managers access to shadowing without giving them permissions to the AMC is to publish the Shadow Taskbar program as a published application.

Troubleshooting the SQL Data Store

If you are using a SQL data store, several troubleshooting tips can assist you in discovering and fixing connectivity problems. The following list consolidates the most common problems encountered with the SQL data store and how to correct these issues:

▼ **The wrong credentials are supplied for SQL authentication.** During the configuration of a SQL data store, a user name and password are entered that are used for accessing the data store database. If the user name or password is changed without updating the DSN used to connect to the data store, connectivity problems will be encountered.

■ **The DSN is configured for NT authentication, not SQL authentication.** Ensure that the DSN file is configured for the proper method of authentication by opening the Data Sources (ODBC) from within Control Panel | Administrative Tools.

■ **The network connection between the SQL server and the XenApp Server is down.** Test connectivity by using the Data Sources (ODBC) utility from within Control Panel | Administrative Tools by selecting the DSN and clicking the Configure button.

- **Control the amount of log space needed on the server.** Ensure you have the Truncate Log At Checkpoint option selected or have adequate backups scheduled to ensure that the logs do not grow unnecessarily.

- **Configure the worker threads.** In larger farms (greater than 256 servers), the number of worker threads needs to be increased for proper operation. This can be achieved by using the SQL Server Enterprise Manager, right-clicking the server name, selecting properties, and then clicking the Processor tab and changing the maximum worker thread count from 256 to a number greater than the number of servers in the farm.

Troubleshooting IMA

The IMA service and underlying subsystems are the core of XenApp Server and must be running on all farm servers for proper operation. The following list consolidates the most common problems encountered with the IMA service and how to correct these issues:

- If an error is received after booting a XenApp server that states one of more services failed to start, and one of the nonstarting services is the IMA service, allow the service more time to start, because the initial load on the IMA service will cause delays past the default six-minute timeout of the Service Manager.

- If a direct connection to the data store is being used, verify that ODBC connectivity exists.

- If the local host cache (imalhc.mdb) is missing, corrupt, or provides incorrect information, start by refreshing the LHC and then move on to re-create the LHC. To refresh the LHC, run the following from a command prompt: dsmaint refreshlhc. If this fails, re-create the LHC with the following command: dsmaint recreatelhc.

- Review the event viewer logs for any errors and research the Citrix Knowledge Center (support.citrix.com), or contact your local Citrix reseller to assist in troubleshooting.

If the ODBC Connection Fails

If you're using direct mode connections to the data store, ODBC connectivity is required for proper operation of the IMA service. If ODBC issues are suspected, try the following:

- Verify the name of the DSN file the IMA service is using by looking in the Registry setting HKEY_LOCAL_MACHINE\SOFTWARE\Citrix\IMA\DataSourceName.

- Reinstall the latest compatible version of MDAC to verify that the correct ODBC files are installed.

- Enable ODBC tracing for further troubleshooting.

Other Common Problems

Some of the most common problems revolve around licensing, such as when servers will not accept product licenses. If problems occur with version and edition compatibility with installed licenses, connect to the AMC, right-click the server, and select All Tasks | Set Server Edition. Verify that the appropriate edition is set for each server that corresponds to the license version purchased. Additional problems related to the ability of the XenApp server to acquire a license on behalf of a client require analysis of Windows event logs and of license server logs. Check the current version of the "Citrix Access Suite Licensing Guide" for detailed information.

OPERATIONS SUPPORT

Whether a network includes on-demand access or not, it is critical to have a support methodology and the appropriate systems in place to ensure user issues can be tracked, resolved, and communicated to those necessary in an appropriate amount of time.

The role that IT support plays in providing efficient and effective customer assistance is continually evolving. Whether a company has a service desk, help desk, or call center, this service is key to bringing customer service to a higher level. Through proper staffing, process development, and the use of tools and technology, the IT support organization must handle the day-to-day problems of the user community, administer the environment, and report back to the business the uptime of the network.

IT management should be treated like a business entity even if it is not revenue-generating. Customers—whether internal staff or outside interests—judge the quality of the entire IT organization by the service they provide. Most companies utilize a three-tier approach to supporting their user communities. The first level is the initial point of contact for user problems. At this level, the support staff should have a basic understanding of Citrix administration. They should be able to log and track problems, provide basic problem resolution (reset sessions, create printer mappings, and so on), notify the company of system outages, and be able to escalate to the second level of support.

The second tier of support is mainly concerned with the day-to-day operation of the Citrix environment. At this level, periodic checks of the system are performed, event logs are processed, backup and core services are verified, licensing levels are monitored, advanced problems are resolved, and the installation and rebuilding of servers are performed. Coordination with the first level of support and escalation of irresolvable problems to the third level of support are also performed. The third level of support ensures the Citrix environment meets the business needs of the organization and adheres to the service-level agreements (SLAs) in place for the company. They are concerned with capacity planning, advanced problem resolution, ensuring that service packs/hotfixes are applied to the environment, reviewing business needs, and escalating problems to authorized Citrix resellers when needed.

It is important that both informal and formal customer surveys be performed regularly to gather objective data about each tier of support. Systems, people, and processes can then be changed and new customer data gathered to ensure constant improvement.

APPENDIX A

XenApp on Windows Terminal Services: A Feature Analysis

Centralized Control

Citrix provides administrators with the tools they need to take control of their Application Delivery infrastructure. This results in more control, less downtime, and a better user experience. Centralized Management features provide administrators the tools they need to manage their entire Application Delivery infrastructure from a centralized location while providing the monitoring and control systems that enterprise deployments need. Printer Management is critical for server-side virtualization. In server-side virtualization, users access their applications on a central server but often have local printers attached to their client device. Seamless integration and performance optimizations ensure that they will experience seamless integration between application and printer.

Centralized Management

CATEGORY/ FEATURE	DESCRIPTION	MICROSOFT WINDOWS SERVER 2003	MICROSOFT WINDOWS SERVER 2008	CITRIX PRESENTATION SERVER 4.5 FP1
Centralized Publishing	Allows administrators to deliver server resources – such as applications, content, and server desktops – to thousands of users from a single wizard-driven console.		Single Server only	✓
Delegated Administration	Allows administration tasks and permissions to be assigned across multiple groups within an IT department. This allows organizations to break up and control management tasks among groups like the help desk, level 2 support, and the Terminal Services administration team.			✓
Centralized Access Policies	Administrators can configure settings for user sessions as policies that can be applied to sessions based on username, group, server name, server management container, client IP address or subnet, zone, or client name (or partial name). Priorities can be applied to these policies depending on specific user session situations.			✓
Administrative Logging	Keeps a running log of changes made to system configurations - for audit trail and root cause analysis purposes.			✓
Basic Server Health Monitoring	Monitor the health of server components and report any failures when they happen.		✓	✓
Advanced Server Health Monitoring	Automatically monitor the health of multiple terminal servers and components and report any failures when they happen. If an issue is detected, initiate automatic server recovery actions, such as restarting the server, or preventing it from accepting user sessions until the problem is resolved.			✓ Enterprise / Platinum Editions only
Integration with Desired Configuration Management	A Configuration Pack is available for Microsoft System Center Configuration Manager 2007 that evaluates configurations against predefined security and best practice guidelines specific to Terminal Services environments. This provides administrators with a tool for automated configuration management.			✓ Enterprise / Platinum Editions only
Integration with Operations Manager	A Management Pack is available for Microsoft System Center Operations Manager 2007 that provides integrated monitoring and alerting capabilities specific to Terminal Services environments.	✓	✓	✓ Enterprise / Platinum Editions only
Integration with Multiple 3rd Party Management Systems	Integration with 3rd party management consoles like Microsoft System Center Operations Manager, IBM Tivoli® NetView, Hewlett-Packard® OpenView®, and Computer Associates® UniCenter® TNG allows administrators to leverage existing infrastructure to manage their application delivery infrastructure.			✓ Enterprise / Platinum Editions only
Centralized Resource Monitoring	Enables monitoring and evaluation of server performance. Custom threshold-based alerts and reports can be generated to enhance management and allow administrators to optimize the Terminal Services farm.			✓ Enterprise / Platinum Editions only

CATEGORY/FEATURE	DESCRIPTION	MICROSOFT WINDOWS SERVER 2003	MICROSOFT WINDOWS SERVER 2008	CITRIX PRESENTATION SERVER 4.5 FP1
Centralized Management continued…				
Application Performance Monitoring	Allow IT to identify poorly performing applications, manage system resources to remove bottlenecks, and report on application utilization. THE CITRIX EDGE: Citrix EdgeSight™ provides administrators with visibility into the end user's perception of application performance allowing them to be proactive instead of reactive.			✓ (Platinum Edition only)
Session Recording and Playback	Provide administrators the ability to monitor user sessions for auditing, regulatory compliance, or troubleshooting needs. THE CITRIX EDGE: Citrix SmartAuditor technology provides a built-in record / playback facility unique to the industry.			✓ (Platinum Edition only)
Printer Management				
Client Printer Redirection				
Client Printer Auto-Creation	Automatically create a mapping of client-attached printers into the user's session when connected to a server-side virtualized application.	✓	✓	✓
Client Printer Session Isolation	Ensure that client-attached printers are isolated to the user's session and not available to other users on the same server.		✓	✓
Inheritance of Printer Properties	Rather than just displaying the default printer settings for auto-created client printers, this provides the ability to inherit the existing printer settings. This provides the user with a seamless experience when printing to their local printer.		✓	✓
User Self-Provisioning	Allows the user to define additional printers available to the Terminal Services session and have them be available in the session without requiring the user to logoff and logon to use the printer.			✓
Retention of Printer Properties	Users can configure settings for client-attached printers and have those settings stored on the client device or in their user profile.			✓
Controlled Security Rights for Client Printers	Provide users with access to the printer device settings for their client-attached printers. The default ACL on redirected printers in Terminal Services does not allow the user to adjust device settings because it would also allow the user access to additional settings like driver, port, etc. With custom security filtering the user can be provided access to manage the printer properties without exposing the full rights.			✓
Universal Printing				
XPS-based Universal Printing	Provide client-side printing support where the Microsoft XML Paper Specification (XPS) protocol is available without requiring a printer driver to be installed on the server.		✓ (XP SP3 or Vista SP1 only)	✓
EMF based Universal Printing	Provide client-side printing support through the Enhanced MetaFile (EMF) print format without requiring a printer driver to be installed on the server.			✓
PCL/Postscript Universal Printing	Provide client-side printing support on non-Windows clients (e.g. Macintosh, Linux, etc.)			✓
Printer Provisioning				
Default Printer Provisioning	Restricts the available client-side printers to only the default printer.		✓	✓

CATEGORY/ FEATURE	DESCRIPTION	MICROSOFT WINDOWS SERVER 2003	MICROSOFT WINDOWS SERVER 2008	CITRIX PRESENTATION SERVER 4.5 FP1
Printer Provisioning continued...				
Client Printer Provisioning	Provides administrators with the ability to control client-side printer auto-creation based on policy.			✓
Network Printer Provisioning	Enables users within a specified IP address range to automatically access the network printing devices that exist within that same range. This increases user productivity and lessens the IT support burden.			✓
Generic Universal Print Driver	Reduces printer creation overhead by allowing a single generic printer to be created in the session that can target any client-side printer.			✓
Printer Driver Management				
Automatic Driver Installation	Automatically install in-box printer drivers when they are needed.	✓	✓	✓
Printer Driver Mapping	Allows an administrator to define a mapping of server printer drivers to use for given client printers.	✓ configured via text file	✓ configured via text file	✓
Fallback Printer Driver	Provides a 'printer driver of last resort' ensuring printer availability with basic printing functions when a matching driver does not exist on the server and a 'universal' print driver is not available.	✓ SP1 and above only	Replaced by TS Easy Print	✓
Driver Replication	Allows administrators to automatically or manually replicate installed print drivers across servers.			✓
Driver Compatibility Control	Allows administrators to manage a list of print drivers that can be used on the server for client-side printers. By supporting both inclusion and exclusion lists administrators have the ability to only allow known 'safe' drivers or to block known 'unsafe' drivers.			✓
Printing Bandwidth and Network Management				
Printer Bandwidth Limit	Control how much network bandwidth print jobs can consume within the ICA channel.			✓
Enhanced Print Stream Compression	Out-of-band pre-compression of print data using large, dedicated compression history buffers provides significant improvements in levels of compression achieved for print data.			✓
Print Traffic Routing	Allows administrators to choose between the traditional network printing path or the ICA printing path when using client printer auto-creation for provisioning of printers. In cases where the client can connect to a network print server for their local printer this can offer significant reduction in bandwidth and overall time required to print. Policies provide administrators the control necessary to ensure this is only applied in situations where it makes sense.			✓

Application Compatibility

Citrix addresses the needs of today's heterogeneous IT environments with technologies that ensure applications can work together in a secure manner on a variety of OS platforms. Flexible Application Delivery means working with a variety of server platforms easily integrating application delivery from anywhere in the data center. Application Virtualization is about allowing the IT administrator to control where and how applications are deployed to provide the best access experience for the end user.

CATEGORY/ FEATURE	DESCRIPTION	MICROSOFT WINDOWS SERVER 2003	MICROSOFT WINDOWS SERVER 2008	CITRIX PRESENTATION SERVER 4.5 FP1
Flexible Application Delivery				
Comprehensive Server Farm Support	Multiple servers can be grouped together as a logical unit even when they are not running the same application delivery or OS platform. Applications can be configured to be delivered from all servers in the farm or any subset easily from the application publishing properties allowing for simple configuration of load balancing across the available platforms.			✓
Unified Application Delivery	Applications can be delivered from multiple server platforms (Windows Server, HP-UX, IBM AIX, or Solaris) in a single view to the end user.			✓
Application Virtualization				
Virtual IP Address Support	Applications that require a unique IP address for each application instance may not work properly in a Terminal Services environment. Virtual IP address support allows an administrator to define a range of IP addresses so that each user session can have a unique IP address. This is especially useful for customer service applications that integrate into VoIP telephony systems. It is also useful when using third-party tools to monitor internet traffic from Terminal Server users.			✓
Server-Side Application Virtualization	Streams applications into an isolated environment running on the server to ensure compatibility between applications. This minimizes or eliminates regression testing for applications and eliminates the need to create server silo's to address application compatibility issues. It is especially useful for applications that require a network connection or for applications that provide access to critical or proprietary business information (e.g. CRM or ERP apps). Server-side application virtualization prevents business data from ever leaving the data center.	Requires Microsoft Application Virtualization for Terminal Services CAL (MAV for TS CAL)	Requires Microsoft Application Virtualization for Terminal Services CAL (MAV for TS CAL)	✓
Client-Side Application Virtualization	Streams applications into an isolated environment running on the user's machine to eliminate potential conflicts between applications. This offloads the resources required to run applications from the server to the user's machine. It is especially useful in Windows environments for applications that can be or must be used while disconnected from the network (e.g. synchronized e-mail, Microsoft Office Suite, etc.)	Available separately with Microsoft Desktop Optimization Pack (MDOP)	Available separately with Microsoft Desktop Optimization Pack (MDOP)	✓ Enterprise / Platinum Editions only
64-bit Platform Support	Allows administrators to deploy application virtualization technology to the latest 64-bit OS platforms for both client-side and server-side virtualization scenarios.	Available separately with MDOP or MAV for TS CAL	Available separately with MDOP or MAV for TS CAL	✓ Enterprise / Platinum Editions only
Support for Complex Application Virtualization Needs	Some applications require access to system components that make them more difficult to stream. Support for the isolation of services, COM+, DCOM access, and printer drivers allow more complex applications (or portions of applications) to be streamed without the need for complex profiling customizations.			

Optimized User Experience

Citrix enhances the usability and performance of applications running on Terminal Services. Simplified Access is about providing the same user experience for applications delivered from Terminal Services as local applications. An Optimized Experience results from a set of technologies that provide significant productivity and performance enhancements for server-based applications. This results in higher user satisfaction and eased support requirements for IT. Web Based Delivery options provide administrators with flexibility in how they provide users with access to their applications, allowing them to easily gain access over the Internet or from existing web portal deployments.

Simplified Access

Local Desktop Integration

CATEGORY/ FEATURE	DESCRIPTION	MICROSOFT WINDOWS SERVER 2003	MICROSOFT WINDOWS SERVER 2008	CITRIX PRESENTATION SERVER 4.5 FP1
Support for High Color	Enables applications running on Terminal Services to display in 24 or 32-bit color depth.	✓ 24-bit	✓ 32-bit	✓ 24-bit
Seamless Applications	Enables applications running on Terminal Services to look and feel as if they are running locally.	✓	✓	✓
Connection Resiliency	Automatically reconnects user sessions when the network connection is temporarily lost.	✓	✓	✓
Session Reconnect	Allows users to reconnect to their Terminal Services sessions without going through the time-consuming logon process again.	✓	✓	✓
Support for Multiple Monitors	Allows applications running on Terminal Services to be displayed across multiple local monitors connected to the client workstation forming a single virtual display.	✓ Requires RDC 6.x on Windows XP / Vista	✓ Requires RDC 6.x on Windows XP / Vista	✓
Audio Playback	Supports audio playback on the client device for audio streams from the server session.	✓	✓	✓
Bi-Directional Audio Support	Supports audio recording and playback on a client desktop, including use of Philips SpeechMike™ transcription devices. Bidirectional audio is a common requirement in medical and legal firms, and provides a foundation to support VoIP soft phones in the future.			✓
Pass-Through Authentication	For Windows clients connected to the company directory, the credentials used for local device logon are passed automatically to sessions running on Terminal Services. This simplifies and speeds up the user's connection process.		Domain-joined Vista clients only	
Extended Support for Multiple Monitors	Provide features that mimic the behavior of applications running locally in a multi-monitor environment including the following key features: ✓ Tested and supported with up to 9 monitors utilizing high resolution displays (up to 64 MB display memory) ✓ Dynamic display configuration – any time the client display environment changes the settings are reconfigured dynamically. ✓ Ensures applications respect multi-monitor boundaries (applications maximize to a single monitor, dialogs center properly, menus and tooltips are positioned so they do not span monitor boundaries, etc.) Multi-monitor support is a common requirement in financial services environments where the typical desktop will have at least 4 high-resolution monitors on the client and often more.			✓

CATEGORY/ FEATURE	DESCRIPTION	MICROSOFT WINDOWS SERVER 2003	MICROSOFT WINDOWS SERVER 2008	CITRIX PRESENTATION SERVER 4.5 FP1
Local Desktop Integration continued...				
Basic Roaming User Support	Allows a user to roam between devices and networks while maintaining the state of their server-based applications. User will be automatically connected to their applications with the display automatically re-configured when the user re-connects.	✓	✓	✓
Advanced Roaming User Support	Simplified controls automatically re-connect to all of the user's applications, even when they are physically running on multiple servers. The user does not need to manually launch each application that is disconnected. THE CITRIX EDGE: Citrix has long been a leader in the industry with the introduction of technologies like SmoothRoaming™, Workspace Control, and Session Reliability providing a natural user experience for roaming users.			✓
Desktop Icon Integration	Allows applications to appear in the start menu or on the local desktop providing a familiar application access experience for users.		Requires distribution of .msi packages	✓
Folder Management	Allows applications to be grouped within folders for easier organization for multiple user groups.		Requires distribution of .msi packages	✓
Client-to-server redirection of file types	Redirects requests for a specific document or file type to a Terminal Server session. For example, clicking on a Visio® document on the client device will launch the document in a Visio application on the Terminal Sever, instead of a local application. This is a useful feature in environments where a particular application may not be installed locally.		✓	✓
Server-to-client URL redirection	When clicking on URL's (such as HTTP or HTTPS links) within an application running on Terminal Services, the link is opened with the local client browser instead of launching the browser on the Terminal Server. This feature enhances support for mixed desktop/Terminal Services environments, and ensures that the local browser and Internet connection is used for web browsing. This can reduce the data center bandwidth requirements, free processing resources on Terminal Services, and improve performance for users. In addition, for environments that track internet usage by IP address, this features preserves the ability to do so using third-party monitoring products.			✓
Client Device Support				
USB Printer Support	Enables users to remotely print to USB printers connected to their client device		✓	✓
USB Storage Device Support	Enables remote access to most USB storage devices connected to their client device		✓	✓
POS for .NET Device Support	Enables support for Microsoft Point of Service for .NET devices.		✓	
Microsoft ActiveSync® Support	Supports the synchronization of client devices via ActiveSync where the software is running in Terminal Services.			✓
Scanner Support	Allows applications running on the server to access TWAIN-compliant scanners connected to the client device.			✓

Optimized Experience

Productivity Enhancements

CATEGORY/ FEATURE	DESCRIPTION	MICROSOFT WINDOWS SERVER 2003	MICROSOFT WINDOWS SERVER 2008	CITRIX PRESENTATION SERVER 4.5 FP1
Small Form-Factor Device Support	Many applications in today's market are not designed to support the screen resolution available on mobile devices. Using scrolling and magnification techniques on the device enables the user to use these applications in their native form without the need for customized applications that support the small form-factor. THE CITRIX EDGE: Citrix Panning (scrolling) and Scaling (magnification) technology provides an improved user experience when viewing full-screen Windows applications on small form-factor devices.			✓
Self-Service Password Reset	Allows users to securely and safely reset their domain password or unlock their Windows account from their PC or web browser, thus reducing help desk costs for password resets.			✓ Platinum Edition only
Enterprise Single Sign-On	Requires users to logon only once with their network credentials and automates subsequent logons to applications accessed through a Web browser, Windows client, or host terminal emulator. Specifies strong password characteristics such as length, character repetition and alphanumeric requirements on a per-application basis – applies to manual and automated password changes.			✓ Platinum Edition only
Click-To-Call	Enables users to initiate a phone call by clicking on a phone number in any application (whether delivered from the server, delivered to the client, or installed locally).			✓ Platinum Edition only

Performance Enhancements

CATEGORY/ FEATURE	DESCRIPTION	MICROSOFT WINDOWS SERVER 2003	MICROSOFT WINDOWS SERVER 2008	CITRIX PRESENTATION SERVER 4.5 FP1
Session Sharing	When a user requests a second application on Terminal Services, the application is launched in the existing user session. This allows the application to start up almost instantly (as opposed to creating a new session) and reduces memory and CPU consumption on the server.		✓	✓
Display Data Prioritization	Offers enhanced application responsiveness with built-in quality of service for graphics applications by controlling how much bandwidth is used for display data as opposed to any other data (e.g. printing, file transfers, etc.)		✓	✓
High Resolution Graphics Enhancements	Improves the delivery of remote applications that contain photographic bitmaps and highly detailed synthetic images. If a bitmap looks as if it is probably photographic or highly detailed, an extra level of lossy JPEG compression is added to reduce the bandwidth required to transmit the image to the client. THE CITRIX EDGE: Citrix SpeedScreen Image Acceleration is a key technology in providing a rich user experience regardless of the underlying connection.			✓
Multimedia Application Support	Provides synchronized audio-video delivery for applications like Windows Media Player (common with computer-based training applications.) THE CITRIX EDGE: Citrix SpeedScreen Multimedia Acceleration intercepts the request for a media file on the server, and streams the media to the client where it can be rendered using local resources.			✓
High-Latency Network Support	Optimizes performance of remote applications presented over high-latency network links (i.e. satellite). These applications may not provide adequate performance with Terminal Services alone. THE CITRIX EDGE: Citrix SpeedScreen Latency Reduction technology provides a far more usable experience for the end user in these scenarios.			✓

Performance Enhancements continued...

CATEGORY/ FEATURE	DESCRIPTION	MICROSOFT WINDOWS SERVER 2003	MICROSOFT WINDOWS SERVER 2008	CITRIX PRESENTATION SERVER 4.5 FP1
Web Browser Performance Optimizations	Provide enhanced performance and usability for Internet Explorer-based web applications when running on Terminal Services. THE CITRIX EDGE: Citrix SpeedScreen Browser Acceleration provides a combination of features that can automatically disable GIF animations, intercept images and pass them on before being uncompressed, dynamically re-compress JPEG images, deliver images in the background, and cache images on the client.			✓
Adobe® Flash® Performance Optimizations	Provide improved performance of web pages containing Flash-based content by improving the compression of the Flash content. THE CITRIX EDGE: Citrix SpeedScreen Flash Acceleration is specifically designed to optimize Flash content in web pages to improve the overall experience for users accessing web sites and applications remotely.			✓
WAN Performance Optimizations	Users can experience significantly improved WAN performance through the automatic application of the right mix of acceleration techniques based on network conditions, data flows, and application mix. These gains can be achieved without requiring any reconfiguration or modification of firewalls, monitoring tools, or applications.			✓
Session Reliability	When a network connection issue occurs, the application window remains visible on the client device and the client continues to accept keystrokes and mouse movement from the user while session re-connection is attempted in the background. For transient network issues, such as where users roam between wireless "hot spots", the user may not even know connectivity was lost.			✓
Graphics Display Optimizations	Dramatically improves the performance and usability of graphics-intensive applications. Enables IT to centrally manage graphics-intensive applications such as PACS (used in Healthcare) and GIS mapping applications, while providing the speed and anywhere-access flexibility that users need. THE CITRIX EDGE: A Tolly Group study showed that Citrix SpeedScreen™ Progressive Display technology can provide up to 15x bandwidth reduction for two-dimensional graphical applications like PACS and GIS systems.			✓

Web-Based Delivery

User Experience

CATEGORY/ FEATURE	DESCRIPTION	MICROSOFT WINDOWS SERVER 2003	MICROSOFT WINDOWS SERVER 2008	CITRIX PRESENTATION SERVER 4.5 FP1
Web Availability	Integrated support for publishing applications to a web portal allows applications to be accessed from any web browser.		✓	✓
Multilingual User Interface	Dynamically changes the locale of the web application portal depending on the user or administrator's preferences.		✓	✓
Broad Client Platform Support	The client view of Web Interface uses standard HTML and is supported on most modern web browsers including IE 6+, Mozilla 1+, Firefox 2+, and Safari 2+ as well as some mobile platforms.			✓
Automated Client Installation	A web-based process walks the user through the process of automatically detecting the needed client software and then automatically installs the appropriate client software for the platform used.			✓
Persistent Bookmarks	Provide users the ability to create persistent browser bookmarks directly to their favorite applications. When using pass-through authentication the user can access their application without the need for additional authentication.			✓

CATEGORY/ FEATURE	DESCRIPTION	MICROSOFT WINDOWS SERVER 2003	MICROSOFT WINDOWS SERVER 2008	CITRIX PRESENTATION SERVER 4.5 FP1
User Experience continued…				
Folder Management	When applications are configured within folders the web interface maintains this grouping enabling easier organization for multiple user groups.			✓
Automatic Reconnection	Automatically re-connects to all disconnected sessions at logon. This provides an automated means of reconnecting to all disconnected applications without user interaction. This functionality works regardless of how many server sessions the user has established. Administrators and users can turn this feature off and also use manual reconnection which still provides a single-click interface for this functionality.			✓
Disconnect or Close All Applications	A single button on the web interface provides a means for the user to suspend or exit all running applications without having to perform this action in each individual application. This functionality works regardless of how many server sessions the user has established. This is especially useful for situations where the user wants to switch devices such as when leaving the office to go home.			✓
User Controlled Network Optimizations	Users can specify their network connection speed and type for application access, thereby providing application performance optimizations based on the user's connection type.			✓
Self-Service Password Change	Provides users notification when their password is about to expire and allows users to change their domain password directly from their browser. This feature is important for remote access scenarios and other situations where user devices do not authenticate to the directory.			✓
Administration and Management				
Custom Branding Support	Provides the ability to easily customize the look and feel of the web application portal through GUI-based wizards in the management tools.			✓
Broad Server Platform Support	Support for IIS, Apache, IBM WebSphere®, BEA WebLogic®, and Sun Java System Application Server provides administrators with the option of hosting the server component on the infrastructure that they already have and are familiar with.			✓
Third-Party Integration				
Basic SharePoint Integration	Provides a web part to integrate Terminal Services application functionality directly within a SharePoint portal.		✓	✓
SharePoint Document Library Integration	Extends Microsoft SharePoint document libraries to include integrated support for accessing the documents in those libraries via an application hosted on Terminal Services. This allows users to view and edit documents in a SharePoint document library even when they do not have the necessary applications installed locally.			✓
IBM WebSphere® Integration	Provides the ability to integrate Terminal Services application functionality natively in an IBM WebSphere portal.			✓
Integration with Multiple Enterprise Information Portals	A reference implementation of a JSR168 portlet provides access to Terminal Services application functionality natively in a BEA WebLogic® Portal. This reference implementation could be used on any system supporting the JSR168 portlet standard.			✓

Comprehensive Access

Security technologies extend the core Terminal Services platform with broader integration and more flexible access scenarios. Policy Management provides the control IT administrators need to ensure that technologies are not abused by users, but rather allow the 'right' level of access. Universal Device Access ensures that users will be able to use their applications regardless of what device they want to use, allowing IT administrators to provide broad access while remaining in control.

Security

CATEGORY/ FEATURE	DESCRIPTION	MICROSOFT WINDOWS SERVER 2003	MICROSOFT WINDOWS SERVER 2008	CITRIX PRESENTATION SERVER 4.5 FP1
Support for Windows Directory Services	Allows role-based access to be provided using either Windows NT domains or Active Directory®.	✓	✓	✓
Support for Novell® eDirectory™	Allows role-based access to be provided using Novell eDirectory (formerly known as Novell Directory Services®).			✓
Secure Access to Server Applications	Provides SSL/TLS encryption and multifactor authentication to provide authorized application access to appropriate users.		✓	✓
Support for Network Access Quarantine Control	Examines and validates the configuration of a remote access computer through an administrator-provided script.	✓	Replaced by NAP	✓
Support for Network Access Protection (NAP)	Allows network administrators to define network access based on who a client is, the groups to which it belongs and the degree of compliance with corporate policy.		✓	
Adaptive User Access	Dynamically determine the access policy through evaluation of multiple factors such as the user role, location, client device information, and client integrity allowing administrators to provide varying degrees of access instead of simply denying access. THE CITRIX EDGE: Citrix SmartAccess technology provides administrators with granular access control of the specific actions that users can take with applications, files, web content, e-mail attachments, and printing. With SmartAccess, access becomes like a dimmer switch, where access is restricted based on the access scenario.			✓ Platinum Edition only
Active Directory Federation Services Support	Supports authentication using credentials from a federated Active Directory forest, thereby increasing the security of applications used by business partners.			✓
Anonymous Access	Provides the ability to grant access to Terminal Services applications without requiring explicit authentication from the user. This can be implemented simply by IT administration and enables support for additional authentication schemes like third party LDAP directories.			✓
Double-Hop DMZ traversal	Provide access to corporate resources from anywhere over SSL. Double-Hop allows the use of SSL end-to-end from the client, through the DMZ, and into the internal corporate network.		Requires ISA Server	✓
Secure Access to All Applications / Protocols	Citrix Access Gateway is a universal SSL VPN appliance that provides a secure, always-on, single point of access to all applications, network resources, and protocols.			✓ Platinum Edition only

CATEGORY/ FEATURE	DESCRIPTION	MICROSOFT WINDOWS SERVER 2003	MICROSOFT WINDOWS SERVER 2008	CITRIX PRESENTATION SERVER 4.5 FP1
Policy Management				
Policy-Based Control of Client Devices	Administrators can enhance security and intellectual property containment by controlling users' ability to connect client devices like printers and local drives.		✓	✓
Policy-Based Control of Bandwidth Usage	Administrators can configure overall session bandwidth limits and also specific limits for audio usage, printing, client storage devices, TWAIN devices, clipboard usage, COM/LPT ports, and OEM virtual channels.			✓
Policy-Based Control of Audio	Administrators can configure policy to manage client audio support, sound quality, and support for client-based microphones for recording audio.			✓
Policy-Based Control of TWAIN Device Support	Administrators can configure policy to control TWAIN device redirection including compression levels.			✓
Policy-Based Control of Application Delivery	Administrators can configure policy to control how applications are delivered – controlling whether the application is virtualized client-side, virtualized server-side, or installed on the server.			✓
Application Launch Limits	Allows administrators to control user access to applications by setting time and instance limits.			✓
Universal Device Access				
Broad client support	Integrated support for client platforms: ✓ **Windows x86 Platforms** Vista, Windows XP, Windows 2003, Windows 2000 ✓ **Windows x64 Platforms** Vista, Windows XP, Windows 2003 ✓ **Macintosh Platforms** OS X, PowerPC, 68030/40 ✓ **Windows Mobile Platforms** Windows Mobile 6, Windows Mobile 5, Windows Mobile 2003, PocketPC, Handheld PC, Windows CE ✓ **Java Platform** J2SE 1.4.x, J2SE 1.5.x ✓ **EPOC / Symbian OS** Series 60 3rd Edition, Series 80, FOMA M1000 ✓ **Unix Platforms** Solaris/Sparc, Solaris x86, IBM AIX, HP-UX, Linux, SGI ✓ **Other Platforms** DOS version 4+, Windows 16-bit platforms, IBM OS/2 Warp	Microsoft Windows® Macintosh OS X (Limited to Remote Desktop only)	Microsoft Windows® Macintosh OS X (Limited to Remote Desktop only)	✓

Enterprise Scalability

Citrix enhances Terminal Services with a set of mature and easy-to-use management and monitoring tools. Simplified Configuration allows administrators to be more productive while industry-leading Performance technologies ensure the best user experience. This increases IT and user productivity while providing additional capabilities not available in the base-level Terminal Services environment.

CATEGORY/FEATURE	DESCRIPTION	MICROSOFT WINDOWS SERVER 2003	MICROSOFT WINDOWS SERVER 2008	CITRIX PRESENTATION SERVER 4.5 FP1
Simplified Configuration				
Comprehensive Server Configuration	The ability to perform actions on a group of servers from a single management point provides administrators the ability to centrally configure application access to a subset of their servers.			✓
Zone Preference and Failover	Establishes user sessions based on their proximity to and availability of a particular server. This feature enables higher performance in farms that span multiple data centers and eases disaster recovery and business continuity.			✓
Broad Database Engine Support	Integrates with existing corporate standards for IT infrastructure by supporting multiple options for the system database (i.e. Microsoft SQL Server, IBM® DB2®, and Oracle®.)			✓
Application Scheduling	Provides the ability to control delivery of applications to users based on time of day and number of sessions or application instances.			✓
Performance				
Enterprise Class Scalability	Supports large server farms that can span wide area networks while maintaining performance and reliability. Proven large deployment support with over 1000 servers.			✓
Enterprise Class Performance	Enterprises employ a large variety of devices, printers, and networks and when deploying Terminal Services for application delivery the end user experience is critical to success. What is necessary is a combination of performance optimizations and bandwidth reduction techniques that have been vetted in large deployments over many years.			✓
Priority Packet Tagging	Enables the prioritization of virtual channel traffic by third-party Quality-of-Service (QoS) network infrastructure providers.			✓
Comprehensive Load Management	Establishes user sessions across a group of load-managed servers based on configurable parameters like session count, application usage, CPU utilization, memory consumption, concurrent logons, IP ranges, time intervals, and more.		Session count only	✓
CPU Utilization Management	In a shared, multi-user Terminal Services environment, one user's activities can adversely affect performance for other users. CPU management ensures that CPU-intensive processes initiated by one user do not degrade performance of other sessions. As a result, additional Terminal Servers do not need to be maintained to assure good user performance.	✓ Enterprise Edition only	✓ with WSRM	✓ Enterprise / Platinum Editions only
Virtual Memory Optimizations	Performs DLL rebasing for applications in order to reduce the amount of memory conflicts when loading DLLs, resulting in a reduction in overall memory requirements for some applications. This enables a single server to support more concurrent users. This results in a reduction of overall server count within a Terminal Services environment.			✓ Enterprise / Platinum Editions only

APPENDIX B

XenApp Comparative Feature Matrix

Application Delivery

FEATURE	DESCRIPTION	EDITION	CITRIX PRESENTATION SERVER™ 4.5	CITRIX PRESENTATION SERVER™ 4.0	CITRIX METAFRAME® PRESENTATION SERVER 3.0™	CITRIX METAFRAME® XP	CITRIX METAFRAME® 1.8
Server-side Application Virtualization	Consolidates applications and data in the datacenter and delivers virtualized applications to users—only screen displays, keyboard entry and mouse movements traverse the network. Provides IT with maximum control, and enables rapid delivery of applications to any location, any device over any network.	P/E/A/S	✓	✓	✓	✓	✓
Client-side Application Virtualization	Centralizes management of desktop applications, and isolates and streams them to users without application and system conflicts. With server-side and client-side application virtualization, Presentation Server can dynamically select the best application delivery method for the user, the application, the device or the network. Stream applications to mobile users who work offline, and for maximum control and security, virtualize applications that access confidential data.	P/E	✓				
Application Hub	Centrally stores isolated applications that you want to deliver to users through either server-side or client-side application virtualization. Rapidly provisions applications and updates to Presentation Server farms without disrupting users or causing application or system conflicts. This feature greatly simplifies delivery and maintenance of applications across any size Presentation Server farm.	P/E	✓				

Editions – Platinum (P); Enterprise (E); Advanced (A); Standard(S). Standard Edition is only available in version 4.0 and earlier.

1

Advanced Application Compatibility

FEATURE	DESCRIPTION	EDITION	CITRIX PRESENTATION SERVER™ 4.5	CITRIX PRESENTATION SERVER™ 4.0	CITRIX METAFRAME® PRESENTATION SERVER 3.0™	CITRIX® METAFRAME® XP	CITRIX® METAFRAME® 1.8
Isolation 2.0	The next generation of isolation technology accelerates performance of isolated applications and expands application compatibility. Isolation 2.0 is leveraged in Application Isolation Environments, Client-side Application Virtualization and the Application Hub.	P/E	✓				
Application Isolation Environment	Provides an isolated environment that contains all the files, registry settings, and named objects for an application, allowing applications that are incompatible with each other to safely run side by side. Also — allows applications that are not compatible to run in a multi-user environment to run on Citrix Presentation Server.	P/E	✓	✓			
Virtual IP Support	Using virtual IP addresses, an administrator can publish applications that require separate IP addresses per session whether for technical or licensing reasons. With virtual IP addresses, you can set aside a block of IP addresses for use by sessions that require them.	P/E/A	✓	✓			
Support for local TWAIN devices	Redirects client-connected TWAIN imaging devices (like document scanners) from the client to the server, regardless of connection type. This allows users to control client-attached imaging devices from applications that run on the server; the redirection is transparent.	P/E/A	✓	✓			
Support for ActiveSync	Allows the synchronization of a client-connected USB PDA device using application software running on the server rather than on the client device. This feature supports USB-tethered and Microsoft Windows powered PDAs that use ActiveSync as a synchronization agent.	P/E/A	✓	✓			
Bidirectional Audio	Bidirectional audio allows the use of client-side audio peripherals such as microphones and dictation hardware.	P/E/A	✓	✓	✓		
Support for UNIX Applications	Presentation Server 4.0 for UNIX ships with Presentation Server 4.5.	P/E	✓				

Editions – Platinum (P); Enterprise (E); Advanced (A); Standard(S). Standard Edition is only available in version 4.0 and earlier.

End-User Experience

FEATURE	DESCRIPTION	EDITION	CITRIX PRESENTATION SERVER 4.5	CITRIX PRESENTATION SERVER 4.0	CITRIX METAFRAME PRESENTATION SERVER 3.0	CITRIX METAFRAME XP	CITRIX METAFRAME 1.8
EasyCall	Powered by Citrix Communication Gateway™, it enables communications within any application running on the PC or on the server — allowing users to 'Click-to-Call' on any telephone number, saving time and money and increasing productivity.	P	✓				
SpeedScreen™ Progressive Display	Dramatically improves the performance and usability of graphics-intensive applications. Centrally manage applications such as healthcare PACS (picture archiving and communication systems) and GIS mapping application, while providing speed and anywhere-access for users.	P/E/A	✓				
SpeedScreen Latency Reduction Manager	Provides mouse click feedback and local text echo, both of which reduce a user's perception of latency when typing and clicking.	P/E/A/S	✓	✓	✓	✓	✓
SpeedScreen Browser Acceleration	Optimizes the responsiveness of graphics-rich HTML pages in published versions of Microsoft Outlook, Outlook Express, and Internet Explorer.	P/E/A/S	✓	✓	✓	✓	
SpeedScreen Multimedia Acceleration	Allows you to control and optimize the way Presentation Server passes streaming audio and video to users.	P/E/A	✓	✓	✓		
SpeedScreen Flash Acceleration	Allows you to control and optimize the way Presentation Server passes Macromedia Flash animations to users.	P/E/A	✓	✓	✓		
SpeedScreen Image Acceleration	Offers you a trade-off between the quality of photographic image files as they appear on client devices and the amount of bandwidth the files consume on their way from the server to the client.	P/E/A/S	✓	✓	✓	✓	✓
Compression	Intelligently compresses data sent across the network for the best possible performance.	P/F/A/S	✓	✓	✓	✓	✓
Priority Packet Tagging	Enables the prioritization of ICA® virtual channel traffic by third-party network infrastructure providers.	P/E/A/S	✓	✓	✓	✓	
Dynamic Session Resizing	Connect to any client with any color depth or resolution and the session will be resized accordingly. Also works when using Tablet PCs when re-orienting the screen.	P/E/A/S	✓	✓	✓		
Workspace Control	Allows users to switch between devices and reconnect to an active or disconnected session on another client device without having to restart applications. The session is automatically transferred from one location and device to the other once the user logs in.	P/E/A	✓	✓	✓		
Session Reliability	Allows work items to remain open when network connectivity is lost, and then seamlessly resumed when connectivity is restored.	P/E/A	✓	✓	✓		
Auto Client Reconnect	In the event that a user connection gets temporarily disconnected, the ICA client will automatically attempt to reconnect to its disconnected, yet still active session.	P/E/A/S	✓	✓	✓	✓	

Editions – Platinum (P); Enterprise (E); Advanced (A); Standard(S). Standard Edition is only available in version 4.0 and earlier.

End-User Experience (Continued)

FEATURE	DESCRIPTION	EDITION	CITRIX PRESENTATION SERVER 4.5	CITRIX PRESENTATION SERVER 4.0	CITRIX METAFRAME PRESENTATION SERVER 3.0	CITRIX METAFRAME XP	CITRIX METAFRAME 1.8
Always-on SSL VPN access	Automatically reconnects sessions after losing a connection or roaming between networks	P	✓				
Application Publishing	Shows end-users which applications are available for use, whether delivered by server-side or client-side application virtualization. User's access published applications through the Web Interface or Program Neighborhood Agent.	P/E/A/S	✓	✓	✓	✓	✓
Content Publishing	Extends the application publishing model to accommodate internal and external content (both documents and web sites) making end user access to information even more seamless.	P/E/A/S	✓	✓	✓	✓	
Content Redirection	Allows administrators to specify whether local or server applications are used to open content, no matter where it is stored. This provides users with tighter integration between local and server-based applications further reducing the need for additional training.	P/E/A/S	✓	✓	✓	✓	
Seamless Windows	Integrates local and remote applications into the local Windows desktop. Users can choose between the local and remote applications on the task bar without having to know anything about the location of those applications.	P/E/A/S	✓	✓	✓	✓	✓
Desktop Integration via Program Neighborhood Agent	Access to published content can be tightly integrated into the end user's Window's desktop Neighborhood Agent so that remote resources are available from the Start menu and leverage the system tray just as local applications do.	P/E/A/S	✓	✓	✓	✓	
Conferencing Manager	Provides online conferencing/sharing of virtualized applications and information.	P/E/A/S	✓	✓			
Pass-Through Authentication	Provides the ability to pass the user's desktop password to the server. This reduces the need for multiple system and application authentication.	P/E/A/S	✓	✓	✓	✓	✓
Microsoft Client Support	Supports all versions of Windows including Win32, WinCE, Pocket PC and Win16.	P/F/A/S	✓	✓	✓	✓	✓
Web Interface for Citrix Presentation Server	Provides secure access over the Internet to published applications and content based on user permissions.	P/E/A/S	✓	✓	✓	✓	
Multi-Lingual User Interface Support for virtualized applications	Provides one client package for all languages and allows user to specify language preference.	P/F/A	✓				
Multi Language Supporting in Web Interface	Language packs are provided to localize the Web Interface into the following languages: English, German, Spanish, French, and Japanese.	P/E/A/S	✓	✓	✓	✓	
Multi-Monitor Support	Allows for spanning of the display across multiple monitors.	P/E/A/S	✓	✓	✓		

Editions – Platinum (P); Enterprise (E); Advanced (A); Standard(S). Standard Edition is only available in version 4.0 and earlier.

FEATURE	DESCRIPTION	EDITION	CITRIX PRESENTATION SERVER™ 4.5	CITRIX PRESENTATION SERVER™ 4.0	CITRIX METAFRAME® PRESENTATION SERVER 3.0™	CITRIX METAFRAME® XP	CITRIX METAFRAME® 1.8
End-User Experience (Continued)							
Local Resource Mapping	Provides ability to redirect most local resources into the session, including clipboard, audio, drives, printers, COM Ports.	P/E/A/S	✓	✓	✓	✓	✓
Local Drive Access	Presentation Server supports local drive access on a variety of platforms (including all versions of Windows, Mac and UNIX) as well as server drive remapping to provide client drives using their native drive letters.	P/E/A/S	✓	✓	✓	✓	✓
Local Printer Access	Provides local printer access on a variety of platforms including native drivers and Universal Printing.	P/E/A/S	✓	✓	✓	✓	✓
Printing							
Universal Printer Driver 3	Enhances all previous versions and enables files to print up to four times faster while using less bandwidth and memory. Users can use advanced printer functions like stapling and trays. Proximity Printing ensures that users will be able to print to their closest printer without having to know the configuration of that printer.	P/E/A/S	✓	✓			
Universal Printer Driver 2	Provides a single print driver for color and high resolution printing.	P/E/A/S	✓		✓	✓	
Universal Printer Driver	Enables consolidation print driver requirements into one universal print driver. Reduces bandwidth requirements for many non-PCL and non-PostScript desktop printers.	P/E/A/S	✓			✓	
Management							
Application Performance Monitoring	Powered by Citrix EdgeSight software, the new monitoring capabilities in Presentation Server enable IT to quickly pinpoint and troubleshoot server, network and application programming issues that impact the user experience.	P	✓				
Health Assistant	Strengthens system resiliency by performing continuous server health checks and automatically initiating recovery procedures, minimizing the need for administrator intervention.	P/E	✓				
Configuration Logging	Tracks changes made to the Presentation Server farm, by whom and at what time to simplify and accelerate troubleshooting. Invaluable for auditing and ensuring accountability when multiple administrators are maintaining Presentation Server.	P/E/A	✓				

Editions – Platinum (P); Enterprise (E); Advanced (A); Standard(S). Standard Edition is only available in version 4.0 and earlier.

Management (Continued)

FEATURE	DESCRIPTION	EDITION	CITRIX PRESENTATION SERVER™ 4.5	CITRIX PRESENTATION SERVER™ 4.0	CITRIX METAFRAME® PRESENTATION SERVER 3.0™	CITRIX METAFRAME® XP	CITRIX METAFRAME® 1.8
Active Directory Federation Services(ADFS) support	Makes it easier to extend application access to trusted partners. No longer is ADFS limited to Web applications–now you can provide federated access to any Windows application delivered by Presentation Server.	P/E/A	✓				
Client Backup URL	Specifies a secondary Web Interface URL and automatically redirects traffic in the event of a primary URL disruption.	P/E/A	✓				
Connection Policies	Provides a comprehensive policy subsystem that allows administrators to control access to Presentation Server resources with policies based on the user, user group, server groups, IP addresses and client names. This enables greater control over bandwidth limits, audio options and printing — helping to ensure that users get consistently good performance.	P/E/A/S	✓	✓	✓		
System Monitoring and Reporting via Resource Manager for Citrix Presentation Server	Administrators can efficiently manage and monitor system resources and generate reports on application and server availability, configuration, performance, capacity and maintenance. Can also be used to generate billing reports for departments using the infrastructure.	P/E	✓	✓	✓	✓	✓
Enhanced Management Experience	Leverages a new comprehensive management interface that enables complete, single-point management of the entire Presentation Server farm including servers, applications, licenses, printers and users from any location. Multiple Citrix products can also be included and managed from a central location.	P/E/A/S	✓	✓	✓		
Extended Shadowing Support	Provides support for a shadowing task bar, a shadowing indicator, one-to-many and many to one shadowing, cross server shadowing and provides support for logging of shadowed sessions.	P/E/A/S	✓	✓	✓	✓	✓
Automatic Client Updates	Ensures that users have the latest version when they connect to the server — saving IT from updating each desktop manually.	P/E/A/S	✓	✓	✓	✓	✓
Directory Support	Native support for Microsoft's Active Directory and Novell's eDirectory means that users logging in with credentials from these directory systems will be recognized and authenticated by Presentation Server.	P/E/A/S	✓	✓	✓	✓	
Installation Manager for Citrix Presentation Server	Includes utilities that ease the burden of installing and uninstalling applications in large server farms across the enterprise by automating the process with centralized configuration and delivery.	P/E	✓	✓	✓	✓	
Integration with Network Management Consoles	Supports SNMP monitoring and integration with third-party network management tools, including: Microsoft Operations Manager, IBM Tivoli, HP OpenView™, CA Unicenter™	P/E	✓	✓	✓	✓	
Delegated Administration	Provides the ability to designate Citrix administrative tasks to users without having to add them to a domain administrative group.	P/E/A/S	✓	✓	✓	✓	✓

Editions – Platinum (P); Enterprise (E); Advanced (A); Standard(S). Standard Edition is only available in version 4.0 and earlier.

Management (Continued)

FEATURE	DESCRIPTION	EDITION	CITRIX PRESENTATION SERVER 4.5	CITRIX PRESENTATION SERVER 4.0	CITRIX METAFRAME PRESENTATION SERVER 3.0	CITRIX METAFRAME XP	CITRIX METAFRAME 1.8
Printer Management	Provides advanced printer management that includes ability to map print drivers to different servers and easily replicate drivers from one server to another. Also, all complexities of dealing with print drivers can be eliminated using Citrix's Universal Printer Driver.	P/E/A/S	✓	✓	✓	✓	
Centralized Management Console	Comprehensive interface that enables complete, single-point management of the entire Presentation Server farm including servers, applications, licenses, printers and users from any location. Provides tight integration with Active Directory®.	P/E/A/S	✓	✓	✓	✓	
System Monitoring and Analysis	Allows administrators to efficiently manage and monitor system resources and to generate billing reports — based on costs such as CPU usage or connection time — for users, departments or domains. The base platform provides Performance Monitor which allows manual configuration of performance data.	P/E	✓	✓	✓		
Report Center	All reports can be created, managed, and analyzed from one location in the MMC console.	P/E	✓	✓	✓		
Remote Server Management	Remotely manage all Presentation Servers directly from an integrated user interface within the Management Console and connect to either the desktop or the console.	P/E/A/S	✓	✓	✓	✓	✓
Connection Control	Allows you set a limit on the number of connections that each user can have simultaneously in the server farm. You can also limit the number of concurrent connections to specified published applications, and you can prevent users from launching more than one instance of the same published application.	P/E/A/S	✓	✓	✓	✓	
Management Pack for Microsoft Operations Manager (MOM) 2005	Enables management of Presentation Server farm through Microsoft's MOM 2005 product using the Microsoft Operations Console.	P/E/A/S	✓	✓	✓		

Performance and Scalability

FEATURE	DESCRIPTION	EDITION	CITRIX PRESENTATION SERVER 4.5	CITRIX PRESENTATION SERVER 4.0	CITRIX METAFRAME PRESENTATION SERVER 3.0	CITRIX METAFRAME XP	CITRIX METAFRAME 1.8
Enterprise-Class Scalability	Citrix has developed and tested Presentation Server in environments with over 1000 servers so that our customers can be assured that they can deploy this product in their enterprise and see the benefits.	P/E/A/S	✓	✓	✓		
Support for Windows Server 2003 x64 Edition	Supports the 64-bit server platform, significantly increasing user density, server consolidation and application performance	P/E/A/S	✓	✓			
Load throttling	Prevents new servers from being overloaded when they first logon to the farm by automatically biasing server load. Creates a consistent, reliable user access experience	P/E/A	✓				

Editions – Platinum (P); Enterprise (E); Advanced (A); Standard(S). Standard Edition is only available in version 4.0 and earlier.

Performance and Scalability (Continued)

FEATURE	DESCRIPTION	EDITION	CITRIX PRESENTATION SERVER 4.5	CITRIX PRESENTATION SERVER 4.0	CITRIX METAFRAME PRESENTATION SERVER 3.0	CITRIX METAFRAME XP	CITRIX METAFRAME 1.8
Enterprise Load Balancing	Built-in load balancing provides the best system performance by allowing administrators to configure balancing rules based on application user load, context switches, CPU utilization, disk data I/O, disk operations, IP address range, memory utilization, page faults, page swapping, schedule, and server user load. This flexibility means that there is no need for third-party load balancing solutions and assures customers of the best possible performance in the enterprise.	P/E/A	✓	✓	✓	✓	✓
CPU Utilization Management	Provides CPU distribution such that individual "power" users will not adversely affect other user son the same server. The technology controls processes from taking too much CPU at any given time, ensuring a consistent performance level for all users on the server.	P/E	✓	✓	✓		
Virtual Memory Optimization	Improves overall performance by rebasing DLLs to better optimize the use of virtual memory. The optimizations attempt to eliminate DLL memory mapping conflicts from process to process (app to app or session to session) which reduces the amount of page swapping.	P/E	✓	✓			
Multiple Farm Support	Supports multiple groups of servers (server farms) to provide customers with the most flexible options for deploying their servers. Farms can be structured to isolate specific applications. Built-in support for aggregation of published content, centralized management, and cross-farm load balancing ensures that almost any scenario can be supported.	P/E/A/S	✓	✓	✓	✓	

Security and Compliance

FEATURE	DESCRIPTION	EDITION	CITRIX PRESENTATION SERVER 4.5	CITRIX PRESENTATION SERVER 4.0	CITRIX METAFRAME PRESENTATION SERVER 3.0	CITRIX METAFRAME XP	CITRIX METAFRAME 1.8
Application User Load	Limits the number of users allowed to connect to a selected published application.	P/E/A	✓	✓	✓	✓	
SmartAuditor	Provides powerful application session recording for improved regulatory compliance, risk mitigation, and accelerated problem resolution.	P	✓				
SmartAccess	Powered by the Citrix Access Gateway product line of SSL VPN appliances, the new secure gateway solution provides SmartAccess granular access control policies and integrated endpoint analysis.	P	✓				
Universal SSL VPN — supports all applications and protocols	Gives users access to any application by supporting all TCP and UDP protocols. Enables administrators to give users access to IT resources without the need for custom development, or the need to maintain both SSL and IPSec VPN infrastructures.	P	✓				
Integrated endpoint scanning and extensible endpoint analysis	Clients are scanned against administrator-defined criteria to enforce proper configurations such as up-to-date security software and operating system versions. Endpoint analysis capabilities can be extended using industry-standard development tools.	P	✓				

Editions – Platinum (P); Enterprise (E); Advanced (A); Standard(S). Standard Edition is only available in version 4.0 and earlier.

Security and Compliance (Continued)

FEATURE	DESCRIPTION	EDITION	CITRIX PRESENTATION SERVER 4.5	CITRIX PRESENTATION SERVER 4.0	CITRIX METAFRAME PRESENTATION SERVER 3.0	CITRIX METAFRAME XP	CITRIX METAFRAME 1.8
Single Sign-On	Secures application logons and enhances the security of all password-protected Windows applications.	P	✓				
Self-service Password Reset and Account Unlock	Allows users to reset their domain password or unlock their Windows account through Web Interface or from the control + alt + delete logon screen.	P	✓				
Hot Desktop	Enables users who share workstations to logon/logoff in seconds instead of using a time-consuming, full Windows or Novell logon/logoff procedure.	P	✓				
Advanced Encryption Standard Support	Provides high performance, standards based encryption security using AES, required by many government agencies and other organizations with strict security requirements	P/E/A	✓				
Trusted Server Configuration	Prevent users from accessing unauthorized servers. Similar to Internet Explorer's "trusted web sites" feature, Trusted Server Configuration helps lock down environments and increases administrator control.	P/E/A	✓				
Two-Factor Authentication Support	Supports RSA SecurID® and SafeWord® Secure Computing tokens for two-factor authentication.	P/E/A/S	✓	✓	✓	✓	
Smartcard Support(including Common Access Card (CAC))	Support for Smart card authentication to Web Interface or Program Neighborhood Agent as well as pass through support for authentication to applications.	P/E/A/S	✓	✓	✓	✓	
Enhanced Smartcard Support	Applications that leverage Smartcards can be more fully supported through the elimination of application specific configurations and better support for a wide range of Smartcard hardware. Better PIN handling helps reduce the need to re-enter Smart Card credentials. Smooth Roaming now enables users to use their smart cards to log on and off automatically through Program Neighborhood Agent.	P/E/A/S	✓	✓	✓		
Secure Gateway for Citrix Presentation Server	Secure Gateway encapsulates Presentation Server traffic in SSL to allow remote users to securely access published content while minimizing the cost & management of certificates. Using industry standards connections can traverse firewalls without the need to open additional ports.	P/E/A/S	✓	✓	✓	✓	
TLS/SSL	Support for TLS/SSL encryption.	P/E/A/S	✓	✓	✓	✓	
Novell Directory Services(NDS) Support	Administrators can publish applications and content to Novell NDS users and groups of users. Support for seamless NDS authentication.	P/E/A/S	✓	✓	✓	✓	
HP Protect Tool Support	User logons and application launches using Win32 Clients or the Web Interface fully operate with HP Protect Tools, greatly enhancing joint solutions with HP.	P/E/A/S	✓	✓			

Editions – Platinum (P); Enterprise (E); Advanced (A); Standard(S). Standard Edition is only available in version 4.0 and earlier.

User Connectivity

FEATURE	DESCRIPTION	EDITION	CITRIX PRESENTATION SERVER™ 4.5	CITRIX PRESENTATION SERVER™ 4.0	CITRIX METAFRAME® PRESENTATION SERVER 3.0™	CITRIX METAFRAME® PRESENTATION SERVER XP	CITRIX METAFRAME® 1.8
Non-Administrator Client Installation	Eliminates the need to give users "Administrator" privileges in order to install the Presentation Server client, making it easier for users to access virtualized applications from any device, such as kiosks and business centers.	P/E/A	✓				
Browser-only SSL VPN access	Allows users to access network file shares, Web email and internal Web sites from devices that are locked down and do not permit the downloading of any software.	P	✓				
Web Interface for Remote Access	Web Interface for Presentation Server provides a rich web portal for end users that provides built-in support for two-factor authentication, offers simple customization through the management console (no coding necessary), and provides dynamic multilingual support. Web interface for Presentation Server is built to leverage the extended features of Presentation Server (like Smooth Roaming™) without any custom coding and integration with most third-party portals is seamless.	P/E/A/S	✓	✓	✓	✓	
Web Interface for Microsoft SharePoint™	Allows organization to publish applications through a SharePoint portal.	P/E/A/S	✓	✓	✓		
Universal Device Access	The Presentation Server client is available for a wide range of platforms including: DOS (16 bit and 32 bit), Windows (16 bit and 32 bit), Windows CE / Pocket PC, UNIX, Linux, Mac OS X, Java, IBM OS/2 Warp, FPOC / Symbian OS.	P/E/A/S	✓	✓	✓	✓	✓
Microsoft Remote Desktop Client Support	Allows users to connect to Presentation Server using Microsoft Remote Desktop Client, enabling access from devices that are locked-down or where restrictions prevent the download of a Citrix client.	P/E/A/S	✓	✓	✓		

Editions – Platinum (P); Enterprise (E); Advanced (A); Standard(S). Standard Edition is only available in version 4.0 and earlier.

INDEX

▼ E